Homeric Receptions Across Generic and Cultural Contexts

Trends in Classics – Supplementary Volumes

Edited by
Franco Montanari and Antonios Rengakos

Scientific Committee
Alberto Bernabé · Margarethe Billerbeck
Claude Calame · Philip R. Hardie · Stephen J. Harrison
Stephen Hinds · Richard Hunter · Christina Kraus
Giuseppe Mastromarco · Gregory Nagy
Theodore D. Papanghelis · Giusto Picone
Kurt Raaflaub · Bernhard Zimmermann

Volume 37

Homeric Receptions Across Generic and Cultural Contexts

Edited by
Athanasios Efstathiou and Ioanna Karamanou

DE GRUYTER

ISBN 978-3-11-061172-4
e-ISBN (PDF) 978-3-11-047979-9
e-ISBN (EPUB) 978-3-11-047918-8
ISSN 1868-4785

Library of Congress Cataloging-in-Publication Data
A CIP catalog record for this book has been applied for at the Library of Congress.

Bibliographic information published by the Deutsche Nationalbibliothek
The Deutsche Nationalbibliothek lists this publication in the Deutsche Nationalbibliografie; detailed bibliographic data are available on the Internet at http://dnb.dn.de.

© 2018 Walter de Gruyter GmbH, Berlin/Boston
This volume is text- and page-identical with the hardback published in 2016.
Logo: Christopher Schneider, Laufen
Printing and binding: CPI books GmbH, Leck
∞ Printed on acid-free paper
Printed in Germany

www.degruyter.com

Preface

This collective volume grew out of an international conference on Homeric Reception held at the Department of History of the Ionian University in Corfu in November 2011. All papers profited by the fruitful interaction between classicists and reception scholars, which gave rise to challenging and refreshing questions, and, subsequently, by the process of peer review for publication. The ensuing revising process took a considerable period of time, but we hope that the revisions made contributed to the focus on the generic and cultural contexts of Homeric reception and, in turn, to the coherence of the volume as a whole. We are extremely grateful to the General Editors of this series, Professor Antonios Rengakos and Professor Franco Montanari, for their brilliant guidance, their scholarly acumen, their great perceptiveness and unfailing patience throughout the publication process.

This conference was made possible thanks to the valuable insight, scholarly vigour and unstinting support of Professor Chris Carey, who has been for us a mentor in the truest sense over the last decades. The debt that we owe him cannot be adequately expressed in words. We are much indebted to Professor Lorna Hardwick for generously offering her valuable advice and great expertise on classical reception during the preparation of the volume for publication and to the four anonymous readers for providing constructive criticism and improving comments. We are truly grateful to Professor Mike Edwards, Professor Ariadne Gartziou-Tatti, Professor Yorgos Kentrotis, Professor Stratis Kyriakidis and Professor Ioannis Perysinakis for their fruitful suggestions as members of the Conference Advisory Board. Special thanks are due to Professor Dimitris Anoyatis-Pelé, Professor Theodosis Pylarinos and Assistant Professor Ilias Yarenis of the Department of History of the Ionian University for their excellent collaboration as members of the conference Organizing Committee.

To our great regret, Professor Daniel Jacob, who was a member of the Conference Advisory Board, brightening the conference with his presence and participating with a significant paper included in this *corpus*, passed away on 21 May 2014, before this volume went to press. Those who were fortunate to have met Daniel Jacob were impressed by his philological vigour, scholarly insight and steadfastness. Younger scholars benefited enormously from his humanity, his kind encouragement and the valuable guidance which he generously offered to them. For young researchers he was and still is a model of academic conduct and scholarly devotion. His academic life formed part of the high scholarly achievements of the Department of Classics of the Aristotle University of Thessaloniki. A remarkable volume dedicated to his memory and edited by his eminent colleagues, Professor Antonios Rengakos and Professor Poulheria Kyriakou, has most recently appeared in this series (*Wisdom and Folly in Euripides*). The editors of the present volume feel the need to honour the memory of Professor Daniel Jacob, gratefully acknowledging his major offer to classical scholarship and his everlasting *aretē*.

Athanasios Efstathiou
Department of History
Ionian University

Ioanna Karamanou
Department of Theatre Studies
University of the Peloponnese

Table of Contents

Preface —— V

Ioanna Karamanou
Introduction: The Contexts of Homeric Reception —— 1

Part I **Framing**

Lorna Hardwick
Homer, Repetition and Reception —— 15

Part II: **Homer In Archaic Ideology**

Margarita Alexandrou
Hipponax and the *Odyssey*: Subverting Text and Intertext —— 31

Andrej Petrovic
Archaic Funerary Epigram and Hector's Imagined *Epitymbia* —— 45

Margarita Sotiriou
Performance, Poetic Identity and Intertextuality in Pindar's *Olympian* 4 —— 59

Chris Carey
Homer and Epic in Herodotus' Book 7 —— 71

Part III **Homeric Echoes in Philosophical and Rhetorical Discourse**

Athanasios Efstathiou
Argumenta Homerica: Homer's Reception by Aeschines —— 93

Eleni Volonaki
Homeric Values in the *Epitaphios Logos* —— 125

Ioannis N. Perysinakis
The Ancient Quarrel between Philosophy and Poetry: Plato's *Hippias Minor* —— 147

Kleanthis Mantzouranis
A Philosophical Reception of Homer: Homeric Courage in Aristotle's Discussion of ἀνδρεία —— 163

Christina-Panagiota Manolea
Homeric Echoes, Pythagorean Flavour: The Reception of Homer in Iamblichus —— 175

Part IV Hellenistic and Later Receptions

Maria Kanellou
Ἑρμιόνην, ἣ εἶδος ἔχε χρυσέης Ἀφροδίτης (*Od.* 4.14): Praising a Female through Aphrodite – From Homer into Hellenistic Epigram —— 189

Karim Arafat
Pausanias and Homer —— 205

Maria Ypsilanti
The Reception of Homeric Vocabulary in Nonnus' *Paraphrase* of St. John's Gospel: Examination of Themes and Formulas in Selected Passages —— 215

Part V Latin Transformations

Helen Peraki-Kyriakidou
Trees and Plants in Poetic Emulation: From the Homeric Epic to Virgil's *Eclogues* —— 227

Sophia Papaioannou
Embracing Homeric Orality in the *Aeneid*: Revisiting the Composition Politics of Virgil's First *Descriptio* —— 249

Charilaos N. Michalopoulos
'*tollite me, Teucri*' (Verg. *Aen.* 3.601): Saving Achaemenides, Saving Homer —— 263

Boris Kayachev
Scylla the Beauty and Scylla the Beast: A Homeric Allusion in the
Ciris —— 277

Andreas N. Michalopoulos
Homer in Love: Homeric Reception in Propertius and Ovid —— 289

Part VI Homeric Scholarship at the Intersection of Traditions

Robert Maltby
Homer in Servius: A Judgement on Servius as a Commentator on
Virgil —— 303

Ivana Petrovic
On Finding Homer: The Impact of Homeric Scholarship on the Perception of
South Slavic Oral Traditional Poetry —— 315

Part VII Homer on the Ancient and Modern Stage

Katerina Mikellidou
Aeschylus reading Homer: The Case of the *Psychagogoi* —— 331

Daniel J. Jacob
Symbolic Remarriage in Homer's *Odyssey* and Euripides' *Alcestis* —— 343

Ioanna Karamanou
Euripides' 'Trojan Trilogy' and the Reception of the Epic Tradition —— 355

Varvara Georgopoulou
Andromache's Tragic *Persona* from the Ancient to the Modern Stage —— 369

Kyriaki Petrakou
Odysseus Satirical: The Merry Dealing of the Homeric Myth in Modern Greek
Theatre —— 379

Part VIII Refiguring Homer in Film and Music

Pantelis Michelakis
The Reception of Homer in Silent Film —— 393

Anastasia Bakogianni
Homeric Shadows on the Silver Screen: Epic Themes in Michael Cacoyannis' Trilogy of Cinematic Receptions —— 405

Hara Thliveri
'Travelling to the Light, Aiming at the Infinite': The *Odyssey* of Mikis Theodorakis —— 417

Bibliography —— 435

Notes on Contributors —— 475

General Index —— 481

Index of Homeric Passages —— 491

Ioanna Karamanou
Introduction: The Contexts of Homeric Reception*

For more than two decades Homeric scholarship has been fruitfully interacting with the increasingly developing field of classical reception studies, by delving into the manner in which Homeric poetry has been transmitted, translated, interpreted, rewritten and represented. A respectable number of studies have investigated the reworkings of Homeric poetry in Greek and Latin literature[1] and in later periods of time,[2] along with the significance of audience and reader response as a trigger for the ancient and subsequent interpretations of Homer.[3]

The purpose of this collective volume is, naturally, not to offer an exhaustive treatment of the fields of Homeric reception; this would be impossible, not least because particular areas, as, for instance, the Hellenistic or Latin transformations of Homeric poetry, may well provide enough material for several volumes. Rather, its objective is quite different. As stated in the title, it seeks to explore how varying aspects of Homeric poetics appeal to and can be mapped on to a diversity of contexts both vertically, that is, over time, and horizontally across different genres of the same period. This key approach is consistent with a fundamental concept of classical reception studies, which is the exploration of the contexts of reception and of the manner in which the reworking of the source text is shaped under different socio-historical, intellectual, literary and artistic conditions.

---

* I am truly grateful to Professor Lorna Hardwick for kindly taking the time to read through this introduction and for providing valuable comments.
1 In a chronological order, see Knauer 1964; Kindstrand 1973; Neitzel 1975; Barchiesi 1984a; Valakas 1987; Rengakos 1993 and 1994; Knight 1995; Rutherford 1996, 20–29; Sotiriou 1998; Zeitlin 2001; Graziosi 2002, ch. 5; Michelakis 2002; Fowler (ed.) 2004, section 5 (esp. Hunter 2004, 234–53 and Farrell 2004, 254–71); Fantuzzi/ Hunter 2004, ch. 2, 3 and 6; Zanetto/ Canavero/ Capra/ Sgobbi (eds.) 2004; Graziosi 2008a; Nagy 2009; Michel 2014; on Homeric reception in ancient philosophy, see Lamberton 1986; Planinc 2003; Manolea 2004.
2 See most importantly Callen King 1987; Beissinger/ Tylus/ Wofford (eds.) 1999; Hardwick 2003, 86–97; Clarke/ Currie/ Lyne (eds.) 2006; Graziosi/ Greenwood (eds.) 2007; Winkler (ed.) 2007a; Hall 2008; Latacz/ Greub/ Blome/ Wieczorek (eds.) 2008; Davis 2008; Most/ Norman/ Rabau (eds.) 2009; Myrsiades (ed.) 2009; Vandiver 2010; Bizer 2011.
3 See especially the chapters by Purkis, Furbank and Hardwick in Emlyn-Jones/Hardwick/Purkis (eds.) 1992; Lamberton/ Keaney (eds.) 1992; Scodel 2002, 173–212; Nagy 2009; Niehoff (ed.) 2012.

The significance of context exploration has been theoretically propounded by Charles Martindale in a chapter entitled 'Framing Contexts' of his seminal work focusing on the hermeneutics of reception.[4] 'Contexts', he argues, 'are not single nor are they found "lying about" as it were; we have to construct them from other texts, which also have to be interpreted (And by text I mean every vehicle of signification, so that in this extended sense a mosaic, or a marriage ceremony, is a "text" as much as a book)'.[5] This concept originates in Jauss's theory of the aesthetics of reception asserting the continuing interaction between source text and the receiving work in conjunction with the receiver's social and cultural context.[6] Reception is thus figured dialogically, as a two-way process of interpretation, backwards and forwards. The relation between the source text and the receiving work is reciprocal, therefore elucidating the former as much as the latter. At the same time, it is essential to look at the routes through which the ancient source text has passed and at the manner in which generic and cultural conditions have shaped later reworkings.

Accordingly, the wide spectrum of Homeric transformations is approached in this volume in the light of their generic and cultural contexts. Genre and culture are intrinsically interrelated and both play a key role in establishing the receiver's 'horizon of expectations'. This notion was introduced by Jauss to refer to the receiver's mind-set determined by his/her literary and socio-cultural milieu and to frame the reciprocal relationship between source text and receiver.[7] In turn, the survey of the contexts of Homeric reworkings presupposes the investigation of the interplay of epic with different genres (literary, scholarly, artistic) and under varying cultural conditions. A major part of this volume naturally covers the echoes of Homer in classical and post-classical literature (sections II-V), as well as exploring the implications of Homeric transmission in Latin and Serbian contexts (section VI) and Homeric refigurations in the performing arts, such as theatre, film and music (sections VII and VIII). At the same time, these contributions seek to evaluate how Homeric referents are appropriated within different cultural contexts and over a wide time span (Ancient Greece, Modern Greece, Rome, Europe and North America). Therefore, the very use of the plural in the title ('receptions' rather than 'reception') aims at drawing attention to the multiformity and diversity pervading the transformations of Homeric poetry.

---

4 Martindale 1993, 11–18; see also Hardwick 2003, esp. ch. 3.
5 Martindale 1993, 13.
6 Jauss 1982. Reception is regarded as a fundamentally 'dialogic' process also in the major theoretical works of Gadamer 1975 and Iser 1978. For a discussion of the impact of these theories, see, for instance, Holub 2003², 57–63; Hardwick 2003, 6–9; Martindale 2006, 3–6.
7 See Jauss 1982, 3–45; Hardwick 2003, 7–8; Holub 2003², 58–63.

As mentioned above, the shared objective of the essays is the exploration of the generic and cultural contexts of Homeric reception. At the same time, this collective volume displays a range of methodological approaches by bringing together internationally acclaimed researchers and acute young scholars in the fields of classics and reception studies. The value of the publication of selected papers originating in an academic conference derives from the engagement of the participants in genuine scholarly 'dialogue', which stimulates careful thought and scholarly interaction about the issues raised in individual papers, thus enhancing the cohesion of the resulting collection of essays. This collaborative attitude constitutes a distinctive feature of the research in the area of classical reception, which invites a variety of voices and a series of theoretical perspectives, testifying to the vitality of debates and to the breadth of possible receptions.[8] Consequently, an effective interdisciplinary collaboration between reception scholars and classicists is required, so that reception studies could benefit from the formal analysis of classical scholarship and, at the same time, a broadly conceived dialectical discipline of classics could be formed to connect the interpretation of texts with their reception history.[9]

This position is brought to the fore by Lorna Hardwick in the first section, which forms a theoretical framework for the analysis of Homeric reception. She argues that the in-depth study of formal structures and conventions provides insight into the cultural power of Homeric reworkings. This approach aims at reconciling the formal and aesthetic appreciation with the cultural interpretation of reception, thus contributing to a long-lasting debate among reception scholars.[10] From this viewpoint, Lorna Hardwick focuses on the transformations of Homeric poetry in the light of the concept of 'repetition', which, as developed by Deleuze, excludes the possibility of exact replication. She investigates the ways in which 'repetition with a difference' appropriates Homeric formal qualities, so that the receiving work enables the reader to experience the processes shaping the continuing dialogue between ancient and modern. It is noteworthy that in the case of Homeric receptions the formal arrangements of the receiving work often implicitly provide a 'commentary' on the source text, thus offering insight into the manner in which Homeric poetry is interpreted and remodelled. As she

---

8 See Hardwick and Stray 2008, 1–9; Kallendorf 2007, 1–4; Bakogianni 2013, I 1–3. The variety of the activators of reception and the vigour of debates are suggestive of the 'democratic' nature of classical reception analysis; on this wide-ranging topic, see recently Hardwick/Harrison (eds.) 2013.
9 On the latter position, see Martindale 1993, xiii and his fresh assessment twenty years later in Martindale 2013; cf. also Brockliss/ Chaudhuri/Haimson Lushkov/Wasdin 2012, 1–4.
10 See, for instance, Goldhill 2010, 56–70 and Martindale 2010, 71–84.

has pointed out in an earlier study, reception (and, in this case, Homeric reception) involves 'a necessary interplay between invention and critique'.[11] Hence, the formal analysis of the source text, the receiving work and the mediating works is significant in evaluating the aesthetic qualities of each production and in investigating the relationships among them in the light of their varying contexts.

The role of reception as a form of 'commentary' is reiterated in the second section by Margarita Alexandrou, who argues that Hipponax's engagement with the *Odyssey* functions as a commentary, in that it sheds light on Odyssean elements which are only implicit in the Homeric oeuvre. Marginality and grotesquery run through Hipponactean poetry, underlined by the fact that events and *persona* were partly modelled on the *Odyssey* to create a sustained metapoetic engagement with the Homeric *epos*, which serves both to undermine the epic and to undercut the authority of the third person narrator. This complex process generates an unusually rich intertextuality, which raises interesting questions about audience response and the contexts of Hipponax's poetry.

From the archaic subversion of the epic we move on to explore Homeric echoes in the equally archaic poetry of *kleos* and praise. The reception of Homer in sepulchral epigrams of the archaic period is investigated by Andrej Petrovic, who looks into two Iliadic passages associated with funerary epigrams by ancient scholiasts and raises the question whether a distinct relation between Homeric 'epigrammatic' passages and early epigrammatic production can be identified. His case study involves the close analysis of two sixth-century BC sepulchral epigrams, which appropriate Homeric structural and stylistic elements and thus seem to have been ideologically and formally chiselled after the Iliadic 'epigrammatic' passages. Likewise, Margarita Sotiriou discusses Pindar's appropriation of formal, thematic and conceptual elements from the eighth book of the *Odyssey* in his *Fourth Olympian Ode* to praise his patron by comparing him with heroic *exempla*. Investigating the performative context of the ode, she argues that Pindar refigures the Homeric scene and the πεῖρα motif in particular, in order to present himself as a '*persona* projected by the poems' and shape his distinct identity as a 'primary narrator' announcing his patron's success with truthfulness and thus establishing the reception of his ode by his audience. Hence, the poet's multifaceted dialogue with his source text provides insight into Pindaric poetics, performance and audience response.

The epic narrator's bestowal of *kleos* and its reception by Herodotus are brought forward by Chris Carey, who delves into the complexity of the historian's

---

11 Hardwick 1992, 248.

appropriation of Homeric elements. Herodotus is placed at a crossroads, as he selects 'those bits and pieces of the oral memory of the archaic period that fit his own literary and ideological agenda',[12] whilst aligning himself with his contemporary Ionic intellectual milieu. His complex relationship with *epos* is prominent in the seventh book locating the Persian Wars within the larger context of hostilities between East and West, for which the epic treatment of the Trojan War serves as an equivalent. Herodotus' interplay with epic is suggestive of the historian's emulation with his source text, as he claims equivalent or greater status for his own narrative, by presenting this Persian invasion as exceeding all of the earlier East-West confrontations.

The third section looks across strands in Homeric reception within philosophical and rhetorical discourse. Philosophy and oratory are brought together in this part of the volume, on the basis of the theoretically propounded essential interaction between knowledge and eloquence.[13] Athanasios Efstathiou considers the implications of the use of Homeric quotations based on the oral learning of poetry in Aeschines' extant speeches, pointing out that Homer is employed as an authority, with the purpose of validating the orator's argumentation and persuasiveness. At the same time, these 'Homeric arguments' form indicators of the audience's *paideia* and 'horizon of expectations' showcasing the cultural contexts of mid-fourth century Athens and the pivotal role that Homeric poetry played in civic processes. Eleni Volonaki then reiterates the key notion of Homeric *kleos* (mainly discussed in the second section) and its ideological transplantation into the genre of funeral oration. To praise their contemporary achievements, orators appropriate epic paradigms and transform the concept of *aretē* (virtue), which becomes imbued with the democratic values represented by the citizen soldier and is associated with the collective glory of the anonymous group within the context of the *polis*, in contrast to the epic praise of individuality.

The reconfiguration of the Homeric notion of *aretē* is similarly brought to the fore in Plato's *Hippias Minor* forming the focus of the analysis by Ioannis Perysinakis. This discussion provides a case study on the ancient philosophical reception of poetry, as it stresses the challenge posed to the values represented in the Homeric epics by Platonic thought, which subjected the poetic *mythos* to *logos* and rejected *mimēsis* for not educating children on *aretē*. This chapter showcases the transformation of Homeric virtue into the Platonic conception

---

[12] Rose 2012, 202.
[13] See, for instance, Pl. *Phdr.* 259e-279c, Arist. *Rh.* 1355a 31–1355b 10, 1356a 31, Cic. *Tusc.* 1.7, 2.6–7, *De or.* esp. 3.71–72, Quint. *Inst.* 2.19–21.

of excellence being particularized in *sophia* (wisdom) and having *dynamis* (ability) as a prerequisite. Subsequently, Kleanthis Mantzouranis reflects on the impact of Aristotle's response to the epic paradigms of martial valour. As he points out, the philosopher's use of Homer is a purposeful act of reception aiming to illustrate by means of concrete examples the forms of courage he describes and to reinforce his argument by adducing the authority of the poet, which could be paralleled, to a certain degree, with the rhetorical practice previously examined by Athanasios Efstathiou. Aristotle uses Homer as a benchmark, refining and developing the epic representation of valour, in order to elucidate his own conception of genuine courage. The implications of the selection of Homer as a source text by the Neoplatonic philosopher Iamblichus are evaluated by Christina-Panagiota Manolea. Iamblichus chose to incorporate Homeric elements in his own discussion of important philosophical matters either directly or indirectly, drawing on his master Porphyry and on Plato, by taking into account his audience's familiarity with Homer. Nonetheless, as she observes, the philosopher appropriates *epos* when he considers it fit to his argumentation, since his aim is not to explain Homer, as his teacher Porphyry did, but to enrich his own Neoplatonic philosophical *exegesis*.

The fourth section highlights the transformation of epic style and motifs, as well as the perception of Homer as a cultural authority from the Hellenistic period to Late Antiquity. Maria Kanellou discusses the refiguration of the Homeric motif of praising female appearance through comparison to the archetypal beauty of Aphrodite in Hellenistic epigrams. She observes that the transformation of this motif has been shaped through a nexus of cross-generic, religious and political factors leading to the literary deification of queens by the Ptolemaic court poets and the heroization of mere mortals. The authority of Homeric poetry as a source text is investigated by Karim Arafat, who argues that Pausanias' affinity with Homer seems to emerge from his perception of the poet as an archetypal periegete. Pausanias' agenda with respect to his approach of the Homeric epics differs from that of his contemporaries, as, for instance, Philostratus, and may also shed light on the reception of Homer as a means of defining the cultural background and intellectual trends of the second sophistic. Subsequently, Maria Ypsilanti's inquiry into the appropriation of Homeric vocabulary, metre and imagery in the *Paraphrase of St. John's Gospel* by Nonnus of Panopolis raises issues of genre, culture and audience response within the Christian milieu of Late Antiquity. She points out that Nonnus' hexameter rephrasing of the Gospel embellishes Johannine prose, highlights and interprets theological notions and doctrinal concepts by addressing an audience both well-versed in the epic tradition and interested in religious matters.

The fifth section brings telling instances of Latin transformations of Homeric poetry to the fore. The chapter by Helen Peraki-Kyriakidou provides an apt transition from the preceding section to the focus of this one, since it showcases the significance of the cross-generic interplay between Hellenistic poetry and Homeric *epos* for the formation of Latin pastoral. The author stresses that Virgil, whose main source text in the *Eclogues* is Theocritus' bucolic poetry, enters into a fertile dialogue with Homer regarding the style, function and symbolism of plant-catalogues, which are, at the same time, naturally imbued with Theocritean features of the pastoral genre. Subsequently, Sophia Papaioannou delves into Virgil's appropriation of the core feature of Homeric orality in the *ekphrases* (*descriptiones*) developed in the *Aeneid*. She argues that Virgil is particularly aware to emphasize the complex intertextuality as the cornerstone at the foundation of the structure of the *Aeneid* ; accordingly, the poet seems to suggest that each *descriptio* may be subjected to multiple possible readings, due to the flexibility of the descriptive technique of visualization, which is an equivalent to the process of motif transference that predominates in Homeric orality.

The metapoetic significance of Virgil's refashioning of the Odyssean Cyclops episode in the Achaemenides scene of the *Aeneid* is investigated by Charilaos Michalopoulos. This chapter contextualizes the impact of this reworking on Virgil's wider poetological programme of Homeric reception, through which he provides a self-definition of his own poetry and its position in the course of continuity and change within the epic tradition. At the same time, the intellectual processes involved in Virgil's strategies of transforming Homeric poetry are indicators of Homer's cultural and ideological assimilation in Rome. The similarly Odyssean figure of Scylla forms the intertext in the narrative of the pseudo-Virgilian *Ciris*. Boris Kayachev sets out to explore the implicit allusion to the Homeric Scylla haunting the *Ciris* as an intertextual *Doppelgänger* of her Roman equivalent. This stealthy intrusion of the Homeric intertext could provide insight into the poetological agenda of the *Ciris* and into allusion as a form of literary reception. This section closes with the examination of the cross-generic transformation of Homeric love themes in Roman elegy by Andreas Michalopoulos. It is stressed that Propertius and Ovid draw parallels between the poetic *persona* and Homeric heroes in their representation of the *militia amoris* motif. In metapoetic terms, the epic system of values is transfigured and filtered through the elegiac-erotic system of values, while the genre of elegy is self-defined by means of its comparison and emulation with *epos*.

The sixth section brings forward the impact of Homeric transmission on different scholarly and cultural traditions, such as Latin scholarship and the edition of Serbian traditional poetry. Robert Maltby's essay pursues the idea propounded by Lorna Hardwick and subsequently by Margarita Alexandrou that commentary is and should be perceived as a form of reception, by investigating the function of Homeric quotations in Servius' commentary on Virgil's *Aeneid*. He focuses on six comparisons of passages in Virgil with their Homeric source text, pointing out that the main criteria applied to evaluate Virgil's reception of Homer are narrative credibility and stylistic appropriateness, which have a long scholarly tradition stretching back to the Alexandrian scholia via earlier Latin commentators. Robert Maltby brings forward the notion of the receiving author's emulation with his source text also stressed by Chris Carey, Charilaos Michalopoulos and Andreas Michalopoulos, by suggesting that Servius is willing to concede that on occasion Virgil manages to surpass his model text. From the purely philological implications of the reception of Homeric scholarship we now move on to explore its cultural power, as well. Ivana Petrovic draws attention to the impact of 18th and 19th century Homeric scholarship on the perception of Serbian oral traditional poetry. She demonstrates that the views of the German scholar Friedrich August Wolf, who regarded the *Iliad* and the *Odyssey* as a collection of popular songs, shaped the conditions of preservation and assessment of Serbian oral poetry. This is a case of cultural exchange involving the appropriation of the renowned figure of Homer to bestow authority to the collection of Serbian folk poems and also his use as a shield to counter the ban on the circulation of this collection in Europe, where traditional Serbian poems were seen as politically charged material. The latter fact showcases a significant dimension of classical reception, which is the potential of ancient texts to be employed as a means of countering censorship and enabling socio-political concerns to be conveyed through the neutral medium of classical culture.[14]

The two last sections of this volume delve into the transformations of Homeric material in the performing arts: theatre, film and music. The seventh section engages with the theatrical reception of *epos* over a wide time-span extending from Greek and Roman drama to European and Modern Greek theatre. Katerina Mikellidou explores the intertextual nexus between the Homeric *Nekyia* and its Aeschylean version in the fragmentarily preserved *Psychagogoi*, pointing out that Aeschylus opens a persistent dialogue with his source text and, as in several aforementioned cases of Homeric reception, he establishes a network of competitive dynamics. As well as regularly recalling the Odyssean archetype, the Aeschylean adaptation challenges it through a process of 'normalization' of the hero bringing him closer to the ordinary man, which is divergent from Homer's treatment of necromancy unfolding the full proportions of Odysseus' boldness.

---

[14] For such examples, see Hardwick 2003, 9, 99–111; van Steen 2001, 133–94; Hardwick 2009, 170–72.

The tragic refiguration of prominent Odyssean motifs is similarly illustrated in Daniel Jacob's essay offering a close analysis of the literary processes which shape the transformation of the archetypal reunion of husband and wife in the *Odyssey* at the end of the *Alcestis*. This intertextual relationship can be deciphered on the basis of the thematic and structural pattern of *nostos*, which has a pivotal position in both the *Odyssey* and the *Alcestis*. Nonetheless, its reception in the *Alcestis* is a complex process, in that the flexible dynamics of the *nostos* motif result in considerable deviations from the source text, thus providing 'a palimpsest, in which parts of the earlier text may be read through the overwritten text'. Likewise, Ioanna Karamanou sets out to explore the cross-generic transformation of Homeric material into tragedy in the 'Trojan trilogy' of Euripides, in the light of fifth-century cultural contexts, which have shaped the dramatic refashioning of the source text. Examining less explored aspects of the Euripidean reception of Homeric ideology from the standpoint of his tragic rhetoric in the formal debates of the *Alexandros* and the *Trojan Women*, she argues that the dramatist engages in a dialogue with Homeric ethics by embedding his epic referents within agonistic contexts. Euripides exploits the dynamics of his tragic rhetoric to juxtapose aspects of Homeric thought to his contemporary ethics, thus showcasing the dialectic, as well as the tension between the ideology of *epos* and fifth-century values.

Moving on to later theatrical receptions of Homer, Varvara Georgopoulou investigates the reception history of Andromache's *persona* and the cultural processes shaping this figure's dramatic transformation. The ancient Greek (Euripides) and Latin tragic treatments of Andromache's legend (Seneca) constitute key stages in the theatrical reception of this Homeric figure, bringing to the fore dominant themes, such as war-violence, militarism and gender issues, which are then reiterated in later theatre: French Classicism (Racine), the Interwar period (Giraudoux) and Modern Greek theatre (Akis Dimou). These theatrical reworkings of Andromache's figure take place within diverse contexts and under varying historical and cultural conditions, which shape the treatment of the aforementioned themes and their ideological implications. The interrelation between classical reception studies and theatre research is brought forward by Kyriaki Petrakou, who offers her perspective on the performance history and critical reception of the parodic treatments of the Odyssean legend in Modern Greek theatre. By employing essential tools of critical analysis of theatre performance, such as theatre criticism and audience response, she delineates the relationship between the theatrical transformation of *epos* and the socio-political and ideological forces shaping the cultural identity of Postwar Greece. This archetypal myth is subversively employed often as a means of political allegory alluding to the intrigues of political power and the misleading rhetoric of persuasion used by the media. In these plays, among which Iakovos Kambanellis' *Odysseus, Come Home* has a pivotal position, Odysseus is transformed into the bearer of a contemporary anti-myth suggesting the illusion of humanity about leadership and touching on crucial ideological issues arising from Postwar circumstances.

From the theatrical receptions of Homer we move on to the cinematic and musical refigurations of *epos* in the eighth section. Pantelis Michelakis' inquiry into the reception history of Homer in silent cinema showcases how these productions engage with a range of narrative modes, technological means and spectatorial practices available to early cinema, raising questions about the historiographical and methodological implications of this research for the reception of Homer in film and popular culture. He revisits the fundamental feature of Homeric orality also highlighted in the chapters by Athanasios Efstathiou, Sophia Papaioannou and Ivana Petrovic, to argue that early film does not merely represent the orality of archaic Greek epic, but also helps define it. The generic diversity of these films breaks down the canonical work of Homer into component parts reconfigured within a number of culturally contingent cinematic modes including not only action and romance but also trick cinematography, fantasy and parody. At the same time, the materiality of these films, which survive in multiple prints differing in terms of preservation conditions, overall length, number and order of scenes, challenges the fixity of the cinematic artwork in ways inviting comparison with the multiformity of Homeric texts. The filmic transformations of the Homeric material are similarly explored by Anastasia Bakogianni, who attempts to 'unmask' elements of Michael Cacoyannis' implicit dialogue with *epos* with regard to narrative and themes in his cinematic reception of Euripides' *Electra, Trojan Women* and *Iphigenia in Aulis*. Her counter-reading of Cacoyannis' trilogy argues for the pivotal role of the viewer's 'horizon of expectations' conditioned by the spectator's familiarity with the Homeric epics, which determines the threads that one can 'discover' in this production and are differently experienced by each viewer and within varying contexts. As she points out, the trilogy is permeable to such interpretations, not least because of the popularity of the genre of epic in cinema, on which Cacoyannis fruitfully drew.

The last section closes with Hara Thliveri's survey on the recent and so far unexplored *Odyssey* by the leading Greek composer Mikis Theodorakis. His work draws freely on the key Odyssean motif of *nostos* —also discussed by Daniel Jacob— to represent the completion of the composer's personal *nostos*. Theodorakis' artistic affinity with Homer also emerges from the fact that throughout his eighty-year career he managed to elevate poetry to a continuing narrative of national Greek myth. His Homerically oriented song-cycle thus provides an incentive to identify the reception of the Odyssean *nostos* pattern in popular discourse, by investigating how ancient symbols may feed collective memory and national awareness and construct cultural identity in conjunction with the composer's literary and artistic milieu.

The lines of inquiry that have been sketched out indicate that the points of convergence and divergence between the Homeric poems and their receptions are to a great extent conditioned by the generic and cultural contexts of both the source text and the receiving work. The approach to reception as a form of 'commentary' reiterated in the chapters of this volume sheds light not only on the receiving work, but also on those very aspects of the source text which have attracted attention in its subsequent reworkings. In more specific terms, Homeric values and patterns are reframed within different contexts elucidating the complex dialectic as well as the tension between source text and reception. This investigation also yields insight into the ideological forces shaping the cross-generic and cross-cultural transplantation of epic concepts into the receiving work. Homer's archetypal figure is regularly employed as an authority, with the purpose of validating narrative, rhetorical argumentation and philosophical exegesis, but also as a means of outwitting censorship. Key features of *epos*, as, for instance, its orality, are appropriated in metapoetic terms, as well as being reconfigured within performative contexts. The receiving author's/artist's trend towards emulation with the source text often functions as a means of generic self-definition providing insight into his/her literary or artistic agenda. All the same, Homeric concepts are also liable to be subversively employed, as in the case of parody, or to be challenged from the standpoint of their philosophical reception.

Overall, the varied strategies of refiguring the Homeric epics form indicators of the generic and cultural conditions defining the receiving work and of the 'horizon of expectations' of readers and audience. At the same time, the wide-ranging 'migration' of Homeric material through time and across place, as shaped by ideological forces, suggests that Homeric reception holds cultural power being instrumental in the construction of new cultural identities.

Part I **Framing**

Lorna Hardwick
Homer, Repetition and Reception

'Slow-striding Achilles, who put the hex on Hector
A swallow twitters in Troy. That's where we start.'

This is an extract from the opening sequence of Derek Walcott's *The Odyssey: A Stage Version*.[1] When I saw the play staged in its opening run at Stratford-upon-Avon, the audience laughed at these lines. Probably laughter was on several levels, but at least some of it was because spectators knew both that Achilles was 'swift-footed' and that the wound to his heel accounted for the actor's limp across the stage. One characteristic of Walcott's use of classical material is the way that he manipulates it to create an irreverent counter-text. The swallow twittering in Troy slyly reminded the spectators of chaos theory and also of the trauma that ensued from Troy. Here, however, my point is that Walcott continued to use the Homeric form, the formulaic epithet. It was part of the joke in which audience recognition was combined with a play on words. Achilles made Hector famous via the hexameters of the *Iliad*. In terms of epic poetics the epithet 'slow-striding is a good example of substitution, where the singer takes a phrase and changes a single word.[2] In Walcott's riff, Homer and Caribbean vernacular intersect.

This essay aims to bring consideration of formal elements back to the centre of analysis of classical receptions. The artificial polarities between studies based on aesthetics and those based on cultural history and its contexts have sometimes precluded study in depth of the role of formal structures and conventions as a nexus between the ancient text and its audiences and between the ancient text and its subsequent receptions.[3]

If the relationship between the ante-text and its receptions is to be genuinely dialogical, that is, if the ancient text and its transmission and appropriations have something to say to one another and if each influences the way that the other is read, then ways have to be found of enabling close reading of the ancient text and the modern to stake out a field of exchange. Steiner calls this relationship one of 'reciprocity'. However, reciprocity is just the fourth stage of his hermeneutic model, a model that is marred by the language of violence which he uses for the second stage – an image of violation of the ante-text by the new.

---

1 Walcott 1993, 1.
2 See further, Hainsworth 1993, 15.
3 For discussion of the aesthetics/cultural history debates, see Martindale/Thomas (eds.) 2006.

I do, however, draw on the initial stage in Steiner's model, that of *trust* – trust that the ante-text has something of value to offer.⁴

The hermeneutic process has been described in different ways: Julia Gaisser has written persuasively of 'accretions', qualities and associations that adhere to the ante-text in the course of its subsequent migrations, re-readings and rewritings. She describes how perceptions of the texts and of their meaning are altered through time. They become 'pliable and sticky artefacts gripped, moulded and stamped with new meanings by every generation of readers and they come to us irreversibly altered by their experiences'.⁵ Equally important, in my view, are the dynamic processes through which poetry travels and survives and becomes an active agent through time, place, language and culture. This 'iterability' of poetry is one of the key aspects that reception scholars have to handle, as they struggle to find ways of describing and explaining how and why ancient texts continue to resurface and to act as artistic and cultural catalysts. Different approaches have characterised the process in different ways. Pucci, drawing on Derrida, has explored the capacity of ancient texts to produce semantic and emotional effects even when the original social and historical co-ordinates are occluded or misunderstood by the subsequent readers and spectators.⁶ Pucci's discussion was grounded in theatre poetry. Poetic responses to Homer are not only a central strand in ancient tragedy but also carriers of the energy that enables the richness and moral and psychological complexities of the performance poetry of the Homeric poems to engage with the new situations into which they are transplanted.⁷ Elizabeth Cook, in her prose poem *Achilles* included a seductive sensory communication of 'A game of Chinese whispers. A hot word thrown into the next lap before it burns. It has not been allowed to set. Each hand that momentarily holds it, weighs it, before depositing it with a neighbour also, inadvertently moulds it ; communicates its own heat' (Cook 2001, 104).

Scholars have rightly turned away from 'universalist' models that kidnap poetic energy and write backwards, in order to permanently inscribe values that are largely invented restrospectively. But the problems of explaining and interpreting transhistorical and transcultural movements are real enough and have to be confronted afresh if classical reception research is to be more than an accumulation of case studies that do not go beyond the particularities and specificities in which they are embedded.

---

4 Steiner 1975, 296–303.
5 Gaisser 2002, 387.
6 Pucci 2007, 107.
7 Hardwick 1992, 248.

In this essay I suggest that the reception histories of the Homeric epics present case studies that are not only important in themselves but also, in combination, benefit from an approach that combines analysis of the formal elements of the ancient texts with close reading of what has been done *with* them. In that way, Homeric receptions can make a special contribution in offering paradigms for other areas of classical reception. There are two main reasons for this. Firstly, the formal elements of epic —such as, for example, formulaic epithets, similes, ring compositions, proems, codas and focalised narratives— provide productive opportunities for close reading of what happens when the formal aspects of the Homeric poems are transmitted and adapted in other literary traditions. Secondly, they also provide a way into the many receptions of Homer which are either not directly lexically-based or use the text in inventive ways. Sometimes formal aspects persist even when the interaction is not primarily lexical. The tensions between formal and non-formal aspects of Homeric reception may provide contrasts not just between different receptions but also sometimes within different aspects of the same work.

To make a start in exploring this challenging area I shall focus on one key area, the practice of repetition. Philosophers such as Deleuze have used the concept of repetition to counter any assumptions that exact replication can ever be possible; repetition is always repetition with a difference.[8] Much has been written by scholars on the importance of cumulative technique in Homer[9] and the directions and tones of the expansiveness that it creates both within the poems and in interactions with listeners and readers. This expansiveness occurs both within the Homeric poems and between the poems and their receptions. For example, in the *Iliad* the image of the reapers, which at 11.67–71 is part of a simile that holds in stark contrast the corn harvest and the mutual destruction of the two armies, is elaborated at 18.550–60 in the scene of harvest plenty on the shield of Achilles. The image of the reapers has echoes in different directions within the poem. Writers responding to Homer can transplant that poetic movement, although they may contextualise it in a different way.[10]

Both within the Homeric poems and in subsequent literature embedded repetition grows into the poetics of difference. Poets such as Derek Mahon have self-reflexively exploited Heraclitus' metaphor of the river, in which it is never possible to step into the same river twice. Not only the river but also the wader is never quite the same.

---

8 Deleuze 1968.
9 Kirk 1985, *passim*.
10 Reynolds 2010, 177.

> *Nobody steps into the same river twice.*
> *The same river is never the same*
> *Because that is the nature of water.*
> *Similarly your changing metabolism*
> *Means that you are no longer you.*
> *[...]*
> *You will tell me that you have executed*
> *A monument more lasting than bronze;*
> *But even bronze is perishable.*
> *Your best poem, you know the one I mean,*
> *The very language in which the poem was written, and the idea of language,*
> *All these things will pass away in time.*
> (Mahon, 'Heraclitus on Rivers' in Mahon 1979, 107)

Mahon's allusion here is to Horace's claim in *Odes* 3.30.1 that '*Exegi monumentum are perennius*' ('I have executed a monument more lasting than bronze', trans. West 2002, 259), but an analogy might equally be made with the notion of *kleos* in Homer, the claim that the reputation of the heroic warriors and their 'good deaths', sung by the poets, will outlive them. One might reply 'yes, but in different ways, in different traditions' and, as Mahon suggests, in a constantly changing poetic.

I want to try to keep the axes of repetition and difference in a creative tension and to trace some examples of how 'repetition with a difference' uses and adapts Homeric formal qualities, with the result that the poetry that emerges helps readers and scholars to experience and to analyze the continual process of dialogue between ancient and modern. In his recent book David Hopkins has called this 'Conversing with Antiquity'. He proposes a reading process which works both backwards and forwards, a process in which reception (and translation) is never a lone encounter between two parties: 'though acts of reception are necessarily made in and by individual minds, those minds are themselves already full of the imaginings, intuitions and emotions of *other* human minds'.[11] My approach is perhaps less gentle, less urbane; it recognizes the sharp edges and the difficulties and disturbances, even the conflicts that may arise from these encounters.

Homeric reception involves a variety of processes: translation, transplantation, re-imagining, rewriting, re-performance. Sometimes these overlap. Often the formal aspects of 'repetition' serve as a metaphor for agencies that transfer poetic energy across time, language and place. As a basis for discussion I have selected four aspects of the Homeric poems and shall briefly mention examples

---

11 Hopkins 2010, 11. Italics original.

of each that bear on the topic of 'repetition'. The four areas are: formal elements; iconic episodes; performance; themes.

a. Formal elements

Formal elements that we have become accustomed to identify with distinctive Homeric poetics include epithets, similes and focalised narrative. Separately and in combination, each of these has an impact in recent literary receptions, shaping readers' perceptions of what is specifically Homeric about the new writing. The aesthetic and cultural power of the new writing both draws on Homer and also remodels Homer. The formal intertextuality becomes a distinctive part of the poetics of the new writer, who is both writing from his or her literary tradition and aiming to create a new dimension to it.

Homeric similes have been drawn into new work in ways that play with perceptions of both the ancient and the modern. For instance in Patrick Kavanagh's 'Epic' (1951), the Irish poet Kavanagh (who was to be an important influence on Seamus Heaney and Michael Longley) transposes into a context of disputes about agricultural land in rural Ireland the simile from *Iliad* 12.421–25, in which there is a stalemate between the two opposing sides. In so doing he draws on the translation by E.V. Rieu that he had recently read: 'they were like two men quarrelling across a fence in the common field with yardsticks in their hands, each of them fighting for his fair share in a narrow strip'.[12]

This is interesting because Kavanagh does not refer to the specific simile nor to the ancient context of the Achaian and Trojan armies. A reader who did not know the *Iliad* (or at least not very well) might miss the repetition.[13] Kavanagh worked from the local to the global. In this case, the global was 'the year of the Munich bother', that is, the events preceding World War II, which were also exercising his mind as he wrote. Only later in the poem does he allude to 'the ghost of Homer' that helped him to see the links between local matters and the world stage. Some of Kavanagh's readers would spot the reversal of the Homeric simile; others would merely have a generalised conception of Homer as a 'poet of war'. In either case, it is the formal movement that is important.

There are many notable examples of the local/global connection being made through the use of short (often very short) Homeric similes in Derek Walcott's

---

[12] Rieu 1950, 232.
[13] See further Hardwick 2011.

Omeros (1990).¹⁴ Such use of similes is part of Walcott's poetic technique, which exploits a variety of classicizing devices, including an ironic *katabasis*.¹⁵ For longer and more expansive similes, we can turn to Michael Longley, who often includes a very close translation as part of his sonnets, into which he interpolates his own specificities of place and linguistic register, drawing on any disjunction that is part of the Homeric simile. An example is his exploitation of the poppy as the image of the death of Gorgythion in 'A Poppy' (2000).¹⁶ In contrast with Kavanagh, the classicist Longley expects his readers to be aware of this. He writes: 'an image Virgil steals …and so do I', thus proclaiming his own status alongside Virgil as a poet energised by Homer (Longley 2006, 255).

However, my argument about the importance of formal elements does not depend just on the examples of transposition of similes. A whole range of framing and detailed devices is involved. In a recent discussion of formalism in Homeric reception, Simon Perris argues that Homeric receptions pointedly use proems and codas to position themselves with respect to genre, theme and literary tradition and that this is a highly charged literary manoeuvre that establishes or rejects a relationship with Homeric epic.¹⁷ Perris' discussion ranges over examples from poetry (Logue and Walcott) to science fiction and the novel. Formal opening and closing devices, as much as similes, position the new works both in relation to Homer and in relation to other works. This suggests that comparison between new works (including between genres) is important in allowing consideration of how they relate to one another, as well as to the Homeric ante-text. Hopkins' concept of 'conversing' has lateral trajectories, as well as diachronic. The triangularity model involved in reading comparative relationships allows close reading and formal analysis to operate without constraining the range of meanings or positioning the ancient text as a closed arbiter of meaning and cultural value.

b. Iconic episodes

These are episodes that 'recur' (sc. are repeated) in many receptions of Homer. They draw on knowledge of the story of the *Iliad* or the *Odyssey*, including stock scenes that are repeated within the poems themselves, and also appeal

---

14 See Hardwick 1997 for discussion of the relationship between Walcott's strategy in *Omeros* 1.1 and the tree-felling simile used in the narrative of the death of Sarpedon in *Iliad* 16.482–85.
15 Hardwick 2002.
16 Discussed in Taplin 2007, 188.
17 Perris 2011.

to a wider audience that may have more generalised perceptions about what sort of poet Homer is. Sometimes the 'repetition with a difference' involves the sequence and arrangement of lines. For example, Michael Longley 'Ceasefire' (1995), which images the supplication scene between Priam and Achilles in *Iliad* 24, moves to the very end of the poem and *after* the meal of reconciliation:

> *I get down on my knees and do what must be done*
> *And kiss Achilles' hand, the killer of my son.*
> (Longley 2006, 225)

Longley's lines thus represent a coda to this variant on the stock scene of supplication rather than a kind of proem and so perhaps bring home to readers what they will have to do in order to live in peace across the sectarian divide at the time of a truce in the north of Ireland.

Recent examples which have taken Homeric repetition with a difference far beyond the circle of classicists have featured the slaughter of the suitors and the hanging of the maids in the *Odyssey*. Michael Longley 'The Butchers' (1991) transposed the slaughter to modern Ireland during 'The Troubles' (Longley 2006, 194). Derek Walcott in *The Odyssey: A Stage Version* (1993) had Penelope prevent the hanging of the maid, probably because Walcott could not stomach the apparent aesthetic validation of a treatment of house slaves that resonated with the history of slavery in the Caribbean. In Walcott, the simile associated with the fluttering of the maids as they hung (*Odyssey* 22.465–72) is transferred to Penelope as an image of her suffering: 'they tried to strangle love…She fluttered. She played dead, but her warm heart still beat'. (Walcott 1993, 158).

The hanging of the maids has come to represent a *topos* in the history of oppression. It underlies the hangings of women in the futuristic fundamentalist patriarchy depicted in Margaret Atwood's *The Handmaid's Tale* (1986) and of the maids in her novella *The Penelopiad* (2005), which was subsequently adapted for the stage and premiered by the Royal Shakespeare Company. The published play text has an image of the maids on the cover (Atwood 2007). In the stage version, the play ends with Penelope's vision of the dead maids who return to haunt her and Odysseus: 'We had no voice/we had no name/we had no choice….we took the blame/it was not fair'. But they resist Penelope's grasp:

> *I hold out my arms to them, my doves, my loveliest ones. But they only run away.*
> *Run isn't quite accurate. Their legs don't move. Their still-twitching feet don't touch the ground.*
> (Atwood, 2007, scene 32, p. 82)

c. Performance

Atwood's staged *Penelopiad* differed in significant respects from the book version that preceded it, notably the arguments presented for and against the hanging of the maids ('The Trial of Odysseus').[18] Performing Homer's performance poetry, rather than reading it on the page, brings together rhapsode, players and audience in ways that are sometimes mediated by expectations about Greek theatre, but which also draw on the interactions that the Homeric poems set up between poem and listeners. In her introductory remarks to the Edinburgh Festival rehearsed readings from her work *Achilles* (Edinburgh Book Festival 2003, 12 August), Elizabeth Cook paid tribute to the actor Greg Hicks because of his experience of classical performance. She said that what made Homer a poet for the present was not just the material shared between antiquity and modernity (fish/spears/shields), but rather the physiology and chemistry of the body, which enabled communication of emotions that enabled moderns to have a rapport with the ancients. These elements were to the fore in Verse Theater Manhattan's 2003 tour of Christopher Logue's 'Account' of the *Iliad*, *War Music* (presented by an all-female cast). I was able to interview the company after their performance in Bristol in March 2003. One actor commented (on Logue's text) that 'it's a very muscular text....there's not a huge thought process between feeling and action. So, I know for myself that the more I could invest in it physically, the better....to understand and really wrap myself around these characters'. She added that 'we had worked with very heavy shields and swords during the fights, so that we learned the weight of these weapons, so *that when we didn't have them we had the physical memory of what it was like to move with that*' (italics added). This placed great demands on the audience because in the actual performance weapons were not used: 'During rehearsal we just had to keep trusting they're going to see what we're going for, without us holding the actual spear'.

Performance poetry, ancient and modern, brings the physical memory of the audience into play. This adds an extra dimension to what Elizabeth Minchin has discussed in her 2007 monograph.[19] (This is a companion work to her *Homer and the Resources of Memory* [2001], which considers the implications of cognitive theory to the Homeric epics.) In her 2007 book Minchin explores the relationship between discourse and memory, which she stresses is multifaceted, including information stored by the senses and also 'world knowledge': that is, information about the physical environment, the social world and the skills needed in those

---

18 See Atwood's comment in Atwood 2007, vii–viii.
19 Minchin 2007.

contexts (Minchin 2007, 9). This, she argues, supports the bard, providing scripts from episodic memory (e.g. on preparing meals, harnessing horses, departing guests). What carries these into the poems are the formal aspects of stylisation and poetic language. One element cues the next and carries into composition. They embrace not only physical acts but also speech acts. Minchin's analysis carries this further and she shows how rhythm, repetition and memory are intertwined in the generation of 'answers' (*op.cit.* 96 ff.). The answers examined by Minchin are mainly those invited in conversation. They involve the respondent taking the words and phrases of the question posed and reusing them in his or her answer (for instance, when Apollo asks Hermes whether he would wish to be in Ares' position in *Od.* 8.335–37). I suggest that this may be a fruitful analogy to use in discussing Homeric receptions. The rewriter responds to the antetext by including the material that has triggered his or her response. And as Minchin points out (*op.cit.* 107), poetic and everyday conversational practices often converge.

d. Themes

The handling of such themes as war and peace in Homeric receptions would require a paper in itself. The assumption that such situations are repeated throughout history enables the themes in Homer to be used as a field for creative interpretation and reflection. War as a theme that links Homer with subsequent human experience and has affinities with theatrical performance in that it requires the bodily co-presence of fighters (military practitioners commonly refer to the area of combat as the 'theatre'). Metaphors and experiences of war are significant activators of the links between the poetry of the *Iliad* and modern readers and listeners. Homeric epic provides experiential parallels and psychological triggers that enable war poetry to communicate across generations, contributing a physical and emotional force to the rhythm, repetition and memory described by Minchin. In her recent study of literary representations of war, from the *Iliad* to Iraq, Kate McLoughlin comments:

> 'The reasons that make war's representation imperative are as multitudinous as those which make it impossible: to impose discursive order on the chaos of conflict.....to keep the record for the self and others (those who were there and can no longer speak for them-

selves and those who were not there and need to be told; to give some meaning to mass death; to memorialise...to provide cathartic relief; to warn; and even, through the warning, to promote peace'.[20]

Multi-faceted aspects of Homeric repetition and reception – formal, performative and thematic—have been brought together in a new poem by Alice Oswald entitled *Memorial* (2011), which Oswald describes as a 'translation of the *Iliad*'s atmosphere, not its story, generated by the *Iliad*'s *enargeia* (which she glosses as 'bright, unbearable reality'). To communicate that *enargeia*, she strips away Homeric narrative to reveal a poem made of similes and short biographies of soldiers, which she thinks derive from the Greek tradition of lament poetry. So her poem presents a 'kind of oral cemetery', an attempt to remember people's names and lives. She paraphrases the biographies but translates the similes. Each is repeated as if in a lament, (with a sometimes incantatory effect) and is also transposed away from its place in Homer's poem, a kind of *parataxis*. She wrote: 'I use them as openings to see what Homer was looking at' (Oswald 2011, 2). The transpositions add to the memorial a lament for those whose names were only recorded in Homer with little or no comment. They are in some ways subversive of the stress on iconic episodes that is found in so many receptions of Homer. So here there is repetition with a difference to make a new poem, but it is a repetition that also draws on the structures in the Homeric poem itself.

Oswald's text starts with a list of names of those killed in the *Iliad*. The names take up seven and a half pages. They are not in alphabetical order, as on most memorials, but in the order of their passing. So the poem begins prosaically: 'The first to die was Protesilaus' (*op.cit.* 13). The descriptions of the men and their deaths use material that is in Homer, but they are interwoven with similes taken from different parts of the poem. Unlike Logue, who uses different names so that there is a disjunction from Homer that can disorientate the reader, Oswald retains the names but expands on their deaths by associating them with the refrains provided by similes that are repeated. In the Catalogue of Ships in the second book of the *Iliad*, Protesilaus is introduced as the first leader to die (2.695–702); there is an allusion to his widow who tears her cheeks with grief, and then the focus returns to his successor as leader. Oswald reworks this: 'His wife rushed out clawing her face' and 'Podarcus his altogether less impressive brother/Took over command, but that was long ago./He's been in the black earth now for thousands of years'. Time is rewritten both forwards and backwards. Then a nine-line simile is repeated twice to give Protesilaus the memorial that he does not achieve in Homer:

---

[20] McLoughlin 2011, 7.

> *Like a wind-murmur*
> *Begins a rumour of waves*
> *One long note getting louder*
> *The water breathes a deep sigh*
> *Like a land – ripple*
> *When the west wind runs through a field*
> *Wishing and Searching*
> *Nothing to be found*
> *The corn stalks shake their green heads.*
> (Oswald 2011, 14)

There are echoes of the simile at *Iliad* 2.144–52, when the assembly of Greeks loses heart and begins to leave for home but there is also a foreshadowing of Glaukos' simile of the leaves, at *Iliad* 6.146–51, in which he likens the generations of humanity to those of the leaves, which are scattered by the wind, but the trees from which they are shaken produce new leaves in the next season. Oswald holds the two similes in tension by the use of the phrase 'shake their green heads' for the corn-stalks that can provide no comfort but nevertheless image the promise of new life. In Homer, the formulaic epithet applied to the grain-giving field in 2.548 (ζείδωρος ἄρουρα) is associated with Erechtheus and autochthony. Oswald takes up the sequence of associations in the next section, which refers to Echepolus, 'known for his cold seed-like concentration', and to Elephenor who dies trying to reclaim his corpse. In contrast with Homer, in Oswald both attract a short simile in lament, again repeated:

> *Like leaves*
> *Sometimes they light their green flames*
> *And are fed by the earth*
> *And sometimes it snuffs them out.*
> (*op.cit.* 15)

The shaking heads of the corn stalks of the previous simile are given a greater ambivalence by juxtaposition with the one that follows it in Oswald.

I hope I have shown that 'repetition' in its various guises also involves movement and difference. At its most effective, it is also developmental. The formal structures in Homer and their transplantation into a new work provide ways of marking and responding to 'time tensions'[21], as well as bringing the repressed to the fore. The most influential aspects of Homeric epic, such as iconic episodes, themes and the poetics of performance need to be considered through the formal structures and practices that transmit and embed them. I suggest that examina-

---

21 I borrow the insight from Taplin 2007, 177.

tion of repetition and difference, both formal and narrative, yields significant insights into how the Homeric poems are subsequently conceived and reconceived. If I am right in my claims that the study of the migration of iconic episodes and themes in Homer necessarily involves formal elements, then the relationship between the textual study of the Homeric poems and the 'idea of Homer' that persists in the popular imagination (e. g. Homer as a poet of war) also becomes part of a lateral conversation, rather than a polarity. This is exemplified in Oswald's poem. There is surely rich work to be done to trace the propensities that different formal elements take with them when they are repeated and varied in new contexts.

Finally, I would like to comment briefly on the issues raised for the 'ethics of reception', a strand of debate in contemporary studies that has particular implications for the status and interpretation of the Homeric poems and the receptions that they have inspired. A recent article by the translation studies scholar Lawrence Venuti was called 'The Poet's Version; or, An ethics of translation'.[22] In this article Venuti revisited some of his early work on 'domesticating' and 'foreignising' models for translation. He argues that 'the poet's version' is a second-order creation that mixes translation and adaptation and that this is a twentieth-century phenomenon that is distinct from early modern notions of 'imitation'. Part of his argument is about the critical impact of creative reworkings on the receiving culture, a relationship that he addresses in terms of ethics. He complains that 'the poets who practise it have not always been forthright about what they have done'.[23] There are several things wrong with this statement. For a start, poets do what poets will do. Practising the art of poetry does not necessarily require the provision of a commentary on their work (despite the usefulness of such metapoetical material as authorial prefaces or the extensive interviews given by poets such as Seamus Heaney and Derek Walcott). However, my main disagreement with Venuti is that in the case of rewritings of Homer the commentary is in the poetry. A 'commentary' is actually often implicitly contained in the new text, in the formal arrangements chosen by the new writer. These are not a mystery, closed to those (including the new writer) who may not know Homeric Greek, but are transparent both on the page and on the stage. They at minimum provide the raw material for comparisons and at maximum introduce an element of self-reflexivity.

Thus, attention to the formal aspects of the relationship between the ante-text, the new text and the mediating texts both implies respect for the aesthetics

---

22 Venuti 2011.
23 Venuti 2011, 230.

of each of the contributions (recognizing the fluidity of recombinations in all the literary traditions that are involved) and as a result enables comparisons within and between texts. Adaptations of form both signal relationships and complicate them, whether the exchanges take place in conversational mode (as Hopkins terms it) or in challenging mode (as Logue practises it and as Oswald explores). Much is talked about the 'new philology' that classical reception research requires. I think it is important that formal analysis and comparison is part of the scrutiny, not solely of literary receptions but also of those that explore other genres. Such investigations imply greater collaboration between reception scholars and specialists in other areas of Classics. The Corfu conference offered us a range of examples and approaches and as we heard about them in the various panels, we experienced a central strand of Homeric poetics and its receptions – repetition, with a difference.[24]

---

[24] I would like to thank the organisers for devising this conference and I am grateful to the Ionian University for its warm welcome and hospitality to visitors from overseas in November 2011. It was an honour and a delight to be in the company of such a gathering of Homer scholars.

Part II: **Homer In Archaic Ideology**

Margarita Alexandrou
Hipponax and the *Odyssey*: Subverting Text and Intertext*

Reception of a text can take multiple forms: citation, imitation, opposition, remodelling, parody. Of all these modes, parody is both the most indicative of authority of the target text and the most interesting play with poetic authority, being arguably the most metapoetic of all literary devices. The 'subversive' reception of the Homeric *Odyssey* by the sixth-century BC iambic poet Hipponax is one such case of a play with poetic authority that has already been explored as parody[1] (on parodic treatments of Odysseus in later periods of time, see Petrakou in this volume).

My aim in this paper is to investigate the engagement of Hipponax with Homer and to revisit the subtle intra-textual and inter-textual dynamics between the receiving and the source texts and their respective genres, *iambos* and *epos*. I hope to show that the *Odyssey* is firmly embedded in the conceptualization of Hipponax's own *iambos*; that the *epos* is there not only as a hypotext[2] of parodic allusion, but as an intertext that is employed particularly at moments where the poetic agenda is articulated. In order to deconstruct and analyze the complexity of Hipponax's reception of the source text, I shall first examine briefly some notable features of his poetry that single him out amongst archaic poets.

Hipponax represents the latest and in a sense most distilled phase of archaic *iambos*. Geographically and chronologically distant from the older exponents of the genre Archilochus and Semonides, Hipponax distances himself from the mainstream *iambos* in many respects by narrowing down its scope and taking some of

---

* I am indebted to Professor Chris Carey for his insightful comments on this paper.
1 For parody in Hipponax, see Degani 1984, 187–205; Pòrtulas 1985; Miralles and Pòrtulas 1988, 77–83; Rosen 1990; Carey 2009, 163–164. Parody is a multifarious phenomenon, therefore a useful but perhaps limited term for the complex intertextual and intergeneric engagement at play in Hipponax. My aim here is not to deny the importance of parody in Hipponax, but to shed some further light on its presence and role. The complex nature of Hipponax's parody fits recent accounts that see parody of one text as revealing of the hypertext's own fictional practices and therefore acting as meta-fiction. On parody as literary criticism, see Dentith 2000, and on parody as metafiction, see Rose 1979 and 1993.
2 Genette (1982) coins the term to indicate the text upon which the secondary work is modelled (the secondary text itself is called hypertext). The intertextual relationship of the hypertext to the hypotext is not necessarily parodic.

its features to extremes.³ Through his poetry Hipponax creates a fictional or semi-fictional world, a very narrow, low and circumscribed world, within which he situates himself and other low characters. This world is one dominated by ugly people, burglars, beggars and gluttons, and humorous episodes of sexual and scatological activity of a farcical and grotesque nature. Recurrent characters and situations across his poems create a sense of coherence: a character named Bupalus is regularly vilified as an enemy, and Arete, another recurring figure, appears to be a woman of sexual license;⁴ even a character named Hipponax regularly figures as a brawler, burglar, beggar or sexual predator, sometimes impotent, involved in all kinds of humiliating activities.⁵ The Hipponactean narrator (implicitly distinct from the Hipponax character) is also an outsider and situates himself among the dregs.⁶

Hipponax's love for ugliness, marginality and grotesquery is also reflected in both diction and form: his linguistic register achieves a degree of crudity which outstrips his predecessors, and the Ionic dialect used contains Lydian and other foreign elements.⁷ His invective is distinctive in the lack of any wider element of reflection or justification for his attacks, and Hipponax constitutes a new and 'uglier' turn for *iambos* even in his use of metre. He uses the choliambic/scazon metre (an iambic metre which ends in a spondee rather than an *iambos*), a 'lame' metre, as its name suggests, whose ending creates a rhythmically limping effect, compatible with the 'ugly' and unorthodox character of Hipponax's poems.

As I shall argue, the extent to which Hipponax uses 'ugliness'⁸ (in language, theme, metre, social register, construction of the poetic *persona*), and the way in which the Homeric intertext is introduced in this world creates more than just a difference within the standard generic range already offered by the 'less elevated' iambic agenda. Hipponax's use of ugliness is embedded in a larger (meta)poetic strat-

---

3 General important studies on Hipponax's iambography are West 1974, 22–39 and 140–9; Degani 1984 and 2007; Miralles-Pòrtulas 1988; Brown 1997, 79–88; Carey 2008, 89–102. For general recent discussions of *iambos* see Bartol 1993; Carey 2009; Kantzios 2005; Rotstein 2010.
4 The name Bupalus occurs in the corpus eleven times: frr. 1 W., 12.2 W., 15 W., 84.18 W., 95.3 W., 95.4 W., 95.15 W., 95a W., 120 W. (also perhaps in frr. 77.4 W., 79.12 W., though the text is very uncertain); the name Arete four: frr. 12.2 W., 14.2 W., 16.1 W., 17.1 W. Another female character, Cypso, with the name perhaps being an obscene distortion of the name Calypso, seems to appear twice in the corpus in frr. 129 W. and 77.1 W. (in the second instance the text is uncertain).
5 See frr. 78 W. and 92 W.
6 On the distinctiveness of the Hipponactean narrator, see Morrison 2007, mainly 285–86. See also Carey 2008, 97–99.
7 On Hipponactean language, see most recently Hawkins 2013.
8 By 'ugliness' I mean the marked deviation from social, physical, aesthetic, poetic, moral ideals and norms, which invites the alienation of the reader/audience.

egy, which uses intertextual dynamics to make an implicit statement about early Greek poetic genres and achieves, as we shall see below, complex effects in terms of characterization of the primary narrator and the received text.

A selection of a number of Hipponactean fragments can illustrate the constant multilayered engagement with the *Odyssey*. Whereas at first glance they appear to present lowlife accounts of frauds, sexual encounters, fights or drinking events, they all seem, however, to be bringing the *Odyssey* to the foreground in a number of ways.[9]

Hipponax uses the *Odyssey* primarily to outline the profile of the iambist/ narrator himself, as it is evident in the following hymnic style poems:

Ἑρμῆ, φίλ' Ἑρμῆ, Μαιαδεῦ, Κυλλήνιε,
ἐπεύχομαί τοι, κάρτα γὰρ κακῶς ῥιγῶ
καὶ βαμβαλύζω ...
δὸς χλαῖναν Ἱππώνακτι καὶ κυπασσίσκον
καὶ σαμβαλίσκα κἀσκερίσκα καὶ χρυσοῦ
στατῆρας ἑξήκοντα τοὐτέρου τοίχου. (fr. 32 W.)[10]

Hermes, dear Hermes, son of Maia, Cyllenian,
I pray to you, for I am shivering violently and terribly
and my teeth are chattering...
Give Hipponax a cloak, tunic, sandals, felt shoes
and sixty gold staters on the other side.

ἐμοὶ γὰρ οὐκ ἔδωκας οὔτέ κω χλαῖναν
δασεῖαν ἐν χειμῶνι φάρμακον ῥίγ<εο>ς,
οὔτ' ἀσκέρῃσι τοὺς πόδας δασείῃσι
ἔκρυψας, ὥς μοι μὴ χίμετλα ῥήγνυται. (fr. 34 W.)

For you haven't yet given me a thick cloak
as a remedy against the cold in winter
nor have you covered my feet with thick felt shoes,
so that my chilblains not burst.

The speaker here claims to be operating from a state of great poverty and makes a number of bold requests to Hermes. The distinctive tone resides both in the ironic irreverence of the narrator and also the intimate relationship that is implied to exist between the narrator and god Hermes, reminiscent of Odysseus' re-

---

[9] By that time, the Homeric epics must have already been the most recognizable Greek cultural artefacts. The poet could therefore rely on his audience to engage in the triangular process necessary for successful intertextuality.
[10] All Hipponactean fragments are quoted according to West *IEG*² 1989–92; translations are from Gerber 1999 with minor adjustments.

lationship with his divine patron Athena (and occasionally Hermes; see also below the discussion of fr. 79 W.). Moreover, the request for a cloak especially enhances identification with Odysseus and simultaneously leads to an undercutting of the iambist by recalling *Od*. 16.78–85,[11] where Telemachus at Eumaeus' place promises to give a cloak, sandals and food to Odysseus. In the requests of the irreverent narrator in the Hipponactean fragments lurks no less irony than in the episode with the disguised king Odysseus in *Odyssey* 16.

Another instance of identification of the Hipponactean narrator with Odysseus occurs in fr. 73 W. with the narrator being involved in a boxing match, which is described in graphic detail and recalls strongly Odysseus' boxing match with Irus in the *Odyssey*.[12]

ὤ]μειξε δ|᾽ αἷμα καὶ χολὴν ἐτίλησεν·
ἐγὼ δεγ[   ]οί δέ μ<εο ὀ>δόντες
ἐν ταῖς γ|νάθοισι πάντες <ἐκ>κεκιν<έα>ται. (fr. 73 W.)

...he pissed blood and shat bile;
but I... and all the teeth
in my jaws have been dislodged...

A Hipponax character, distinct from the Hipponactean narrator, is often involved in low narratives and is also modelled on the figure of Odysseus. We are better served in this respect by fr. 79 W., which preserves a more substantial narrative. Here, the Hipponax character is assimilated to Odysseus again by evoking recognizable incidents from the *Odyssey*:

ἀ]λοιᾶσθα[ι
τῆς] ἀνοίης ταύτη[ς
τὴ]ν γνάθον παρα.[
    ]ι κηρίνους ἐποι[5
]κἀνετίλησε[
]χρυσολαμπέτωι ῥάβδωι
]αν ἐγγὺς ἑρμῖνος·
Ἑρμῆς δ᾽ ἐς Ἱππών]ακτος ἀκολουθήσας
το]ῦ κυνὸς τὸν φιλήτην   10
]ὡς ἔχιδνα συρίζει
]αξ δὲ νυκτὶ βου[...(.)].[
]καὶ κατεφράσθη[

---

11 *Od*. 16.78–81: ἀλλ᾽ ἦ τοι τὸν ξεῖνον, ἐπεὶ τεὸν ἵκετο δῶμα,/ ἕσσω μιν χλαῖνάν τε χιτῶνά τε εἵματα καλά,/ δώσω δὲ ξίφος ἄμφηκες καὶ ποσσὶ πέδιλα,/ πέμψω δ᾽, ὅππη μιν κραδίη θυμός τε κελεύει.
12 *Od*. 18.28: κόπτων ἀμφοτέρῃσι χαμαί, δέ κε πάντας ὀδόντας/ γναθμῶν ἐξελάσαιμι. For a discussion of the relation between Hipponax and the Homeric Odysseus, see Rosen 1990.

]δευς κατεσκη.[
ἐμερ]μήριξε· τῶι δὲ κ[η]λητ[ῆι   15
]ς παῦνι, μυῖαν .[
ὁ δ' αὐτίκ' ἐλθ]ὼν σὺν τριοῖσι μ[άρτυσιν
ὅκου τὸν ἔρπιν ὁ σκότος καπηλεύει,
ἄνθρωπον εὗρε τὴν στέγην ὀφέλλοντα –
οὐ γὰρ παρῆν ὄφελμα – πυθμένι στοιβῆς.   20

... to be cudgelled...
... of this foolishness...
...(striking?) his jaw...
...made of wax...
...and he shat upon...
...staff gleaming with gold...
...near the bed post,
And Hermes providing an escort to the house of Hipponax
...the dog-stealer... ...hisses like a viper...
...(Hipponax deliberating?) at night...
...and devised...
...
...pondered; and to the charmer...
...small(?), (like?) a fly...
With three witnesses he went at once
to the place where the swindler sells wine
and found a fellow sweeping the room
with a stock of thorn, since no broom was at hand.

This obscure and quite complicated narrative is typically Hipponactean in style, in that it is broadly realistic, vivid and racy, concerning probably an act of theft, in which a number of characters are involved (Hermes and the Hipponax character at l. 9, the recurring Bupalus perhaps at l. 12 and three witnesses at l. 17). Hermes' intervention betrays that the narrative is more than just a story about lowlifes and invites us to notice the interaction with *epos* and see this as a parallel to Athena's divine patronage to Odysseus.[13] Hipponax seems to act as the hero of his own narrative with his own divine patron and is simultaneously also a lowlife trickster: this presentation has a bearing on Odysseus.[14] One recalls also specifically *Od.* 10.275–301, where the disguised Odysseus meets Hermes on his way to Circe, and the god gives him the potion that will later protect him from her.

---

[13] See Carey 2009, 164.
[14] On Odysseus as the archetypal trickster, see, for instance, Pucci 1987.

Moreover, Hipponax 'populates' his poetry with 'Odyssean' characters (Arete, Cypso).¹⁵ Their presence and the very fact that they are taken from the fairytale world of Odysseus' adventures described in the *Odyssey* is in marked contrast to the arguably different kind of ugly fairytale world suggested by the Hipponactean contexts.

Frr. 13 and 14 W., which probably formed parts of a single poem, present a drinking party of people of the low orders (notice that they they are drinking wine from a milk pail). Arete is presiding over this party, so the scene parodically recalls the Phaeacian Arete's presence and presiding role in Alcinous' palace in *Od.* 7.53 ff.

ἐκ πελλίδος πίνοντες· οὐ γὰρ ἦν αὐτῆι
κύλιξ, ὁ παῖς γὰρ ἐμπεσὼν κατήραξε (fr. 13 W.)

drinking from a pail;
for she had no cup, since the slave had fallen on it
and smashed it

ἐκ δὲ τῆς πέλλης
ἔπινον· ἄλλοτ' αὐτός, ἄλλοτ' Ἀρήτη
προύπινεν. (fr. 14 W.)

they were drinking from the pail; now
he and now Arete were drinking a toast.

Less straightforward in its Odyssean overtones is fr. 12 W., in which the recurring figures of Bupalus and Arete seem to be involved in what looks to be an act of theft or fraud.¹⁶ Apart from Arete here being set in yet another lowlife story, parody is enhanced on another level. Despite the low content, we have use of high style language (Ἐρυθραίων παῖδας, δυσώνυμον; cf. e.g. *Il* .6.255: δυσώνυμοι υἷες Ἀχαιῶν), which creates this mock stylistic effect typical of Hipponax.¹⁷ Here (at least in the remnants of this poem), one steps back from very specific engagement with Odysseus to a more pervasive sort of epic feel.

τούτοισι θηπ<έω>ν τοὺς Ἐρυθραίων παῖδας
ὁ μητροκοίτης Βούπαλος σὺν Ἀρήτηι
†καὶ ὑφέλξων τὸν δυσώνυμον †ἄρτον. (fr. 12 W.)

---

15 See above, n. 4.
16 The majority of scholars read this passage as an erotic one: see Masson 1962, *ad loc.;* Degani 2007, *ad loc;* Rosen 1990. However, for reasons that are beyond the scope of this paper I take it as a narrative of an act of theft.
17 We sporadically find other mock epic diction in the Hipponactean corpus, e.g. fr. 3a W., fr.32 W. and 38 W., 35 W. and 39 W. (which are specifically parodying the hymnic form); see also fr. 128 W. and fr. 129 W.

Bupalus, the mother-fucker with Arete,
fooling with these words (by these means?) the Erythraeans,
preparing to draw back the damnable loaf.

Apart from fleeting/subtle evocations of the *Odyssey* in the scazon poems, there is some scanty evidence that Hipponax may have composed more substantial mock-epic narratives, as suggested in frr. 74–77 W.:

   οδυ[.
    .[
   ω[
    .[(fr. 74 W.)

...Odysseus?....

×– ∪]ωλῆν.[
×– ∪].ζων φυκι[
×–]αν αὐτὸν ὅστις ε[
×–]ἐπεὶ τὸν ψωμὸ[ν
  ]ερεῦσι τὴν γενὴ[ν   (fr. 75 W.)

...
...seaweed/razor-fish?...
...him who...
...since/when the nibbles...
...they ask questions about his/my family...

×– ∪–]υψου.[
×– ∪ (–)].αιηκασ[
×– ∪]επλοωσεν[
×]ασιος ὥσπερ βου[
  ]υτο φρενώλης τ[5
×]θεν διδάξων γ[
×–]ο κορσιππ[
×– ∪]λυκρον κ[
×– ∪]εκτησ[
×–]ενειδα[10
 ×– ∪]αλλα· τ[(fr. 77 W.)

...(C)ypso (?)...
...(Ph)aeacians(?)...
...
...like (Bupalus?)...
...frenzied...
...(came?) to predict?...
...lotus root...

Although the condition of these fragments is desperate, they seem to have constituted (on grounds of content and position on the papyrus) either a single poem or adjacent poems as parts of a single Odyssean narrative sequence. Hipponax seems to mainly draw again his refashioned material specifically from the Phaeacian rhapsodies of the *Odyssey*.[18] A number of narrative details would fit a distorted version of Odysseus' adventures related in a very condensed manner: references to seaweed (fr. 75.2 W.), to the Phaeacians asking questions about family (fr. 75.5 W.) and τὸν ψωμό[ν ('morsel' or 'nibbles' in fr. 75.4 W.) may point either to the Cyclops incident (linguistically) or, more likely, to a distorted allusion to the Phaeacian dinner of Odysseus.[19]

The transformation of the Homeric episode seems substantial: firstly, there is perhaps admixture with other contemporary themes and characters (perhaps a reference to Bupalus in fr. 77.4 W.). Secondly, the poem would appear to be quite long for the Hipponactean standards, though still much shorter than the epic. Thirdly, it may have moved quite rapidly between incidents, which would make it visibly different from epic, and may have also displayed some of the changes of scene and pace that we find elsewhere in Hipponax.[20]

The third person singular narrative raises important questions regarding the narrator; either the regular Hipponactean narrator tells the story of an Odysseus as an extra-diegetic narrator, or even Odysseus himself assumes the role of the narrator as in the *Odyssey* and narrates a distorted version of his well-known adventures. This in turn makes one wonder if Odysseus here was modelled on the character of Hipponax (as Hipponax is elsewhere modelled on Odysseus).

The most crucial indication of an Odyssean narrative is that fr. 74 W. preserves what seems to be a title relating to Odysseus or *Odyssey* (οδυ[), most likely the only Hipponactean title preserved in the whole of the corpus. It may be that the distinctive Odyssean/ mythical content of this poem justified the attribution of a title as well as its scale. In fact, if frr. 74–77 W. belonged to a first person narrative entitled Ὀδυσσεύς, we are probably indeed before a little mock mini-epic.[21] The mock-epic content of this set of fragments and the title could even point to a type of perform-

---

[18] See Rosen 2007, 117–72, who regards Odysseus as figuring as a satirist already in Homer and then becoming a favourite iambic and comic theme.
[19] The occurrence of διδάξων (fr. 77.6 W.) suggests that we may even have a reference to a prophecy.
[20] Perhaps the pronounced narrative element of *iambos* in comparison to the rest of lyric, acknowledged by Bowie 2001, 1–27, allowed Hipponax to elaborate in this kind of reception of the epic, as the narrative element is a distinctive feature of the *epos* as well, and may have enabled the Hipponactean narrator to align or contrast himself with the Homeric one.
[21] Of course, it may also be that Hipponax's predilection for the *Odyssey* reflects the penchant of the author and of his generic agenda for mythological narratives in general. For a more detailed discussion of this set of fragments along with another set of Hipponactean fragments (frr. 102–103 W.) that seem to relate mythical narrative, see Alexandrou 2016.

ance different from that of the rest of the Hipponactean material, perhaps festive rather than sympotic, something which has a bearing on the implications of the narrative style and intertext.[22]

Parodic transformation of the Homeric model by Hipponax takes also another form. It accommodates the hexameter and Homeric formulae. Fr. 128 W. constitutes a satire of the grandiose Homeric metre used to satirize the exceeding appetite of a voracious glutton, but also constitutes a very concentrated parody of the beginning lines of the *Odyssey*:[23]

Μοῦσά μοι Εὐρυμεδοντιάδ<εα> τὴν ποντοχάρυβδιν,
τὴν ἐν γαστρὶ μάχαιραν, ὃς ἐσθίει οὐ κατὰ κόσμον,
ἔννεφ', ὅπως ψηφῖδι < > κακὸν οἶτον ὀλεῖται
βουλῆι δημοσίηι παρὰ θῖν' ἁλὸς ἀτρυγέτοιο.   (fr. 128 W.)

Tell me, Muse, of the sea swallowing,
the stomach carving of Eurymedontiades who eats in no orderly manner,
so that through a baneful vote determined by the people
he may die a wretched death along the shore of the undraining (?) sea.

Hipponax, however, departs from Homer's word-order to enhance the parodic effect and parades a number of Homeric/epic motifs: the invocation to the Muse, the interposition of the first person, the request to sing, the epic dialectal forms, the long compound Homeric style words in appropriate metrical positions, the use of Homeric formulae and allusion to Charybdis.[24] It may be that hexametrical parody was a significant strand in the corpus which is unfortunately lost to us.[25]

In frr. 72 W. and 16 W. we seem to digress from the *Odyssey* and have a reference to the famous Rhesus story of *Iliad* 10:

ἐπ' |ἁρμάτων τε καὶ Θρεϊκίων πώλων
λε|υκῶν †οείους κατεγγυς† Ἰλίου πύργων
ἀπ|ηναρίσθη Ῥῆσος, Αἰνειῶν πάλμυς   (fr. 72.5–7 W.)

---

[22] There is much dispute in scholarship about the performance of Hipponactean poetry. I incline to the view that much of the material is sympotic and that public performance was possible only for part of the corpus. For the different views on Hipponactean performance, see West *OCD*⁴ s.v. 'iambic poetry, Greek' (for festive performance) and Bowie 2001 (for sympotic performance).
[23] Fr. 129 W. mentioning Cypso scans in hexameter and enhances the possibility that there may have been more poems written in hexameters designed to be parodies of the *epos*, as in the case of fr. 128 W., or poems with a mixture of rhythms.
[24] For comic parody of the epic invocation, see also Archil. fr. 117 W.: τὸν κεροπλάστην ἄειδε Γλαῦκον.
[25] See below the testimonium of Athenaeus 15.698b.

> (while sleeping near?) the towers of
> Ilium by his chariot and white Thracian foals,
> Rhesus, sultan of the Aeneians,
> was despoiled of them...

> ἐγὼ δὲ δεξιῶι παρ' Ἀρήτην
> κνεφαῖος ἐλθὼν 'ρωιδιῶι κατηυλίσθην. (fr. 16 W.)

> with a heron on the right I went to Arete
> in the dark and took up lodging.

However, the two clear references of Hipponax to the *Iliad* come from the *Doloneia* and take us back to the Odysseus territory again and his famous *dolos* against Rhesus. This could imply that Hipponax's interest may have been Odysseus (including Iliadic references to him) and not exclusively or predominantly the *Odyssey*, and that the accident of the tradition may have distorted our perspective.[26]

In fr. 16 W. Hipponax draws on the portent and prodigies of Homeric narrative (*Il.* 10.274 ff.) and the military language more generally, in a predictably erotic content. The reference to the heron takes us firmly to the *Doloneia* again.[27]

Lastly, Homeric echoes are also present in the more serious strand of Hipponax's corpus. If the highly disputed with reference to their authorship Strasbourg epodes were actually composed by Hipponax, as I take them, then they would further attest to his reception of Homeric language and imagery in compositions that conform to the lyric composed for the aristocratic *hetereia*.[28] More specifically, in fr. 115 W. the figure of Odysseus seems once again to be the main intertext: the poem anticipates a fateful castaway end for an enemy drawing on the archetypal castaway and recalling also Homeric linguistic, syntactical and stylistic elements.

> κύμ[ατι] πλα[ζόμ]ενος·
> κἀν Σαλμυδ[ησσ]ῶι γυμνὸν εὐφρονε.[5
> Θρήϊκες ἀκρό[κ]ομοι
> λάβοιεν – ἔνθα πόλλ' ἀναπλῆσαι κακὰ
> δούλιον ἄρτον ἔδων –
> ῥίγει πεπηγότ' αὐτόν· ἐκ δὲ τοῦ χνόου
> φυκία πόλλ' ἐπέχοι, 10

---

[26] It is certainly reasonable to suppose that this reference to the *Iliad* was not isolated; see Steiner 2008, 89 ff., who has argued that Hipponax seems to have drawn his diction and imagery from the *Iliad* also in the case of fr. 92 W.
[27] See the discussion of Pòrtulas 1988.
[28] On this, see most recently the thorough discussions of Nicolosi 2007 and Carey 2009, 166–67, who take the Strasbourg Epodes as Hipponactean.

κροτ<έοι> δ' ὀδόντας, ὡς [κ]ὐων ἐπὶ στόμα
  κείμενος ἀκρασίηι
ἄκρον παρὰ ῥηγμῖνα κυμα....δọụ·
ταῦτ' ἐθέλοιμ' ἂν ἰδεῖν,
ὅς μ' ἠδίκησε, λ[ὰ]ξ δ' ἐπ' ὁρκίοις ἔβη,   15
τὸ πρὶν ἑταῖρος [ἐ]ών. (fr. 115.4–16 W.)

...drifting about on the wave.
And at Salmydessus may the top-knotted
Thracians give him naked
a most kindly reception- there he will have full measure of a multitude of woes,
eating the bread of slaves-
stiff from cold. As he comes out from the foam
may he vomit much seaweed
and may his teeth chatter while he lies on his face like a dog
at the edge of the surf,
his strength spent...
This is what I'd like him to experience,
who treated me unjustly by trampling on his oaths,
he who was formerly my friend.

Despite the scantily preserved Hipponactean corpus, it is possible to distinguish a number of different strands: long narratives of the narrator's demi-monde activities, poems imitating the hymnic style, long mythological narratives, as well as hexametric ones, and perhaps even more mainstream lyric compositions; in all of them strikingly there lurks the *Odyssey* and the figure of Odysseus.

What Hipponax's interaction with *epos* creates is then quite remarkable. We are before a two-directional receptive process, which is revealed and conveyed by setting up contrasting worlds. Hipponax's engagement with *epos* has an impact on our perception both of the speaker and of the narratives (as more than just lowlife stories) and also functions as commentary on the *Odyssey/epos*, since it sheds light on elements of the *Odyssey* that are only implicit in the *epos* (for reception as 'commentary' on the source text, see Hardwick in this volume). On such a reading Hipponax's love for 'ugliness' goes beyond a simple selection within the range of opportunities offered by the iambic genre. We note a tendency to subvert epic by means of substituting ugliness, cowardice and low status for all that is implicit in the very notion of the heroic epic. We also note the fundamental ambiguity which underlies this engagement, in that the appeal to epic simultaneously underlines the antinomian character, world and storyline of the Hipponactean narrator. The intertextual play thus creates a text which is subversion in both directions: it serves both to undermine epic and also to undercut the authority of the third-person narrator. Just as the epic looks slightly preposterous in the way in which it is brought into a new context, the speaker himself is placed under question, as he presents himself as a trickster and a low-life, being able, however, to compose most sophisticated allusive fiction and blur two poetic traditions. This complex two-directional effect generates an unusually rich and demanding intertextuality, which in turn raises interesting questions about audience and context of the Hipponactean poetry.

It therefore emerges that the reception of the Homeric *epos* by Hipponax amounts to (among other things) an exercise in poetics. The increased level both of fictionality and appropriation of, and interplay with, earlier poetry gives his work a pronounced metapoetic dimension as well—an aspect which has received only limited attention from recent scholarship mostly focusing on the pervasive presence of parody of the Homeric *epos*.[29]

This sense of Hipponax's unusual poetic stance and the pervasive presence of parody is reflected also in the tradition which credits him with its invention (Ath. 15.698b);[30] though the claim of the invention is suspect, the point about parody remains suggestive for the way Hipponax was read in later ages:

> Πολέμων δ' ἐν τῷ δωδεκάτῳ τῶν πρὸς Τίμαιον περὶ τῶν τὰς παρῳδίας γεγραφότων ἱστορῶν τάδε γράφει· 'καὶ τὸν Βοιωτὸν δὲ καὶ τὸν Εὔβοιον τοὺς τὰς παρῳδίας γράψαντας λογίους ἂν φήσαιμι διὰ τὸ παίζειν ἀμφιδεξίως καὶ τῶν προγενεστέρων ποιητῶν ὑπερέχειν ἐπιγεγονότας. εὑρετὴν μὲν οὖν τοῦ γένους Ἱππώνακτα φατέον τὸν ἰαμβοποιόν. λέγει γὰρ οὗτος ἐν τοῖς ἑξαμέτροις.
>
> Polemon inquiring into the composers of parody, writes as follows in the twelfth book of his 'Address to Timaeus': 'I should say that both Boeotus and Euboeus who composed parodies are skilled in words because they play with double meanings and, although born later, outstrip the poets who preceded them. It must be said however, that the iambic poet Hipponax was the founder of the genre. For he speaks as follows in hexameters.

The importance of the *Odyssey* in Hipponax's work may actually have been more profound than the Hipponactean fragments allow us to evaluate, as revealed by the fact that it seems to have been built into what was probably Hipponax's poetic initiation scene. According to an anecdote by Choeroboscus, in one of his poems Hipponax relates a meeting of him with an old woman named Iambe, who is washing wool by the shore.[31]

---

29 For parody as metafiction, see references in n. 1.
30 Aristotle in *Poet.* 1448a 12, contrary to the above testimonium, calls Hegemon of Thasos the inventor of parody, but by this he probably means that Hegemon made parody a profession. See Gerber 1999, 459, n. 4.
31 For discussion of this anecdote see Rosen 1988b; Brown 1988, 478–81; Brown 1997, 83–84 and Fowler 1990 who adds to the line quoted by Choeroboscus two more lines found in a

εἴρηται (scil. ἴαμβος) ἤτοι ἀπὸ Ἰάμβης τῆς Κελεοῦ θεραπαίνης, ἥτις τὴν Δήμητρα λυπουμένην ἠνάγκασε γελάσαι γέλοιόν τι εἰποῦσα, τῷ ῥυθμῷ τούτου τοῦ ποδὸς αὐτομάτως χρησαμένη. ἢ ἀπὸ Ἰάμβης τινὸς ἑτέρας, γραός, ᾗ Ἱππῶναξ ὁ ἰαμβοποιὸς παρὰ θάλασσαν ἔρια πλυνούσῃ συντυχὼν ἤκουσε τῆς σκάφης ἐφαψάμενος, ἐφ' ἧς ἔπλυνεν ἡ γραῦς,
    ἄνθρωπ', ἄπελθε, τὴν σκάφην ἀνατρέπεις.
καὶ συλλαβὼν τὸ ῥηθὲν οὕτως ὠνόμασε τὸ μέτρον. ἄλλοι δὲ περὶ τοῦ χωλιάμβου τὴν ἱστορίαν ταύτην ἀναφέρουσι, γράφοντες τὸ τέλος τοῦ στίχου
    τὴν σκάφην ἀνατρέψεις. (Choerob. in Heph. 3.1)

It derived its name (scil. iambos) either from Iambe, Celeus' maidservant, who compelled the grieving Demeter to laugh by saying something in jest and spontaneously using the rhythm of this metre, or from some other Iambe, an old woman, whom Hipponax the iambic poet met as she was washing wool by the sea and heard her say, as he touched the trough at which the old woman was washing:
    'Sir, be gone, you are upsetting the trough'.
And grasping what had been said, he named the metre after her. But others refer this narrative to the choliambus writing as the end of the line:
    'you will upset the trough'.

If it is accurately presented by our later source, this story was probably a combination of a highly adapted version of Archilochus' own initiation scene (his very famous meeting with the Muses inspired by Hesiodean *Dichterweihe*)[32] with the Homeric meeting of Odysseus and Nausicaa by the shore (*Od.* 6.149 ff.). The significance of this is twofold; firstly, the story was probably a programmatic statement by Hipponax on his relation to the *Odyssey*, which would reveal how highly influential the Homeric intertext was to his poetry to have presumably even influenced his own story of poetic initiation. Secondly, the kind of distortion of the Homeric story perhaps also illustrates that the use of the Homeric intertext within Hipponax's poetry in general was of a similar kind: distorted, allusive, parodic (and perhaps sustained throughout much of the corpus). Particularly important in the passage is the substitution of the ugly old woman of low status for the beautiful young virgin princess.

If Hipponax used both metrical forms (iambic and scazon) attested by the anecdote in his possible relation to the Iambe incident, then, it is as if he is almost enacting a double ἀνατροπή: this sense of turning over of the trough wittily points to the fact that he is inverting the rhythm of his predecessor Archilochus (from iambic to scazons). We may be here before a highly metapoetic moment, as

---
fourteenth century manuscript. On Iambe and her relation to *iambos*, see West 1974, 23 – 24; Richardson 1974, 213 ff.; Brown 1997, 16 – 25; Rosen 2007, 47 – 57; Rotstein 2010, 167 – 182.
32 Mnesiepes inscription *SEG* 15.517 (E1 col ii 23 ff.= Archil. Test. 4 Tarditi): see Miralles 1981, 29 – 46; Clay 2004, 10 – 16. On the ancient tradition of *Dichterweihe*, see Kambylis 1965; West 1966, 158 – 61.

what is evidently at issue is an attempt to define his oeuvre in relation to the iambic genre, by enacting an adjustment of the rhythm traditionally associated with *iambos*, while also aligning his own *iambos* with the *Odyssey*.

Thus, what one gets in Hipponax arguably amounts to a poetics and aesthetics of the ugly. The case of Hipponactean reception of Homer brings to mind the case of the geographically and chronologically adjacent *Margites,* which is another example of epic subversion, of a different kind however (as it focuses on an intellectual anti-hero rather than a moral anti-hero, which is the case of the Hipponactean narrator), suggesting that we should see this multilayered engagement with other texts (and especially *epos*) in Hipponax as something probably generated by chronology and geography. In the *Margites* certain features, such as its length, its extra-diegetic third-person narrative and its epic metre, suggest affinities with epic and define it generically up to a point. On the other hand, certain aspects of narrative technique, the juxtaposition of high and low, the parodic tone and the importance of an anti-hero align it with the Hipponactean *iambos*. Even rhythmically some of the effects are suggestive of Hipponax. The *Margites* begins with hexameters and then moves to iambics; if this is happening constantly, then it lacks the fluency of the Homeric hexameter, and has a halting quality to it, which aligns it once again with the Hipponactean scazon and the various asynartetic metres that one gets in *iambos*. The *Margites*, therefore, seems to be placing itself ambiguously in terms of genre categories; it has very strong literary cultural affinities with Hipponax, something which, combined with the geographical proximity, is very suggestive indeed of the fact that what one gets a glance into with Hipponax is both the distinctive oeuvre of a single poet, as well as the product of a cultural milieu.

Hence, one can see that a careful reading of the scanty corpus of Hipponax could be quite insightful. We are dealing with an archaic poet who is stretching the boundaries of Greek *iambos*, Greek poetic fiction and idea of aesthetics to extremes. His poetry has a metapoetic dimension and, to some extent, is an experiment with form in extracting a particular aspect of the *iambos*, turning it into the essence of the corpus and setting up a mirror for epic poetry.

In conclusion, the complexity and allusiveness of Hipponax's poetry justifies why it aroused the fascination of Hellenistic poets, such as Callimachus and Herodas, who were, as Hipponax himself, very fond of intertextual play and unusual modes of poetry. Hipponax has, therefore, arguably been characterized occasionally as a 'proto-Hellenistic poet'. However, as he was wronged by the tradition (his work has been very fragmentarily preserved), we can only glimpse what could probably have been a most fascinating reworking of the Homeric *Odyssey*.

Andrej Petrovic
Archaic Funerary Epigram and Hector's Imagined *Epitymbia**

From its very beginnings Greek epigram displays literary features associated with epic language, metre and motifs. A glance through some 460 verse inscriptions from the period between the eighth and fifth century BC reveals a wealth of lexemic, morphological, dialectal, syntactical and even narrative elements, which early Greek epigram shares with the *Iliad* and the *Odyssey*:[1] *epigram*, whose lit-

---

* I would like to express my gratitude to the organizers of the conference, the beacons of Greek *filoxenia*, dear friends and editors of this volume, Ioanna Karamanou and Athanasios Efstathiou for their support, criticism and patience, as well as my thanks to the audience at the Ionian University in Corfu for their suggestions and observations. As always, I am deeply grateful to Ivana Petrovic for her critique, encouragement and the many insightful remarks which she provided on several drafts of this paper. My earlier Durham colleague, Don Lavigne, contributed greatly to this paper in many ways, in particular concerning the form of the argument. The anonymous reviewers have both corroborated this paper and have helpfully suggested several improvements and clarifications: I am indebted to all of them, but I should like to highlight in particular an Italian reader's knowledgeable contribution to my comments on scholia.

Finally, I owe much to serendipity: a chance encounter of Jenny Strauss Clay and Ivana Petrovic at a Berlin conference made the author of these lines realize that Jenny and I were working on exactly the same Iliadic material simultaneously. Even if we relied on different approaches, the findings of our papers agree and complement each other to a great extent: I am deeply indebted to the generosity of Jenny Strauss Clay, who shared her persuasive and refined paper ('Homer's Epigraph: *Iliad* 7.87–91', forthcoming in *Philologus*) with me in advance of its publication and suggested several improvements to mine; I acknowledge my debt to this *chariessa amoibē* in the main text and the footnotes.

1 Abbreviations of epigraphic corpora follow the guidelines of *SEG*. The standard edition of verse inscriptions of this period is *CEG* 1; *DAA*, *FH*, *GV* and *LSAG* (with Poinikastas: http://poinikastas.csad.ox.ac.uk) remain useful resources for the study of early Greek verse inscriptions. Much work remains to be done on the intersection and interaction between *epos* and *epigram*; here I am pointing out a selection of the most influential and useful studies: Bowie 2010 discusses narrative traits in early Greek epigram and their similarities with *epos*; Gutzwiller 2010 discusses Homeric echoes in heroic epitaphs of the classical age; Skiadas 1965 analyzed the influence of Homer on later literary epigram; Harder 2007 is concerned with epic legacy and the appropriations of Trojan myths within Hellenistic epigrams; Trümpy 2010 investigates the language and dialect of early dedicatory and sepulchral verse inscriptions; Tsagalis (2008a, 64–132) explores the imagery of Attic sepulchral epigram of the fourth century BC, also in the light of epic influences; Muth/Petrovic 2013 investigate the impact of Homeric ideology on archaic monumental representations and epigrams.

erary history starts in the last quarter of the eighth century BC,[2] and *epos*, the oldest orally transmitted genre, seem to have been closely connected in multiple ways during the first three centuries of Greek literary history.[3]

In this paper I shall explore the early traces of intertextual references between the two genres and collect remnants of epigrammatic language explicitly recognized as such by the ancient commentators of the epics. Then, I shall investigate aspects of the appropriation of epic passages in the funerary epigrams of the archaic period. Did passages from the Homeric epics which were understood in antiquity as 'epigrammatic' leave traces on the inscriptional material of the archaic period? My aim is, therefore, to look into the surviving epigrammatic material of the archaic period, with the purpose of throwing more light on elements of distinctly *Homeric* (as opposed to the more general, and infinitely more elusive *epic*) tradition identifiable in early Greek sepulchral epigram.

However, there are several underlying methodological issues which impose limits to the scope of the conclusions one can reach: if two entities, clearly discernible as separate (as epigram and the Homeric epics are), demonstrate the same properties at the same time (e.g. formulas),[4] and possess the same features (e.g. hexameter), need we analyze their notional *influence* or their notional *concurrence*? Did they impinge on each-other or did they both draw from the same reservoir, an epic reservoir once fresh and luscious, now dry and dusty? The likeliest answer seems to be that both possibilities may have occurred, even if complex difficulties associated with contingencies of early Greek literature hinder any simple solution[5] – especially so, when it comes to the relationship between lost epic traditions, Homeric epics, and archaic sepulchral epigram.

Therefore, I shall investigate their marked, that is, distinctive features, by focusing first on Homeric passages with traits of verse inscriptions and then on verse inscriptions, in particular sepulchral, with distinctive Homeric features,

---

[2] Häusle (1979, 39-46) labelled it for that reason as 'the oldest literary genre of European history'.
[3] Allusions to the epics occur as early as in eighth-century BC verse inscriptions; see *CEG* 432 ('Dipylon vase'), *CEG* 454 ('Ischia cup') and the discussion in Fantuzzi/Hunter 2004, 285–88.
[4] On the genesis, fixation and transformations of Homeric texts in the archaic period, see Nagy 1996, 29–63. On the alleged formulaic character of early Greek epigram, see Baumbach/A. Petrovic/ I. Petrovic 2010, 1–8; on methodological approaches in the study of epigrammatic reception, see Fantuzzi/Hunter 2004, ch. 7 and Hunter 2010, 265.
[5] The situation is as complex in the case of the reception of Homer in non-inscriptional early Greek poetry: for a discussion, see the bibliographical survey in Giangrande 1968. In a recent talk at Oxford (Stesichorus conference, March 2012), Adrian Kelly argued that it is only with Stesichorus that we find the first unambiguous case of literary reception of the *Iliad* and the *Odyssey*, whilst epic traits identifiable in earlier authors stem from a shared pool of epic traditions. For an insightful discussion, see Scodel 1992.

as far as these can be found. The reason for the focus on sepulchral epigram as object of the present investigation is first and foremost the nature of genres recognized in epics as 'epigrammatic' and the corresponding epigrammatic material surviving from the archaic period, as ought to become immediately obvious.

a. Epigrams in Homer

The history of Greek epigram is inextricably intertwined with epic, also because both the *Iliad* and the *Odyssey* contain passages, six in number, which were read in antiquity with epigrammatic conventions and functions in mind. In 1975 Onofrio Vox gathered and analyzed five such passages from the *Iliad*. Ancient commentators explicitly labelled all five as 'epigrammatic',[6] identifying them variously as 'epigrams' and 'epigrammatic' or even using the generic term 'epikedeia' sometimes used of funerary epigrams. In 2005 David Elmer added to the material assembled by Vox an Odyssean passage relating *Ich-Rede* of Athena disguised as Mentes, which was also labelled as an 'epigram' by a scholiast (1.180–81).

Of the six epic 'epigrams' three come from *teichoskopia* scenes (*Il.* 3.156–58; 3.178–80; 3.200–02).[7] These textual segments, along with the newcomer, 'the epigram' of Athena/Mentes, are in form and function closely reminiscent of epi-

---

[6] For explicit references in the scholia, see below. See also Scodel 1992; Dinter (2005, 153–56) discusses further 'epitaphic gestures' in the *Iliad* and points out that the portrayal of Iphion's death adheres to epigraphic conventions (*Il.* 20.389–92).

[7] See Elmer 2005: 'Helen's epigrams' followed by ancient labels in square brackets: (a) *Il.* 3.156–8: οὐ νέμεσις Τρῶας καὶ ἐϋκνήμιδας Ἀχαιοὺς/ τοιῇδ᾽ ἀμφὶ γυναικὶ πολὺν χρόνον ἄλγεα πάσχειν· / αἰνῶς ἀθανάτῃσι θεῇς εἰς ὦπα ἔοικεν· [τρίγωνον ἐπίγραμμα πρῶτος Ὅμηρος γέγραφε τὸ "οὐ νέμεσις Τρῶας"· ἀφ᾽ οἵου γὰρ τῶν τριῶν στίχων ἀρξόμεθα, ἀδιάφορον. Scholia AT]; (b) *Il.* 3.178–80: οὗτός γ᾽ Ἀτρεΐδης εὐρὺ κρείων Ἀγαμέμνων,/ ἀμφότερον βασιλεύς τ᾽ ἀγαθὸς κρατερός τ᾽ αἰχμητής·/δαὴρ αὖτ᾽ ἐμὸς ἔσκε κυνώπιδος, εἴ ποτ᾽ ἔην γε. [ὡς ἐνὶ λόγῳ ἐπιγραμματικῶς αὐτὸν δηλοῖ. Scholium T]; (c) *Il.* 3.200–02: οὗτος δ᾽ αὖ Λαερτιάδης πολύμητις Ὀδυσσεύς, / ὃς τράφη ἐν δήμῳ Ἰθάκης κραναῆς περ ἐούσῃ /εἰδὼς παντοίους τε δόλους καὶ μήδεα πυκνά. [ἐν βραχεῖ τὸ ἐπίγραμμα πάντα ἔχει. μετὰ ἐπαίνων δὲ περὶ ἑκάστου ἐκτίθεται διὰ τὸ προσπεπονθέναι τῷ Ἑλληνικῷ. Scholia AbT]. Three passages relating to Helen are found in the third book of the *Iliad*, gathered within some 50 lines and displaying characteristics which are shared, to an extent, by both early inscriptional and later literary epigram. These are the features due to which Vox (1975, 69) believed that the poems cannot function as epigrams *qua* epigrams: (i) in two of the cases [(a) 3.156–8 and (c) 3.200–02], the epigrams were understood by critics, ancient and modern, as 'trigōna epigrammata', that is, 'three angled epigrams': such three-liners whose poetic architecture allows for verses to be read in any sequence (be it a-b-c, or a-c-b, or any of the other four possibilities), and (ii) all three have descriptive features unattested in the epigraphic context of the early period. For a critique of these views, see Elmer 2005, 10–11.

grammatic *Beischriften*, as Elmer persuasively demonstrated. Such epigrams are explanatory (this is to avoid the anachronistic use of the term 'ekphrastic') in nature and used to accompany works of art from the archaic period onwards. I shall leave aside the *Beischriften* because they were recently the subject of Elmer's detailed investigation and because both the epigraphic and the literary material of the archaic period furnish only limited *comparanda* for this epigrammatic subgenre.[8]

Instead, I shall focus on the remaining two Homeric passages, both of which can be read as funerary epigrams stemming from Hector's imagination.[9] These are an *epitaphion* for a fallen warrior envisaged by Hector (*Il.* 7.89–90), and an *epitaphion* imagined both for Hector and, as I suggest, for his widow (*Il.* 6.460–61). I shall suggest that they both employ generic features that we recognize in archaic sepulchral epigrams for fallen warriors and ladies of high birth respectively. Furthermore, I shall argue that certain archaic epigrams may well have been composed with Hector's imaginary epigrams in mind.

b. Hector as composer of a sepulchral epigram

I shall start with the most famous of the epic 'epigrams', an Iliadic passage in which Hector challenges the Greeks to select the best and strongest among them to fight a duel with him. Even though his opponent is only yet to be selected and Hector's victory uncertain, he already envisages his victory and a tomb with a monument, which will preserve the *kleos* of this duel (7.84–91):[10]

> τὸν δὲ νέκυν ἐπὶ νῆας ἐϋσσέλμους ἀποδώσω,/ ὄφρα ἑ ταρχύσωσι κάρη κομόωντες Ἀχαιοί / σῆμά τέ οἱ χεύωσιν ἐπὶ πλατεῖ Ἑλλησπόντωι./ καί ποτέ τις εἴπησι καὶ ὀψιγόνων ἀνθρώπων, / νηὶ πολυκληΐδι πλέων ἐπὶ οἴνοπα πόντον·
> 'ἀνδρὸς μὲν τόδε σῆμα πάλαι κατατεθνηῶτος,
> ὅν ποτ' ἀριστεύοντα κατέκτανε φαίδιμος Ἕκτωρ.'
> ὣς ποτέ τις ἐρέει, τὸ δ' ἐμὸν κλέος οὔ ποτ' ὀλεῖται.

---

8 See Elmer 2005; the closest parallels for such epigrams are those from the chest of Kypselos (allegedly coming from the sixth century BC) quoted by Pausanias. For a recent analysis, also in respect to their relationship to epics, see Borg 2010 (with further literature). To the functional parallels adduced by Elmer one could add interesting cases of sepulchral epigrams used as *Beischriften* on vases of the classical period (see Gutzwiller 2010, 219–26).
9 See Elmer 2005, 5: 'An overtly sepulchral character distinguishes the two epigrams of the "Hectorad"'.
10 For an analysis of graves (and material objects) as transmitters of historical memory ('archaeology of the past') in the epics, see Grethlein 2008, 27–51, with 28–32 on graves as 'time-marks' and spatial marks.

> But his corpse I shall give back among the strong-benched vessels,/ so that the flowing-haired Achaeans may give him due burial/ and heap up a mound upon him beside the broad passage of Hellespont./ And some day one of the men to come will say, as he sees it,/one who in his benched ship sails on the wine-blue water:
> 'This is the mound of a man who died long ago in battle,
> who was one of the bravest, and glorious Hector killed him'.
> So will he speak some day, and my glory will not be forgotten.
> (trans. based on Lattimore 1951)

Do these lines refer to inscribed texts? The epigrammatic character of Hector's words projected onto the *sēma* of a fallen warrior was recognized as such by ancient scholiasts, possibly already in the Hellenistic period: the bT scholia on the *Iliad*, parts of which are of Alexandrian and parts of late antique origin, state that Hector, as if he has already won the duel, is writing (*epigraphei*) his praises on the grave. This praise, the scholiast remarks, is self-praise rather than praise of the fallen and takes the form of an *epikēdeion* even before there is a corpse (τὸ ἐπικήδειον πρὸ τοῦ θανάτου διατιθείς).[11] Since *epikēdeion* is a term used of sepulchral epigrams and sepulchral elegies and dirges alike[12] and given that the scholiast associates it with Hector's act of *writing* on the grave, it follows that the scholiast's contemporaries envisaged it as an actual inscribed funerary text.

Scholium T, on the other hand, picking up the first words of the 'epigram' (ἀνδρὸς μὲν τόδε σῆμα), asserts that these words are uttered 'in contrast to the discovery of the script',[13] which would imply that vv. 89–90 do not designate an actual inscription. However, this statement ought not to be taken at face value, as what the scholiast is apparently attempting to do is to correct the (widespread?) view that the passage indeed *was* a reference to an inscribed monu-

---

11 Cf. Dickey 2007, 19–20 on the date and origin of the bT scholia; b(BCE3E4)T (ad *Il.* 89): ἀνδρὸς μὲν τόδε σῆμα: ὡς ἤδη νενικηκὼς ἐπιγράφει τῷ τάφῳ †τὸν† ἐπινίκιον, οὐκ ἐπὶ τεθνηκότι, ἀλλ' οὐδὲ γιγνωσκομένῳ τῷ μέλλοντι μονομαχεῖν τὸ ἐπικήδειον πρὸ τοῦ θανάτου διατιθείς. See also scholia b and T ad v. 90 for a criticism of Hector's behaviour and his characterization as vain, boastful and barbarian.
12 See *LSJ* s.v., Plu. *Mor.* 1030a 7 and *IMEGR* 42.
13 T ad 89: ἀνδρὸς μὲν τόδε σῆμα: πρὸς τὴν τῶν γραμμάτων εὕρεσιν. I need to stress here my debt to the anonymous reader, who pointed out deficiencies in my original (and, as I came to realize, unlikely) interpretation of the preposition πρός: 'Credo che si debba mantenere il significato letterale *contro / in contrasto con l'invenzione della scrittura* e, seguendo le indicazioni di H. Erbse nell'ed. e nell'apparato, mettere questo scolio in rapporto con lo *schol.* Ariston. *Il.* 6. 169a, relativo alle famose tavolette incise affidate da Preto a Bellerofonte (Aristonico [Aristarco] interpreta *grapsai* come *xesai*, *encharaxai*, "incidere", "intagliare"). D'altra parte, la conclusione di Petrovic resta valida: lo *schol.* T *Il.* 7.89 conferma *e contrario* l'esistenza dell'altra interpretazione antica (secondo la quale Ettore ha in mente un vero e proprio *epitymbion* inciso).'

ment, as scholia bT clearly state: there would have been no need for the scholiast to state that Hector's epigram was composed 'πρὸς τὴν τῶν γραμμάτων εὕρεσιν', had it not been believed, at least by some, that Hector envisaged an actual inscription. Hence, this remark, together with the use of the verb *epigraphei* in the bT scholia, confirms that the scholiasts' contemporaries could well conceive Hector's words as an actual sepulchral inscription.[14]

Modern scholars, too, have recognized the epigrammatic character of Hector's utterance, conducting studies in terms of the function of the passage within the Iliadic narrative, the origin of epigrammatic intimations in epics and genre-specific characteristics of the passage.[15] In a forthcoming essay Jenny Strauss Clay investigates epic's awareness of writing, revisits previous scholarship and tackles the vexed issues of literacy in Homer. Her persuasive conclusion is that '[Hector's epitaph] attests not only to the existence of writing, but also to a sophisticated understanding of its potential: how writing can be exploited, and even subverted and manipulated in shaping a narrative. In addition, its goal coincides with the aim of the *Iliad* itself: the conferring of *kleos* on the heroes of long ago.' If Hector's epitaph attests the existence of an epitaphic tradition known to Homer and bears testimony to Hector's particular spin (Strauss Clay's exploitation, subversion, and manipulation), then, like in a game of ping-pong, let us take a look at its possible impact on the epigrammatic habit of the archaic period: if Hector's words were understood in antiquity as an *epi-kēdeion*, did they leave any trace in the early epigrammatic material?

The reasons for the ancient conceptualization of 7.89–90 as a sepulchral epigram are transparent: the form of a hexametric two-liner for an inscribed *epitymbion* is very common in the archaic period, and this will change only in mid-sixth century BC under the influence of elegy (and the emergence of Panathenaea), when elegiac distichon will become a prevalent form.[16] In terms of con-

---

[14] Ivana Petrovic points out to me that scholia T might also be implying here that Homer knew about epigram as a genre, but since he is referring to a time when script was not yet invented, this would render Hector's statement an anachronism. Furthermore, the scholium might be implying that Homer composed epigrams before they were even invented, according to the tradition that viewed Homer as the originator of all literary genres.
[15] I can offer only a selection of relevant literature here: on these issues in general, see Scodel 1992 and Elmer 2005 (with observations on the relative chronology of the Homeric passages viz. the emergence of sepulchral epigram in the archaic period). On its function in the *Iliadic* narrative: Bing 2009, 127–29; Nagy 1983, 35–55 and 1990, 19; epitymbic language appropriated by the epics from the Near East along with the script: *FH* 1987, 7; generic characteristics: Thomas 1998, 206.
[16] On the formal characteristics of archaic and classical epigram, see Petrovic 2007, 4–9. On the circumstances of the change to elegiac disticha as a dominant form, see Wallace 1984, 307–14.

tent, the Iliadic passage contains a master-model of early epitymbic expression: line one contains the statement that X is dead and line two denotes the circumstances under which X died. The formulas and the language employed by Hector correspond closely to inscriptions on tombs of warriors of the archaic and classical period: name of the deceased in the genitive, followed or preceded by τόδε σῆμα, praise of the heroic death (ἀριστεύοντα) and an outline of the circumstances of his death.[17]

For these reasons, several scholars pointed to one particular inscriptional epigram that seems to be picking up on Hector's words. Hans-Martin Lumpp was, as far as I can see, the first one to argue that the late seventh-century BC sepulchral epigram from Corcyra, the well-known Arniadas epigram, contains a direct allusion to the Iliadic passage (CEG 145 = FH 25):

σᾶμα τόδε Ἀρνιάδα· χαροπὸς τόνδ᾽ ὄλε|σεν Ἄρες
βαρνάμενον παρὰ ναυσ|ὶν ἐπ᾽ Ἀράθθοιο ῥοFαῖσι
πολλὸ|ν ἀριστεύ<F>οντα κατὰ στονόFεσσαν ἀFυτάν

This is the marker of Arniadas. This man fierce-eyed Ares destroyed
battling by the ships beside the streams of the Aratthos
achieving great excellence and the battle-roar that brings mourning.
(trans. Bowie 2010, 356–57)

Is this a direct allusion to Hector's words or is this epigram indebted, more generally, to the epic tradition? Taking a cue from Lumpp, Anthony Raubitschek describes the epigrams as being 'extraordinary similar' to Hector's words, and concisely states that a comparison provides a 'general overlap' between the texts.[18] The views of Paul Friedländer and Herbert B. Hoffleit that the epigram 'is the masterpiece among ... sepulchral [epigrams] in epic manner' appear more appropriate and are confirmed by the findings which Ewen Bowie advanced in his analysis of epic elements in the poem.[19]

As it happens, χαροπός is never used as an epithet of Ares in the epics, and as Christos Tsagalis points out, it is in direct contrast with the usual epithets known from the epics and early Greek poetry more generally.[20] The general overlap between the poems seems to be exhausted in the generic marker σᾶμα τόδε,

---

[17] See Thomas 1998, 206; on the narrative technique in early epigram, Bowie 2010.
[18] Lumpp 1963; Raubitschek 1968, 6–7 ('ausserordentliche Ähnlichkeit'; 'ein Vergleich [zeigt] weitgehende Übereinstimmungen').
[19] FH: 30 (who consider possible influences of Eumelos); Bowie 2010: 356–57: 'it is hard not to see here some impact of performed battle poetry, whether hexameter epic or hortatory elegy'.
[20] Tsagalis 2008a, 89–90. See also Hunter 2010, 281–82, with n. 42 for a refutation of Lumpp's views.

the mention of Ares as a slayer[21] and ἀριστεύ<F>οντα, thus rendering any close association of this epigram with the Iliadic passage somewhat fragile.

There is, however, another famous epigram adduced as a parallel, but not further discussed by Raubitschek,[22] which may indeed provide a very close comparison to Hector's words. This epigram, both when considered on its own and in its monumental context, is strongly influenced by the Iliadic ideology, as Muth/ Petrovic recently argued.[23] In my view, it shows particular resemblance to the passage from the seventh book of the *Iliad*. This is the grave-complex of Croesus, which consists of an over-life-sized representation of a naked warrior, placed on a basis on which two verses of the epigram are inscribed in four lines. I print the text in metrical transcription, followed by representation of the text as inscribed on the basis (Athens, ca. 530 BC [*CEG* 27 = *IG* I³ 1240, *GV* I, 1224, *SEG* 24 70]):

*στέθι καὶ οἴκτιρον Κροίσο παρὰ σέμα θανόντος
hόν ποτ' ἐνὶ προμάχοις ὄλεσε θôρος Ἄρες.*

Halt and show pity beside the monument of dead Croesus,
whom raging Ares once destroyed in the front rank of the battle.
(trans. Baumbach/ A. Petrovic/ I. Petrovic 2010, 14)

*στέθι : καὶ οἴκτιρον : Κροίσο
παρὰ σέμα θανόντος : hόν
ποτ' ἐνὶ προμάχοις : ὄλεσε
θôρος : Ἄρες.*

It is worth exploring the texts in isolation, before we move on to a comparison of the Croesus epigram in its monumental setting with the epic passage. The parallels between Hector's imagined *epitymbion* for the anonymous opponent and the inscription from the grave of Croesus are striking: the structure of the second line of each epigram is identical. The first two words which dislocate death into a timeless dimension (*hόν ποτ'*),[24] are followed by praise of the heroic death of the warrior (ἐνὶ προμάχοις vs. ἀριστεύοντα). After these the verb denoting killing follows (ὄλεσε vs. κατέκτανε), and both lines end with the names of the slayers with identical grammatical disposition in the verse, i.e. as grammatical subjects θοῦρος Ἄρες and φαίδιμος Ἕκτωρ). Furthermore, in terms of diction, every single word from the

---

21 On the epic parallels for this technique, see below.
22 Raubitschek 1968, 6 regards it as 'eng verbunden' with the Iliadic passage.
23 Muth/Petrovic 2013, see below.
24 On this, see Young 1983, 31–48; Day 1989, 18–19.

Croesus epigram is attested in the epics, together with the epithet of Ares (θοῦρος), which predominantly appears in the same *sedes* in Homeric verses.[25]

But this is not where the similarities end. One of the reasons Hector's words attracted the interest of ancient readers and modern critics is that he composed a sepulchral epigram for the opponent he was about to kill as a monument (*sēma*) to himself, rather than the deceased. Thus, he is modifying the most elementary function of an *epitymbion*. A focus on the slayer, rather than the slain, is also present in the case of the Croesus epigram, and not only because of the marked position of the name of the slayer at the end of the verse. Susanne Muth und Ivana Petrovic have recently argued that the Croesus monument, together with the inscription on its base, *intentionally* incites an interpretative ambiguity in its reception:[26] The supra-human representation of a naked muscular body captured mid-motion is placed on a base on which the name of the god, θοῦρος Ἄρες, appears in a single line, separated from the rest of the poem. Its legibility is further facilitated through use of interpunction, separating the epithet from the name of the god. As Muth/Petrovic stress, for a recipient, ancient as well as modern, the first impulse may well be to interpret the statue as a representation of the divinity, rather than of the fallen warrior.[27] By this token the statue with its inscription might be taken to reflect, at first glance, the functional modification attested also in Hector's epigram: instead of being a *geras thanontōn*, as a recipient would infer from its position and original surrounding, the monument appears, initially, to be a representation of the war-god.

Upon reading the epigram, however, although the recipient will be prompted to adjust his understanding of the monument, some similarities will persist: the identity of the representation might become less puzzling, but the extraordinary emphasis on the slayer remains. Being killed by Hector, like being killed by Ares, is understood on its own as a source and verification of the virtue of the fallen. In such a constellation, Muth/Petrovic argue, Croesus appears himself as a Homeric hero – as a man similar or equal to divinities, who, correspondingly, could be conquered and felled only through divine agency.

If the Croesus epigram reflects both epic ideology and language to the point that it is modeled upon Hector's imagined *epitymbion*, as seems likely in my view, then the substitution of Hector with Ares is a logical and appropriate

---

25 Ares accompanied with the epithet θοῦρος appears eleven times in the *Iliad* (not attested in the *Odyssey*), of which it is found seven times at the end of the hexameter (5.30; 5.35; 5.355; 5.830; 5.904; 15.127; 15.142).
26 Muth/Petrovic 2013.
27 Muth/Petrovic 2013, 298–306. On idealized representations of fallen warriors in archaic Attic, see Day 1989, 21–22 and on the reception of the Croesus epigram, Lorenz 2010, 143–45.

one. Ares as a slayer of Croesus provides a convenient and appropriate metaphor for the death of a warrior on the battlefield, which is well attested in the Iliadic narrative: when a warrior is felled by a human enemy, he is described as having been killed by Ares himself.[28] Furthermore, Hector is represented as a (literal) incarnation of Ares, since Ares is described as entering Hector's body – the only mortal whose body the god of war entered in the *Iliad*: Ἕκτορι δ᾽ ἥρμοσε τεύχε᾽ ἐπὶ χροΐ, δῦ δέ μιν Ἄρης / δεινὸς ἐνυάλιος, πλῆσθεν δ᾽ ἄρα οἱ μέλε᾽ ἐντὸς / ἀλκῆς καὶ σθένεος.[29] Hence, Croesus' appropriation of Hector's epigram can render Hector as Ares, not just for the sake of appropriate epic convention, but also because Hector was, at least temporarily, the embodiment of Ares.[30]

c. Andromache as a sepulchral epigram and Andromache's own sepulchral epigram

In a moving scene towards the end of the sixth book of the *Iliad*, Hector sinisterly predicts the fall of Troy, the deaths of its defenders, and the subsequent enslavement of his wife, addressing Andromache directly with the following words (*Il*. 6.459–65):

καί ποτέ τις εἴπῃσιν ἰδὼν κατὰ δάκρυ χέουσαν
   "Ἕκτορος ἥδε γυνὴ ὃς ἀριστεύεσκε μάχεσθαι
   Τρώων ἱπποδάμων ὅτε Ἴλιον ἀμφεμάχοντο'.
ὥς ποτέ τις ἐρέει· σοὶ δ᾽ αὖ νέον ἔσσεται ἄλγος / χήτεϊ τοιοῦδ᾽ ἀνδρὸς ἀμύνειν δούλιον ἦμαρ.
ἀλλά με τεθνηῶτα χυτὴ κατὰ γαῖα καλύπτοι/ πρίν γέ τι σῆς τε βοῆς σοῦ θ᾽ ἑλκηθμοῖο πυθέσθαι.

and once, someone is to say having seen you weeping:
   'This is the wife of Hector, who kept excelling in battle

---

28 See *Il*. 24.260, 498 and Redfield 1994², 225–26. Cf. also *Il*. 9.239, where Diomedes states that *lussa* enters Hector's body. Note that the Arniadas epigram discussed above (*CEG* 145) appropriates the same technique.
29 *Il*. 17.210–13.
30 There is a further possibility: in her forthcoming paper, Jenny Strauss Clay takes into account my suggestion and remarks: 'However – although all such matters are speculative – the presence of Ares attested also in the Arniades' epitaph, as well as the *Iliad's façon de parler*, might allow for the possibility that Hector has inserted his name in the place traditionally reserved for Ares. Such a possibility would, I think, strengthen the claim for the need for a written label whereby Hector identifies himself as the slayer of the Greek whom his epigraph has consigned to anonymity.'

among the horse-taming Trojans, when they fought about Ilion'.
so will one say once, and grief will beset you anew, lacking this man here to avert the day of slavery. But let the heaped up soil cover my corpse, before I should hear your shrieks as they carry you off.
(trans. based on Lattimore 1951)

Ruth Scodel, as well as several scholars afterwards, has observed that in this scene Andromache is assigned the function of a living memorial of Hector's virtue, and that she represents, in a way, a living female *mnēma*, an encapsulation of the memory of the fallen hero.[31] When analyzed in the context of the Iliadic narrative, this is indeed likely to be the case: Hector imagines for himself only a sepulchral mound, there is no mention of a *sēma* he envisaged for his opponent in the epigram from book seven, and it is only his wife who is hoped to preserve the memory of his virtue.

Commenting on the words Ἕκτορος ἥδε γυνὴ ὃς ἀριστεύεσκε μάχεσθαι, scholia bT remark cursorily that the line displays epigrammatic features or epigrammatic character: ἐπιγραμματικὸν ἔχει τύπον ὁ στίχος.[32] This comment may well be motivated by the use of the deictic following a genitive and could be interpreted as a variation on the formulaic expression we might expect on Hector's monument, such as Ἕκτορος τόδε σῆμα or similar, as Scodel remarks.[33]

Nevertheless, when observed in isolation and outside the Iliadic context, the lines uttered by Hector could also be conceptualized as an *epitymbion* not necessarily only for himself, but also for Andromache: Hector does mention his own envisaged death, but only after he has composed the 'epigram' – an epigram that he introduced with a vivid depiction of Andromache's enslavement and a gloomy vision of her future toils.[34] Given that enslavement in Homeric ideology corresponds closely to social death and enslavement of aristocratic women to 'blame-

---

31 See the discussion in Scodel 1992 and Elmer 2005, 5 and esp. 25: 'Hector's auto-epitaph at 6.460–61, by which he transforms Andromache into his funeral monument –a *stēlē*, that is, the place of writing'; Graziosi/Haubold 2010, commentary *ad loc.*
32 See b(BCE3)T ad v. 6.460 (Erbse). Here too, I would like to acknowledge the encouragement of the anonymous reviewer, and simultaneously express my regret that the scope of the contribution does not allow me to pursue her/ his suggestion further: 'Potrebbe essere utile analizzare anche lo *schol. ex.* 460a (che, nei manoscritti, è direttamente congiunto al 460b: cf. Erbse, apparato), dove, se capisco bene, si commenta lo stile del verso omerico facendo riferimento proprio alla concisione e all'allusività tipiche dello stile epigrammatico'.
33 On this, see Scodel 1992, 58–60; Elmer 2005, 25.
34 Il. 6.454–59: ὅσσον σεῦ, ὅτε κέν τις Ἀχαιῶν χαλκοχιτώνων / δακρυόεσσαν ἄγηται ἐλεύθερον ἦμαρ ἀπούρας· / καί κεν ἐν Ἄργει ἐοῦσα πρὸς ἄλλης ἱστὸν ὑφαίνοις,/ καί κεν ὕδωρ φορέοις Μεσσηΐδος ἢ Ὑπερείης· / πόλλ' ἀεκαζομένη, κρατερὴ δ' ἐπικείσετ' ἀνάγκη.

less catastrophe',[35] it is in my view possible that the scholiast had in mind some of the famous *epitymbia* for ladies of noble birth, when he remarked on the epigrammatic character of the first line of Hector's utterance.

The fact that Andromache's life would be characterized entirely through her relationship to her husband is no obstacle to this interpretation. I adduce two striking examples of such depiction of queens and aristocratic women in sepulchral epigrams. The first case involves one of the most famous *epitymbia* of the archaic period. This is the epigram composed for Archedike of Lampsakos, daughter of Peisistratus' son Hippias, the last tyrant of Athens, and wife of the tyrant of Lampsakos, Aiantides. As a noble-woman, she is praised for having been a daughter, a wife and a mother of tyrants (in the neutral rather than pejorative sense). The epigram was quoted by both Thucydides and Aristotle and was hence available and, very likely, familiar to Hellenistic (and later) scholiasts (*EG* Sim. 26a = Petrovic 2007 Ep. 12):[36]

> ἀνδρὸς ἀριστεύσαντος ἐν Ἑλλάδι τῶν ἐφ' ἑαυτοῦ
> Ἱππίου Ἀρχεδίκην ἥδε κέκευθε κόνις,
> ἣ πατρός τε καὶ ἀνδρὸς ἀδελφῶν τ' οὖσα τυράννων
> παίδων τ' οὐκ ἤρθη νοῦν ἐς ἀτασθαλίην.

> Archedike, daughter of the man who excelled in Hellas of his day,
> of Hippias, is covered by this soil.
> She, who was a daughter, wife, sister and mother of tyrants,
> did not raise her mind to arrogance.

The second example is the sepulchral epigram for no lesser a figure than Olympias, wife of Philip II and mother of Alexander the Great, quoted only by Plutarch without any further remarks regarding the queen in *Mor.* 747f–748a (*Quaest. Conv.*):

> τῆσδε πατὴρ καὶ ἀνὴρ καὶ παῖς βασιλεῖς, καὶ ἀδελφοί,
> καὶ πρόγονοι. κλῄζει δ' Ἑλλὰς Ὀλυμπιάδα.

> Her father and husband and son were kings, as were her brothers
> and ancestors. Hellas calls her Olympias.[37]

It is difficult to determine whether this epigram was a genuine inscription or a later literary composition.[38] The deictic τῆσδε would certainly favour the former

---

35 On female enslavement in Homer, see the overview in Hunt 2011, 25–28.
36 Th. 6.59.2; Arist. *Rh.* 1.9.20 (=1367b); see also Isid. Pelus. 3.224 and Petrovic 2007: commentary on epigram no. 12.
37 For a discussion of this epigram, see Fantuzzi 2005, 256–57.
38 On issues of authenticity of the couplet, see Carney 2006, 187 and 195 (Olympias).

possibility. Furthermore, given that Plutarch had a keen epigraphic interest, firmly believing in the reliability of inscriptional evidence, and extensively praised the virtues of epigraphy in the very work from which the sepulchral epigram derives, there is little that might stand in the way of its authenticity.[39]

Yet, what most matters here is that in this epigram, too, we encounter the portrayal of queens conveyed through their relationship to the excellence of the men who surround them: the sepulchral inscriptions of Archedike and Olympias do not encapsulate their own achievements or virtues, but rather commemorate the virtue of their closest male kin, as in the case of Andromache's commemoration through Hector. Thucydides famously quipped that women's greatest virtue was not to be talked about by men, neither for good nor ill (2.45.2), and these sepulchral epigrams show that this was the case in death as well – women are not to be talked about, save as a reason to talk about their men.

Concluding remarks

Alexandrian and later scholiasts, who labelled and analyzed passages from the *Iliad* as epigrammatic or sepulchral in nature, are very likely to have had solid knowledge of epigrammatic collections and anthologies with their developed generic typologies. This may have prompted their use of terminology, such as ἐπικήδειον and ἐπιγραμματικὸς τύπος, and epigrammatic extrapolations of Homeric passages – sepulchral epigrams were for them, of course, both inscriptional and literary artifacts with clearly defined generic conventions and forms.

However, I hope to have highlighted the possible early impact of these passages on Greek archaic sepulchral epigrams: the Croesus and Archedike epigrams seem to closely resemble Hector's 'epigrams': the epigrams for Croesus and Archedike do not seem to be simply drawing from the linguistic and literary pool of general 'epic' traditions, but rather appear to be ideologically and formally chiselled after respective Homeric passages. Therefore, in my view, the answer to the question of whether the Croesus and Archedike epigrams mirror anonymous authors' awareness of Hector's epigrams ought to be a blunt yes.

---

[39] On Plutarch's use of inscriptions generally and in the *Quaestiones Convivales*, see Liddel 2008, 128–29. I wonder if Plutarch, who in the *Quaestiones Convivales* explicitly acknowledges familiarity with the work of Polemon Periegetes, derived the sepulchral epigram for Olympias from Polemon's *On the epigrams according to a city* (FHG III, T79–80).

How early does emulation of Hector's epigrams in verse inscriptions start? We cannot know for certain whether epigrammatic sections in the *Iliad* entered the epic narrative during the later period of its fixation, when sepulchral epigrams were no longer a novelty, or whether they belonged to the earlier stages in the evolution and fixation of the epics. The *epitaphia* for Archedike and Croesus (coming from late sixth century) postdate the Peisistratid redaction of the epics[40] and are thus more likely to reflect epic passages, than to have provided models for them.

Were there any earlier models that did? We cannot know this. In Madeline Miller's beautiful novel *The Song of Achilles*, the shadowy soul of Patroclus finds no peace until a sepulchral inscription is set up on his tomb. Homer's *Iliad*, on the other hand, provides us only with shadows of sepulchral inscriptions, yet the epic echoes, attested in the language and form of sepulchral epigram, are resounding.

---

[40] See Nagy 1996, 41–43 and 99–100 on possible *modi* and chronologies of textualization.

Margarita Sotiriou
Performance, Poetic Identity and Intertextuality in Pindar's *Olympian* 4*

The relation of Pindar's lyric tradition to the epic past has been since years a subject of philological research. Frank Nisetich's *Pindar and Homer* published in 1989 and one year later Gregory Nagy's *Pindar's Homer: The Lyric Possession of an Epic Past* both illustrate the function of the heroic tradition in Pindar's melic environment.[1]

In what follows I shall attempt to provide a new suggestion about Pindar's creative adaptation[2] of the Homeric flavour in his *Olympian* 4 and the subtle way in which he develops his epic model, carefully preserving traditional elements of the Homeric athletic scenes or intentionally varying specific aspects of them, in order to serve his own epinician purpose. I shall also attempt to reveal the relationship between intention and expression and explore the manner in which Pindar reworks the Homeric source text, in order to praise lavishly the victor, as well as to present himself in public as a 'primary narrator' and a skillful professional 'panegyrist'.

Pindar's *Olympian* 4 celebrates Psaumis from the Sicilian state of Camarina[3] and his Olympic victory in chariot-race (452 BC).[4] It is a rather short ode chorally performed (l. 9) in Olympia immediately after the end of the contest:[5]

---

* Very special thanks to Dr Ioanna Karamanou and Dr Athanasios Efstathiou for their invitation to give a paper (from which this contribution developed) at the International Conference *Homeric Receptions in Literature and the Performing Arts*, organized by the Department of History, Ionian University in Corfu (7–9 November 2011). I am deeply indebted to Dr Ioanna Karamanou and Dr Sophia Kapetanaki for many important linguistic improvements that they suggested.
1 All Pindaric citations are taken from the edition of Snell/ Maehler 1987. For Homer I used the edition of Allen (Oxford). For further bibliography concerning Homeric reception in the epinician songs of Pindar, cf. Sotiriou 1998. On the same issue in general with the latest bibliographical references, see Graziosi 2008a, 26–37.
2 Cf. the definition of the term 'adaptation' in Hardwick 2003, 9.
3 On a detailed overview of the political history of the state, see Hornblower 2004, 186–92.
4 Gerber 1987, 8; Schmitz 1992, 142–47.
5 Gelzer 1985, 100. The performance place of the Ode has been since years a subject of controversial discussion. See particularly Gerber 1987, 7–9, who insists on the performance of the Ode during a festive procession in honour of Zeus in Camarina. In favour of a choral performance of the Ode instead of a *solo*, see the convincing argumentation of Calame 2004, 427–31.

Ἐλατὴρ ὑπέρτατε βροντᾶς ἀκαμαντόποδος
Ζεῦ· τεαὶ γὰρ Ὧραι
ὑπὸ ποικιλοφόρμιγγος ἀοιδᾶς ἑλισσόμεναί μ' ἔπεμψαν
ὑψηλοτάτων μάρτυρ' ἀέθλων·
ξείνων δ' εὖ πρασσόντων
ἔσαναν αὐτίκ' ἀγγελίαν ποτὶ γλυκεῖαν ἐσλοί·   5
ἀλλ', ὦ Κρόνου παῖ, ὃς Αἴτναν ἔχεις,
ἷπον ἀνεμόεσσαν ἑκατουκεφάλα
Τυφῶνος ὀβρίμου,
Οὐλυμπιονίκαν
δέξαι Χαρίτων ἕκατι τόνδε κῶμον
χρονιώτατον φάος εὐρυσθενέων ἀρετᾶν.   10
Ψαύμιος γὰρ ἵκει
ὀχέων, ὅς, ἐλαίᾳ στεφανωθεὶς Πισάτιδι, κῦδος ὄρσαι
σπεύδει Καμαρίνᾳ. θεὸς εὔφρων
εἴη λοιπαῖς εὐχαῖς·
ἐπεί νιν αἰνέω μάλα μὲν τροφαῖς ἑτοῖμον ἵππων,
χαίροντά τε ξενίαις πανδόκοις   15
καὶ πρὸς ἀσυχίαν φιλόπολιν καθαρᾷ
γνώμᾳ τετραμμένον.

Driver most high of thunder with unwearied foot Zeus
on you I am calling, for your Horai
in their circling round have sent me with song on varied lyre
as a witness of the most lofty games.
When guest-friends are successful,
good men are immediately cheered at the sweet news.
And so, son of Cronus, you who rule Aetna,
windy burden for hundred-headed
Typhos the mighty,
receive an Olympic victor
and, for the sake of the Games, this celebration,
longest-lasting light for deeds of great strength.
For it comes with the chariot of Psaumis,
who is crowned with olive from Pisa and is eager to arouse glory
for Camarina. May heaven look kindly
on his future prayers,
for I praise him, very earnest in his raising horses,
delighting in receiving guests from everywhere,
and devoted to city-loving Hesychia
with a sincere mind.
(trans. Race 1990 with minor adjustments)

The mythical narrative creates the epilogue of the Ode (ll. 19–27). The story refers to the Argonaut Erginus (l. 19), who won the race of armour at the Games put on by the women of Lemnos, when the Argonauts stopped there. Mocked by the Lemnians because of his grey hair during the prize-giving by the queen of the island Hypsipyle, Erginus proudly declared himself capable to win also in other disciplines:[6]

> οὐ ψεύδεϊ τέγξω
> λόγον· διάπειρά τοι βροτῶν ἔλεγχος·
> ἅπερ Κλυμένοιο παῖδα
> Λαμνιάδων γυναικῶν   20
> ἔλυσεν ἐξ ἀτιμίας.
> χαλκέοισι δ' ἐν ἔντεσι νικῶν δρόμον
> ἔειπεν Ὑψιπυλείᾳ μετὰ στέφανον ἰών·
> 'οὗτος ἐγὼ ταχυτᾶτι·
> χεῖρες δὲ καὶ ἦτορ ἴσον. φύονται δὲ καὶ νέοις   25
> ἐν ἀνδράσιν πολιαὶ
> θαμάκι παρὰ τὸν ἁλικίας ἐοικότα χρόνον .'

> I shall not tinge my praise with a lie;
> the trial to the end is the (true) test for men.
> This it was that released son of Clymenus
> from the dishonour of the Lemnian women.
> After winning the race in bronze armour
> and going to Hypsipyle to receive his crown, he said:
> 'You have seen me in speed;
> my hands and spirit are equally strong. Even young men
> have often grey hair
> before the time they are (normally) expected to appear'.

In 1994 the German scholar Thomas Schmitz drew attention to a nexus of affinities between the Pindaric description and the Homeric presentation of the athletic games in Scheria in the eighth book of the *Odyssey*.[7] After a banquet accompanied by Demodocus' song (ll. 1–96), Odysseus attends the athletic games organized at Alcinous' palace (ll. 97–253). Laodamas' exhortation to Odysseus to take part in the games and Euryalus' mockery of him forced him to demonstrate his superiority by throwing the discus far away, over the pegs:

> τὸν δ' ἀπαμειβόμενος προσέφη πολύμητις Ὀδυσσεύς·   152
> 'Λαοδάμαν, τί με ταῦτα κελεύετε κερτομέοντες;'

> Odysseus, always thinking, answered him in this way:
> 'Laodamus, why are you provoking me like this?'

> [...] τὸν δ' αὖτ' Εὐρύαλος ἀπαμείβετο νείκεσέ τ' ἄντην   158

---

[6] On the Argonaut myth, see schol. A.R. 1.185–188a (Wendel); for the Games in Lemnos, see Pi. P. 4.253 and schol. Pi. P. 4.451 (Drachmann); on the legend before Pindar, see further Braswell 1988, 6–23; Gerber 1987, 21.
[7] Schmitz 1994, 142–47.

And Euryalus answered him:

[...]ἀλλὰ καὶ ὥς, κακὰ πολλὰ παθών, πειρήσομ' ἀέθλων·
θυμοδακὴς γὰρ μῦθος, ἐπότρυνας δέ με εἰπών.   185
ἦ ῥα, καὶ αὐτῷ φάρει ἀναΐξας λάβε δίσκον
μείζονα καὶ πάχετον, στιβαρώτερον οὐκ ὀλίγον περ
ἢ οἵῳ Φαίηκες ἐδίσκεον ἀλλήλοισι.
τόν ῥα περιστρέψας ἧκε στιβαρῆς ἀπὸ χειρός,
βόμβησεν δὲ λίθος· κατὰ δ' ἔπτηξαν ποτὶ γαίῃ   190
Φαίηκες δολιχήρετμοι, ναυσίκλυτοι ἄνδρες,
λᾶος ὑπὸ ῥιπῆς· ὁ δ' ὑπέρπτατο σήματα πάντων
ῥίμφα θέων ἀπὸ χειρός. ἔθηκε δὲ τέρματ' Ἀθήνη
ἀνδρὶ δέμας ἐικυῖα, ἔπος τ' ἔφατ' ἔκ τ' ὀνόμαζεν·

'Even so, even with all I have been through, I shall give your games a try.
Your words are biting my heart, and now you have got me going'.
He jumped up, with his cloak still on, and grabbed a discus
larger than the others, thicker and much heavier
than the one that the Phaeacians used for their contests.
Winding up, he let it fly, and the stone,
launched with incredible force from his hand, hummed as it flew.
The Phaeacians ducked as the discus zoomed overhead
and finally landed far beyond the other marks.
The goddess Athena, who looked like a man now,
marked the spot where it came down, and she called out to him.

[...]ὣς φάτο, γήθησεν δὲ πολύτλας δῖος Ὀδυσσεύς,
χαίρων, οὕνεχ' ἑταῖρον ἐνηέα λεῦσσ' ἐν ἀγῶνι.   200
καὶ τότε κουφότερον μετεφώνεε Φαιήκεσσι·
'τοῦτον νῦν ἀφίκεσθε, νέοι· τάχα δ' ὕστερον ἄλλον
ἤσειν ἢ τοσσοῦτον ὀίομαι ἢ ἔτι μᾶσσον.
τῶν δ' ἄλλων ὅτινα κραδίη θυμός τε κελεύει,
δεῦρ' ἄγε πειρηθήτω, ἐπεί μ' ἐχολώσατε λίην,   205
ἢ πὺξ ἠὲ πάλῃ ἢ καὶ ποσίν, οὔ τι μεγαίρω,
πάντων Φαιήκων, πλήν γ' αὐτοῦ Λαοδάμαντος.

Odysseus cheered up at this,
Glad to see a loyal supporter out of the field.
In a lighter mood now, he spoke to the Phaeacians:
'Match that if you can, boys. In a minute
I shall get another one out just as far or farther.
And if anyone else has the urge to try me,
step right up –I am angry now–
I do not care if it is boxing, wrestling or even running.
Come one, come all – except Laodamas'.

[...]πάντα γὰρ οὐ κακός εἰμι, μετ' ἀνδράσιν ὅσσοι ἄεθλοι.
εὖ μὲν τόξον οἶδα ἐύξοον ἀμφαφάασθαι·   215

*I am not weak in any athletic activity
and I really know how to handle the bow.*

[...]δουρὶ δ' ἀκοντίζω ὅσον οὐκ ἄλλος τις ὀϊστῷ.   229

*I am always the first to hit my man in the enemy lines, no matter how
many archers are standing with me and getting shots.*
(trans. Lombardo 2000 with minor adjustments)

The verbal affinities between Pindar and his Homeric model are evident:
(i) While in Homer the mockery against the athlete occurs in the provocative speeches of Laodamas and Euryalus, in Pindar it is initiated by the crowd of Lemnian women (*Od.* 8.153, 158, 185, 205 and *O.* 4.20).
(ii) In both descriptions there is a reference to discipline: Odysseus wins in discus, Erginus wins in race in armour. They both claim that they are able to win also in other disciplines (*Od.* 8.206, also 8.214 and *O.* 4.24–25).
(iii) Both protagonists use demonstrative pronouns to highlight their triumph (*Od.* 8.202 and *O.* 4.23).
(iv) Odysseus emphasizes his superiority in war as an archer (*Od.* 8.215–18) and a spearman (*Od.* 8.229–31), while Erginus argues that his strength derives from his spirit (l. 24: ἦτορ)— a term that is often used in martial contexts.[8]
(v) Odysseus and Erginus are probably middle-aged men. In Homer the hero addresses his competitors with the term νέοι (*Od.* 8.202), apparently because he wants to stress the age difference between him and the some twenty years younger Phaeacians, who seem to be at the same age with Telemachus. Accordingly, Laodamas addresses him as ξεῖνε πάτερ (*Od.* 8.145).[9] Erginus in Pindar expresses the same thought: after testing his legs (*O.* 4.23), he talks about the power of his arms and heart. Then, he refers to the contrast between his physical power and his appearance with the following words: 'Even young men have *often* grey hair before the time they are expected to appear'. While scholars have pointed out that the passage refers to young Erginus, who has prematurely grey hair,[10] I strongly believe that the use of the Homeric text enables us to adopt an alternative interpretation of the Pindaric speech. Youth is always associated with physical strength, whereas old age is a synonym of weakness. In this case, the athletic test shows that older men (i.e. grey haired) are often strong (i.e. 'young'), whereas young men are often 'weak' (i.e. 'grey haired'). Erginus is an eloquent example in support of this view. A young man

---

[8] Schmitz 1994, 216 n. 34; Gerber 1987, 23.
[9] Cf. also *Od.* 23.790–91, where Antilochus addresses Odysseus as ὠμογέρων (*LSJ*[9]: 'fresh, active old man'). See also Stanford 1963, 256.
[10] See, for instance, Schmitz 1994, 210–11.

can be as weak as an older one, whereas an older man can be as strong as a young one, 'against the external sign of the age' (l. 27). Though the age reference is consciously cryptic, such an interpretation highlights a logically explained metaphorical sense of the passage. The older men, Erginus and Odysseus, proved their strength against their younger competitors, who have been as weak as the real grey haired men.[11]

(vi) Pindar's reception of Homer also emerges from the so called πεῖρα motif (O. 4.18: διάπειρα and Od. 8.184: πειρήσομαι ἀέθλων), indicating the proof of the physical strength in the athletic contest: 'the trial to the end (διάπειρα) is the true test/proof for men' (ἔλεγχος βροτῶν).[12] The term πεῖρα occurs several times throughout the eighth Book of the *Odyssey* in the form of a verb (πειράω: 'attempt, endeavour, try, make proof or trial of') or a noun; though it is sometimes referred to the young Phaeacians who participate in the games, the word is mainly associated with Odysseus and the proof of his strength during the contest.[13]

Pindar's reworking of the motif deserves closer scrutiny. Since years the majority of commentators has claimed that the emphasis of the passage is on the 'perseverance' or 'endurance' of the athlete as main factors (such as πόνος, μόχθος, κάματος, τόλμα) leading him to success according to his mythical *exempla*.[14] Undeniably, Pindar's use of the Homeric pattern has an important bearing on the question about the way he receives the epic material in a verbal and a conceptual level. However, I believe that the relation of the lyric creator to his source is no more conventional, as Schmitz and others have suggested. It rather goes beyond the simplicity of a verbal affinity or a phrasal echo, which just confirms the meaning of the mythical narrative. In that sense a second, more crucial and rather cryptic level of Homeric reception in O. 4 is detected through this motif, which has not been sufficiently explored. My purpose, therefore, is to investigate this motif within the structural, thematic and performative context of the Ode.

---

11 Bowra 1964, 178; Mader 1990, 54; Krischer 1991, 158.
12 Schol. O. 4.29a–c, 32b (Drachmann). Διάπειρα is a synonym of πεῖρα (schol. Nem. 3.122e Drachmann) and, in a way, even stronger than merely πεῖρα (Thom. Mag. Ecl. δ 83.13). In Plutarch (*Thes.* 30.1.4), in oratory ([D.] 44.58.5, 56.18.10, Aeschin. 1.184.5) as well as in historiography (Hdt. 2.15, 28, 77), the term διάπειρα bears the meaning of 'crucial experiment, trial, proof'.
13 Od. 8.100, 120, 126, 145, 149, 184, 205, 213.
14 In that sense, Odysseus, Erginus and Psaumis have proved their superiority during the athletic contest.

Surprisingly, the motif is not included in the mythical narrative of the Ode.[15] Instead, it is incorporated in an enunciative self-reference about Pindar's encomiastic task and the principles of his art, which functions as a proem to the mythical narrative (ll. 17–18: οὐ ψεύδεϊ τέγξω λόγον· διάπειρά τοι βροτῶν ἔλεγχος, 'I shall not tinge my praise with lies; the test till the end is the proof for the men').

Two other, rather similar, first person declarations occur in the poem.[16] At the proem (ll. 1–3) Pindar mentions that he has been personally sent here (μ' ἔπεμψαν ... μάρτυρ' ἀέθλων) with his song as a witness to the games, instead of merely sending his song as a gift to the victor.[17] The background of the image is Homeric. Twice in the Hymns (6.12–13 and 3.189–196) the Horae, daughters of Zeus and Themis, are presented as dancing along with Harmonia, Hebe and Aphrodite to the accompaniment of choral song and lyre:[18]

Ὧραι κοσμείσθην χρυσάμπυκες ὁππότ' ἴοιεν
ἐς χορὸν ἱμερόεντα θεῶν καὶ δώματα πατρός. (6.12–13)

Adorned [...] with golden necklaces like those that grace the Horai wearing golden tiaras, when they fly to the dance of the gods and their father's house.

Μοῦσαι μέν θ' ἅμα πᾶσαι ἀμειβόμεναι ὀπὶ καλῇ
ὑμνεῦσίν ῥα θεῶν δῶρ' ἄμβροτα
[...]αὐτὰρ ἐϋπλόκαμοι Χάριτες καὶ εὔφρονες Ὧραι
Ἁρμονίη θ' Ἥβη τε Διὸς θυγάτηρ τ' Ἀφροδίτη
ὀρχεῦντ' ἀλλήλων ἐπὶ καρπῷ χεῖρας ἔχουσαι· (3.189–96)

*The Muses respond as one, their rich voices
singing the immortal gifts of the gods.
[...] Then the rich-haired Graces, gracious Horai,
Harmonia, Hebe and Zeus' daughter, Aphrodite,
all dance together joining hands at their wrists.*

(trans. Rayor 2004 with minor adjustments)

---

15 The mythical narrative is inserted in the form of direct speech (*oratio recta*). According to Dornseiff 1921, 121, this technique indicates Pindar's literary model as activating the audience's awareness of the source text, in order to impart them information that is essential for their knowledge and understanding.

16 Carey 1995, 92–93: 'in Pindar, as distinct from other choral lyric poets, references to the poet are distributed throughout the poem'.

17 Gerber 1987, 11–12. It is not necessary to assume that the poet has been actually present in the location of the games. The statement can be equally a rhetorical stance for the poet's prominence in praising lavishly the victor and his success.

18 On the relationship between Horae and Graces, see further Hes. *Op.* 72–76, *Th.* 901–911, *Cypr.* fr. 4 Bernabé. Cf. also *Orph. H.* 43.5–9. Their cult in ancient Greece is discussed in Pirenne-Delforge 1996, 198–201.

The next lines (ll. 4–5) are also devoted to Pindar's personal relationship to Psaumis and their friendship in conjunction with his encomiastic task.[19] Thanks to Psaumis' liberality the poet finds his place among other guests of that celebration.[20] Pindar frequently describes his task with terms such as ἀγγελίαν or ἀγγέλλειν, 'a conventional mode of discourse associated with athletic competition, the formal announcement of the athlete's victory'.[21] Zeus is, then, invoked by the speaker 'to receive this victorious procession at Olympia, a longest-shining light of mighty deeds' (ll. 6–10), in order to sing Psaumis' athletic *aretā* (ll. 10–13). The sentence stops at a semi-colon and the point goes on with a causal ἐπεί (l. 14) in the form of an emphatic first person statement (the second one of the poem) justifying Pindar's encomiastic task: 'for I praise him for his horsemanship, hospitality and the civic harmony in the state'.

At this point we come to the third and final first person statement of the Ode (l. 17: οὐ ψεύδεϊ τέγξω λόγον). In a brief personalized moral judgment introduced by an *asyndeton* Pindar stresses the truthfulness of his praise enhancing, in this manner, a prominent aspect of his personal style in art.[22] The sentence stops at a semi-colon and the speaker goes on to the next clause to justify his declaration: 'because I praise him for his values, I shall tell (you) the truth; for (I tell you) the test till the end is the proof for the men'.[23] The poet addresses his public not only to reveal the meaning of the following myth (l. 19: ἅπερ), but also to establish once again the technique which he follows, the medium of his poetry.[24] Speaking of himself as a professional for the third time Pindar stands in the centre of his procession (l. 9), in order to bring in public the message of glory, thus securing the continuity of his addressee's fame. This message embodies the epinician αἶνος, which is in fact

---

19 Race (1990, 92–93) noted that the poet is not the only one to personally feel joy at Psaumis' achievement, but 'in general, all good men should take delight in his host's victory'.
20 Bundy 1962, 89.
21 Wells 2009, 34–35.
22 Carey 1995, 97. Cf. also Pratt 1993, 120–21, who claims that Pindar always associates truth with his own praise and lying with the blame of slanders.
23 Cf. Denniston 1954, 541–42, who claims that one of the nuances of τοι is to reveal 'the speaker's emotional or intellectual state (present or past) [...] With a proverb or general reflection, far commoner in serious poetry than in comedy or prose, τοι is used to point the applicability of a universal truth to the special matter in hand: it forces the general truth upon the consciousness of the individual addressed: "Don't forget, please"'.
24 Cf. the function of τοι according to Denniston 1954, 537: 'its primary function is to bring home to the comprehension of the person addressed a truth of which he is ignorant, or temporarily oblivious: to establish, in fact, a close rapport between the mind of the speaker and the mind of another person'. See also τοι in Pi. *I.* 1.6 (in his address to the victor) and *O.* 2.90 (addressing his own θυμός).

the justification of the truth.²⁵ The common denominator of the first person statements in the poem is the reference to the public. 'Good men' (l. 5: ἐσλοί, i.e. the local people of the small Camarina or the panhellenic audience at Olympia) are delighted to hear the message of Psaumis' victory, as do the 'mortals' (l. 18: βροτῶν), who also expect Pindar to communicate the glorious event.

Therefore, the διάπειρα motif, though Homeric in nature, is refigured with regard to its function. It is consciously placed at the peak of a series of the performative 'I', right at the beginning of the mythical narrative, which enables Pindar to reveal to the audience his professional profile as a lyric creator, 'his distinct identity'.²⁶ The motif belongs, then, to the programmatic content of the poem, at the *hic et nunc* of the epinician performance. As with Odysseus, Erginus and Psaumis, Pindar proves his own superiority to the public. He presents himself as a '*persona* projected by the poems',²⁷ a speaker in singular accompanied by a group of dancers (l. 9), whose task is to announce with truthfulness Psaumis' success and establish it through a mythical example.

What is particularly significant for our interpretation is the manner in which Homer presents Odysseus throughout his work. Not only does the hero appear as an athlete who gains victories in different disciplines (discus, spear, archery) in the athletic games in Scheria and later in Ithaca,²⁸ but also as a story-teller, a skillful narrator, who communicates his past adventures to the Phaeacians.²⁹ This aspect of the hero is particularly interesting, mainly because Odysseus, unlike other Homeric professional singers, such as Phemius or Demodocus, is often depicted as a trickster, an arch-liar, whose descriptions often combine true and fictional elements of his past (on Odysseus' refigurations, see also Alexandrou and Petrakou in this volume).³⁰ It is exactly this aspect of Odysseus that Pindar wants to suppress, and the combination of διάπειρα with the truth as a preliminary remark in his narrative helps to convey such a view. As a 'primary narrator' he aims at distinguishing himself from the Homeric Odysseus by providing im-

---

25 Nagy 1990, 314 observes that the term sums up a moral message demonstrating the authority of its creator. Cf. also Race 1990, 93, n. 18.
26 Carey 1995, 93.
27 *op.cit*. 92.
28 In *Il*. 23.859 Odysseus appears as a spearman.
29 Odysseus narrates his wanderings and experiences to the Phaeacians in the four books of his Ἀπόλογοι (*Od*. 9–12). As regards this aspect of the function of the Homeric text in Pindar, I am deeply indebted to Lucia Athanassaki for our fruitful and stimulating private discussion on the subject.
30 See Pucci 1987; Goldhill 1991, esp. ch. 1; De Jong 1997, 306, with further literature in n. 6. For Odysseus as a lying narrator, cf. also the interesting discussion of Pratt 1993, 62–63.

mediately the necessary guarantees about the truthfulness of his story.³¹ Eventually, he anticipates the false conclusions of his audience and then narrates his story suggesting analogies between past and present, according to the common epinician practice.

Concluding remarks

The appropriation of Homer in Pindar's *Olympian* 4 is developed in two levels. The first one concerns the verbal affinities to the epic source and serves primarily to praise the victor by comparing him with heroes of the past.³² Pindar's handling of Erginus' myth is entirely Homeric in diction and subject-matter. Glimpses of the *Odyssey* provide his audience with the factual data that define the celebrated victory and enhance Psaumis' glory by likening his accomplishment to the exploits of the Homeric heroes. Epic is refigured within Pindar's medium, while Erginus (from the Argonaut myth) and Odysseus (from the Homeric *Odyssey*) are treated as equivalent or 'parallel variants' to highlight the same idea: the comparison between the heroic past and the present.³³

The second level of Homeric reception is more crucial and complex. It concerns the adaptation of a specific element of the Homeric narrative. The so-called πεῖρα motif³⁴ is now developed into one of Pindar's prominent communicative strategies. The motif constitutes a medium of his epideictic rhetoric within a defined performative context. Διάπειρα then belongs to 'the current composer-audience interaction'. In a way it indicates Pindar's 'speech-plan', according to the ethnographic analysis of Wells.³⁵ Thus, the motif is not simply employed to praise the victor, as it is till now commonly assumed, but, primarily, to detect *in public* Pindar's professional task and to underline the epinician bond between him and his patron. Like other terms in the Ode, such as μαρτυρία, ἀγγελία and αἶνος, διάπειρα refers not only to the victor but also to the poet himself and to his 'overt and visible' professional role, while he comments openly upon his story.³⁶

---

31 For Odysseus as 'secondary narrator' among other Homeric characters, see de Jong 1997, 309–10.
32 Graziosi/Haubold 2009, 107 argued that Pindar's epinicia must be explored as 'elaborate attempts to link the (suitably doctored) past and the present circumstance in which he performs'.
33 Nagy 1990, 414–16.
34 Behind the variation of the πεῖρα motif its function is revealed, which mainly concerns the performative context of the poem.
35 Wells 2009, 68–73.
36 Pfeijffer 2004, 215–19.

Combined with the virtue of truthfulness in the frame of a gnomic authoritative declaration, διάπειρα establishes the true message of victory, while the poet attempts to 'convince' his public, by conveying the importance of the narrated event.[37] The matter is, then, not only about the narration of a story, but also about its *reception by the public* (διάπειρά τοι βροτῶν ἔλεγχος).[38]

From a narratological point of view, Pindar differentiates himself from the Homeric Odysseus. He anchors himself to the present occasion of the celebration, creating *ēthos*. Being conscious about the expectations of his audience the poet aims at persuading about the truth of his attitude and praise, by narrating the story of a similar situation.[39] The Homeric reflection of the (δια)πειρα motif infuses Pindar's speech with authority. It is a poetic strategy showcasing a multilayered adaptation of the epic source text and the manner in which it is reworked to meet the needs of a lyric performance.

---

37 Pfeijffer 2004, 219; Carey 1995, 93.
38 It seems like the poet intrudes into his own story, in order to add to it credibility and value. The Ode is 'Homeric' not only in terms of its narrative, but also with regard to its introduction, which is made in Homeric colours. In the form of a gnomic, authoritative declaration the Homeric πεῖρα motif combined with the truth signals not only the mythical *exemplum*, but the narrator as well.
39 Nagy 1990, 437 mentions: 'The presence of heroic narrative in Pindar is the continuation of a living tradition, not the preservation of references to lost epic texts. Recognizing the Homeric source text is essential for the understanding of the denotation of the text and for the appreciation of the poem as a meaningful work of art'.

Chris Carey
Homer and Epic in Herodotus' Book 7

Herodotus' relationship with Homer, already a commonplace in antiquity,[1] is both complex and shifting. It is a cliché, but like most clichés true, that Herodotus overtly place himself at a crossroads in European literary history. While his broadly rationalizing approach to his world and his insistence on explaining causation align him with developments in contemporary Ionia,[2] his programmatic opening also firmly aligns him with the epic hero's quest for, and the epic narrator's bestowal of, *kleos aphthiton*, undying renown:

> Ἡροδότου Ἁλικαρνασσέος ἱστορίης ἀπόδεξις ἥδε, ὡς μήτε τὰ γενόμενα ἐξ ἀνθρώπων τῷ χρόνῳ ἐξίτηλα γένηται, μήτε ἔργα μεγάλα τε καὶ θωμαστά, τὰ μὲν Ἕλλησι, τὰ δὲ βαρβάροισι ἀποδεχθέντα, ἀκλέα γένηται, τά τε ἄλλα καὶ δι' ἣν αἰτίην ἐπολέμησαν ἀλλήλοισι.
>
> *This is the exposition of the research of Herodotus of Halicarnassus, so that events may not be lost to mankind through time nor great and marvellous deeds, some performed by Greeks and others by barbarians, may not lose their glory, including the reason why they went to war with each other.*[3]

The debt to epic is overtly advertised at the level of form. It appears as a generic debt in the archaizing dialect which Herodotus shares with other Ionian logographers and in the presence of words otherwise attested only in poetry, and as a specifically Homeric debt in the pervasive presence of direct speech, a feature which Aristotle singled out as especially associated with the *Iliad* and the *Odyssey*.[4] More generally, in locating the Persian Wars within the larger context of hostilities between East and West he associates his narrative closely with the Trojan War as the salient predecessor of the westward aggression of 490 and 480 BC. At the same time, as so often when one creative work engaged with another, the encounter with epic always carries an implied or explicit distancing.[5] Thus Herodotus' 'Homeric' dialect is resolutely Ionic; it is a *Kunstsprache* but not the epic Ionic-Aeolic

---

1 [Longin.] De sublim.13.3: μόνος Ἡρόδοτος Ὁμηρικώτατος ἐγένετο· Στησίχορος ἔτι πρότερον ὅ τε Ἀρχίλοχος...
2 For Herodotus' relationship with contemporary intellectual trends, see in general Thomas 2000.
3 Translations of Herodotus are based on the Loeb of A.D. Godley 1920–25 with revisions of my own, those of Homer ultimately are based on the Loeb of A.T. Murray 1924–25, with my own (often radical) revisions. Other translations are my own unless otherwise indicated.
4 *Poet.* 1460a.
5 See on this especially Pelling 2006.

Kunstsprache. And when he explicitly approaches Homer, Herodotus pointedly distances himself from and questions the authority of the Homeric text.

This complex relationship is omnipresent in Herodotus. But it is not uniformly present. There are highs and lows of interaction. Herodotus' use of Homer and of epic more generally reaches its highest point in book 7, which engages with the Homeric text to a degree unparalleled in the *History*. My present purpose is simply to chart this engagement.

The engagement with Homer first surfaces explicitly at §20 with the assertion that the invasion of 480 exceeded all of the early East-West confrontations put together.

> στόλων γὰρ τῶν ἡμεῖς ἴδμεν πολλῷ δὴ μέγιστος οὗτος ἐγένετο, ὥστε μήτε τὸν Δαρείου τὸν ἐπὶ Σκύθας παρὰ τοῦτον μηδένα φαίνεσθαι μήτε τῶν Σκυθέων ὅτε Σκύθαι Κιμμερίους διώκοντες ἐς τὴν Μηδικὴν χώρην ἐσβαλόντες σχεδὸν πάντα τὰ ἄνω τῆς Ἀσίης καταστρεψάμενοι ἐνέμοντο, τῶν εἵνεκεν ὕστερον Δαρεῖος ἐτιμωρέετο, μήτε κατὰ τὰ λεγόμενα τὸν Ἀτρειδέων ἐς Ἴλιον μήτε τὸν Μυσῶν τε καὶ Τευκρῶν τὸν πρὸ τῶν Τρωικῶν γενόμενον, οἳ διαβάντες ἐς τὴν Εὐρώπην κατὰ Βόσπορον τούς τε Θρήικας κατεστρέψαντο πάντας καὶ ἐπὶ τὸν Ἰόνιον πόντον κατέβησαν μέχρι τε Πηνειοῦ ποταμοῦ τὸ πρὸς μεσαμβρίης ἤλασαν. αὗται αἱ πᾶσαι οὐδ' ἕτεραι πρὸς ταύτῃσι γενόμεναι στρατηλασίαι μιῆς τῆσδε οὐκ ἄξιαι.

> *This was by far the greatest of all expeditions of which we know. The one that Darius led against the Scythians is nothing compared to this; nor is the Scythian expedition, when they invaded Median territory in pursuit of the Cimmerians and conquered and held almost all the upper lands of Asia (for which Darius afterwards attempted to punish them); nor according to the reports, the expedition led by the sons of Atreus against Troy; nor the expedition of the Mysians and Teucrians, who before the Trojan War crossed the Bosporus into Europe, conquered all the Thracians, and came down to the Ionian sea, driving southward as far as the river Peneus. Not all these nor all the others added to them equal this single expedition.*

Though Herodotus gives a list of the earlier invasions, only one receives a comment on its source. That is the Trojan War, where (in a milder way than his suspicion of Homer in book 2)[6] he qualifies the reference to Troy with a disclaimer about the tradition. The comment is revealing. Troy and epic are the main competitors for his theme and the passage insists that in scale and significance Herodotus' story dwarfs that of Homer. The position of this assertion is highly signif-

---

[6] 2.116.1: Ἑλένης μὲν ταύτην ἄπιξιν παρὰ Πρωτέα ἔλεγον οἱ ἱρέες γενέσθαι. Δοκέει δέ μοι καὶ Ὅμηρος τὸν λόγον τοῦτον πυθέσθαι· ἀλλ', οὐ γὰρ ὁμοίως ἐς τὴν ἐποποιίην εὐπρεπὴς ἦν τῷ ἑτέρῳ τῷ περ ἐχρήσατο, μετῆκε αὐτόν, δηλώσας ὡς καὶ τοῦτον ἐπίσταιτο τὸν λόγον.

This is the way the priests narrate the arrival of Helen to the court of Proteus. I think that Homer heard of this account; but seeing that it was not so well suited to epic poetry as the tale of which he made use, he rejected it, while showing that he knew it.

icant. It is placed very early in (what for us is) book 7 of the *History*, immediately after the ratification of the decision to go to war but before the army begins to mobilize. As such it serves as a second *prooimion*, introducing a new and climactic phase in the narrative. This book follows the specifically Athenian *aristeia* at Marathon in book 6, which is the climax of the pre-invasion narrative. In contrast to Marathon, presented by Herodotus as a Persian punitive expedition against targeted enemies, the invasion in book 7 is a threat to the whole of Greece; Herodotus has already signalled Darius' escalation of his ambitions from targeted *tisis* to a more general intention to take Greece,[7] and the prospect of a Persian conquest of Greece had figured as an implied counter-factual as early as book 3, when Atossa playing the familiar role of tempter tries to divert Darius from the Scythian campaign to an attack on Greece.[8] But in the case of Xerxes the target is from the start the whole of Greece. And more than Greece. For Herodotus the ultimate goal is Europe.[9] This is for Herodotus a conflict on a scale unprecedented in the history of the world; not all the East-West conflicts combined equal it. As such it is an epic contest, and one which surpasses all epic narrative.

In fact of course this *prooimion* is simply making explicit an engagement with Homer visible to the original audience in the preceding narrative. The dream which tempts Xerxes draws on an established narrative role for dreams in epic, lyric and drama (and indeed in real life) as the prompters to action. One text lurking in the background is almost certainly Aeschylus' *Persians*, whose influence is palpable throughout book 7. But far more important as an influence is the epic background. The generic affinity with epic is visible in the behaviour of the dream. Unlike those dreams where people see something while asleep (the more usual form in Herodotus), this dream is a figure who comes and stands over the sleeping Xerxes in the manner of epic apparition dreams.[10]

---

7 6.43–44, 7.1.1.
8 3.133–34.
9 7.5.3.
10 7.12.1: ταῦτα μὲν ἐπὶ τοσοῦτο ἐλέγετο. μετὰ δὲ εὐφρόνη τε ἐγίνετο καὶ Ξέρξην ἔκνιζε ἡ Ἀρταβάνου γνώμη· νυκτὶ δὲ βουλὴν διδοὺς πάγχυ εὕρισκέ οἱ οὐ πρῆγμα εἶναι στρατεύεσθαι ἐπὶ τὴν Ἑλλάδα. δεδογμένων δέ οἱ αὖτις τούτων κατύπνωσε. καὶ δή κου ἐν τῇ νυκτὶ εἶδε ὄψιν τοιήνδε, ὡς λέγεται ὑπὸ Περσέων· ἐδόκεε ὁ Ξέρξης ἄνδρα οἱ ἐπιστάντα μέγαν τε καὶ εὐειδέα εἰπεῖν· "μετὰ δὴ βουλεύεαι, ὦ Πέρσα, στράτευμα μὴ ἄγειν ἐπὶ τὴν Ἑλλάδα, προείπας ἁλίζειν Πέρσῃσι στρατόν; οὔτε ὦν μεταβουλευόμενος ποιέεις εὖ, οὔτε ὁ συγγνωσόμενός τοι πάρα· ἀλλ' ὥσπερ τῆς ἡμέρης ἐβουλεύσαο ποιέειν, ταύτην ἴθι τῶν ὁδῶν." τὸν μὲν ταῦτα εἴπαντα ἐδόκεε ὁ Ξέρξης ἀποπτάσθαι.

The discussion went that far; then night came, and Xerxes was pricked by the advice of Artabanus. Giving over the night to reflection, he concluded that to send an army against Hellas was not his affair. He made this second resolve and fell asleep; then (so the Persians say) in the night he saw a

But there is a very specific intertext here in the account of the dream sent by Zeus to Agamemnon in book 2 of the *Iliad*, a text which is regularly cited in this context.¹¹ The presence of other dreams in both the *Iliad* and the *Odyssey* indicates that they were a regular narrative motif in epic texts. So we should avoid the automatic assumption that an intertext which strikes us immediately with our very small sample of early Greek poetry would have been as obvious to a Greek, with a whole tradition potentially available. But in this case the similarities are striking and numerous enough to rule out coincidence.

The position immediately invites comparison. In both cases after a narrated or implied interval in the hostilities a renewal of the fighting is prompted by a divine dream. In Homer the dream is explicitly sent by Zeus. This is a more tricky situation for Herodotus to manage. The historian never adopts the omniscient stance of the epic poet; his account comes from research,¹² not as a gift from the Muses. So divine origin cannot be a narrative fact. But the narrative, while carefully avoiding anything which might count as an explicit authorial validation of the dream figure, strongly invites us to take it seriously as something supernatural. This is achieved both with the amount of space devoted to the narrative and with the subtle shift in focalization. Though we begin with explicit distancing of author from story through the reference to Persian sources (7.12.1: λέγεται ὑπὸ Περσέων¹³), the demurrer is not repeat-

---

vision like this: it seemed to Xerxes that a tall and handsome man stood over him and said: 'Are you then changing your mind, Persian, and not intending to lead an expedition against Hellas, although you have proclaimed the mustering of the army? It is not good for you to change your mind, and there will be no one here to pardon you for it; but continue along the path you resolved upon yesterday.' With these words the figure seemed to Xerxes to flit away.

For Herodotean parallels, see 1.34.1, 38.1, 2.139.1, 141.3, 5.56.1. Stein (1889, *ad loc.*) speaks of 'das nach homerischer Art gedachte Traumbild'. Macan 1908 remarks: 'the analogy with the dream of Agamemnon, *Il.* 2 ad init., has been often pointed out'. Immerwahr (1954, 34) never actually justifies his brisk: 'it is also not very enlightening to compare the dreams to the famous dream of Agamemnon of *Iliad* 2'. West (1987, 264) is a little less brisk, but ignores the similarity in narrative context and purpose (of the dream). See n.17 below.

11 *Il.* 2.16–34.

12 The most succinct statement of method is 2.99.1: μέχρι μὲν τούτου ὄψις τε ἐμὴ καὶ γνώμη καὶ ἱστορίη ταῦτα λέγουσά ἐστι, τὸ δὲ ἀπὸ τοῦδε αἰγυπτίους ἔρχομαι λόγους ἐρέων κατὰ [τὰ] ἤκουον· προσέσται δέ τι αὐτοῖσι καὶ τῆς ἐμῆς ὄψιος.

So far is said by my own autopsy and judgment and inquiry. In what follows I shall record Egyptian accounts, according to what I have heard, and will add something of what I myself have seen.

13 See Ophuisen/Stork 1999, *ad loc.*

ed. Instead, we are offered authorial statements of fact and a degree of circumstantial detail, which further invites belief.[14]

The status of the dream is also boosted by the form taken by the dream figure, who has superhuman stature and beauty. This is not unique (it happens in the case of Hipparchus in book 5[15]). But here the sense that we are in the presence of something superhuman is further emphasized by the test which refutes the rationalist incredulity of Artabanus. As Harrison notes,[16] these doubts are clearly introduced into the narrative specifically to be quashed by the sequel. Finally, its immediate context also aligns it with Homer. Both are intimately tied to councils. Agamemnon's dream prompts two meetings, a council of the elite and a general *agora* of the army. Xerxes' dream visions are interspersed with meetings of his council (this time three). Finally, both are false. The falsity of the Iliadic dream is explicit; Zeus misleads Agamemnon with a dream which offers instant success, though the aim is in fact to further the impact of Achilles' withdrawal from battle. Again it is more difficult for the historian to flag the intent to deceive, and scholars have often been less ready to see the dream to Xerxes as aimed at deceiving. But the apparition emphatically tells Xerxes that the alternative to the expedition is ruin and diminution, when in fact it is the expedition which will be ruinous.[17] The dream means to deceive.[18]

However, while visibly drawing on Homer, the text also visibly goes beyond Homer. Agamemnon receives a single dream vision. Xerxes' dream figure comes not just once but three times. There are two dreamers.[19] And there are three councils, not two. There is a process of expansion here, which gives the Herodotean narrative an element of hyperbole in comparison with its antecedent, commensurate with the claim which follows that this campaign was unprecedented in scale. A unique expedition like this requires divine prompting on a scale unprecedented even in epic.

The other visibly Homeric element is the expanded catalogue. Catalogues of combatants are a recurrent and distinguishing feature of the invasion narrative.

---

[14] The tacit narrator validation of the dream is marked by the narrative shift from subject impression here (ἐδόκεε) to authorial statement (4.1: ἔλεγε, 17.1: ἦλθε with Macan) and back (7.18.1).
[15] 5.56.1.
[16] Harrison 2000, 135.
[17] Contra e.g. West 1987, 264–65: 'Despite the widespread assumption that these dreams are sent to mislead the king, there is no reason to question their message that it would be personally disastrous for Xerxes to change his mind at this point'. Nothing in the text suggests the latter; and the net result (contrary to the dream) is humiliation for Xerxes, in the narrative if not in real life.
[18] See especially Harrison 2000, 136–37.
[19] Dodson 2009, 92 rightly refers to 'the dreams of Xerxes and Artabanus'.

It is interesting here to compare the account of Marathon. Though a catalogue on the Greek side is ruled out by the simple fact that only Athenians and Plataeans fight, a Persian catalogue was always a possibility and Marathon receives none. In contrast, the invasion narrative is rich in catalogues. They recur at 8.1–2 (Artemisium), 43–48 (Salamis), and finally 9.28–32 (Plataea). But the present is by far the longest. Since only the Iranian contingents listed play any part in the subseqent account of the fighting,[20] the list mainly serves to retard the narrative, in order to create suspense and to continue Herodotus' emphasis on the unprecedented scale of the army descending on Greece. But again the epic intertext is an important part of the rhetoric. For the detailed catalogue of forces at Doriscus the obvious antecedent was the catalogue of ships in *Iliad* book 2. Again, of course, we need to bear in mind that with so much more epic available to author and audience intertexts which we perceive unhesitatingly may have had less salience. There must have been many catalogues in epic war narratives. But equally we should note that the scale of Homer's list invites comparison and that the East-West axis of the conflict gives *Iliad* 2 a salience which is not the result of modern Homerocentrism nor of the accident of survival.

There are, of course, some obvious differences. Herodotus carefully integrates his catalogue into his narrative by locating it in the marshalling of the troops at Doriscus. So it has a natural role in his narrative. He also lists his Greeks when they enter his narrative as fighters. So there is no mechanical insertion of the Homeric motif. Herodotus is also at pains to vary his model. Thus, where the Homeric text gives first place to the Greeks both in position and in scale (the Greeks in Homer receive 276 lines, the Trojans 61), Herodotus reverses the relationship. His Greeks, as the more familiar combatants and the smaller force, receive relatively little space and enter the narrative later (7.202–03), while his Asiatics receive in total approximately one sixth of the book.

But as well as varying his model Herodotus outdoes it in the way he chooses to present his Asiatics. Where Homer notes only in passing the polyglot nature of his Trojans and their allies[21] in a narrative which generally assimilates them cul-

---

20 Burn 1984², 320.
21 *Il.* 2.867–69:
   Νάστης αὖ Καρῶν ἡγήσατο βαρβαροφώνων,
   οἳ Μίλητον ἔχον Φθιρῶν τ' ὄρος ἀκριτόφυλλον
   Μαιάνδρου τε ῥοὰς Μυκάλης τ' αἰπεινὰ κάρηνα

   And Nastes again led the Carians, barbarian speakers,
   who held Miletus and the mountain of Phthires, with its boundless leaves,
   and the streams of Maeander, and the steep peaks of Mycale.

turally to each other and to the Greeks, Herodotus is at pains to emphasize diversity as well as scale. Not only do these forces come from everywhere in the empire, they are consistently exotic (with few exceptions) and often as different from each other as they are from the Greeks. It is in fact very unlikely that most of these troops were marshalled by Xerxes or set foot in Greece, and (as observed already) almost all of them disappear from the subsequent narrative. It is probable that the bulk of the troops were the Iranian core of the Persian army, the Persians, Medes and Saka (known to the Greeks as Scythians). Herodotus seems to be following a Persian source for the composition of the army contingents from the empire as a whole rather than a muster list for the invasion of 480. This reflects in part the difficulty he experienced in obtaining information specific to the expedition. He admits that he has no detailed source for scale of the individual components[22] and this in turn invites us to conclude that he did not have access to a list of the forces engaged in the campaign. But in filling the gap he has been influenced by Aeschylus' understanding of the Persian army as one which empties the empire of men and draws on peoples from every

---

Cf. *Il.* 3.1–9:
αὐτὰρ ἐπεὶ κόσμηθεν ἅμ' ἡγεμόνεσσιν ἕκαστοι,
Τρῶες μὲν κλαγγῇ τ' ἐνοπῇ τ' ἴσαν ὄρνιθες ὣς
ἠΰτε περ κλαγγὴ γεράνων πέλει οὐρανόθι πρό·
αἵ τ' ἐπεὶ οὖν χειμῶνα φύγον καὶ ἀθέσφατον ὄμβρον
κλαγγῇ ταί γε πέτονται ἐπ' ὠκεανοῖο ῥοάων
ἀνδράσι Πυγμαίοισι φόνον καὶ κῆρα φέρουσαι·
ἠέριαι δ' ἄρα ταί γε κακὴν ἔριδα προφέρονται.
οἳ δ' ἄρ' ἴσαν σιγῇ μένεα πνείοντες Ἀχαιοὶ
ἐν θυμῷ μεμαῶτες ἀλεξέμεν ἀλλήλοισιν.

Now when they were marshalled, each with their leaders,
the Trojans advanced with clamour and cries like birds,
like the clamour of cranes before heaven,
who when they have fled wintry storms and rain beyond measure,
with clamour fly toward the streams of Ocean,
bringing slaughter and death to the Pigmy men,
and in the early dawn offer grim battle.
But the Achaeans advanced in silence, breathing courage,
eager at heart to defend each other.

22 7.60.9: ὅσον μέν νυν ἕκαστοι παρεῖχον πλῆθος ἐς ἀριθμόν, οὐκ ἔχω εἰπεῖν τὸ ἀτρεκές (οὐ γὰρ λέγεται πρὸς οὐδαμῶν ἀνθρώπων), σύμπαντος δὲ τοῦ στρατοῦ τοῦ πεζοῦ τὸ πλῆθος ἐφάνη ἑβδομήκοντα καὶ ἑκατὸν μυριάδες.

I cannot give the precise number that each group contributed to the total, for there is no one who tells us; but the total of the whole land army turned out as one million and seven hundred thousand.

region.²³ The effect (apart from increasing the emphasis throughout the narrative on the dramatic disparity between the Greek and Persian forces) is again to stress the unprecedented nature of the invasion. So once more Herodotus uses Homeric motifs to recall and at the same time distance himself from Homer.

Again it is worth stressing that this is not Herodotus' only catalogue. But it has no equal in what precedes and even the catalogue of combatants in the climactic battle of Plataea in book 9 is much smaller in scale and lacking in the cumulative exoticism of this catalogue. This catalogue also advertises its Homeric origin in a way that the subsequent catalogues do not in its structural similarity to that of the *Iliad*; it lists both contingents and commanders, where subsequent catalogues are happy to list contingents.

There is one further aspect of the narrative of the decision to go to war, which is worth stressing. Xerxes too is shaped by Herodotus on the model of the epic hero, with all its ambiguity, in the grandeur of his ambitions and the motives which take him to war. He is invited by Mardonius, the ultimate tempter, to think of the renown which he will win if he conquers Greece,²⁴ as well as the territory and the opportunity for revenge. He himself stresses in council that glory is one of the things he seeks. In conversation with Mardonius he praises the life of action and risk²⁵ in a manner which (as Angus Bowie has noted) would be fitting in the mouth of a Homeric hero.²⁶ And Herodotus stresses

---

23 A. *Pers.* 12–15, 718:
πᾶσα γὰρ ἰσχὺς Ἀσιατογενὴς
οἴχωκε, νέον δ' ἄνδρα βαΰζει,
κοὔτε τις ἄγγελος οὔτε τις ἱππεὺς
ἄστυ τὸ Περσῶν ἀφικνεῖται·
[...] θούριος Ξέρξης, κενώσας πᾶσαν ἠπείρου πλάκα.
For the whole strength of Asia
has gone, and yelps around the young man,
and no messenger or horseman
reaches the city of the Persians.
[...] Rushing Xerxes, emptying the whole plain of the mainland.
24 7.5.2: ἀλλ' εἰ τὸ μὲν νῦν ταῦτα πρήσσοις τά περ ἐν χερσὶ ἔχεις· ἡμερώσας δὲ Αἴγυπτον τὴν ἐξυβρίσασαν στρατηλάτεε ἐπὶ τὰς Ἀθήνας, ἵνα λόγος τέ σε ἔχῃ πρὸς ἀνθρώπων ἀγαθὸς καί τις ὕστερον φυλάσσηται ἐπὶ γῆν τὴν σὴν στρατεύεσθαι.

For now you should do what you have in hand; then, when you have tamed the arrogance of Egypt, lead your armies against Athens, so that you may have fair fame among men, and others may beware of invading your land in future.
25 7.50.3: μεγάλα γὰρ πρήγματα μεγάλοισι κινδύνοισι ἐθέλει καταιρέεσθαι.
Great causes are usually achieved with great risks.
26 Bowie 2007, 10.

(not entirely correctly) that his decision to build the canal was down to his *megalophrosynē*.²⁷ The desire for glory was Persian as well as Greek. And the epic hero is not the only influence at work, since Herodotus' account of Xerxes' decision also draws on Aeschylus' version of his psychology in the *Persians*. But the values of the epic hero, as formulated resoundingly by Homer, are there as part of the (complex) presentation of Xerxes:

αὐτίκα δὲ Γλαῦκον προσέφη παῖδ' Ἱππολόχοιο·
Γλαῦκε τί ἢ δὴ νῶϊ τετιμήμεσθα μάλιστα
ἕδρῃ τε κρέασίν τε ἰδὲ πλείοις δεπάεσσιν
ἐν Λυκίῃ, πάντες δὲ θεοὺς ὣς εἰσορόωσι,
καὶ τέμενος νεμόμεσθα μέγα Ξάνθοιο παρ' ὄχθας
καλὸν φυταλιῆς καὶ ἀρούρης πυροφόροιο;
τὼ νῦν χρὴ Λυκίοισι μέτα πρώτοισιν ἐόντας
ἑστάμεν ἠδὲ μάχης καυστείρης ἀντιβολῆσαι,
ὄφρά τις ὧδ' εἴπῃ Λυκίων πύκα θωρηκτάων·
οὐ μὰν ἀκλεέες Λυκίην κάτα κοιρανέουσιν
ἡμέτεροι βασιλῆες, ἔδουσί τε πίονα μῆλα
οἶνόν τ' ἔξαιτον μελιηδέα· ἀλλ' ἄρα καὶ ἲς

---

27 7.24: ὡς μὲν ἐμὲ συμβαλλόμενον εὑρίσκειν, μεγαλοφροσύνης εἵνεκεν αὐτὸ Ξέρξης ὀρύσσειν ἐκέλευε, ἐθέλων τε δύναμιν ἀποδείκνυσθαι καὶ μνημόσυνα λιπέσθαι. παρεὸν γὰρ μηδένα πόνον λαβόντας τὸν ἰσθμὸν τὰς νέας διειρύσαι, ὀρύσσειν ἐκέλευε διώρυχα τῇ θαλάσσῃ εὖρος ὡς δύο τριήρεας πλέειν ὁμοῦ ἐλαστρεομένας.

As far as I can determine by reasoning, Xerxes ordered this digging out of pride, wishing to display his power and leave a memorial; though with no trouble they could have drawn their ships across the isthmus, he ordered them to dig a canal from sea to sea, wide enough to float two triremes rowed abreast.

Like μεγαλοφροσύνη, μηδένα πόνον λαβόντας captures the ambiguity of Herodotus' presentation, for it hovers somewhere between needless labour and the readiness of the Pindaric athlete to undergo *ponos* for the sake of renown (*O*. 5.15, 6.9–11, 8.7, 9.22–23, 10.91–93, 11.4, *P*. 8.73–80, *N*. 1.32–33, 4.1–2, 5.48–49, 6.24, 7.14–16, 10.24, 30–31, *I*. 1.45–46, 4.45–47, 5.22–25, 57–59, 6.10–11). Herodotus' objection that it would have been feasible to drag the ships overland across the peninsula is only superficially persuasive. As Macan notes *ad loc.*, the Greeks occasionally moved small forces short distances in this way (Th. 2.3, 2.81, 4.8.2); but it would be an enormous task to use this method to move (and reinforce) a large fleet on a major expedition (despite Herodotus' μηδένα πόνον λαβόντας). The canal would offer advantages for provisioning as well as movement of warships, if it was deep enough for barges or small cargo vessels. Herodotus is not however entirely wrong. The Chalouf *stēlē* (DZc, Brosius 2000 no 52, p.47. Kuhrt 2007 no. 11, 6, pp. 485–6) says: 'King Darius says: I am a Persian. From Persia I seized Egypt. I ordered this canal dug from a river that is called Nile and flows in Egypt, to the sea which begins in Persia. Therefore, this canal was dug as I had ordered, and ships went from Egypt through this canal to Persia, as I wished'. The Egytian canal was evidently a source of pride for Darius (as well as practical politics) and Xerxes was probably motivated in part by a desire to emulate his father (as Stein 1889 notes).

ἐσθλή, ἐπεὶ Λυκίοισι μέτα πρώτοισι μάχονται.
ὦ πέπον εἰ μὲν γὰρ πόλεμον περὶ τόνδε φυγόντε
αἰεὶ δὴ μέλλοιμεν ἀγήρω τ' ἀθανάτω τε
ἔσσεσθ', οὔτέ κεν αὐτὸς ἐνὶ πρώτοισι μαχοίμην
οὔτέ κε σὲ στέλλοιμι μάχην ἐς κυδιάνειραν·
νῦν δ' ἔμπης γὰρ κῆρες ἐφεστᾶσιν θανάτοιο
μυρίαι, ἃς οὐκ ἔστι φυγεῖν βροτὸν οὐδ' ὑπαλύξαι,
ἴομεν ἠέ τῳ εὖχος ὀρέξομεν ἠέ τις ἡμῖν.
(Il. 12.309–28)

At once he spoke to Glaucus, son of Hippolochus:
'Glaucus, why is it you and I are honoured above others
with pride of place, and meats and filled wine cups
in Lycia, and all men look on us as if we were immortals,
and we have our allocated land by the banks of Xanthus,
good land, orchard and vineyard, and fields for growing wheat?
So now it is our duty in the forefront of the Lycians
to take our stand, and go to meet blazing battle,
so that a man of the close-armoured Lycians may say of us:
"Indeed, these are no inglorious men who are lords of Lycia,
these kings of ours, who feed upon the fat sheep
and drink the exquisite sweet wine, but there is noble
valour in them, since they fight in the forefront of the Lycians."
Friend, supposing you and I, escaping this battle,
Could go on to live on forever, ageless, immortal,
I would not myself be fighting in the foremost
nor would I send you into battle where men win glory.
But now, seeing that the spirits of death stand close about us
countless, and no man can turn aside or escape them,
let us go on and give someone cause to boast or he to us.'
(trans. Lattimore 1951 adapted)

Like the other motifs, it aligns the invasion with the themes of epic and stresses both its significance and the climactic nature of the last three books. There is, however, an irony in all of this. Although I have stressed the unique salience of epic in book 7, and the book does have a neat wholeness to it in the narrative arc that takes us from the decision to invade through to the first major encounter, the account of the invasion has to be read as a fluent whole; the books are not free-standing. Xerxes will in the end prove to be entirely unheroic. Where the pre-Salamis narrative places emphasis on Greek fears and the Greek readiness to flee, the decisive victory at Salamis transfers these emotions to Xerxes. His response to defeat is to enact a flight, which reverses the morale ratio between Greek and Persian:[28]

> Ξέρξης δὲ ὡς ἔμαθε τὸ γεγονὸς πάθος, δείσας μή τις τῶν Ἰώνων ὑποθῆται τοῖσι Ἕλλησι ἢ αὐτοὶ νοήσωσι πλέειν ἐς τὸν Ἑλλήσποντον λύσοντες τὰς γεφύρας καὶ ἀπολαμφθεὶς ἐν τῇ Εὐρώπῃ κινδυνεύσῃ ἀπολέσθαι, δρησμὸν ἐβούλευε (8.97.1)
>
> When Xerxes understood the calamity which had taken place, he feared that some of the Ionians might advise the Hellenes, or that they might decide themselves, to sail to the Hellespont and destroy the bridges, and he would be trapped in Europe and in danger of destruction, he resolved on flight.

The epic stance in book 7 is in part a preparation for this *peripeteia*.

The scale of the invasion is not the only reason for the dense indebtedness to Homer in book 7. The other reason is the nature of the culminating battle of the book at Thermopylae. The tradition which Herodotus inherited already stressed the dramatic disparity of the forces and the courageous choice made by the Greek fighters. This is all there in the epigram for the fallen set up at the site with its emphasis on overwhelming odds (7.228.1):

> μυριάσιν ποτὲ τᾷδε τριακοσίαις ἐμάχοντο
> ἐκ Πελοποννάσου χιλιάδες τέτορες.
>
> Against three million here fought
> Four thousand from the Peloponnese.

The poetic tradition had expanded this aspect. Simonides' fragmentary lyric celebration of the dead rings a number of changes on the epic notion of *kleos aphthiton*, immortal renown (*PMG* 531):

> τῶν ἐν Θερμοπύλαις θανόντων
> εὐκλεὴς μὲν ἁ τύχα, καλὸς δ' ὁ πότμος,
> βωμὸς δ' ὁ τάφος, πρὸ γόων δὲ μνᾶστις, ὁ δ' οἶκτος ἔπαινος·
> ἐντάφιον δὲ τοιοῦτον οὔτ' εὐρὼς
> οὔθ' ὁ πανδαμάτωρ ἀμαυρώσει χρόνος.
> ἀνδρῶν ἀγαθῶν ὅδε σηκὸς οἰκέταν εὐδοξίαν
> Ἑλλάδος εἵλετο· μαρτυρεῖ δὲ καὶ Λεωνίδας,
> Σπάρτας βασιλεύς, ἀρετᾶς μέγαν λελοιπὼς
> κόσμον ἀέναόν τε κλέος.
>
> Of those who died at Thermopylae
> the fate is glorious, fine is the destiny,
> the tomb an altar, for lamentation there is remembrance, their pity is praise.

---

28 See 8.4.1, 18, 74–75 of the Greeks.

A shroud like this not mould
nor all-conquering time will erase.
This precinct of brave men received as dweller renown
throughout Greece. Witness is Leonidas,
king of Sparta, who left behind the great ornament of valour
and glory without end.

The link with the heroic quest for *kleos* becomes explicit in Herodotus' account of the decision of Leonidas to send away the allies. They had no enthusiasm for the fight, while for him it was not *kalon* to withdraw. Herodotus' own comment on the decision associates it firmly with the value system of the epic poems:

ταύτῃ καὶ μᾶλλον τὴν γνώμην πλεῖστός εἰμι· Λεωνίδην, ἐπείτε ᾔσθετο τοὺς συμμάχους ἐόντας ἀπροθύμους καὶ οὐκ ἐθέλοντας συνδιακινδυνεύειν, κελεῦσαί σφεας ἀπαλλάσσεσθαι, αὐτῷ δὲ ἀπιέναι οὐ καλῶς ἔχειν· μένοντι δὲ αὐτοῦ κλέος μέγα ἐλείπετο, καὶ ἡ Σπάρτης εὐδαιμονίη οὐκ ἐξηλείφετο. (7.220.2)

I, however, firmly believe that when Leonidas perceived that the allies were dispirited and unwilling to share all risks with him, he told then to depart. For himself, however, it was not good to leave; if he remained, he would leave a name of great glory, and the prosperity of Sparta would not be erased.

And again:

ταῦτά τε δὴ ἐπιλεγόμενον Λεωνίδην καὶ βουλόμενον κλέος καταθέσθαι μούνων Σπαρτιητέων, ἀποπέμψαι τοὺς συμμάχους μᾶλλον ἢ γνώμῃ διενειχθέντας οὕτω ἀκόσμως οἴχεσθαι τοὺς οἰχομένους. (7.220.4)

Considering this and wishing to win glory for the Spartans alone, Leonidas sent away the allies rather than have them leave in disorder because of a difference of opinion.

This sense of Leonidas as both distinct and superlative is prepared by his (re)-entry into the narrative at 7.204:

τούτοισι ἦσαν μέν νυν καὶ ἄλλοι στρατηγοὶ κατὰ πόλις ἑκάστων, ὁ δὲ θωμαζόμενος μάλιστα καὶ παντὸς τοῦ στρατεύματος ἡγεόμενος Λακεδαιμόνιος ἦν Λεωνίδης ὁ Ἀναξανδρίδεω τοῦ Λέοντος τοῦ Εὐρυκρατίδεω τοῦ Ἀναξάνδρου τοῦ Εὐρυκράτεος τοῦ Πολυδώρου τοῦ Ἀλκαμένεος τοῦ Τηλέκλου τοῦ Ἀρχέλεω τοῦ Ἡγησίλεω τοῦ Δορύσσου τοῦ Λεωβώτεω τοῦ Ἐχεστράτου τοῦ Ἤγιος τοῦ Εὐρυσθένεος τοῦ Ἀριστοδήμου τοῦ Ἀριστομάχου τοῦ Κλεοδαίου τοῦ Ὕλλου τοῦ Ἡρακλέος ...

There was a general for each contingent, but the one most admired and the leader of the whole army was a Lacedaemonian, Leonidas, son of Anaxandrides, son of Leon, son of Eurycratides, son of Anaxandrus, son of Eurycrates, son of Polydorus, son of Alcamenes, son of Teleclus, son of Archelaus, son of Hegesilaus, son of Doryssus, son of Leobotes, son of Echestratus, son of Agis, son of Eurysthenes, son of Aristodemus, son of Aristomachus, son of Cleodaeus, son of Hyllus, son of Heracles.

Though he commands a conventional Greek army, Leonidas is set apart not just by the elementary fact that he alone of the Greeks is singled out for naming at this point (unlike the Persian catalogue),[29] but by the elaborate genealogy and by his presentation as an object of awe/amazement/admiration.[30] In his singularity he resembles Xerxes (7.187.2):

> ἀνδρῶν δ' ἐουσέων τοσουτέων μυριάδων κάλλεός τε εἵνεκα καὶ μεγάθεος οὐδεὶς αὐτῶν ἀξιονικότερος ἦν αὐτοῦ Ξέρξεω ἔχειν τοῦτο τὸ κράτος.
>
> *Of all those tens of thousands of men, for beauty and grandeur there was not one worthier than Xerxes himself to hold that command.*

The way the spotlight singles out both leaders presents the encounter almost as a duel, one which (at least at the level of *kleos*) Leonidas will win.

It is of course true that Leonidas is not simply assimilated to the Homeric hero. There are complications to his motivation,[31] which reflect the fact that these events belong to contemporary history, not epic. Herodotus was too firmly aware of the unrecoverability of the past to be seduced by a facile assimilation of the war to the heroic world.[32] But it is equally true that Leonidas is presented in glorious isolation by the narrative, despite the fact that until they run out of weaponry the Spartans fight a recognizably contemporary (if slightly unconventional) battle against the Persians, not a series of individual encounters of the stylized Homeric kind. And it is also true that the Greeks saw at the time and continued to see in Thermopylae a remarkable example of courage and devotion both to country and to duty.

The dialogue with epic is also visible in the account of the fighting. The death of Leonidas occasions the first of two instances of the epic motif of the fight over a prize corpse. The second is the fight over the corpse of Masistios at Plataea in book 9 (22.3–23.2). Even here, however, book 7 is distinctive, in that Herodotus has the fighting ebb and flow four times, with the Greeks in the ascendant until the arrival of Ephialtes:

---

29 The effect is repeated in the announcement of his death at 7.224.1, where after noting that Leonidas died ἀνὴρ γενόμενος ἄριστος Herodotus withholds the names of the other Spartans who died with him, while insisting that he knows the names.
30 He is also selected for separate mention in Simonides *PMG* 531, cited above.
31 Pelling 2006, 95 notes that even in deciding to lay down glory for Sparta Leonidas acknowledges that the alternative risks having his mixed force quarrel and disperse. Real life is more grimy than the heroic ideal. See also Baragwanath 2008, 68, who notes the way his suspicions of Theban medizing undercut the heroic atmosphere. She also notes (65) the way Leonidas like many characters in the *History* seems to mirror the intellectual curiosity of the narrator.
32 See especially 1.5.4.

Ξέρξεώ τε δὴ δύο ἀδελφεοὶ ἐνθαῦτα πίπτουσι μαχόμενοι, <καὶ> ὑπὲρ τοῦ νεκροῦ τοῦ Λεωνίδεω Περσέων τε καὶ Λακεδαιμονίων ὠθισμὸς ἐγίνετο πολλός, ἐς ὃ τοῦτόν τε ἀρετῇ οἱ Ἕλληνες ὑπεξείρυσαν καὶ ἐτρέψαντο τοὺς ἐναντίους τετράκις. Τοῦτο δὲ συνεστήκεε μέχρι οὗ οἱ σὺν Ἐπιάλτῃ παρεγένοντο. (7.225.1)

Two brothers of Xerxes fought and fell there. There was a great struggle between the Persians and Lacedaemonians over Leonidas' body, until the Hellenes by their prowess rescued it and routed their enemies four times. The battle went on until the men with Epialtes arrived.

It is difficult not to sense a contest such as the fight over Patroclus behind the historical narrative.[33] Fighting over bodies was not just a literary device, of course. And battles ebb and flow, especially hard-fought battles like this one. The body of a commander has a value which justifies a fight to deny it to the enemy, just as its capture has enormous implications for morale. This is not invention. The question, however, is (as often) not 'what happened?' but 'what are we told and how?' The narrator is free to include or exclude, to extend and contract, to elaborate or not; and this kind of narrative detail is normally withheld by Herodotus. Its inclusion here recalls narrative moments in Homer or epic more generally and gives Leonidas something of the stature of a Homeric warrior. The impression is enhanced by the play with Leonidas' name. The effect of the word play is to summon up the lion of the Homeric simile, the ideal symbol of the warrior at his most courageous and lethal. The play lurks behind the oracle at 7.220.4:

ὑμῖν δ', ὦ Σπάρτης οἰκήτορες εὐρυχόροιο,
ἢ μέγα ἄστυ ἐρικυδὲς ὑπ' ἀνδράσι Περσεΐδῃσι
πέρθεται, ἢ τὸ μὲν οὐχί, ἀφ' Ἡρακλέους δὲ γενέθλης
πενθήσει βασιλῆ φθίμενον Λακεδαίμονος οὖρος·

---

[33] Il. 17.1–6:
οὐδ' ἔλαθ' Ἀτρέος υἱὸν ἀρηΐφιλον Μενέλαον
Πάτροκλος Τρώεσσι δαμεὶς ἐν δηϊοτῆτι.
βῆ δὲ διὰ προμάχων κεκορυθμένος αἴθοπι χαλκῷ,
ἀμφὶ δ' ἄρ' αὐτῷ βαῖν' ὥς τις περὶ πόρτακι μήτηρ
πρωτοτόκος κινυρὴ οὐ πρὶν εἰδυῖα τόκοιο·
ὣς περὶ Πατρόκλῳ βαῖνε ξανθὸς Μενέλαος...

*Nor did Atreus' son, Menelaus, dear to Ares,
fail to note Patroclus slain by the Trojans in the fight.
He went through the front ranks, armed in flaming bronze
and bestrode him, as its mother stands over a calf
lowing plaintively for her first-born,
who has not known motherhood before.
So over Patroclus strode fair-haired Menelaus.*
Cf. Boedeker 2003, 34–36.

οὐ γὰρ τὸν ταύρων σχήσει μένος οὐδὲ λεόντων
ἀντιβίην· Ζηνὸς γὰρ ἔχει μένος· οὐδέ ἕ φημι
σχήσεσθαι, πρὶν τῶνδ' ἕτερον διὰ πάντα δάσηται.

For you, inhabitants of spacious Sparta,
either your great and glorious city is wasted by Persian men,
or if not that, then the boundary of Lacedaemon
will mourn a dead king, from Heracles' line.
The might of bulls or lions will not check him
with opposing strength; for he has the might of Zeus. I affirm
he will not stop until he rends one of these utterly.

It also emerges at 7.225.2 with the mention of the lion at his tomb. Herodotus did not invent this. The lion predates him and indicates that the etymological play with the first two syllables of his name was traditional. But he did choose to include the implied symbolism of Leonidas as lion.

The rapprochement with the Homeric hero may also apply to the treatment of the body by Xerxes, where Herodotus goes out of his way to emphasize the departure from Persian behaviour in his treatment of a brave enemy.[34] Here we are on weaker ground, since an incident like this could scarcely have been omitted irrespective of the engagement with epic. But the epic abuse which comes to mind is the mistreatment of the body of Hector in Homer. We cannot say whether this parallel would have occurred to all or most or even any of Herodotus' original audience. But the parallel was an apt one, since both died fighting bravely for a lost cause.

The epic background also seems to lie behind a detail of timing (§223) in Herodotus' battle narrative. The timing of the final attack is noted by a detail which like the Homeric simile takes us into the normal world of peaceful activities[35] in the midst of bloodshed:

---

34 7.238: ταῦτα εἴπας Ξέρξης διεξήιε διὰ τῶν νεκρῶν καὶ Λεωνίδεω, ἀκηκοὼς ὅτι βασιλεύς τε ἦν καὶ στρατηγὸς Λακεδαιμονίων, ἐκέλευσε ἀποταμόντας τὴν κεφαλὴν ἀνασταυρῶσαι. δῆλά μοι πολλοῖσι μὲν καὶ ἄλλοισι τεκμηρίοισι, ἐν δὲ καὶ τῷδε οὐκ ἥκιστα γέγονε, ὅτι βασιλεὺς Ξέρξης πάντων δὴ μάλιστα ἀνδρῶν ἐθυμώθη ζώοντι Λεωνίδῃ· οὐ γὰρ ἄν κοτε ἐς τὸν νεκρὸν ταῦτα παρενόμησε, ἐπεὶ τιμᾶν μάλιστα νομίζουσι τῶν ἐγὼ οἶδα ἀνθρώπων Πέρσαι ἄνδρας ἀγαθοὺς τὰ πολέμια.

Having spoken in this way, Xerxes passed over the place where the dead lay and hearing that Leonidas had been king and general of the Lacedaemonians, he gave orders to cut off his head and impale it. It is plain to me by this piece of evidence among many others, that while Leonidas lived, king Xerxes was more incensed against him than against all others; otherwise he would never have dealt so outrageously with his dead body, for the Persians are beyond all men known in the habit of honoring valiant warriors.

35 Cf. for instance *Il.* 12.432–38.

> Ξέρξης δὲ ἐπεὶ ἡλίου ἀνατείλαντος σπονδὰς ἐποιήσατο, ἐπισχὼν χρόνον ἐς ἀγορῆς κου μάλιστα πληθώρην πρόσοδον ἐποιέετο· καὶ γὰρ ἐπέσταλτο ἐξ Ἐπιάλτεω οὕτω·
>
> *Xerxes poured a libation at sunrise and after holding back for a while till the time the market fills he made his advance. This was Ephialtes' instruction.*

Perhaps closer still than the simile is the time indicator at *Il.* 11.86–91:

> ἦμος δὲ δρυτόμος περ ἀνὴρ ὁπλίσσατο δεῖπνον
> οὔρεος ἐν βήσσῃσιν, ἐπεί τ' ἐκορέσσατο χεῖρας
> τάμνων δένδρεα μακρά, ἄδος τέ μιν ἵκετο θυμόν,
> σίτου τε γλυκεροῖο περὶ φρένας ἵμερος αἱρεῖ,
> τῆμος σφῇ ἀρετῇ Δαναοὶ ῥήξαντο φάλαγγας
> κεκλόμενοι ἑτάροισι κατὰ στίχας·
>
> *But at the time a woodman prepares his meal*
> *in the glades of a mountain, when he has tired his arms*
> *felling tall trees, and weariness comes upon his spirit,*
> *and desire of sweet food seizes his mind,*
> *at that time the Danaans by their valour broke the enemy lines*
> *calling to comrades in the ranks.*

The effect in the present case is to add here an element of *pathos* in reminding us of the continuity of normal life, now about to be lost forever to the Greek fighters.[36] There is a good antecedent for this in the climactic duel in *Iliad* 22, as Hector races for his life, where we are taken back to the peaceful activities of Troy in a world which he is about to leave:

> κρουνὼ δ' ἵκανον καλλιρρόω· ἔνθα δὲ πηγαὶ
> δοιαὶ ἀναΐσσουσι Σκαμάνδρου δινήεντος.
> ἣ μὲν γάρ θ' ὕδατι λιαρῷ ῥέει, ἀμφὶ δὲ καπνὸς
> γίγνεται ἐξ αὐτῆς ὡς εἰ πυρὸς αἰθομένοιο·
> ἣ δ' ἑτέρη θέρεϊ προρέει ἐϊκυῖα χαλάζῃ,
> ἢ χιόνι ψυχρῇ ἢ ἐξ ὕδατος κρυστάλλῳ.
> ἔνθα δ' ἐπ' αὐτάων πλυνοὶ εὐρέες ἐγγὺς ἔασι
> καλοὶ λαΐνεοι, ὅθι εἵματα σιγαλόεντα
> πλύνεσκον Τρώων ἄλοχοι καλαί τε θύγατρες
> τὸ πρὶν ἐπ' εἰρήνης πρὶν ἐλθεῖν υἷας Ἀχαιῶν.
> τῇ ῥα παραδραμέτην φεύγων ὃ δ' ὄπισθε διώκων·
> (*Il.* 22.147–57)
>
> *They came to the fair-flowing springs, the two sources*
> *of the river Scamander which bubble up.*
> *One of these flows with warm water, and all about smoke*

---

36 This point I owe to Simon Hornblower.

Rises from it as from a burning fire,
but the other even in summer is like hail
or snow, or the ice that forms on water.
Here, hard by the springs, are the broad washing-troughs
fine, of stone, where the wives and fair daughters of Troy
used to wash their bright clothes
before in the time of peace before the Achaeans came
Past these they sped, the one in flight and the other pursuing behind.

Alongside such specific and general glances toward Homer and Troy Herodotus also draws on other epic cycles to shape his narrative. Especially important is the march of the Seven against Thebes. From the *Thebaid* onward the campaign of the Seven was the archetypal ill-fated expedition. It was pursued in direct opposition to the will of the gods as expressed in portents:

ἤτοι μὲν γὰρ ἄτερ πολέμου εἰσῆλθε Μυκήνας
ξεῖνος ἅμ' ἀντιθέῳ Πολυνείκεϊ λαὸν ἀγείρων·
οἳ δὲ τότ' ἐστρατόωνθ' ἱερὰ πρὸς τείχεα Θήβης,
καί ῥα μάλα λίσσοντο δόμεν κλειτοὺς ἐπικούρους·
οἳ δ' ἔθελον δόμεναι καὶ ἐπῄνεον ὡς ἐκέλευον·
ἀλλὰ Ζεὺς ἔτρεψε παραίσια σήματα φαίνων.
(Il. 4.376 – 81)

He came once to Mycenae, not in war
but as a guest, with godlike Polynices to gather forces;
for they were going to war against the sacred walls of Thebes,
and prayed our people to give picked men to help them.
The people were minded to let give them,
but Zeus discouraged them, showing unfavourable omens.

The expedition even had its own prophet, Amphiaraus, who read the signs and warned the army of ruin to come. In Herodotus too the march of Xerxes is rich in signs, large and small, indicating the hostility of the gods. This creates a complex narrative in which the recurrent drumbeats are unprecedented scale (the rivers drunk dry) and unnoticed pointers to defeat. The sense of impending destruction is there from the moment Xerxes commits to the expedition. Modern scholarship focuses not unreasonably on the lying dream which sends Xerxes to war. But the text stresses that he has an alternative. There is a dream which Xerxes and his advisers misinterpret, which points (for an audience which knows the outcome) to final defeat (7.19). We find it in portents on the way; the cautionary tale implied by the fate of Marsyas (7.26.3); the *stēlē* of Croesus at the beginning of the narrative of the march which shows the limits of the Lydian territory, long since absorbed into the next empire, that of the Persians (7.30.2); the eclipse (misdated by

Herodotus) which occurs as the Persians leave Sardis (7.37.2); the disastrous experiences in the Troad (7.42–3); the unnatural birth and inverted animal behaviour encountered in Asia (7.57) and the strangely selective diet of the Greek lions, which devour only the creatures unknown in Greece (7.125–6). Some of these signs are made explicit to Xerxes, while others speak to the reader over the head of the human participants in the action. Perhaps the most interesting of the signs is the pair which frame Xerxes' visit to Troy:

> καὶ πρῶτα μέν οἱ ὑπὸ τῇ Ἴδῃ νύκτα ἀναμείναντι βρονταί τε καὶ πρηστῆρες ἐπεσπίπτουσι καί τινα αὐτοῦ ταύτῃ συχνὸν ὅμιλον διέφθειραν. Ἀπικομένου δὲ τοῦ στρατοῦ ἐπὶ ποταμὸν Σκάμανδρον, ὃς πρῶτος ποταμῶν ἐπείτε ἐκ Σαρδίων ὁρμηθέντες ἐπεχείρησαν τῇ ὁδῷ ἐπέλιπε τὸ ῥέεθρον οὐδ' ἀπέχρησε τῇ στρατιῇ τε καὶ τοῖσι κτήνεσι πινόμενος, ἐπὶ τοῦτον δὴ τὸν ποταμὸν ὡς ἀπίκετο Ξέρξης, ἐς τὸ Πριάμου Πέργαμον ἀνέβη, ἵμερον ἔχων θεήσασθαι. θεησάμενος δὲ καὶ πυθόμενος ἐκείνων ἕκαστα, τῇ Ἀθηναίῃ τῇ Ἰλιάδι ἔθυσε βοῦς χιλίας· χοὰς δὲ οἱ μάγοι τοῖσι ἥρωσι ἐχέαντο. ταῦτα δὲ ποιησαμένοισι νυκτὸς φόβος ἐς τὸ στρατόπεδον ἐνέπεσε.

> *And firstly, when they had halted for the night at the foot of Ida, a storm of thunder and lightning fell upon them, killing a great number right there. When the army had come to the river Scamander, which was the first river after the beginning of their march from Sardis that fell short and was not sufficient for the army and the cattle to drink—when Xerxes arrived at this river, he ascended to the citadel of Priam, having a desire to see it. After he saw it and asked about everything there, he sacrificed a thousand cattle to Athena of Ilium, and the Magi offered libations to the heroes. After they did this, a panic fell upon the camp in the night.*

As he camps near Ida thunderstorms destroy part of his army. Arriving at Troy he makes offerings to the heroes; the aftermath is a panic in the army by night and the implication of the text is that the offerings are rejected. Here Herodotus draws together the two epic traditions, the ill-fated army marching to destruction against the will of the gods and in defiance of the signs and the Graeco-Asiatic tensions of which the Trojan War was the most celebrated. These signs are reinforced for the reader by authorial *prolepses* such as the reference to Artayktes at the first mention of the bridge (7.33). Artayktes was eventually executed by the Athenians at a spot overlooking the bridges and explicitly for his abuses in relation to the cult of Protesilaus. The mention of this comes just before Xerxes commits against the Hellespont an act which Herodotus himself condemns as 'barbarous and sinful' (7.35.2) and it invites us to look toward the end even as we admire the greatness of the Persian engineering.

The final gesture toward this tradition (perhaps) comes in the death of Megistias, who like Amphiaraus at Thebes is a prophet who fights in the knowledge that his cause is doomed (7.219.1, 228.3).[37] Here the motif (if it is present and not just in my imagination) is transferred to the other doomed army, the Spartans.

The engagement with epic in this section of the narrative has a density marked both by the sheer number of features and the degree of elaboration which each (or at least some of them) receives. This reflects in part its pivotal position. The constant play with epic is not just an embellishment (though it does embellish), but a way of marking the escalation in the action and emphasizing the factors which made the new theme to which he now turns unique and the unusual scale of its demands on the narrator. But the engagement is also triggered by the sharpness with which this book sets out some of the key themes of the war as a whole because of the non-negotiable facts of chronology. The first encounter of Greeks with barbarians in this invasion – at Thermopylae– was one which juxtaposed seemingly unstoppable mass with individual and collective courage of an unusual sort. Between them they set the scene for a narrative which gave Herodotus the opportunity more explicitly than anywhere else to evoke the status of epic in general and Homer in particular, to emphasize the superiority of his theme and to claim equivalent or greater status for his narrative. There is throughout the book a vacillation between mirroring ideas, motifs and moments from Homer and visibly going beyond the original. Though Herodotus can be dismissive of Homer on occasion, the iconic status of the Homeric epics was an inescapable fact by the time he was writing. This status is in fact of fundamental importance for Herodotus' project, which is both to claim the Homeric legacy and simultaneously compete with the status of the original, both in terms of genre and in terms of his own individual narrative.

---

37 7.219.1: τοῖσι δὲ ἐν Θερμοπύλῃσι ἐοῦσι Ἑλλήνων πρῶτον μὲν ὁ μάντις Μεγιστίης ἐσιδὼν ἐς τὰ ἱρὰ ἔφρασε τὸν μέλλοντα ἔσεσθαι ἅμα ἠοῖ σφι θάνατον, ἐπὶ δὲ καὶ αὐτόμολοι ἦσαν οἱ ἐξαγγείλαντες τῶν Περσέων τὴν περίοδον·

It was the seer Megistias, examining the sacrifices, who first told the Hellenes at Thermopylae that death was coming to them with the dawn. Then deserters came who announced the circuit made by the Persians.

7.228.3: Μνῆμα τόδε κλεινοῖο Μεγιστία, ὅν ποτε Μῆδοι
Σπερχειὸν ποταμὸν κτεῖναν ἀμειψάμενοι,
μάντιος, ὃς τότε Κῆρας ἐπερχομένας σάφα εἰδὼς
οὐκ ἔτλη Σπάρτης ἡγεμόνας προλιπεῖν.

*This is a monument to glorious Megistias, whom the Medes
who crossed the Spercheius river slew,
a seer, who knowing well his coming doom,
refused to abandon the leaders of Sparta.*

Part III **Homeric Echoes in Philosophical and Rhetorical Discourse**

Athanasios Efstathiou
Argumenta Homerica:
Homer's Reception by Aeschines*

Following a broadly traditional scheme of reading oratorical texts as pieces of literature pursuing persuasion, poetic quotations, which are found within speeches and originated in the bulk of Greek poetic tradition, build arguments by themselves or most commonly support orator's argumentation through appropriate use. The purpose of this paper is to discuss the Homeric material adapted or appropriated by Aeschines in his speeches in such a way as to support his argument with the widely accepted authority of Homer. Aeschines' use of Homer forms part of a mid-4th century phenomenon, when poetry is mainly used especially in public speeches. Poetic quotations are used by Demosthenes in his speeches *On the Crown* and *On the False Embassy*, by Aeschines in his three extant speeches (i.e. *Against Timarchus, On the False Embassy, Against Ctesiphon*)[1], as well as by Lycurgus in his speech *Against Leocrates*. Aeschines, well-known as a former actor of tragic plays, quotes in his speeches a good deal of poetic passages from Hesiod, from Euripides, and especially from Homer; he recites by himself or asks the clerk to do so in case of long passages (coming only from the *Iliad*) running up to eighteen lines.[2]

It is evident that the main way people got to know literature in the period of late 5th and the first half of 4th century BC was oral performances and not written texts (on Homeric orality, see also Papaioannou, I. Petrovic and Michelakis in this volume). Moreover, it seems supportive to the idea of oral learning of poetry that Socrates within his discussions and dialogues quotes poetry very often, for example Homer, but he is based not on his reading of certain poets but on oral recitations.[3] In the short dialogue of Plato *Ion*, the homonymous rhapsodist (Pl. *Ion* 530a–531a)

---

* I am grateful to Professor Chris Carey for his valuable comments on this paper.
1 The three speeches of Aeschines are abbreviated as follows: *Against Timarchus*=1, *On the False Embassy*=2, *Against Ctesiphon*=3; when one of these speeches is discussed, I do not use the number of the speech, only the number of the paragraph.
2 As for the Homeric quotations of the pre-Aristarchan period, which are accounted to twenty-nine separate writers quoting 152 portions, they amount to about 480 lines. The most interesting issue is the plus-verses which are not more than nine to eleven lines. For the original investigation see Ludwich 1898, 138 ff.
3 See Russo/Fernández-Galiano/Heubeck 1992 and Steiner 2010 on *Od.* 17.578, 246, 347; cf. Pl. *La.* 201a–b, *Chrm.* 161a with *Od.* 17.578 (κακὸς δ' αἰδοῖος ἀλήτης); Hoekstra 1957, 193–225, esp. 199–201.

is a winner of the Homer contest in Epidaurus; Ion boasts that he can recite very long Homeric passages or even that he knows everything about Homer and no other poet. Aristotle himself, while quoting a lot of seemingly Homeric excerpts in his works (e.g. in the *Rhetoric* and in the *Nicomachean Ethics*), recalls them from memory or rather based on solid knowledge of the widespread epic tradition, he reshapes epic material in order to present it as Homeric.[4]

Finally, Aeschines himself confirms children's learning of poets' thoughts by heart in their early age, in order to use them when they become of age (3.135). In that case, the discussion concerns Hesiod, but a close reading of Aeschines' comments on Hesiod's advice brings forth an element of casual approach from the part of Aeschines saying that 'He (scil. Hesiod) says somewhere (που), since he attempts to instruct the masses and advise the cities, that they should not tolerate corrupt politicians'.

Using Homer as a supportive material for his arguments, Aeschines follows his own batch of methodological principles, which we need to single out in order to come close to the intertextual relation developed between the two texts and to assort the various levels of reference to the original or primary text, which is Homer.

Eventually, it is the primary text which is of high importance. It seems to encounter a case of 'literary palimpsest'; when, similarly, in manuscript transmission, we come across a palimpsest, the interest always goes to the original text covered by a new one. So, one needs to look closely at the cited passage, so as to decide what kind of citation we have and then to collate the two texts, the primary text and the reporting source, in order to signify the differences between them. It is obvious that the reporting source has a specific agenda, according to which the intermediary author makes selection of specific texts to support its content.

Thus, the selection of the primary text made by the intermediary author offers the opportunity to examine closely the purpose of the orator to use a specific poetic example, the intratextual[5] function of the original text within the reporting source and thus the expectation of the orator for its persuasive power. Evidently, poetry quoted in various ways is applied by Aeschines to the current situation in such a way as to create a new effect, supporting his political proposals and enhancing his claims. Sometimes, the way of quoting a primary text (direct quotation, paraphrase, summary of the primary text etc.), the particular selection of excerpts and the use of this citation within the reporting text can be characterized as a mere padding, when the quotation does not enhance the quality of the secondary text, adds almost nothing to the author's argument and simply

---

4 See Haslam 1997, 76.
5 For more on intratexuality, see Sharrock/Morales 2000.

creates a cumulative effect; this is the case of Aeschines' repeating the same points when in advance he summarizes the content of the cited text, he comments on this and finally he himself or the clerk reads out the quotation (e. g. 1.143 with 1.144; also 1.145 f.).

Moreover, intervention by the reporting author ranges from a selective citation of the primary text to a heavy distortion of it. To reconstruct the procedure of quoting a primary text, we have to start with the ascertainment that the secondary author makes use of what is needed for his specific argumentation strategy; the selection of the cited text may lead us to understand the method and the causes for the inclusion of these particular texts. The orator, Aeschines in this case, having designed his broad argumentation strategy, makes proper selections from the original source, and usually forms excerpts from the original text, so as to cite what only matters for the immediate purpose.[6]

Quoting from memory is often a common cause of distortion; this habit reflects confidence or implies the popularity of a text used in education or recited orally in public festivals (e. g. Homeric poems) or even points out the lack of supportive means to form a citation properly (e. g. no access to the papyrus containing the text).

However, defective memory, in case of an original like Homer, sometimes coexists with heavier intervention with use of alternative formulaic phrases or even invented formulas, transposition of verses with due syntactical modifications, which may be found in the wide spectrum of the intertextual relation of the two texts. In such a case, it is important for the study of the primary text and its transmission to treat the excerpt in isolation from its context, thus decontextualizing it. Decontextualization is also necessary when the reporting source tends to make generalizations based on the primary texts. A scholar working on such texts is not facilitated to resemble the original content from which the primary text derives. Certainly, in a thorough study of two texts, original and conduit, together with decontextualization we may use contextualization, which is important to trace the intermediary author's intervention upon the primary source, by taking into account the social, political, economic and cultural factors surrounding the conduit text.

Aeschines, as a secondary source quoting Homer, interferes with our perception of the primary text in a variety of ways. It is evident that the focus of Aeschines (as in the cases of the citing authors) determines what is cited and why and this in turn shapes our perception of the cited text. The selection of the particular cited text reveals the literary preferences of the orator and his audience.

---

6 See also Perlman 1964, 161.

a. The speech Against Timarchus

The speech *Against Timarchus* is an accusation presented by Aeschines in the Athenian court against his opponent Timarchus, a close political friend of Demosthenes, in 345 BC. It is a case in which Timarchus' credentials as a public speaker (*rhētōr*) in the Ecclesia are contested before being involved in public policy in the Assembly.[7]

Aeschines' prosecution of Timarchus was intended to block Demosthenes' attack on Aeschines (in the case *On the False Embassy*) and through him his associates and their overall policy.

The main issue which Aeschines has to work on and form an argument is his opponent's scandalous private life, that is, Timarchus' allegedly sexual homoerotic preferences in connection with his habit to sell himself, which was incompatible and illegitimate for an Athenian citizen. Thus, the sale of sexual gratification was by itself the issue and could bring an automatic penalty of disfranchisement in case that an individual so barred pursued to exercise citizen rights.

In the *refutatio* part (paragraphs 117–76), Aeschines opts for anticipating several possible arguments which his opponents may present; among them we must single out his discussion of *Phēmē* ('report') in paragraphs 125–31 and the use of poetry and especially Homer in paragraphs 141–54; the latter follows the crucial debate on noble or chaste love in Athenian culture (paragraphs 132–40).[8] Aeschines in this speech as Lycurgus in the speech *Against Leocrates* do not confine themselves in legal arguments, but tend to use poetry as literary evidence supplementing their rhetorical means of persuasion.[9]

b. Reference to *Phēmē*: an invented Homeric quotation

In paragraphs 125–131, Aeschines attempts to move from evidence to rumour, making noise by using mainly the mockery of Timarchus' sexual activity; he needs *Phēmē* to be divine and thus worthy of respect.

---

[7] Democracy provided the special legal procedure *of dokimasia tōn rhētorōn* ('scrutiny of public speakers') purporting to remove from influence those citizens who were proved to be unworthy. On this procedure, see recently Efstathiou 2014, 231–54.

[8] In this speech Aeschines quotes Hesiod once, while Euripides is quoted three times: 128 tragedy unknown; 151: *Stheneboea* (fr. 661.24–25 K.); 152: *Phoenix* (fr. 812 K.).

[9] See also Perlman 1964, 168.

Thus, Aeschines' references to *Phēmē*, presented as being sprung from Homer are followed by an unidentified Euripidean verse (128), which comments on *Phēmē*'s ability to show forth the good man, even if he is hidden in the interiors of the earth; Aeschines claims that Euripides supports even further his own view according to which *Phēmē* is a goddess and he does so by attributing to Euripides the view that *Phēmē* makes known not only the living men by revealing their own characters, but also the dead people. This statement is neither of poetic form nor of identifiable poetic origin.[10] Finally, this *Phēmē*'s poetic anthology culminates with Hesiod's two verses coming from *Op.* 763f. (see 129), which comes to a conclusion on *Phēmē*'s divinity, further supported by the idea that *Phēmē* never dies, if many men utter it.

Therefore, this quasi-Homeric quote on *Phēmē* presented by Aeschines in 128:

[...] καὶ τὸν Ὅμηρον πολλάκις ἐν τῇ Ἰλιάδι λέγοντα πρὸ τοῦ τι τῶν μελλόντων γενέσθαι·
φήμη δ' εἰς στρατὸν ἦλθε [...]

You will find that Homer often says in the Iliad before some event which is about to happen: 'Report came to the host'.[11]

can only be compared with an Iliadic poetic two-verse passage, which does not mention *Phēmē* but *Ossa*, 'rumour' (*Il.* 2.93–94), who calls the Greeks to assembly:

ἰλαδὸν εἰς ἀγορήν· μετὰ δέ σφισιν ὄσσα δεδήει
ὀτρύνουσ' ἰέναι Διὸς ἄγγελος· οἳ δ' ἀγέροντο.

with them blazed, Zeus' messenger,
urging them on, while they gathered together.[12]

The poetic phrase which Aeschines quotes instead seems to have no real connection with the context and adds almost nothing to his own argument; the reference to *Phēmē* seems superficial. Moreover, the phrase, a semi-formula, half of an hexameter verse, although it recalls roughly the meaning of the *Iliad* (2.93–94), is far from being Homeric.

Trying to trace this poetic quote, we soon realize that it may belong to a lost corpus of early epic poetry and Homer's name is used as popular denomination.[13] Alternatively, it could be an invention of Aeschines himself,

---

10 See E. fr. inc. 865 K.
11 All cited passages from Aeschines follow the translation of Carey 2000 with adjustments.
12 All cited Iliadic passages follow the translation of Murray/ Wyatt 1999 with adjustments.
13 See also Perlman 1964, 165 with n. 59, where among others he refers to Thucydides (3.104.4–6); in that case Thucydides quotes from the *Hymn to Apollo*, which may have been composed by Homer.

who tries to support his statements with Homer's authority. The passage displays his cavalier but also the commonly encountered way of using poets' thoughts in a form of quasi-quotations or paraphrases within his speeches (cf. also 3.135).

Although the habit of rough quoting by recalling the original from memory reflects confidence, the issue also hints at the nature of the ancient book, which in the form of papyrus involves a certain amount of difficulty and imperfection for the procedure of citing a text; unrolling a papyrus to consult a written text was not the easiest thing to do, while a commonly encountered phenomenon of absence of page numbers made the job of accurate quoting particularly hard.[14]

Thus, we could perceive this kind of quotations as sprung from an immanent knowledge created by oral recitations of Homeric or other epic songs. It seems convincing that the poems which were later included in the Epic Cycle were formed by a long-lasting interactive oral process, embracing and reshaping a slew of traditional material confirmed by more or less consistent bardic performances.[15]

c. Achilles and Patroclus: lovers or friends? A distinction on chaste or unlawful sexual relations

The most important literary material for the argumentative arsenal of all the contestants of Timarchus' trial is the relationship of Achilles and Patroclus. Both sides attempt to exploit it in their own terms and strategic demands, in order to form an argument against the opponent. Aeschines first starts from the love affair of Harmodius and Aristogeiton; the invocation of the two distinguished heroes of democracy purports to support Aeschines' interpretation of the friendship of Patroclus and Achilles as an erotic relationship; thus, Aeschines skilfully manages to sanction the *eros* of Patroclus and Achilles through a widely accepted democratic stereotype.

Aeschines reaches 133, where the main issue, the relationship of Patroclus and Achilles, is brought forth; he argues that their friendship was caused by *eros*, while in 135, he has to anticipate the opponents' claims on his own history as the lover of young men, which seem to become more bitter by referring to him as a poet of erotic poetry inspired by passion. In the end, Aeschines must play on

---

14 See also Carey forthcoming.
15 Tsagalis 2008b, xi ff. and Burgess 2001, 173, where it is noted that: '[…] the Cycle would have been prefigured by rhapsodic performance of material from different epics (not necessarily the ones of the Epic Cycle)'.

the same terrain and he does that at 136 by acknowledging the notion of honourable-chaste love, admitting his love affairs of the past, while he acknowledges some of the erotic poems as his but not the rest, which may be fabricated by the opponents for obvious reasons. Finally, he comes to a definition of chaste love and love sold for money making a clear distinction between them (137).

In 141 the passage runs as follows:

Ἐπειδὴ δὲ Ἀχιλλέως καὶ Πατρόκλου μέμνησθε καὶ Ὁμήρου καὶ ἑτέρων ποιητῶν, ὡς τῶν μὲν δικαστῶν ἀνηκόων παιδείας ὄντων, ὑμεῖς δὲ εὐσχήμονές τινες προσποιεῖσθε εἶναι καὶ ὑπερφρονοῦντες ἱστορίᾳ τὸν δῆμον, ἵν᾽ εἰδῆτε ὅτι καὶ ἡμεῖς τι ἤδη ἠκούσαμεν καὶ ἐμάθομεν, λέξομέν τι καὶ ἡμεῖς περὶ τούτων. Ἐπειδὴ γὰρ ἐπιχειροῦσι φιλοσόφων ἀνδρῶν μεμνῆσθαι καὶ καταφεύγειν ἐπὶ τοὺς εἰρημένους ἐν τῷ μέτρῳ λόγους, θεωρήσατε ἀποβλέψαντες, ὦ Ἀθηναῖοι, εἰς τοὺς ὁμολογουμένως ἀγαθοὺς καὶ χρηστοὺς ποιητάς, ὅσον κεχωρίσθαι ἐνόμισαν τοὺς σώφρονας καὶ τῶν ὁμοίων ἐρῶντας, καὶ τοὺς ἀκρατεῖς ὧν οὐ χρὴ καὶ τοὺς ὑβριστάς.

But since you have come to mention of Achilles and Patroclus and of Homer and other poets, as though the jury were men without education, while you represent yourselves as men of superior rank, whose erudition allows you look down on the people, to show you that we too have already acquired a little knowledge and learning, we too shall say a word on this subject. For since they undertake to cite wise men and take refuge in tales expressed in verse, look, men of Athens, at those who are acknowledged to be good and edifying and see how far apart they considered chaste men, lovers of their equals, and those whose love is illicit, men who recognize no limits.

Teaching the mass by quoting poets becomes a risky matter, since the orator may be offensive when putting on a show and enlivening his speech; the speaker presenting himself as over clever, as a man of distinctive erudition, above the average Athenian, therefore above the jurors can cause harm to himself. Noteworthy, here in 141, there is the term ἱστορία used by Aeschines, which may be equivalent to *paideia*, 'education', or even 'general or encyclopaedic knowledge'.[16] The term is possibly used with the latter of the proposed meanings highlighting the arrogant posture of his opponents justified by their pretension of comprehensive-encyclopaedic knowledge.

A delicate balance is demanded from *rhētores* using poetry in their speeches: the Athenians expected from them a highly qualified speaking and thinking, their sincere advice, while they felt particularly cautious towards expertise, professionalism and preparation, all of them pointing to a kind of deceptive communication.[17] Sophistry and its notable product, deception, usually connected with various forms of trickery and delusion of the audience fabricated by

---
16 On ἱστορία, see also the discussion in Fowler 2006, 33 and 42, n. 18.
17 Ober/ Strauss 1990, 237–70, esp. 250–58.

magic arts and alien methods became a *topos* in the context of public oratory. The description of the opponent as γόης ('wizard') and βάσκανος ('sorcerer', 'slanderer') points to a deceptive speaking with dangerous results for the *dēmos*. Demosthenes, as Aeschines argues, represents the prototype of sophistic speaker, who controls his speech in an absolute way; his sophistry allows him to speak only according to his targets and purposes speaking the truth only when he intends to create a favourable result. That is a depiction of a professional sophist performing an art with deceptive potential and no moral or other constraints, in order to achieve his end to persuade people. Thus, distinguished knowledge of poetry in a sophistic way of speaking might hide deception and, even more, may be associated with un-Athenian identity and behaviour, since everything originating in sophists could be exotic and of foreign origin, thus alien and incompatible to the Athenian identity.[18]

All in all, Aeschines, taking the necessary precautions against the risk to look like a highly educated public speaker using tricks and poetry in his speech, a real wiseacre, tries to do his best by adopting the first person plural in order to present himself as one of audience and jurors; in detail, he accepts the value of Homeric poetry, which is going to be used by his opponents, although he declares that he has taken aback to hear that his opponents have managed to rally even Homer's spirit, as the verb μέμνησθε may mean;[19] even more by associating himself with the audience he hits upon the opponents with a charge for arrogant and slighting behaviour towards the jurors.[20] In 142 Aeschines refers to Homer, making an attempt to begin his argumentative procedure from the widely accepted acknowledgement of his value as a poet, which is an easy point to make.

The text precisely states:

λέξω δὲ πρῶτον μὲν περὶ Ὁμήρου, ὃν ἐν τοῖς πρεσβυτάτοις καὶ σοφωτάτοις τῶν ποιητῶν εἶναι τάττομεν. ἐκεῖνος γὰρ πολλαχοῦ μεμνημένος περὶ Πατρόκλου καὶ Ἀχιλλέως, τὸν μὲν ἔρωτα καὶ τὴν ἐπωνυμίαν αὐτῶν τῆς φιλίας ἀποκρύπτεται, ἡγούμενος τὰς τῆς εὐνοίας ὑπερβολὰς καταφανεῖς εἶναι τοῖς πεπαιδευμένοις τῶν ἀκροατῶν.

---

18 For the concept of deception in Athenian public speaking, see Hesk 1990, 212 – 13 and Hesk 2000, 213 ff.; Burkert 1962, 36 – 55, esp. 55; Bowie 1993, 114 – 15.
19 The verb here may mean: 'you after all now have discovered or rather you have now brought Achilles, Patroclus, the poets and especially Homer into play', thus pointing again to sophistic manipulation.
20 See also Ober 1989, 178 – 79; for Demosthenes' attempt to denote that his knowledge of poetry is not superior to that of his audience, see 19.243 and 245.

> *I shall start with Homer, whom we rank among the oldest and wisest of the poets. Although he often speaks of Patroclus and Achilles, he keeps love and the name of their friendship concealed, since he thinks that the exceeding strength of their affection is manifest to the cultivated among his hearers.*

Thus, Aeschines enumerates Homer's real and indisputable qualities by saying that he is classified among the senior and wisest poets. Homer, as an intellectual authority, could perfectly confirm the relationship between Patroclus and Achilles, although, as Aeschines notes, Homer avoids identifying their friendship as love. According to Aeschines, Homer does not mention the name of love due to 'cultivated sensitivity',[21] since it was manifested that such an affection between them could be easily understood as love by the well-educated hearers, namely the most of the jurors, as he has already pointed out in 141.

The long-standing discussion on the nature of the relationship between Achilles and Patroclus as accounted in the *Iliad* starts from the interpretation of Homer's text and followed by consecutive attempts of later authors to rework the Iliadic text, a lasting process which pervades antiquity. Certainly, Homer does not depict Patroclus and Achilles as lovers at least in an explicit manner. Aeschines argues that even Homer, although he believes that their relationship was an erotic one, for his own reasons – he does not specify which— he avoids naming it as such. Homer's silence on homoerotic relationship, followed by Hesiod and Archilochus, makes us believe that in the archaic period homosexual behaviour was not institutionalized and was not acceptable in Greek societies. However, the ravishing of Ganymede, 'the most beautiful of the mortals' to be Zeus' cupbearer may point to Zeus' homosexual desire (see Ibycus fr. 289), if it is combined with Dawn's rape of Tithonus as well as Aphrodite's affair with Anchises; they are all brought forth in the same context of erotic passion.

In the classical period Aeschylus' trilogy *Myrmidones, Nereides* and *Phrygians* was made a subject for discussion in Plato's *Symposium* 180a, where Phaedrus appears to say that:

> ὅθεν δὴ καὶ ὑπεραγασθέντες οἱ θεοὶ διαφερόντως αὐτὸν ἐτίμησαν, ὅτι τὸν ἐραστὴν οὕτω περὶ πολλοῦ ἐποιεῖτο. Αἰσχύλος δὲ φλυαρεῖ φάσκων Ἀχιλλέα Πατρόκλου ἐρᾶν, ὃς ἦν καλλίων οὐ μόνον Πατρόκλου ἀλλ' ἅμα καὶ τῶν ἡρώων ἁπάντων, καὶ ἔτι ἀγένειος, ἔπειτα νεώτερος πολύ, ὥς φησιν Ὅμηρος.

> *Therefore, the gods admired him (scil. Achilles) so much that they gave him distinguished honour, since he took so much care of his lover. Aeschylus talks nonsense in saying that Achilles was in love with Patroclus. Achilles was more beautiful not only than Patroclus alone but than all the heroes, being still beardless and, moreover, much the younger, as Homer says.*

---

21 The expression comes from Dover 1978, 197.

Obviously, Phaedrus based on Homer (*Il.* 11.786) rightly claims that Achilles was younger than Patroclus, while he argues that the relationship was one of love between Achilles as *erōmenos* and Patroclus as *erastēs*; devotion highlights passion, since Achilles was ready to die in avenging Patroclus' death.[22] Coming back to Aeschylus' fragments (frr. 135, 136 Radt[23]), we realize that the language used when referring to the two companions is explicit enough for their homoerotic relationship:

<'ΑΧΙΛΛ.>: σέβας δὲ μηρῶν ἁγνὸν οὐκ ἐπῃδέσω,
     ὦ δυσχάριστε τῶν πυκνῶν φιλημάτων
(*Myrmidones* fr. 135 Radt)

And you felt no compunction for (sc. my?) pure reverence of (sc. your?) thighs—
O, what an ill return you have made for so many kisses!

μηρῶν τε τῶν σῶν εὐσεβὴς ὁμιλία
(*Myrmidones* fr. 136 Radt)

god-fearing converse with your thighs[24]

On the other hand, Xenophon's Socrates in *Smp.* 8.31 opts for a real friendship developed between the two men.[25]

Eventually, apart from the issue concerning the kind of relationship which was developed between Achilles and Patroclus, Aeschines' view of both the nature of this relationship and of Homer's real opinion may represent the dominant attitude of the Athenian society of the period. Aeschines' representation of Homeric values and ideas tends to restore the Athenian society of his period, making conclusions on the education he had received but also the education of the audience, the cultural atmosphere in Athens towards the last decades of the fourth century; in general terms, it is a matter of Homeric reception within antiquity, which allows us to find connections between Homeric material and creativity; the orator by using Homer in his speeches appears as an intelligent reader whose views correspond

---

[22] It has been stated by Weil (1955, xii) that the discussion of the relationship between Achilles and Patroclus in Plato's *Protagoras* shows us that Aeschines knew the text of Plato; as Fisher (1991, 289) rightly comments, this topic may be discussed widely in oral debates, in which Aeschines must have participated.
[23] Radt 2009².
[24] Both fragments as translated by Dover 1978, 197; for fr. 137, see also Lobel/Roberts/Wegener 1952, 51.
[25] See also Dover 1978, 196–97 and 1988, 130; Clarke 1978, 381–96; Poole 1990, 108–50; Ogden 1996.

with those of the ordinary person; he undertakes the duty to interpret and finally appropriate the poetic material in order to offer it to the public.²⁶

Moreover, conventions of speaking and reticence of language may be an issue, when the orator has to give an account of such a thorny matter which was the homoerotic relationship of the most important hero of Greek history, Achilles. The hero comes out of the idealizing framework of Homeric epics, but for Aeschines' own rhetorical needs it must function as a prototype of homoerotic relationship applied to the case of Timarchus. Even though Aeschines needs to present the relationship in this particular way, he skips the Aeschylean version, which would have been particularly supportive of his own thesis, opting for a specific reading of Homer which focuses on the emotional aspect of desire rather than the physical dimension; he also has to be careful in interpreting a text presented before an educated audience and not breaking with traditions of restraint in public speaking, as well as maintaining decorum of language. Explicit words, excessive obscenity, reference to distasteful matters may offend the audience; Aeschines has at least to pretend that he respects the audience by using the right language being a man of ethical values.²⁷

In 143 the Athenian orator moves to another point: he tries to corroborate his claim that the relationship between the two men was clearly a passionate love, since Achilles accepted the duty to take care of Patroclus.

The text runs as follows:

λέγει γάρ που Ἀχιλλεὺς ὀδυρόμενος τὸν τοῦ Πατρόκλου θάνατον, ὡς ἕν τι τοῦτο τῶν λυπηροτάτων ἀναμιμνησκόμενος, ὅτι τὴν ὑπόσχεσιν τὴν πρὸς τὸν πατέρα τὸν Πατρόκλου Μενοίτιον ἄκων ἐψεύσατο· ἐπαγγείλασθαι γὰρ εἰς Ὀποῦντα σῶν ἀπάξειν, εἰ συμπέμψειεν αὐτὸν εἰς τὴν Τροίαν καὶ παρακατατεθεῖτο αὐτῷ. ᾧ καταφανής ἐστιν ὡς δι' ἔρωτα τὴν ἐπιμέλειαν αὐτοῦ παρέλαβεν.

Homer says somewhere that Achilles in the course of his lament for Patroclus' death mentions, as one of his greatest painful memories, that he has unwillingly betrayed his promise given to Patroclus' father Menoetius; he had declared he would bring the son safe back to Opus, if the father would send him along with him to Troy, and entrust him to his care. And this makes it quite evident that it was because of love that he had taken responsibility for his care.

---

26 Hardwick/Stray 2008, 8.
27 See Alex. *De Figuris* 8.432 Walz: παρέχει δὲ καὶ ἔμφασιν ἤθους χρηστοῦ. Theon (*Prog.* 1.170 Walz) commenting on the same technique, he says that the dignity of the speech is gained when the speaker does not express shameful things in a straightforward way, but by using allusions. Theon names this technique of Aeschines ἀρρητοποιία ('speaking of unspeakable things'). Hermogenes (*Id.* 2.6.343 Rabe) expresses his doubt about this technique and thinks that 'if you give an advance indication of what you are doing [...] you will not be as persuasive and you will appear to be someone who enjoys slander' (trans. Wooten 1987, 93).

Aeschines in this paragraph tries to give a prose account, a paraphrase of the forthcoming quotation of *Il.* 18.324–29, which follows in 144; this paraphrase anticipating the direct quotation of the Iliadic passage purports to predispose the audience in such a way as to focus on the points which Aeschines singles out.[28] Worthy of note is the way of introducing the Homeric text using the adverb of place with indefinite meaning *που* ('somewhere'); this mode of rough quoting brings into discussion the issue of citations from memory common even for well-known authors like Aristotle.

Achilles' unspeakable sorrow due to Patroclus' death caused him double harm, firstly because he lost his love companion and secondly because he unwillingly had broken his promise to Menoetius, father of Patroclus, that he would bring his son back safe to Opus, if he entrusted him to Achilles. Aeschines' personal view of the subject is expressed in the phrase ᾧ καταφανής ἐστιν ὡς δι' ἔρωτα τὴν ἐπιμέλειαν αὐτοῦ παρέλαβεν, i.e. that the duty of Achilles to take care of Patroclus makes evident the erotic nature of their affection, though the syllogism is based on a logical fallacy.

In 144 Aeschines continues his argument by referring directly to *Il.* 18.324–29; it is the same point which comes back, the betrayal of Achilles' promise to bring Patroclus back to Opus safely.

> ὢ πόποι, ἦ ῥ' ἅλιον ἔπος ἔκβαλον ἤματι κείνωι
> θαρσύνων ἥρωα Μενοίτιον ἐν μεγάροισιν.
> φῆν δέ οἱ εἰς Ὀπόεντα περικλυτὸν υἱὸν ἀπάξειν
> Ἴλιον ἐκπέρσαντα λαχόντά τε ληΐδος αἶσαν.
> ἀλλ' οὐ Ζεὺς ἄνδρεσσι νοήματα πάντα τελευτᾷ·
> ἄμφω γὰρ πέπρωται ὁμοίην γαῖαν ἐρεύθειν.

> *Alas, vain words I uttered that day,*
> *when I assured the hero Menoetius in his halls.*
> *I told I would surely bring his glorious son back to Opus again*
> *as sacker of Troy having taken the due share of spoil.*
> *But Zeus does not fulfil to men all intents;*
> *for it is fated that both (scil. Achilles and Patroclus) of us make red one spot of earth.*

Nowhere in the Iliadic text is there any hint to the relationship between the two men; certainly, as Homer avoids naming their relationship as love, something which Aeschines himself has noticed (142), it would not be expected to go even further by saying that Achilles' acceptance of the duty to take care of Patroclus points to a homoerotic love relationship.

---

[28] See also 2.67–68, where Aeschines in a similar way anticipates the testimony of Amyntor, the sole witness called upon in the case *On the False Embassy*.

The text of the *Iliad* which is quoted by Aeschines in 144 is almost identical with the text transmitted by the mss; the only difference is that Aeschines gives the verb ἐρεύθειν, while mss (especially Bibl. Brit. Add. ms. 17210, 6th c. AD, P. Bibl. Brit. inv. 107, 1st–2nd c. AD, testimonia cetera and mss Z and Ω)[29] opt for ἐρεῦσαι; the exact reference to the fate of Achilles and Patroclus is better served by an aorist infinitive, and also the syntax with πέπρωται needs a future expression as predicate; the infinitive of present tense found in Aeschines' text may be influenced by τελευτᾶι of verse 328; however, from 328 to 329 there is a shift from general to specific.[30]

Coming to 145, we encounter Aeschines' summary of an extensive section of book 18 of the *Iliad*, the dialogue of Achilles and Thetis, which starts from v. 65 ff. The main parts of this section from the *Iliad* are the arrival and departure speeches of Thetis (73–77 and 128–37), the two speeches of Achilles (79–93 and 98–126) and certainly the crucial announcement of Achilles' fate by Thetis (95–96). Achilles' decision to avenge Patroclus' death brings Thetis to tears and leaves no room for optimism (90–93); Thetis declares that Achilles' fate would be speedy and his death prompt following Hector's death (95–96).

Aeschines, on the other hand, focuses on Achilles' grief, his solid faith with the dead friend, which forced him to avenge his death and to prefer death instead of survival. Thetis' appeal to Achilles to abandon his plan is left unfulfilled. His noble strength of purpose was such that he hastened to punish his friend's killer, and though everyone urged him to bathe and take food, he swore that he would do none of them until he brings Hector's head to Patroclus' tomb. However, detailed description and elements of brutality concerning Hector's death are omitted from Aeschines' idealizing[31] account (cf. *Il.* 18.91–93).

In 146 Aeschines presents a short prose version of *Il.* 23.65 ff., the appearance of Patroclus' ghost to Achilles (65–68) preceding Patroclus' speech (69–92); Aeschines' account in 146 ends up with a summary of scattered Homeric verses: ὥσπερ καὶ ἐτράφησαν καὶ ἐβίωσαν ἐν τῷ αὐτῷ, οὕτω καὶ τελευτησάντων αὐτῶν τὰ ὀστᾶ ἐν τῇ αὐτῇ σορῷ κείσεται ('in just the same way that they had grown up and lived together, in death too their bones should lie in the same coffer'); his summary comes from 23.77–91, especially v. 84 (ἀλλ' ὁμοῦ, ὡς τράφομέν περ ἐν ὑμετέροισι δόμοισιν) and 91 (ὡς δὲ καὶ ὀστέα νῶϊν ὁμὴ σορὸς ἀμφικαλύπτοι) closely echoing the wording of the Homeric verses. Again, Aeschines'

---

29 Reference to the sigla of M. West's edition of the *Iliad* (1998–2000); this edition is followed throughout.
30 For the use of πέπρωται with the infinitive of aorist, see also E. *Alc.* 21, [A.] *PV* 815, D.C. 55.1.3.
31 The term is used by Fisher 2001, 290.

main purpose is to underline the strong bond of the two men in life and death hinting at a passionate love. Two techniques are used by Aeschines here, repetition and anticipation. The above stated idea expressed by these verses, identical or in an adjusted form, permeates almost all Homer-based arguments of Aeschines aiming at a cumulative effect. Moreover, it is Aeschines' usual technique of anticipation, by which he comments in his own way on a forthcoming quotation of Homeric text (in this case in 149), attempting to predispose the audience (see below 147).

In paragraph 147, Aeschines moves from summarizing the Homeric scenes and ideas sprung from *Iliad* book 18 to a prose paraphrase of an allegedly Homeric passage: the introductory lines of Patroclus' ghost speech, when Achilles was sleeping by the funeral pyre. Patroclus is referred to be saying in direct speech the following:

οὐκέτι περὶ τῶν μεγίστων, ὥσπερ τὸ πρότερον, καθεζόμενοι μετ' ἀλλήλων μόνοι ἄπωθεν τῶν ἄλλων φίλων βουλευσόμεθα.

We are not going to sit together alone anymore, as in the old days, apart from our friends, and deliberate on the most serious matters.

Aeschines enriches this paraphrase of the Homeric text with his comment on the core meaning of the passage, which, in his opinion, is the loss of loyalty and affection, the most characteristic virtues of the relationship between the two men (τὴν πίστιν οἶμαι καὶ τὴν εὔνοιαν ποθεινοτάτην ἡγούμενος εἶναι).[32] He probably aims at a 'romantic' presentation of affection, loyalty and mutual exclusiveness featuring the relationship of the two men. This seemingly Homeric quotation given in an anticipatory way purports to predispose the audience and recognize throughout the forthcoming direct quotation of 18.333–35 (in 148) the points which Aeschines singles out.[33]

Indeed, in 148 the Athenian orator calls upon the clerk to read the actual Homeric verses concerning the vengeance of Hector (*Il*. 18.333–35). This quotation belongs to Achilles' lament in which he promises Patroclus to honour his burial with the armour and head of his killer, Hector, together with the sacrifice of twelve Trojans and the long-lasting lamentation of captive women.

λέγε πρῶτον τὰ περὶ τῆς Ἕκτορος τιμωρίας.
ἀλλ' ἐπεὶ οὖν, φίλ' ἑταῖρε, σεῦ ὕστερος εἶμ' ὑπὸ γαῖαν,
οὔ σε πρὶν κτεριῶ, πρίν γ' Ἕκτορος ἐνθάδ' ἐνεῖκαι
τεύχεα καὶ κεφαλήν, μεγαθύμου σεῖο φονῆος.

---

[32] I believe that he (Patroclus) considers that the loss most keenly felt is loyalty and affection.
[33] See also n. 28 above.

Read the verses first about the vengeance on Hector.[34]
But since, dear comrade, I shall go beneath the earth after you,
I shall not bury you until I bring here
the armour and head of Hector, the killer of you, the great-hearted.

The Homeric text runs as follows:

νῦν δ' ἐπεὶ οὖν, Πάτροκλε, σέ' ὕστερος εἴμ' ὑπὸ γαῖαν,
οὔ σε πρὶν κτεριῶ, πρὶν Ἕκτορος ἐνθάδ' ἐνεῖκαι
τεύχεα καὶ κεφαλὴν, μεγαθύμου σεῖο φονῆος·
(*Il.* 18.333–35)

But now, Patroclus, since I shall go beneath the earth after you,
I shall not bury you until I bring here the armour and head of Hector,
the killer of you, the great-hearted.

Divergences from Homer's text are the following: (i) major alteration, change of a whole phrase; in v. 333 the vocative Πάτροκλε has been replaced by the address φίλ' ἑταῖρε. Obviously, it is a deliberate alteration emphasizing the erotic relationship between the two men.[35] The suggestion which has been prompted that may have been caused by slip of memory falls down, since the phrase is unique in surviving epic poetry.[36] (ii) Minor alterations concerning grammatical or metrical alternatives: in v. 334 the use of the Ionic or Attic contracted future κτεριῶ instead of the ancient form κτερίω[37] and the particle γ'.

The important conclusion again is that Aeschines, for his argumentative needs, reforms his Homeric quotation with slight alterations, so as to make it mean something quite different from what Homer implies in the *Iliad*.

Paragraph 149 is devoted to the direct quotation of *Il.* 23.77–91. This time it is not Aeschines himself who reads the poetic quotation, but the clerk of the court, who is called by the orator to read out what Patroclus says:

ἀναγίγνωσκε δὴ τὰ περὶ τοῦ ὁμοτάφους αὐτοὺς γενέσθαι καὶ περὶ τῶν διατριβῶν ἃς συν-
διέτριβον ἀλλήλοις.
77 οὐ γὰρ ἔτι ζωοί γε φίλων ἀπάνευθεν ἑταίρων
βουλὰς ἑζόμενοι βουλεύσομεν· ἀλλ' ἐμὲ μὲν κὴρ
ἀμφέχανε στυγερή, ἥπερ λάχε γεινόμενόν περ·
καὶ δὲ σοὶ αὐτῷ μοῖρα, θεοῖς ἐπιείκελ' Ἀχιλλεῦ,
81 τείχει ὕπο Τρώων εὐηγενέων ἀπολέσθαι,

---

34 *Il.* 18.333–35.
35 Van der Valk 1963–64, II 328–29.
36 Edwards 1991, 185–86.
37 Chantraine 1942, I 451.

81a μαρνάμενον δηίοις Ἑλένης[38] ἕνεκ' ἠυκόμοιο.
81b ἄλλο δέ τοι ἐρέω, σὺ δ' ἐνὶ φρεσὶ βάλλεο σῇσιν·
     μὴ ἐμὰ σῶν ἀπάνευθε τιθήμεναι ὀστέ', Ἀχιλλεῦ,
83a ἀλλ' ἵνα πέρ σε καὶ αὐτὸν ὁμοίη γαῖα κεκεύθῃ,
83b χρυσέῳ ἐν ἀμφιφορεῖ, τόν τοι πόρε πότνια μήτηρ,
84   ὡς ὁμοῦ ἐτράφεμέν περ ἐν ὑμετέροισι δόμοισιν,
     εὖτέ με τυτθὸν ἐόντα Μενοίτιος ἐξ Ὀπόεντος
     ἤγαγεν ὑμέτερόνδ' ἀνδροκτασίης ὕπο λυγρῆς,
     ἤματι τῷ, ὅτε παῖδα κατέκτανον Ἀμφιδάμαντος,
     νήπιος, οὐκ ἐθέλων, ἀμφ' ἀστραγάλοισι χολωθείς·
     ἔνθα με δεξάμενος ἐν δώμασιν ἱππότα Πηλεὺς
     ἔτρεφέ τ' ἐνδυκέως καὶ σὸν θεράποντ' ὀνόμηνεν·
91   ὣς δὲ καὶ ὀστέα νῶιν ὁμὴ σορὸς ἀμφικαλύπτοι.

In modern editions of the *Iliad* (see West *ad loc.*) v. 83b is edited as v. 92:

92   χρυσέος ἀμφιφορεύς, τόν τοι πόρε πότνια μήτηρ

> Now read out what Patroclus says in the dream about their burial together and the pursuits
> they once had in life with one another.
> Never more in life shall we sit apart from our dear comrades
> and take counsel together. No, the hated fate
> has gapped around me, the fate which was appointed me at my birth.
> And for you yourself too, godlike Achilles, it is fated
> to die beneath the walls of the noble Trojans,
> fighting with the enemy for fair-haired Helen's sake.
> More shall I tell you, and fix it in your heart.
> Let not my bones be laid apart from your own, Achilles,
> but that you and I may lie in common earth,
> in the golden casket your queenly mother gave you,
> just as we were reared together in your chambers/home,
> when as a small child still Menoetius from Opus
> brought me to your house because of sad man-slaying,
> on that day, when I slew Amphidamas' son,
> in childish wrath, all unwitting, angered over dice.
> There in his halls Peleus the knight welcomed me,
> kindly reared me and called me your companion.
> So to let the same vessel cover our bones.

The above lengthy direct quotation from Homer (23.77–91) seems to stand quite apart from the Homeric text as it is transmitted by the mss; we encounter significant variations such as: (i) major additions: a) of the verse 81a (μαρνάμενον δηί-

---

[38] The type Ἐλήνης in Dilts' text must be an orthographic error.

οις Ἑλένης ἕνεκ' ἠϋκόμοιο) made by two Homeric formulaic parts found elsewhere (μάρνασθαι δηίοις in Il. 9.317, 11.190, 205, 17.148... and Ἑλένης ἕνεκ' ἠϋκόμοιο in Il. 9.339), b) of the verse 83a ἀλλ' ἵνα πέρ σε καὶ αὐτὸν ὁμοίη γαῖα κεκεύθῃ, which retains a somehow formulaic character resembling Il. 18.329 ἄμφω γὰρ πέπρωται ὁμοίην γαῖαν ἐρεῦσαι; (ii) a transposition of verse: since Aeschines' quotation stops at v. 91, the transposition of v. 83b in effect corresponds to v. 92 of Homer's text with some due amendments: χρυσέῳ ἐν ἀμφιφορεῖ, τόν τοι πόρε πότνια μήτηρ; (iii) major alterations: the latter part of v. 82 σὺ δ' ἐνὶ φρεσὶ βάλλεο σῇσιν replaces the Homeric formula καὶ ἐφήσομαι, αἴ κε πίθηαι; αἴ κε πίθηαι is found in Il. 1.207, 21.293 and Od. 1.279; (iv) minor alterations: in v. 77 Aeschines ('and some of the city- texts', Did/A)[39] prefers the wording οὐ γὰρ ἔτι ζωοί γε, while the mss read οὐ μὲν γὰρ ζωοί γε.

In 150 Aeschines opts for quoting five other Iliadic verses coming from 18.95–99. Again he asks the clerk to read the verses marked in the 'Aeschinian' version of the text:

ὡς τοίνυν ἐξῆν αὐτῷ σωθῆναι μὴ τιμωρησαμένῳ
τὸν τοῦ Πατρόκλου θάνατον, ἀνάγνωθι ἃ λέγει ἡ Θέτις.
95 ὠκύμορος δή μοι τέκος ἔσσεαι, οἷ' ἀγορεύεις·
αὐτίκα γάρ τοι ἔπειτα μεθ' Ἕκτορα πότμος ἑτοῖμος.
Τὴν δ' αὖτε προσέειπε ποδάρκης δῖος Ἀχιλλεύς·
αὐτίκα τεθναίην, ἐπεὶ οὐκ ἄρ' ἔμελλον ἑταίρῳ
99 κτεινομένῳ ἐπαμῦναι, ὅ μοι πολὺ φίλτατος ἔσκεν.

Now to show that he could have been saved if he had not avenged Patroclus' death, read out what Thetis says:
'Swift will fall your fate, my child, from what you say.
For immediately after Hector, your doom is waiting.'
To her in turn made answer swift-footed divine Achilles:
'Let me die straight-away, since it seems I was not to rescue
my friend from death, he who was far dearest to me.'

Il. 18.95–100:
95 "ὠκύμορος δή μοι, τέκος, ἔσσεαι, οἷ' ἀγορεύεις·
αὐτίκα γάρ τοι ἔπειτα μεθ' Ἕκτορα πότμος ἑτοῖμος."
τὴν δὲ μέγ' ὀχθήσας προσέφη πόδας ὠκὺς Ἀχιλλεύς·
"αὐτίκα τεθναίην, ἐπεὶ οὐκ ἄρ' ἔμελλον ἑταίρῳ
κτεινομένωι ἐπαμῦναι· ὃ μὲν μάλα τηλόθι πάτρης
100 ἔφθιτ', ἐμέο δ' ἐδέησεν ἀρῆς ἀλκτῆρα γενέσθαι.

---

39 Richardson 1993, 173 referring to Did.= Didymus and A= Marc. gr. 822 (olim 454), saec. x.

Comparing Aeschines' text to *Il.* 18.95–99, we can specify the following variations: (i) selective quotation: Aeschines quotes the first two lines (95–96) from the dialogue of Thetis and Achilles and then chooses only vv. 98–99 from Achilles' extensive answer (in *Il.* 18.98–126); (ii) major alterations: a) the latter part of v. 99 ὅ μοι πολὺ φίλτατος ἔσκεν is Aeschines' invention, b) in v. 97 a major change has been made by Aeschines introducing the phrase αὖτε προσέειπε ποδάρκης δῖος instead of μέγ' ὀχθήσας προσέφη πόδας ὠκύς.

Homer's *Iliad* 18.95–99 provides a very useful material for Aeschines to compose an argument in poetic form this time, which corroborates his thesis. It is the result of an apt reworking of the Homeric text with slight changes in wording and use of two variant phrases: a) ὅ μοι πολὺ φίλτατος ἔσκεν and b) αὖτε προσέειπε ποδάρκης δῖος. The first phrase emphasizes the close relationship between Achilles and Patroclus alluding to a homoerotic bond, while the second one is used to fit the current situation and context: the original phrase μέγ' ὀχθήσας might have caused a misunderstanding, since it could have taken to point to the anger of Achilles towards Thetis, which is really not the case. Leaving aside v. 100f. from the *Iliad* and making these alterations Aeschines turns his quotation neatly and gives an impression of completeness.

Socrates in Plato's *Apology* 28c–d supporting the decision to abandon his way of life uses the same episode from the *Iliad* as an *exemplum* for heroic thinking and behaviour. However, this does not prove in any sense that Aeschines knew and used Plato's text; Homer would have been well known to the Athenians of the fourth century through numerous oral recitations.

This conspectus of the readings of both texts (original and conduit) may lead us to several conclusions focusing on the changes which Aeschines has made.

Aeschines' quotations diverge quite significantly from the text transmitted by the Homeric mss: he adds, alters and transposes verses. However, especially in 149, which gives scope for further investigation, it is most unfortunate that this specific manuscript (papyrus fragments noted as P12 in West's edition) does not contain vv. 2–84 to give us a safe idea how Aeschines' quotations (and especially the plus-verses 81a, 83a and 83b)[40] can be connected with the pre-Aristarchan tradition of the text.[41] The long-standing scholarly discussion on the value of

---

[40] As for the plus-verse 81a again the old papyrus P12 (=P. Grenf. 2.4, P. Hib.22, P. Heid.1262–66) does not help; this plus-verse does not exist in later papyri (as P9, 23, 257 and Ω ms) either, but this is out of the question in the pre-Aristarchan tradition; on P12, see also West 1967, 136–91.

[41] As we were fortunate enough to check [Plu.] *Consol. ad Apoll.* 117c, where *Il.* 23. 222–223b (with two plus-verses) is quoted; in that case we were helped by the papyrus edited by Grenfell and Hunt (1897, 11), which came into light to verify Plutarch's quotation; for more detail, Allen 1899, 39–41, esp. 41.

plus-verses and minus-verses found in quotations of ancient authors seems to be inconclusive.

Dué after a thorough analysis of Aeschines' variants and based also on Aldo di Luzio[42] supports the inclusion of these verses in the text arguing that we can 'find ways of including them in a multi-text that embraces the fluidity of the textual traditions of the *Iliad* and *Odyssey*',[43] which certainly helps us by creating a full picture of the variants, but still does not separate out the different traditions pointing to the pre-Aristarchan tradition.

However, a critical approach of the Homeric excerpts cited by Aeschines forces us to make a decision on these readings through rhetorical judgement, mainly due to the lack of other evidence from the pre-Aristarchan period, such as papyrus fragments. Lapse of Aeschines' memory as a cause to all these variations must be excluded, and on this point I agree with Dué.[44] By examining the cited texts in comparison to the original text, the way in which they rhetorically function within the overall corpus of the reporting text, how they fit to various arguments marshalled by Aeschines, we may conclude that the changes might more safely represent his personal version of the text rather than a distinct tradition of the Homeric text: most of the departures from the Homeric text (see edition by West) may have been made to form or better to create a text that best supports Aeschines' argument in which the relationship of Patroclus and Achilles was one of chaste homoerotic love. Aeschines' job was quite difficult, since Homer's presentation of the relationship at issue was quite different, and this was well understood by the Athenian society of the fourth century BC. The twofold target, to use Homer but also to adapt his ideas in such a way as to serve his rhetorical purpose was for Aeschines a challenging job giving him the opportunity to function like an experienced reader, who has to play with a text, its wording, its phrasing, its poetic formulaic identity and structure with a final target to produce his own version in a convenient form. All his changes had to abide by the ideas of fourth-century society on homoerotic relations. Aeschines provided the clerk of the court with this 'interpolated' version of the text after having marked it with the relevant passages. It is a text for official use in the court but not 'official' by itself. Poetry used in court may be regarded rhetorically and procedurally as a kind of witness (see Arist. *Rh.* 1375b 28 ff), obtaining a really authoritative character; teaching poetry and teaching law from

---

42 Di Luzio 1969, 3–152.
43 Dué 2001, 33–47, quotation from 47.
44 Dué 2001, 36.

the rostrum were two parallel and equally important procedures in the Athenian court, Ford has proved.⁴⁵

Moreover, the Homeric text cited by Aeschines in the speech *Against Timarchus* seems to be the text delivered during the hearing of the case; it is probably not a product of later revision, simply because it is organically connected with the arguments of the orator:⁴⁶ the way the speech is structured in 141–54 is Aeschines' way; it is really the way in which Aeschines also predisposes the audience with comments before the clerk reads out a testimony or a document (e. g. in the speech *On the False Embassy* the testimony of Amyntor follows a proleptic exposition given by Aeschines in six paragraphs [63–68] or in the same speech, paragraph 60, where Aeschines presents a partial, possibly modified, quotation of the Allies' *dogma* given in an anticipatory way, in order to corroborate his own arguments).

In all these cases, Aeschines reworks a text of Homer and makes slight modifications trying to support his case. At the same time, he avoids significant deviations.

d. The Speech *Against Ctesiphon*

In this political trial presented before the law court in 330, the accused, Ctesiphon, who was a political friend of Demosthenes, had to defend himself. He was also helped by Demosthenes who acted as his *synēgoros*; the reason for the prosecution of Aeschines against Ctesiphon was the latter's proposal —illegal, according to Aeschines— suggesting that the city should offer a crown to Demosthenes as a reward for his lifetime service and efforts offered to the city.

However, the real target of Aeschines' accusation was political, since he had to dispute over Ctesiphon's justification of the award, which was based on a long argumentation that Demosthenes has showed concern for and loyalty to the city all his life. Thus, Aeschines moves to a real evaluation of Demosthenes' political career attempting to impose his unfavourable view for Demosthenes' political record. The prosecution was not successful for the part of Aeschines, who failed to get the one-fifth of the votes. He was then fined and he left Athens.

We encounter in this speech of Aeschines an indirect quotation or allusion to the Homeric text through the epigram of the Stoa of Hermai in paragraph 185.⁴⁷

---

45 Ford 1999, 231–56.
46 Van der Valk 1964, II 329; Dué 2001, 36 and n.17.
47 It is also Hesiod (*Op.* 240–45) that is quoted in 3.135.

In 190 an epigram in honour of the democrats from Phyle is also quoted. The purpose of setting up these three *stēlai* was to honour Cimon's victory at Eion in 476 (Hdt. 7.107, Th. 1.98.1). Aeschines by quoting these inscriptions demands to support his case that Demosthenes' asking to be crowned by the *dēmos* does not comply with the glorious Athenian past; Athens promotes collective and not personal deeds.

> ἐπὶ δὲ τῷ τρίτῳ ἐπιγέγραπται Ἑρμῇ·
> ἔκ ποτε τῆσδε πόλησς ἅμ' Ἀτρείδῃσι Μενεσθεὺς
> ἠγεῖτο ζάθεον Τρωικὸν ἂμ πεδίον,
> ὅν ποθ' Ὅμηρος ἔφη Δαναῶν πύκα χαλκοχιτώνων
> κοσμητῆρα μάχης ἔξοχον ἄνδρα μολεῖν.
> οὕτως οὐδὲν ἀεικὲς Ἀθηναίοισι καλεῖσθαι
> κοσμητὰς πολέμου τ' ἀμφὶ καὶ ἠνορέης.
> ἔστι που τὸ τῶν στρατηγῶν ὄνομα; οὐδαμοῦ, ἀλλὰ τὸ τοῦ δήμου.
> (Aeschin. 3.185)
>
> *And on the third of Hermai is inscribed:*
> *When Menestheus from this city led his men on the holy plain of Troy to join Atreus' sons,*
> *Homer once said, of the linen clad Danaans*
> *he was supreme in ordering the battle.*
> *Fittingly then shall the Athenians be all*
> *honoured, and called*
> *marshals and leaders of war, heroes in combat of arms.*
> *Is the name of the generals anywhere? Nowhere; just the name of the people.*

The inscription recalls a passage from *Il.* 2.552–54:

> τῶν αὖθ' ἡγεμόνευ' υἱὸς Πετεῶιο Μενεσθεύς.
> τῶι δ' οὔ πώ τις ὁμοῖος ἐπιχθόνιος γένετ' ἀνήρ
> κοσμῆσαι ἵππους τε καὶ ἀνέρας ἀσπιδιώτας·
>
> *The leader of those (scil. the Athenians) was Menestheus, son of Peteos.*
> *Like him was no other man upon the earth for*
> *the marshalling of chariots and of warriors that bear the shield.*

In fact, we have a case of a two-stage reception of Homer: first, the reception of the *Iliad* by the Athenians in the 470s producing this epigram and second, the reception of the epigram and indirectly of the *Iliad* by Aeschines in his speech.

The third inscription mentioned here by Aeschines makes reference to the Athenian contingent for the Trojan War. Menestheus, appearing as son of Peteos in this text, was the Athenian army leader; his role in the Trojan War was probably minor.[48] Theseus is totally absent from the Homeric passage, although the reference to Athens only and not to Marathon, Aphidna, Eleusis, Thoricos may mean that this concerns an age after the synoecism attributed to Theseus.

The content of both texts (*Il.* 2.552–54 and *Against Ctesiphon* 185) presents a close similarity; the wording resembles in a way the Homeric original (e.g. κοσμῆσαι in Homer, κοσμητῆρα and κοσμητάς in the inscription cited by Aeschines). Nevertheless, the addition of the two verses οὕτως οὐδὲν ἀεικὲς [...] καὶ ἠνορέης, which overstates Athenian virtues, may be a slight distortion of the Iliadic text.

This inscription is in effect an attempt of a retrospective reworking of Homer's verses concerning Athens' engagement with the Trojan War. It is simply the association technique employed in this 'Stoa of the Hermai' in such a way as to place the recent prominent victory against Persia within a broader historical context, including the War against Troy.

Eventually, concerning the question of the edition of the Homeric text in the age of Peisistratus, the issue of Athens' role in the Trojan War may help draw conclusions on the overall interpolations by the Athenians. Moreover, as a corpus, the three inscriptions of the 'Stoa of Hermai' of the early classical age point to a dynamic or creative reception of Homer by the Athenians, once they quote their engagement— though not eminent—in the Trojan War, backing their deeds of the recent past. What really interests the city in the 470s is a sole reference to their presence in Troy enriched by the authority of Homer, overlooking the minor character of this participation. This may be the reason why they do not distort the source so much, since it is again a matter of rhetorical use.

Important to this discussion on the inscription of the 'Stoa of Hermai' is that the text quoted by Aeschines in 3.185 is also used with the same order and almost the same wording by Plutarch (*Cimon* 7) followed by Plutarch's phrasing immediately afterwards (*Cimon* 8).[49] Although Wade-Gery supports the idea of a multiple source for Plutarch's text (including Hypereides and Demosthenes *Against Leptines* 112), Plutarch's conclusion that ταῦτα καίπερ οὐδαμοῦ τὸ Κίμωνος ὄνομα δηλοῦντα τιμῆς ὑπερβολὴν ἔχειν ἐδόκει τοῖς τότ' ἀνθρώποις ('although these inscriptions nowhere mentioned the name of Cimon, his contemporaries regarded them to be an honour of distinction for him') connects the two texts, Aeschines' and Plutarch's, very closely.[50] However, it is beyond the scope of our discussion to go to a more de-

---

[48] For more detail, see Kirk 1985, 179–80, 206–07.
[49] For the divergences of Plutarch's text from Aeschines, see Wade-Gery 1933, 93.
[50] See Wade-Gery 1933, 71–104, esp. 87–95; see also Jacoby 1945, 185–211, where it is noted that Aeschines copied them from D. 20.112 (*Against Leptines*); recently Robertson 1999, 167–72; Petrovic 2013, 197–213.

tailed analysis of these epigrams making comments on the 'Stoa of Hermai' and the bulk of inscriptions that may have been kept there.

Nevertheless, I feel quite confident that Aeschines, presenting these three epigrams within his text had made a selection among more than three epigrams reversing the order and making the epigram from Eion first and the Menestheus epigram third. The typical motif of 'our ancestors, our fathers, ourselves' used also in funeral orations is probably reversed here (see Th. 2.36.1–4).[51]

e. Thersites: the symbolic language of rhetoric

Θερσίτης δ' ἔτι μοῦνος ἀμετροεπὴς ἐκολώια,
ὃς ἔπεα φρεσὶν ᾗσιν ἄκοσμά τε πολλά τε εἴδη
μάψ, ἀτὰρ οὐ κατὰ κόσμον, ἐριζέμεναι βασιλεῦσιν,
ἀλλ' ὅ τί οἱ εἴσαιτο γελοίιον Ἀργείοισιν
ἔμμεναι· αἴσχιστος δὲ ἀνὴρ ὑπὸ Ἴλιον ἦλθε·
φολκὸς ἔην, χωλὸς δ' ἕτερον πόδα, τὼ δέ οἱ ὤμω
κυρτώ, ἐπὶ στῆθος συνοκωχότε· αὐτὰρ ὕπερθεν
φοξὸς ἔην κεφαλήν, ψεδνὴ δ' ἐπενήνοθε λάχνη.
ἔχθιστος δ' Ἀχιλῆϊ μάλιστ' ἦν ἠδ' Ὀδυσῆϊ·
τὼ γὰρ νεικείεσκε· τότ' αὖτ' Ἀγαμέμνονι δίωι
ὀξέα κεκληγὼς λέγ' ὀνείδεα· τῶι δ' ἄρ' Ἀχαιοὶ
ἐκπάγλως κοτέοντο νεμέσσηθέν τ' ἐνὶ θυμῶι.
αὐτὰρ ὃ μακρὰ βοῶν Ἀγαμέμνονα νείκεε μύθωι·
(*Il*. 2.212–24)

Only Thersites still kept chattering, unmeasured in speech,
being adept at disorderly words
with which to revile the kings, recklessly, in no due order
whatever he thought would raise a laugh among the Argives;
the ugliest of men who came to Ilion.
He was bandy-legged, dragging the foot, with two rounded shoulders,
hunching together over his chest and above them
his head was pointed and a sparse stubble flowered on it.
Hateful was he to Achilles above all, and to Odysseus,
for both of them he was in the habit of reviling; but now
with shrill cries he uttered abuse against noble Agamemnon. With him were the Achaeans
exceedingly angry and indignant in their hearts.
Thus, shouting loudly he reviled Agamemnon.

καὶ εἰ μέν τις τῶν τραγικῶν ποιητῶν τῶν μετὰ ταῦτα ἐπεισαγόντων ποιήσειεν ἐν τραγωιδίᾳ τὸν Θερσίτην ὑπὸ τῶν Ἑλλήνων στεφανούμενον, οὐδεὶς ἂν ὑμῶν ὑπομείνειεν, ὅτι φησὶν Ὅμηρος ἄνανδρον αὐτὸν εἶναι καὶ συκοφάντην· αὐτοὶ δ' ὅταν τὸν τοιοῦτον ἄνθρωπον στεφανῶτε,

---

51 Cf. Loraux 1986, 120–21.

οὐκ <ἂν> οἴεσθε ἐν ταῖς τῶν Ἑλλήνων δόξαις συρίττεσθαι; οἱ μὲν γὰρ πατέρες ὑμῶν τὰ μὲν ἔνδοξα καὶ λαμπρὰ τῶν πραγμάτων ἀνετίθεσαν τῷ δήμῳ, τὰ δὲ ταπεινὰ καὶ καταδεέστερα εἰς τοὺς ῥήτορας τοὺς φαύλους ἔτρεπον· Κτησιφῶν δ' ὑμᾶς οἴεται δεῖν ἀφελόντας τὴν ἀδοξίαν ἀπὸ Δημοσθένους περιθεῖναι τῷ δήμῳ.
(Aeschin. 3.231)

And if any of the tragic poets who are to bring on their plays afterwards, in a tragedy, were to represent Thersites as crowned by the Greeks, no one of you would tolerate it, because Homer says he was a coward and a slanderer (sykophantēs); but when you yourselves crown such a man as this, don't you think you are being hissed in the minds of the Greeks? Your fathers gave a tribute for the glorious and brilliant achievements to the people but mean and unworthy acts threw upon the incompetent politicians; however, Ctesiphon thinks you should remove the stigma from Demosthenes and place it on the people.

Aeschines in his attempt to evaluate not only Demosthenes' political career but also his overall personality takes refuge to Homer, this time in an alternative way; he attacks Demosthenes' character trying to convince the jurors that such a personality is not worthy of being crowned; to support this claim and to add more strength and credit to this, he makes a direct comparison between Demosthenes and Thersites, the infamous man mentioned by Homer in *Il.* 2.221,[52] to criticize Agamemnon being punished by Odysseus afterwards. Thersites' name is obviously a 'speaking' name (originating in θέρσος, the Aeolic form of Ionic θάρσος),[53] since it carries an apparent meaning of over-boldness, recklessness, rashness. Thus, the comparison attempted by Aeschines purports to assimilate the present to the past and transfer the features of unmanliness (see ἄνανδρον[54]) and sycophancy (συκοφάντην[55]) and even other characteristics (being nastily

---

[52] Cf. Aeschin. 3.212, where an implicit comparison between Demosthenes and Ajax is attempted; this echoes the epic cycle in a way (cf. Proclus' summary of the *Little Iliad*). In 212 the tone is ironic (Demosthenes is characterized as μεγαλόψυχος καὶ τὰ πολεμικὰ διαφέρων), but the reference to the intentional wounding by Demosthenes to himself (see the case *Against Meidias*) and the overall content of the passage are leading to a conclusion that Demosthenes uses even his body (his head, in this passage, his mouth in the speech *On the False Embassy* 23 and 88) for gaining profit.
[53] Kirk 1985, 138.
[54] For the feature of unmanliness (ἄνανδρος, ἀνανδρία) given to Demosthenes by Aeschines in various occasions, see also 1.131; the whole context in this passage refers to an association of passive homosexuality and womanly clothing.
[55] The term συκοφάντης hints at the social and civic sphere; it may mean the person who brings an unjust prosecution, one not based on solid ground (cf. also D.57.34). Despite the frequent references of litigants to their opponents as sycophants, the meaning and etymology of the word remain obscure; see Harvey 1990, 120–21 for various meanings of the word and numerous references. In some cases, it means a professional informer (Ar. *Ach.* 559, 725, 825), in

abusive, disgusting, repulsive and distinguished for impropriety) from Thersites to Demosthenes, but not only these: Aeschines intends to ascribe to Demosthenes all these features coming directly from Thersites and, moreover, to prompt an identification of both men in terms of character and posture, since visible personality and character must be consistent.[56]

However, Thersites' courage is never really discussed in Homer or other epic; Aeschines does discuss Demosthenes' courage or lack of it, rewriting Thersites in the image of Demosthenes as he himself presents him. In that sense, Aeschines reworks Thersites in terms of fifth and fourth-century language and concepts.

Similarly, the initial statement of the paragraph 'if any of the tragic poets [...] a slanderer (*sykophantēs*)' seems important. Indeed, this clearly brings forth the cultural atmosphere of the period, in which proclamation of honours upon citizens or non-citizens for distinctive service to Athens was organized during tragic festivals and especially City Dionysia;[57] more than this, within this cultural atmosphere, it is Homer who is recognized as one of the favourite authors, reworked by the tragic poets of the time through the myths and ideas which he offers; however, Homer has already established his ideas and even his characters with a certain profile in the Athenian audience; adaptation of Homeric material was a usual phenomenon and sometimes a routine process for classical literature; in the fourth century Thersites' character was reworked by Chaeremon in a tragedy entitled *Achilles Thersitoktonos* ('Slayer of Thersites'). It seems as though that such an unpopular character like Thersites is a risky venture, if a tragic poet or even an orator attempts a representation of him.[58] It is also the famous case of Phrynichus' *Capture of Miletos* (see Hdt. 6.21.2) along with various other anecdotes and vivid accounts presenting cases of conflicts between tragic performances and Athenians' moral and political sentiments in tandem with the audience's frightened reaction.[59]

---

others, a prosecutor who seeks financial reward from public action or by blackmailing his opponent; it can also mean, generally, a citizen who uses his legal expertise to escape conviction.
56 See Russell 1990, 199.
57 Pickard-Cambridge 1988², 59.
58 See also Lowry 1991; cf. the vase-painting related to the *Achilles Thersitoktonos* (Boston, Museum of Fine Arts 03.804).
59 See further Pickard-Cambridge 1988², 274–75.

f. Reference to Margites

In 3.160 Demosthenes is presented by Aeschines to give to Alexander the nickname 'Margites':

> Ἐπειδὴ δ' ἐτελεύτησε μὲν Φίλιππος, Ἀλέξανδρος δ' εἰς τὴν ἀρχὴν κατέστη, πάλιν αὖ τερατευόμενος ἱερὰ μὲν ἱδρύσατο Παυσανίου, εἰς αἰτίαν δὲ εὐαγγελίων θυσίας τὴν βουλὴν κατέστησεν, ἐπωνυμίαν δ' Ἀλεξάνδρῳ Μαργίτην ἐτίθετο, ἀπετόλμα δὲ λέγειν ὡς οὐ κινηθήσεται ἐκ Μακεδονίας. ἀγαπᾶν γὰρ αὐτὸν ἔφη ἐν Πέλλῃ περιπατοῦντα καὶ τὰ σπλάγχνα φυλάττοντα. Καὶ ταυτὶ λέγειν ἔφη οὐκ εἰκάζων, ἀλλ' ἀκριβῶς εἰδὼς ὅτι αἵματός ἐστιν ἡ ἀρετὴ ὠνία, αὐτὸς οὐκ ἔχων αἷμα, καὶ θεωρῶν τὸν Ἀλέξανδρον οὐκ ἐκ τῆς Ἀλεξάνδρου φύσεως, ἀλλ' ἐκ τῆς ἑαυτοῦ ἀνανδρίας.

> But when Philip died and Alexander had come to rule, Demosthenes still presenting himself with an imposing air, he caused a shrine to be dedicated to Pausanias and involved with the Council in the charge of making sacrifice for good news; he gave Alexander the nickname 'Margites' and had the effrontery to maintain that he would not stir from Macedonia, because he was content, he said, to stroll around[60] in Pella observing the omens.[61] He said this was not based on conjecture, but on accurate knowledge that the price of valour is blood, though he himself having no blood in him and formed his judgement of Alexander not by Alexander's nature but by his own cowardice.

This reference to Margites is clearly from a mock-epic named after the eponymous character. Margites is featured by proverbial stupidity, madness and lust, lack of experience, immaturity, indecision; the name Margites is a 'speaking' name coming from μάργος (see also LSJ⁹ s.v. Μαργίτης).

Demosthenes' reference to Margites cannot be found anywhere in his published speeches and may have been obelized after revision. However, Plutarch (*Dem.* 23.2) repeats the statement as follows: καὶ τὸ βῆμα κατεῖχε Δημοσθένης, καὶ πρὸς τοὺς [...] παῖδα καὶ Μαργίτην ἀποκαλῶν αὐτὸν ('Demosthenes reigned supreme in the Assembly and wrote to the generals of the King, who were in Asia attempting to stir them up to start a war against Alexander from there, while he called Alexander a boy and a Margites'). In addition, Philotas, the son of Parmenio, called contemptuously Alexander a stripling (μειράκιον), who enjoyed the title of king through Philotas' and Parmenio's efforts (see Plu. *Alex.* 48.5).

---

60 The word περιπατοῦντα has been regarded (see Carey 2000, 219, n. 177) as sneering at Alexander's training in the school of Aristotle, which was called *Peripatos*.

61 Τὰ σπλάγχνα φυλάττοντα is likelier to mean 'guarding the sacrificial entrails' hinting at his indecision, like Margites, to proceed to further action, although he had made all the necessary preparations (see also above: οὐ κινηθήσεται ἐκ Μακεδονίας).

It seems quite possible to have a genuine reference here and a truthful allegation from the part of Aeschines for the attribution of the nickname to Alexander by Demosthenes (cf. Plu. *Alex.* 11.3), which is in tune with Demosthenes' policy against Alexander; especially in the first years of Alexander's reign, Demosthenes tried to form a stubborn opposition against him, he firmly supported Thebes in their attempt to resist the Macedonians and made ironic and disdainful comments on Alexander's personality (see also Marsyas of Pella *FGrH* 135 F3). It may be the case that Demosthenes trying to make a clear distinction between Alexander and Achilles, who is the prototype of heroic character and a model that Alexander wished to imitate, identifies Alexander to Margites, who was the very opposite model.[62]

A single reference to a comic hero like Margites without any other comment simply means that the person referred to and, more importantly, the parodic epic poem were really well-known to the Athenian audience of the mid fourth century. Indeed, the poem is discussed in *Poetics* 1448b, where Aristotle argues that it must be credited to Homer, who was the first poet delineating the forms of comedy by composing the *Margites*. According to Aristotle, Homer in the case of the *Margites* dramatized the laughable avoiding invective, and the *Margites* became a predecessor of comedy as the *Iliad* and the *Odyssey* of tragedy (1448b 35 – 40).[63] Moreover, the pseudo-Platonic dialogue *Alcibiades* II (147b) makes reference to the *Margites* as Homeric.[64]

Once again, fourth-century political oratory uses epic themes and symbols with or without reference to Homer and transfers them as *rhetorica exempla*[65] into political discussion. Moreover, in the third century BC the popularity of the mock-epic poem *Margites* continues to be high, since it enjoys the admiration of Callimachus (see fr. 397 Pf.).

---

[62] See Plu. *Per.* 1.6, where Alexander is presented as playing *kithara*, a hint at his attempt to imitate Achilles.

[63] For modern scholarly views on the authorship of the *Margites*, see Jacob 1993, 275 – 79; Rotstein 2010, esp. 98 – 104; Bossi 1986.

[64] According to Eustratius on Arist. *EN* 6.7.2 (*Comm. in Arist. Gr.* xx, p. 320, 38 Heylbut), the attribution of the name *Margites* to a poem of Homer is accepted also by Archilochus (fr. 153 B4) and Cratinus (fr. 368 K.-A.); see Pfeiffer 1949, 1. 325; see also Hyp. *Lyc.* 7 presenting Margites as ἀβελτερώτατος; for more ancient references to the *Margites*, see West *IEG*² 1989 – 1992, II 69 – 78.

[65] See Quint. *Inst.* 5.11.6 (*est in exemplus allegoria, si non praedicta ratione ponantur*) with Lausberg 1960, §421.

g. Reference to the Sirens

Another point in anticipation is Aeschines' reference to the Sirens, though this point is not included in the speech *On the Crown* omitted possibly after revision, although it is equally possible that this reference could be an invention by Aeschines to introduce his attack on Demosthenes. It is an allusion to the *Odyssey*:

> Καὶ νὴ τοὺς θεοὺς τοὺς Ὀλυμπίους, ὧν ἐγὼ πυνθάνομαι Δημοσθένην λέξειν, ἐφ' ᾧ νυνὶ μέλλω λέγειν ἀγανακτῶ μάλιστα. Ἀφομοιοῖ γάρ μου τὴν φύσιν ταῖς Σειρῆσιν ὡς ἔοικε. Καὶ γὰρ ὑπ' ἐκείνων οὐ κηλεῖσθαί φησι τοὺς ἀκροωμένους, ἀλλ' ἀπόλλυσθαι, διόπερ οὐδ' εὐδοκιμεῖν τὴν τῶν Σειρήνων μουσικήν· καὶ δὴ καὶ τὴν τῶν ἐμῶν εὐπορίαν λόγων καὶ τὴν φύσιν μου γεγενῆσθαι ἐπὶ βλάβῃ τῶν ἀκουόντων. Καίτοι τὸν λόγον τοῦτον ὅλως μὲν ἔγωγε οὐδενὶ πρέπειν ἡγοῦμαι περὶ ἐμοῦ λέγειν·τῆς γὰρ αἰτίας αἰσχρὸν τὸν αἰτιώμενόν ἐστι τὸ ἔργον μὴ ἔχειν ἐπιδεῖξαι·

(Aeschin. 3.228)

And by the Olympian gods, of all the things, which I hear Demosthenes will say, the one I am about to tell you makes me most indignant the most. For he likens my natural gifts to the Sirens. He says that their hearers were not enchanted but destroyed by them and that therefore the Siren-song has no good repute; and that in like manner the smooth flow of my way of speaking and my natural talent have proved disastrous for those who listened to me. And yet I think this claim is one that nobody under any circumstances can properly make against me; it is a shame when someone makes an accusation and is not able to show the ground for the accusation.

Though the Sirens must have occurred in a lot of poetry in the interim, the reference may point to Homer without mention of Homer or can be regarded as a specific detail which would point to Homer's *Odyssey* 12.39–54 (Circe's foretelling account on the Sirens) and 158–200 (the episode with the Sirens), where these supernatural female sea-creatures (soul-birds or otherworld enchantresses) singing with the sweetest voice lure sailors to their doom.[66]

Demosthenes –through Aeschines– compared the sweet but destructive sounding of the Sirens to Aeschines' skilful and allegedly destructive speaking. Thus, Aeschines' voice is at issue here, a theme which could also be encountered in various other passages in Demosthenes' speeches contra Aeschines (see, for example, 18.259, 308, 19.337; cf. Demochares *FGrH* 75 F6c with [Plu.] *Mor.* 840e). But in 19.216–17 Demosthenes attempts to reverse the situation arguing that the jurors' job must not be dependent on the speakers' talent and the quality of speeches. This idea can be found in 18.287, where Demosthenes argues that he was chosen

---

[66] For an account of the Sirens' scene in the *Odyssey* and this literary motif, see Heubeck/Hoekstra 1989, 118 ff.

–and not Aeschines—as a speaker for the funeral speech over the war dead after Chaeronea, since the Athenians looked for a speaker to express the mourning of his soul and not to lament their fate with the pretended voice of an actor; see also 18.291, where Aeschines is presented as λαρυγγίζων, i.e. roaring.[67]

The charge in its generic form is not uncommon in rhetorical exchanges: the orator is suspect of rhetorical skill and manipulation trying to captivate the jurors and audience with pleasurable speaking.[68] Even more, an actor-orator like Aeschines is able to transfer his acting experience, skilful delivery, gestures and fine voice from acting stages to political stages becoming πάνδεινος ('dreadful'), γόης ('wizard'), σοφιστής ('sophistēs'), φέναξ ('rogue');[69] this hints at the idea of deception, a rhetorical motif used elsewhere in oratory with the terms ψυχαγωγέω and ψυχαγωγία.[70] This is also what Philocleon at Aristophanes' *Wasps* (see esp. 566f.) presents as entertainment and pleasures enjoyed by a juror; Philocleon among other things makes reference to Aesop's funny tales and other jokes, which make jurors laugh and lay aside their wrath. The last point on jokes is made also by Demosthenes (23.206), who claims that the jurors acquit criminals who have proved guilty, if they make witty remarks in court.

Eventually, the motif of the Odyssean Sirens moves the discussion from lawcourt to theatre, from argument to performance, from logic to seductive means. Aeschines' fine voice represents the histrionic power which enables the orator to seize the audience and leads the jurors to accept the thesis of the speaker, which is manipulated through illusion and deception. But not only this: the discussion on Aeschines' voice is levelled as an important argument, since, as Easterling has observed,[71] it is placed at a climactic point with the perorations in both speeches *On the False Embassy* and *On the Crown*.

---

[67] See Harpocration s.v. λαρυγγίζων meaning 'full throatened with mouth wide open'.
[68] For references to good speakers, see Aeschin. 3.139 (a description of Leodamas the Acharnian) and D. 18.219, a description of Callistratus of Aphidna, who enjoyed widespread fame as an orator: see Plu. *Dem.* 5 ff. with [Plu.] *Mor.* 844b; it was Callistratus who inspired Demosthenes (see Plu. *loc.cit.*).
[69] See Lada-Richards 2002, 416–17.
[70] See also *Lex. Vind.* (Nauck) s.v. ψυχαγωγός; D.H. *Dem.* 44.13. For the relation between lawcourts and theatre, see Hall 1995, 39–58; Ober/Strauss 1990, 238.
[71] Easterling 1999, 158; Lada-Richards 2002, 416.

Concluding remarks

In the period of 345–330 BC, when the opposition between Athens and Macedon reached a high point, we find three men of great significance, Demosthenes, Aeschines and Lycurgus, who enrich their argumentative weapons with poetry. With the authority of Homer (together with Euripides and Hesiod) Aeschines anticipates the main arguments of his opponent, Demosthenes, in the case *Against Timarchus*, while Homer provides him with material to deconstruct Demosthenes' image in the case *Against Ctesiphon*. It is worthy of note that Homer is used mainly in these two speeches; this raises issues on personal and political behaviour, where personal life and public sphere are seen as two sides of the same coin.[72]

The interesting outcome is that all the poetic quotations, paraphrases and summaries are found in speeches (of the three orators mentioned) delivered in a short period of 15 years, from 345 to 330.[73] This is an issue (educational, political or otherwise) that needs further investigation, since we have a bulk of speeches, political or not, of the late fifth and the first half of the fourth century, which would have included poetic texts in their corpus.

Consequently, one may ask what forces Demosthenes, Aeschines and Lycurgus to use poetry? And also: was that a rhetorical variation or a new cultural phenomenon traced in this specific period? To answer these questions, we have to point to the cultural features and the overall political trend of the period, especially the third quarter of the fourth century BC, including the 'Lycurgan Era' (338–322 BC); in this period political initiatives and significant cultural measures offered Athens the opportunity to reaffirm its dominant cultural role in the Greek world. It seems that this cultural policy (Kulturpolitik) functions as an alternative to the political and military policy now in decline.[74] I held that the encounter of poetry in oratory of this period may lead us to believe that it was not only the revival of tragedy and the three tragedians (Aeschylus, Sophocles and Euripides) and their plays which came to be presented again in the Athenian theatre. More than this it was a revival in arts, literature and generally in culture, which was spread around using theatre industry as a starting point and influenced all kind of poetry and Homer among them. This procedure seems to have already started from the period of Eubulus' administration after

---

[72] However, poetry in general can be found in more public speeches of the same period, as Demosthenes' *On the Crown* and *On the False Embassy* and Lycurgus' *Against Leocrates*.
[73] See Petrovic 2013, 199–200 for an analogous note on the use of epigrams within oratory which is placed in 330.
[74] See Hintzen-Bohlen 1995.

the Social War (355 BC). It is not accidental that both Eubulus and Lycurgus became heads of the city's Theoric fund.

In a period of crisis, as the Lycurgan era, when Athens faces the question of its independence in the future, a re-evaluation of institutions, traditions, cultural and historical heritage is needed. The Athenians seek to assure the past, in order to form a reworked identity with future perspective. The term 'intentional history' used by Gehrke and interpreted as 'projection in time of the elements of subjective, self-conscious self-categorization, which construct the identity of a group as a group' is telling of the policy adopted by Lycurgus in this period.[75] Homer, Hesiod and the tragedians were surely in the agenda of the old idealized heritage worthy of modern adaptation.

In his two speeches (*Against Timarchus* and *Against Ctesiphon*) Aeschines opts for a creative reception of Homer, appropriating the poet's ideas and values through his modernized perspective but also tentatively with due respect to a sanctioned text. In the speech *Against Timarchus* he feels certain that he is adapting the issue of the relationship of Achilles and Patroclus to his argumentative needs, namely speaking of chaste love as distinctively different from the sale of sexual gratification allegedly characterizing Timarchus.

In the speech *Against Ctesiphon*, again, Aeschines has to play with the idea of a glorious past with such values and principles that check the present situation of the allegedly unlawful crowning of his opponent, Demosthenes. Homer conveys all the necessary literary material to support Aeschines, i.e. a reference to the Athenian contingent to the Trojan War embedded in an inscription of the 470s and figures of symbolic power like Thersites, the Sirens and Margites.

However, while the rhetorical scope was served well, the citations of the Homeric text which are used should not be regarded as a safe indicator for the transmission of this text. Divergences from what was regarded as Homeric text in the fourth century BC were made to form freestanding excerpts, and this has been made on purpose and not to represent a distinct part of the transmission of the text.

All in all, in the third quarter of the fourth century BC Homer is not a text for public recitations or for educational use only; it is transformed into a powerful rhetorical tool with influence on the *dēmos*.

---

[75] For 'intentional history' and its interpretation, see Hanink 2014, 5 and n. 14 quoting Luraghi/Foxhall 2010, 9–14. However, to the above interpretation I feel that a creative process is missing as an aspect of 'intentional history'.

Eleni Volonaki
Homeric Values in the *Epitaphios Logos*

a. Moral values in the Homeric poems

The specific character of Homeric values has been the subject of considerable debate during the last half-century and more. Two are the most influential approaches that have been introduced to describe the sense of morality in the Homeric poems; firstly, Dodds made the distinction between 'shame culture' and 'guilt culture'[1] and later Adkins advocated the 'competitive' and the 'co-operative' values.[2] In particular, Adkins argued that the Greeks from Homer onwards consistently attributed supreme value to those virtues of which success rather than intention is the criterion, and on this view, competition would count far more than co-operation.[3]

Adkins' views have generally been adopted in scholarly literature,[4] although they have encountered some acute criticism. As Lloyd-Jones (1987, 308) noted, Adkins approached Greek religion from a distance, in the manner of an anthropologist, his own ethical standpoint being that 'duty and responsibility are the central concepts of ethics'.[5]

Adkins favours the study of values of societies as wholes and has also equated the system of values as a whole with the morality of the society.[6] Long has objected to the interpretation of many Homeric contexts as if they reflected the values of an autonomous existent society outside the poems, and argues that any inferences drawn purely from Homer about ethical language cannot be assumed as 'historical axioms'.[7] Hence, heroic *aretē*, as depicted in the Homeric poems, should not be taken to represent accurately the life and values of any actual society. Objections to Adkins' approach have mainly concentrated on his denial of 'co-operative values' and the centrality of his thesis to Homer's ethics of the so-called 'competitive

---

1 Dodds 1951, 28–63.
2 Adkins 1960, 30–85.
3 Adkins 1960, 152, 185. He also maintained that the most powerful terms of value continued in the fifth century to be what they had been in Homeric times *aretē*, *agathos* and *kakos* used of men and *aischron* used of actions that diminished *aretē*.
4 As well as in general philosophical discussions of Greek ethics; cf. Finkelberg 1998, 14, n. 3.
5 Adkins 1960, 2.
6 Adkins 1987, 311.
7 Long 1997, 122.

values'.[8] His treatment assumes a rigidity of structure in the behaviour of certain Greek moral terms; for example, he seems to exaggerate the extent to which *agathos* applies to qualities of courage and capacity.[9]

Gagarin uses the term morality to designate a sense of consideration for others not closely related to rational self-interest, but not either the status of pure morality; based on this approach he distinguishes three categories of rules, the legal rules between two or more full members of a community, the religious rules which influence the behaviour of a mortal toward a god and the moral rules which influence the behaviour toward another person who is unprotected.[10] In reply, Adkins disputes the distinction of these three types of rules, on the grounds that the same vocabulary of evaluation (e.g. *aretē*, *timē*, *hybris* etc) is used for all kinds of relationships.[11]

The purpose of this paper is not to examine all the issues that have been raised, but to focus on the significance of the Homeric values of *aretē* (bravery) and *timē* (honour) as central to the representation of the hero/warrior. Based on the assumption that there is a continuity in the application of heroic *aretē* as a fundamental value of success attached to the *agathos* from Homer until the fifth century,[12] we shall explore the context in which *aretē* and the associated Greek values are employed in the funeral orations of late 5th and 4th centuries BC and the extent to which these have functioned as an inspiration for the praise of the dead. As will be shown, there is a shift in the emphasis placed upon the warrior's heroic *aretē* in the funeral orations of the democratic *polis*, when addressing the whole of the Athenian *dēmos*, in contrast to the aristocratic connotations reflected in the Homeric poems.

Aretē as a Homeric value is closely related to the warrior's greatness in battle. It is a power necessary to and valued by the society. *Aretē* is far more impor-

---

8 Long (1997, 121–39) explores the link between *timē*, which is a competitive standard, and the unfavourable evaluation of certain kinds of aggressive or unco-operative behaviour; as for the use of the adjective *agathos* in Homer to make the most powerful commendation, as Adkins rightly argued, Long notes that only the context will decide whether in the use of *agathos* is the evaluative or rather the descriptive aspect which prevails. For other arguments from objection to Adkins' approach, cf. also Lloyd-Jones 1983, 12–20; Schofield 1986, 6–31; Williams 1993, 81–84, 100–02; Cairns 1993, 50–146; Zanker 1994, 1–45.
9 Creed (1973, 213–17) argued that there is a tendency to use the word in relation to these qualities in certain contexts and questions whether in these cases *agathos* retains the automatically overriding force with which Adkins invests it.
10 Gagarin 1987, 285–306.
11 Adkins 1987, 311–22. Lloyd-Jones (1987, 307–10) criticizes Gagarin's attempt to establish a *via media* between Adkins and himself as not successful.
12 Generally on the continuity and persistence of Greek values, cf. Walcot 1996.

tant than any other social value and is firmly attached to the individual *agathos*, denoting the significance of his achievements in war. The adjective *agathos*, which corresponds to the noun *aretē*, indicates the basic qualification required in order that one may be recognized as a possessor of this value, which is not just success, but the very fact of participating in the competition.[13]

The *agathos* man has been traditionally characterized as the one who can more effectively secure the stability, safety and welfare of the social group, both in war and in peace. The Homeric warrior is driven to action by a need for social validation. The noble men are honoured by their people because they achieve fame – *kleos*. The warrior's greatness in battle ensures his continued prestige during his life, so that his identity persists among future generations by the tale of his deeds. In the *Iliad* the heroic excellence is prominent, but it is also explored in terms of its underlying bitterness. In the *Odyssey* the poet moves beyond the glamour of heroism to a standard level of human condition, where the hero succeeds only by accepting his own weakness.[14] Thus, the heroism in the two epics is based upon the success and personal achievement within competition.

Honour is generally assumed to be a competitive value. However, as Frinkelber (1998, 16) points out, the only Homeric formula in which the word *timē* occurs is ἔμμορε τιμῆς; the use of this formula and its modifications in the Homeric corpus show that 'the idea of allotment of *timē* rather than gaining it in fair competition was deeply rooted in the epic tradition'.[15] In this view, *timē* (honour) should be regarded as a distributive rather than a competitive value; moreover, the distribution of *timē* in Homer appears to follow a person's social status, which is determined by the superiority in birth and wealth. On the other hand, the function of *agathos* and *aretē* in Homer to commend achievement and status is consistent with a standard of appropriateness which condemns excess and deficiency.[16]

On balance, the limits between what scholars define as 'competitive', 'distributive' and 'co-operative' values are not clear-cut. Most scholars, however, agree that the hero's *aretē* and *timē* involve prowess in war, status, birth and observation of social conventions. Achievement on the battlefield does play a fundamental role to those who possess *aretē* and *timē*, even though it may not necessarily constitute qualification for possessing these values. In effect, the values of *aretē* and *timē* in the Homeric poems are closely related to the aristocratic

---

[13] Finkelberg 1998, 15.
[14] On the heroism as displayed and used in the two epics, cf. Clarke 2004, 77–90.
[15] *Ibid.* 16, n.16.
[16] Long 1997, 139.

background of the Homeric hero and the society to which he belonged. In this context, *kleos* (glory), *andreia* (bravery), *auto-thusia* (self-sacrifice) and *hysterophēmia* (posthumous fame) are essential and natural qualities of the *agathos* hero and warrior who is being allotted prizes (*timē*) for his excellence and expertise.

b. The praise of the dead (*egkōmion*) in the funeral oration

In Homeric epic the *thrēnos* (lament) is sung by the bard over the hero's body creating a sort of contrasted mourning between the members of the family and the crowd.[17] The heroes of epic appear to play the primary role to the family mourning, since they did not regard tears as incompatible to their virility as warriors. Appeals for pity were frequent in the aristocratic epitaphs celebrating a warrior. A typical example of epic lamentation comes from *Iliad* 23, where Achilles is mourning in tears over the dead body of his friend Patroclus. The glorious complement to the hero's lamentation is the organization of the funeral games in respect for the dead friend. In honour of Patroclus, Achilles institutes the following games: the chariot-race, the fight of the caestus, the wrestling, the footrace, the single combat, the discus, the shooting with arrows and darting the javelin. The funeral games essentially function as a sort of diversion from grief, celebrating Patroclus' life. Furthermore, the funeral games of Patroclus represent one of the most significant values of Greek aristocratic life: individual honour.

The original place of the funeral oration should be assigned between the two poles of the lament and the eulogy, which in aristocratic society expressed the relationship between the living and the dead. The classical city abandoned the conception of mourning and the funeral oration excludes the lamentation (*thrēnos*) of epic and lyric poetry, since it involves the relationship between a community –the democratic *polis*– and its dead and, through these dead, its connection with its present and its past.[18] The funeral oration constitutes a eulogy, containing the elements of praise (*egkōmion*), exhortation (*parainesis*) and consolation (*paramythia*). The preference of praise over lamentation is stated in Plato's *Menexenus* 248c:

---

[17] Loraux 1986, 78.
[18] *Ibid.* 75–78; in the classical period, *thrēnos* is regarded as simply a synonym of *gōos*, the general term for any kind of lamentation.

τὰ μὲν γὰρ ἡμέτερα τελευτὴν ἤδη ἕξει ἥπερ καλλίστη γίγνεται ἀνθρώποις, ὥστε πρέπει αὐτὰ μᾶλλον κοσμεῖν ἢ θρηνεῖν.

The end of our lives will be very noble for mankind, and praise will be more appropriate than lamentation.[19]

In the classical period the Athenian city left room for women's lamentation, since weeping was women's lot at the time, while it chose a man to deliver the praise of the men that it was burying.[20] As a purely military and political speech, the funeral oration reflected only male values and therefore rejected the *thrēnos* and any appeals for pity. The democratic city was identified with its army and was able to accept the death of its men with greater peacefulness. However, the official orator was inspired by the epic tradition so that he was mediating in the community's relationship with its dead.[21]

All funeral orations reflect a democratic reading of Athenian history; in Homer's world, funeral ceremonies were restricted to the individual aristocrat, but in democratic Athens they were anonymous and collective, since they represented ordinary Athenian soldiers (particularly hoplites) and not their leaders. The notion of the 'posthumous glory and memory of the name' of the dead is the most substantial in the funeral oration, dominated by the rule of anonymity. In the *epitaphioi* the citizens are given no other name than that of Athenians and a collective glory. A gap can be noticed between the catalogue of the dead and the funeral oration, between the hymn and the eulogy, the funeral or heroic lament; two dimensions coexist in the national funeral oration and should be viewed as such, the religious and the political context.[22]

Funeral speeches reviewed the achievements of the mythical and historical past of the city of Athens, setting thus an example of virtue in political life. A speaker on a burial ceremony is encouraged to say something significant and

---

[19] The translation of all cited passages is based on Herrman 2004 with minor adjustments.
[20] The funeral orations (*epitaphioi*) were delivered as part of a state burial ceremony. Thucydides, in his introduction to Pericles' funeral oration (2.34), informs us of this traditional custom which was presumably celebrated annually, whenever there were Athenian war-dead to bury. According to Thucydides 2.34.1 and 2.47.1, the ceremony was dated in the winter, a time most appropriate for the Athenians to gather and bury their dead, after the battle operations had ended and the dead bodies had been brought to Athens. The ceremony consisted of four stages, the *prothesis*, where the remains of the dead bodies were brought in the coffins, one for each of the ten Athenian tribes, the *ekphora*, a formal procession to the public cemetery named Kerameikos, the burial at the *dēmosion sēma* and finally the funeral oration delivered by a chosen, distinguished orator.
[21] Loraux 1986, 82; Hardwick 1992, 232–35.
[22] Loraux 1986, 75.

original. On the other hand, he needs to satisfy audience expectations, which involve the traditional cultural ideals, such as patriotism, freedom under the law, self-confidence and public democratic debate.[23] All surviving speeches display a common structure, and later rhetoricians refer to these same typical elements for funeral orations. In the proem the speaker explains that his words are inadequate to the occasion. The *epainos* or 'praise' section follows, which included standard mythological and historical exploits, one of which was the praise of the ancestors and their accomplishments. In the final section, the speaker should give some consolation to the relatives of the dead.

The orations did not aim to inform, but to apply common ideals, values and attitudes of the citizens. To that end they sought to resolve the conflict between a cultural ideal of Panhellenic altruism and the Athenian superiority at any cost (*philonikia*) or desire for honour (*philotimia*).[24] The claims to Athenian primacy and uniqueness are frequent in the funeral orations with a hyperbolic and self-praise rhetorical emphasis transforming Athenian aggression into noble self-sacrifice. In this context, the orators praise *aretē* and prowess of the dead Athenian soldiers, in such a way that the purely historical events may be distorted or deliberately misinterpreted.[25]

c. Moral values in the *epitaphioi*

Among the surviving *epitaphioi* each one is distinctive, despite all the traditional elements of structure; each one serves its own goal addressing a different audience.[26] Moreover, the *epitaphioi* cannot be included in one and the same group since they were not all delivered at a public burial nor are they all dated to the same period. The central themes of all speeches are 'noble death' and the 'freedom' of Greece due to the achievements of the ancestors and the dead in specific battles. The achievements derived from *aretē* and all relevant qualities of the Athenian warriors as well as of their ancestors. Our emphasis will be placed upon these qualities and the distinctive skills that contributed to their own private but also to the common freedom and welfare (*eudaimonia*).

---

[23] Cf. Kennedy 1994, 21–22.
[24] Walters 1980, 2.
[25] *Ibid.* 3–5.
[26] The tone of funeral orations is both educative and deliberative (*symbouleutic*), since the orators attempt to influence public opinion for resistance and continuation of the war.

d. Thucydides: Pericles' *Epitaphios* 2.34 – 46

Thucydides' *epitaphios* was a reworking of the funeral oration delivered by Pericles at the end of the first year of the Peloponnesian War in 431.[27] It had a specific political goal: to glorify the Athenian democracy in the time of Pericles. The *epainos* begins with praise of the *progonoi* (ancestors) by asserting:

> ἄρξομαι δὲ ἀπὸ τῶν προγόνων πρῶτον· δίκαιον γὰρ αὐτοῖς καὶ πρέπον δὲ ἅμα ἐν τῷ τοιῷδε τὴν τιμὴν ταύτην τῆς μνήμης δίδοσθαι. τὴν γὰρ χώραν οἱ αὐτοὶ αἰεὶ οἰκοῦντες διαδοχῇ τῶν ἐπιγιγνομένων μέχρι τοῦδε ἐλευθέραν δι' ἀρετὴν παρέδοσαν (2.36.1).
>
> *I shall begin with our ancestors: it is both just and appropriate that they should have the honour of the first reference on an occasion like the present. They dwelt in the country without break in the succession from generation to generation, and it is because of their excellence that the state we have inherited is free.*

The ancestors deserve to be honoured through the funeral oration. Their virtue as excellence has guaranteed freedom for later generations. Here, the term *aretē* does not explicitly denote the military excellence and bravery of the ancestors but it does imply that their efforts on the battlefield established freedom for that time and the future. The notion of freedom in Thucydides is closely related to happiness and valour (2.43.4).[28]

The real subject of the praise in Pericles' *epitaphios* is the Athenian way of life, without offering any specific examples.[29] However, Thucydides later exemplifies their audacity, performance of duty and feeling of shame at the moment of fighting as virtues of all Athenian warriors (2.43.1). *Aretē* is also designated as the criterion of electing public officials, in particular their good deeds (2.371: ἔχων γέ τι ἀγαθὸν δρᾶσαι τὴν πόλιν). It becomes obvious that *aretē* in Thucydides is assigned with men's achievements and needs to be proved in practice either in war or in peace.

---

27 Thucydides (1.22.1) explains in the introduction to his history that the speeches are reconstructed on the basis of probability with an attempt to hold as closely as possible to what was actually said. He also describes how difficult it was for him to remember exactly what was said and therefore needed to talk to witnesses about the speeches.

28 Further on the idea of freedom and its use in Thucydides, cf. Hornblower 2003, 297.

29 Pericles avoids referring to the achievements of the ancestors, since 431BC had been a year of invasion and destruction; the first year of the War was marked by lack of military and political success. Therefore, any comparison between the past and the present would open negative reactions and criticism. The remarkable rhetorical technique of Pericles lies in the way he blends the past and the present in a 'timeless encomium of the city'; the city of Athens is praised as a city worth dying for. On the historical context of Thucydides' funeral oration, see Bosworth 2000, 216.

Orators tend to suggest that their praise is distinct, in particular from that of the poets. Thucydides rejects the need for a poetic eulogy of Athens, on the grounds that poets exaggerate and distort the truth:

> καὶ οὐδὲν προσδεόμενοι οὔτε Ὁμήρου ἐπαινέτου οὔτε ὅστις ἔπεσι μὲν τὸ αὐτίκα τέρψει, τῶν δ' ἔργων τὴν ὑπόνοιαν ἡ ἀλήθεια βλάψει, ἀλλὰ πᾶσαν μὲν θάλασσαν καὶ γῆν ἐσβατὸν τῇ ἡμετέρᾳ τόλμῃ καταναγκάσαντες γενέσθαι, πανταχοῦ δὲ μνημεῖα κακῶν τε κἀγαθῶν ἀίδια ξυγκατοικίσαντες. (2.41.4)
>
> *We shall not need the praises of Homer or of any other rhapsodist, whose poetry may please for the moment, but the truth of action will work against his intention. We have made all of the sea and the earth accessible for our daring and we have established jointly everlasting memorials to our harmful and good deeds.*

The dead do not need the Homeric praise, but their own fights have left eternal memorials to their deeds.[30] The contrast here indicates that prizes for poetic competitions were designed for the immediate moment, whereas Thucydides' work is permanent but superficially unpleasing.[31] Elsewhere, Thucydides also makes a distinction between literary genres, implying for example that he is neither a poet nor a logographer (1.21.2) or that his work is not to be recited because such a recitation might have been a joyless occasion (1.22.4).[32] In this context, Thucydides may not wish to devalue the Homeric praise but drawing on its reception, as was commonly and widely accepted, he rather uses it to describe his own work. Thus, his own praise is solely based upon historical deeds and achievements either bad or good which reveal the truth. By the mid-fifth century, Homeric eulogy has been connected with a joyful recitation, giving only pleasure. There is a shift in the emphasis of the praise by Thucydides, which does not exaggerate for the readers' pleasure but employs proofs for its credibility:

> καὶ τὴν εὐλογίαν ἅμα ἐφ' οἷς νῦν λέγω φανερὰν σημείοις καθιστάς. (2.42.1)
>
> *The funeral for the men over whom I am now speaking should be by proofs manifestly established.*

---

[30] On the issue whether this downgrading of Homer should be attributed to Pericles or to Thucydides, cf. Loraux 1986, 110.
[31] Hornblower 2003, 309.
[32] In 1.22.4 Thucydides says that his aim is purely intellectual and that he does not intend to improve his readers by making them morally better people, like doctors who wish to make 'their patients better'. Here the distinction does not involve literary genres but rather scientific approaches to people.

Noble death rather than a disgraceful life is a Homeric ideal reflected in the praise of Thucydides' funeral oration. Their death is presented to have occurred at a moment of glory and not fear:

καὶ ἐν αὐτῷ τῷ ἀμύνεσθαι καὶ παθεῖν μᾶλλον ἡγησάμενοι ἢ [τὸ] ἐνδόντες σῴζεσθαι, τὸ μὲν αἰσχρὸν τοῦ λόγου ἔφυγον, τὸ δ' ἔργον τῷ σώματι ὑπέμειναν καὶ δι' ἐλαχίστου καιροῦ τύχης ἅμα ἀκμῇ τῆς δόξης μᾶλλον ἢ τοῦ δέους ἀπηλλάγησαν. (2.42.4)

Since they thought that fighting and suffering were more appropriate than yielding and surviving, they avoided any shameful talk with their act of physical resistance and in an instance, at the height of their fortune, they passed away from the scene, not of their fear but of their glory.

Thucydides also argues that death occurring at a moment of patriotism and strength is to be preferred to humiliation, which follows cowardice:

ἀλγεινοτέρα γὰρ ἀνδρί γε φρόνημα ἔχοντι ἡ μετὰ τοῦ [ἐν τῷ] μαλακισθῆναι κάκωσις ἢ ὁ μετὰ ῥώμης καὶ κοινῆς ἐλπίδος ἅμα γιγνόμενος ἀναίσθητος θάνατος. (2.43.6)

And surely, to a man of spirit, the degradation of cowardice must be considerably more painful than the unfelt death striking him in the midst of his strength and patriotism![33]

Immortal glory for the dead is a Homeric idea (*hysterophēmia*), which is emphatically used in the funeral oration. It is striking that Thucydides refers to the common glory which will be eternally remembered upon every occasion (2.43.2). Because they gave their lives for the common good, they received ageless praise individually and a tomb most distinctive. They don't rest there; instead their glory eternally awaits any occasion for speech or action that may arise. Moreover, the glory of the dead constitutes a relief for the living (2.44.4).

Pericles' funeral oration closes with the identification of *aretē* as the bravery shown by excellent men and honoured by prizes: ἆθλα γὰρ οἷς κεῖται ἀρετῆς μέγιστα, τοῖς δὲ καὶ ἄνδρες ἄριστοι πολιτεύουσιν (2.46.1). The conception of courage in the Periclean funeral oration is closely tied to Athenian democratic ideology. Thucydides emphasizes that 'Athenian courage was grounded in rational deliberation' (2.40.3).[34] As has been shown, virtue has been presented by Thucydides mainly as a 'competitive' value, according to Adkins' terminology, though it involves the achievements of the whole group of warriors rather than of each hero individually.

---

33 For a discussion on the young age of the dead, cf. Hornblower 2003, 312–13. For the association of a noble and good death with happiness (*eudaimonia*) in life, see Th. 2.44.1.
34 Herrman 2009, 62.

e. Gorgias' *Epitaphios*

During the Peloponnesian War another funeral oration was composed by Gorgias, the famous sophist from Leontini (480–380 BC), which survives only in fragments. In the best preserved fragment of the funeral oration Gorgias describes *aretē* as divine, whereas the mortality of the dead as human:

> οὗτοι γὰρ ἐκέκτηντο ἔνθεον μὲν τὴν ἀρετήν, ἀνθρώπινον δὲ τὸ θνητόν, πολλὰ μὲν δὴ τὸ πρᾶον ἐπιεικὲς τοῦ αὐθάδους δικαίου προκρίνοντες... (DK86 B6)

In this funeral oration, which was most probably written as a kind of demonstration speech for students of rhetoric,[35] the praise of the dead is exaggerated to such an extent that they are even deified. Moreover, the deification of their *aretē* implies an excellence of achievements.

Further below in the same fragment, the *epainos* of the dead refers to their noble death and the sacrifice of their lives, in order to benefit their country; proof of their courage is that they fought against greater numbers of the enemy and endured. The honourable behaviour of the dead is specified as respect towards the gods, care for their parents and justice towards their fellow citizens. Such a conduct resulted into their immortality: τοιγαροῦν αὐτῶν ἀποθανόντων ὁ πόθος οὐ συναπέθανεν, ἀλλ' ἀθάνατος οὐκ ἐν ἀθανάτοις σώμασι ᾖ οὐ ζώντων.

The emphasis placed upon their excellent behaviour both in private and public life is intended to offer an exemplary way of political life. Thus, the dead deserve the honour and praise of all the living; in effect, the citizens are encouraged to imitate their choice and virtue. As can be seen, moral and civic values are here interrelated for the educational purposes of a reading audience.

f. Lysias 2: *Epitaphios* for those who died assisting the Corinthians

The *epitaphios* attributed to Lysias was composed during the Corinthian War of 395–387 for those who died 'assisting the Corinthians'. Lysias' *epitaphios* presents a clear divergence from the rest of the corpus, and therefore its authorship has been considerably doubted.[36] Lysias, however, would most likely be the one to have such

---

[35] It is unlikely that Gorgias actually delivered this funeral oration, since he was not an Athenian citizen.
[36] Usher/Najock 1982, 85–105.

good reasons for 'highlighting the contribution played by *xenoi* (foreigners) in the democratic counter-revolution of 403/2 (Lys. 2.66)'.[37] Moreover, the funeral oration may seem the sort of patriotic speech Lysias would be expected to write.[38] Lysias himself could not have delivered the speech since he was not an Athenian citizen and therefore this specific funeral oration must have been designed as a model to be used for rhetorical training addressing in any case a reading audience.[39]

Lysias' *epainos* is taken almost completely from the *genos* and extends over sixty sections. Such a lengthy mythical-historical narrative is often considered to be the most typical and important part of classical funeral orations.[40] Lysias develops the *epainos* chronologically according to three broad divisions: the ancestors (§§ 3–19), their descendants (§§ 20–66) and those now being buried (§§ 67–70).

In the opening of the speech Lysias states that the virtues as denoting the achievements of the dead are celebrated by the living who are mourning for their sufferings (2.2: πανταχῇ δὲ καὶ παρὰ πᾶσιν ἀνθρώποις οἱ τὰ αὐτῶν πενθοῦντες κακὰ τὰς τούτων ἀρετὰς ὑμνοῦσι). The verb *hymnein* (celebrate) attributes a heroic tone, since it implies a connection with hero-cult.[41] The heroic element of the praise is complemented with the didactic purpose of the funeral oration; the funeral practice consists of 'the celebration of the dead in songs, making speeches at memorials for the brave men, honouring the dead at these sorts of occasions and teaching the living the deeds of the dead' (2.3).[42] In this educational context, virtue is also associated with *sōphrosynē* (discretion) and opportunity to exercise good judgement, while extending a great deal of self-control and respect to all people (2.57). The *aretē* of the dead is also connected with the idea of competitiveness, which here serves to emphasize the limitation of

---

37 Todd 2007, 157–64.
38 Cf. Kahn 1963, 231.
39 Modern scholars view Lysias' *epitaphios* as a typical funeral oration of the period; cf. Ziolkowski 1981, 78–79; Herrman 2004, 27–28; Todd 2009, 163–64; Loraux 1986, 136–39.
40 Cf. Ziolkowski 1981, 78–79.
41 Todd (2009, 212) refers to the stereotype connected with hero-cult: ὑμνοῦνται δὲ ὡς ἀθάνατοι διὰ τὴν ἀρετήν ('they are praised like immortals on account of their bravery').
42 On *paideusis* playing an important role in *epitaphioi* and predicated not just of those being buried but also of their ancestors, cf. *ibid*. 215. For the educative role of the *epitaphioi*, cf. also 2.69: ἄνδρες δὲ γενόμενοι τήν τε ἐκείνων δόξαν διασώσαντες καὶ τὴν αὐτῶν ἀρετὴν ἐπιδείξαντες ('these men are to be envied both in their life and in death, because they were schooled in the good qualities of their ancestors, and as adults they preserved the glory of those generations and displayed their own virtue').

Athenian military action.⁴³ In effect, *aretē* has been introduced as a heroic, competitive value rhetorically employed for educative purposes.

Aretē explicitly denotes the bravery shown on the battlefield within a patriotic context: ἄνδρες δ' ἀγαθοὶ γενόμενοι, καὶ τῶν μὲν σωμάτων ἀφειδήσαντες, ὑπὲρ δὲ τῆς ἀρετῆς οὐ φιλοψυχήσαντες (2.25: 'they proved to be brave without sparing their lives and they did not choose life over virtue').⁴⁴ *Aretē* is also associated with freedom and as such is preferable to enslavement accompanied by reproach and wealth (2.33). The exaggeration that the dead exceeded their contemporaries or even their ancestors in virtue is consistent with the heroic representation of the warriors and their glorious self-sacrifice (2.40). It is striking that virtue as bravery is identified with fatherland itself for which the warriors fought and died (2.66); from such a display of virtue the living can benefit and enjoy their life (2.74).

The choice of a glorious and immortal death is a common theme in funeral orations and is also used by Lysias to portray the bravery and virtue of the dead (2.23). As Loraux (1986, 98–118) argued, it is characteristic of funeral speeches to praise not the lives of the citizens but their choice of death. The concept of the 'beautiful death' of the heroic warrior is a Homeric ideal; for example in *Iliad* 22 the Greeks admire the physical beauty of the dead Hector even as they take turns to disfigure it. Moreover, the Homeric hero chooses to die in honour of his homeland and comrades rather than live in shame.⁴⁵ An extension of this concept is the choice of freedom as consequent to the choice of death; as Lysias states, the ancestral virtue was proved by the choice of a death with freedom rather than a life with slavery (2.62). On this view, the funeral oration distances from the Homeric ideal of a beautiful death to emphasize the freedom of the community, a city-state and the whole of Greece.

g. Plato's *Menexenus* 234a–249d

Socrates presents another funeral oration by Aspasia, the well-known mistress of Pericles, which has been incorporated in Plato's dialogue *Menexenus*; the historical detail in the speech indicates that it was written after the Corinthian War and Lysias'

---

43 Ibid. 221; cf. Lys. 2.10: ἀλλ' ἐκείνοις μὲν ἀντὶ τῆς ἀσεβείας τὴν ἑαυτῶν ἀρετὴν ἐπεδείξαντο, αὐτοὶ δὲ λαβόντες τὰ ἆθλα ὧνπερ ἕνεκα ἀφίκοντο ('They demonstrated to them their own virtue in place of impiety. They themselves took the prizes for which they had come').
44 For showing bravery on the battlefield, cf. also 2.47; on the importance of *aretē* for making the memory immortal, cf. 2.81; for the rhetoric on *aretē* as a whole, cf. 2.54.
45 For Hector's views on the performance of duty, even if this implies self-sacrifice, cf. *Il.* 6.381–502.

funeral oration, in 386 BC. The ascription to Aspasia establishes a connection between Plato's *Menexenus* and the famous Periclean funeral oration by Thucydides.

Scholars differ in their interpretation of the dialogue.[46] Many parallels can be observed between Plato's and Thucydides' orations, such as the antithesis of word and deed (*logos* and *ergon*), the tradition of the funeral oration and the emphasis placed upon the *paideia* and *politeia*.[47] There are, however, differences between the two orations concerning the individual and collective ideal of virtue, the vocabulary, the tone and the approach of the audience.[48] Despite the polemic relationship between the two orations, the *Menexenus* can be seen as an alternative and an answer to the Periclean oration in two aspects, the rhetoric and the politics. It offers an analysis of the faults of rhetoric by recognizing the falsehood of the idealized portrayal of Athens, which in effect becomes object of parody in Socrates' funeral oration.[49] Thus, Plato takes the opportunity to demonstrate how a funeral oration should be written.[50] In terms of politics, the contrast between the two figures, Pericles and Socrates, is obvious; the former represents the prestige of the Athenian empire and naval power, whereas the latter reflects the ideals of virtue (Socratic *aretē*) and justice. Plato's target is the construction of Pericles as a symbol, and he criticizes Thucydides' portrayal and the Athenian practice, particularly in the funeral oration, to exemplify Pericles, his leadership and his policy.[51] Thus, the appeals to the traditions of Athenian history are presented to offer a judgement against Pericles' imperial policy.

Plato's *epainos* (239a6–246b2) is treated in a long section that included the stories of the mythical background and a survey of Athenian history from the Persian Wars down to the Peace of Antalcidas in 387 BC. Plato makes no distinction between the deeds of the present dead and the deeds of their ancestors. He praises the dead for their virtue, as they set an example to imitate in the later battles (240d), which reflects the didactic purpose of the funeral oration. They are more spe-

---

46 Some view the speech as an antagonistic response to Thucydides' idealized view of Athenian democracy under Pericles, whereas others see it as a sort of parody that adopts an ironic tone on Lysias' *epitaphios*. For a detailed discussion of scholarly views, cf. Herrman 2004, 45–47.
47 For an analysis of these parallels, cf. Kahn 1963, 221–22; Monoson 1998, 491–92.
48 Cf. Salkever 1993, 134–35.
49 Cf. Coventry 1989, 4–10.
50 Plato praises the city of Athens as it should be praised, but departures from historical accuracy can be observed. A funeral oration is certainly not a work of historical research, and therefore the historical distortions, especially in details, such as the role of Sparta to the Persian Wars and the supposed alliance between Athens and Sparta against Persia in the Corinthian War, should not be looked for further analysis and explanation; cf. Kahn 1963, 225; Salkever 1993, 138–39.
51 Cf. Monoson 1998, 492–500.

cifically praised for their nobility of birth, upbringing and education and their deeds (237a). Virtue is here associated with education, noble nature and freedom (239a–b), as well as *sōphrosynē* (243a: 'moderation'). Plato identifies military with civic *aretē*, by praising the virtue of the warriors as causing not only the victory, but also the glory and good reputation of the city (243c–d). The concept of justice co-existing with virtue is stressed by Plato and is consistent with his philosophical approach of *aretē* as a system of values that sets limitations for the common good (247a).

The choice of a glorious death rather than a shameful life is also stressed in Plato's *Menexenus*, but focuses upon the consequences for the relatives, friends and citizens (246d);[52] it is striking, however, that the dead are described as brave and glorious but not immortal (247d).[53]

Plato refers to funeral games as a part of the funeral together with the performance of the oration, recalling the Homeric funeral games in honour of Patroclus (*Iliad* 23) and enhancing the competitive nature of moral values praised for the dead: πρὸς δὲ τούτοις ἀγῶνας γυμνικοὺς καὶ ἱππικοὺς τιθεῖσα καὶ μουσικῆς πάσης (249b: 'In addition, the city enacts competitions in gymnastics, horses and all sorts of music').[54]

h. Demosthenes 60: *Epitaphios*

In 338 Demosthenes was chosen by the Athenians to deliver the funeral oration over those Athenians who had died fighting Philip II at the Battle at Chaeronea.[55] Despite the dispute about the authenticity of the funeral speech, it cannot be discarded as a non-genuine work of Demosthenes on grounds of style and structure.[56] The *epitaphios* had to deal with a terrible defeat, which involved an enemy who was not Greek and signalled the beginning of the end for the independent Greek city-states of the classical periods. In this context, the *epainos* of the dead is not limited to their achievements on the battlefield, but expands to their virtue in life. Thus, *aretē* is presented both as a co-operative value attached to birth, education, way of life and justice (60.3) and as a competitive value tied to manhood, bravery, self-sacrifice, courage and success (60.17–18). The co-ex-

---

[52] On the theme of a 'glorious death', cf. above the discussion on the *epitaphios* attributed to Lysias.
[53] For the immortality of the dead that compasses the living parents, cf. Lys. 2.78.
[54] Cf. Th. 2.46.1.
[55] D. 18.285; Plu. *Dem.* 21.2.
[56] For a detailed analysis of the authenticity of Demosthenes 60, cf. Worthington 2003, 152–57.

istence of excellence and justice is reflected in the praise of the ancestors as καλοῖς κἀγαθοῖς καὶ δικαιοτάτοις εἶναι (60.7).

Demosthenes departs from the tradition outlined in the previously described speeches by praising the men as children and adults before their service as soldiers (60.15–24); we can thus deduct the *topoi paideia and epitēdeusis*. *Sōphrosynē* (moderation) was the primary focus in the education of young Athenians,[57] and within this context Demosthenes' definition of complete virtue is placed, consisting first of learning and then of bravery (60.17). In order to prevent from any bad feelings, Demosthenes states that all those who die in battle have no share in defeat, but should all equally share in victory (60.19) and accuses the Theban commanders for their performance in the battle-field (60.18, 22). The *epainos* may be directed upon the present rather than the historical past of the Athenians, but Demosthenes connects the eulogy for both the ancestors and the dead by depicting the latter related to their ancestors by birth (60.12). Demosthenes' *epitaphios* contains the sad immediacy of the recent defeat, and a gap opens between the legendary past and the present.[58]

It is striking that Demosthenes states in the beginning of his funeral speech that he will avoid using the myth or heroic element in his praise of the achievements of the dead (60.9):

> ἃ δὲ τῇ μὲν ἀξίᾳ τῶν ἔργων οὐδέν ἐστι τούτων ἐλάττω, τῷ δ' ὑπογυώτερ' εἶναι τοῖς χρόνοις οὔπω μεμυθολόγηται, οὐδ' εἰς τὴν ἡρωϊκὴν ἐπανῆκται τάξιν, ταῦτ' ἤδη λέξω.
>
> *Now I shall speak of other achievements, in no way inferior to those earlier deeds in worth, though they have not yet been shaped into myth or elevated to the heroic rank, as they are more recent.*

However, at a later point of his speech Demosthenes exemplifies the qualities of courage and self-sacrifice through mythical paradigms; in particular, he mentions Acamas who had sailed for Troy for the sake of his mother Aethra (60.29). Aethra is mentioned in *Il.* 3.144, but the rest of the story is not Homeric.[59] The distance from the Homeric tradition may reflect Demostenes' own differentiation from earlier versions of the myth, though his use of courage and self-sacrifice for the depiction of the dead obviously derives from the heroic code.

---

57 Aeschin. 1.6–7; cf. Herrman 2009, 74.
58 Loraux 1986, 181.
59 This Acamas is unknown to Homer, though he mentions two other individuals of the same name. It was later myths that told of the rescue of Aethra after the fall of Troy by her two grandsons, not sons, Acamas and Demophon.

A common place in the funeral oration is the freedom of the whole of Greece as an achievement of the virtue of the dead;[60] Demosthenes also stresses this theme by identifying the virtue of the dead with the very life of Greece (60.23). The reference to individual and common achievements is enhanced by the rhetoric of common freedom as a kind of motivation for the choice of death (60.28):

> δεινὸν οὖν ἡγοῦντο τὴν ἐκείνου προδοῦναι προαίρεσιν, καὶ τεθνάναι μᾶλλον ᾑροῦνθ' ἢ καταλυομένης ταύτης παρὰ τοῖς Ἕλλησιν ζῆν φιλοψυχήσαντες.
>
> They regarded it, therefore, as a dreadful thing to betray the principles of that ancestor and preferred to be dead, rather than through love of life to survive among the Greeks with this equality lost.

Another common rhetorical theme in funeral orations is the choice of death, a glorious, good, noble or just death.[61] Demosthenes, in particular, praises noble death over disgraceful life (60.26: καὶ θάνατον καλὸν εἵλοντο μᾶλλον ἢ βίον αἰσχρόν). Shame is an important quality closely tied with life as opposed to nobility and death.[62] Demosthenes underlines the factors that have contributed to the choice of a noble death: birth, education, habituation to high standards of conduct and the underlying principles of the Athenian form of government (60.27: ἃ μὲν οὖν κοινῇ πᾶσιν ὑπῆρχεν τοῖσδε τοῖς ἀνδράσιν εἰς τὸ καλῶς ἐθέλειν ἀποθνῄσκειν, εἴρηται, γένος, παιδεία, χρηστῶν ἐπιτηδευμάτων συνήθεια, τῆς ὅλης πολιτείας ὑπόθεσις). Aristocratic background has thus been merged with the civic values of Athenian democratic ideology to praise death.

Two common themes closely associated with the good death in Homeric poetry and funeral orations are the superiority of immortal glory over physical death (60.27) and the *hysterophēmia* brought upon the families of the dead, together with relief and happiness (60.35–36).

In conclusion, Demosthenes applies certain ideas and terminology for *aretē*, nobility, shame, immortality and glory from an aristocratic point of view; he also praises the civic values of Athenian democratic ideology, such as freedom and common good, moderation with education as a prerequisite to the actual display of bravery.

---

60 cf. D. 60.28; Lys. 2.33, 44; Hyp. 6.16.
61 cf. Th. 2.42.4, 2.43.6, 2.44.1; Lys. 2,23; Pl. *Mx*.246d.
62 This view is further reflected in the speaker's statement that the dead considered either a life worthy of their heritage or a noble death (60.31).

i. Hypereides 6: *Epitaphios* fr. 1b, 1–43

Hypereides' *epitaphios*, in the form in which it has been transmitted to us,[63] was delivered at a burial ceremony in 322 BC, at the end of the first season of the so-called Lamian War. This war was largely successful for the Greeks, though the general Leosthenes, a friend of Hypereides, was killed. The speech was presented after the initial victory in Boeotia, the siege at Lamia and the defeat of Leonnatus (6.12–14). Later that year the Athenian fleet suffered two major losses and the army was defeated soon afterwards. The battle was a complete failure for the Greeks. More than one thousand Athenians died and two thousand were taken hostage; the rest of the Greeks also suffered losses. As a result, the Athenians had to submit to Macedonian terms, whereas Hypereides and Demosthenes, the leading opponents of Macedonian involvement in Greek affairs, were condemned to death by the Athenian *dēmos*.[64] Hypereides' funeral oration highlights the Athenian policy of resistance to Macedon.[65]

Hypereides gives more details about the occasion of death than the earlier speakers. He underlines that Leosthenes deserves more praise than his predecessors, whereas earlier *epitaphioi* praise the deeds of the dead as equivalent to those of their ancestors.[66] Hypereides brings an innovation to the traditional themes and structure of the *epitaphioi logoi* by inserting a picture of the present.[67] He emphasizes the virtues of the Athenians of the present, wishing probably to encourage and mobilize them to fight, though the war was at the end unsuccessful.

Despite the innovation in content and structure of his funeral oration, Hypereides is employing aristocratic terms to describe the deeds of the fallen soldiers, such as *megaloprepeia* (1: οὔτε ἄνδρας ἀμείνους τῶν τετελευτηκότων οὔτε πράξεις μεγαλοπρεπεστέρας) – a virtue that motivated Athenian aristocrats to participate in liturgies.[68] *Aretē* is generally applied in the speech to describe

---

[63] Hypereides' delivery of the funeral oration is attested by Diodorus of Sicily (18.13.5), Ps.Plutarch (*Decem Oratorum Vitae* 849f) and Ps.Longinus (*De Subl.*34.2); cf. Herrman 2004, 77.
[64] For details about the arrest and death of Demosthenes and Hypereides, cf. Plu. *Phoc.* 28.1; Plu. *Dem.* 28.2–4.
[65] Herrman 2009, 3.
[66] A description of the war in which the men commemorated in the *epitaphios* died is uncommon in funeral speeches, let alone the focus so exclusively on one person. For the unusual element of narrative, cf. Ziolkowski 1981, 88; Herrman 2009, 77.
[67] Loraux 1986, 182.
[68] Herrman 2009, 60.

purely military excellence and is used in the plural to denote specific virtuous accomplishments on the battlefield (3):

> ἄξιον δέ ἐστιν ἐπαινεῖν τὴν μὲν πόλιν ἡμῶν τῆς προαιρέσεως ἕνεκεν, τὸ προελέσθαι ὅμοια καὶ ἔτι σεμνότερα καὶ καλλίω τῶν πρότερον αὐτῇ πεπραγμένων, τοὺς δὲ τετελευτηκότας τῆς ἀνδρείας τῆς ἐν τῷ πολέμῳ, τὸ μὴ καταισχῦναι τὰς τῶν προγόνων ἀρετάς.
>
> *Our city is worthy of praise for the choice it made, a policy that suited and even surpassed the proud and noble deeds it accomplished in the past; the dead men deserve praise for their courage in battle, courage that did not disgrace the valour of their ancestors.*

Similarly to the other funeral orations,[69] Hypereides pairs intellectual ability and martial courage. As Loraux (1986, 109–10) has argued, Hypereides here follows a time-honoured definition of *aretē*, and this kind of narrow conception may be a reaction against current trends in civic funeral orations, in which *aretē* is equated with other qualities, more importantly *sōphrosynē* ('moderation'). Hypereides, however, later states that the soldiers as children have learned qualities such as *sōphrosynē* and *dikaiosynē* ('justice'), and when they went to war they demonstrated their military skill (28: τότε μὲν γὰρ παῖδες ὄντες ἄφρονες ἦσαν, νῦν δ' ἄνδρες ἀγαθοὶ γεγόνασιν).[70] Education (*paideia*) was essential to the upbringing of the soldiers, in order to demonstrate their military excellence and bravery in war.[71] A common honourific phrase describing soldiers' death in funeral orations and other patriotic literature is employed here (28) as well as in §8 (ἵνα ἄνδρες ἀγαθοὶ γένωνται). Hypereides contrasts the heroic death of the soldiers with their childhood and presents their death on the battlefield as the decisive moment of their adulthood.[72]

For the praise of victory Hypereides uses the verb *epainein*, whereas for the praise of the virtue of Leosthenes and his soldiers he uses the verb *egkōmiazein*. The repeated usage of *egkōmion* in Hypereides' funeral oration may reflect the development of the prose genre of *egkōmia* praising contemporary individuals and, in this case, Leosthenes.[73]

The slogan 'freedom for the Greeks' –a commonplace in the funeral oration –depicts the Greek alliance as a kind of reincarnation of the Greek unification

---

[69] Th. 2.40.3; D. 60.17.
[70] For the use of *aretē* to denote military excellence and echo the description of the Marathon battle, cf. Hyp. 6.19, 23.
[71] For the interest in the education of the soldiers as reflecting contemporary institutional reforms in mid-fourth century Athens, such as the *ephēbeia*, cf. Herrman 2009, 74.
[72] Ibid. 75.
[73] According to Arist. *Rh.* 1367b 18–32, the distinction between the two terms corresponds to the contrast between virtue (*epainos*) and accomplishment (*egkōmion*); cf. Herrman 2009, 80–81.

against the Persians in 480/479 BC (16: οἳ τὰς ἑαυτῶν ψυχὰς ἔδωκαν ὑπὲρ τῆς τῶν Ἑλλήνων ἐλευθερίας). The choice of death is presented as associated with the concept of freedom (24: οἵτινες θνητοῦ σώματος ἀθάνατον δόξαν ἐκτήσαντο, καὶ διὰ τὴν ἰδίαν ἀρετὴν τὴν κοινὴν ἐλευθερίαν τοῖς Ἕλλησιν ἐβεβαίωσαν). This passage distinguishes the soldiers from the Athenian citizens, whereas in §5 (τοῖς δὲ ἰδίοις κινδύνοις καὶ δαπάναις κοινὴν ἄδειαν τοῖς Ἕλλησιν παρασκευάζουσα) and in §19 (καὶ τὴν μὲν ἐλευθερίαν εἰς τὸ κοινὸν πᾶσιν κατέθεσαν) a distinction is made between Athens as a collective whole and the rest of Greece. Immortality (27) and glory (42) are themes closely tied with the choice of death.

A new element in Hypereides' approach of *aretē* is the *andragathia* (29: μνημονευτοὺς διὰ ἀνδραγαθίαν γεγονέναι, 40: ὑπερβαλλούσης δὲ ἀρετῆς καὶ ἀνδραγαθίας τῆς ἐν τοῖς κινδύνοις). In his discussion of the development of the concept of *andragathia* in the late fifth century, Whitehead (1993, 57–62) concludes that *andragathia* praised men for 'what they had done rather than who they were' and was often used to describe military valour or more specifically death on the battlefield.[74] Hypereides links the two terms, *aretē* and *andragathia*, to denote both the qualities acquired through education as well as the deeds or the moment of death. The combination of the two concepts may reflect Hypereides' use of traditional and innovative elements in his funeral oration, as well as the development of the Athenian democratic and civic ideology in the fourth century.

Concluding remarks

Funeral orations display commonplaces in the praise of the dead refiguring the Homeric heroic code either in the use of terminology or in content. Homeric *aretē* as a competitive value denoting success on the battlefield and purely military excellence is prominent in the praise of funeral orations. In this context, the choice of a noble, glorious and immortal death of the hero is widely employed in funeral oration to depict the bravery and glory of the Athenian warriors and citizens;[75] in effect, heroic fame and immortality are frequently used for the praise of the dead, both ancestors and current soldiers.[76]

Orators may use mythical paradigms in their *epainos* of the dead, but they appear to draw a line in rejecting the poetic *epainos*; they focus on the history

---

[74] For the use of *andragathia* in decrees awarding Athenian citizenship to foreigners, cf. Kapparis 1999, 364–65.
[75] Th. 2.43.6; Lys. 2.33, 41, 62; Pl. *Mx.* 236d; Hyp. 6.40.
[76] Th. 2.41.4, 42.4; Lys. 2.2,3,5,22; Pl. *Mx.* 241c, 243d, 247d; D. 60.2, 32.

of Athens, and their commendation is based upon the Athenian and civic identity of the dead. For Pericles, as well as the other orators, Athens was a model of political and military *aretē*. Even when the funeral speech serves a Panhellenic propaganda, this is apparently linked with Athenian nationalism (e. g. Lys. 2.47); the *epitaphioi* lay claim on the honour of the warriors for the salvation and freedom of Greece.[77]

New civic and political qualities develop in the praise of funeral oration throughout the fifth and fourth centuries, in relation with the changes of the Athenian constitution. *Sōphrosynē* and education are central to the acquisition of virtue, as well as the subsequent display of bravery and courage in life and war in adulthood. *Dikaiosynē* is also fundamental to the description of *aretē* and freedom of the city and the whole of Greece. The pair of individual and common achievements is stressed in funeral orations to show the superiority of the city of Athens but also its contribution to the common good of the rest of Greece.

Our close examination of the surviving funeral orations dating from the second half of the fifth century until the end of the fourth century reflects, on the one hand, a common praise of both moral and civic values and, on the other hand, a development in structure and content of the rhetoric of praise influencing respectively the didactic purpose of the funeral oration. Thucydides' funeral oration focuses on the competitive civic *aretē* that brings success and superiority as indicative of the Athenian democratic ideology. Gorgias identifies moral and civic values in the context of excellence in all kinds of achievements. Lysias combines the heroic and patriotic element in the praise of citizens both in war and life; he also stresses the importance of the ancestors' virtue for justice and democracy. Plato's funeral oration emphasizes the significance of *dikaiosynē* ('justice') and *sōphrosynē* ('moderation') in the education of the Athenian citizens. The role of education to the acquisition of *aretē* is further explored and developed in the last two funeral orations, which were the only two speeches actually delivered in the last half of the fourth century BC. It is to be noted that both orations by Demosthenes and Hypereides were performed on occasions of Athenian defeat. Hence, one can notice a shift in the emphasis from the praise of the past to the praise of the present. Demosthenes' praise focuses on the virtues in present life referring back to the childhood of the Athenian citizens. Hypereides played a significant role to the change of *epainos* of the virtues of the whole body of the soldiers to an *egkōmion* of an individual. Although he draws on aristocratic terminology and views, he gives more details on the moment of

---

[77] Ibid. 114.

death creating thus a picture of the present. *Aretē* is complemented and closely tied with *andragathia*.

On balance, civic *aretē* is mainly honoured in public commemoration in fifth and fourth-century funeral orations, which assumed their educative function by linking the present of Athens to its past and future. The Homeric hero is *agathos*, but the dead praised in the funeral oration is described as *agathos gignesthai*. The term *agathos gignesthai* implies that the citizen's *aretē* is not an immanent quality; in a city a man must become *anēr agathos*, he is not *agathos* by essence. In contrast to the epic praise of individuality the funeral oration celebrates the anonymous group. No one receives the honour of a special mention with the exception of the general Leosthenes, praised by Hypereides, who is nevertheless taken to represent the whole group.

Ioannis N. Perysinakis
The Ancient Quarrel between Philosophy and Poetry: Plato's *Hippias Minor*

a. The Dialogue

In the *Hippias Minor* Hippias has just delivered a public lecture on Homer (*epideixis*), and Socrates is invited by Eudicus to comment on it. Hippias' position is that Achilles is ἀληθής τε καὶ ἁπλοῦς ('true and simple'), while Odysseus is πολύτροπός τε καὶ ψευδής ('resourceful and false'). The discussion originates in *Iliad* 9.308–13, where Achilles addresses Odysseus after the latter's speech in the Embassy: 'Without consideration for you I must make my answer [...] For as I detest the gates of Hades, I detest that man who hides one thing in his mind and says another'.[1] The conclusion in the first section (363a 1–369b 7) is that the true man and the false man are the same, and therefore Achilles and Odysseus are the same. Before that it had been accepted that 'the false man is the man with the power, ability and the wisdom to be false in the matters in which he is false' ('the false is he who has the wisdom and the power to speak falsely'), 'the true man is the man with the power, ability and wisdom to speak truthfully' and 'the expert is ἄριστος in the matters he is most capable and wisest of men'.

In the second section (up to 373c), Hippias denies the conclusion they have reached, and Socrates quotes several Homeric passages: *Il.* 9.312–13, 9.357–63, Achilles' first answer to Odysseus ('tomorrow you will see early in the morning my ships sailing over the fishy Hellespont, and on the third day I shall reach fertile Phthia') and 1.169–71 ('Now I am returning to Phthia'), as well as 9.650–55, Achilles' third answer to Ajax ('I shall not think again of the bloody fighting until such time as the son of wise Priam... comes... to the ships of the Myrmidons, and their shelters'). All these passages, he claims, support the conclusion they came to and show that Achilles is resourceful and false. Hippias argues that Achilles acts involuntarily, induced by the kindness of his heart (371e 5 ff.), but this seems to lead to the conclusion that those who voluntarily deceive (371e 7–8) are better than those who do so involuntarily. Hippias denies this, since he finds it incredible to think that people voluntarily doing wrong (371e 7–8) could be better than those involuntarily doing so.

---

[1] The translation of the Iliadic passages is based on Lattimore 1951 with adjustments.

In the third section (up to the end) Socrates and Hippias consider whether people voluntarily or involuntarily doing wrong or failing (ἁμαρτάνειν) are better in each in a long series of human activities and, finally, in the area of justice—justice being both power and science, and therefore the soul which has the greater power is also the more just, and the wiser soul will be the juster soul (375d 7 ff.). Their conclusion always seems to be that the one voluntarily 'doing bad' in an area is better, and, in fact, that the person who voluntarily fails and voluntarily does shameful and unjust things would have to be the good person, if such a good person even exists (376b 5–6). Both Socrates and Hippias deny the conclusion, but neither is able to explain how they have gone wrong, and so the dialogue ends without their being able to come to a satisfactory conclusion.

b. Homer, *Iliad* 9

According to Socrates, Achilles 'dares to contradict himself in front of Odysseus, who does not notice it; he does not appear to have said anything to him which would indicate that he noticed his falsehood' (371a, trans. Jowett 1953[4] with adjustments). It has been said that we are never closer to Plato as a writer than when we are reading Plato reading.[2]

Analyzing Achilles' evolution as a hero in the ninth book of the *Iliad*, C.H. Whitman[3] finds that the embassy does not fail entirely to move Achilles, and that his rejection of Agamemnon's offer is not based upon mere sulky passion, but upon the half-realized inward conception of honour. When Odysseus has finished his speech, Achilles in his final words to him announces that 'tomorrow [...] you will see, if you wish and if it concerns you, my ships at early dawn sailing over Hellespont [...] on the third day thereafter we might reach generous Phthia' (357–63). After the long emotional speech of Phoenix, Achilles is less sure and in his final words to Phoenix he says 'we shall decide tomorrow, as dawn shows, whether to go back home again or stay here' (618–19). Finally, after the short and straight targeted speech of Ajax, Achilles says nothing about going home, but he announces that 'I shall not think again of bloody war until such time as [...] Hector comes to the ships of the Myrmidons [...] But around my own shelter, I think, and beside my black ship Hector will be held, though being eager for battle' (650–55). Achilles' reply to fight only when the fire reached his own ships constitutes the active terms in which he has framed the absolute for himself: this

---

2 O'Connor 2007, 56.
3 Whitman 1958, 190–91; Perysinakis 2004.

is the heroic paradigm which he embraced from the story of Meleager. These three points in Achilles' replies to the envoys and to Phoenix have already since antiquity been recognized as three stages of Achilles' decision making. But scholars have failed to see a gradual withdrawal in Achilles' refusal to participate in the war and its function.

When the envoys go back, at the end of the ninth book, Odysseus reports only Achilles' reply to him and that he threatened to go home, and hence the whole venture seems to have failed. Odysseus, the great diplomat, reports Achilles' position quite erroneously, for dramatic reasons and for the sake of the plot. This inconsistency has been observed as early as the scholia. The strategy of the Embassy is consumed; the Achaeans are found in a worse position than before and Achilles is going to meet his fate.

c. *Hippias Minor*

(i) Literature on the *Hippias Minor*

Many scholars have written papers on the *Hippias Minor* (Weiss 1981; Mulhern 1968; Hoerber 1962; Phillips 1987; Zembaty 1989; Lévystone 2005; Balaban 2011; Lampert 2002; Blundell 1992; Rudolph 2010), and others have occasionally referred to the dialogue (Taylor 1926; Guthrie 1962–1981, IV 191–99; Vlastos 1991; Friedländer 1964; Blondell 2002; Hobbs 2000; Cormack 2006; see recently Destrée/ Herrmann eds. 2011 and on Plato's response to poetry from the viewpoint of classical reception theory, see Emlyn-Jones 2008).

In more specific terms, Vlastos believes that Plato presents in the *Hippias Minor* the historical Socrates in an authentic situation of confession of uncertainty and vacillation unparalleled in the elenctic dialogues, accepting in this way indirectly the view alluded to in the second part of his additional note 'The *Hippias Minor*-Sophistry or Perplexity'.[4]

Behind the sudden uncertainty of Socrates, 'if there be such a man' (376b) and his refusal to be reconciled with the necessary conclusion, what follows from our argument, and the final *aporia* of the dialogue, stands the entire solution, the idea of good, in which the whole Platonic belief in the necessity of the knowledge of bad and good has been invested.[5]

---

4 Vlastos 1991, 275–80, esp. 277–78.
5 Skouteropoulos 1985, 24.

In Mulhern's terms, the argument fails because of a confusion of *dynamis*-terms, i.e. terms which denote ability, and *tropos*-terms, i.e. terms which denote typical behaviour. Thus, the statement that 'those who do wrong voluntarily are better' may mean either of two things: those who have it in their power to do wrong are better; or those who normally wish or desire to do wrong are better. Of course, in the first case 'better' means 'good at something', while in the second 'better' means 'morally good'.[6] Mulhern's starting point was Sprague's monograph,[7] which drew attention to the fact that large parts of the argument of Plato's *Hippias Minor* turn on the equivocal use of 'wiliness' (for both 'shiftiness', and 'intellectual ability'), 'power' (for both 'power for good' and 'power for evil'), 'good' (for both 'good at something' and 'morally good') and 'voluntary' (for both 'what is in our power' and 'what we normally wish or desire').

Roslyn Weiss's interpretation[8] constitutes an attempt to maintain the integrity of the dialogue by viewing all its parts as related to a single topic: who is the truly superior man. She concludes that the ἀγαθός of the *Hippias Minor* is thus not the standard ἀγαθός, who is judged on the basis of his actions. Since the agent in this dialogue is judged solely on the basis of his skill, things may be said with impunity about this man that could not be said so freely about the ordinary ἀγαθός. The arguments of both stage I and III of the dialogue go no further than to assert that the better man in all τέχναι and ἐπιστῆμαι is the one who is δυνατός and σοφός. We need only bear in mind that the ἀγαθός here is the man *skilled* at justice—not 'the just man'.

Hoerber argues that it is clear from several aspects that Plato is challenging his readers to work out a solution to the perplexing propositions of the *Hippias Minor*, especially since Socrates himself admits perplexity both in the course of the discussion and at the conclusion of the dialogue (372d – e, 376b – c). Another warning Plato presents to the reader concerning the argumentation, which is not to be taken as final, is the statement of Socrates on the concluding page εἴπερ τίς ἐστιν οὗτος (376b); for Plato employs such a phrase in other dialogues (cf. *Euthyphro* 8e, *Gorgias* 480e) to show his personal disagreement. The doublets and professed confusion within the dialogue seem to be dramatic clues pointing the reader to two famous propositions of Socrates, that virtue is knowledge, and that no one does wrong voluntarily. The dramatic technique of the dialogue, finally, is manifest from the play on the word πολύτροπος. The term first becomes prominent in the discussion of the Homeric characters Odysseus and Achilles;

---

6 Mulhern 1968, 288.
7 Sprague 1962, 67 – 68, 74 – 76.
8 Weiss 1981, 288, 304.

then in the sense of clever or skillful, the adjective becomes the chief characteristic of the polymath Hippias; and at the conclusion of the dialogue, it is Socrates who is πολύτροπος.⁹

Similarly, Cormack suggests that instead of interpreting the *Hippias Minor* as Plato's criticism of the craft analogy and the earlier Socratic method of doing philosophy, one should treat the ending of the dialogue as a puzzle that Plato has left to be worked out by the reader.[10]

The word *polytropia* is ambiguous; according to Antisthenes, it means either 'diversity of styles and discourses' or 'diversity of dispositions, characters or souls' (fr. 51 Caizzi). Lévystone argued that the same distinction is implicitly at work in Plato's *Hippias Minor*, where Socrates defends Odysseus' *polytropia* against the pseudo-'simplicity' of Hippias' favourite hero, Achilles. However, whereas Antisthenes tries to clarify these different meanings, Plato's Socrates exploits the ambiguity to confuse his interlocutor. Such a distinction sheds a new light on the *Hippias Minor*; Odysseus is *polytropos* in the first positive sense, while the simplicity of Achilles should be understood as a bad kind of *polytropia*. It provides an explanation for the first paradoxical thesis of the dialogue: that he who voluntary deceives is better than he who errs, for falsehood is, in one case, only in words, while in the other, it is falsehood in the soul itself. It is thus proposed that Odysseus' skill in adapting his *logos* to his hearers was probably a model for Socrates himself. The analogy between the hero and Socrates is especially clear in Plato's dialogues, which show the philosopher in an *Odyssey* for knowledge.[11]

Blondell uses the *Hippias Minor* to show how Plato puts characterization to work in various ways. She chose, as she says, this dialogue as exemplary not only because of its elenctic character and its vividly characterized participants, but also because of its concern on the discursive level with the educational value of traditional literary figures.[12]

Hobbs argues that the *Apology*, *Hippias Major* and *Hippias Minor* show unequivocally that the old Homeric heroes like Achilles and Odysseus are still powerful influences in classical Athens, and that they also show that reflection on the heroes and their code of conduct raises ethical and psychological issues of the greatest importance.[13]

---

9 Hoerber 1962, 128–31, *passim*.
10 Cormack 2006, 48.
11 Lévystone 2005.
12 Blondell 2002, 113–64, especially the sections 'Hippias and Homer' (128–37) and 'Rewriting Homer' (154–63).
13 Hobbs 2000, 198.

After reviewing Weiss's position, Jane Zembatty argues that Socrates' perplexity in the dialogue should not be seen merely as an ironic ploy. Rather, it should be seen as reflecting Plato's awareness of the problems endemic to the Socratic attempt to define virtue simply in terms of some characteristic of the agent *psychē*.[14]

Arguing that liars are better than the unenlightened, Socrates concludes that there are no liars. Instead, there are only those who know and those who do not. The unenlightened cannot lie, and alien volitions, desires or emotions are unlikely to mislead and deceive those who know, i.e. the wise.[15]

Why does Socrates argue for the superiority of Odysseus? Why does he insist on a repellant conclusion? And why does he say he vacillates? The answer to these questions points to an essential element of Socrates' political philosophy.[16]

Blundell's reading of the *Hippias Minor* argues first that Socratic argument is intrinsically *ad hominem* rather than a preliminary sketch for a universal moral theory; second, that the dialogues must be situated in their local context (in this case, the *Hippias Minor* needs to be seen as Plato's response to the educational programmes of Homerists and Sophists); and third, that it is necessary both to consider the possibility that weak Socratic argument is an intrinsic part of the design of the dialogue rather than Plato's oversight and to recognize that this unavoidable question can never be resolved with absolute certainty.[17]

For Rudolph, finding Hippias incompetent as a Homeric interpreter, Socrates takes up the task of interpreting the poetic basis for Hippias' moral position. By so doing, he makes a larger point that the liar and the truth-teller are the same man or that unintentional wrongdoers are worse than deliberate wrongdoers. By re-appropriating the language of rhapsody, Socrates subverts the Homeric content in a way that it is reminiscent of Plato's *Ion*. She concludes that by mastering the rhapsodic skill, Plato shows that the supposedly authoritative interpretations of Homer lead to moral dilemmas from which even Socratic dialectic cannot free us.[18]

(ii) My suggestion

According to Aristotle's *Metaphysics* (995a 7–8), there are people who will take seriously the arguments of a speaker (including those of a philosopher) only if a poet can be cited as a witness in support of them. Hippias uses Homer to support

---

14 Zembatty 1989, 51.
15 Balaban 2011.
16 Lampert 2002.
17 Blundell 1992.
18 Rudolph 2010.

his arguments. Socrates does the same for his purposes. The *Hippias Minor* is concerned on the discursive level with the educational value of traditional literary figures. Plato has to contend not only against the *mythos* of poetry but also against the power of rhetoric.

The following interpretation constitutes an attempt to discover unnoticed threads of thought in the *Hippias Minor*, especially the transformation of Homeric moral values and political behaviour that Plato is making in his dialogues, the formation of some of Socrates' (or Plato's) main principles and propositions, and the relationship of thought with other dialogues.

In composing the *Hippias Minor* Plato's aim seems to be twofold: first, to determine what is *agathos* and the meaning of *aretē* and second, to blame poetry for using plots and *mimēsis* by means of which it cannot educate the children on *aretē*. Plato aimed at subjecting *mythos* to *logos*. That the conclusion 'must follow from our argument' (*ek tou logou*) is part of the same strategy; 'reason proves or persuades' (*logos hairei*) is a standard expression in Plato (*R.* 604c, 607b, *Lg.* 663d). Achilles, 'the best of the Achaeans', cannot behave in the way he does in the *Iliad*, as it is described, apart from the *Hippias Minor*, in the *Republic* (336e, 390e, 391c, 386c, 388a, 516d; but cf. *Apol.* 28c) and other dialogues (*Lg.* 628c–d, 728a). The traditional *agathos* has been led to deadlock. Justice is the final point in the *Hippias Minor* and constitutes the main subject of the *Republic*; the main themes of the dialogue are also addressed in the *Apology, Protagoras, Menon* and the first book of the *Republic*. Hippias is treated (and mistreated) in a dramatic way (as often with other Platonic dialogues); he is one of the 'dramatis personae'. Socrates' intrusion into the sophists' arena could be described as a critique of the Athenian performance culture and was itself a drama, in which Socrates' 'performance philosophy' gave conviction to Plato's critique of the institutions of his *polis* and force to his 'alternative dramatic stage'. The Platonic dialogues constitute 'metatheatrical prose dramas'. What we hear are philosophical voices in action, a poetic and philosophic call to the philosophic life. In Socrates' interlocutions with the sophists Plato is dramatizing the reception and the contest of cultural values as a physical reality.[19] The absence of Plato himself, either as author or as character in his dialogues, strengthens more than anything else the generic link between the dialogues and Athenian drama—and validates ironically Socrates' complaints (or Plato's himself) about the poets. Finally, in the *Hippias Minor* we have a chapter in the history

---

19 Emlyn-Jones 2008, 38, 41, 49. Cf. also Goldhill/von Reden 1999; Ferrari 1989, 145, 148. The term 'metatheatrical prose dramas' is adopted by Charalabopoulos 2012, esp. 22–29. For other explanations why Plato wrote dialogues cf. Griswold 1995, Kahn 1981 and 1998, ch. 2.

of the ancient quarrel between philosophy and poetry (on which I am currently working)—without offering a definition of the quarrel or further chapters.[20]

(ii a) *Republic*: *mythos* ('plot') and *mimēsis*

The verb used for Homer in the *Hippias Minor* and the *Republic* is *poiei, pepoiēkenai, pepoiēken, pepoiētai*, and it is the verb which denotes poetry from the fifth century BC onwards. The poet's own voice can be heard in and through all the elements of his poem; it is no more than a technical distinction whether we take him to be 'making' his characters act/speak in certain ways or 'speaking' himself.[21] But the verb *poiein* serves to convey implicit responsibility in such passages as the following from the *Republic* and the *Hippias Minor*; and this is what Plato criticizes.

Homer and the poets are banished from the city both on the basis of their *mythos* (plots and myths) and the *mimēsis* which they employ. Plato believed that one becomes the kind of person one is portraying, and this led to the conclusion that drama has a bad moral and psychological effect on performers who, in their turn, pass the influence on to their audience (cf. *Ion* 535d). The poet and later the recipient assimilates himself to the figures of poetry. The battle of the gods that Homer made (*pepoiēken*) must not be admitted into the city. 'A child cannot distinguish what is and what is not allegory, and the ideas he takes in at that age are likely to become indelibly fixed; for this reason, it is very important to see that the first stories he hears should be composed to produce the best possible effect on his character' (ὅτι κάλλιστα μεμυθολογημένα πρὸς ἀρετήν, *R.* 378d–e, trans. Cornford 1941 with adjustments). Socrates and Adeimantus will not let the guardians believe that Achilles, who was the son of a goddess and of the wise Peleus, and the pupil of the sage Chiron, was so disordered that his heart was a prey to two contrary maladies, mean covetousness and arrogant contempt of gods and men (*R.* 391c; cf. also *R.* 388a, 516d, *Hippias Minor* 371d). Needless to say that there is neither covetousness nor arrogant contempt on the part of Achilles; it is a matter of honour and the plot of the *Iliad*, which Plato criticizes. The truth-content of myths and stories must be judged principally in terms of their implicit *logos*. Achilles' character is also rejected because it is

---

[20] Cf. Most 2011, 3–20. This is a wide theme, and I am mentioning only the monographs under the same or similar title: Barfield 2011; Edmundson 1995; Gould 1990; Kannicht 1988; Levin 2001; Rosen 1988; Naddaff 2002; Ramphos 1978. To these I must add the seminal study by Nightingale 1995, which reassesses Plato's quarrel with poetry and rhetoric as well as the debt he owes to these 'unphilosophical' adversaries.
[21] Cf. Halliwell 2000, 103.

associated with grief and lamentation both in his first appearance in book two (383b) and in the final book of the *Republic* (605d – e). His lamentation poses a great threat to the well-being of the citizens of Plato's ideal state. Homer, tragedy, lamentation and 'womanish' behaviour are all to be eliminated from the lives of the guardians, as from the city as a whole. Some themes of Plato's critique of poetry are already prefigured in the first and second book of the *Republic*, as the first definition of justice by Simonides (331d – e) and Cephalus' words about old age and the Underworld, which are echoed in the view that the gods can be propitiated (364c – d, 365e).[22]

Besides, falsehood and deceptiveness are two main points of the *Hippias Minor*; they must be connected to Plato's arguments on Greek poetry in the *Republic*: 'To be deceived about the truth of things and so to be blindly ignorant and harbour untruth in the soul is what all men would least of all accept. Falsehood in that case is abhorred above everything'. Therefore, 'this ignorance in the soul of the man deceived is what really deserves to be called the true falsehood' (382b, trans. Cornford 1941 with adjustments). But, since we do not know the truth about events in the past, by making something as close as possible to the truth, we make it useful (382d). Deceptiveness of poetry is the subject of the tenth book of the *Republic*.[23]

Where Homer is delivering a speech in character, he tries to make his manner resemble that of the person he has introduced as speaker. In the Embassy scene Homer speaks in the character of the participating persons and tries to make us feel that the words come, not from him, but from the speakers. Homer does not speak in his own person, but he makes Odysseus, Phoenix, Ajax and Achilles speak each in his own character (*R*. 393). Plato is blaming Homer for the very point for which Aristotle praises him (*Poet*. 1460a 5 – 11): after a short proem he represents his characters as speaking and acting. Homer is praised, because his poems have so little narrative and so much speech or because only in the proems he speaks in his own voice.[24] Plato criticizes Homer for speaking in the character of Chryses and tries to make us feel that the words come, not from Homer, but from an aged priest.

---

[22] Perysinakis 2006, 82 – 84, 87; Michelakis 2002, 9, n. 37 and 39, 98, 182, n. 89; Murray 2011, 182 – 83; Hobbs 2000, 199 – 219; Janaway 1995, 80 – 105 and 2006, 389 – 91; Halliwell 1997, 314 – 16, 322.
[23] Cf. Gill 1993 and Belfiore 1985; Halliwell 1997, 318 – 9. Belfiore first suggested that in *R*. 382d Plato echoes Hes. *Th*. 27 and *Od*. 19.203. Plato concludes that the poet creates only 'lies unlike the truth', not 'lies like the truth'; Partee 1981, 69 – 70.
[24] On this point, cf. the discussion in De Jong 2005, 616 – 21. For poetic imitation in *R*. 3, cf. Dyson 1988.

The metaphysical argument of the tenth book on poetry and *mimēsis* (in particular 598d–599e) is an expansion of the point adumbrated in the third (393a). The tragic poets and their master, Homer, we are told, understand not only all technical matters but also all about goodness and badness and about the gods; 'for a good poet must understand the issues he writes about, if his writing is to be successful, otherwise he could not write about them' (598e). The tragic poet, as well as the other poets, since he is a representer, comes third from the king and the truth (597e). *Aretē* retains much of its Homeric sense but with a Platonic twist. Homer sings the claims of the *agathos* 'to be the bravest' and 'the lays of men'. Plato accepts the traditional view that tragic poetry is concerned with *aretē* in the sense of the important and memorable actions recorded by the singers of the glorious deeds of men. However, he insists that, because *aretē* depends on use, true *aretē* requires craft knowledge of what is useful (601d).[25] The poet, or the singer, has no knowledge of a craft; he is possessed by divine portion (luck) and power (*Ion* 534c). *Aretē* in Plato refers to the order in the soul, in which each of the parts of the soul does its own job as a ruler or subject (443b, 444d–e); *agathos politēs* is one who knows both how to govern and to be governed in accordance with *dikē* (*Lg.* 643e).

The moral point is clear: if the chief purpose of representation is to create an impression, then the representer does not have to know about the moral value of his work (*R.* 599d). He lacks knowledge, and knowledge is always in some sense knowledge of goodness. 'Imitative poetry copies appearances of human affairs and of human excellence in particular. But these appearances differ drastically from reality: being varied and contradictory instead of stable and uniform, the apparently excellent character is in fact a model of vice'.[26] Poetry corrupts, because it is a form of imitation copying appearances instead of reality. The poet imitates *eidola* of excellence instead of genuine excellence; this is to say that the poet imitates apparently excellent characters and actions, that is, whichever characters and actions appear excellent to the ignorant many. The poet creates the illusion of forms based on the deceptions of the material world and the flattery of the lower part of the soul. Thus, mimetic art encourages the soul to rest content with the shadow world of the becoming. Plato's argument against poetry involves, firstly the opposition of reason to the irrational parts of the soul; secondly, it involves the opposition between two aspects of reasoning, which is involved in explaining why one can be tempted to act

---

[25] Cf. Belfiore 2006, 112–13; Woodruff 1982, 145–47; Janaway 2006, 392–94.
[26] Moss 2007, 443 and *passim*. Cf. Urmson 1982, 131, 135; Janaway 1995, 133–57, esp. 136–40; Marusic 2011, esp. 239–40.

even on what one knows not to be correct. Besides, Plato's repudiation of the tragic is a vital dimension of his own philosophy.[27]

Therefore, Plato banishes Achilles and Homer, because in his character Achilles appears to lie; Homer makes his characters speak in accordance with the plot and for the dramatic purposes of the *Iliad*. We must keep in mind that according to Aristotle the poet must be a maker of plots (*Poet.* 1451b 28–9; cf. Pl. *Phd.* 61b, where *mythos* has a different meaning). Achilles, 'who was the son of a goddess and of the wise Peleus, and the pupil of the sage Chiron', and in the main 'the best (ἄριστος) of the Achaeans', cannot behave in this way, and Homer must not make him false. The acceptable poet is described as 'the unmixed imitator of the good man' and as 'one who will imitate for us the speech of the good man' (397d, 398b); Achilles does not meet the presuppositions. Plot, *mimēsis*, virtue (*aretē*) and *agathos*, falsehood and deceptiveness, all of them are questioned in the *Republic* and Plato's other dialogues and all of them are found in the *Hippias Minor*. Of course, Achilles' replies serve the plot of the epic; Homer makes Achilles speak in his own dramatic character; but Plato criticizes this. And since he is *aristos*, it is time (Plato seems to say) to find out what *aristos* means; and to transform the traditional *aretē* in terms of morals. As Diotima says in the *Symposium*, 'if someone got to see the beautiful itself, only then will it become possible for him to give birth not to images of virtue but to true virtue' (211e–212a). 'If we recall that in the *Republic* Plato applies the phrase "images of virtue" to poets, a particular contrast suggests itself. While the poet makes only images and understands only images, the philosopher, who strives for and encounters the eternal unchanging beauty, can bring genuine goods into the world, because he understands what virtue is'.[28]

(ii b) *Agathos-aretē*

Throughout the dialogue Achilles is called ἀμείνων or ἄριστος; at the beginning of their conversation Socrates asks Hippias 'in what particular' he thinks Achilles is ἀμείνων (364d). The first thing to be noticed, therefore, is that Plato continues the particularization of *aretē*, begun already in Homer with expressions such as 'good in battle-cry'; the standard meaning of *aretē* is excellence of every kind. A second observation is the agreement between Socrates and Hippias: the wisest

---

[27] Nehamas 1982, 68; cf. Murdoch 1977, 1–32; Halliwell 1996; Lear 2011; Annas (1981, 94–101, 336–44 and Annas 1982) criticizes Plato for his account of poetry and argues for the differences between the third and the tenth book of the *Republic*.
[28] Janaway 2006, 399; Janaway 1995, 76–79.

and the ablest of men is also the best (ἄριστος) in these matters (366d), which means that wisdom, science, is identified with *aretē*; i.e. *aretē* is particularized in wisdom, and *dynamis* ('ability') is also identified with *aretē*. *Dynamis*, generally speaking, is the presupposition of excellence/*aretē*. In the *Republic* Plato speaks of the power and capacity of the crafts or of the limbs of the body, i.e. the specific virtue (*oikeia aretē*, 346a, 353b–c, 433d).

In the first part of the dialogue it has been accepted that 'the false are they who have the wisdom and the power to speak falsely' (366b), in the second part that 'the voluntary liars are better than the involuntary' (371e), in the third part, 'better are those who err voluntarily' (373c), and the conclusion is that the one voluntarily 'doing bad' in an area is better, and in fact that the person who voluntarily fails and voluntarily does shameful and unjust things would have to be the good person, if such a good person even exists (376b 5–6). In fact, what is under discussion in these judgments is the old Socratic *dictum* 'no one does wrong voluntarily' (or 'no one wishes evil') and 'virtue is knowledge'; the man who errs involuntarily lacks knowledge and is at a disadvantage. The *agathos* is the man who errs voluntarily, while the *kakos* errs involuntarily and does wrong against his own will; the *kakos* who errs involuntarily has no knowledge and therefore he is not *kakos* voluntarily. It is a typical feature of the traditional *agathos* to do wrong voluntarily and of the traditional *kakos* to do wrong involuntarily. This statement mirrors the historical situation for the traditional *agathos*, who is in a position to do wrong against the *kakos* and to fall into *hybris*. This is 'the might is right' principle of the *agathos*. The runner who runs slowly voluntarily is better (373d), because he has both the ability and the knowledge to run quickly, if he decides to do so. The *agathos* has the ability to do wrong, because he has the *dynamis*, ability, which is an element of *aretē*. It has been shown that 'the soul which has the greater power (*dynamis*) and wisdom (*sophia*) is better' (375e), because the former is the presupposition of *aretē* and the latter is (part of the) *aretē* itself.[29] A third doctrine, 'I neither know nor think that I know' (*Ap.* 21d, 29a–b, cf. *Hp.Ma.* 298c), related to Socrates' ignorance and method, may be found in the dialogue: he who knows the truth can deceive better than he who does not, and he who deceives voluntarily (as Socrates does) is better than he who does so involuntarily. In the *Hippias Minor*, as in other Platonic dialogues, we have to know every

---

[29] Aristotle criticizes Socrates' doctrine that virtue is knowledge in the seventh book of the *EN* (1146b 31–1147b 6). At the end of the sixth he says epigrammatically: 'Socrates, then, thought that the virtues are instances of reason, because he thought that they are all instances of knowledge. We, on the other hand, think that they involve reason' (1144b 28–30, trans. Irwin 1999² with adjustments). Cf. Guthrie 1962–1981, III 2, 130–38.

time whether Plato uses *agathos* in the traditional political and social meaning or in the moral meaning he wants to attach to the word.

(ii c) *Hippias Minor, Protagoras* and other Platonic Dialogues

The Socratic principle 'no one does wrong voluntarily' is also found in the *Protagoras* (345d – e) and, as it is well known, in other Platonic dialogues.[30] There are, also, a number of minor topics which may be found in the *Hippias Minor* and in other dialogues of Plato. In the *Protagoras* Socrates argues that 'Simonides was not so uneducated as to say that he praised a person who willingly did no evil, as if there were some people who did evil willingly' and that 'no wise man believes that anyone does wrong willingly or acts shamefully and badly of his own free will' (345d – e, trans. Taylor 1991 with adjustments). This is what Socrates is talking about in the *Hippias Minor*, and this is what is included in the conditional statement of the final conclusion: 'if there be such a man'.

When in the first section of the *Hippias Minor* the interlocutors agree that 'the false is he who has the wisdom and the power to speak falsely' (366b) and that 'every man has power who does that which he wishes at the time when he wishes', Socrates feels the need to add 'I am not speaking of any special case in which he is prevented by disease or something of that sort' (366c). Similarly, in the *Protagoras* Socrates argues that an *agathos* ('good man') could sometimes become *kakos* ('bad'), 'through the effect of either age or toil or disease or some other misfortune—for doing badly is nothing other than being deprived of knowledge' (345b, trans. Taylor 1991 with adjustments).

In the *Protagoras*, since a most important part of a man's education is being knowledgeable about poetry, the title-character and Socrates decide to analyze Simonides' poem to Scopas, concerning the very thing that they are discussing, namely excellence, with the only difference that it is transferred to the sphere of poetry. At the end of the discussion the analysis fails, and they leave aside the discussion of lyric and other kinds of poetry; they do not need poets, because 'one cannot question them on the sense of what they say, but in most of the cases when people quote them, one says the poet means one thing and one another' (347e, trans. Taylor 1991 with adjustments). At the end of the dialogue Protagoras and Socrates exchange their views on the teachability of virtue. In the *Hippias Minor* the title-character

---

30 *Cr.* 49a, *Ap.* 25d – 26a, 37a, *Meno* 77b – 78b, *Prt.* 345d – e, 358c – d, *R.* 589c, *Lg.* 731c, 734b, 860d, *Ti.* 86d. For the recurrent theme οὐδεὶς ἑκὼν ἁμαρτάνει, see Mackenzy 1981, ch. 9.

has given a lecture on Homer and uses certain Homeric passages to support his views. In the middle of the dialogue they decide to leave aside Homer, 'as there is no possibility of asking Homer what he meant in these verses of his' (365d) and at the end they result in a paradox. The paradox 'if there be such a man' is what follows from the argument, in accordance with the *logos* (376e).[31]

Finally, as in the *Protagoras*, *Menon* and the *Republic*, Socrates starts the conversation in the *Hippias Minor* inductively from various arts and professions, from the limbs of the body and the soul's capacity, to result in general conclusions.

(ii d) *Hippias Minor*, Aristotle's and Xenophon's works

There are a number of topics which may be found in the *Hippias Minor* and in the works of Aristotle and Xenophon. Without the explicit testimony of Aristotle, probably few critics would consider the *Hippias Minor* a genuine Platonic work.[32] Aristotle says: 'Hence, the argument in the *Hippias* that the same man is false and true is misleading; for it takes him to be false who is able to deceive, though he is discerning and intelligent, and takes him to be better who is willingly bad' (*Metaph.* 1025a 6–9, trans. Hope 1960 with adjustments).

The distinction between ethics and other areas of human *epistēmē* and *dynamis* seems to be clear from Aristotle's reception of the *Hippias Minor*.[33] Two passages from the *Nicomachean Ethics* are extremely pertinent. In the first passage, justice is prescribed as a state of character (*hexis*), and since justice is a state, its relation to just actions is different from the relation of a capacity to its character: 'We see that the state (*hexis*) everyone means in speaking of justice is the state that makes us doers of just actions, that makes us do justice and wish what is just. In the same way they mean by injustice the state that makes us do injustice and wish what is unjust [...] For what is of sciences (*epistēmē*) and capacities (*dynamis*) is not true of states. For while one and the same capacity or science seems to have contrary activities, a state that is a contrary has no contrary activities' (1129a 6–17, trans. Irwin 1999²).

In the second passage, in defining intelligence Aristotle recognizes the connection between temperance and intelligence, that intelligence cannot be misused and cannot be forgotten: 'Hence, intelligence must be a state grasping the truth, involv-

---

[31] On the interlocutors not having the possibility of asking the poet and, in general, on the difference between oral and written discourse, cf. *Ap.* 22b, *Phdr.* 275d–e, *Ep.* VII 343a, 344c.
[32] Friedländer 1964, 146.
[33] Hoerber 1962, 130–31.

ing reason and concerned with action about human goods. Moreover, there is the virtue of craft, but not of intelligence. Furthermore, in a craft, someone who errs willingly is more choiceworthy; but with intelligence, as with virtue, the reverse is true. Clearly, then, intelligence is a virtue, not craft-knowledge. There are two parts of the soul that have reason. Intelligence is a virtue of one of them, of the part that has belief; for belief is concerned, as intelligence is, with what admits of being otherwise. Moreover, it is not only a state involving reason. A proof of this is the fact that such a state can be forgotten, but intelligence cannot' (1140a 20 – 30, trans. Irwin 1999^2 with minor adjustments).

Aristotle's reception of the *Hippias Minor* emerges from each of these passages. From the first citation it seems that the prior portion of the *Hippias Minor* led Aristotle to the definition between *hexis* versus *dynamis* and *epistēmē*, thus solving the riddle of the first perplexing proposition. In the second citation Aristotle appears to have the latter portion of the *Hippias Minor* in mind in distinguishing between voluntary error in ethics as contrasted with error in the crafts.

Finally, there is a long passage in Xenophon's *Memorabilia* (4.2.1–40) which, in view of its similarity to Plato's *Hippias Minor*, has been discussed in connection with that dialogue. Various claims have been made about the relationship of the two works, including that Plato copied Xenophon.[34] Though there are clearly some similarities between this section of the *Memorabilia* and the *Hippias Minor*, the differences are more striking and more important. In Hippias' position, the arrogant professional teacher who charges others for teaching them what he knows is Euthydemus, who is not only not teaching others, but has not even reached full maturity. Since the Platonic material is entirely dramatic, with no external 'explanations' by a narrator, and so no explicit statement of purpose, the interpretation is left to the reader. In the *Memorabilia* (4.2.19 ff.), Xenophon allows the discussion to end with Socrates apparently agreeing that justice is exactly like the other crafts and that the knowing wrongdoer is better. In the dialogue not only Hippias directly denies this conclusion, but Socrates himself expresses his grave doubts. It is the identification of craft and justice—being explicit in the *Memorabilia* but problematic in the *Hippias Minor*— that some critics take to be Plato's point in the *Hippias Minor* and what they accordingly take him to task for.[35]

---

[34] Phillips 1989, 369 – 70; cf. Phillips 1987; Weiss 1981, 304, n. 53.
[35] I am grateful to Prof. M. Edwards who read this paper and improved on its English; for whatever blemishes remaining the responsibility is mine.

Kleanthis Mantzouranis
A Philosophical Reception of Homer: Homeric Courage in Aristotle's Discussion of ἀνδρεία

Homer's representation of the heroic warriors of the *Iliad* bequeathed to the Greeks paradigmatic examples of martial valour as models for emulation and comparison: heroic figures such as Achilles, Hector, and Diomedes became a benchmark for subsequent discussions of courage and military prowess by poets, prose authors and even philosophers. This paper explores how Homeric courage forms part of τὰ ἔνδοξα, that is, the reputable views that inform Aristotle's discussion of ἀνδρεία in the *Nicomachean Ethics*. I aim to show how Aristotle responds to the Homeric idea of courage and how he appropriates Homer to elucidate his own conception of genuine ἀνδρεία. I shall start by briefly summarizing Aristotle's position.

Aristotle's discussion of ἀνδρεία as a particular virtue of character (*EN* III 6–9) can be divided into two parts. In the main body of his exposition (*EN* 1115a 6–1116a 15, 1117a 29–1117b 22), Aristotle discusses what we may describe as ἀνδρεία proper or genuine ἀνδρεία, which he defines as a mean state with regard to fear and confidence (*EN* 1115a 6–7). Aristotle places ἀνδρεία exclusively in the field of battle and thus narrows its scope in comparison to Plato.[1] For Aristotle, to display ἀνδρεία is to show the appropriate amount of fear and confidence and act accordingly when faced with the dangers and the fear-inspiring circumstances of the battlefield (*EN* 1115a 28–35). The performance of one or more courageous actions, however, does not necessarily make one courageous. According to Aristotle, an action qualifies as a genuine manifestation of the relevant virtue only if the agent acts with the proper motivation. Courage, therefore, like other virtues of character, should be displayed 'for the sake of the noble', τοῦ καλοῦ ἕνεκα (*EN* 1115b 11–13, 23–24; 1122b 7).

In the remaining of his discussion (*EN* 1116a 15–1117a 28), Aristotle describes and examines certain states which are commonly thought to conduce

---

[1] By narrowing ἀνδρεία to its most paradigmatic manifestation, namely courage displayed in the battlefield, Aristotle responds to Plato's Socrates, who in the *Laches* (191d–e) extends the field of ἀνδρεία to include one's courageous stance in the face of various adversities, such as poverty, disease or sea-danger. For Aristotle, the application of ἀνδρεῖος in such cases is a metaphorical use of the word (καθ' ὁμοιότητα, *EN* 1115a 19), which extends ἀνδρεία beyond its proper field; cf. Stewart 1892, I 283–84. On the different methodology that Plato and Aristotle employ in their treatment of the particular virtues, see Joachim 1951, 113–14.

to courageous behaviour. The discussion of these states aims to show how ordinary conceptions of courage fail to qualify as proper ἀνδρεία in the Aristotelian sense. At the same time, by contrasting his own understanding of courage with popular views about it, Aristotle elucidates the true nature and scope of this virtue. It is this part of Aristotle's exposition that is most relevant for the examination of his reception and use of Homer.

Aristotle discusses five defective forms of courage. First, πολιτικὴ ἀνδρεία, 'citizen courage', is the kind of courage displayed by citizen soldiers, who are motivated by a desire to win honour and avoid disgrace and the penalties imposed by the laws (*EN* 1116a 17–1116b 3). The second form is the kind of courage resulting from experience in certain conditions (ἐμπειρία), such as the courage displayed by mercenary soldiers (*EN* 1116b 3–23). Third comes the courage that results from spirit or passion, θυμός, which resembles the ferocity of wild beasts (*EN* 1116b 23–1117a 9). Courage can also be displayed, fourth, by hopeful people (εὐέλπιδες), who feel confident because of past successes (*EN* 1117a 9–22). Finally, one can display courage as a result of ignorance of the impending danger (*EN* 1117a 22–28).

It has long been observed by Aristotle scholars that the classification of the defective forms of courage has its roots in Plato.[2] The role of technical expertise or skill (τέχνη) in the display of courage and the connection between courage and the spirited part of the human soul (τὸ θυμοειδές) are recurrent ideas in the discussions of ἀνδρεία in the Platonic dialogues.[3] Even the term πολιτικὴ ἀνδρεία that Aristotle uses (*EN* 1116a 17) seems to have been borrowed from Plato.[4]

These Platonic resonances, however, are only part of the picture of Aristotle's sources. In his discussion of the defective forms of courage, Aristotle explicitly establishes Homer as a source for two of these forms, namely πολιτικὴ ἀνδρεία and the ἀνδρεία of θυμός. In each case, Aristotle develops his argument

---

[2] Already in Grant 1885, II 37.
[3] Experience in a certain skill and courage: *La.* 192d–193e, *Prt.* 349e–351b; θυμός and courage: *R.* 410d–412a.
[4] Grant 1885, II 37; Joachim 1951, 120. At *R.* 430b–c πολιτικὴ ἀνδρεία is defined as the 'power to preserve through everything the correct and law-inculcated belief about what is to be feared and what isn't' (trans. Grube, rev. Reeve 1992). Plato uses the term πολιτικὴ ἀνδρεία to distinguish the courage of the civilized man from the impetus of animals or slaves, who may *appear* to act courageously when driven by their natural instincts, but in truth they are not, since their actions are not the result of education inculcated by law. The idea that true courage should be cultural, not natural, and a result of rational choice is formulated already in fifth-century political discourse. Athenian democratic ideology, in its attempt for self-definition, presented Athenian courage as a result of free choice and rational thought in contrast to Spartan courage which was a result of constant hardship, enforced discipline, and external pressure; see Bassi 2003, 47–48; Balot 2004.

in two steps. He first describes the nature of the defective form of courage in question, and then furnishes his discussion with citations of, and/or allusions to, Homer. Aristotle's use of Homer in this part of the discussion is a purposeful act of reception with a twofold aim: firstly, to illustrate by means of concrete examples the form of courage described; secondly, to reinforce his argument by adducing the authority of the poet.[5] This use of Homer to elucidate and strengthen a philosophical argument reveals something about the context of reception and Aristotle's attitude towards the source text itself. On the one hand, for an example to achieve its purpose it must be immediately recognizable by those to whom it is addressed. The use of Homeric examples, therefore, suggests that Aristotle's audience was (or was expected to be) able to identify these examples and understand how they can help illustrate the point just made. On the other hand, the very fact that Aristotle adduces Homer to reinforce his argument suggests that in his view the two defective forms of courage in question are evidenced already in the epics. In other words, in Aristotle's mind Homer has already grasped an essential truth about the nature of courage.

Let us then describe the two defective forms of courage as 'Homeric' and assess their status *vis-à-vis* Aristotle's genuine ἀνδρεία. This discussion will show how Aristotle responds to the Homeric conception of courage and how he reworks the Homeric material in accordance with his philosophical outlook.

a. The courage of θυμός

In the epics θυμός is the seat of the affective life, it is therefore the physical basis that produces, among other things, the passion that prompts one to act courageously.[6] Aristotle endorses this prevalent conception of θυμός and argues that θυμός is 'most eager' (ἰτητικώτατον) to rush into dangers (*EN* 1116b 26–27).[7]

---

[5] For the Greek practice of citing poetry in general and Homer in particular to illustrate or reinforce a point of view, see Halliwell 2000, 95–99.
[6] *Il.* 3.8–9; 5.792; 15.561–64; 19.164–66; *Od.* 1.320–22. On Homeric θυμός, see Redfield 1994², 173–74; Hobbs 2000, 8.
[7] Stewart 1892, I 296 points to *Prt.* 349e, where Protagoras says of courageous men that they are confident and ready for action (ἴτας) in circumstances in which most men would be fearful. As has already been stressed, the Homeric idea that θυμός contributes to courage is discussed and elaborated in Plato's *Republic*. Although Plato's conception of θυμός is not identical to the Homeric one, Plato endorses the Homeric insight about the connection between θυμός and martial valour and links closely the spirited part of human soul (τὸ θυμοειδές) to the virtue of courage. For an extensive discussion of the Platonic conception of ἀνδρεία and its relation to

To elucidate this form of courage Aristotle uses two sets of Homeric examples. One set comprises quotations of Homeric formulaic phrases which describe the rousing of a hero's spirit, usually as a result of the intervention of some god:

> ἰτητικώτατον γὰρ ὁ θυμὸς πρὸς τοὺς κινδύνους, ὅθεν καὶ Ὅμηρος "σθένος ἔμβαλε θυμῷ" καὶ "μένος καὶ θυμὸν ἔγειρε" καὶ "δριμὺ δ' ἀνὰ ῥῖνας μένος" καὶ "ἔζεσεν αἷμα·" πάντα γὰρ τὰ τοιαῦτα ἔοικε σημαίνειν τὴν τοῦ θυμοῦ ἔγερσιν καὶ ὁρμήν.[8]
> (EN 1116b 26–30)

> For spirit is something which especially spurs people on to face dangers; hence, we have in Homer 'he cast strength into his spirit' and 'he stirred up rage and spirit' and 'fierce rage breathed through his nostrils' and 'his blood boiled'. All such expressions seem to stand for impetus and the rousing of spirit.[9]

The second set of examples builds on the familiar comparison of courageous men with wild beasts.[10] Here Aristotle does not cite, but rather alludes to, Homeric lines and, in particular, to Homeric similes, where a warrior's courageous behaviour is compared to the sturdy boldness of some animal in a situation of danger. Aristotle comments on the bold behaviour of animals:

> οὐ δή ἐστιν ἀνδρεῖα διὰ τὸ ὑπ' ἀλγηδόνος καὶ θυμοῦ ἐξελαυνόμενα πρὸς τὸν κίνδυνον ὁρμᾶν, οὐθὲν τῶν δεινῶν προορῶντα, ἐπεὶ οὕτω γε κἂν οἱ ὄνοι ἀνδρεῖοι εἶεν πεινῶντες· τυπτόμενοι γὰρ οὐκ ἀφίστανται τῆς νομῆς·
> (EN 1116b 33–1117a 1)

> Now rushing into danger because one is driven on by pain and spirit without any sense in advance of the frightening things one has to face is not courage, because on that score even donkeys would be courageous when hungry, since they don't stop grazing even when they are beaten.

Aristotle's image is an allusion to the famous Homeric simile where Telamonian Ajax, in his slow and unwilling retreat in the face of a Trojan assault, is compared to an ass who does not stop feeding itself, although it is being incessantly beaten by children (Il. 11.558–65).[11] From the very beginning of the discussion of

---

θυμός or τὸ θυμοειδές, see Hobbs 2000. For a discussion of ἠνορέη ('manliness', the Homeric precursor of ἀνδρεία), see Graziosi/ Haubold 2003.

8 Aristotle quotes from memory and, as a result, inaccurately from (a) Il. 11.11–12 (μέγα σθένος ἔμβαλ' ἑκάστῳ καρδίῃ) and 16.528–29 (μένος δέ οἱ ἔμβαλε θυμῷ), (b) Il. 15.594–95 (ἔγειρε μένος μέγα, θέλγε δὲ θυμόν), (c) Od. 24.318–19 (τοῦ δ' ὠρίνετο θυμός, ἀνὰ ῥῖνας δέ οἱ ἤδη / δριμὺ μένος...), (d) the expression ἔζεσεν αἷμα does not occur in Homer; cf. Stewart 1892, I 297; Burnet 1900, 148, 150; Irwin 1999², 213.
9 All the translations of the *Nicomachean Ethics* are taken from Taylor 2006 with minor adjustments.
10 Cf. Pl. *La.* 196e; *R.* 430b8.
11 Cf. Stewart 1892, I 297; Burnet 1900, 150; Irwin 1999², 213.

the ἀνδρεία of θυμός Aristotle compares this form of courage to the fury and ferocious spirit of animals:

> καὶ τὸν θυμὸν δ' ἐπὶ τὴν ἀνδρείαν φέρουσιν· ἀνδρεῖοι γὰρ εἶναι δοκοῦσι καὶ οἱ διὰ θυμὸν ὥσπερ τὰ θηρία ἐπὶ τοὺς τρώσαντας φερόμενα, ὅτι καὶ οἱ ἀνδρεῖοι θυμοειδεῖς·
> (EN 1116b 24–26)
>
> People also bring spirit under the heading of courage. Those who from spirit rush like wild beasts against those who have injured them also seem courageous, since for their part courageous people are spirited.

The image of wounded beasts attacking their pursuers, to which Aristotle compares those driven by their spirit into acting courageously, is less specific than the aforementioned example of the ass. Nonetheless, given the recurrence of the references to Homer in this part of the *EN*, I argue that we can read this image as another allusion to a Homeric simile. When the Trojan Agenor decides to hold his ground and face the raging Achilles, his bold determination is compared to that of a leopard, which, though wounded, does not give up its fight against those who attack it:

> ἠΰτε πάρδαλις εἶσι βαθείης ἐκ ξυλόχοιο
> ἀνδρὸς θηρητῆρος ἐναντίον, οὐδέ τι θυμῷ
> ταρβεῖ οὐδὲ φοβεῖται, ἐπεί κεν ὑλαγμὸν ἀκούσῃ·
> εἴ περ γὰρ φθάμενός μιν ἢ οὐτάσῃ ἠὲ βάλῃσιν,
> ἀλλά τε καὶ περὶ δουρὶ πεπαρμένη οὐκ ἀπολήγει
> ἀλκῆς, πρίν γ' ἠὲ ξυμβλήμεναι ἠὲ δαμῆναι·
> ὣς Ἀντήνορος υἱὸς ἀγαυοῦ δῖος Ἀγήνωρ
> οὐκ ἔθελεν φεύγειν, πρὶν πειρήσαιτ' Ἀχιλῆος.
> (*Il.* 21.573–80)
>
> But as a leopard emerges out of her timbered cover
> to face the man who is hunting her and is neither afraid
> at heart nor runs away when she hears them baying against her;
> and even though one be too quick for her with spear thrust or spear thrown stuck with the shaft though she be, she will not cease
> her fighting fury, till she has closed with one of them or is overthrown;
> so proud Antenor's son, brilliant Agenor,
> refused to run away until he had tested Achilles.
> (trans. Lattimore 1951 with adjustments)[12]

---

[12] Note the reference to the θυμός of the leopard (574) as well as to its ἀλκή (578), which does not cease although the animal is hurt: at *EN* 1115b 4–5, Aristotle concludes his response to the Socratic widening of ἀνδρεία by arguing that people show courage (ἀνδρίζονται) in circumstances which admit of ἀλκή or in which it is καλόν to die. In the *EE* discussion of courage, Aristotle compares the courage of θυμός to the fury of wild boars (ἄγριοι σύες), which display such behav-

This form of courage can be understood as a sudden emotional impulse that emerges as a reaction to a certain stimulus and urges one onto unreflective engagement with some danger. According to Aristotle, it is the most natural type of ἀνδρεία (φυσικωτάτη, EN 1117a 4): it is an irrational, purely physical type of courage, which owes more to natural instincts than to cultural norms or experience. People who display this type of courage, like wild beasts, act because of pain (διὰ λύπην, EN 1116b 32) and from their passion (διὰ πάθος, EN 1117a 8–9), without any appreciation of the danger they face. By contrasting the Homeric ἀνδρεία of θυμός to genuine ἀνδρεία, Aristotle does not aim to question the role of θυμός in courage altogether. In Aristotle's view, the spirited element of human nature does contribute to the display of courage (συνεργεῖ, EN 1116b 31), but its role in promoting courageous behaviour must be subsidiary, not primary. This is precisely why wild beasts and θυμός-driven humans fail to qualify as properly courageous: their spirit is the *primary* motivational force that incites their courageous behaviour. For Aristotle, θυμός provides only the natural basis required for courageous action and is inadequate by itself to produce genuine ἀνδρεία:

> φυσικωτάτη δ' ἔοικεν ἡ διὰ τὸν θυμὸν εἶναι, καὶ προσλαβοῦσα προαίρεσιν καὶ τὸ οὗ ἕνεκα ἀνδρεία εἶναι. καὶ οἱ ἄνθρωποι δὴ ὀργιζόμενοι μὲν ἀλγοῦσι, τιμωρούμενοι δ' ἥδονται· οἱ δὲ διὰ ταῦτα μαχόμενοι μάχιμοι μέν, οὐκ ἀνδρεῖοι δέ· οὐ γὰρ διὰ τὸ καλὸν οὐδ' ὡς ὁ λόγος, ἀλλὰ διὰ πάθος·
> (EN 1117a 4–9)

> *Now courage prompted by spirit seems to be something purely natural, but it is when in addition it includes choice and the goal that it is courage. And people feel distress when they are roused to anger, and pleasure when they retaliate; people who fight for these reasons are combative, but not courageous; for they do not do it for the sake of the noble or as reason prescribes, but from feeling.*

The courage of spirit requires two additional elements to become genuine ἀνδρεία: deliberate choice (προαίρεσις) and proper motivation or direction towards the proper goal (τὸ οὗ ἕνεκα). Courageous actions do not consist in rushing foolhardily into every danger. They must be rationally chosen and dictated by reason (λόγος), after calculating the nature of the impending danger, the alternative courses of action open to one, and what one puts at stake by risking one's life in battle. Furthermore, genuine ἀνδρεία requires proper motivation on the part of the agent. In Aristotle's theory of virtue, performing virtuous actions is

---

iour when they are beside themselves (*EE* 1229a 25–27). Again, the image of the distraught wild boar seems to be an allusion to a Homeric simile: at *Il.* 13.471–74, Idomeneus is compared to a wild boar (σῦς), whose back bristles and whose eyes are 'shining with fire', as it stands up to a group of men attacking it.

not enough for making one truly virtuous; one must also act for a certain *reason*. Courageous behaviour motivated by pain or passion does not count as genuine ἀνδρεία. The truly courageous man is expected to act 'for the sake of the noble' (διὰ τὸ καλόν or τοῦ καλοῦ ἕνεκα).[13]

b. πολιτικὴ ἀνδρεία, 'citizen courage'

Aristotle distinguishes between two forms of πολιτικὴ ἀνδρεία, one of which ranks higher than the other. The lower form of πολιτικὴ ἀνδρεία is a result of compulsion and fear. It is displayed by soldiers who maintain their posts and fight because their commanders use coercive means, such as punishments and beatings, to enforce their obedience. Again, Aristotle chooses a Homeric example to elucidate this form of courage: he cites Agamemnon's words to his troops, by means of which Agamemnon threatens with death anyone who stays by the ships and avoids fighting (*EN* 1116a 29 – 35).[14] In its higher form, πολιτικὴ ἀνδρεία is motivated by a sense of shame towards the opinion of others (δι' αἰδῶ, *EN* 1116a 28). This latter form of πολιτικὴ ἀνδρεία ranks higher than the former, for in Aristotle's view shame is superior to fear as an incentive to action. Fear is what the many (οἱ πολλοί) respond to: such people do the right thing only to avoid the pain of punishment. On the other hand, responsiveness to shame is a mark of better upbringing and of having already acquired a sense of what is noble and truly pleasant (*EN* 1179b 10 – 16). Acting out of shame and the desire to avoid doing what is considered disgraceful suggests that one pays due respect to the opinion of others and has been properly habituated in acting in accordance with the values of the community. In other words, whereas fear implies blind conformity to the precepts of others with a view to avoiding external sanctions, shame requires the internalization by the agent of the values of the community: one who acts out of shame has made the values of the community one's own.[15]

This higher form of 'citizen courage', Aristotle says, is mostly displayed in societies where the complementary concepts of honour and shame weigh heavily and are regarded as major motivational factors. Aristotle finds that the society which best fits this description is the society depicted in the epics, so he adduces

---

13 On the two requirements, see Joachim 1951, 121; Deslauriers 2003, 189 – 90.
14 The reference is to *Il.* 2.391 – 93, but Aristotle wrongly attributes these words to Hector instead of Agamemnon; cf. Stewart 1892, I 293.
15 Cf. Williams 1993, 78 – 85 and Cairns 1993, 16 – 17, 43 – 44, 80 – 81, who respond to Dodds' famous description of Homeric society as a 'shame culture' (Dodds 1951, 17 – 18).

Homer once again to reinforce his argument and elucidate it by means of two concrete examples:

> δοκοῦσι γὰρ ὑπομένειν τοὺς κινδύνους οἱ πολῖται διὰ τὰ ἐκ τῶν νόμων ἐπιτίμια καὶ τὰ ὀνείδη καὶ διὰ τὰς τιμάς· καὶ διὰ τοῦτο ἀνδρειότατοι δοκοῦσιν εἶναι παρ' οἷς οἱ δειλοὶ ἄτιμοι καὶ οἱ ἀνδρεῖοι ἔντιμοι. τοιούτους δὲ καὶ Ὅμηρος ποιεῖ, οἷον τὸν Διομήδην καὶ τὸν Ἕκτορα·
> Πουλυδάμας μοι πρῶτος ἐλεγχείην ἀναθήσει·
> καὶ {Διομήδης}
> Ἕκτωρ γάρ ποτε φήσει ἐνὶ Τρώεσσ' ἀγορεύων
> "Τυδείδης ὑπ' ἐμεῖο."
> (EN 1116a 18–26)
>
> Citizens seem to face dangers because of the penalties of the law and public disgrace and honour, and therefore the most courageous seem to be those among whom the cowardly are disgraced and the courageous honoured. Homer depicts people of that kind, such as Diomede and Hector, who say
> Polydamas will be the first to heap reproach on me
> and
> Hector will say when he speaks to the Trojans
> 'The son of Tydeus has fled from me.'

Aristotle's knowledge of Homer becomes evident in this context, since the examples he chooses to use from the *Iliad* are particularly successful in showing how one's sense of shame can generate courageous behaviour. The first is derived from Hector's famous monologue before his final battle with Achilles. Hector anticipates the heavy criticism he will incur from Polydamas for not heeding his prudent advice and decides to remain outside the walls of Troy and confront the raging Achilles (*Il.* 22.99–110). In the second example, Diomedes, forced by Zeus' thunderbolt to abandon his advance, complains that should he listen to Nestor's advice and retreat before Hector, Hector's boast would inflict upon him an insufferable loss of face (*Il.* 8.146–50).

Having clearly illustrated the nature of πολιτικὴ ἀνδρεία, Aristotle then goes on to describe its workings and explain how it relates to genuine ἀνδρεία:

> ὡμοίωται δ' αὕτη μάλιστα τῇ πρότερον εἰρημένῃ,[16] ὅτι δι' ἀρετὴν γίνεται· δι' αἰδῶ γὰρ καὶ διὰ καλοῦ ὄρεξιν (τιμῆς γάρ) καὶ φυγὴν ὀνείδους, αἰσχροῦ ὄντος.
> (EN 1116a 27–29)
>
> This sort most closely resembles the one previously discussed [i. e. genuine courage], because it comes about from virtue, i. e. from shame and the desire for a noble thing (namely honour) and the avoidance of disgrace, as something shameful.

---

[16] Cf. *EN* 1116a 17: μάλιστα ἔοικεν.

Aristotle's construal of πολιτικὴ ἀνδρεία fits perfectly in the Homeric framework and captures the epic representation of military prowess, its motivation and its scope. The martial valour of a Homeric hero is the most evident manifestation of his ἀρετή,[17] which is motivated by his sense of αἰδώς towards his milieu: in battle circumstances, the single cry for αἰδώς is the most common way to prompt slacking or discouraged men back into action.[18] By displaying his prowess in battle, the Homeric hero seeks to secure for himself τιμή, which entails both respect and a good name among his peers and the more concrete material possessions and privileges that accompany his superior status and social position.[19] Failure or unwillingness to display courage besmirches one's τιμή and results in the disgraceful condition of being open to the reproach of others.[20] Thus, the higher form of Aristotle's 'citizen courage' corresponds to the most typical form of Homeric courage, namely courage motivated by a sense of shame in the face of public criticism.

This form of courage, Aristotle says, is most akin, but not tantamount, to genuine ἀνδρεία. This is due to the status of honour (τιμή), the complementary concept of shame, as a motive for action. Aristotle classifies honour as 'the greatest of the external goods' (*EN* 1123b 20–21), but rejects the view of those who consider it the supreme good of human life (*EN* 1095b 22–26). Honour is indeed a noble motive, since it is not distributed haphazardly, but is bestowed only upon those who promote, or are in a position to promote, the community's well-being (*Rh.* 1361a 28–30). In this light, displaying courage with a view to honour is finer than being courageous for the sake of acquiring less admirable goods, such as power or wealth. In Aristotle's theory of virtue, however, honour does not constitute the proper motivation for a truly virtuous action. If one fights bravely being primarily motivated by the honour that customarily ensues from such actions, then one is motivated by external rewards rather than by the nature of the action itself. In Aristotelian terms, this amounts to performing an action for an *external* end, which violates one of the requirements of virtuous actions, namely that the action must be chosen *for its own sake* (προαιρούμενος δι' αὐτά, *EN* 1105a 32). Aristotle's principle that the courageous man should act 'for the sake of the noble' (τοῦ καλοῦ ἕνεκα, *EN* 1115b 12–13, 23–24) redirects the

---

17 *Il.* 8.535–36, 11.90–91, 11.407–10, 11.762–64, 13.276–86, 22.268–69.
18 *Il.* 5.529–32, 5.787, 8.228.
19 *Il.*12.310–21, 8.161–66, 9.601–05.
20 *Il.* 2.119–22, 2.295–98, 4.242–46, 11.313–15.

order of priority and focuses on the intrinsic value of the action, rather than on the external rewards that accompany it.[21]

c. 'For the sake of the noble'

Performing an action τοῦ καλοῦ ἕνεκα implies that the agent chooses to act in the way he does because he fully appreciates, and is motivated by, the intrinsic beauty or goodness of his action.[22] The man of citizen courage (in its higher form) and the man of genuine ἀνδρεία may indeed prove equally courageous in action. In addition, by displaying courage they act in a way that their social *milieu*, and they themselves, regard as καλόν. The man of genuine ἀνδρεία, however, rationally grasps that what renders courageous actions καλόν is their intrinsic goodness not the praise or honour that customarily ensues from them. Unlike the man of citizen courage, who acts with a view to honour, the man of genuine ἀνδρεία is motivated by the intrinsic value of his action. What prompts him is the understanding that such an action is worth doing in itself, just because it is the kind of action it is, regardless of any favourable consequences or rewards.[23] When the cause justifies the risk, the man of genuine courage risks his life in battle even if no honour is to be gained by his action, or even if his decision to act courageously is shared by no one but himself.

Aristotle's analysis, therefore, shows that πολιτικὴ ἀνδρεία, the most typical form of Homeric courage, ranks lower than genuine ἀνδρεία. Nonetheless, Aristotle does not overlook or underrate the value of the Homeric conception of courage. Aristotle often reiterates that becoming truly virtuous, and so acting 'for the sake of the noble', is not an easy task: few people are endowed with the moral and mental capacities that would enable them to achieve this ideal. But the city still needs protection and ordinary men to defend it and risk their lives for its sake. Therein lies the

---

[21] There is no tension or incompatibility between doing an action 'for the sake of the noble' and doing it 'for its own sake'; a courageous action is seen as noble in virtue of its being courageous: see Rogers 1994, 311; Lear 2004, 124–25; Taylor 2006, 86–87.

[22] This is only one of the attributes that Aristotle's conception of τὸ καλόν entails. I focus on this aspect of τὸ καλόν, because it is the one most relevant to the distinction that Aristotle draws between 'citizen courage' and genuine courage. Actions described as καλόν are also rationally chosen, demanding, praiseworthy, fitting or appropriate to the circumstances in which they are performed, and (more often than not) other-regarding. Actions of genuine ἀνδρεία display, of course, all these characteristics. For Aristotle's conception of τὸ καλόν, see Owens 1981; Broadie 1991, 92–94; Rogers 1993; Nisters 2000, 52–67; Irwin 2010. For a detailed discussion of the motivation of Aristotelian ἀνδρεία, see Rogers 1994.

[23] Cf. Cairns 1993, 420, 427, n. 254; Taylor 2006, 187.

value of honour and shame as motivational factors: being more applicable to ordinary people than the rational appreciation of τὸ καλόν, the desire for honour and a sense of shame in the face of public criticism ensure that the city will not be left without protection. As Aristotle observes, while professional soldiers are the first to flee, citizen soldiers hold their ground and sacrifice themselves, because they prefer death to the disgrace of a shameful flight (*EN* 1116b 17–20). 'Citizen courage' preserves the city, even when the citizens are not so philosophically oriented as to fulfil the requirements of τὸ καλόν. This pragmatic form of courage, though defective in philosophical terms, is according to Aristotle the form that most closely resembles genuine ἀνδρεία.

Concluding remarks

Homer occupies a prominent place in the part of Aristotle's discussion where genuine ἀνδρεία is contrasted to five commonly held but defective conceptions of courage. Aristotle finds that two of these endoxic conceptions, πολιτικὴ ἀνδρεία and the courage of θυμός, are formulated already in the epics. He therefore appropriates Homer to elucidate and reinforce his argument, by citing and alluding to Homeric examples which provide concrete evidence of the forms of courage in question. Aristotle singles out these two 'Homeric' forms as being closer to genuine ἀνδρεία than the rest and explains why they are defective and how they can be transformed into genuine ἀνδρεία. Like Homer and Plato, Aristotle sees a connection between θυμός and courage and argues that in order to become true courage the ἀνδρεία of θυμός requires deliberation (προαίρεσις) and proper motivation. Courageous actions must be the product of rational choice and must be performed with a view to a certain goal. Motivation is what distinguishes πολιτικὴ ἀνδρεία from genuine ἀνδρεία as well. 'Citizen courage' aims at honour, which *is* a noble thing, but it does not aim at 'the noble', τὸ καλόν, itself.

Aristotle's conception of genuine ἀνδρεία underlines the importance of proper motivation for virtuous action and therefore refines, develops, and deepens the Homeric representation of courage. Nevertheless, throughout his discussion Aristotle acknowledges the validity and value of the Homeric outlook. By ranking the courage of a Hector or a Diomedes as second-best next to his conception of genuine ἀνδρεία, Aristotle does justice to the authority of the poet and at the same time propounds his own view on what it means to be truly courageous by acting 'for the sake of the noble'.

Christina-Panagiota Manolea
Homeric Echoes, Pythagorean Flavour: The Reception of Homer in Iamblichus

Introduction

The Neoplatonic philosopher Porphyry (3rd century AD) has included valuable exegetic material in his work *Quaestiones Homericae* that is based on Aristarch's principle *"Ὅμηρον ἐξ Ὁμήρου σαφηνίζειν*' in terms of methodology.[1] The work in question is part of a long tradition of commentary that goes back at least to Aristotle and was enormously appropriated in the Byzantine Homeric scholia, but, nonetheless, is up to now relatively unexplored.[2] Moreover, Porphyry's short monograph *De antro Nympharum* is also a text of the utmost importance, as it interprets a certain passage of the *Odyssey* (13.102–12) allegorically and is regarded as a major text of ancient literary criticism.[3] Both works show the Neoplatonic philosopher's knowledge and esteem for Homer and also render Porphyry a major figure in the history of Homeric reception.

Such was the situation with Homer's reception by Porphyry when his student Iamblichus of Chalcis (3rd–4th century AD) appeared. Iamblichus was a prolific Neoplatonic philosopher, who elaborated the Platonic system propounded by Plotinus and Porphyry, widely receiving the Pythagorean pseudepigrapha and the Chaldean Oracles, and also gave a prominent role to theurgical theory and practice.[4] But he was also the man who influenced Athenian Neoplatonism more than any other and also a figure that was hagiographized by posteriors,

---

[1] For Porphyry's work, see Lamberton 1986, 108–13; cf. Smith 2010, 328. For Aristarchus a brief yet inclusive account is found in Janko 1992, 25–29; cf. Manolea 2004, 35–36.
[2] See Lamberton 1986, 112; cf. Manolea 2004, 41.
[3] See Lamberton 1986, 119–33. This analysis of the work in question, pioneering in its time, is still valuable, especially as a starting point on the work's study. Moreover, A. Smith (2010, 328) rightly remarks that the style of approach and presentation found in this work is to be found in many other works of Porphyry, as well. He also rightly stresses the philosophical content of the *De Antro Nympharum*.
[4] For an introduction to Iamblichus' philosophy see Dillon 2010, 358–74. We should note that Dillon is of the opinion that the role of theurgical theory and practice in the thought of Iamblichus has been given too prominent a role in the past (2010, 373). Nevertheless this element did exist and was also important in Iamblichus' and his students' thought and everyday practice.

who called him 'divine'.⁵ Nevertheless, Iamblichus' attitude towards Homer is not identical with Porphyry's. In his existing works he has not provided us with an appropriation of the Homeric tradition as rich and as elaborate as his master's.⁶ Therefore, it is not surprising to see a lack of attention on the scholars' part as far as Iamblichus' Homeric passages are concerned.

However, this does not mean that the Homeric tradition is absent from Iamblichus' works or that Homer is particularly underestimated by the Neoplatonic philosopher in question. In this paper we shall try to answer a series of questions:⁷ How was Homer's text received by Iamblichus? What are the artistic and intellectual processes involved in his –admittedly limited– selection of the Homeric material? Did the receivers' knowledge of Homer play a role in Iamblichus' choice? What is the purpose for Homer's presence in Iamblichus' philosophical works? It will be demonstrated that quotations from both the *Iliad* and the *Odyssey* do appear in some surviving philosophical works of Iamblichus that primarily aimed not at the Homeric text's elaboration, but at the expression of Iamblichus' own Neoplatonic beliefs. The existing Homeric passages (traced in only three extant philosophical works of Iamblichus, namely the *De vita Pythagorica*, the *Protrepticus* and the *De mysteriis*) will be examined and briefly analyzed, in order to demonstrate that the Homeric tradition is employed in some cases for anecdotological purposes; moreover, it will be shown that Homeric references are rather well placed in Iamblichus' philosophical discussions on cosmology and metaphysics and bear a distinctly Pythagorean flavour.

a. *De Vita Pythagorica*

(i) At 9.11–13 Iamblichus says that Pythagoras left Samos by night with a certain Hermodamas surnamed 'the Creophylian' and said to descend from Creophylus, who was Homer's host.⁸ Iamblichus had already mentioned Creophylus as one

---

5 We shall only mention the sophist Eunapius, whose *Vita Iamblichi* is hagiographical, though ill informed, as Dillon rightly remarks (2010, 358). The expression 'ὁ θεῖος Ἰάμβλιχος' is found in Syrianus and Proclus (Neoplatonic School of Athens, 5th century AD), as well as in writers of the School of Ammonius (Neoplatonic School of Alexandria, 6th century AD).
6 For instance, Lamberton 1986, 134 has argued that Iamblichus paid little attention to the interpretation of Homer—in his own words: 'more important [...] is the almost complete lack of concern for the interpretation of early poetry that characterizes Iamblichus and his immediate cycle'.
7 See Hardwick 2003, 5.
8 *De vita Pyth*. 9.9–15: νύκτωρ λαθὼν πάντας μετὰ τοῦ Ἑρμοδάμαντος μὲν τὸ ὄνομα, Κρεοφυλείου δὲ ἐπικαλουμένου, ὃς ἐλέγετο Κρεοφύλου ἀπόγονος εἶναι, Ὁμήρου δὲ ξένου τοῦ ποιητοῦ

of the eminent teachers of Pythagoras (8.8–11). Creophylus is known from many ancient sources to have been closely related to Homer, although in a rather blurred way.[9] But given the fact that Pythagoras himself was by birth and studentship personally involved in the Samos/Creophylus tradition of the transmission of the Homeric text,[10] Iamblichus could not but have treated Creophylus favourably, thus showing, consciously or unconsciously, a quite early close relation between Pythagoras and Homer. Now, as to the descendant of Creophylus, Hermodamas, who is called 'the Creophylian', Iamblichus in the passage that we are discussing mentions him as the man who taught Pythagoras and travelled with him to see Pherecydes, Anaximander and Thales. We therefore see how Homeric tradition and philosophy are encountered in this Pythagoras-Hermodamas relation.

<οὗ δεῖ δοκεῖ > γενέσθαι φίλος καὶ διδάσκαλος τῶν ἁπάντων, μετὰ τούτου πρὸς τὸν Φερεκύδην διεπόρθμευε καὶ πρὸς Ἀναξίμανδρον τὸν φυσικὸν καὶ πρὸς Θαλῆν εἰς Μίλητον.

9 For information on Creophylus, Burkert 1972, 74–85 is still useful. Yet Creophylus' relation to Homer is challenging in itself. There is an ancient discussion on the authorship of the poem *Oechaliae Halosis* as to whether it should be attributed to Creophylus rather than Homer. For a recent brief yet illuminating account of this complex issue see Graziosi 2002, 164–200. Graziosi rightly remarks that there is a group of authors (Stasinus, Lesches and Creophylus) who are clearly subordinated to Homer, are presented as his relatives or friends and are said to have been given by Homer some of his poems as gifts. To speak only of Creophylus, ancient sources refer to him as Homer's host (Sextus Empiricus, *Adv. Math.* 1.48.4–5: Κρεοφύλου πόνος εἰμί, δόμῳ ποτὲ θεῖον ἀοιδὸν δεξαμένου), while Aelius Aristides describes him as an ἑταῖρος of Homer (Πρὸς Καπίτωνα 328.3–4: ὁ γὰρ Κρεόφυλος [...] ὁ τοῦ Ὁμήρου ἑταῖρος). It is Strabo who informs us that *Oechaliae Halosis* is said to have been given to Creophylus by Homer as a gift, but also mentions that Callimachus states the opposite and links the whole issue with the story of the hospitality (Strabo 14.1.18: Κρεώφυλος, ὅν φασι δεξάμενον ξενίᾳ ποτὲ Ὅμηρον λαβεῖν δῶρον τὴν ἐπιγραφὴν τοῦ ποιήματος ὃ καλοῦσιν Οἰχαλίας ἅλωσιν. Καλλίμαχος δὲ τοὐναντίον ἐμφαίνει δι' ἐπιγράμματος τινος ὡς ἐκείνου μὲν ποιήσαντος λεγομένου δ' Ὁμήρου διὰ τὴν λεγομένην ξενίαν). It is indeed Callimachus who in *Epigram* 6 attributes the *Oechaliae Halosis* to Creophylus. For a discussion of Strabo and Callimachus' evidence see Graziosi 2002, 190–93. We should not forget, either, that Plato does not have a positive opinion about Creophylus (*R.* 600a–b). Nevertheless, Graziosi seems to consider that negative evidence for Creophylus was not influential in antiquity. In our case, Iamblichus does not seem willing to speak of the authorship of the *Oechaliae Halosis* or to speak negatively of Creophylus in general. Iamblichus was in all probability familiar with the Platonic opinion about Creophylus and maybe with Callimachus' opinion, as well. He nevertheless does not choose to touch the issue in question.

10 There is a discussion in modern scholarship concerning what seems to be a double tradition in the Homeric text transmission, namely the Samos/Creophylus tradition and the Chios/Homeridae tradition. For an account of the double traditions, the disagreement between scholars and what seems to be a rather convincing conclusion, see Graziosi 2002, 201–34.

What is important, however, is the fact that Iamblichus' teacher Porphyry mentioned Hermodamas' association with Pythagoras in his own *De vita Pythagorica*.[11] We should not forget that the two works bearing the same title and written by the master and the student present many similarities and often use the same sources, but they also display considerable differences as to their aim and context.[12]

(ii) At 64.14–15 we have a Pythagorean reading of epic poetry, as selected passages from Hesiod and Homer are reported to have been used by Pythagoras in order to cure the soul.[13] Furthermore, we cannot but observe the epithet ἐξειλεγμένοις ('selected'), as it places Iamblichus in the tradition not only of Pythagoras, but also of Plato, who actually in the *Republic* expressed severe reservations on poetry and art in general, but in the end accepted the use of selected poems that would undeniably result in the proper education of the youth.[14] Iamblichus repeats his opinion on the use of selected passages at 92.20–22 using almost identical words with his first reference.[15] What is important is the fact that the Homeric tradition is used in order to cure the soul (πρὸς ἐπανόρθωσιν ψυχῆς). We are dealing with the healing power of the epics of Homer and Hesiod, or, as has been noted,[16] with a ritual use of Homeric poems. Iamblichus has

---

11 Porphyry, *De vita Pyth.* 1.13–2.1 (ἐπανελθόντα δ' εἰς τὴν Ἰωνίαν ἐντεῦθεν τὸν Πυθαγόραν πρῶτον μὲν Φερεκύδῃ τῷ Συρίῳ ὁμιλῆσαι, δεύτερον δ' Ἑρμοδάμαντι τῷ Κρεοφυλείῳ ἐν Σάμῳ ἤδη γηράσκοντι) and 15.5–8 (νοσήσαντα δὲ τὸν Φερεκύδην ἐν Δήλῳ θεραπεύσας ὁ Πυθαγόρας καὶ ἀποθανόντα θάψας εἰς Σάμον ἐπανῆλθεν πόθῳ τοῦ συγγενέσθαι Ἑρμοδάμαντι τῷ Κρεοφυλείῳ). For both passages, see Makris 2001, *ad loc.*
12 See Makris 2001, 37–45.
13 *De vita Pyth.* 64.14–15: χρῆσθαι δὲ καὶ Ὁμήρου καὶ Ἡσιόδου λέξεσιν ἐξειλεγμέναις πρὸς ἐπανόρθωσιν ψυχῆς. The use of the epic tradition by early Pythagoreans has been adequately stressed by Delatte 1915, 109–36; Boyancé 1937, 121ff.; Buffière 1956, 58–59; Detienne 1962, 18–36. According to Lamberton's analysis (1986, 31–43), the evidence for early Pythagorean concern with Homer is considerable, but we should nevertheless bear in mind that when we refer to their allegories we should not insist too strongly on distinct categories of physical, moral and mystical allegory. For all those issues, cf. Makris 2001, 158–59, n. 7; cf. also Manolea 2004, 26–28.
14 For a discussion on Plato's attitude towards art in general and poetry in particular the bibliographical references are numerous and date from the 19th century. In fact, the matter is far from being closed. From the huge bibliography on Plato's attitude towards art in general it is worth mentioning T. Gould's influential article (Gould 1964). For Plato's attitude towards poetry an interesting account is to be found in Murray 1996, 1–24. Furthermore, a brief but nice discussion on Plato's attitude towards Homer in particular can be found in Richardson 1993, 30–33. On this issue, cf. Murray 1996, 19–24; Manolea 2004, 28–33.
15 *De vita Pyth.* 92.20–22: ὑπελάμβανον δὲ καὶ τὴν μουσικὴν μεγάλα συμβάλλεσθαι πρὸς ὑγείαν, ἄν τις αὐτῇ χρῆται κατὰ τοὺς προσήκοντας τρόπους. ἐχρῶντο δὲ καὶ Ὁμήρου καὶ Ἡσιόδου λέξεσι διειλεγμέναις πρὸς ἐπανόρθωσιν ψυχῆς.
16 Lamberton 1986, 35.

probably taken the whole idea from Porphyry, who in his *De vita Pythagorica*[17] sustains exactly the same thing.

(iii) At 22.20 – 26 Homer is acknowledged to have done the right thing when he exalted the king of the gods with the title 'father of gods and mortals'.[18] The poet is immediately afterwards described as a myth maker; nevertheless Iamblichus points out that the characteristics he ascribed to Zeus were right from a Pythagorean point of view. In these words of Iamblichus we realize a clearly Pythagorizing attempt at giving a solution to the Platonic reservations towards poetry.[19]

(iv) Moreover, at 23.27– 24.7[20] we find an interesting moralizing interpretation of the *Iliad:* the whole poem deals with nothing less than the disastrous consequences of ἀκρασία ('lack of self-control') of a single man. Lamberton[21] has taken the man to be meant to have been Paris. According to this interpretation, had the younger son of Priam had some self-control, neither the barbarians (Trojans) nor the Greeks would have suffered terribly, as they did. If we follow this interpretation, Iamblichus claimed that the Trojans faced the consequence of war, i.e. the defeat and the destruction of their city. The Greeks in their turn faced difficulties when they sailed back home and were also granted with a ten-year and a thousand-year punishment. As far as the Trojans are concerned, the interpretation is fine, but in the case of the Greeks we have some problems. Why is the sailing back home mentioned? It has nothing to do with Paris, who had already been killed by Neoptolemus. And what about the ten-year and the thousand-year sentence as well as the maidens from Locroi?

It seems that each of the two parties suffered because of one man, but it was not the same man for both parties. For the Trojans it was Paris, but for the Greeks it was Ajax. We know that the rape of Cassandra by Ajax the Locrian took place at the altar of Athena, where Cassandra had sought refuge, and that it was

---

17 *De vita Pyth.* 32: καὶ ἐπῇδε τῶν Ὁμήρου καὶ Ἡσιόδου ὅσα καθημεροῦν τὴν ψυχὴν ἐδοκίμαζε. Cf. Makris 2001, *ad loc.*

18 *De vita Pyth.* 22.20 – 26: ὅθεν καὶ τὸν Ὅμηρον τῇ αὐτῇ προσηγορίᾳ τὸν βασιλέα τῶν θεῶν αὔξειν, ὀνομάζοντα πατέρα τῶν θεῶν καὶ τῶν θνητῶν, πολλοὺς δὲ καὶ τῶν ἄλλων μυθοποιῶν παραδεδωκέναι τοὺς βασιλεύοντας τῶν θεῶν τὴν μεριζομένην φιλοστοργίαν παρὰ τῶν τέκνων πρὸς τὴν ὑπάρχουσαν συζυγίαν τῶν γονέων καθ' αὐτοὺς περιποιήσασθαι πεφιλοτετιμημένους.

19 See above, n. 14.

20 *De vita Pyth.* 23.27 – 24.7: φανερὸν δὲ εἶναι καὶ διὰ τῆς ἀντικειμένης ἀντιθέσεως· τῶν γὰρ βαρβάρων καὶ τῶν Ἑλλήνων περὶ τὴν Τροίαν ἀντιταξαμένων ἑκατέρους δι'ἑνὸς ἀκρασίαν ταῖς δεινοτάταις περιπεσεῖν συμφοραῖς, τοὺς μὲν ἐν τῷ πολέμῳ, τοὺς δὲ κατὰ τὸν ἀνάπλουν, καὶ μόνης ⸢ταύτης⸣ τῆς ἀδικίας τὸν θεὸν δεκαετῆ καὶ χιλιετῆ τάξαι τὴν τιμωρίαν, χρησμῳδήσαντα τήν τε τῆς Τροίας ἅλωσιν καὶ τὴν τῶν παρθένων ἀποστολὴν παρὰ τῶν Λοκρῶν εἰς τὸ τῆς Ἀθηνᾶς τῆς Ἰλιάδος ἱερόν.

21 Lamberton 1986, 35.

avenged afterwards by Poseidon.[22] So, if in the case of the Greeks we perceive the man who did not control himself to have been Ajax, we interpret the passage correctly. Iamblichus is clearly referring to the sentence imposed on the habitants of Locroi and the maidens' account for the Locrian custom to send every year two virgins of their noblest families to serve in the temple of Athena Ilias. Therefore, Lamberton's interpretation of the audacious man is incomplete as to the Greeks (actually it was Ajax and not Paris).

Iamblichus thus proves himself to have been undoubtedly familiar with Cassandra's story. In any case, we should bear in mind that we are dealing with a moralizing interpretation of the Trojan War, which can well be characterized as Pythagorean.[23]

(v) At 31.10 – 16[24] Iamblichus mentions the effort of Calypso to bribe Odysseus, by giving him immortality, at the cost of forgetting and abandoning his legal wife Penelope. This *Odyssey* element is nicely exploited in the tradition of Pythagoras' teaching, as he is supposed to have been the one who made use of the episode and stressed that it took place near Croton. We may welcome this moralizing, Pythagorean use of a Homeric heroine as a clear shift from Plotinus, who at *Enn.* I 6.8.16 – 21 did not even make the distinction between Circe and Calypso.[25]

(vi) At 34.7–35.8[26] Pythagoras is reported to have claimed and proven that he himself in a previous life had been Euphorbus, son of Panthoos (the one who

---

22 This is a story of the wider tradition of the Trojan War. It is found in the *Iliou Persis* and the *Ilias Parva* cited in Proclus' account. For Cassandra as a prophetic figure and for her bad fate, see Davreux 1942, *passim*; Mason 1959, 80–93; Aélion 1983, 217–18. Cassandra's rape has also been depicted in art (for example, in fifth-century pottery Cassandra is often depicted at the moment that she clutches the image of Athena and Ajax seizes her).
23 See Lamberton 1986, 35.
24 *De vita Pyth.* 31.10–16: λέγεται δὲ καὶ τοιοῦτόν τι διελθεῖν, ὅτι περὶ τὴν χώραν τῶν Κροτωνιατῶν ἀνδρὸς μὲν ἀρετὴ πρὸς γυναῖκα διαβεβόηται, Ὀδυσσέως οὐ δεξαμένου παρὰ τῆς Καλυψοῦς ἀθανασίαν ἐπὶ τῷ τὴν Πηνελόπην καταλιπεῖν, ὑπολείποιτο δὲ ταῖς γυναιξὶν εἰς τοὺς ἄνδρας ἀποδείξασθαι τὴν καλοκαγαθίαν, ὅπως εἰς ἴσον καταστήσωσι τὴν εὐλογίαν.
25 See Lamberton 1986, 106–07.
26 *De vita Pyth.* 34.7–35.8: Ἀλλὰ μὴν τῆς γε τῶν ἀνθρώπων ἐπιμελείας ἀρχὴν ἐποιεῖτο τὴν ἀρίστην, ἥνπερ ἔδει προειληφέναι τοὺς μέλλοντας καὶ περὶ τῶν ἄλλων τὰ ἀληθῆ μαθήσεσθαι. ἐναργέστατα γὰρ καὶ σαφῶς ἀνεμίμνησκε τῶν ἐντυγχανόντων πολλοὺς τοῦ προτέρου βίου, ὃν αὐτῶν ἡ ψυχὴ πρὸ τοῦ τῷδε τῷ σώματι ἐνδεθῆναι πάλαι ποτὲ ἐβίωσε, καὶ ἑαυτὸν δὲ ἀναμφιλέκτοις τεκμηρίοις ἀπέφαινεν Εὔφορβον γεγονέναι Πάνθου υἱόν, τὸν Πατρόκλου καταγωνιστήν, καὶ τῶν Ὁμηρικῶν στίχων μάλιστα ἐκείνους ἐξύμνει καὶ μετὰ λύρας ἐμμελέστατα ἀνέμελπε καὶ πυκνῶς ἀνεφώνει, τοὺς ἐπιταφίους ἑαυτοῦ,

αἵματί οἱ δεύοντο κόμαι Χαρίτεσσιν ὁμοῖαι
πλοχμοί θ᾽ οἳ χρυσῷ τε καὶ ἀργύρῳ εὖ ἤσκηντο.
οἷον δὲ τρέφει ἔρνος ἀνὴρ ἐριθηλὲς ἐλαίης

wounded Patroclus[27] and later got killed by Menelaus).[28] Pythagoras is also reported to have cited and sung along with his lyre the corresponding Homeric passage (*Il.* 17.51–60). We notice that he is reported to have sung it more frequently than any other Homeric passage. The Pythagorean flavour of the context of the episode is evident.[29] What is more, exactly the same story appears at Porphyry's *De vita Pythagorica* 26.4–17,[30] whereas the fact that Euphorbus was the first in the line of Pythagoras' lives is also briefly mentioned at 45.4–5 of the same work.[31]

(vii) At 65.5–15[32] the line from *Od.* 4.221 is quoted in an anecdotological reference: Iamblichus holds that Empedocles sat, turned his lyre, played a soothing, calming melody and sang the aforementioned verse, which actually reports a soothing drug being prepared by Helen.[33] The result was that Empedocles saved both his host Anchitus from being murdered and a young man from committing the murder! Pythagoras is reported to have done more or less the same. It should be noted that both Porphyry and Iamblichus mention that Pythagoras ac-

---

χώρῳ ἐν οἰοπόλῳ, ὅθ' ἅλις ἀναβέβρυχεν ὕδωρ,
καλὸν τηλεθάον, τὸ δέ τε πνοιαὶ δονέουσι
παντοίων ἀνέμων, καί τε βρύει ἄνθεϊ λευκῷ,
ἐλθὼν δ' ἐξαπίνης ἄνεμος σὺν λαίλαπι πολλῇ
βόθρου τ' ἐξέστρεψε καὶ ἐξετάνυσσ' ἐπὶ γαίης·
τοῖον Πάνθου υἱὸν ἐυμελίην Εὔφορβον
Ἀτρείδης Μενέλαος, ἐπεὶ κτάνε, τεύχε' ἐσύλα.

27 *Il.* 16.806–15, where Euphorbus cowardly hits the disarmed Patroclus with a spear hurled at the small of his back and then retreats to the ranks. For an analysis of the passage, see Janko 1992, *ad loc.*
28 *Il.* 17.51–60. For a brief presentation of all the Homeric passages that include Euphorbus, see Edwards 1991, *ad loc.*
29 For a discussion of the issue of Pythagoras' own metempsychosis that includes many references to ancient sources, as well as to secondary bibliography, see Makris 2001, *ad loc.*
30 Porphyry, *De vita Pyth.* 26.4–17. The only difference is that instead of ἀπέφαινε Εὔφορβον τὸν Πάνθου Iamblichus wrote ἀπέφαινε Εὔφορβον γεγονέναι Πάνθου υἱόν, τὸν Πατρόκλου καταγωνιστήν. The rest of the quotation is exactly the same. It is evident that in an era of intertextuality Iamblichus used his master's work without bothering to change the exact words of the passage in question.
31 *Ibid.* 45.4–5: ἀνέφερεν δ' αὐτὸν εἰς τοὺς πρότερον γεγονότας, πρῶτον μὲν Εὔφορβος λέγων γενέσθαι.
32 *Ibid.* 65.5–15: Ἐμπεδοκλῆς δὲ σπασαμένου τὸ ξίφος ἤδη νεανίου τινὸς ἐπὶ τὸν αὐτοῦ ξενοδόχον Ἄγχιτον, ἐπεὶ δικάσας δημοσίᾳ τὸν τοῦ νεανίου πατέρα ἐθανάτωσε, καὶ ἀίξαντος, ὡς εἶχε συγχύσεως καὶ θυμοῦ, ξιφήρους παῖσαι τὸν τοῦ πατρὸς καταδικαστήν, ὡσανεὶ φονέα, Ἄγχιτον, μεθαρμοσάμενος ὡς εἶχε τὴν λύραν καὶ πεπαντικόν τι μέλος καὶ κατασταλτικὸν μεταχειρισάμενος εὐθὺς ἀνεκρούσατο τὸ νηπενθὲς ἄχολόν τε, κακῶν ἐπίληθον ἁπάντων κατὰ τὸν ποιητήν, καὶ τόν τε ἑαυτοῦ ξενοδόχον Ἄγχιτον θανάτου ἐρρύσατο καὶ τὸν νεανίαν ἀνδροφονίας.
33 For the verse in question, see Heubeck/ West/ Hainsworth 1997, *ad loc.*

tually used the healing power of music.[34] In the case we are discussing, though, it is Homer that both Empedocles and Pythagoras were reported to have sung. We regard the passage as evidence on the prestige and usefulness which certain Homeric material used to have in Pythagoras' circle. We should also mention that Plutarch interpreted the verse in question as allegory of Helen's bewitching eloquence.[35] It seems that both Empedocles and Pythagoras had realized this fact and, according to Iamblichus' account, used the verse appropriately.

(viii) An echo of *Il.* 13.13 (οὐ μέν με κτενέεις, ἐπεὶ οὔ τοι μόρσιμός εἰμι) is traced at 117.26–29.[36] Pythagoras is reported to have had suspicions that Phalaris wants to murder him, but at the same time knows that he is not fated to die at the hands of Phalaris. The whole concept of fate that dominates people's lives is a *topos* in ancient Greek tradition. Iamblichus' use presupposes its knowledge by the reader. We should perhaps add that the verse in question was used by ancient writers, such as Flavius Philostratus,[37] Eusebius[38] and also Eustathius Archbishop of Thessalonica.[39]

(ix) At 131.18–22 there is a reference to *Od.* 11.582–92, where Odysseus meets Tantalus during his journey to the Underworld.[40] It has been pointed out[41] that in

---

34 For the corresponding passages in both Porphyry and Iamblichus' *De vita Pyth.*, as well as for relevant bibliography, see Makris 2001, 280–81, n. 113.
35 See Plutarch *Mor.* 614b; cf. Heubeck/ West/ Hainsworth 1988, *ad loc.*
36 *De vita Pyth.* 117.26–29: ὁ δὲ Φάλαρις καὶ πρὸς ταῦτα ἠναισχύντει τε καὶ ἀπεθρασύνετο. αὖθις οὖν ὁ Πυθαγόρας, ὑποπτεύων μὲν ὅτι Φάλαρις αὐτῷ ῥάπτοι θάνατον, ὅμως δὲ εἰδὼς ὡς οὐκ εἴη Φαλάριδι μόρσιμος, ἐξουσιαστικῶς ἐπεχείρει λέγειν.
37 Philostr. *VA* 8.5.46–50: δός, εἰ βούλοιο, κἀμοὶ τόπον, εἰ δὲ μή, πέμπε τὸν ληψόμενόν μου τὸ σῶμα, τὴν γὰρ ψυχὴν ἀδύνατον μᾶλλον δὲ οὐδ' ἂν τὸ σῶμα τοὐμὸν λάβοις,

οὐ γάρ με κτενέεις, ἐπεὶ οὔτοι μόρσιμός εἰμι.

Cf. also *ibid.* 8.8.1–5: ὧδε μὲν δὴ τῷ ἀνδρὶ τὰ ἐκ παρασκευῆς εἶχεν, επι τελευτῃ δ' εὗρον τοῦ λόγου τὰ τελευταῖα τοῦ προτέρου τὸ

οὐ γάρ με κτενέεις, ἐπεὶ οὔτοι μόρσιμός εἰμι,

καὶ τὰ πρὸ τούτου ἔτι, ἀφ'ὧν τοῦτο.
38 Eus. *Contra Ieroclem* 401.12–21: ἐν τῷ δικαστηρίῳ αὐτὰ δὴ ταῦτα ἀναφωνῆσαι "δός, εἰ βούλει, κἀμοὶ τόπον, εἰ δὲ μή, πέμπε τὸν ληψόμενόν μου τὸ σῶμα, τὴν γὰρ ψυχὴν ἀδύνατον. μᾶλλον δὲ οὐδ' ἂν τὸ σῶμα τοὐμὸν λάβοις·

οὐ γάρ με κτενέεις, ἐπεὶ οὔτοι μόρσιμός εἰμι",

καὶ δὴ ἐπὶ τούτῳ τῷ περιβοήτῳ ῥήματι ἀφανισθῆναι τοῦ δικαστηρίου φησὶν αὐτόν, καὶ ἐν τούτοις τὸ περὶ αὑτοῦ καταστρέφει δρᾶμα.
39 Schol. Eust. on *Il.* 4.563.2 (van der Valk): λέγει δὲ μόρσιμον ἀπολύτως ἐνταῦθα ὁ ποιητὴς τὸν μοίρᾳ ὑποκείμενον.
40 *De vita Pyth.* 131.18–22: αὐτὸν δὲ συνεπικρύπτεσθαι πολὺ τῶν λεγομένων, ὅπως οἱ μὲν καθαρῶς παιδευόμενοι σαφῶς αὐτῶν μεταλαμβάνωσιν, οἱ δ' ὥσπερ Ὅμηρός φησι τὸν Τάνταλον, λυπῶνται παρόντων αὐτῶν ἐν μέσῳ τῶν ἀκουσμάτων μηδὲν ἀπολαύοντες.
41 Heubeck/ Hoekstra 1989, *ad loc.*

the *Odyssey* no reason for Tantalus' punishment is given – the poet takes for granted his audience's knowledge of the cause of these sufferings. Iamblichus' point is the following: as Tantalus could neither eat nor drink, despite the fact that everything was placed around him, this was exactly the case with Pythagoras' teachings, which were all around, yet those who were not trained could not profit from them. We see the criticism Iamblichus addresses to those who have not made the same choice. The readers' familiarity with Tantalus story has undoubtedly played its role to Iamblichus' choice to place it in this context.

(x) At 137.17–23[42] Iamblichus says that no Pythagorean called Pythagoras by his name; when they wanted to refer to him in his lifetime, they called him divine ('godlike': τὸν θεῖον), whereas after his death 'That Man' (ἄνδρα). Iamblichus rightly mentions that in the *Odyssey* the shepherd Eumaios is embarrassed to utter the name of Odysseus, in spite of the fact that the king is absent. Then, the corresponding verses are quoted (*Od.* 14.144–45). We are dealing with the well-known issue of how the Pythagoreans showed their respect towards Pythagoras through sacred silence (εὐφημία), an element common in many mystic cults.[43] The fact that a Homeric parallel is being used in the context of such an important issue speaks of Homer's prestige in the Pythagoreans.

(xi) At 139.21[44] the common Homeric expression ποιμὴν λαῶν[45] is reported to have been used by the Pythagoreans, in order to denote that ordinary people are nothing less than cattle which need a shepherd. In fact, Iamblichus holds that Homer actually denoted a preference towards oligarchy by using this expression. This view about ordinary people did, of course, fit to the oligarchic character of the Pythagorean societies. Thus, this passage is a rather interesting testimony of

---

42 *De vita Pyth.* 137.17–23: ἐπὶ μὲν γὰρ τῷ μηδένα τῶν Πυθαγορείων ὀνομάζειν Πυθαγόραν, ἀλλὰ ζῶντα μέν, ὁπότε βούλοιντο δηλῶσαι, καλεῖν αὐτὸν θεῖον, ἐπεὶ δὲ ἐτελεύτησεν, ἐκεῖνον τὸν ἄνδρα, καθάπερ Ὅμηρος ἀποφαίνει τὸν Εὔμαιον ὑπὲρ Ὀδυσσέως μεμνημένον·

τὸν μὲν ἐγών, ὦ ξεῖνε, καὶ οὐ παρεόντ' ὀνομάζειν
αἰδέομαι· πέρι γάρ μ' ἐφίλει καὶ ἐκήδετο λίην.

43 For the sacred silence (εὐφημία) in general, see Burkert 1985, 73, 199, 248, 273. For the sacred silence in the Pythagoreans, as well as for Pythagoras' authority for the antecedents, see Barnes 1982, 100 03.

44 *De vita Pyth.* 139.17–23: τὴν αὐτὴν ταύτην γνώμην ὑπὲρ Πυθαγόρου μεμνημένους ἐν μέτρῳ τοὺς μαθητὰς λέγειν·

τοὺς μὲν ἑταίρους ἦγεν ἴσον μακάρεσσι θεοῖσι,
τοὺς δ' ἄλλους ἡγεῖτ' οὔτ' ἐν λόγῳ οὔτ' ἐν ἀριθμῷ.

τὸν Ὅμηρον μάλιστ' ἐπαινεῖν ἐν οἷς εἴρηκε ποιμένα λαῶν· ἐμφανίσκειν γὰρ βοσκήματα τοὺς ἄλλους ὄντας, ὀλιγαρχικὸν ὄντα.

45 See, for example, *Il.* 1.226, 2.85, 2.105, 2.243, 2.254, 2.772, 4.173, 4.176.

how any work of art and its elements may be used freely by antecedents, so as to serve not only artistic but also political purposes.

b. *Protrepticus*

In the *Protrepticus*, a work in which Pythagorean and Platonic elements play a major role,[46] we find two references that actually refer to well-known episodes from the *Odyssey* – yet their transmission is an indirect one.

(i) At 69.22–70.9[47] we read that the famous weaving trick of Penelope (*Od.* 2.92–95) is a useless activity of the irrational man, whose passions imprison it during the night, while philosophy frees it during the day. What is important is that we are dealing with an indirect reception of Homer through Plato, as the *Protrepticus* passage which we are discussing (69.22–70.9) actually belongs to the section 67.18–70.9, where *Phaedo* 82b–84b is quoted, and reproduces *Phaedo* 84a–b. In this case, then, the Homeric reference is actually Plato's choice. The latter, as we have noted, is treated by Iamblichus as being in harmony with Pythagoras' spirit.

(ii) Similarly, the reference to Achilles' words that he would rather be the last man on earth but still alive than a king in Hades, as he currently is (*Od.* 11.489– 90), actually belongs to a passage where the *Republic* is used by Iamblichus. *Protrepticus* 78.1–82.4 actually quotes *R.* 514a–517c. To be more specific, the reference to Achilles' words is found at *Protrepticus* 80.23–81.6[48] and actually repeats

---

[46] Iamblichus' *Protrepticus* has been characterized as an anthology of Platonic philosophy. Many of its passages are no other than known Platonic passages carefully chosen and elaborately interwoven between one another, as L. Benakis notes (Benakis 2012, 19), but still Plato's passages are believed to be in harmony with Pythagoras' spirit (Benakis 2012, 15). The work also contains a major part of Aristotle's *Protrepticus*. For the work's relation to Aristotle's *Protrepticus*, see P. Kotzia-Panteli 2002, 111–32.

[47] *Protrepticus* 69.22–70.9: ἀλλ' οὕτω λογίσαιτ' ἂν ψυχὴ ἀνδρὸς φιλοσόφου, καὶ οὐκ ἂν οἰηθείη τὴν μὲν φιλοσοφίαν χρῆναι ἑαυτὴν λύειν λυούσης δὲ ἐκείνης αὐτὴν παραδιδόναι ταῖς ἡδοναῖς καὶ λύπαις ἑαυτὴν πάλιν αὖ ἐγκαταδεῖν καὶ ἀνήνυτον ἔργον πράττειν, Πενελόπης τινὰ ἐναντίως ἱστὸν μεταχειριζομένης· ἀλλὰ γαλήνην τούτων παρασκευάζουσα, ἑπομένη τῷ λογισμῷ καὶ ἀεὶ ἐν τούτῳ οὖσα, τὸ ἀληθὲς καὶ τὸ θεῖον καὶ τὸ ἀδόξαστον θεωμένη καὶ ὑπ' ἐκείνου τρεφομένη, ζῆν τε οἴεται οὕτω δεῖν ἕως ἂν ζῇ, καὶ ἐπειδὰν τελευτήσῃ εἰς τὸ ξυγγενὲς καὶ εἰς τὸ τοιοῦτον ἀφικομένη ἀπηλλάχθαι τῶν ἀνθρωπίνων κακῶν.

[48] *Protrepticus* 80.23–81.6: τιμαὶ δὲ καὶ ἔπαινοι εἴ τινες ἦσαν αὐτοῖς τότε παρ' ἀλλήλων καὶ γέρα τῷ ὀξύτατα καθορῶντι τὰ παριόντα, καὶ μνημονεύοντι μάλιστα ὅσα τε πρότερα αὐτῶν καὶ ὕστερα εἴωθε καὶ ἅμα πορεύεσθαι, καὶ ἐκ τούτων δὴ δυνατώτατα ἀπομαντευομένῳ τὸ μέλλον ἥξειν, δοκεῖς ἂν αὐτὸν ἐπιθυμητικῶς αὐτῶν ἔχειν καὶ ζηλοῦν τοὺς παρ' ἐκείνοις τιμωμένους τε καὶ ἐνδυναστεύοντας, ἢ τὸ τοῦ Ὁμήρου ἂν πεπονθέναι καὶ σφόδρα βούλεσθαι ἐπάρουρον ἐόντα θητευέμεν ἄλλῳ

R. 516d–e. Nonetheless, it is worth noticing that, although Plato himself had condemned and censored the Homeric verses in question at *R.* 386c, he used them at 516d–e without reservation–and so did Iamblichus, without saying anything on the matter. We therefore conclude that we are dealing with another indirect transmission of Homer through Plato, who used the famous words of Achilles in his discussion of the cave myth. We should not forget either that in Iamblichus' work in question Plato is employed in a Pythagorean perspective.

c. *De Mysteriis*

At *De mysteriis* 8.18.18[49] there is a negative reference to Homeric gods: according to the philosopher, it is not appropriate to refer to Homeric gods, as they may be turned by prayer. The latter characteristic is clearly stated at *Il.* 9.497. Iamblichus obviously expresses his disagreement with a common feature of Homeric gods, thus placing himself in the chain of the philosophers who criticized Homer on the image of the gods he provides his audience or his readers.

Concluding remarks

On the basis of the exploration of the Homeric passages in Iamblichus, the first thing to remark is that Iamblichus in some cases of his *De vita Pythagorica* seems to have taken the Homeric material directly from Porphyry's *De vita Pythagorica*, whereas in the *Protrepticus* he used Platonic material which contained Homeric elements. But still, all Homeric passages in Iamblichus have not been indirectly transmitted. We have a rather satisfying number of passages where Iamblichus himself chose to include Homer. Moreover, we should mention the fact that in Iamblichus' existing works the number of passages from the *Odyssey* are not considerably less in number compared to those from the *Iliad*. This is something to note, as in most writers of the Hellenistic age and Late Antiquity the quotations from the *Iliad* are considerably more numerous. This may be attributed to the possibility of Iamblichus' having an ear towards the *Odyssey*. After all, the adherence to the text of the *Odyssey* might well be attributed to Porphyry's influence. In any case, Iamblichus was certain that his own audience would

---

ἀνδρὶ παρ' ἀκλήρῳ καὶ ὁτιοῦν ἂν πεπονθέναι μᾶλλον ἢ ἐκεῖνά τε δοξάζειν καὶ ἐκείνως ζῆν; οὕτως ἔγωγε οἶμαι, πᾶν μᾶλλον πεπονθέναι ἂν δέξασθαι ἢ ζῆν ἐκείνως.

49 *De mysteriis* 8.18.18: ὥστε οὐδ' ὅπερ ἐκ τῶν Ὁμηρικῶν σὺ παρέθηκας, τὸ στρεπτοὺς εἶναι τοὺς θεούς, ὅσιόν ἐστι φθέγγεσθαι.

be familiar with both Homeric poems, and so he would be free to choose whatever material he saw fit for his own purposes.

We should also point out that the majority of Homeric references are to be found in the *De vita Pythagorica,* a work that actually aims at providing the reader with a Pythagorean way of living and thinking, while the *Protrepticus* seems to bear Platonic elements, which are considered in a Pythagorean perspective. Of course, as a proper Neoplatonist Iamblichus widely receives Platonic philosophy, and this might account for the only negative reference to Homer in the *De mysteriis*. In any case, the Pythagorean flavour of the Homeric reception actually shows that Homer's prestige in Iamblichus' eyes was far from being negligible.

Moreover, Iamblichus' reception of Homer is developed in the context of his own Neoplatonic philosophy that bears Pythagorean elements. The selection of Homer as a source text in cases where philosophical matters are discussed is by no means accidental. Having undoubtedly a sound knowledge of Homer, as his education denotes, Iamblichus does not refer to Homer much; he nevertheless does so in cases where his master used to do so or when he considers it fit to his argumentation. He knows his audience to be familiar with the Homeric text–nevertheless, his aim is not to explain Homer, as his teacher Porphyry did, but to enrich his own Neoplatonic philosophical *exegesis*.

Part IV **Hellenistic and Later Receptions**

Maria Kanellou
Ἑρμιόνην, ἣ εἶδος ἔχε χρυσέης Ἀφροδίτης (*Od.* 4.14): Praising a Female through Aphrodite – From Homer into Hellenistic Epigram*

It is firstly in the Homeric epics that one finds the idea of a woman being praised through her comparison to one of the goddesses, especially Aphrodite, the archetype of beauty and sexuality; formulas of the type εἶδος ἔχε χρυσέης Ἀφροδίτης (*Od.* 4.14) are usually employed for this purpose.[1] My aim in this chapter is to examine the reception of this motif in the surviving poems of the Hellenistic epigrammatists and to exemplify how its transformations are closely connected to and influenced by several factors: changes in the religious practices that took place during the Hellenistic era, the use of the goddess Aphrodite within the framework of the Ptolemaic political propaganda and the generic characteristics of specific sub-categories of epigrams. An appreciation of the motif's reuse in the poetry of the archaic and classical era is essential, because it enables the identification of the advances which the Hellenistic epigrammatists brought about.

With the exception of the Homeric epics, no surviving poetic text that dates to the archaic and classical periods openly equates a mortal's charms with a goddess' beauty: as we shall see through characteristic case-studies, the praise is always somehow restrained, and the gap between mortals and gods is always maintained. On the contrary, in the Hellenistic era, and especially in the Meleagrean epigrams (first century BC), the motif is transformed in manners that transcend the gap between deities and humans. Let us first examine two Sapphic fragments (frr. 96.4–5 and 31.1–5 Voigt) which exemplify the restraint in the reception of the motif during the archaic times:

---

* I would like to thank S. Budin, A. Griffiths, S. Chatzikosta, L. Floridi, R. Höschele and above all C. Carey for the critical reading and comments on earlier drafts of this chapter. It goes without saying that any views expressed are mine alone.
[1] See the Homeric formulae ἰκέλη χρυσέῃ Ἀφροδίτῃ (*Od.* 17.37, 19.54, *Il.* 19.282, 24.699) and οὐδ' εἰ χρυσείῃ Ἀφροδίτῃ κάλλος ἐρίζοι (*Il.* 9.389). In a similar vein, in *Od.* 18.190–96, Athena bestows on queen Penelope irresistible, divine attractiveness. In *Od.* 6.149–57, Odysseus extols Nausicaa's godlike virginal beauty by asking her whether she is a goddess or a mortal, and then, by comparing her to Artemis in stature and comeliness. His praise is restrained because he entertains the possibility of the girl being a goddess and never states that she is a goddess (cf. *Od.* 6.16). For the topic of the comparison of men with gods, see Bieler 1935/1936, *passim*.

σε θέαι σ' ἰκέλαν ἀρι-
γνώται, σᾶι δὲ μάλιστ' ἔχαιρε μόλπαι.
(fr. 96.4–5)

*(She honoured) you as being an easily
recognized goddess, and took most delight in your song.*[2]

φαίνεταί μοι κῆνος ἴσος θέοισιν
ἔμμεν' ὤνηρ, ὄττις ἐνάντιός τοι
ἰσδάνει καὶ πλάσιον ἆδυ φωνεί-
σας ὐπακούει
καὶ γελαίσας ἰμέροεν...
(fr. 31.1–5)

*He seems as equal to the gods to me
the one who sits opposite you
and listens nearby to your sweet voice
and lovely laughter...*
(trans. Campbell 2002 with minor adjustments)

In fr. 96.4–5 Atthis is commended for resembling a goddess. In fr. 31.1–2 the man who sits opposite to a woman and listens to her voice and laughter is said to be 'equal to the gods'. This phrase either denotes that the man is blessed to see the woman or extols his ability to resist her attractiveness; in either case, it simultaneously praises her beauty indirectly. In both fragments, the hyperbole is controlled as the statements are expressed as forming subjective thoughts, and not an objective, incontrovertible truth. The reason for this caution in the formulation of praise lies in the religious considerations of Sappho's era: expressing superiority over the gods would be profoundly dangerous, because it would provoke their wrath.[3] Sappho herself highlights the religious beliefs of her time when she says in fr. 96 21–23: 'it is not suitable for us to rival goddesses in loveliness of figure'. In Homer, the hyperbole is permitted, as the epics praise mythic heroes and heroines, not living contemporaries.

Ibycus fr. 288 Davies proves that similar modes of praise were used for the male beloved, and moreover, preserves a variation of the motif which, as we shall see, was widely imitated and refreshed by the Hellenistic epigrammatists: the boy's seductive charms are extolled as deriving from the co-operation of a group of deities.

---

2 For the supplement ἔτι]σε and the interpretation of the MS σεθεασϊκελαν, see Page 1979, 89.
3 See e.g. Hdt.7.10, Pi. P. 8.15–20, I. 5.14–16. See also Call. *Ap.* 25 and Williams 1978, 35–36 for further relevant passages.

Εὐρύαλε γλαυκέων Χαρίτων θάλος < >
καλλικόμων μελέδημα, σὲ μὲν Κύπρις
ἅ τ' ἀγανοβλέφαρος Πει-
θὼ ῥοδέοισιν ἐν ἄνθεσι θρέψαν.

Euryalus, offshoot of the blue-eyed Graces,
darling of the beautiful-haired (Seasons), the Cyprian
and soft-lidded Peitho
nursed you among rose-blossoms.
(trans. Campbell 2001 with minor adjustments)

It should be stressed that Ibycus does not equate Euryalus either to Aphrodite or her attendants; his beauty is definitely idealized, but he is not portrayed as excelling his patron deities.[4] The precise means through which each deity makes him irresistible is left vague, but the audience can easily envisage a chain of attributes.[5]

From the relevant poetic texts of the classical era, I use as my case-study (due to space limitations) Aristophanes *Ec.* 973–75.[6] The motif is here used in a burlesque of lyric love songs, especially of the *paraclausithyron*:[7] a girl is extolled through her association with multiple deities:

ὦ χρυσοδαίδαλτον ἐμὸν
μέλημα, Κύπριδος ἔρνος,
μέλιττα Μούσης, Χαρίτων

---

[4] Breitenberger (2007, 186) is wrong to suggest that Euryalus 'in his beauty [...] seems equal to these divine beings, or even superior since, due to his origin, he combines all of their qualities'. What the poem does is to make him a favourite of the gods; his beauty and charm reflect divine favour.
[5] Elsewhere, the Graces and the Seasons adorn Aphrodite, and their role implies the granting of alluring beauty and seductiveness: *H.Hom.Ven.* 61–66 and *Od.* 8.362–66 (after her affair with Ares), and *Cypr.* fr. 4.1–7 Davies/Bernabé (before Paris' Judgment). As far as Peitho is concerned, she can confer physical attraction, the power of persuasion, and alluring talk (cf. e.g. Rufinus *AP* 5.70.1 = 26.1 Page, Meleager *AP* 5.137.1 = 43.1 GP, Meleager *AP* 5.195.6 = 39.6 GP and Leontius Scholasticus *APl* 288.1). Aphrodite can be thought of as bequeathing various charms, such as beauty and seductiveness (cf. e.g. Hes. *Th.* 203–06 describing Aphrodite's province and referring to these attributes). Similar is the tenor of Ibycus S257 (a) 6–12 Davies.
[6] Another interesting passage is E. *Hec.*354–56, where Polyxena says that among young girls she was conspicuous, like the gods in all but her mortality. Here, the hyperbole is explicitly tempered by a firm statement of the unbridgeable boundary between mortals and immortal gods. Cf. *Od.* 6.15–17, where Nausicaa is said to resemble the immortal goddesses in stature and beauty. The princess is mortal while the goddesses are deathless, and this maintains strict boundaries between them.
[7] For the 'love-duet' (Ar. *Ec.* 952–75) as a sophisticated literary parody of the *paraclausithyron*, see Olson 1988, 328–30.

θρέμμα, Τρυφῆς πρόσωπον,
ἄνοιξον, ἀσπάζου με·
διά τοι σὲ πόνους ἔχω.

Oh my golden work of art,
my darling, scion of Cypris,
honeybee of the Muses, nursling
of the Graces, the image of Delight,
open – welcome me;
it's for you that I am suffering so.
(ed. and trans. Sommerstein 2007 with minor adjustments)

As far as Aphrodite is concerned, a metaphorical relationship is implied between the girl and the goddess (through the use of the term ἔρνος) with the praise stressing the former's beauty and sexuality.[8] Her characterization as the honeybee of the Muse(s) extols her singing skills (a bee produces honey),[9] but also points to the distress that she has caused the boy because of his longing for her (a bee can also sting, cf. *Ec.* 968–70). Her description as 'the very image of Delight' is also ambiguous, both stressing the softness of her skin and implying her luxuriousness.[10] So, as in Ibycus' fr. 288 Davies, the girl is not equated with and does not surpass her benefactors; the praise is restrained and mortals remain at arm's length from the divine.

When we now move on to the epigrams, at the first stages of the genre's development as a literary genre and throughout the third century BC, no clear and unambiguous comparison between a common mortal woman and the goddess exists. I start my analysis of the epigrammatic material with Nossis, whose collection dates from 280 or 270 BC.[11] *AP* 6.275 (= 5 GP) and *AP* 9.332 (= 4 GP) exemplify this tendency for maintaining a clear boundary between mortals and gods: in both of them, only very indirect links are created between the devotees and Aphrodite; the poems toy very discreetly with the idea of a mortal woman resembling the deity, in that they all share the same qualities of beauty and/or slyness:[12]

---

[8] See *LSJ*[9], s.v. ἔρνος I 1, II 1. One can compare γλαυκέων Χαρίτων θάλος in Ibycus fr. 288.1.
[9] Cf. Ussher 1973, 211.
[10] See *LSJ*[9], s.v. τρυφή I, II. Cf. Sommerstein 2007, 222.
[11] See Gutzwiller 1998, 74–75.
[12] Gutzwiller (1998, 83) is fundamental for the interpretation of these epigrams. She argues that the women and Aphrodite are linked together by shared qualities 'in both external appearance and its internal reflection'. Her analysis focuses on the thematic links among the devotees and not between them and Aphrodite. I revisit the epigrams with the aim to show the special link that is created between the women and the goddess. For the interrelation between Aphrodite and her devotees, as expressed in votive epigrams, see also Natsina 2012, 249–79.

ἐλθοῖσαι ποτὶ ναὸν ἰδώμεθα τᾶς Ἀφροδίτας
  τὸ βρέτας ὡς χρυσῷ δαιδαλόεν τελέθει.
εἵσατό μιν Πολυαρχὶς ἐπαυρομένα μάλα πολλάν
  κτῆσιν ἀπ' οἰκείου σώματος ἀγλαΐας.
(AP 9.332 = 4 GP)

Let us go to the temple and see Aphrodite's statue,
how intricately it is adorned with gold.
Polyarchis set it up, enjoying the benefits of the great wealth
that she has from the beauty of her own body.

χαίροισάν τοι ἔοικε κομᾶν ἄπο τὰν Ἀφροδίταν
  ἄνθεμα κεκρύφαλον τόνδε λαβεῖν Σαμύθας,
δαιδάλεός τε γάρ ἐστι καὶ ἁδύ τι νέκταρος ὄσδει·
  τούτῳ καὶ τήνα καλὸν Ἄδωνα χρίει.
(AP 6.275 = 5 GP)

With joy, I think, Aphrodite has received this gift,
a headband from Samytha's hair.
For it is variegated and smells somewhat of sweet nectar;
with this she, too, anoints handsome Adonis.
(trans. Gutzwiller 1998 with minor adjustments)

In *AP* 9.332 Nossis plays with the natural assumption that, since Aphrodite is the goddess of seduction, and seduction is the trade of the hetaerae, she and her devotee share the same qualities. Implicit clues suggest a certain degree of resemblance between Polyarchis and Aphrodite. Specifically, it is the adjectives χρυσῷ and δαιδαλόεν (l.2), describing the statue, that hint at these shared qualities, as they create a triangular link between the goddess, her devotee and the devoted object. At a first glance, the epithet χρυσῷ refers to the gilt surface of the statue (or to the metal from which it is made[13]) and δαιδαλόεν to an elaborate pattern on its surface (perhaps to the garment that covers the statue's body).[14] But χρυσῷ also encapsulates the goddess's beauty, which is mirrored in her statue,[15] and anticipates the explanation provided for the source of Polyarchis'

---

[13] We can take the statue to be gilted (cf. Gow-Page 1965, ii 438, Gutzwiller 1998, 82), or (less likely) follow the lemmatist (C) and take it to be made entirely of gold — this hyperbole would highlight Polyarchis' wealth.
[14] Derivatives of δαιδάλλω are often used in the praise of objects that are decorated with intricate motifs, see e.g. *Il.* 18.481–82 of the shield made by Hephaestus; A.R. 1.728–29 of the mantle that Athena gave to Jason; Mosch. 43 of Europa's golden basket. Cf. Ar. *Ec.* 973.
[15] The adjective constitutes Aphrodite's most common characterization from archaic times onwards. See e.g. *Od.* 8.337, 8.342, 17.37, *Il.* 3.64, 5.427, 9.389, 19.282, 22.470, 24.699. For the characterization of Aphrodite as 'golden', see Friedrich 1978, 77–79. For a funny reading of the Homeric epithet, see Luc. *J. Tr.* 10. Other poets, in a sceptic context, link the epithet with prostitution

wealth; it was the beauty of her body that enabled her to make such an offering (l. 4).¹⁶ Similarly, the adjective δαιδαλόεν can be interpreted as a *double-entendre* that indicates the 'cunning' nature both of Aphrodite, whose figure the statue represents,¹⁷ and of Polyarchis who devoted the object to the goddess. One may juxtapose the adjective's use in the epigram to Hes. *Th.* 574–75, where the word stands for the embroidered design of Pandora's veil, but, most importantly, hints at the cunning of its wearer and of the gods who created Pandora to wreak vengeance upon humans: ζῶσε δὲ καὶ κόσμησε θεὰ γλαυκῶπις Ἀθήνη/ ἀργυφέῃ ἐσθῆτι· κατὰ κρῆθεν δὲ καλύπτρην/ δαιδαλέην χείρεσσι κατέσχεθε, θαῦμα ἰδέσθαι ('...and with her hands she [i.e. Athena] hung an intricately wrought veil from her head, a wonder to see').¹⁸

Nossis *AP* 6.275 illustrates the dedication of another object, i.e. of a headband by a woman called Samytha. The adjective δαιδάλεος (l. 3) describing the object¹⁹ most probably creates a verbal link with δαιδαλόεν in *AP* 9.332.2 and can be considered as a pointer towards the woman's crafty nature, a characteristic that she shares with Aphrodite. Moreover, the nectar used by Samytha links her to Aphrodite, since it is (supposedly) the same one with the nectar that the goddess used to anoint Adonis' body (see the emphatic use of τούτῳ in l.4). This hyperbolic statement accentuates the praise of the sensual appeal of the dedicated object, and incidentally implies that it is worthy of its recipient. It praises Samytha, embellishing her with divine beauty and sexuality. A comparison with Sappho fr. 94.18–20 Voigt discloses the development in the mode of praise: καὶ π.....[ ]. μύρωι/ βρενθείωι. [ ]ρυ[..]ν/ ἐξαλ<ε>ίψαο κα[ὶ βασ]ιληίωι. In the Sapphic fragment the girl's sexuality is praised through the idea that she anoints herself with flowery myrrh, the customary means for beautifying queens. In the epigram, in a more hyperbolic manner, Samytha uses nectar. However, de-

---

(an easy association as Aphrodite was the patroness of the hetaerae), see e. g. *AP* 5.30 = 6 GPh and *AP* 5.31 = 112 GPh (Antipater of Thessalonica). For the association between the gods and gold, see Williams 1978, 39.

16 Gutzwiller 1998, 82–83.

17 There is rich intertextual background on Aphrodite's wily nature. E. g. in Hes. *Th.* 205 deceits (ἐξαπάτας) form part of her realm of power; in *H.Hom.*5.249–51 she herself connects her power over gods with skills that have to do with seduction and trickery; in lyric poetry she is characterized as 'wile-weaving': Sapph. fr.1.2 Voigt: παῖ Δ[ί]ος δολ[όπλοκε, Simon. fr. 541.9–10 *PMG*: ἢ δολοπλ[όκου ...'Ἀφροδίτ[ας and fr. 575.1 *PMG*: ... δολομήδεος Ἀφροδίτας, Bacch. *Dith.* 17.116: ... δόλιος Ἀφροδίτα.

18 Hes.*Th.* 574–75 is also noted by Gutzwiller 1998, 82. Translation by Most 2006, 49, slightly altered.

19 The term δαιδάλεος denotes that the headband was embroidered or that it consisted of various colours (Gow-Page 1965, ii 438).

spite the exaggeration, Samytha is only indirectly linked to the goddess, and a clear boundary is maintained between them.

By examining now the epigrams of Posidippus and Callimachus, who flourished during the third century BC, we detect that these court poets associated only the Hellenistic queens to Aphrodite, and did not openly compare any other woman to the goddess. Only *AP* 5.194 (= 34 GP), which might have been written by a court poet,[20] associates a girl with Aphrodite. However, as we shall see, there is no effort to identify the girl with the deity. Three Posidippean epigrams openly equate Arsinoe II (316 BC–270 BC or 268 BC[21]) with Aphrodite and refer to the queen's cult at her temple on Cape Zephyrium:[22]

> ἔνθα με Καλλικράτης ἱδρύσατο καὶ βασιλίσσης
> ἱερὸν Ἀρσινόης Κύπριδος ὠνόμασεν.
> ἀλλ' ἐπὶ τὴν Ζεφυρῖτιν ἀκουσομένην Ἀφροδίτην,
> Ἑλλήνων ἁγναί, βαίνετε, θυγατέρες,
> οἵ θ' ἁλὸς ἐργάται ἄνδρες· ὁ γὰρ ναύαρχος ἔτευξεν
> τοῦθ' ἱερὸν παντὸς κύματος εὐλίμενον.
> (116.5–10 AB = 12 GP)

Here Callicrates set me up and called me
the shrine of Queen Arsinoe-Aphrodite.
So, then, to her who will be called Zephyritis-Aphrodite,
come, you pure daughters of the Greeks,
and you too toilers on the sea. For the captain built
this shrine to be a harbour safe from every wave.

> τοῦτο καὶ ἐν πόντῳ καὶ ἐπὶ χθονὶ τῆς Φιλαδέλφου
> Κύπριδος ἱλάσκεσθ' ἱερὸν Ἀρσινόης,
> ἣν ἀνακοιρανέουσαν ἐπὶ Ζεφυρίτιδος ἀκτῆς
> πρῶτος ὁ ναύαρχος θήκατο Καλλικράτης·
> ἡ δὲ καὶ εὐπλοίην δώσει καὶ χείματι μέσσῳ
> τὸ πλατὺ λισσομένοις ἐκλιπανεῖ πέλαγος.
> (119 AB = 13 GP)

---

20 i.e. Posidippus, who was definitely a court poet, or Asclepiades, for whom it is uncertain whether he worked under Ptolemaic patronage or not. For the ascription of the epigram, see Guichard 2004, 383–85, Sens 2011, 228. No firm conclusion can be drawn for the authorship.
21 Arsinoe's death is dated to 270 BC (see Cadell 1998, 1–3), but the alternative date of 268 BC has been proposed as well (Grzybeck 1990, 103–12).
22 The temple was erected by Callicrates, the naval admiral of the Ptolemies. For Callicrates, see Bing 2002/2003, 243–66. Cf. Stephens 2004, 163–70 for the identification of the armed Arsinoe with Athena in 36 AB; Bing 2002/2003 identifies the goddess in this epigram with Aphrodite. *APl* (A) 68 = 39 GP (Asclepiades/Posidippus) also praises a Ptolemaic queen, most probably Berenice I, by associating her with Aphrodite. I am not analyzing this epigram due to space limitations.

*Both on the sea and on land make offerings to this shrine
of Cypris Arsinoe Philadelphus.
She it was, ruling over the Zephyrian promontory,
whom Callicrates, the captain, was the first to consecrate.
And she will grant safe sailing and in the middle of the storm
will smooth the vast sea for those who entreat her.*

καὶ μέλλων ἅλα νηΐ περᾶν καὶ πεῖσμα καθάπτειν
 χερσόθεν, Εὐπλοίᾳ 'χαῖρε' δὸς Ἀρσινόῃ,
πό]τνιαν ἐκ νηοῦ καλέων θεόν, ἣν ὁ Βοΐσκου
 ναυαρχῶν Σάμιος θήκατο Καλλικράτης,
ναυτίλε, σοὶ τὰ μάλιστα·
(39.1–5 AB)

*Whether you are ready to cross the sea in a ship or to fasten the cable
to shore, say 'greetings' to Arsinoe of fair sailing,
invoking the reverend goddess from her temple, which was dedicated
by the Samian captain Callicrates son of Boiscus,
especially for you, sailor.*
(ed. and trans. Austin/Bastianini 2002 with minor adjustments)

The epigrams mirror Ptolemaic self-fashioning. After gathering together the cult titles which reflect Arsinoe's identification with the deity, I investigate the religious implications of this representation of the queen.[23] In 116 AB Arsinoe's name is juxtaposed with that of the goddess (l. 6) and then it is suppressed, as she is called 'Zephyritis Aphrodite' (l. 7); in 119.1–2 AB it is used along with Aphrodite's title 'Cypris', and the appellation is preceded by the cult title Philadelphus, which, as Fraser states, softens the incestuous nature of Arsinoe's marriage to her brother and lays emphasis on their mutual power;[24] in 39.2 AB the queen takes on Aphrodite's cult title *Euploia*.[25] Although it is uncertain to what extent these cult titles reveal different degrees of association to Aphrodite, it is likely that the main factor is a desire for variation.

---

[23] Fraser (1972, i 237–46) discerns three modes of identification of the Hellenistic kings and queens with the gods: (i) identification by adoption of their attributes, (ii) identification by juxtaposition and (iii) complete identification, in which the royal name is suppressed.
[24] Fraser 1972, i 217.
[25] For Aphrodite *Euploia*, see Pirenne-Delforge 1994, *passim*. I believe that this mode of identification with the divine does not compartmentalize the diverse powers of the deified queen; it provides her worshippers with a way of invoking particular powers of the deified queen. For Arsinoe *Euploia*, see Robert 1966, 175–211. Cf. also the anonymous Chic.Lit.Pap. no.II, col.ii 14 (Powell 1925, 82–89), where Arsinoe is said to 'govern the sea' (κρατοῦσα σὺ πόντον). For this papyrus, see Barbantani 2004, 137–53.

All three poems commemorate directly or indirectly the role of Arsinoe II as a marine deity at Cape Zephyrium; Callicrates' dedication aimed to promote the queen as the patroness of the maritime empire, and this formed part of his plan to expand the influence of the Ptolemaic navy throughout the Mediterranean.[26] Moreover, it is possible that 116.8 AB, where the chaste daughters of the Greeks are invited to worship Arsinoe, evokes her role as a goddess of marriage. In fact, the queen has the same double cultic function in Callimachus Ath. 7.318b (= 5.1–4Pf. = 14 GP), where Selenaia's dedication of a nautilus to Arsinoe II is both an offering for the protection of sailors by the deified queen and a symbol of the girl's hope for a good marriage.[27] Similarly to the epigrams quoted above, in Callimachus fr. 5 Pf. Arsinoe is concisely addressed as 'Cypris' (l.2), the appellation emphatically identifying her with Aphrodite: ...ἀλλὰ σὺ νῦν με,/ Κύπρι, Σεληναίης ἄνθεμα πρῶτον ἔχεις ('but Cypris I am yours, a first offering from Selenaea'). In addition, in 116.10 AB the temple is projected as offering sanctuary from any sort of adversity (εὐλίμενον); the adjective παντός opens up the semantic field of the term κύματος, which thus symbolizes any kind of adversity and misfortune. The ambiguity of the phrase also allows for the possibility that the queen was worshipped at Cape Zephyrium under additional roles — the lack of further sources relating to the nature of her worship there may have led us to mistakenly narrow the spectrum of her actual religious functions. A papyrus of 252/1 BC, which preserves the names of various streets in Alexandria deriving from Arsinoe's diverse religious roles, includes the appellation 'Arsinoe Eleēmon' ('Arsinoe of pity'). Another papyrus, dating from the second century BC, contains the cult title 'Arsinoe Sōzousa' ('Arsinoe the Saviour'). Both titles project the queen's benevolence, and it is intriguing that 'Eleēmon' ('The Merciful') was also a cult title for Aphrodite.[28] It is exactly her kindness that the Posidippean epigrams also stress at their closure (116.9–10 AB, 119.5–6 AB and 39.7–8 AB).[29] Along with the papyri, they exemplify that this was a feature of her deified *persona*, which she shared with Aphrodite.[30]

---

26 Robert 1966, 201 02.
27 Gutzwiller 1992, 199.
28 Cf. Fraser 1972, i 237–38, ii 386–87. Note also that Posidippus 38 AB implies Arsinoe's benevolence, since a dedication is offered to her by a manumitted slave woman (see Stephens 2004, 163).
29 For the projection of Arsinoe's benevolence in Posidippus' epigrams, cf. Stephens 2004, 171–73.
30 Cf. *APl* (A) 68 = 39 GP (Asclepiades or Posidippus) which also praises a Ptolemaic queen (most probably Berenice I) by associating her with Aphrodite.

Leaving aside Arsinoe II, I turn our attention to *AP* 5.194 = 34 GP, since it is essential to examine the motif's transformation in this poem, given that it might have been written by a court poet (Posidippus/Asclepiades):

αὐτοὶ τὴν ἁπαλὴν Εἰρήνιον εἶδον Ἔρωτες
  Κύπριδος ἐκ χρυσέων ἐρχόμενοι θαλάμων
ἐκ τριχὸς ἄχρι ποδῶν ἱερὸν θάλος οἷά τε λύγδου
  γλυπτήν, παρθενίων βριθομένην χαρίτων·
καὶ πολλοὺς τότε χερσὶν ἐπ' ἠιθέοισιν ὀιστούς
  τόξου πορφυρέης ἧκαν ἀφ' ἀρπεδόνης.

The Erotes themselves looked on soft Eirenion
whilst leaving Cypris' golden chambers,
a sacred shoot from head to feet, as if
carved from white marble, laden with a virgin's graces;
and then they let fly from their hands many arrows
against young men, sent from the purple bow-strings.
(trans. Paton 1999 with minor adjustments)

Similarly to Ibycus fr. 288 Davies, Eirenion is only indirectly associated to Aphrodite. Her praise starts immediately with the use of the adjective ἁπαλήν, a common laudatory description in erotic poetry.[31] The image of the Erotes coming out of Aphrodite's chamber is a natural one, since they are her children.[32] They form the intermediaries between Eirenion and Aphrodite, connecting the girl with the goddess. Aphrodite is not the one meeting her, but it is her children who see Eirenion by chance and start shooting men as soon as they gaze upon her. According to this interpretation, the praise of Eirenion is accentuated, because it is as if the Erotes themselves fall prey to her attractiveness. The notion highlights her impact on male viewers.[33]

In addition, Eirenion is a ἱερὸν θάλος (l. 3), the characterization emphasizing her supernatural beauty.[34] It is the adjective ἱερόν, meaning 'filled with or manifesting divine power, supernatural',[35] which adds an element of hyperbole; the girl exhibits divine beauty from head to toe. As in Ibycus fr. 288 Davies, the phrase implies a special bond between Eirenion and a deity (or the deities) responsible for her supreme

---
[31] For the use of ἁπαλός in poetry, see Sens 2011, 134.
[32] The mss reading ἐρχόμενοι has been emended into ἐρχομένην; see Sens 2011, 227–34. The participle ἐρχόμενοι can be defended, since the distich makes perfect sense as transmitted.
[33] Sens (2011, 227) also notes that the Erotes act as surrogates for men and adds that their gaze stands for that of the youths.
[34] For her other characterizations within the distich, see Guichard 2004, 386–87; Sens 2011, 231–33.
[35] *LSJ*⁹, s.v. ἱερός I.

beauty. While these benefactors remain unnamed, Aphrodite naturally comes to the reader's mind, as she is mentioned in the first distich.[36] So, if indeed the poem was written by a court poet, it is in line with the pronounced reluctance observed in their corpus to equate commoners with Aphrodite.

This narrow and highly specialized range of application of the motif within the work of the court poets is very interesting. I suggest that it can be directly related to the proximity of these poets to the centre of power and their role as disseminators of the Ptolemaic propaganda. Since we are at the first stages of the dissemination of the official propaganda equating the Hellenistic queens with Aphrodite, the indiscriminate, random and repeated comparison of ordinary mortals to the goddess could have the potential of diluting this propaganda.

Outside now of the Ptolemaic court, and later in time (second century BC), the motif is employed by Antipater of Sidon in *AP* 9.567 (= 61 GP), in which a theatrical artist called Antiodemis is praised as 'the nursling of Aphrodite' (l. 2: *Παφίης νοσσίς*), and *AP* 7.218 (= 23 GP), where the dead hetaera Lais is eulogised by her tomb with a series of hyperboles that involve Aphrodite. As *AP* 9.567.2 has similar implications to Ibycus fr. 288 Davies, I focus on *AP* 7.218 (= 23 GP) that articulates the praise in a much more open, emphatic, and hyperbolic way:

> τὴν καὶ ἅμα χρυσῷ καὶ ἀλουργίδι καὶ σὺν Ἔρωτι
> θρυπτομένην, ἁπαλῆς Κύπριδος ἁβροτέρην,
> Λαΐδ' ἔχω, πολιῆτιν ἁλιζώνοιο Κορίνθου,
> Πειρήνης λευκῶν φαιδροτέρην λιβάδων,
> τὴν θνητὴν Κυθέρειαν, ἐφ' ᾗ μνηστῆρες ἀγαυοί
> πλείονες ἢ νύμφης εἵνεκα Τυνδαρίδος
> δρεπτόμενοι Χάριτάς τε καὶ ὠνητὴν Ἀφροδίτην,
> ἧς καὶ ὑπ' εὐώδει τύμβος ὄδωδε κρόκῳ,
> ἧς ἔτι κηώεντι μύρῳ τὸ διάβροχον ὀστεῦν
> καὶ λιπαραὶ θυόεν ἆσθμα πνέουσι κόμαι,
> ᾗ ἔπι καλὸν ἄμυξε κατὰ ῥέθος Ἀφρογένεια
> καὶ γοερὸν λύζων ἐστονάχησεν Ἔρως.
> εἰ δ' οὐ πάγκοινον δούλην θέτο κέρδεος εὐνήν,
> Ἑλλὰς ἂν ὡς Ἑλένης τῆσδ' ὕπερ ἔσχε πόνον.

> *I hold Lais, who exalted in her wealth and her purple dress and in her amours/*
> *with the power of Eros, more delicate than tender Cypris,*
> *the citizen of sea-girt Corinth,*
> *more sparkling than the white water of Peirene,*
> *the mortal Cytherea, who had more noble suitors*
> *than Tyndareus' daughter,*

---

[36] Cf. Sens 2011, 230–31.

plucking her charms and mercenary favours.[37]
Her very tomb smells of sweet-scented saffron,
her skull is still soaked with fragrant ointment,
and her anointed locks still breathe a perfume as of frankincense.
For her the Foam-born tore her lovely face,
and sobbing Eros groaned and wailed.
If she had not made her bed the public slave of gain,
Greece would have pains for her as for Helen.
(ed. and trans. Gutzwiller 1998[38] with minor adjustments)

In this poem, the tomb speaks as if it was Lais' last and perpetual lover. Already in the second line, the hetaera is praised as being 'more delicate than tender Cypris'. The hyperbolic phrase obviously presents her as superior to the goddess in softness of the skin. This development in the reception of the motif can be attributed to the generic characteristics of the sub-genre of fictitious sepulchral epigrams (to which our epigram belongs), since extravagant statements are a common feature of praises of the dead.[39] Also, as we shall see later on in detail, there is a sceptic element in the epigram which inevitably undermines the praise of Lais' beauty. It is quite interesting that there is flexibility in the employment of the motif, since the epigrammatist (in the voice of the tomb) moves between over-exaggerated praises and more restrained ones. In l. 5 the expression τὴν θνητὴν Κυθέρειαν limits the hyperbole of the praise, as it emphasizes Lais' mortality, stressing human limits and firmly binding her superiority to the human world. In parallel, the hetaera is eulogized as being superior to 'Tyndareus' daughter/bride' in beauty (ll. 5–6). The phrase is ambiguous since νύμφη can mean both 'bride' and 'maiden', and therefore can refer either to Leda or Helen. It is the second comparison with Helen in the epigram's closure which will lead the reader to interpret this phrase as referring to Helen as well. After all, in general terms, the disloyal Helen is a better yardstick for comparison

---

[37] For the metonymic use of the Graces and Aphrodite, see the analysis of the epigram. For the defence of the mss reading ἀγανοί, altered by Gow-Page (1965, ii 53) into ἄγερθεν, see White 1985, 77–79.
[38] I alter the translation slightly and in the original I print Ἔρωτι (l.1), Χάριτάς and Ἀφροδίτην (l.7).
[39] For Lais, cf. Ath.589b. Supposedly, in an engraved epigram on a stone hydria marking her tomb in Thessaly, Greece is said to have been enslaved by her divine beauty; Eros begot her and Corinth reared her. On the narratives on her death, see McClure 2003, 148–49. For the heroization of the deceased and their association with the gods in funerary epigrams of the 1st–3rd century AD, see Wypustek 2013, *passim*. In sarcophagi and tomb statues of the second century AD, the deceased themselves appear in the form of gods: e.g. the depiction of a wife can allude to Aphrodite/Venus (especially to 'Capitoline Venus'), the allusion stressing her beauty and womanly virtues including sexual modesty. For this topic, see Zanker/Ewald 2012, 175–244.

with a hetaera than her mother, Leda.⁴⁰ Lais is more beautiful than Helen since, as the tomb says, more men were subjugated to her beauty, as opposed to the Spartan princess. The formula μνηστῆρες ἀγαυοί, reserved in Homer for Penelope,⁴¹ is attached here to Helen. Lines 11–12 also praise the hetaera. Aphrodite and Eros are depicted as mourning her death. The description of their bereavement reflects great pathos and sorrow (Aphrodite tears her face and Eros groans and weeps).

However, the encomium of Lais' beauty constitutes only one side of the epigram; the paradoxes included in Lais' hyperbolic praise point towards the humour: the tomb speaks as if Lais retains her beauty in death, as if her body is not decayed, but able to preserve in the grave the scent of the saffron perfume and myrrh. This incompatibility between her praise (ll. 9–10) and the realistic image of a decayed body in a grave⁴² makes the praise seem almost grotesque. There are two further points which reduce the hetaera from a high class courtesan to a simple prostitute, thus creating a melange of praise and satire. In l. 7 the metonymic use of the goddess and her companions praises Lais' charms, beauty, sexual skills, and attractiveness. However, the use of ὠνητήν highlights the venality of this divine beauty, and the idea suggests a slight, under-hand irony against Lais. Moreover, the phrase 'plucking her charms and mercenary favours' is placed at the end of her comparison with Helen, which seems to suggest that the commercialization of her splendour provided Lais with more suitors than the princess. The last distich expresses this idea in a much more open and emphatic way. The concept of Lais having 'made her bed the public slave to profit' emphasizes her venality; πάγκοινον and δούλην, characterizing her bed, degrade her to a common prostitute, available to anyone who was able to pay.⁴³ In addition, the idea of going to war for a prostitute is in itself paradoxical and has a double effect. On the one hand, it undercuts the comparison with Helen and suggests that the comparison should be taken humorously. On the other hand, it potentially cuts Helen down to size, since it is stressed that Helen created *ponos* for Greece.⁴⁴

---

40 For the parody of Helen in sceptic poems (based on her common use as a symbol of disloyalty or an archetype of beauty), see e.g. *AP* 11.278 and *AP* 11.408 (Lucilius) with Floridi 2014, 480–81 and 547–51, and *AP* 9.166 (Palladas), where Penelope and Helen are employed to stress that all women are disastrous for men.
41 See *Od.* 2.209, 4.681, 14.180, 18.99, 21.174 and 21.232.
42 Cf. *AP* 7.217 = 41 GP (with Gutzwiller 1998, 255): if we take the verb ἕζετ' as present and not as imperfect (l. 2: ἇς καὶ ἐπὶ ῥυτίδων ὁ γλυκὺς ἕζετ' Ἔρως), then the image of Archeanassa as preserving her beauty in tomb is incongruous with the realistic state of bodies in graves.
43 As Penzel (2006, 103) notes, there is an indirect allusion to Aphrodite *Pandemos*.
44 For a different reading of the epigram, see Gutzwiller 1998, 255–57.

It is, therefore, Meleager who breaks new ground in the reception of the motif within epigrams. In *AP* 5.137 (= 43 GP), within a purely erotic context, Heliodora is emphatically associated and metaphorically identified with Aphrodite, Grace and Peitho:

> ἔγχει τᾶς Πειθοῦς καὶ Κύπριδος Ἡλιοδώρας
>   καὶ πάλι τᾶς αὐτᾶς ἁδυλόγου Χάριτος·
> αὐτὰ γὰρ μί᾽ ἐμοὶ γράφεται θεός, ἇς τὸ ποθεινόν
>   οὔνομ᾽ ἐν ἀκρήτῳ συγκεράσας πίομαι.

> *Pour in (wine) for Heliodora Peitho and for Heliodora Cypris,*
> *and again for the same Heliodora the sweet-speaking Grace.*
> *Because for me she herself is inscribed as the one goddess, whose desirable*
> *name I drink mixed with pure wine.*[45]

The lover's toasts acquire a special meaning, which derives from the form of the toasts themselves that imitates official cult titles. The phrase τᾶς Πειθοῦς καὶ Κύπριδος Ἡλιοδώρας mimics cult titles, in which the names of queens and kings were placed in juxtaposition with that of a god to express identification with the specific deity (e.g. Ἀρσινόης Κύπριδος in 116.6 AB). In the same vein, the characterization τᾶς αὐτᾶς ἁδυλόγου Χάριτος imitates cult titles where the name of the queen/king is fully repressed. This phraseology constitutes a hyperbolic praise of the beloved that (metaphorically) apotheosizes her: Heliodora is glorified as a goddess who combines the (erotic) powers of the three female goddesses. If we compare this epigram to e.g. Ibycus fr. 288 Davies and Ar. *Ec.* 973–75, both passages exalting a person for combining attributes offered by a group of deities, the difference in the degree of hyperbole is obvious. Here, Heliodora is not the protégée of the goddesses, but she is identified with them. This hyperbolic praise has a double application: on the one hand, it stresses the lover's complete infatuation for Heliodora; on the other hand, it highlights the woman's preeminence in beauty and all methods of allurement: 'Peitho Heliodora' denotes her expertise in persuasive speech; 'Cypris Heliodora', having multiple associations, alludes *inter alia* to her supernatural beauty, attractiveness, expertise in seductiveness and sexual pleasure; in the same manner, 'Grace' underlines her beauty, sweet voice (this attribute is emphasized by the adjective ἁδυλόγου), charm and attractiveness. In this context, it is noteworthy that Heliodora's voice is also praised in *AP* 5.141 (= 44 GP) via hyperbolic phraseology that includes comparison with the divine. The lover (Meleager) swears in the name of Eros that he prefers to hear a whisper from Heliodora than Apollo's lyre-playing:

---

[45] My translation.

ναὶ τὸν Ἔρωτα, θέλω τὸ παρ' οὔασιν Ἡλιοδώρας/ φθέγμα κλύειν ἢ τὰς Λατοΐδεω κιθάρας ('By Eros I swear, I had rather hear Heliodora's whisper in my ear than the harp of the son of Leto').[46]

The phrase αὐτὰ γὰρ μί' ἐμοὶ γράφεται θεός (l. 3) carries on this idea of Heliodora's metaphorical apotheosis. What is more, the phrase has a metapoetic function. The verb γράφεται alludes to the act of writing poetry and suggests that Heliodora's apotheosis stands for her prominent position within the Meleagrean corpus (17 epigrams are devoted to her).[47] Moreover, the verb, both through its allusion to the act of writing and of inscribing epigrams, implies the perpetuality that this 'goddess' gains through Meleager's poetry. It can further act as an intratextual marker, which points towards the other Meleagrean epigrams that link the girl with the divine world (AP 5.140, 5.195, 5.196).

Garrison attributes the beloved's apotheosis to Meleager's 'erotic extremism' that 'robs man of his reason, his independence, and his individuality'. In Meleager, Garrison argues, we have the image of the extreme lover, whose 'erotic state becomes a part of him and it emerges in religious images'.[48] Garrison's explanation is useful for appreciating the effect of this kind of hyperbole, which underlines the lover's passion for and infatuation with the object of his desire. However, it does not get us any closer to understanding how Meleager was able to use such a degree of hyperbole. I believe that the answer is to be found in specific changes that concern the religious beliefs and practices of the Hellenistic era. Firstly, the cultic practice of the deification and assimilation of kings and queens to the Greek Olympian gods, which was added to the traditional religious practices of the Greeks, blurred the boundaries between mortals and gods. People became gradually more accustomed to the idea of mortals (albeit their rulers) being deified. This change certainly did not happen overnight; as the surviving material suggests, earlier Hellenistic poets were reluctant to present the beloved as equal or superior to a god, and only the court poets assimilated their queens and kings with the Olympian gods. But the use of the motif within the frame of Ptolemaic propaganda probably enabled its transfer to the erotic domain with the passing of time.

What is more, from the second century BC at the latest, ordinary men and women, recently dead, were offered cultic honours and were spoken of as 'heroes/ heroines'. For instance, the citizens of Amorgos established (at the end of the second century BC) in honour of Aleximachus, who died at a young

---

46 Cf. Gutzwiller 1997, 179. Trans. Paton 1999, 197.
47 Gutzwiller 1997, 177.
48 Garrison 1978, 84.

age, monthly public contests that started with a sacrifice in front of his statue and were followed by a public feast. In addition, Artemidorus from Perge, after decades of service to the Thereans and their deities, received himself after his death cultic honours appropriated to a hero.[49] These cases exemplify the broadening of the scope of people to whom cultic honours were offered. During the classical era this meant heroes, athletes, and famous poets (such as Archilochus). However, by the second century BC, mere mortals could likewise receive such honours. This change in cult practice could have enabled the blurring of boundaries between mortal and divine in poetry. In other words, the praise in poetry of a mortal as being equal or superior to a god gradually stopped being connected with the idea of expressing disrespect towards gods and impiety. Since by Meleager's time these cult practices were well-established (and not new cultic phenomena), this can explain why the poet 'apotheosized' his beloveds more systematically than his predecessors; why Heliodora is praised as 'one goddess'.

To sum up, we cannot draw a homogeneous picture of the reception of the Homeric motif in poetry. There is a gradual development in the degree of hyperbole employed that depends upon a nexus of factors. Within the genre of epigrams Nossis' dedicatory poems simply create indirect links between Aphrodite and her devotees. In the hands of the court poets the motif acquires religious and political implications, and its application within the frame of Ptolemaic propaganda led to a reluctance on the part of the court poets to openly compare any other female with the goddess. A more adventurous transformation of the motif takes place in Antipater's *AP* 7.218 (= 23 GP), and it is the fact that this is a sepulchral epigram and the underlying humour that permits the hyperbole. Meleager's *AP* 5.137 (= 43 GP) constitutes the apex in the motif's reception in the epigrams of the Hellenistic period.[50] The comparison and (metaphorical) assimilation of a beloved to Aphrodite, a concept that would be inconceivable during the archaic and classical times, is attributed to the religious changes that took place during the Hellenistic era, and which had become established cult practices by Meleager's time, allowing a gradual closing between the Greeks and their gods.

---

49 Cf. Jones 2010 48–65; Mikalson 2005, 214–18.
50 In the post-Meleagrean epigrammatists it becomes common to openly compare and/or assimilate women with the goddess, and this fact confirms the changes in the reception of the motif during the Hellenistic era. See e.g. *AP* 5.102 = 5 GPh (Marcus Argentarius), *AP* 5.70 = 26 Page, *AP* 5.73 = 27 Page and *AP* 5.94 = 35 Page (Rufinus). The motif was further adapted by the poets of the *Cycle* of Agathias (6th century AD): see e.g. *AP* 7.599 (Julianus of Egypt).

Karim Arafat
Pausanias and Homer

The second-century AD traveller and writer Pausanias was *dianooumenos* or an intellectual.[1] Not a self-promoting sophist like many of his time – I think first of Aelius Aristides, the 'star sophist' in Ruth Webb's description[2] – but someone who showed his knowledge of literature and art when he felt it necessary and on occasion refrained from expressing his views, something no self-respecting sophist would do. Thus, he says: 'though I have investigated very carefully the dates of Hesiod and Homer, I do not like to state my results, knowing as I do the carping disposition [...] especially of the professors of poetry at the present day' (9.30.3). Similarly, he says of the *Theogony* that 'some' believe it to be by Hesiod (8.18.1) and he casts doubt on attributions to poets such as Eumelus (2.1.1).

One manifestation of his learning is the frequency with which he refers to, or quotes from, earlier authors, some 125 in total.[3] Although his prototype is Herodotus, it is the poets whom he cites most often. Above all, he refers, and defers, to Homer, of whom he calls himself 'an attentive reader' (2.4.2). He quotes Homer over 20 times and cites him another 250; Hesiod is quoted eight times and cited 50, while Pindar is quoted 23 times and cited five times, and Stesichorus is quoted 13 times.[4] It is clear that Homer, more than any other writer, dominates Pausanias' thinking. In this article, I shall look behind the headline statistics and get a sense of how Pausanias saw and used Homer and why. Characteristically, he does not tell us much, but I think we can make some safe inferences.

First, why Homer, not, for example, Hesiod or Pindar? Partly because authority comes from chronological primacy and from the sense that Homer is the original source and not a derivative one. Pausanias does not explicitly say that he sees Homer as the first poet, but it is often implicit. It is repeatedly clear from his writings on art that for him antiquity confers sanctity and, similarly, the very remoteness in time of Homer conferred on him an unmatchable authority.

Then there is Pausanias' belief that the *Iliad* and the *Odyssey* are the supreme poems in terms of quality. Consistent with this is his view of the epic *Thebaid*. He quotes the seventh-century Ephesian poet Callinus as saying that the

---

[1] References to the text of Pausanias are from the Teubner edition of Rocha-Pereira 1989–90².
Translations are from Frazer 1913², Vol. I, with minor adjustments.
[2] Webb 2009, 65.
[3] Habicht 1985, 132.
[4] *op.cit.* 133.

author was Homer, and adds 'many respectable persons have shared his opinion. Next to the *Iliad* and *Odyssey* there is certainly no poem which I esteem so highly' (9.9.5). He speaks similarly of the 'hymns of Orpheus': 'for poetical beauty they may rank next to the hymns of Homer and they have received still higher marks of divine favour' (9.30.12, cf. 1.14.3). In both these cases, the poems are ranked below Homer, but enhanced by approaching the quality of Homer. Pausanias refers to many other epics—such as the *Cypria* (3.16.1, 4.2.7, 10.26.1, 4, 10.31.2), *Little Iliad* (3.26.9), *Minyad* (4.33.7, 10.28.2, 7, 10.31.3) and *Naupactia* (10.38.11)–but he uses them purely as resources for information on, for example, mythology or heroic genealogy, commenting on their authorship, but not on their quality, which is precisely what sets the Homeric poems apart in his opinion.

I think there is also something more personal in Pausanias' reverence for Homer. There may be a natural geographical sympathy, as Homer's traditional home island of Chios is not far from Pausanias' apparent own home-city of Magnesia ad Sipylum in Lydia in Asia Minor.[5] He says he has heard different stories about the origins of Homer–and of his mother– but that he will not give his opinion on Homer's native land (10.24.3). It is striking that he rejects here an opportunity to claim broadly common origins with Homer of all people. Similarly, as I mentioned, he 'investigated very carefully the dates of Hesiod and Homer' (9.30.3). This is reminiscent of Herodotus' phrase: 'I suppose Hesiod and Homer flourished not more than four hundred years earlier than I' (2.53.2). Pausanias may here simply be imitating Herodotus, as he often does, although it is extremely unlikely that he would not have his own views; in any case, the claim shows the importance of Homeric scholarship to an intellectual of Pausanias' time. I see this as precisely the sort of occasion when he differs strikingly from other writers of the second sophistic in *not* showing off his knowledge–one might say, in making a show of not showing off, unless, of course, he is bluffing and knows less than he claims.

Another reason I would suggest for Pausanias' reverence for Homer is that, as he says, Homer 'had travelled into far countries' (1.2.3), and Pausanias may well have seen him as a fellow-geographer and even as a prototype periegete, therefore as a model for his own travels and descriptions. Pausanias' work is after all centred on descriptions of places and what they contain. Homer mentions nearly 350 places in the *Iliad* alone, and the use of the *Odyssey* as a geographical manual continues to our own day with the recently-revived debate

---

5 Arafat 1996, 8 and n.11.

over the identity of the Homeric Ithaca.[6] Pausanias uses Homer as the (not 'an') authority for the foundation or names of cities or their belonging to a particular territory or people (e.g. 4.1.3–4 etc). Thus, he gives us the Homeric names of the islands of Aeolus (10.11.3) and of Delphi (10.6.5). Still in Phocis, he mentions that the cities which in his day no longer existed were once renowned 'chiefly through the verses of Homer' (10.3.2). In discussing the most Homeric of mainland Greek cities, Mycenae (2.15.4–16.7), 'the city which led the Greeks in the Trojan War', he does not use Homer for his description of the site–despite noting that the walls were Cyclopean, as at Tiryns-beyond mentioning the tombs of the Atreids and of those returning from Troy, and even then he does not directly mention Homer. But he would hardly need to, as he is making the safe assumption that his readers would know the connection. Where he does mention Homer is in explaining that the city was named after a woman called Mycene (2.16.4).

It is his view of rivers as natural boundaries defining and separating places and yet linking them, that reflects the broadest scope of Pausanias' geography, real or imagined. Thus the Argolid is linked with Asia Minor through the river Asopos which 'they say' comes from the river Maiander (2.5.3), and the western Peloponnese is linked with Magna Graecia through the waters of the Alpheios (5.7.2–3, 8.54.2–3, cf. 7.23.2). Rivers and seas are central to Pausanias' work and here, too, Homer has a key role as a source for many names of rivers and for stories associated with them. Most references are purely recording, with Homer again seen as authoritative: e.g. in book 1 (1.17.5) Pausanias mentions the Acherusian Lake and the rivers Acheron and Kokytos, calling the latter 'a joyless stream' and adding: 'it appears to me that Homer had seen these things, and boldly modelled his descriptions of hell on them and that in particular he bestowed on the rivers of hell the names of the rivers in Thesprotis'. In book 8 he says that Homer introduced the name of Styx into his poetry, citing the oath of Hera in *Il.* 15 (36–37), where Homer says: 'Witness me now, earth and the broad heaven above and the down-trickling water of Styx'. Pausanias concludes: 'this passage is composed as if the poet had himself seen the water of the Styx dripping' (8.18.2). Incidentally, he opts for Homer's account after rejecting those of Hesiod, Linus and Epimenides (8.18.1–2). Both these passages emphasize the importance of travelling and of autopsy, of seeing for oneself, both themes central to Pausanias' methodology.

Thus it is clear that Pausanias sees Homer as a prototype geographer and traveller and therefore as a model for his own work. The same criteria apply

---

[6] E.g. Bittlestone/Diggle/Underhill 2005; Graziosi 2008b.

also to Herodotus, and it is interesting that Pausanias makes what is in many respects parallel use of a historian and an epic poet.

As geography is central to Pausanias' work, so are two further areas for which he finds information in Homer, namely religion and art. Pausanias gives no critique of Homer's view of the gods and makes surprisingly little explicit use of him, but, as so often, he still sees him as a supremely influential and authoritative figure: to give a small example, he says that the poems of Homer determine how Hermes and Heracles are viewed (8.32.4). On occasion, he uses Homer to clarify a cult practice, as at Olympia, where he says: 'I forgot to ask what they do with the boar after the athletes have taken the oath. With the ancients it was a rule that a sacrificed animal on which an oath had been taken should not be eaten by man. Homer proves this clearly. For the boar, on the cut pieces of which Agamemnon swore that Briseis was a stranger to his bed, is represented by Homer as being cast by the herald into the sea' (5.24.10–11; see *Il.* 19.266–68).

I turn now to art, much of which is mythological and therefore narrative, and so inevitably lends itself to comparison with written accounts, those of Homer above all. Pausanias' primary use of Homer is again as an authority, usually for identification of figures or narrative details. The lost wall-paintings of the Classical period are the obvious examples, particularly those of the Painted Stoa at Athens and the Cnidian Lesche at Delphi, described in detail by Pausanias. Here I shall say nothing of the Homeric influence on, or 'accuracy' of, the paintings – that has been assessed by many scholars already.[7] Instead, I mention a lesser-known painting, which Pausanias saw at Plataea, by Onasias of the mid-fifth century, showing Euryganea, who, Pausanias alone (as far as I know) tells us, was known to be the mother of Oedipus' children from 'the author of the poem they call the *Oedipodia*' (9.5.11). Euryganea is shown 'bowed with grief at the battle between her children'. The unnamed author Pausanias cites seems not to be sufficient authority, since he starts by citing Homer as proof that Oedipus had no children by Iocaste (*Od.* 11.271–73). Pausanias has strong views on Oedipus, finding Sophocles' version of his death 'incredible' (1.28.7) and citing Homer's differing account as his sole authority, apparently without second thought; indeed, he never disagrees with Homer. The nearest he comes is when he says (10.31.3) that the *Ehoiai* and the *Minyad* give different accounts

---

[7] The commentary of Sir James Frazer (1913², V 356–92) is still invaluable in this respect. Most scholarship on the wall-paintings is concerned with reconstructing them from Pausanias' account, e.g. Stansbury-O'Donnell 1989 and 1990, although he does discuss their relationship to Homer particularly in his 1990 article (e.g. 217–18, 222–26, 230).

of the death of Meleager from Homer. He simply states the disagreement without giving an opinion.

So far, I have spoken of lost works, where we are at an obvious disadvantage in assessing Pausanias' accuracy in general and specifically in his use of Homer. Of surviving works, where we would hope to be on more solid ground, probably the best-known example is the central figure of the west pediment of the temple of Zeus at Olympia, the huge, dominant figure with his right hand stretched out to quieten the fighting Lapiths and Centaurs. Pausanias calls him Peirithous, at whose wedding the fight erupted (5.10.8). Scholars almost universally agree that this is, rather, Apollo, primarily on the grounds that the centre should be held by a god, that the figure is much taller than the other figures, that Peirithous should be the same size as Theseus, who is also depicted, and that Peirithous should be more agitated considering that it is his bride whose abduction is being attempted before his eyes.[8] All good reasons; why, then, does Pausanias call him Peirithous? Simply because, he says, Peirithous was a son of Zeus, to whom the temple was dedicated and who was depicted in the centre of the east pediment. At Delphi, describing the paintings of the Cnidian Lesche, he notes (10.29.10) that Homer calls Theseus and Peirithous 'children of the gods' (*Od.* 11.631). In the same way, the Seasons are depicted on the throne of the statue of Zeus at Olympia, because 'in poetry the Seasons are described as daughters of Zeus' (5.11.7). The logic for identifying Peirithous at Olympia is unimpeachable in literary and genealogical terms, but incompatible with sculptural conventions, of which we are, I think, rather more conscious than Pausanias would have been, although he does say he has read what he calls 'the historians of sculpture' (5.23.3).

Homer is also called upon in the intriguing case of the necklace of Eriphyle, which Pausanias tells us was said to be preserved in his time in the sanctuary of Adonis and Aphrodite at Amathos in Cyprus. Pausanias denies that the necklace at Amathos is genuine, because it 'is of green stones fastened together with gold' (9.41.3), whereas Homer in the *Odyssey* says Eriphyle's necklace was simply 'precious gold' (*Od.* 11.327). At first this looks like precision on the part of someone as interested in materials and techniques as Pausanias, but sheer fussiness in terms of literary criticism. However, Pausanias strengthens his case by adding: 'not that Homer was ignorant of the necklaces composed of various materials'. Thus, he cites two references in the *Odyssey* to 'golden necklaces [...] strung at

---

8 E.g. Ashmole/Yalouris (1967, 17–18) say that Apollo is the 'patron of all the arts and of all that makes life humane and decent. His presence ensures that civilized man shall prevail'; Rolley (1994, 365) says that this is Pausanias' 'seule erreur inexcusable ... Apollon, qui n'a aucune place dans le sanctuaire, répond a la règle qu'un dieu se dresse au centre des frontons'; Boardman (1985, 36) calls Apollo 'dispenser of law and order'; see also Stewart 1990, 144 and others.

intervals with amber beads', one of them a gift to Penelope from one of her suitors. Pausanias concludes that Homer knew of necklaces made of gold and beads and would have described the necklace of Eriphyle as such if it had been; since he calls it simply 'precious gold', it cannot be the one Pausanias saw in Amathos. Thus, Pausanias is led to a reasoned conclusion by the synthesis of his technical and literary knowledge, rather than the unthinking adherence to Homer of which he is often accused. Incidentally, Pausanias' often-expressed interest in technique extends to the period of the Trojan War, when he denies, for example, that a bronze statue of Athena was from the Trojan spoils and that a bronze Poseidon was dedicated by Achilles because bronze-casting had not yet been invented (8.14.7, 10.38.5–7). Conversely, he deduces from his reading of Homer that 'weapons in the Heroic Age were all of bronze' and finds confirmation of this in the spear of Achilles, which he saw at Phaselis, and the sword of Memnon, which he saw at Nicomedia, since 'the blade and the spike at the butt-end of the spear and the whole of the sword are of bronze' (3.3.8). Clearly, there is some wishful thinking in this conclusion, but it demonstrates his belief in the literal truth of Homer.

Homer personifies chronological remoteness, and Pausanias uses him to approach as nearly as possible the art and artists of earliest antiquity. Here I think of Hephaestus and Daedalus, works by both of whom Pausanias claims to have seen, citing Homer in his support in both cases. An obvious example is the shield of Achilles made by Hephaestus and described in detail by Homer (*Il.* 18.478–608). Pausanias has to rely on his literary source for his description of this lost masterpiece exactly as we have to rely on Pausanias for our understanding of, for example, the lost wall-paintings from Athens and Delphi. If we make more of our source than we should, it is because we have no other source, no means of forming a truly independent, objective judgement. Another factor is relevant and, indeed, central here, namely Pausanias' insistence on autopsy, which I mentioned earlier apropos of Homer's own travels. Wherever possible, he went to see the places or works of art that he described, on occasion going to great lengths to do so, and he is reluctant to comment on works he has not seen. It may be for this reason that his one extended passage about the shield of Achilles–concerning Linus, who was killed by Apollo for vying with him in song– has more literary and historical than artistic content, citing Pamphus, 'author of the oldest Athenian hymns' (9.29.8, cf. 7.21.9), and Sappho, and ending with the removal of the bones of Linus to Macedonia by Philip II, and his subsequently sending them back to Thebes (9.29.6–9).

Pausanias describes only one work he believes to be by Hephaestus, in this passage from book 9: 'the god whom the Chaeroneans honour most is the sceptre which Homer says Hephaestus made for Zeus, and Zeus gave to Hermes, and

Hermes to Pelops, and Pelops bequeathed to Atreus, and Atreus to Thyestes, from whom Agamemnon had it. This sceptre they worship naming it a spear; and that there is something divine about it is proved especially by the distinction it confers on its owners [...] it was brought to Phocis by Electra, daughter of Agamemnon. There is no public temple built for it, but the man who acts as priest keeps the sceptre in his house for the year, and sacrifices are offered to it daily, and a table is set beside it covered with all sorts of flesh and cakes' (9.40.11–12). He concludes 'of all the objects which poets have declared and public opinion has believed to be works of Hephaestus, none is genuine save the sceptre of Agamemnon' (9.41.1).[9]

This strongly expressed sentiment is interesting for showing that Pausanias is willing to disagree with writers, including poets, on principle; and that he will also disagree with, and distance himself from, 'public opinion', unsurprisingly for someone who is *dianooumenos* and has studied sculpture books. An example of a work which he sees as wrongly attributed to Hephaestus is the third, bronze, temple at Delphi (10.5.11–12), although he does not say who *does* believe it was by Hephaestus; perhaps he is again referring to 'public opinion'. Still on the bronze temple, he adds that he does not believe 'the story about the golden songstresses which the poet Pindar mentions in speaking of this particular temple'. He means *Paean* 8: 'brazen were the walls and of bronze were the supporting pillars, and over its pediment sang six enchantresses made of gold' (68–71) and adds: 'here, it seems to me, Pindar merely imitated the Sirens in Homer'— effectively a double denigration of Pindar compared to Homer.

On one occasion, Pausanias approaches Hephaestus the artist indirectly, saying that Homer 'compares the dance wrought by Hephaestus on the shield of Achilles to a dance wrought by Daedalus, never having seen finer works of art' (8.16.3, ref. *Il.* 18.590–604). I presume that this is the dance of Ariadne which Daedalus carved in white marble and which Pausanias saw at Knossos (9.40.3–4). He tells us nothing else about it. Elsewhere, he mentions that 'Homer says Daedalus made images for Minos and his daughters' (7.4.6).

One final observation on Homer and art: Pausanias mentions many statues of poets, such as those of Corinna at Thebes (9.22.3) and Pindar at Athens (1.8.3), but it is striking that he mentions only one 'likeness' (*eikona*) of Homer (10.24.2). One might have expected Homer to have been honoured with more statues, although one might equally recall Pausanias' words that 'in [Homer's] days they did not yet know how to make bronze images' (8.14.7), an observation which applies equally to stone images. However that may be, the likeness of Homer that

---

9 Most recently on the sceptre, Pirenne-Delforge 2010, 138.

Pausanias mentions has rare *kudos* from its positioning 'on a monument' in the *pronaos* of the temple of Apollo at Delphi and from its being accompanied by the text of an oracle given to Homer:

> *Blest and unhappy, for thou were born to be both,*
> *Thou seekest thy father-land; but thou hast a mother-land and no fatherland.*
> *The isle of Ios is the father-land of thy mother, and it in death*
> *Shall receive thee; but beware of the riddle of young children.*

The first line of this oracle, pithily stating the lot that Fate had given Homer, may serve to remind us that Pausanias gives no other writer the human dimension he gives Homer. Otherwise, he only very occasionally gives writers characteristics, notably describing Tyrtaeus as 'a school-master, generally thought to be a poor-witted creature' (4.15.6), perhaps unsurprising given that 'in all the wide world there is no people so dead to poetry and poetic fame as the Spartans' (3.8.2). Pausanias visited the grotto in the territory of Smyrna 'where they say that Homer composed his poems' (7.5.12) and he visited his tomb, as he did those of Pindar and Corinna. Where he sets Homer apart is in his references to his ill-fortune: 'Never, I think, did fortune show her spiteful nature so plainly as in her treatment of Homer. For Homer was first struck blind, and then, as if this great calamity were not enough, came pinching poverty, and drove him forth to wander the wide world a beggar' (2.33.2–3). This poverty may be related to the humility Pausanias attributes to Homer, saying that he 'esteemed the largess of princes less than the applause of the people' (1.2.3). In spite of this, Pausanias says Homer 'bore up against his misfortune and continued to compose poetry to the last' (4.33.7). I wonder if Pausanias identified with him, whether he wandered unappreciated in his own lifetime. Did Pausanias have an infirmity, too, perhaps as a result of age, given the length of his travels, variously estimated as around twice or even three times the length of Odysseus' wanderings? His fear, expressed towards the end of his travels, that he may not get as far as Delphi (8.37.1), perhaps hints that he did.

Whatever Pausanias' reasons, his affinity with Homer is evident, and, as I mentioned earlier, he never disagrees with him. This absolute faith in Homer causes problems: for example, to quote William Hutton on a passage of book 1 (1.12.5), 'Pausanias' source for the state of the Epeirote naval and culinary expertise in the third century BC is none other than Homer'.[10] Jas Elsner draws this contrast between Pausanias' and Philostratus' view of Homer: 'For Pausanias, Homer is a sanctification of Greece to be followed with respect and an arbiter

---

10 Hutton 2005, 286.

in matters of interpretation. For Philostratus, Homer is an excuse to display learning and an appropriate springboard from which to launch into his own creative interpretation'.[11] This is fair, but inevitable given Pausanias' and Philostratus' very different approaches and agendas. To quote Ruth Webb on the *Eikones* of Philostratus, 'its sophistication makes it a special use of *ekphrasis* that should be ranked alongside the novels for its conscious play with fiction',[12] something one could not say of Pausanias. I do think, though, that there is a Procrustean touch to Elsner's criticism of Pausanias; for example, he says of a passage in book 9: 'Homer can prove that a pile of stones at Thebes (9.18.2) is the tomb of Tydeus'.[13] In fact, Pausanias simply reports the use made of Homer (*Il.* 14.11) by what he calls 'the Theban antiquaries', as often elsewhere he refers to local writers or *exegetes* (local guides). He does not comment on the passage of Homer nor does he express an opinion on whether the stones he sees at Thebes are the tomb of Tydeus.

The uses Pausanias makes of Homer are many and varied, but he is aware of Homer's wider value, summarizing his thoughts by saying: 'Homer's ideas have proved useful to mankind in all manner of ways' (4.28.8). Quite so.

---

[11] Elsner 1995, 317, n. 30.
[12] Webb 2009, 187.
[13] Elsner 1995, 317, n. 30.

Maria Ypsilanti
The Reception of Homeric Vocabulary in Nonnus' *Paraphrase* of St. John's Gospel: Examination of Themes and Formulas in Selected Passages

The work of the fifth century AD poet Nonnus of Panopolis in Egypt entitled *Paraphrase* or *Metabole* of the Gospel of St. John is a poem in hexameters, which versifies the prose narration of the Fourth Gospel. It is the only extant Greek poem paraphrasing a text of the New Testament, although in Latin there are several surviving samples.[1] In fact, as is attested mainly by church historians, the fourth and, principally, the fifth-century Christian paraphrases flourished. These are rewritings either of Biblical texts or of Acts of Saints, probably written in various poetic metres.[2] The paraphrase expands upon the original, employing the rhetorical process of *amplificatio* to do so. This is achieved mainly through embellishment of the original text with verbal abundance (*copia verborum*), tropes and figures (*ornatus*) and variation (*variatio*) of the original vocabulary and phrases, as Roberts points out, drawing on Quintilian's account of the paraphrase as a genre.[3] The dactylic verse employed by Nonnus in his paraphrase naturally invites the use of epic diction in this process of expanding Biblical prose. The poem is in fact full of Homeric vocabulary and formulas in variation. However, the poet does not merely employ epic poems as his source texts. He

---

[1] Juvencus' *Evangeliorum Libri IV*, Arator's *Historia Apostolica*, Sedulius' *Carmen Paschale* (New Testament); verse-paraphrases of the Old Testament are Claudius Marius Victorius' *Alethia*, Cyprianus' *Heptateuch*, Avitus' *De Spiritalis Historiae Gestis*. Dracontius' *Laudes Dei* is a poem part of which is a paraphrase of the *Genesis*. The other major extant Christian Greek poetic paraphrase is Pseudo-Apollinaris' hexameter *Paraphrase* of David's *Psalms*, dealing with an Old Testament text. The less important hexameter Greek texts based on the Bible known as the *Codex Visionum* should be also here mentioned.
[2] See further Whitby 2007, 195.
[3] Roberts 1985, 21, 27 – 29. Cf. Quint. *Inst.* 10.5.8: *sua brevitati gratia, sua copiae, alia tralatis virtus, alia propriis, hoc oratio recta, illud figura declinata commendat* and 10.5.11: *illud virtutis indicium est, fundere quae natura contracta sunt, augere parva, varietatem similibus voluptatem expositis dare, et bene dicere multa de paucis.* Cf. also 10.5.4: *neque ego paraphrasin esse interpretationem tantum volo, sed circa eosdem sensus certamen atque aemulationem.*

also enriches his work with vocabulary and expressions taken from tragedy and other poetry as well.[4]

It is a remarkable feature, although perhaps not surprising given the infinite possibilities offered by the text of Homer, that it is used by later authors of works of widely varying subject-matter and styles. Poets who compose hexameters on epic themes, such as Quintus Smyrnaeus, Triphiodorus, Colluthus and Nonnus in his *Dionysiaca*, not surprisingly incorporate in their verses Homeric references adapted to their work in accord with the specific requirements of each scene, their personal taste and their ideas of literary *imitatio/variatio*.[5] As for Nonnus' *Paraphrase*, scholars have indeed occasionally traced reminiscences of certain scenes and settings of earlier poetry in this work.[6] However, the subject-matter of the *Paraphrase*, i.e. the narration of Biblical episodes, does not generally allow systematic echoes of more extensive passages, images and motifs drawn from the poetic past, since consistent mythological allusion is not appropriate for the task that Nonnus is undertaking. Thus, the reception of epic and other poetry in the *Paraphrase* occurs mainly on the lexical level and consists in the creative adaptation of phrases. Still, at times the poet makes use of some wider motif that tradition offers him, developing it to the extent that his narrative and the spirit of his work let him. An important aspect of the use of Homer by authors of Late Antiquity, and especially by Christian authors, is the process of philosophical or religious interpretation whereby these authors use Homeric terms and passages, now, however, endowed with new meaning and/or 'metaphysical' depth.[7] In adapting Homeric vocabulary in his *Paraphrase*, Nonnus can either remain on a more 'superficial' level, as it were, employing the Homeric diction for purely decorative purposes, or endow these terms with theological significance, according to the needs of religious exegesis that obviously arose in the procedure of paraphrasing a biblical text. Furthermore, it has been argued

---

4 For example, the Wedding at Cana has been regarded as described in terms of a Bacchic feast, and echoes from the *Bacchae* of Euripides have been also traced in it; see Bogner 1934, 320. For Homeric echoes and for similarities between the *Dionysiaca* and the *Paraphrase* in this scene, see Shorrock 2011, 58–67. For echoes from Callimachus' *Hecale* and from Euphorion, see Hollis 1994, 58–59.
5 For examples of this much-discussed matter, see Maciver 2012, 26–29 (with reference to Quintus and Nonnus and with further bibliography). For Homeric adaptation in Quintus, see, for instance, Maciver 2012, *passim*.
6 For instance, the Feeding of the Five Thousand has been seen as recalling a Homeric φιλοξενία; see MacCoull 2003, 492f. For Dionysiac elements of the imagery of *Par.* 2 (including also resemblances with verses from the *Dionysiaca*), see also Livrea on *Par.* 2.15.
7 See Agosti 2005. The basic work on this handling of Homer, mainly by Neoplatonists, is Lamberton 1986.

that elements of everyday Christianity of fifth-century Egypt were incorporated in the Nonnian biblical reformulation of the Homeric diction. Having the presence of the Church in mind, Nonnus addresses an educated audience that recognizes and appreciates the combination of epic language with religious practice.[8] Nonnus, of course, employs the Hellenistic technique of variation, deftly adjusting the various poetic echoes in his text, rather than merely stitching together verses and half-verses borrowed from the epic, so that his poem is by no means a Homeric cento.[9] Examples of the Nonnian incorporation of Homeric vocabulary in the *Paraphrase* and the consequent attainment of multiple poetic aims will be examined in the present paper.

A very common Homeric formula, υἶες Ἀχαιῶν (for instance *Il.* 1.162, 2.281, 4.114, 6.255), is readily adjusted by Nonnus to a Biblical context. Just as in Homer the 'sons of the Achaeans' are the Ἀχαιοί themselves, so Nonnus uses υἶες Ἰουδαίων (7.6) to denote the Jews, which is exactly what the Gospel also says: Ἰουδαῖοι in 7.1. The transfer of epic words bearing heavy pagan overtones to a Christian context is especially noticeable, when terms describing divinities and their qualities or activities in the epic are applied to the Trinitarian God or to a super-human creature in Nonnus. Characteristic is the use of ὀμφή, the typical term for the voice of the gods in Homer (for instance *Il.* 2.41: θείη... ὀμφή, 20.129: θεῶν...ὀμφῆς, *Od.* 3.215 and 16.96: θεοῦ ὀμφῇ) always at verse-end. In the *Paraphrase* the noun appears in the Homeric metrical position, usually accompanied by an adjective manifesting its divine provenance, exactly as happens in the epic: 1.93: θεοδινέος...ὀμφῆς, 3.49, 5.106, 8.139 and 15.103: θέσκελος/ον ὀμφή(ν), 3.53: θεσπεσίης...ὀμφῆς,[10] 5.127: θεοδέγμονος...ὀμφῆς, 5.141: ὑπέρτερον ὀμφήν, 7.162: θεηγόρος...ὀμφή, 12.166 and 14.116: ἔνθεον ὀμφήν. Nonnus is not the only writer who transfers this epic noun to a Christian context. The fact that it occurs elsewhere in Christian literature designating the divine voice[11] clearly illustrates the adaptation of such pagan terminology to texts of the new religion. Now, to describe what in John is simply called δαιμόνιον (the Jews stating that it is a δαιμόνιον which dictates Christ's words), Nonnus uses vo-

---

[8] It has been suggested, more specifically, that for the Feeding of the Five Thousand Nonnus transfers liturgical elements into Homeric vocabulary and style: MacCoull 2003.
[9] For an examination of the same Biblical episode in Nonnus' *Paraphrase* and in Eudocia's *Homeric Centos* and for the consequent demonstration of their differences, see Whitby 2007.
[10] For the adjective θεσπέσιος, often used by Cyril, whose commentary on St. John's Gospel Nonnus used systematically, see Agosti on *Par.* 5.140. For ὀμφή as the divine voice in Nonnus, see also Stegemann 1930, 146, n. 52.
[11] For instance, in the Vision of Dorotheus (P. Bodmer 29, 220) Christ is referred to as πατέρ' ὀμφῆς; see further Agosti on *Par.* 5.141. Cf. also Christodorus *AP* 2.1, 245: θέσπιδος ὀμφῆς.

cabulary borrowed from Homer and from tragedy, so sketching this daemon imaginatively and with exaggeration, as is to be expected. In 8.158f. δαιμόνιον is conceived as a gad-fly who drives people crazy: ὅττι σε λύσσης / δαίμονος ἠερόφοιτος ἀλάστορος οἶστρος ἐλαύνει. Here the image is created by combining the famous Aeschylean ἀλάστωρ δαίμων (for instance *Pers.* 354, *Ag.* 1501[12]), together with a Homeric touch realized through the word ἠερόφοιτος, an adjective that Nonnus is particularly fond of,[13] and which is, in a slightly varied form, a Homeric rarity: in both Iliadic passages where it appears, it is attributed to the chthonian deity Erinys (*Il.* 9.571 and 19.87: ἠεροφοῖτις Ἐρινύς). It has been argued that in Homer the epithet describes a movement in the darkness, rather than a movement in the air.[14] In Nonnus the adjective has simply the sense of 'moving in the air'[15] and does not convey any negative connotation. In fact, in Book One of the *Paraphrase*, ἠεροφοίτης describes the throng of angels moving up and down the sky (1.215). It is remarkable that after Homer there is no other passage in extant literature where this adjective occurs, except for one instance in Aeschylus (fr. 282 R.: ἀερόφοιτος). Much later, it appears again. In addition to Nonnus, other poets who employ ἠερόφοιτος are Oppian, Manetho and Paul the Silentiary, the adjective being comparable to οὐρανοφοίτης, frequently used by Gregory of Nazianzus who attributes it to St. John and to St. Paul *inter alios*.[16] As regards the fact that in Book One of the *Paraphrase* the adjective is associated with movement of angels and in Book Eight it qualifies a daemonic power, it is evident that Nonnus uses the terms offered by the poetic past with a freedom and flexibility that do not prevent him from putting such terms in even completely contrasting contexts.[17]

Descriptions creating visual and acoustic stimulus inspired by Homer are occasionally used by Nonnus to elaborate a brief or plain phrase in the Gospel. The poet refers repeatedly to death as an ἀχλυόεν βέρεθρον (6.157, 11.184: ἀχλυό-

---

[12] For this Aeschylean motif, see further Fraenkel on *Ag.* 1501.
[13] Ἠερόφοιτος or ἠεροφοίτης: see, for instance, *D.* 5.492, 6.368, 10.262, 11.132, 12.63, 18.32, 21.333.
[14] See Hainsworth on *Il.* 9.571.
[15] See Vian on *D.* 25.86.
[16] See further De Stefani on *Par.* 1.215.
[17] A *variatio* of this adjective, again applied on the δαιμόνιον attributed to Christ by the Jews (John 7.20: δαιμόνιον ἔχεις), appears in *Par.* 7.75, δαίμονος ἠερίοιο. Ἥέριος in Homer describes the cranes (*Il.* 3.7), the tribe of the Cicones (*Od.* 9.52), and twice Thetis (*Il.* 1.497, 1.557). This adjective appears again like ἠερόφοιτος/ης very frequently in Nonnus' poetry. In the *Dionysiaca* it seldom qualifies a divinity, but in the *Paraphrase*, apart from accompanying the daemon in 7.75, it is also employed for the voice of the Holy Spirit (3.43 φωνῆς ἠερίης θεοδινέα βόμβον); in its only other occurrence in the *Paraphrase* it is attributed to the winds: see 3.91.

εντος...βερέθρου, 12.44: ἀχλυόεντι...βερέθρῳ). In other instances, Hades is a βέρεθρον without return (2.104: κόλπον ἀνοστήτοιο βερέθρου, occurring in the *Dionysiaca* as well[18]) or simply a βέρεθρον (8.56 and in 11.155). The image of the dark chasm is the result of the combination of two themes. Leaving aside the commonplace that the Underworld is dark, again ultimately Homeric (*Il.* 15.191: Ἀΐδης δ' ἔλαχε ζόφον ἠερόεντα), when one looks at ἀχλύς with death in mind, reminiscence of Homeric passages emerges once more. The first motif used in the Nonnian verses in discussion is that of death (or fainting) as a mist, ἀχλύς, falling on one's eyes: cf. *Il.* 5.696, 16.344: κατὰ δ' ὀφθαλμῶν κέχυτ' ἀχλύς, 20.421, *Od.* 22.88. On the other hand, Hades as a βέρεθρον is also a variation of the Iliadic description of Tartarus as an abyss in the depths of the earth, even lower than Hades (*Il.* 8.13f. ἤ μιν ἑλὼν ῥίψω ἐς Τάρταρον ἠερόεντα / τῆλε μάλ', ἧχι βάθιστον ὑπὸ χθονός ἐστι βέρεθρον, a passage discussed by Plato in *Phaedo* 112a). Nonnus is moreover probably recalling the idea that Hades is a βέρεθρον, which appears in other epic poets, namely Apollonius and Quintus Smyrnaeus, who also modelled their phrases on the Iliadic line.[19] It is remarkable that Christian poetry, too, exploited this theme, as is evident in the poetry of Romanus the Melodist, who says, when speaking of the fall of the Devil (33.20.7): καὶ ἐν βαράθρῳ κατηνέχθη Ἅιδου. Now, the origin of this presentation of the noise of thunder, described as βροντή in the Gospel (12.29: καὶ ἀκούσας ἔλεγεν, ὅτι βροντὴ γέγονεν), is clearly Homeric. The Gospel here narrates how some took God's voice for thunder from heaven. Nonnus takes the opportunity offered by the text itself and adorns his diction with vocabulary that bears clear epic overtones, when he says (12.116f.) λαὸς ἐπεσμαράγησεν, ὅτι ζαθέων ἀπὸ κόλπων/ βρονταίη βαρύδουπος ἐπέκτυπεν αἴθριος ἠχώ ('and the people roared, because a thunder-like, loud heavenly echo resounded'). Firstly, the poet replaces the simple ἔλεγεν of the Gospel with ἐπεσμαράγησεν, a variation of the verb σμαραγέω. This denotes inarticulate noises caused by the elements, such as thunder or the sea breaking on the shore or birds, and appears three times in Homer (*Il.* 2.210, 2.463, 21.199).[20] In the last passage σμαραγέω designates the noise of Zeus' thunder: Διὸς μεγάλοιο κεραυνόν/ δεινήν τε βροντήν, ὅτ' ἀπ' οὐρανόθεν σμαραγήσῃ. Nonnus transfers the verb to a similar context, but interesting-

---

18 D. 30.159: εἰ πέλε νόστιμος οἶμος ἀνοστήτοιο βερέθρου.
19 A.R. 2.642: διὲξ Ἀΐδαο βερέθρων, Q.S. 6.490 and 12.179: μέχρις ἐπ' Ἀϊδωνῆος ὑπερθύμοιο βέρεθρον, see Campbell 1981, ad loc.; cf. 6.264: ὑπ' ἠερόεντι βερέθρῳ.
20 Nonnus uses (ἐπι)σμαραγεῖν also in the *Dionysiaca* to render various noises and clamour and in [Oppian] the verb is used for the echo of the forest (*Cyn.* 2.78) and of the waters (*Cyn.* 4.170). For the verb meaning 'resound', rather than 'gleam', as some thought, having confused its root with that of σμάραγδος ('emerald'), see Kirk 1985 on *Il.* 2.462–63.

ly attributes it to human voices, this accomplishing an impressive *variatio*, since, quite unexpectedly, it is not the thunder itself that σμαραγέει, but the people who *think* they hear a thunder. It should be here added that in the only other instance in which σμαραγέω appears in the *Paraphrase* it describes the voice of Christ, who addresses Lazarus and commands him to come out of the tomb (11.157: εἶπε καὶ ἐσμαράγησε διαπρυσίῃ τινὶ φωνῇ). The use of the verb is again exceptional and striking, here enhancing the notion of the supernatural character that the words of Christ possess. Now, the adjective Nonnus attributes to the thunder, βαρύδουπος, in *Par.* 12.117, is a word first found in Moschus,[21] which the Panopolite poet uses very frequently in the *Dionysiaca* of various deities and noises.[22] In the present passage, combined as it is with the following verb ἐπέκτυπεν, it is a variation of βαρύκτυπος,[23] which qualifies Zeus in the Homeric hymn to Demeter (*Cer.* 3, 334, 441, 460) and in Hesiod (*Th.* 388, *Op.* 79);[24] at the same time, the adjective further recalls the Homeric ἐρίγδουπος for 'the husband of Hera' (ἐρίγδουπος πόσις Ἥρης in *Il.* 7.411, 10.329, 13.154, 16.88, *Od.* 15.180; Ζηνὸς [...] ἐριγδούποιο in *Il.* 12.235, 15.293). Thus Nonnus evokes in a manifold fashion the Homeric notion of Zeus who thunders when the poet speaks of the Jews, who assume they hear a βροντή. The *doctum* audience is once more invited to recognize the transfer of a memorable epic pattern to an entirely different environment and the sophistication the author employs as he adapts it to a Christian narrative.

Variation can be achieved in a particularly subtle way by exploiting the potential of a Homeric image in a highly allusive manner, in what is a purely Hellenistic fashion. In Book 21 of the *Paraphrase* Nonnus narrates the scene where the disciples meet Christ while they are fishing in Lake Tiberias. The net is called either δίκτυον,[25] as in the Gospel, or λίνον,[26] and the net imagery is recurrent, even when it is absent from the original, as typically happens in the *Paraphrase*. The fish-net is called λίνον once in Homer, in *Il.* 5.487. It is interesting to observe that Peter's garment, τὸν ἐπενδύτην in the Gospel (21.7), is conceived of as a linen veil by Nonnus and is depicted as πολύτρητος (21.39: καὶ λινέῳ πεπύκαστο πολυτρήτῳ χρόα πέπλῳ, 'and covered his body with a linen robe, full of holes').

---

[21] Moschus uses the adjective for Poseidon (*Eur.* 120).
[22] For instance *D.* 5.387, 17.92, 20.347, 27.91, 29.241, 36.371.
[23] There is also a self-variation with *D.* 7.276f. (ἐρωτοτόκῳ δὲ φαρέτρῃ / βρονταίης βαρύδουπος ἐδουλώθη κτύπος ἠχοῦς) on the arrow of Eros which strikes Semele.
[24] For the adjective, see West on Hes. *Th.* 388 and 441.
[25] 21.43, 21.50.
[26] 21.17f.: Σίμων / ...ὑπηνέμιον λίνον ἕλκων, 21.30f.: λίνα κολπώσαντες... / πόντιον αὐτοκύλιστον ἀνείρυον ἑσμὸν ἀλήτην, 21.33: οὐκέτι δὲ σθένος εἶχον ὑποβρύχιον λίνον ἕλκειν, 21.67f.: καὶ οὐ λίνον ἔνδοθι πόντου / σχίζετο τοσσατίων νεπόδων βεβαρημένον ὄγκῳ.

In this description the poet is playing with the Homeric image of the fish-nets, which are 'full of holes' (*Od.* 22.386: δικτύῳ...πολυωπῷ). Having presented Peter's garment as λίνεον, whose cognate λίνον[27] qualified the nets a little earlier, and having further attributed to it an adjective (πολύτρητος) similar to that describing the nets in Homer (πολυωπός), Nonnus uses words playfully reminiscent of the Homeric idea of the πολυωπὸν δίκτυον, which is also taken up by Oppian (*Hal.* 3.579) as λίνου πολυωπὸν ὄλεθρον (on the dangerousness of the net for the fish). In fact, Nonnus transfers the image of the epic nets to the clothes of Peter through the semantic transition offered by the meanings of λίνον. Πολύτρητος is also Homeric, appearing three times in the *Odyssey* and typically attributed to the sponge,[28] and both Suda and Eustathius underline its likeness to πολυωπός.[29] A λίνεος πέπλος, described as fine-crafted and suitable for warriors to be worn under the breast-plate, dresses the fighter Morrheus in *D.* 35.197 f.: καὶ λινέῳ κόσμησε δέμας χιονώδεϊ πέπλῳ, / οἷον ἔσω θώρηκος ἀεὶ φορέουσι μαχηταί. Thus, Nonnus produces a self-variation, which is emphasized in that it holds the same metrical position where adjective and noun stand in both poems. In the *Dionysiaca* the λίνεος πέπλος is decorative, as is emphasized by the verb κόσμησε and the adjective 'white like snow', and by the fact that it is found in a heroic environment; in the *Paraphrase* it is, on the other hand, a cloth imagined as ragged and of extremely poor quality, indeed suitable for fishermen. Nonnus' phrase is anyway somewhat paradoxical, since linen is usually the material of the *chiton*, a masculine garment, while *peplos* is the feminine garment, more embellished and luxurious.[30] This identification, however, is not always retained by Nonnus, since elsewhere he invariably uses πέπλος and χιτών.[31] In any case, πέπλος still bears epic connotations of luxury and fineness,[32] and forms a

---

[27] See, for instance, Chantraine s.v. λίνον; the thread of linen was originally used for fishing.
[28] *Od.* 1.111, 22.439 and 453: σπόγγοισι πολυτρήτοισι.
[29] Eustathius puts in parallel πολύτρητος and πολυωπός in his comment on *Od.* 1.111 (1.30,8 f.: ὅρα δὲ τὸ πολύτρητον οἰκειότατον ὂν σπόγγοις ὥσπερ δικτύοις τὸ πολυωπόν) and on 22.439 (2.289,21: πολύτρητοι δὲ σπόγγοι πρός τινα ἴσως ὁμοιότητα τοῦ, πολυωπὸν δίκτυον); see also Suda s.v. πολυωπόν· τὸ πολύτρητον δίκτυον.
[30] *Et. Gud.* s.v. πέπλος: διαφέρει πέπλος καὶ χιτών· χιτών λέγεται τὸ ἁπλοῦν καὶ λινοῦν περιβόλαιον· πέπλος δὲ τὸ ποικίλον καὶ γυναίκιον ἱμάτιον; cf. *EM* s.v. χιτών: ἐπὶ μὲν γὰρ ἀνδρῶν λέγεται χιτών· ἐπὶ δὲ γυναικῶν, πέπλος.
[31] *D.* 41.295, where the cloth woven on the loom is called πέπλος and χιτών in the same line.
[32] For instance, *Il.* 6.90, where the πέπλος is χαριέστατος and μέγιστος, *Od.* 7.96 f., where the πέπλοι are λεπτοὶ εὔννητοι, 15.105, where they are παμποίκιλοι, 18.292, where the πέπλος is called περικαλλέα. In the two other instances where πέπλος is used in the *Paraphrase*, the word has connotations of splendour, literal (20.82: θεοκμήτῳ τινὶ πέπλῳ, on the shining garment of the resurrected Christ), or supposed (19.9 f.: ἐπὶ χροΐ πέπλα βαλόντες/ Σιδονίης στίλβοντα

sharp contrast with its adjective, 'full of holes', and its position in a context of poverty and deprivation.

The following example demonstrates Homeric *variatio* in the service of religious *exegesis*. Nonnus renders the Gospel's σκηνοπηγία (7.2) with a combination of words which both remains very close to the original and at the same time bears clear Homeric overtones: the phrase πηγνυμέναις κλισίησιν (7.8), which occurs in variation also in *D.* 24.125 (κλισίας πήξαντες), retains the etymology of the noun employed in the Gospel, keeping πήγνυμι and only changing σκηνή to κλισίη, its Homeric equivalent, and is also, by a happy coincidence, reminiscent of Homer's εὔπηκτος κλισίη (*Il.* 9.663 and 24.675: μυχῷ κλισίης εὐπήκτου). Nonnus playfully uses a phrase recalling the Iliadic setting, but applies it to a different context. The σκηναί of the Jews rendered by the term κλισίαι are not 'tents' like those of the Iliadic warriors, but rather huts made from branches of trees (the Hebrew term is 'soukkot'), as befits a rural festival that σκηνοπηγία is. Moreover, πήγνυμι in the word σκηνοπηγία expresses the fact that the branches are pushed into the ground, while in Homer the tents are εὔπηκτοι, because the pieces of wood which support them are strong, well-made, εὐπαγῆ, as Eustathius notes on *Il.* 9.663.[33] It is interesting to observe that κλισίην πήγνυμι occurs again in the other Greek biblical poem, Ps. Apollinaris' *Paraphrase* of the Psalms, to render the verb κατασκηνόω used in the *Septuagint*.[34] It is evident that κλισίη offers the most convenient solution for the poetic transformation of the common σκηνή and its cognates for authors who chose the epic style for their paraphrase. The learned audience of both Ps. Apollinaris and Nonnus appreciates the transfer of a standard Iliadic expression to a totally dissimilar context, in which the Homeric terminology can be still present, albeit endowed with a different meaning and describing acts belonging to a totally diverse cultural environment. In Nonnus this transfer is all the more successful, since his participle πηγνύμεναι functioning as an adjective directly and powerfully recalls the Homeric adjective of the κλισίη from the same root, εὔπηκτος. Yet, Nonnus' capacity for variety can go further and deeper still. In *Par.* 7.32f. Jesus refuses to participate in the festival

---

σοφῷ σπινθῆρι θαλάσσης, concerning the ἱμάτιον πορφυροῦν with which the soldiers dressed Christ in mockery, as it is described in the Gospel in 19.2).
33 Schol. Eust. *Il.* 2.832, 5 ff. (van der Valk): ὅτι οἴκου μὲν οἰκεῖον ἐπίθετον τὸ εὔδμητον ἤτοι εὐδόμητον, κλισίας δὲ μάλιστα τὸ εὔπηκτον διὰ τὸ εὐπαγὲς τῶν ἐρειδόντων αὐτὴν ξύλων. Ἀχιλλεὺς οὖν εὗδε μυχῷ κλισίης εὐπήκτου. οὕτω που καὶ πηκτὸν ἄροτρον λέγεται. δῆλον δὲ ὅτι καὶ μέγαρόν που εὔπηκτον, ὥσπερ καὶ εὔτυκτον (cf. also *Il.* 13.240, *Od.* 4.123: κλισίην εὔτυκτον).
34 PG vol. 33 Migne: in *Par.* 64.8 (σοῖσι παρ' αὐλείοις κλισίην πήξοιτο μελάθροις, rendering David's κατασκηνώσει ἐν ταῖς αὐλαῖς σου in Psalm 64.5) and in 67.40 (κλισίην σθεναρήν ἐο πάντοτε πήξει, rendering David's καὶ γὰρ ὁ κύριος κατασκηνώσει εἰς τέλος in Psalm 67.17).

and Nonnus describes this statement by once more employing κλισίη and attributing to it a cognate of πήγνυμι as an adjective: οὔπω ἐγὼ κλισίας νεοπηγέας ἄρτι γεραίρων / εἰς τελετὴν ὁσίην ἐπιβήσομαι (to render the Johannine ἐγὼ οὐκ ἀναβαίνω εἰς τὴν ἑορτὴν ταύτην in 7.8). With κλισίας νεοπηγέας Nonnus again achieves a creative adaptation of the Homeric εὔπηκτος κλισίη, but this time is also moving in the realm of biblical *interpretatio*, as he adds to the text terms that further clarify the content: νεοπηγέας, in addition to being one more *variatio* of εὔπηκτος, lends an eschatological dimension to Christ's words, as the 'new' rite will replace the old Jewish one, since the new religion is to surpass and renew outdated Judaism and its rituals.[35]

Another noteworthy Homeric adaptation occurs at *Par*. 11.188f. Here the act of the high-priests in coming and meeting in council is rendered with the sentence καὶ ἄφρονες ἀρχιερῆες / εἰς ἀγορὴν ἀγέροντο πολύθροον, ἧχι γερόντων/ εἰς ἓν ἀγειρομένων πρωτόθρονος ἕζετο βουλή ('and the senseless high-priests gathered in the clamorous assembly, where the elders sitting in the first thrones used to come together in council'), rendering the simple Johannine συνέδριον (11.47). Several Homeric expressions are blended in this image and the spirit of the Homeric settings echoed in this passage is reversed. First we have a *verbatim* reproduction of the *figura etymologica* ἐς δ' ἀγορὴν ἀγέροντο of *Il*. 18.245,[36] which stands also in the same metrical *sedes* occupying the first hemistich. Nonnus further enhances this figure by the ἀγειρομένων of the next line, which multiplies the etymological play. This triple occurrence of cognates is partly parallel to the passage just mentioned, where ἀγορήν reappears in the next line (*Il*. 18.246: ὀρθῶν δ' ἑσταότων ἀγορὴ γένετ'), but, even more notably, it is parallel to the Iliadic οἳ δ' ἀγορὰς ἀγόρευον ἐπὶ Πριάμοιο θύρῃσι / πάντες ὁμηγερέες ἠμὲν νέοι ἠδὲ γέροντες (2.788–89: 'they were speaking in public, at the doors of Priam, all gathered together, young and old people'). Moreover, the image of the elders' sitting in council is a variation on *Il*. 2.53 βουλὴν δὲ πρῶτον μεγαθύμων ἷζε γερόντων, and the ἀγορὴ πολύθροος is a variation on the ἀγορὴν πολύφημον of *Od*. 2.150.[37] The notion of wisdom and prudence inherent in the

---

35 See Caprara 1999, 201.
36 Cf. Eustathius *ad loc*. (4.169,4f.): ἐτυμολογικὸς δὲ συνήθης τρόπος τὸ ἐς ἀγορὰν ἀγέροντο. Apollonius Rhodius also uses the phrase in the same *sedes* in 4.214. Although this phrase does not recur in Homer, in order to justify Eustathius' description of it as 'usual', we have similar etymological schemas like οἳ δ' ἐπεὶ οὖν ἤγερθεν ὁμηγερέες τε γένοντο in *Il*. 1.57 and αὐτὰρ ἐπεί ῥ' ἤγερθεν ὁμηγερέες τ' ἐγένοντο in *Il*. 24.790, *Od*. 2.9, 8.24 and 24.421. See also Kirk 1985 on *Il*. 2.788–89.
37 The creative use of *Il*. 2.53 and *Od*. 2.150 by Nonnus, who further combines them with other Homeric lines, can be contrasted with the use made of them by Eudocia, who integrates them *verbatim* in her cento (1.1492, 1.1276 and 2.1288).

Homeric image of the leaders' assembly, stressed by Nonnus' explicit statement that the meeting is principally made by the γέροντες, is contrasted with the foolishness of the ἄφρονες high-priests, who plan to kill Jesus. This is an illustrative case of Homeric imitation through opposition and also yet one more example of Nonnus' hostile attitude toward the Jews, a stance influenced by Cyril of Alexandria.[38]

These are only a few examples of the reception and adaptation of Homeric vocabulary and formulas in the *Metabole* of the Gospel by Nonnus. It is evident that the poet is repeatedly echoing epic phrases and achieves expected *variatio*, by changing such phrases slightly or even considerably and by modifying the context in which these reminiscences appear. Thus, he creates a poem written in Homeric style, rather than merely a Homeric cento. He frequently enhances the sophistication of his work by combining more than one source in his text, so that a Homeric phrase can find its way in the work of Nonnus through its use in some later epic author. In addition, epic motifs can be combined with themes from other poetry, e.g. tragedy, and result into new images creatively adjusted into Nonnian narration, according to the Alexandrian literary practice. The poet incorporates in his verses terms and imagery drawn from the poetic past with an extraordinary flexibility, being ready to place them in a pagan or in a Christian context and in opposite settings with equal ease. Interestingly, biblical *interpretatio* is moreover occasionally realized through the employment of epic phraseology. Characteristic passages from both Nonnus and other Christian poets demonstrate that narratives wholly alien to the mythical heroic world can be vested with the elaboration of epic splendour, and, furthermore, that Homeric language and Homeric allusion can even be used to articulate ideological positions and to convey fundamental theological notions and doctrinal concepts.

---

38 See Caprara 1999, *passim*; cf. also above, with n. 35. For the Jews' deranged state of mind, in particular, cf. *Par.* 5.57: Ἑβραῖοι μανιωδέες ἄφρονι θυμῷ, 10.130: ὑμεῖς ἄφρονα μῦθον ἐπεφθέγξασθε μανέντες, 11.28: Ἰουδαίης μανιώδεες ἄρτι πολῖται. See further Agosti 2003, 410–11.

Part V **Latin Transformations**

Helen Peraki-Kyriakidou
Trees and Plants in Poetic Emulation: From the Homeric Epic to Virgil's *Eclogues*

It is obvious that a brief list of two or three lines in length cannot have the same function as an epic-sized catalogue – such as a battle-catalogue – of, say, ten lines or longer. It is true that in a catalogue each name may gain a place in human memory.[1] In a long catalogue, however, the portion of that memory each name holds may be indeed meagre. Things function differently in a small list of names: each constituent—whether a proper name or not—proportionately holds a more prestigious position in the poetic text; even more so if that list belongs to the pastoral genre, like the *Eclogues*. Considering the size of a bucolic work, a short catalogue is no longer short. In such catalogues each part retains its value; what matters, however, is not only the entry of an item but also with what other similar items the catalogue is formed and, above all, what the aim of each catalogue is. In this paper we shall deal with short lists of two to three lines more or less consisting of names of trees and plants. Homer has given us a number of such catalogues.

In the *Iliad* there are five such catalogues.[2] Three of them are found in epic similes and display a purely epic character, portraying the tension and force of the fight. One of them appears in two occasions with exactly the same *comparatum* and *comparandum* and with the same aim. It is found at 13.389–93=16.482–86. In both instances the fall of a hero at the time of the fight is likened to the felling of trees by the hands of carpenters (τέκτονες ἄνδρες, 13.390 = 16.483).[3] The third one appears at 16.765–71, where the fierceness of the battle is compared with the strong winds in a wood and the noise the tall trees make as they clash each other.[4] The tension[5] thus created is such that the listener/reader is under the impression that each fallen tree represents nothing more than a brief moment in the phase of destruction. Each tree of the simile – usually a

---

[1] Minchin 2001, 77 ff.; Kyriakidis 2007, xiv–xvi.
[2] At least three names distributed in two or more lines should be regarded as a catalogue: Kyriakidis 2007, xiii. In the present case, however, I would like to bring into the discussion also some instances of one-line catalogues; see n. 4, below.
[3] Cf. *Il.* 23.114 ff. which, according to Skutsch (1985, 341, fr. 115) and Elliott (2013, 290), is the model of Enn. *Ann.* 177–79 Sk. (see below, p. 239).
[4] In this case, the catalogue itself covers only one line (16.767). It is useful though to include it into our discussion. See below, p. 240.
[5] Kyriakidis 2007, *passim*, mainly Part I: 'Structure and Contents'.

tall tree– falls. The poetic purpose is similar in the fourth catalogue occurring at 21.350 – 52, when Hephaestus burns everything together with Achilles' victims:

καίοντο πτελέαι τε καὶ ἰτέαι ἠδὲ μυρῖκαι,
καίετο δὲ λωτός τε ἰδὲ θρύον ἠδὲ κύπειρον,
τὰ περὶ καλὰ ῥέεθρα ἅλις ποταμοῖο πεφύκει.

Burned were the elms and the willows and the tamarisks,
burned were the lotus and the rushes and the galingale
which grew abundantly round the fair streams of the river.[6]

The trees are the victims of divine wrath in a fashion similar to the human victims of Achilles, since the true perpetrator was Hera scheming against the Trojans. The character of these catalogues is purely epic: there is tension and magnitude; the slayers and the slain are also there.

In the *Iliad*, however, there is one instance of a vignette-catalogue which could draw the attention of a bucolic poet.[7] It is from the scene where Zeus makes love to Hera:

Ἦ ῥα καὶ ἀγκὰς ἔμαρπτε Κρόνου παῖς ἣν παράκοιτιν·
τοῖσι δ' ὑπὸ χθὼν δῖα φύεν νεοθηλέα ποίην,
λωτόν θ' ἑρσήεντα ἰδὲ κρόκον ἠδ' ὑάκινθον
πυκνὸν καὶ μαλακόν, ὃς ἀπὸ χθονὸς ὑψόσ' ἔεργε.
(*Il.* 14.346 – 49)

At that Cronus' son clasped his wife in his arms,
and beneath them the bright earth made fresh-sprung grass to grow,
and dewy lotus and crocus and hyacinth,
thick and soft, that kept them from the ground.

No large trees are mentioned, and the violence is absent. The scene has the characteristics of springtime;[8] it is almost a *locus amoenus*, a creation of the poetic imagination which – according to scholars– has its roots in the same epic work.[9] This catalogue is different in nature and significance from the previous ones. If there is anything epic in it, it is the divine nature of the participants. Here, as in the Virgilian catalogue which will be discussed below, 'the earth un-

---

6 In the Iliadic passages I follow the translation of Murray/Wyatt 1999 with minor adjustments.
7 Janko 1992 on 347 – 48: 'Verses 347 f. are richly paralleled in post-Homeric *epos*.'
8 Janko (1992 on 347 – 48) commenting on the word ποίη recognizes spring flowers in the scene, such as the hyacinth.
9 Elliger 1975; Griffin 1992, 192, 200.

asked, throws up a carpet of spring flowers beneath the lovers'.[10] Virgil perhaps saw in this catalogue elements pertaining to his imagery in *Eclogue* 4, when nature itself brings gifts to the *puer, nullo .... cultu* (4.18).[11]

In our discussion, however, the *Odyssey* proves to be more revealing. At 4.602–04 Telemachus compares Laconia, fit for horsemanship (ἱππήλατος), with rugged Ithaca:

> σὺ γὰρ πεδίοιο ἀνάσσεις
> εὐρέος, ᾧ ἔνι μὲν λωτὸς πολύς, ἐν δὲ κύπειρον
> πυροί τε ζειαί τε ἰδ' εὐρυφυὲς κρῖ λευκόν.
> (Od. 4.602–04)
>
> *For you are lord of a wide plain,*
> *where there is abundant lotus and galingale*
> *and wheat and spelt and broad-eared white barley.*[12]

With this catalogue Telemachus claims that Ithaca cannot be ἱππήλατος (4.607). The very plants contained in the catalogue define the qualities of the place.

In Book 7 the surroundings of Alcinous' palace are described. It is full of trees yielding fruit all year round:

> ἔκτοσθεν δ' αὐλῆς μέγας ὄρχατος ἄγχι θυράων
> τετράγυος· περὶ δ' ἕρκος ἐλήλαται ἀμφοτέρωθεν.
> ἔνθα δὲ δένδρεα μακρὰ πεφύκασι τηλεθάοντα,
> ὄγχναι καὶ ῥοιαὶ καὶ μηλέαι ἀγλαόκαρποι   115
> συκέαι τε γλυκεραὶ καὶ ἐλαῖαι τηλεθόωσαι.
> τάων οὔ ποτε καρπὸς ἀπόλλυται οὐδ' ἀπολείπει
> χείματος οὐδὲ θέρευς, ἐπετήσιος· ἀλλὰ μάλ' αἰεὶ
> Ζεφυρίη πνείουσα τὰ μὲν φύει, ἄλλα δὲ πέσσει.
> ὄγχνη ἐπ' ὄγχνῃ γηράσκει, μῆλον δ' ἐπὶ μήλῳ,   120
> αὐτὰρ ἐπὶ σταφυλῇ σταφυλή, σῦκον δ' ἐπὶ σύκῳ.[13]

---

10 Janko 1992 on 14.346–53.
11 See below, p. 245.
12 The translation of the passages from the *Odyssey* is based on Murray/Dimock 1995 with minor adjustments.
13 Equally simple is the imagery in Theocr. *Id.* 23.28–31:
> καὶ τὸ ῥόδον καλόν ἐστι, καὶ ὁ χρόνος αὐτὸ μαραίνει·
> καὶ τὸ ἴον καλόν ἐστιν ἐν εἴαρι, καὶ ταχὺ γηρᾷ·
> [λευκὸν τὸ κρίνον ἐστί, μαραίνεται ἁνίκα πίπτει·
> ἁ δὲ χιὼν λευκά, καὶ τάκεται ἁνίκα † παχθῇ·]
>
> *Fair is the rose too, yet time withers it;*
> *fair in spring is the stock, but ages fast;*

> ἔνθα δέ οἱ πολύκαρπος ἀλωὴ ἐρρίζωται,
> τῆς ἕτερον μέν θ' εἰλόπεδον λευρῷ ἐνὶ χώρῳ
> τέρσεται ἠελίῳ, ἑτέρας δ' ἄρα τε τρυγόωσιν,
> ἄλλας δὲ τραπέουσι· πάροιθε δέ τ' ὄμφακές εἰσιν   125
> ἄνθος ἀφιεῖσαι, ἕτεραι δ' ὑποπερκάζουσιν.
> ἔνθα δὲ κοσμηταὶ πρασιαὶ παρὰ νείατον ὄρχον
> παντοῖαι πεφύασιν, ἐπηετανὸν γανόωσαι.
> ἐν δὲ δύω κρῆναι ἡ μέν τ' ἀνὰ κῆπον ἅπαντα
> σκίδναται, ἡ δ' ἑτέρωθεν ὑπ' αὐλῆς οὐδὸν ἵησι   130
> πρὸς δόμον ὑψηλόν, ὅθεν ὑδρεύοντο πολῖται.
> τοῖ' ἄρ' ἐν Ἀλκινόοιο θεῶν ἔσαν ἀγλαὰ δῶρα.
> (Od. 7.112–32)
>
> But outside the courtyard, close to the doors,
> there is a great orchard of four acres, and a hedge runs about it on either side.
> In it grow trees, tall and luxuriant,
> pears and pomegranates and apple-trees with their bright fruit,
> and sweet figs, and luxuriant olives.
> The fruit of these neither perishes nor fails
> in winter or in summer, but lasts throughout the year;
> and continually the West Wind, as it blows, quickens to life some fruits, and ripens
> others; pear upon pear waxes ripe, apple upon apple,
> cluster upon cluster, and fig upon fig.
> There, too, is his fruitful vineyard planted,
> one part of which, a warm spot on level ground,
> is being dried in the sun, while other grapes men are gathering,
> and others, too, they are treading; but in front are unripe grapes
> that are shedding the blossom, and others that are turning purple.
> There again, by the last row of the vines,
> grow trim garden beds of every sort, blooming the year through,
> and in the orchard there are two springs, one of which sends its water throughout all the garden, while the other, opposite to it, flows beneath the threshold of the court
> toward the high house; from this the townsfolk drew their water.
> Such were the glorious gifts of the gods in the palace of Alcinous.

The orchard (ὄρχατος, 7.112) has a specific size (τετράγυος) and well-set boundaries (113: περὶ δ' ἕρκος ἐλήλαται ἀμφοτέρωθεν). The trees and fruits of the two catalogues (to the degree to which the second corresponds to the first) do not seem to have any other distinct presence in the epic outside the catalogue in

---

[white is the lily but it withers in a short while,
and white is the snow, but it wastes away on the ground]. (trans. Gow 1952[2] with minor adjustments)

See also Id. 27.10 (ΔΑΦΝΙΣ): ἀ σταφυλὶς σταφὶς ἔσται· ὃ νῦν ῥόδον, αὖον ὀλεῖται ('The grape will become a raisin, and what is now a rose will wither and die', trans. Gow 1952[2]).

all its versions, as we shall see; they have no role, therefore, in the feasts of the aristocracy at the palace of Alcinous. Although in the *Odyssey* there is no scene in which men are fed with this kind of fruits, nevertheless the scene described[14] gives a sense of opulence. Indeed Alcinous' society[15] bears the characteristics of an affluent aristocratic society.[16] The passage closes with the reminder that whatever the orchard contains, trees, plants, springs, are the gifts of the gods to Alcinous (132: τοῖ᾽ ἄρ᾽ ἐν Ἀλκινόοιο θεῶν ἔσαν ἀγλαὰ δῶρα).[17]

Again the description consists of pieces contained in a sort of *locus amoenus*, a *utopia*, according to Schein,[18] suitable to a bucolic environment: trees, water, springs. This kind of description, according to Hunter, is characterized by a 'typicality' to the degree that 'all landscape description in literature is more or less "typical"'.[19] This 'typicality' facilitates the catalogue's accommodation in different contexts. Furthermore, the double –of a sort– appearance of the catalogue within the same narrative unit and its reappearance in very different parts of the epic, as we shall see below, denotes its formulaic character, which means that it can serve different poetic aims in different poetic environments. One element which enhances the dynamics of repetitiveness is the absence of human activity or of human toil, as Edwards (1993) notes, with the exception, of course, of the verbs τρυγόωσιν (7.124) and τραπέουσιν (7.125) in our passage, where the subject remains an abstraction. This latter point, as Edwards acknowledges, is a non-Homeric characteristic and transfers the focus from the action to the result.[20] All these elements permit us to say that the description of the orchard seems to have characteristics of a rather generic value.

---

14 The passage can be considered to be part of court poetry. For Theocritus or Virgil, however, the description of the surrounding space contains elements that could be recognized as pastoral. At the same time we should not forget that Theocritus has served court poetry within the frame of his pastoral (e.g. *Id.* 16, 17).
15 According to John Rundin (1996, 203, n. 40), as the trees bear fruits all the year round, 'the net result of this is summed up in the observation that, because they have unfailing supplies, the Phaeacians like to sit around on expensive coverlets eating and drinking (*Od.* 7.95–99).'
16 Dalby (1995, 277) doubts that the *Odyssey* refers to an 'aristocratic' society and that the poets used to sing only for its members. One of his examples is the garden of Alcinous with its fruits where at no time is there anybody who eats any of its fruits.
17 It is rather similar to what Virgil would have described as the gifts of the Earth, in *Eclogue* 4 when the *puer* is born (see below, p. 245).
18 Schein 1995, 48.
19 Hunter 1999, 13.
20 Edwards 1993, 47: 'The passage exhibits the same careful and orderly division of space noted in the descriptions of Achilles' Shield and of the founding of Scheria, with perhaps the same cosmogonic implications. The beauty, order, and continuous fertility of the garden, warmed by gentle Zephyr, distinguish Alcinous's garden as an example of the enchanted

In the description of Alcinous' palace, besides trees and running water (7.129–30) we have the blowing wind, Zephyrus (119), which helps the fruits ripen. The presence of Zephyrus in particular is noteworthy, for elsewhere this very wind is described as δυσαής (stormy) as in *Il.* 23.200,[21] whereas here it is a favourable, mild wind, as again in the *Odyssey* in the Elysian fields (*Od.* 4.563) at line 4.567.[22]

> οὐ νιφετός, οὔτ' ἄρ χειμὼν πολὺς οὔτε ποτ' ὄμβρος,
> ἀλλ' αἰεὶ Ζεφύροιο λιγὺ πνείοντος ἀήτας
> Ὠκεανὸς ἀνίησιν ἀναψύχειν ἀνθρώπους.
> (*Od.* 4.566–68)

> *There is no snow, nor heavy storm, nor even rain,*
> *but Ocean always sends up blasts of the shrill-blowing West Wind,*
> *that they may give cooling to men.*

We cannot but notice that the space of the palace, therefore, shares some details with the description of the Underworld. As a matter of fact, in the palace of Alcinous the hero will immerse himself in his past and revive it with his narrative to the Phaeacians, as though he is experiencing a form of *katabasis*.

This overlapping between features of the palace and the Netherworld is confirmed at *Nekyia* 11.588–90.[23] There Tantalus is punished for the *hybris* he has shown in life (not registered in the epic). He strives to drink water but always

---

locus amoenus as much as it is a working farm. This distinction is emphasized by the strange absence of any reference to labor and laborers from the garden precinct. In the entire passage only the subjectless τρυγόωσιν (124) and τραπέουσιν (125), referring to the harvesting and crushing of the grapes, adumbrate the necessity of labor in this description, which otherwise eclipses an entire class of the population (the vast majority) and a fundamental social relationship. Such a complete ellipsis of a verb's subject is uncharacteristic of Homer and distracts attention from the activity itself to its result. The processes of cultivation, dressing and irrigation, moreover, are submerged in the passage as are those of gathering the fruits of the orchard or harvesting the vegetables'.

21 Strab. 1.2.21. See also *Il.* 11.305–06 and Stanford 1959 on *Od.* 7.119.
22 West 1988 on 4.563 ff.
23 As expected, the reappearance of the catalogue from the orchards of Alcinous' palace in the Underworld has been discussed on the basis of epic orality. This repetition is what Combellack (1965, 53) calls 'formulary illogicalities': 'As usual, the poet shows no concern to modify the phraseology designed for a normal situation, so as to make it appropriate for the abnormal situation he happens to describe.' Orality, however, should not have been in the priorities of a Latin poet. Nonetheless, one cannot ignore the fact that every time a passage is in a new environment, it should retain a functional role there contextually. This catalogue of trees repeated in the narrative of the Underworld should be read as an integral part of the description there.

fails. At the same time, every attempt of this poor man to grasp the fruits of the trees with rich foliage over the pond fails, as the wind tosses them away to the clouds (591–92):

> δένδρεα δ' ὑψιπέτηλα κατὰ κρῆθεν χέε καρπόν,
> ὄγχναι καὶ ῥοιαὶ καὶ μηλέαι ἀγλαόκαρποι
> συκέαι τε γλυκεραὶ καὶ ἐλαῖαι τηλεθόωσαι·
> τῶν ὁπότ' ἰθύσει' ὁ γέρων ἐπὶ χερσὶ μάσασθαι
> τὰς δ' ἄνεμος ῥίπτασκε ποτὶ νέφεα σκιόεντα.
> (Od. 11.588–92)
>
> *And trees, high and leafy, let dangle their fruits from their tops,*
> *pears and pomegranates and apple trees with their bright fruit*
> *and sweet figs and luxuriant olives.*
> *But as often as that old man would reach out towards these, to clutch them*
> *with his hands, the wind would toss them to the shadowy clouds.*

The transference of the scene is perfectly served by the formulaic character of the catalogue retaining once again features of a *locus amoenus*[24] (trees/water) that the dead man cannot enjoy; he cannot even approach the trees. Furthermore, as in the palace of Alcinous, but more emphatically in this case, human labour connected with the cultivation of these trees is absent.[25]

The catalogue of Alcinous' orchard after its reappearance in the Netherworld appears again- although in a variant form- in Book 24 of the *Odyssey*:

> ὦ γέρον, οὐκ ἀδαημονίη σ' ἔχει ἀμφιπολεύειν
> ὄρχατον, ἀλλ' εὖ τοι κομιδὴ ἔχει, οὐδέ τι πάμπαν,
> οὐ φυτόν, οὐ συκῆ, οὐκ ἄμπελος, οὐ μὲν ἐλαίη,
> οὐκ ὄγχνη, οὐ πρασιή τοι ἄνευ κομιδῆς κατὰ κῆπον.
> ἄλλο δέ τοι ἐρέω, σὺ δὲ μὴ χόλον ἔνθεο θυμῷ·
> αὐτόν σ' οὐκ ἀγαθὴ κομιδὴ ἔχει, ἀλλ' ἅμα γῆρας
> λυγρὸν ἔχεις αὐχμεῖς τε κακῶς καὶ ἀεικέα ἔσσαι.
> (Od. 24.244–50)
>
> *Old man, no lack of skill in tending a garden besets you;*
> *But your care is good, and there is nothing whatsoever,*
> *either plant or fig tree or vine or olive*
> *or pear or garden-plot in all the field that lacks care.*

---

24 See also Edwards 1993, 47, who uses the term with some reservations (passage quoted above, n. 20).
25 See Combellac 1965, 53 on the similarity between this passage and the description of Alcinous' orchard.

> But something else I shall tell you, and do not take offence.
> You yourself do not enjoy good care, but you bear woeful old age,
> and you are sadly squalid and wear wretched clothes.

It is the moment Odysseus pretends that he does not recognize his father Laertes (a pretence that he will abandon a little later). In sharp contrast, however, with the previous occurrences of the catalogue, the human effort Odysseus' father has exerted in cultivating his garden is stressed. This detail is important, as it differentiates this use of the catalogue from its previous uses. There is a further point, though, which is particularly stressed here. It is the value *each* kind of tree has: Odysseus names them all *one by one* in order to stress that not a single one of them is deprived of his father's special attention (οὐδέ, οὐ, οὐ, οὐκ, οὐ, οὐκ, οὐ). The element of bestowing separate value to every single item of the catalogue is particularly enhanced in the last appearance of the same list further down. It is when Odysseus speaking to Laertes uses the contents of the catalogue together with a reference to the wound (24.331: οὐλή) as a sign to the father to *recognize* his son after a lapse of long years (340–41):

> σὺ δέ με προΐεις καὶ πότνια μήτηρ
> ἐς πατέρ' Αὐτόλυκον μητρὸς φίλον, ὄφρ' ἂν ἑλοίμην
> δῶρα, τὰ δεῦρο μολών μοι ὑπέσχετο καὶ κατένευσεν.
> εἰ δ' ἄγε τοι καὶ δένδρε' ἐϋκτιμένην κατ' ἀλῳὴν
> εἴπω, ἅ μοί ποτ' ἔδωκας, ἐγὼ δ' ᾔτευν σε ἕκαστα
> παιδνὸς ἐών, κατὰ κῆπον ἐπισπόμενος· διὰ δ' αὐτῶν
> ἱκνεύμεσθα, σὺ δ' ὠνόμασας καὶ ἔειπες ἕκαστα.
> ὄγχνας μοι δῶκας τρεισκαίδεκα καὶ δέκα μηλέας,
> συκέας τεσσαράκοντ'· ὄρχους δέ μοι ὧδ' ὀνόμηνας
> δώσειν πεντήκοντα, διατρύγιος δὲ ἕκαστος
> ἤην; ἔνθα δ' ἀνὰ σταφυλαὶ παντοῖαι ἔασιν,
> ὁππότε δὴ Διὸς ὧραι ἐπιβρίσειαν ὕπερθεν.
> (Od. 24.333–44)

> It was you who sent me, you and my honoured mother,
> to Autolycus, my mother's father, that I could get
> the gifts which, when he came here, he promised and agreed to give me.
> And come, I shall tell you also the trees in the well-ordered garden
> which you once gave me, and I, who was only a child,
> was following you through the garden, and asking you for this and that.
> It was through these trees that we passed, and you named them, and told me of
> each one. You gave me thirteen pear-trees and ten apple-trees
> and forty fig-trees. And you also promised to give me rows of vines,
> even as I say, fifty of them, which ripened one by one at different times
> — and upon them are clusters of all sorts—
> whenever the seasons of Zeus weighed them down from above.

In the frame of this catalogue (337–39)[26], the poet gives special attention to the value of *each tree separately*. The word ἕκαστος used twice (337, 339) and the phrase διὰ δ' αὐτῶν (338) contribute to it. Laertes did not give to Odysseus any old piece of land but a well-ordered space (336: ἐϋκτιμένην κατ' ἀλῳήν)[27] with a specific number of trees of each kind, which he names separately. It is these very trees which Odysseus had learnt *one by one* and which became the second token for his recognition; hence, these trees constitute a proof for his identity, a sort of referent or even a symbol of his youth.

The above catalogue repeated in various versions in different parts of the epic, as well as the other short catalogues of plants and trees in the Homeric text show that:

(i) Most of the above descriptions function outside the sphere of human labour.
(ii) The items in the above catalogues are added one by one in a paratactic and linear way (things will change to a great extent in Theocritus and Virgil).
(iii) Not only the last catalogue but the others as well, except for the three (=four) 'epic' catalogues of the *Iliad* that we examined at the beginning of this paper, contain some details from the imagery of a *locus amoenus*. Such a description, according to scholars, contains some 'typical' components which evidently contribute to its potentials of repetitiveness facilitating the catalogue's accommodation in different environments within the epic (or in different genres).
(iv) Considering the last catalogues of the *Odyssey* especially in Book 24, we saw that the separate value of every single item seems to be stressed, even though each one is pertinent to collectivity. Each one represents either human labour (at 24.244–50) or particulars of the hero's identity, as at 24.333–44. It is precisely this power of representation of each plant or tree which has the dynamism to develop into a symbol and which in turn –centuries later and together with the other characteristics of the catalogue– found the proper conditions for development in the pastoral.

In Virgil's *Eclogues* there are short catalogues of two to three lines, similar to the Homeric ones as regards both form and content. It is clear that Homeric epics have been significantly employed as a source text. There are, however, major differences. First of all, the plants included in Virgil's short catalogues differ to a

---

[26] Kyriakidis 2007 shows the importance of the frame for the reception of a catalogue: Part II: 'Catalogues in Context'.
[27] Cf. *Od.* 7.112–13 (Alcinous' garden, for which see above, pp. 229–30).

great extent from their Homeric counterparts; in this instance the Roman poet seems to have received Theocritus rather than Homer. Another major difference is that a considerable number of these plants are related in tradition in one way or another to a certain god, especially to gods of poetry, culture and civilization. Such cases are already attested in Theocritus. The reader can therefore easily conceive the symbolic power[28] of such plants. An obvious example is the vignette-catalogue of *Idyll* 2:

> ἧνθον γάρ κεν ἐγώ, ναὶ τὸν γλυκὺν ἧνθον Ἔρωτα,
> ἢ τρίτος ἠὲ τέταρτος ἐὼν φίλος αὐτίκα νυκτός,
> μᾶλα μὲν ἐν κόλποισι Διωνύσοιο φυλάσσων,
> κρατὶ δ' ἔχων λεύκαν, Ἡρακλέος ἱερὸν ἔρνος,
> πάντοθι πορφυρέαισι περὶ ζώστραισιν ἑλικτάν.[29]
> (*Id.* 2.118–22)[30]
>
> *For I would have come, by sweet Love,*
> *I would, at early nightfall, with two or three friends,*
> *bearing in my bosom apples of Dionysus,*
> *and on my brows the white poplar, the holy plant of Heracles,*
> *twined all about with crimson bands.*[31]

Given that the *Eclogues*, as a whole, lend themselves to a metapoetic reading, many of the plants mentioned in such catalogues, such as, for instance, the laurel, the ivy or the vine, function very much as cultural or metaliterary symbols.[32]

I would like to start with a catalogue[33] where things are made very clear by the poet himself. As in Theocritus, Virgil, in a direct way, relates a plant or a tree to a specific god,[34] who in tradition has a well-recognized cultural and metalit-

---

28 'The symbol as divine accoutrement occupies a mediating position between the divine and human realms. It is a thing from this world that is affiliated with a being from beyond' (Struck 2004, 146).
29 Cf. below (*Id.* 3.23; 1.29, 31).
30 Cf. *Epigr.* 1.1–3.
31 The translation of Theocritus' *Idylls* is based on Gow 1952² with minor adjustments.
32 E.g. Saunders 2008, 146 and n. 44.
33 Comparing the length of the Homeric text with that of the *Eclogues*, the frequency of this sort of catalogue in the pastoral poetry of Virgil is very high; some one-line catalogues are equally interesting: e.g. *Ecl.* 3.63, 7.38.
34 Later Phaedrus (3.17) will form a similar catalogue of plants and trees in relation to certain gods:

> *olim quas uellent esse in tutela sua,*
> *diui legerunt arbores. Quercus Iovi*
> *et myrtus Veneri placuit, Phoebo laurea,*
> *pinus Cybebae, populus celsa Herculi.*

erary significance: at *Ecl.* 7 we have the competition between Corydon and Thyrsis. Through a short catalogue of plants and trees, each of them declares their love for, and faith in their beloved. At lines 7.61–64 Corydon, the eventual winner, associates certain plants and trees with specific deities and concludes that his beloved Phyllis, who loves hazels (*corylos*) will, in the end, defeat the myrtle of Venus[35] and the laurel of Apollo:

> *Populus Alcidae gratissima, vitis Iaccho,*
> *formosae myrtus Veneri, sua laurea Phoebo:*
> *Phyllis amat corylos; illas dum Phyllis amabit,*
> *nec myrtus vincet corylos nec laurea Phoebi.*
> (*Ecl.* 7.61–64)
>
> *Dearest is poplar to Alcides, vines to Bacchus,*
> *Myrtle to lovely Venus, to Phoebus his own bay.*
> *Phyllis loves hazels, and, while Phyllis loves them,*
> *Hazels will never lose to myrtle or Phoebus' bay.*
> (trans. Lee 1980 with minor adjustments)

All four plants of the two-line catalogue represent gods who in one way or another were associated with poetry and culture in myth and literature. Further to each god's individual contribution, however, the relation between Dionysus and Apollo,[36] as well as that between Venus and Dionysus is well known; also well-known is Hercules' contribution to culture and civilization and his relation to the Muses.[37] This is not the time to discuss the number of instances where these deities were worshipped together or had overlapping interests. What is of importance to us is that Phyllis who loves hazels[38] does not have to compete only with one god and his or her symbolic plant, but with what the four of them together represent. Corydon, through Phyllis' *corylos* (a word which can be regarded as an etymology of his own name),[39] seems to contend that his poetry

---

> Once the gods chose the trees they wanted
> to have under their protection. Jupiter liked the oak,
> Venus liked the myrtle, Apollo the laurel,
> and Cybele liked the pine; Hercules liked the tall poplar.

[35] On the relation between Venus and the myrtle, see Ov. *Fast.* 4.15; also Plin. *NH* 15.124–26; Serv. on *Ecl.* 7.62, *Geor.* 2.64, *Aen.* 1.720. See Vollgraff 1921, 246–50 (esp. 250).
[36] On this relation in Virgil, see the seminal article by Mac Góráin 2012–13.
[37] See below, n. 40.
[38] In *Geor.* 2.299 the poet advises the farmer: *neve inter vitis corylum sere* (nor plant the hazel among the vines).
[39] Egan 1996, 235; on her name, *ibid.* 236; on Corydon's name: Lipka 2001, 178 ff.; Peraki-Kyriakidou 2010, 564 f.; Cucchiarelli 2012 on 7.63.

is better than that which is considered the quintessence of poetic production characterized by Apollonian along with Dionysiac elements[40] *cum venustate*[41] in the Muses' realm. The relation of *populus* to Hercules in the first position of the catalogue is not without significance. The Muses and Hercules had established their connection long ago. Highly important for this connection was the erection of the *Aedes Herculis Musarum* by M. Fulvius Nobilior.[42] However, only in Corydon's song is this tree related to Hercules,[43] not in Thyrsis' song.

In his response Thyrsis employs another catalogue of trees,[44] which closes by claiming that if his beloved Lycidas visits him more often, nature will reward him. In this short catalogue any connection of the trees with corresponding deities is absent:

fraxinus in silvis pulcherrima, pinus in hortis,
populus in fluviis, abies in montibus altis.
saepius at si me Lycida formose revisas
fraxinus in silvis cedat tibi, pinus in hortis.
(*Ecl.* 7.65 – 68)

Fairest the ash in forest, in pleasure-gardens pine,
poplars by streams and on high mountains silver fir.
But, lovely Lycidas, visit me more often,
and forest ash and garden pine will honour you.
(trans. Lee 1980 with minor adjustments)

Here I would like to add some further thoughts to what I have already discussed in an earlier paper with regard to this *certamen*.[45] Lycidas himself, unlike Phyllis, does not have some favourite plant which would stand as representative of him. Furthermore, Corydon includes in his catalogue plants and trees which were directly related to certain gods and were also acknowledged as symbols of essential constituents of poetry and civilization. Only the poplar appears in both qua-

---

40 On the co-existence of Apollonian and Dionysiac features in the song, see Mac Góráin 2012 – 13, 211: 'Apollo and Dionysus are both gods of poetic inspiration and as such often paired, and it is hardly to be imagined that an ancient poet would subordinate one to the other in a poetic context.'
41 Cf. Peraki-Kyriakidou 2013, 225 – 26.
42 Fowler 2002 on 2.13; Hardie 2007.
43 Theocritus was obviously the model (see *Id.* 2.118 – 22 cited above, p. 236). Cucchiarelli (2012 on 7.61) stresses the fact that in the aforementioned verses of Theocritus λεύκα is clearly associated also with Dionysus.
44 At *Geor.* 2.63 – 72 the catalogue has much in common with the two aforementioned catalogues. For *populus* at l. 66 (*Herculeaeque arbos umbrosa coronae*), see Thomas 1988, *ad loc.*
45 Peraki-Kyriakidou 2010.

trains. In Thyrsis' catalogue, however, it is dissociated from Hercules. Under such circumstances it will not be in a position to give enough drive to his song to compete with that of Corydon's.[46]

In this contest Corydon is the winner, one of the reasons being that his poetics, as represented by his beloved Phyllis and her *corylos,* has the ambition to go beyond the standards of the day, based on the synthesis of what the above trees symbolize. In this *Eclogue* Corydon's catalogue does not function in the sense of accommodating different items one next to the other, in order to form a general picture. Each plant or tree carries an indisputable and widely-known symbolic value related to poetry and culture. Even if the above plants or trees are accommodated in a linear fashion, it is obvious to the reader that they represent qualities and values of poetry and civilization in a synthetic way. Virgil's poetry receives Homeric poetry only to a degree; there the corresponding catalogues were linear catalogues without any obvious symbolic power of each plant separately.

According to Macrobius (*Sat.* 6.2.27) Thyrsis' catalogue has its model in the *Annales* of Ennius,[47] where the poet describes the felling of the same kind of tree in catalogue-form and with the significant exception of the poplar:

Percellunt magnas quercus, exciditur ilex,
fraxinus frangitur atque abies consternitur alta,
pinus proceras pervortunt (Ann. 177–79 Sk.)

They throw down great oaks, down falls the holm,
the ash is subdued, the high fir tree is levelled
and the tall pines are overthrown.

The Ennian catalogue is possibly related to the preparations for the funeral of the victims of the battle at Heraclea, where Pyrrhus suffered heavy losses in 280 BC. It is quite obvious that the content of this catalogue is inappropriate for the bucolic environment. Besides, as Lipka points out, *abies* is an 'unbucolic tree, occurring nowhere in any Greek bucolic poet'. Thyrsis may well stress the positive relation of each kind of tree to a certain environment, but this in no way means that the reader does not recollect the unbucolic features of its ancient model. In Ennius the prevailing imagery is that of felling and death. Accordingly, in Thyrsis' response, the bucolic pattern seems to collapse. If, as I think we

---

[46] As Egan 1996 observes: 'The trees which Thyrsis names have no apparent associations with divinity nor with love or song. In general, while Thyrsis formally and superficially responds to most of the elements in Corydon's quatrain, his words and phrases are unidimensional.'
[47] Lipka 2001, 118f.

should, we accept Ennius as the immediate Roman model, then we should perhaps take it as a 'window reference' to the earlier Iliadic[48] 'epic' catalogues which we mentioned briefly above, since they similarly could not offer any incentive for a pastoral reading. I am referring to the two catalogues of purely epic flavour from Book 16 at 482–86 and 765–70. Their aim in the Greek epic was to highlight the tension and the violence of the battle. The first one was also a word for word repetition of *Il.* 13.389–93:

> ἤριπεν δ' ὡς ὅτε τις δρῦς ἢ ἀχερωῒς
> ἠὲ πίτυς βλωθρή, τήν τ' οὔρεσι τέκτονες ἄνδρες
> ἐξέταμον πελέκεσσι νεήκεσι νήϊον εἶναι·
> ὡς ὃ πρόσθ' ἵππων καὶ δίφρου κεῖτο τανυσθεὶς
> βεβρυχὼς κόνιος δεδραγμένος αἱματοέσσης.
> (*Il.* 13.389–93 = *Il.* 16.482–86)
>
> *And he fell as an oak falls or a poplar*
> *or a high pine, that among the mountains shipwrights fell*
> *with whetted axes to be a ship's timber;*
> *so he lay outstretched in front of his horses and chariot,*
> *moaning aloud and clutching at the bloody dust.*

The above description has obviously much in common with the description of battle in Book 16.765–70, although in this case the names of the trees are accommodated in only one line:[49]

> ὡς δ' Εὖρός τε Νότος τ' ἐριδαίνετον ἀλλήλοιιν
> οὔρεος ἐν βήσσῃς βαθέην πελεμιζέμεν ὕλην
> φηγόν τε μελίην τε τανύφλοιόν τε κράνειαν,
> αἵ τε πρὸς ἀλλήλας ἔβαλον τανυήκεας ὄζους
> ἠχῇ θεσπεσίῃ, πάταγος δέ τε ἀγνυμενάων,
> ὣς Τρῶες καὶ Ἀχαιοὶ ἐπ' ἀλλήλοισι θορόντες
> δῄουν, οὐδ' ἕτεροι μνώοντ' ὀλοοῖο φόβοιο.
> (*Il.* 16.765–70)
>
> *And as the East and the South Wind strive with each other*
> *in shaking a deep wood in the glades of a mountain,*
> *– a wood of beech and ash and smooth-barked cornel,*
> *and these dash one against the other their long boughs with a wondrous din,*
> *and there is a crack of broken branches –*
> *so the Trojans and the Achaeans leapt one on another*
> *and slaughtered, nor did either side think of destructive flight.*

---

48 Cf. above, n. 4.
49 See above, nn. 2 and 3.

Since δρῦς and φηγός seem to be the same tree, then of the 5 (=6) trees of the above-cited Homeric catalogues, three also appear in the catalogue of Thyrsis. However, in a bucolic song, such catalogues have no place. The imagery of the felled trees, like the victims of war in the archaic text and the imagery of manic destruction, do not suit pastoral diction. Some of these trees may have their own independent presence[50] in the pastoral, but their grouping together creates different associations. In Corydon's piece, each plant, because of its symbolic possibility, had to add its own contribution to poetry and song. In that of Thyrsis, the grouping together of these trees functions only as an 'unpastoral' reminiscence. Thyrsis has justly yielded to Corydon, since the Iliadic imagery is ill-suited to being generically transplanted.

Theocritus could be a better model for Thyrsis. In *Dioscuri* (*Id.* 22) there is a similar catalogue, as some of the trees coincide with those employed by Thyrsis:

εὗρον δ' ἀέναον κρήνην ὑπὸ λισσάδι πέτρῃ,
ὕδατι πεπληθυῖαν ἀκηράτῳ· αἱ δ' ὑπένερθε
λάλλαι κρυστάλλῳ ἠδ' ἀργύρῳ ἰνδάλλοντο
ἐκ βυθοῦ· ὑψηλαὶ δὲ πεφύκεσαν ἀγχόθι πεῦκαι
λεῦκαί τε πλάτανοί τε καὶ ἀκρόκομοι κυπάρισσοι
ἄνθεά τ' εὐώδη, λασίαις φίλα ἔργα μελίσσαις,
ὅσσ' ἔαρος λήγοντος ἐπιβρύει ἂν λειμῶνας.
(*Id.* 22.37–43)

Under a smooth rock they found a perennial spring
brimming with pure water, the pebbles in its depths
showing like crystal or silver.
High pines were growing nearby,
poplars and planes and tufted cypresses,
and fragrant flowers farmed gladly by the shaggy bees
–all flowers that teem in the meadows as spring fades away.

What the reader notices, however, is that the overall imagery in Thyrsis' song is a much lowered pastoral description, denuded, one might say, of its bucolic elements. Thyrsis was unsuccessful in constructing a truly bucolic catalogue. His catalogue was generically ill-suited, a rather 'unidimensional' presentation of trees, as Egan rightly says,[51] and deprived of any obvious symbolic value

---

50 *Pinus* also appears in other passages of the *Eclogues* either as a metonymy for a boat or as a metonymy for the Pan-pipe (8.22). However, its listing along with *fraxinus* and *abies* (trees with no other presence in the *Bucolics*) seems to be a rather direct allusion to the catalogues of tall trees of the Homeric past, thus creating a rift in the bucolic discourse.
51 See above, n. 46.

which could contribute to the formation of an overall idea.[52] Synthesis of symbols created by the symbolic dynamics of different trees or plants was not a recognized feature in the short catalogues of plants and trees in the Homeric epics.

This feature does not appear only at *Ecl.* 7.61–64. It seems to be an established characteristic in this Virgilian work: in *Eclogue* 2 Corydon tries to attract Alexis.

> huc ades, o formose puer: tibi lilia plenis   45
> ecce ferunt Nymphae calathis; tibi candida Nais,
> pallentis violas et summa papavera carpens,
> narcissum et florem iungit bene olentis anethi;
> tum casia atque aliis intexens suavibus herbis
> mollia luteola pingit vaccinia calta.   50
> ipse ego cana legam tenera lanugine mala
> castaneasque nuces, mea quas Amaryllis amabat;
> addam cerea pruna (honos erit huic quoque pomo),
> et vos, o lauri, carpam et te, proxima myrte,
> sic positae quoniam suavis miscetis odores.   55
> (*Ecl.* 2.45–55)

> Come here, O lovely boy: for you the Nymphs bring lilies,
> look, in baskets full; for you the Naiad fair,
> plucking pale violets and poppy heads, combines them
> with narcissus and flower of fragrant dill;
> then, weaving marjoram in, and other pleasant herbs,
> colours soft bilberries with yellow marigold.
> Myself, I shall pick the grey-white apples with tender down
> and chestnuts, which my Amaryllis loved;
> I shall add the waxy plum (this fruit too shall be honoured).
> I shall pluck you, O laurels, and you, neighbour myrtle,
> for so arranged you mingle attractive fragrances.
> (trans. Lee 1980 with minor adjustments)

His words to Alexis form a double catalogue: the list of plants and flowers the Naiad and the Nymphs offer in baskets (45–50), and the list of what Corydon himself is offering (51–55). Although this double catalogue is beyond the group of short catalogues we are discussing in this paper because of its length (even in its separate parts), I believe that it deserves to be taken into consideration, in order to see the

---

52 Mac Góráin (2012–13, 212), who reads these verses from their political aspect, comes very near to what we understand here as 'unidimensional', to use Egan's term: 'Thyrsis responds almost as if to seal his loss referring to plants and trees only with no sensitivity to their religious dimension, seemingly unaware that if we are to sing of woods, then these woods should be worthy of a consul, and thus unaware of his own inferior political sophistication'.

poet's inclinations in his *Eclogues:* the flowers and plants of the first part (45–50) are put together in baskets (46: *calathis*). The second (51–55) is a selection (45: *legam*) of Corydon's himself. What we have here is not the mere presentation of plants in a linear way but rather an arrangement of them in verse as well as in the basket or even in Corydon's arms. Similar– but still different– was the notion of arrangement of plants and trees in well-ordered areas in Homer, as in *Od.* 24.336 (see above, p. 234). Here, in Virgil, it is not only the separate beauty (or even the [separate] symbolism) of each one plant that matters, but the synthesis of *all* the flowers *together:* in the first part, the Nymphs offer the flowers in baskets, *calathis* (46). This word is Greek– though rarely used in Greek poetry– and usually denotes a basket used in rituals. This is the first word in the Callimachean *Hymn to Demeter.*[53] By using this word– instead of the Latin synonym *fiscella* (which at the end of the *Eclogues* seems to represent the whole of the work[54])– Virgil at this point shows his Hellenistic inclinations.[55] There is agreement that Meleager (*AP* 5.147) is the model for these lines. In that epigram the main verb is πλέκω ('to plait'), a verb related to the making of a wreath or of a basket. In *Eclogue* 2 the Naiad combines (48: *jungit*) the flowers she gathers *weaving* (49: *intexens*) them in an array.[56] Theocritus has shown the way; in *Id.* 3.21–23 the poet talks about the wreath he has prepared to Amaryllis:

τὸν στέφανον τῖλαί με κατ' αὐτίκα λεπτὰ ποησεῖς,
τόν τοι ἐγών, Ἀμαρυλλὶ φίλα, κισσοῖο φυλάσσω,
ἀμπλέξας καλύκεσσι καὶ εὐόδμοισι σελίνοις.

You will make me shred my wreath to pieces,
the wreath of ivy which I twined with rosebuds
and fragrant celery, and wear for you, my dear Amaryllis.

Plants and flowers are mixed and interwoven, arranged in this way in a synthesis: each plant is one part of the synthesis, one factor of an imagery pertaining to the formation of a whole. This same idea is adopted by Virgil in his description of the cup in *Ecl.* 3, as πλοκή and synthesis are at its centre. The notion of ἀμπλέξας also appears in the description of Alcimedon's cups:

Et nobis idem Alcimedon duo pocula fecit
et molli circum est ansas amplexus acantho (*Ecl.* 3.45)

---

53 Hopkinson 1984, 41–42 and his comment on l. 1. The word was used by Virgil also at *Ecl.* 5.71, *Geor.* 3.402 and at *Aen.* 7.805: Cucchiarelli 2012 on 2.45–46.
54 Saunders 2008, 118–19.
55 Clausen 1994 on l. 46.
56 Berg 1974, 111.

The same Alcimedon also created two cups for us
and twining soft acanthus leaves around the handles.
(trans. Lee 1980 with minor adjustments)

The Theocritean origins of the description of the κισσύβιον are more than obvious:

καὶ βαθὺ κισσύβιον κεκλυσμένον ἁδέι κηρῷ,
ἀμφῶες, νεοτευχές, ἔτι γλυφάνοιο ποτόσδον.
τῶ ποτὶ μὲν χείλη μαρύεται ὑψόθι κισσός,
κισσὸς ἑλιχρύσῳ κεκονιμένος· ἁ δὲ κατ' αὐτόν
καρπῷ ἕλιξ εἰλεῖται ἀγαλλομένα κροκόεντι.
(*Id.* 1.27–31)

And I shall give you a deep cup, washed over with sweet wax,
two-handled, and newly fashioned, still fragrant from the knife.
Along the lips above trails ivy,
ivy dotted with golden clusters,
and along it winds the tendril exalting in its yellow fruit.

In the second part of the double catalogue of *Eclogue* 2, Corydon makes his own choices (51: *legam*) closing his list with two plants, symbols of poetry and love *par excellence*, the laurel and the myrtle, the sacred plants of Apollo and Aphrodite respectively. These were precisely the plants with which Corydon again, the winner of the song-contest, closed his list at *Ecl.* 7 (62).[57] Here these two plants are *mixed* (55: *miscetis*), to become parts of a synthesis with their beautiful odours. The metapoetic significance strengthened by the vocabulary– not only in this specific passage but in the whole poem[58]– is obvious to all. It is further enhanced by the fact that this synthesis has nothing to do with the descriptions of nature at the beginning and the end of the *Eclogue*.[59] What is important for the poet at this stage is to talk metapoetically, in order to disclose and promote his stance regarding poetry. In this *Eclogue* through Corydon 'Virgil directs attention to a theoretical consideration of pastoral poetry.'[60] Our poet seems to claim that his poetry should not be considered to be a product of a uniform tradition but rather the eclectic product and mixture of various and different literary experiences.

---

[57] Leach 1966, 436 with reference to Pfeiffer 1933, 17.
[58] Leach 1966, 436 (on *fontibus*: 59 and n. 24). See also Papanghelis 1995, 56; Saunders 2008, 117–18.
[59] Leach 1966, 430: 'As the singer pursues his evangelical discourse, he transforms the pastoral life into something more fantastic than real.'
[60] Leach 1966, 427.

From *Eclogue* 2 we turn our attention to *Ecl.* 4: the poet extols the birth of the *puer* who will bring the New Golden Era in the world. At his coming, Earth celebrates and offers abundantly her gifts *nullo cultu* (18).

At tibi prima, puer, nullo munuscula cultu
errantis hederas passim cum baccare tellus
mixtaque ridenti colocasia fundet acantho.[61]   20
[...]
ipsa tibi blandos fundent cunabula flores.[62]

But first, child, as small gifts for you, Earth untilled
will pour the straying ivy rife and baccaris
and colocasia mingling them with acanthus' smile.
[...]
your very cradle will pour forth caressing flowers.
(trans. Lee 1980 with minor adjustments)

I have dealt with this really interesting catalogue elsewhere.[63] But let us confine ourselves to the recognition of the symbolism of the plants included and the way they are presented: the Bacchic element with the ivy and the baccar[64] has a strong presence, while the Apollonian is represented by the acanthus.[65] These two elements, however, are not presented next to one another, but are interwined, are *mixed*. *Miscere* (20) is used again, as in *Ecl.* 2.55 which we saw above, bringing forth the importance of the synthesis which depicts the first experiences of the child: the Bacchic element is *mixed* with the Apollonian. The first experiences are not 'unidimensional';[66] they are a synthesis of major elements of culture and poetry. Although everything is under Apollo's sway (10: *tuus iam regnat Apollo*),[67] no element can stand alone.

---

61 Acanthus is present also at *Geor.* 2.119, 4.123; *Aen.* 1.649, 1.711; cf. Stat. *Theb.* 6.64: *medio Linus intertextus acantho*. See Arnold 1994–95, 147; Saunders 2008, 146–47 with notes; Cucchiarelli 2012 on 3.45 and on 4.20 (*ridenti acantho*).
62 Mynors' text; Harrison (2007, 42) prefers to read line 23 as 21.
63 Peraki-Kyriakidou 2014, 91.
64 Coleman 1977 on 4.19; Hardie 2009a; Peraki-Kyriakidou 2013, 218; Peraki-Kyriakidou 2014, 92 and n. 8.
65 Elderkin 1941 has the evidence; Mac Góráin 2012–13: Acanthus may also be a Bacchic symbol. I am most grateful to Fiachra Mac Góráin for sending me his paper before publication. His analysis on how Apollonian and Dionysiac elements were blended in the *Eclogues* is of high interest and very insightful; see also Peraki-Kyriakidou 2014, 94–95, 97–98 and nn. 3, 10.
66 This is different from what happens in Thyrsis' song (see above, n. 46).
67 Peraki-Kyriakidou 2013, 218.

With such a cultural background, the boy will bring in the New Golden Era which will be realized when, according to the poet, he will have read (*legere*) the praise (26: *laudes*) of the heroic past along with the achievements of his ancestor(s) (26: *facta parentis*) and have recognized their virtues (27). Then, in the world of nature new phenomena will take place, which will indicate the coming of a new period:

> *at simul heroum laudes et facta parentis*
> *iam legere et quae sit poteris cognoscere virtus*
> *molli paulatimflauescet campus arista*
> *incultisque rubens pendebit sentibus uva*
> *et durae quercus sudabunt roscida mella.* (Ecl. 4.26–30)
>
> *But as soon as you can read of the praise of the heroes*
> *and of your father's deeds and know what virtue means,*
> *then tender spikes of grain will turn the field yellow*
> *and reddening grapes will hang from a wild thornbush*
> *and hard oak-trees will sweat out dewy honey.*
> (trans. Lee 1980 with minor adjustments)

What is important in this passage is that the gifts of Nature are produced with the notion of novelty to predominate: *uva* will come out from uncultivated thornbush, being something different and new, like honey which will be produced from tough oak-trees. The new is not any more the same as the old. In the first proem to the *Georgics* there is a corresponding description, where *arista*[68] and *uva* obviously represent the new phase of the development of civilization.

> *Liber et alma Ceres, vestro si munere tellus*
> *Chaoniam pingui glandem mutavit arista,*
> *Poculaque inventis Acheloia miscuit uvis* (Geor. 1.7–9)
>
> *Liber and nourishing Ceres, if by your grace the earth*
> *changed the Chaonian acorn for ripe ears of corn*
> *and mingled Acheloan water with new-found wine...*[69]

Virgil shows his intention of relating these two passages by putting *arista* and *uva* at the same metrical position and in a more or less similar context. Both in the *Eclogues* and the *Georgics* civilization does not develop with the mere succession of one period after another nor does one age simply substitute for another, but it is the result of synthesis; the new comes from the old. It is like the de-

---

[68] On *arista* as a cultural symbol: Zissos 2008 on l. 70.
[69] Peraki-Kyriakidou 2006, 85 with notes.

velopment of the *puer* in the *Eclogues* who will bring in the New Era after delving into the deeds and virtues of Man in the past. Nature, in a similar manner, will bring the new era out of the old. The manifestation of nature will show that it finally is the mirror of human spirit and civilization. The aspirations of the Roman poet are rather different from what is highlighted in the Homeric text:

> ὄγχνη ἐπ' ὄγχνῃ γηράσκει, μῆλον δ' ἐπὶ μήλῳ,
> αὐτὰρ ἐπὶ σταφυλῇ σταφυλή, σῦκον δ' ἐπὶ σύκῳ.
> (*Od.* 7.120 – 21: translated above, p. 229 – 30)

In Homer the new does not seem to promise anything novel. In Virgil from the uncultivated (*incultis ... sentibus*)[70] something new will come about. In Homer the quality of the past experiences seems to be repeated in the future. Man in the age of Virgil, through his more complex experiences, looks forward to a new –possibly better– life, but this in itself is an *adynaton*.

---

[70] Cf. *Aen.* 6.461 with Serv. *ad loc.* As Papanghelis (1995, 278 – 79) notes, the word *incultus* in the *Eclogues* oscillates between the 'uncultivated' in agriculture and the intellectually 'uncultivated'.

Sophia Papaioannou
Embracing Homeric Orality in the *Aeneid*: Revisiting the Composition Politics of Virgil's First *Descriptio*

An important dimension of the antagonistic attitude that marks Virgil's reception of Homer and has escaped in-depth critical study is the 'oral' character of the *Aeneid* and the poetics of antagonism behind it; specifically, Virgil's realization that Homeric orality was a literary technique as much as a means of literary expression, and his systematic effort to appropriate it by embracing tropes and mechanisms of orality fundamental and conspicuous in the composition of the Homeric narrative. It is the goal of the present study to assess Virgil's sophisticated engagement with the Homeric methodology of text composition. I shall explain how the complexity in the texture of the Homeric poems, which relies on the recollection and interfusion of different traditional accounts, is mirrored in the composition of the *Aeneid*. As case study for Virgil's simulation of Homeric orality I have chosen the first *ekphrasis* of the *Aeneid*, the narrative of the Trojan battle on the Carthaginian murals in *Aen*. 1.430 ff.

A seminal passage that governs the reading of the *Aeneid* in many respects, the Carthaginian *descriptio* has received scholarly interest since the dawn of New Criticism. Scholars, however, have focused almost exclusively on the interaction between the scenes on the murals and the plot of the *Aeneid*. My discussion, on the contrary, will focus on the method of introducing the *descriptio* to an audience that does not have visual access to it; my reading aspires to serve as methodological introduction to the assessment of a literary (epic) *ekphrasis* and the politics that govern the composition made available to the audience. A final goal is to illustrate the deep involvement of the technology of orality in the complexity and sophistication of a narrative that originates in a literacy-governed culture.

Seemingly antithetical, orality and literacy as ways of human interaction in reality are complementary. Orality serves to enhance, refine and systematize literacy, firstly, as an expression of human communication, secondly, as a way of memory enhancement, thirdly, as a form of literary expression and fourthly, as a means of fashioning the past in the broadest sense (from inventing to discovering to editing and revising) and recording the present.[1] Similar interdependence

---

1 Cf. the words of Susan Niditch, a leading critic of oral traditions, and the ways these are

marks the concepts of orality and literacy with relation to literary expression. This calls for redefining one's research priorities: for the field of orality studies, oralists are strongly encouraged to move beyond the task of determining which traditions are genuinely oral, which are anterior or posterior, more or less widely known and influential, and onto an investigation of how oral tradition and writing substitute one another across a spectrum of stories originally articulated orally and in different versions but later prescribed and formalized in writing. The phenomenon of the literary *ekphrasis* as articulated in the *Aeneid* projects ideally a comparable cognitive process of 'open text' narrative composition-in-performance in a literacy-determined environment.

'Oral performance' in terms of Homeric poetry communication is a system as much as a theoretical concept; at once a mechanism of poetic production and a technical term of literary criticism, defined within the field of Homeric interpretation studies as the major rival to neoanalysis[2] and situated at the core of the Homeric Question.[3] Though neither Virgil nor any other Roman poet prior to him acknowledge the Homeric Question explicitly, Virgil's antagonistic embrace of Homer among other things fused creatively the poetics surrounding the thematic typology of oral tradition and the systematic sharing of motif dissemination espoused by neoanalysis. For Virgil, Homer is a model for the *Aeneid:* Virgil's narrative, not unlike the Homeric epics, is flexible and fluid enough to sustain variant readings of an interactive subtext of ever evolving character within a long tradition of epic composition.[4] This composition to a considerable extent has developed orally, and as such has subconsciously maintained aspects of orality. The narrative context of a pictorial description, which is widely acknowledged as a self-reflection of the entire epic in many respects, is further determined by the focalization of the narrator at the time; as such it constitutes a narrative-in-performance, and so encapsulates how the technology of orality manifests itself in the context of literacy

---

reflected in the Hebrew Bible and the ancient Israelite written texts: 'Scholars are now [contrary to earlier claims among Biblical scholars that in ancient Israelite literary tradition "simple oral works gave way to sophisticated written works produced by a literate elite"] beginning to see that orality and literacy exist on a continuum and that there is an interplay between the two modalities, a feedback loop of sorts' (Niditch 1983, 43). The same interplay manifests itself in Greco-Roman literature and is the ongoing preoccupation of criticism in recent decades.

2 For definitions of neoanalysis, see Rutherford 1996, 91–93; Willcock 1997, 174–75.

3 The foundational work on the Homeric Question is that of Milman Parry (= Parry 1971), developed by Albert Lord (Lord 1995; 2000²); succinct overviews are offered also in Rutherford 1996; and more recently Fowler 2004, 220–32.

4 A recent concise discussion on the parameters that determined the character of Virgil's reception of Homer as part of the long and complex process of Homeric reception in Greek and Roman antiquity (Homer being the source of inspiration for most major ancient literature) is Graziosi 2006.

(on Homeric orality and its subsequent transformations, see also Efstathiou, I. Petrovic and Michelakis in this volume).

Etymologically deriving from *scribere*, 'to write, note, record in writing, draw, mark (within a pictorial representation)', the term *descriptio* literally means a 'detailed recording, transcript', it implies a process that involves writing,[5] literal or metaphorical, or both, but more importantly it firmly communicates an ideology of literacy. The employment of a term that signifies writing to translate a term that means oral articulation (i.e. the Greek term '*ekphrasis*') suggests further that the Latin term was fashioned inside a literacy-determined environment, in the sense that one produced a detailed, complete description when one could record it in writing, 'transcribed' it, set certain limitations for the audience who would receive (audibly or visually) the written description and would try to reproduce the described object (in the broader sense, be it a single item of a synthesis of items) in their imagination. The Carthaginian *descriptio* relayed in *Aeneid* 1, it will be argued presently, is a composition that toys with the technology of orality, for it is presented by someone who has been personally and intimately affected by the events reproduced on the depiction. Aeneas' intimacy with the theme on the murals shapes the way of his reproducing the *descriptio*, for the verbal reconstruction of the artifact is directed (i) by Aeneas' personal Trojan-War memories, and (ii) by his subjective interpretation of the various details on pictorial material captured in the actual *descriptio* on the murals. In short, Aeneas narrates as much as describes —interprets the *descriptio* for the audience rather than reproducing it faithfully for the audience to interpret.

Indeed, during the action described in most of these panels Aeneas was not present to witness the events. This deliberate distancing of the narrator from the action in the narrative is significant, in order to assess Aeneas' ekphrastic reading as an oral epic-in-performance, because it tampers with the notion of poetic memory, both with its literal meaning formed within the context of oral poetics as the memory of the epic bard who composes from memory, and in its metapoetic, Contean meaning that is defined within the context of literacy and denotes a demiurge's acknowledgment and embrace of the preexisting literary tradition. For, like an epic performer (even any oral storyteller) Aeneas does not compose *from* memory as much as he composes *with* memory.[6] He does not recall events that he actually sees on the murals and tries to report them as accurately as possible, but he has in mind the various traditional accounts of each of

---

[5] See also Webb 2009, 9: 'Although it is the nearest equivalent to ancient *ekphrasis* (*descriptio* in Latin)..., its connotations are very different, as is only to be expected of a term that has been defined and discussed with reference to the written word rather than live, oral performance'.
[6] E.g. Rubin 1995; Minchin 1999.

the epic events narrated on the panels, which may include the Homeric epics, the other epics of the Epic Cycle, and not least, the treatments of the Trojan legend throughout the post-archaic, largely literate, literary tradition, including the early Roman tradition.

The politics of introducing a pictorial description outlined above draws directly on the methodology of artificial memory and the construction of the 'palace of memory' for the most detailed and accurate memorization. This 'palace of memory' system was a Roman memory-training technique particularly favoured among the orators in the ancient and medieval worlds.[7] In all likeness it was widely employed by the technology of memorization available to the archaic bards, as well. I propose that Virgil is aware of the implementation of mnemotechnics by archaic oral poets and aspires to emulate the methodology in his *Aeneid*. The simulation of Homeric mnemotechnics is particularly evident in the composition of the Virgilian *descriptiones*, with that of the Carthaginian murals in *Aeneid* 1 standing out given that thematically it reproduces yet another focalized account of the Trojan War.

The actual text of the Carthaginian *descriptio* reproduces a series of episodes, mostly battle-scenes, from the Trojan War with an emphasis on Greek, primarily Achilles' victories or Trojan defeats.[8] The proper assessment of the narrative composition of the panels constitutes a challenge for the interpreter, because the 'reading' of the murals produced is guided by Aeneas' marveling gaze, which means that the selection of panels and their serial arrangement is directed by Aeneas' perspective (*Aen.* 1.456–57):

> videt Iliacas ex ordine pugnas / bellaque iam fama totum vulgata per orbem.
>
> He sees the battles of Troy in order, and wars already spread by fama through the entire world.

This epigraph operates as the introduction to the pictorial synthesis, and it notes that all panels represent depictions of Trojan-War episodes; the intriguing detail, however, is their specified arrangement 'in order' (*ex ordine*). As the content of the artwork unfolds, however, it becomes increasingly difficult to understand what sort of 'order' is meant. In all probability the episodes recorded do not fol-

---

[7] Carruthers 1990; Carruthers and Ziolkowski 2002; Yates 1966.
[8] Smith 1997, 26–43.

low chronological order, because Aeneas' reading arranges the panels in a way that violates the chronology of the Trojan legend.[9]

Indeed, the *descriptio* opens with two scenes of war (1.466–68), one featuring the Trojans on the attack and the Greeks fleeing, the other reversely Achilles' pursuing the fleeing Trojan army. The two scenes are generic Trojan battles, impossible to locate specifically in the chronological course of the Trojan War. The next scene, the first referring to a specific episode of the Trojan War, records the death of Rhesus by Diomedes (469–73). This event constitutes the culminating moment of the Doloneia episode and is recorded in *Iliad* 10.[10] Nonetheless, the panel introduced immediately afterwards regresses to the early years of the war, as it depicts the death and mutilation of Troilus (474–78), which according to the sources had been related in the *Cypria*. Next the pictorial narrative returns to Iliadic time: the episode from the *Cypria* is followed by a well-known scene from *Iliad* 6, the peplos-offering to Minerva by a procession of Trojan women (479–82); and immediately afterwards comes the mutilation and ransom of Hector's corpse (483–87), the leading theme of the last three books of the *Iliad*. The sixth panel to be introduced merits the most economic as well as the most vague description: it centers on Aeneas, whom he portrays 'among the Achaeans' (488)—an epic moment impossible to place with specificity in Trojan-War time, and, as we shall see, deliberately so. The two panels Aeneas admires last, before Dido's arrival interrupts his study, depict scenes from the *Aethiopis*, the epic detailing the events of the Trojan War following the death of Hector and the end of the *Iliad*. The former of the two panels, according to Aeneas' reading order, features the Ethiopian king Memnon (489), while the latter captures the Amazon queen Penthesilea (490–93); both warriors are set amidst their troops in a similar fashion, as to allude to their similar roles as champions of the Trojan cause in the place of Hector, but also to their similar tragic deaths at the hand of Achilles. Notably, Aeneas' narrative order once again clashes against the chronology of the Epic Cycle, for Penthesilea's arrival and death preceded those of Memnon in the *Aethiopis*.

---

9 On the chronologically inconsistent seriality of the murals, see Clay 1988, 195–205; other readings of the anachronous sequence of the murals include Lowenstam 1993, 43–44 and La Penna 2000.

10 The 'oral' character of the descriptive synthesis of the Carthaginian murals is evidenced in the placement of the Rhesus episode from the allegedly spurious *Iliad* 10 at the head of the specific stories of the Trojan War accounted on the murals and, more prominently, in the integration of elements in the Virgilian account of Rhesus that do not come from the *Iliad*; see now Dué and Ebbott 2010, 89–152.

It becomes clear from the above that Aeneas' violation of the Epic Cycle chronology, obvious even to a less experienced reader of archaic epic, signifies a different type of 'order'; and so does the employment of the term *ordo*, which on occasion may refer equally to both time and space.[11] Putnam and others have argued that the phrase *ex ordine* (*Aen.* 1.456) more likely represents spatial order (the way the panels are arranged on the walls),[12] but the text does not justify this argument either. The *descriptio* conspicuously lacks modifiers of distinct location, and the vagueness of the local adverbs that do exist and allegedly mark this *ordo* argues against such a spatially determined arrangement. Only two of the panels are introduced with some information regarding a spatial placement: the Rhesus panel (469: *nec procul hinc...*) and the Troilus panel (474: *parte alia...*); the information, however, is hardly specific, while the employment of modifiers of space does not continue. The panel of the Trojan suppliants coming next is introduced with a modifier of time, *interea...* (479), and so is the panel depicting Priam's supplication of Achilles, *tum...* (485).[13]

It is logical, then, to accept that *ordo* is used to denote some other perception of order, determined by Aeneas' point of view.[14] This more complex type of *ordo* is endorsed by the testimony of Servius (ad *Aen.* 1.456):

> EX ORDINE hoc loco ostendit omnem pugnam esse depictam, sed haec tantum dicit quae aut Diomedes gessit aut Achilles, per quod excusatur Aeneas, si est a fortioribus victus.

---

[11] According to the *OLD* s.v. 1e, *ex ordine* can refer to chronological sequence ('in [chronological] order') but also to spatial arrangement ('in a row'). On the ambiguity of the phrase, see Clay 1988, 202 and Barchiesi 1999, 333–35.

[12] In his classic treatment of Dido's murals, Putnam (1998, 26) endorses the spatial meaning: Aeneas sees 'the scenes of battle in a row..., the smaller spacings of Carthaginian art (*ordo*) taking their restricted place in the grander sphere (*orbis*) [*Aeneid* 1.457] of what humankind as a whole knows'.

[13] Such constrictions lead Putnam to rather enforced compromises, as e.g. in his discussion of *interea*, the temporal adverb that introduces the middle panel of the frieze, the supplication of the Trojan women before Minerva; cf. Putnam 1998, 32; Thomas 1983, 180 n. 17 influenced by the spatial modifiers at the beginning of the *descriptio*, *nec procul hinc* and especially *parte alia* embraces the spatial argument and assumes that the pictures are arranged simply in a line.

[14] Aeneas is the so-defined (by Fowler 1992) 'watching character', who serves the narratees/ Virgil's audience with a first alike presentation and assessment of the *descriptio*. I agree with Boyd 1995, 80, that the chronological reversal of the Memnon and Penthesilea episodes in the end of the *ekphrasis* narrative can alert the reader to suspect of bias Aeneas' selective gaze, yet, I do not understand why the flag of suspicion over a compromised reading is not raised much earlier in the course of the reading.

> EX ORDINE: in this passage [Virgil] shows that every battle has been depicted, but he mentions only the deeds of either Diomedes or Achilles, so that Aeneas is excused for being defeated by stronger men.

Servius states that 'every battle has been depicted', but he implicitly takes the phrase *omnem pugnam* to include only the episodes identified by Aeneas. Since all these episodes revolve around either Achilles or Diomedes, it is implied that these battles represent the essence of the entire war for Aeneas.[15] Servius, in other words, here realizes that Aeneas is initiating a selective reading of the murals, a reading that includes primarily panels which revolve around Achilles and Diomedes; that the so-called 'order' is subjective, is thematically set and is determined by the personal criteria of the viewer at the time—in the given instance Aeneas (on Servius as a commentator on Virgil, see Maltby in this volume).

The interests of the viewer/reader, then, determine the character and operation of multitextuality; it is the organizing principle behind the composition of the Carthaginian *ekphrasis* whose reading is a cognitive process. Virgil invites his audience to produce a critical assessment of the set-piece depiction's content introduced by Aeneas. This invitation raises expectations of two different sorts. First, the Virgilian audience is called to embrace Aeneas' point of view and decode the criteria by which the Trojan hero chooses to identify the specific panels from the Carthaginian murals and not others. Subsequently, this vicarious critical reading on the audience's part is expected to stimulate their own literary memories and cause them to produce and visualize new material from the Trojan War story, not visibly present on the *descriptio* but implicitly present in the alternative versions of the episodes identified already by Aeneas. This new material could include aspects of the depicted story that are not explicitly articulated, the broader myth the depicted story belongs to, alternative versions of the story, significant omissions or changes to the version of the story depicted; it may also include real images, that is, various other monumental depictions of the same story, and even parallel stories, namely other stories of kindred theme or about the same protagonists etc.[16] Upon 'collecting' this material newly disclosed to them from the depths of their memories, Virgil's 'readers' across time could

---

[15] The suggestion of Petrain (2006, 265–66) that Servius 'takes ex *ordine* as a reference to chronological sequence and he treats this sequence as a comprehensive, faithful transcript of the epic tradition', where 'the pictures on the temple display "every battle" of the Trojan War in order (*omnem pugnam esse depictam*) and thus require no further justification' seems to me unjustified on the basis of the textual evidence provided in the *Aeneid*.

[16] My understanding of an *ekphrasis* as a subjective and elliptic verbal reproduction of a *descriptio* is inspired by the distinction between description and narrative (or focalization) introduced in Fowler 1992.

build their own version (or narrative or ekphrastic expression) of the depiction, which means that they were becoming actively and personally involved in the process not only of the interpretation but of the actual composition; their personal visualization is projected on Aeneas' own and competes against it. To recall readily this rich material, however, Virgil's audience should have developed a technique to facilitate their memorization and ready recollection of stored memories. Pointing them to such a technique of memorization, Virgil organizes the theme-based narrative sequence on the murals by drawing on the composition methodology of an oral epic performer.[17] This epic performer in the *descriptio* at hand is the character of Aeneas.

With Servius' suggestion to look for thematic narrative lines, in order to rationalize Aeneas' particular ordering of the panels and assess his interpretation of the Trojan War, Aeneas' initial reaction to the sight of the murals calls for careful consideration anew (*Aen.* 1.453–57):

Namque sub ingenti lustrat dum singula templo
reginam opperiens, dum quae fortuna sit urbi
artificumque manus inter se operumque laborem
miratur videt Iliacas ex ordine pugnas
bellaque iam fama totum vulgata per orbem.

For, while waiting for the queen and studying everything there was to see
under the roof of this huge temple, as he admired the good fortune of the city,
the skill of the workmen and all the work of their hands,
he suddenly saw, laid out in order, depictions of the battles fought at Troy.
The Trojan War was already famous throughout the world.
(trans. West 1990 with minor adjustments)

The panels Aeneas chooses to identify put together *part* of the pictorial synthesis, a fact that it is clearly revealed to the careful reader of *Aen.* 1.453 ff. Upon entering the temple, Virgil reports, Aeneas is immediately confronted with a series of independently standing works of art (*singula*) and he immediately sets out to study them carefully (*lustrat*). *Lustrat* along with *videt* and *miratur* are the finite verbs in the passage: it is hardly a coincidence that all three signify the same activity of 'seeing, viewing'. As the description of the ekphrastic unit put together

---

[17] I agree with Petrain 2006, 266 that Servius' commentary on the content of the temple panels allegedly balances his omission to take clear stance on the meaning of *ordo* regarding the sequence of the scenes narrated in the *ekphrasis*. Petrain's Servius interprets Virgil's particular selection process as an effort 'to preserve Aeneas' reputation', while the criterion that underwrites the thematically determined narrative of Aeneas is the presence in the selected panels of either Diomedes or Achilles.

by Aeneas proceeds in the following lines, more verbs of 'viewing' and 'seeing' appear: *videbat* (466), *agnoscit* (470), *conspexit* (487), *se... agnovit* (488). The strong emphasis on vision and visual activity splits the readers' focus between the panels on the one hand and the act of viewing them on the other.

The repetition of vocabulary—viewing-related terminology in the case at hand—at the opening of the Virgilian *descriptio* introduces an unmistakable mark of epic orality and as such emulates a typical practice of epic descriptions of artifacts. The latter are presented compartmentalized, and the description of each segment begins with some verbal expression that recurs henceforth systematically. The classic case study is of course the Homeric Shield of Achilles, which constitutes the model for all epic pictorial narratives following the *Iliad*. In the Shield ekphrasis the key verb is ποιεῖν, 'to fashion'. The description of the Shield itself is introduced with ποίει (478)—which happens to be a leading metapoetic term as well.[18] The Homeric narrator uses ποιεῖν in a variety of (usually past) tenses and forms, and the synonyms to ποιεῖν, to introduce each new panel/episode on the surface of the Shield.[19] The reader thus receives the impression that the Shield is just being crafted panel by panel, and that he/she is watching the process unraveling before his/her own eyes. This is crucial from the perspective of the oral epic poet who wishes to maintain undiminished the impression of a process that involves the description of a material object and, at the same time, to combine each panel with a non-describable narrative. To accomplish such a continuous sensation of visual observation, Virgil's collective employment of signposts of pseudo-viewing in the opening of the description is enforced through the introduction of the individual panels with adverbial expressions of place and time continuity (469: *nec procul hinc...*, 474: *parte alia...*, 479: *interea...*, 485: *tum...*); in this way he creates for his readers the illusion that they watch along with Aeneas the pictorial series on the murals unraveling before their eyes.

The instructive process of constructing selectively a mentally visualized pictorial narrative and reproducing it verbally in a way that would enable the evaluators of the *ekphrasis* to visualize it themselves, too, might well be inspired by the methodology of a mnemonic system that is based on the architecture or geography of space. This method of spatially determined memorization was famously credited to Simonides of Ceos by Cicero in *De oratore* 2.74, where he tells the story of how Simonides uses his ability to memorize by using specific, topographically tied signifiers in a particular scene to locate the bodies of his dinner companions,

---

18 On the Shield of Achilles as *mise en abyme* of the *Iliad*, see Hardie 1985; Hardie 1986, 336–76; Taplin 1980.
19 See *Il.* 18.478, 482, 483, 490, 541, 550, 561, 573, 587, 590, 607.

when the building they were dining had collapsed during the poet's absence. Roman orators and those among the Roman elite trained in oratory, like Virgil, had studied how to enhance the faculties of their memories to remember visual impressions. As a result of methodical training that observed key rules, memories could be visually imprinted and impressions could be held in the mind with vividness resistant to the passage of time. Depending on the orator's experience to resist the distorting influence of emotions, second thoughts and current events, these memories could be recalled more or less unaltered. The Roman process of artificial memory, structured around the premise that remembering retrieved information stored in the mind, involved identifying certain places where the memories desired from preservation could be securely stored. The places where these memories would be stored were arranged in the mind in a way as to be readily traversable once the need for the recollection of a series of memories arose; these places would famously comprise what Matteo Ricci would later call 'palace of memory', an imaginary architecture of orderly synthesized physical spaces and mental imagery.[20] According to Ricci, memory was to be thought of as a palace which existed in the mind. In the different rooms and corridors which comprised the palace, one would place a series of images/signifiers of the different concepts/signifieds that needed to be remembered.[21]

The construction and the operational management of these 'memory palaces' is already conceived and ideally described prior to Cicero, in the anonymous rhetorical treatise known as *Rhetorica ad Herennium* dating from the middle 80s BC,[22] the first systematic effort in Rome to describe and assess artificial memory training. According to the author of the *ad Herennium*, this 'palace' was the comprehensive background against which all memories were to be situated in arranged fashion.[23] The arrangement had to follow specific, well-defined serial

---

[20] On artificial memory in antiquity with special emphasis on the pioneering contribution of Roman oratory to the cultivation and professionalization of the architectonics of memory, see Small 1995; *id.* 1997, ch. 8: "The Roman Contribution"; very useful also is Vasaly 1993.

[21] On Ricci's 'palace of memory' theory, see Spence 1984—a book notably listed among the New York Times Best Books of the Year—along with Brook 1986. The great popularity of memory enhancement techniques is best illustrated in the most recent (February 2011) article by Joshua Foer in the *New York Times Sunday Magazine* (=Foer 2011), essentially a personal diary of the journalist's own one-year-long memory training that resulted to his winning the USA Memory Championship.

[22] *Ad Herennium* 3.16–24 is the section devoted to the description and training of artificial memory; the text is taken from Caplan 1954; the reference commentary to date is Calboli 1969 (Calboli attributes the text to Cornificus).

[23] For the Roman art of artificial memory, on the basis of a comparative discussion of the systematization and methodology of the technology of memorization as detailed in the anonymous

order. Seriality would be determined on the basis of criteria subjectively devised to facilitate individual recollection. For the author of the *ad Herennium*, seriality (though not identified as such) is best visualized mentally as a physical familiar space, like a housing complex, with multiple compartments in terms of architectural features inside, such as an intercolumniation, a corner, an arch etc.; memories would be located in orderly (serial) fashion on each of these spaces:

> Constat igitur artificiosa memoria ex locis et imaginibus. Locos appellamus eos qui breviter, perfecte, insignite aut natura aut manu sunt absoluti, ut eos facile naturali memoria conprehendere et amplecti queamus: ut aedes, intercolumnium, angulum, fornicem, et alia quae his similia sunt. (*ad Herennium* 3.16)
>
> Artificial memory consists of physical places and mental images. We call places those things which by nature or by artifice are for a short distance, totally and strikingly complete, so that we can understand and embrace them easily with natural memory—such as a house, an intercolumniation, a corner, an arch and other things which are similar to these.
> (trans. Small 1997 with minor adjustments)

The memories would be captured as images (*imagines*) and impressed on these specific locations (*loci*) according to some order sensible to and readily recalled by the individual interested in recalling them in the future in the exact same condition as when they had been originally stored and in the particular order that facilitated their personal recollection process: *imagines eorum locis certis conlocare oportebit*, 'it will be necessary to set the mental images of them [the different information which needs remembering] in specific places'. By traversing mentally through this orderly arrangement the orator would be able to recall the desired images/memories.

The philosophy of artificial memory-training is particularly applicable to the description of the operation of the epic poet's memory. For an epic poet, either a Homeric bard, who composes exclusively from memory, or Virgil, the epitome of sophisticated epic literacy, '*imagines*' are the various available traditions (literary or oral); these traditions were constantly subjected to manipulated recollection depending on the narrative context embracing them at the time. Accordingly, an epic 'memory' is defined ideally as the recording of all available traditions, even though authorial predilection may opt for the memorization of a single—the preferred—tradition, and excluding the rest from preservation inside the palace of memory, effectively resulting to their marginalization, even gradual disappearance. Each panel of the Carthaginian mural composition is trailed after by several different ver-

---

Rhetorica ad Herennium, in Cicero's *De Oratore* and in Quintilian's *Institutiones*, see Scarth 2008, 44–53.

sions of the visualized Trojan War story; Aeneas' perspective of the 'epic composer', however, has stored in his memory only one version, which may be memorized more readily than the rest, because it touches Aeneas' personal interests and feelings more than the others. Upon recognizing the unifying subject of the depicted narratives on the murals, he proceeds to identify and provide details for those among them (we are never specifically told that Aeneas' description covers all the panels depicted on the mural of Juno's temple) that seem the most appropriately addressing the trail of thoughts (sorrow, desperation and pain for Trojan suffering and fate; attachment to the Trojan heroic past) and concerns (fear of the unknown and of possible treacherousness) running through Aeneas' mind at the moment he enters the temple of Juno. He also proceeds to determine: (i) his selection of the specific panels and not others and (ii) his description/'reading' of them by stressing the particular details instead of others. Further, in accordance with the directions of the *Auctor ad Herennium*, Aeneas has stored in his memory carefully selected details of the action unraveling in the episodes/*imagines* he readily recalls—details that makes these narrative episodes striking, and as such easy to recall, even though some of them do not appear anywhere in the surviving literary tradition: Polites' mutilated body on the ground trailing behind his chariot leaving his trace on the ground (and in Aeneas' memory path), which is there in order to duplicate (and anticipate later in the *descriptio*) Hector's similar mutilation behind Achilles' chariot, given that Troilus' mutilation as reported in the murals has no precedent in the pre-Virgilian tradition, Greek and Roman alike; the impressive mixing of red and white in the fierce (lit. 'fiery', *ardentis*) horses of Rhesus next to the snow white (*nivea*) tents of the Thracian army and to the blood-drenched (*cruentus*) Diomedes by the rivers of Troy; the *Iliades* with their hair down; the eyes of Minerva's statue fixed on the ground immovable; the shiny gold in the middle of the encounter between Achilles and Priam; the supplication of the Trojan women that leads naturally Aeneas' memory to recall (and turn his gaze next to) the supplication gesture of Priam to Achilles; the *niger* Memnon; Penthesilea with the golden breast band. Unusual postures and gestures, impressive and impressionable colours, weapons, gold, in other words, specific subject matter or items (*res*), which contribute to making a panel easier to remember and more permanently retained; which leads one back to the *Rhetorica ad Herennium* warmly encouraging the aspiring orator to 'set up images that are not many or vague, but are doing something' (*non multas nec vagas, sed aliquid agentes imagines ponemus*), because:

> *si egregiam pulcritudinem aut unicam turpitudinem eis adtribuemus; si aliquas exornabimus, ut si coronis aut veste purpurea, quo nobis notatior sit simulitudo; aut si qua re deformabimus, ut si cruentam aut caeno oblitam aut rubrica delibutam inducamus, quo magis insignita sit forma, ... nam ea res quoque faciet ut facilius meminisse valeamus.* (ad Herennium 3.22)

If we bestow extraordinary beauty or singular ugliness on them; if we dress others as if in crowns or purple cloaks, so that the similarity may be more distinct to us; or if we disfigure them somehow, as if we presented one stained with blood, covered with mud or smeared with red ochre, so that its appearance is more distinct, ... these things will ensure that we will be able to remember them more easily.
(trans. Small 1997 with minor adjustments)

And these recollections, importantly, are reproduced by Aeneas *ex ordine*, because *this is how he has memorized them:* the advice offered by the professorial author of the *ad Herennium* is once again crucial. The *loci* (or background frames in terms of the *ekphrasis*) must be kept in order, *ex ordine*, to avoid any confusion when following the sequence of the images (the narratives depicted on these backgrounds). An order is especially important, so that an individual might be able to recall the stored information from start to finish, backwards or from the middle of any of the *loci: Item putamus oportere <ex ordine hos locos habere,> ne quando perturbatione ordinis inpediamur*, 'I likewise think it obligatory to have these backgrounds in a series, so that we never by confusion in their order be prevented from following the images' (*Ad Her.* 3.17, trans. Small 1997). In this light, the order in which Aeneas reproduces his Trojan memories has already been predetermined in his mind, emerging instinctively in accordance with the recollections he will identify in the pictures of the murals and hence reproduce, and depending on which of these recollections he will first identify—since each recollection is part of a different concatenation of *imagines*/episodes.

The readers of the *descriptio*, then, are made aware that it is their visual perception, the way themselves in their individual exclusiveness envision mentally the set-piece descriptive composition on the murals that gives shape and meaning to the *descriptio*; that there are as many visual representations as many gazes, just as, in oral epic composition, there are as many verbal renderings of a typical scene (a description of a recurrent action sequence) as many times this is rendered, either in a single epic synthesis or in different epic performances and by multiple performers; and the mental re-composition of a visually described picture is no less a hypertext, as complex and elusive as the composition of an epic poem that exists and circulates only orally. Thus, the study of the Carthaginian description discloses the two linking threads, one thematic, one structural, both fundamental in the composition mechanism of archaic epic, behind Aeneas' narrative composition/interpretation of the *descriptio*.

Charilaos N. Michalopoulos
'tollite me, Teucri' (Verg. Aen. 3.601): Saving Achaemenides, Saving Homer

In the third book of the *Aeneid* wandering Aeneas and his crew land on Sicily, the island of the Cyclops Polyphemus, where they come across a totally unexpected spectacle. They are approached by a Robinson Crusoe-like figure rushing towards them with hands stretched out in supplication. This emaciated and disheveled figure is identified with Achaemenides, a member of Ulysses' crew, who has been inadvertently abandoned by his fellow shipmates. After being assured his safety the left-behind Greek gives his account of the disastrous meeting of Ulysses with the ferocious Cyclops. The Trojans listen to his story and Aeneas offers him the much desired salvation by taking him on board (see also the relevant discussion by Kayachev in this volume).

The intertextual nature of this so-called 'Achaemenides episode' (3.588–691) has long now been discussed (on its reception in Latin scholarship, see Maltby's chapter in the next section of this volume).[1] Much ink has already been spilt in an attempt to map out Virgil's probable –and less probable– literary models for what Stephen Hinds has aptly called 'a remake-with-sequel'[2] of the Homeric Cyclops episode (*Od.* 9.177–566).[3] Virgil's intertextual arsenal comprises a rich and dense network of multiple allusions, intersections and transformations of prior literature ranging from the Homeric epics[4] and Greek tragedy[5] to Roman tragedy[6] via the decisive influence of Hellenistic poetry[7] (Apollonius Rhodius, in particular).[8] The metaliterary nature of this episode has also been acknowledged.[9] So far, however, emphasis has been put primarily (if not entirely) on the temporal and spatial intersection of the *Aeneid* with the Homeric *Odys-*

---

[1] For a concise overview of the critical work on the episode, see Horsfall 2006 on Verg. *Aen.* 3.588–691.
[2] Hinds 1998, 111.
[3] For Aeneas' legend prior to Virgil's *Aeneid* and its many ramifications, see Lloyd 1957.
[4] See Williams 1980b; Knauer 1981, 871–90; Harrison 1986; Ramminger 1991, 64–66; Barchiesi 2001, 134.
[5] See Ramminger 1991, 66.
[6] See Wigodsky 1972, 87; Flores *EV* IV, s.v. 'Polifemo' 165–66.
[7] So Glenn 1972; Flores *EV* IV, s.v. 'Polifemo' 165; Geymonat 1993; Barchiesi 2001, 134; Nelis 2001, 50.
[8] So Quinn 1969, 132; Heinze 1993, 82–83; Ramminger 1991, 66–69; Nelis 2001, 51–59.
[9] For various aspects of the episode's metaliterariness, see Papanghelis 1999.

sey. In addition, there seems to be a long standing debate regarding the structural and thematic relevance of the Achaemenides episode with the rest of the poem; more specifically, its correspondence with Sinon's episode in book 2.[10] It is not my intention to get involved into this discussion, even though –for reasons which I hope to prove below– I believe that the episode was meant to survive the poet's *ultima manus*.[11] The aim of this paper, instead, is to investigate the episode's metaliterary self-consciousness and to contextualize its impact on Virgil's wider poetological program of Homeric reception. In particular, I want to examine how Virgil manipulates Homer not only as a text but also as a cultural and ideological reservoir for his own epic.

The importance of Homer (and, for that matter, of all that was considered 'Homeric')[12] for the Roman elite from the early Republic to the late Empire hardly needs any justification. The active engagement of the Roman poets with the Homeric epics, as early as the first 'translation' of the *Odyssey* into Latin by Livius Andronicus, is yet another cliché in the study of Homeric reception in Rome.[13] Moreover, the fact that both the *Iliad* and the *Odyssey* constituted for centuries an indispensable part of the curriculum of the children of the Roman elite is symptomatic of the Romans' unfailing concern for the relevance of the Homeric values to their own culture.[14] Still, despite the importance of literary exchange, Homer's impact at Rome needs not be confined solely to literature; it should be assessed also on grounds of material culture and social practice.[15] The role of the visual arts (i.e. sculpture, wall-painting, painting, artifacts) must be taken into consideration at all times. Hence, my investigation, even though primarily concerned with intertextual correspondences and linguistic exchanges, proves to

---

10 For more details on this, see Lloyd 1957, 398 n. 52; Williams 1962 on Verg. *Aen.* 3.588 ff. with bibliography; Quinn 1969, 134; Wigodsky 1972, 87–88; Kinsey 1979, 111, n. 5 with bibliography *ad loc.*; Cova *EV* I, s.v. 'Achemenide' 22; Moskalew 1988, 26–27; Hershkowitz 1991, 74–75, n. 18 with bibliography *ad loc.*, Ramminger 1991, 55–64; Heinze 1993, 83; Papanghelis 1999, 282, n. 23; Papaioannou 2005, 81, n.12 with bibliography.
11 *pace* Williams 1962 on Verg. *Aen.* 3.588 ff.
12 Graziosi 2008a, 27–32 offers an informative discussion of the different meanings acquired by 'Homer' and the 'Homeric epic tradition' in antiquity (both Greek and Roman).
13 Homer was of vital importance for the Roman poets of early Rome (Livius Andronicus, Naevius, Ennius) and their claim of 'Hellenizing innovation'. For more on this, see Hinds 1998, 52–63 and Graziosi 2008a, 35. See also the useful bibliography on the relationship between Homer and the Roman epic poets compiled by Farrell 2004, 271.
14 See Farrell 2004, 266 n. 33 with bibliography *ad loc.*
15 Both Farrell 2004 and Graziosi 2008a argue against any linear (mostly literary) models of Homeric reception and stress the need to discuss Homer's presence throughout Roman culture from the viewpoint of a wider engagement with the Homeric epics in their entity.

be equally aware of the wider intellectual processes involved in Virgil's varied strategies of refiguring the Homeric epics. For practical reasons my paper is organized in the following sections: (a) Achaemenides' physical appearance and supplication, (b) Achaemenides' (self-)presentation, (c) the Sicilian shore and (d) the Cyclops and his brothers.

a. Achaemenides' physical appearance and supplication

Achaemenides presents a pitiful sight (Verg. *Aen.* 3.590–99): he is disgustingly filthy (593: *dira inluuies*), he has an overgrown beard (593: *inmissa barba*), and he is frail from starvation and suffering (590: *macie confecta suprema*). His pathetic appearance is complemented by a reference to the rags he is wearing, which are sewn together with thorns (594: *consertum tegumen spinis*). A close reading of Achaemenides' description reveals how well chosen Virgil's vocabulary is, as it abounds with terms of metaliterary output. The emphatic accumulation in one line of terms like *ignoti* (591), *noua forma* (591), *cultu* (591) aims at underscoring further its metaliterary implications. It is true that Achaemenides' appearance owes much to a long standing tradition of similar descriptions, whose archetype seems to have been Ulysses' appearance before Nausicaa (*Od.* 6.128–29);[16] also, let us not forget that Ulysses upon arrival on Ithaca was dressed in beggar's rags (miraculously transformed as such by goddess Athena, cf. *Od.* 13.397–403, 430–38). Nevertheless, Virgil's detailed reference to Achaemenides' spin-sewed rags seems to be looking towards a completely different direction, given that clothes in Roman poetry are often employed as poetological markers.[17] A reader well equipped to seize on such hints must have appreciated the metaliterary implications behind the poet's reference to Achaemenides' Greek attire (596: *Dardanios habitus*) as opposed to the Trojans' armour (595–96: *Troia ... / arma*), which in turn works as a subtle allusion to the opening of the *Aeneid* (1.1: *Arma uirumque cano...*). The overgrown beard underscores both Achaemenides' Greekness (by attributing to him a rather unpopular and old-fashioned –at least for Roman standards– appearance)[18] and his wretchedness. The emaciated Greek is very close to death as a result of exhaustion and suffering (590: *macie confecta suprema*).

---

16 So Ramminger 1991, 69.
17 Cf. e.g. Keith 1994, 27, 30; Miller 2001, 140; Wyke 2002, 149–50; Gibson 2007, 89–90.
18 Papanghelis 1999, 281 with n. 21; Horsfall 2006 on Verg. *Aen.* 3.593.

But what are we supposed to make out of all these? It is my contention that Virgil through his use of this carefully chosen vocabulary manages to refigure Achaemenides from a miserable shipwrecked Greek sailor into a living incarnation of the pitiful state of the post-Homeric epic production. Achaemenides is not merely 'the relic of an archaic past',[19] but more importantly he is a metaphor for the literary remains of the so-called ὁμηρίζοντες, whose poor literary output was a barren and unimaginative imitation of Homer's work. The hero's almost terminal condition in life (590: *macie confecta suprema*) is suggestive of the almost terminal condition of that literary production. In this light, the remark by Nicholas Horsfall that Achaemenides' beard could perhaps 'suggest the age and authority of Homer'[20] becomes all the more meaningful. Virgil's *noua forma* (591) sounds doubly programmatic: firstly, it underscores the fact that Achaemenides is (in all probability) a Virgilian invention;[21] and secondly, it puts forward the claim for something new, for something fresh, which will help him overcome his own (nearly) terminal condition.[22]

Granting this thread of thought Achaemenides' desperate cry for rescue at line 601, *tollite me, Teucri; quascumque abducite terras,* receives further metaliterary significance by essentially becoming a desperate cry for the rescue of the Homeric epic tradition by Virgil's Roman epic. Achaemenides, the living impersonation of a decadent and dying tradition, begs for deliverance. He urges the recently arrived Trojans to remove him from the Odyssean island of the Cyclops and take him to another literary land, whichever that may be (601: *quascumque abducite terras*). Achaemenides' imminent death is twofold, both corporeal and literary. The hero fears both his biological death and the potential absence of his textual body from the long line of epic production (both Greek and Roman). In this light, his wish to 'happily die at the hands of a human' (606: *si pereo, hominum manibus periisse iuuabit*) receives an intriguing metaliterary resonance, since *manus* apart from 'hand'[23] can additionally be taken here 'as the instrument with which writing is done'.[24] The metaliterary impact of *manibus periisse* is further enhanced by the fact that *manus* also appears in phrases referring to

---

19 So Papanghelis 1999, 281.
20 Horsfall 2006 on Verg. *Aen.* 593.
21 So Lloyd 1957, 397; Williams 1962 on Verg. *Aen.* 3.588ff.; Cova *EV* I, s.v. 'Achemenide' 22; Heinze 1993, 83 with n. 43; Papanghelis 1999, 280 with n. 19; Nelis 2001, 51.
22 Papaioannou 2005, 93 acutely remarks that Achaemenides' *noua...forma* in Virgil's *Aeneid* facilitates the hero's assimilation in Ovid's *Metamorphoses*, where shapes change into new bodies (1.1: *in noua...mutatas...formas corpora*).
23 *OLD* s.v. 'manus' 1.
24 *Ibid.* 19.

the use and handling of books (e. g. *in manibus esse, in manibus uersari, in manibus habere*)²⁵ or the transmission of texts (e. g. *per manus tradere*).²⁶

b. Achaemenides' (self-)presentation

Achaemenides' self-definition as a 'comrade of unfortunate Ulysses' at the very first line of his speech (613: *sum patria ex Ithaca, comes infelicis Ulixi*) should be read as yet another Virgilian attempt to establish continuity within the epic tradition.²⁷ It is surely not haphazard that the whole episode is rounded off with the repetition of the same formula; the second time, however, the formula comes from the mouth of Aeneas (691: *comes infelicis Ulixi*).²⁸ Achaemenides right from the very beginning also defines himself as one of the Danaan fleet (602: *Danais e classibus unum*). I am inclined to read here more than a reference to ethnic descent. *Classis*, which means 'fleet',²⁹ also carries implications of order and class which 'are essential to the notion of canon and literary succession'.³⁰ In this light, Achaemenides' ethnic self-definition becomes a matter of generic appropriation, as the hero effectively subscribes himself to the long literary tradition of the Homeric epics. The metaliterary suggestiveness of *classis* has already been detected behind Virgil's use of the noun to describe Achaemenides' unspeakable joy at his first sight of the approaching Trojan fleet (651–52: *hanc primum ad litora classem/ conspexi venientem*). In this case, 'the *Aeneid* is the first modern epic to revisit the Cyclops episode after the *Odyssey*, just as Aeneas' ships are the first to approach the land of the Cyclops after Odysseus'.³¹

---

25 *Ibid.* 12.
26 *OLD* s.v. 'manus' 18.
27 The exact meaning of *infelix* (ranging from 'cursed'or 'hateful' to implying [authorial] sympathy) has caused considerable confusion to commentators ever since Servius (see Williams 1962 and Horfall 2006 on Verg. *Aen.* 3.613). *Infelix* should preferably be associated with κάμμορος and δύστηνος, two Homeric adjectives exclusively attributed to Ulysses. So Papaioannou 2005, 87–88 discussing Virgil's emphasis on the hero's suffering.
28 For the repetition of *comes infelicis Ulixi* by Aeneas (a rarity in Virgil) as a sign of the Trojan hero's recognition of common humanity with his former hated enemy see Kinsey 1979, 114. I cannot agree with Williams 1983, 263–64, who finds the repetition 'ironical' and 'totally alien to his tone [...] an authorial sympathy that is inappropriate in the mouth of Aeneas.'
29 *OLD* s.v. 'classis' 3.
30 Papanghelis 1999, 284.
31 *loc. cit.*

Achaemenides' reference to his father, which follows immediately his association with Ulysses, also calls for attention.[32] The hero's reference to his humble descent from poor Adamastus (614–15: *Adamasto/paupere*) is much more than a 'superfluous' account 're-used ... in a less suitable context' compared with the similar details used by Sinon in Book 2.[33] As I shall try to show, Virgil's reference to the father and his poverty is intrinsically related with Achaemenides' metaliterary status. To begin with, *Adamastus* as a proper name appears nowhere else in classical literature (either Greek or Roman), thus highlighting the fact that Achaemenides is a Virgilian coinage.[34] Horsfall finds the name 'extremely appropriate for a warrior from rugged Ithaca (...), but equally true of the Trojans who prove just as *indomiti* in defeat.'[35] True this may be, I contend that, given the episode's highly metaliterary texture, *Adamastus* in the sense of 'unsubdued, unconquered'[36] could well be read as an allusion to the poetic material of the Homeric heritage, which the decadent and technically flawed post-Homeric production of the ὁμηρίζοντες (to which Achaemenides belongs) failed to conquer. The particular reference to Adamastus' poverty (615: *pauper*), which belongs to the 'poor father' *topos*,[37] offers further support to my claim with its implications of 'poor quality' and 'lack of technical resources'.[38] Through this manipulation of language Virgil manages to portray Achaemenides as the genuine offspring of a technically poor and artistically deficient poetry.

c. The Sicilian shore

Despite Virgil's laborious efforts to avoid the encounter of his *Aeneid* with Homer's *Odyssey*, it is the temporal and spatial proximity of the two epics which often brings the footsteps of Aeneas really close to the footsteps of Ulysses.[39] As has already been argued, during this intertextual seafaring 'the voyage [becomes]

---

32 Verg. Aen. 3.613–15: *sum patria ex Ithaca, comes infelicis Vlixi, / nomine Achaemenides, Troiam genitore Adamasto / paupere (mansissetque utinam fortuna!) profectus.*
33 So Ramminger 1991, 62. Cf. also Williams 1962 on Verg. Aen. 3.614–15.
34 Nelis 2001, 51–52 argues for the influence of four different rescue stories from Apollonius Rhodius' *Argonautica* on the story of Achaemenides. One of these stories is Jason's rescue of the sons of Phrixus (2.1093–1230). Nelis 2001, 52 suspects behind the use of *Adamastus* an allusion to *Athamas*, whose wealth the sons of Phrixus are urged to take possession of.
35 Horsfall 2006 on Verg. Aen. 3.614.
36 LSJ^9 s.v. 'ἀδάμαστος'.
37 Horsfall 2006 on Verg, Aen. 3.614–15.
38 Cf. *OLD* s.v. 'pauper' 3,4.
39 For more on the spatio-temporal intersection of the two epics, see Barchiesi 2001, 16–17.

a trope for intensive self-reflexivity' with 'sailing past/close' a shore or arriving to a certain Odyssean shore regulating the degree of *Aeneid's* avoidance, proximity or coincidence with the Odyssean intertext.[40] The very fact that the encounter between the left-behind Homeric hero and the Trojan crew takes place on the shore of Sicily ultimately transforms this shore from a borderline between land and sea into a metaliterary borderline between the Greek epic tradition (represented by the pitiful and decadent sight of Achaemenides) and the new, still undefined and unmapped, Roman epic tradition (represented by Aeneas' equally unmapped sea route). Right from the very beginning, Achaemenides desperately urges the Trojans to remove him from the Cyclopean shore to any other land (600–01)—a claim which he repeats near the end of his speech, when he urges the Trojans to violently cut off the ropes of their ships.[41] The repeated imperative (639: *fugite...fugite*) is indicative of the urgency of his appeal. It seems that the danger involved is not so much the death at the hands of the Cyclops but rather the entrapment of Aeneas' boat, i.e. of the new epic, in the safety of the harbour of a badly written epic poetry. By cutting off the ropes the Trojans are practically urged to cut off the umbilical cord with the sad remains of a decadent literary tradition. At the far opposite of the harbour's failed safety stands the challenge of the open sea, where the ship of the new Roman epic sails with its canvas open to favourable winds (683: *uentis intendere uela secundis*).[42]

d. The Cyclops and his brothers

The reworking of the adventure of Odysseus in *Aeneid* 3 provide Virgil with ample opportunity to enrich his narrative with three episodes (namely Charybdis, mount Aetna and Polyphemus) of hyperbolic narratives, which, as Philip Hardie has shown, are artfully contextualized in *Aeneid*'s wider poetological program.[43] As I shall try to prove, Virgil's depiction of Polyphemus adds further to the metaliterary texture of the whole episode. Achaemenides' story is introduced by a description of mount Aetna and its volcanic eruptions, both fine ex-

---

40 Papanghelis 1999, 279.
41 Verg. *Aen.* 3.639–40: *sed fugite, o miseri, fugite atque ab litore funem / rumpite*. Cf. also 667: *taciti incidere funem*.
42 The open sea and the ship traveling with sails open to the wind constitute stock poetic metaphors for literary pursuits in both Greek and Latin poetry.
43 Hardie 1986, 259–67.

amples of hyperbolic writing.[44] At first sight both descriptions seem to facilitate the geographical localization of the episode. Mount Aetna, as we already hear from Lucretius,[45] is traditionally considered to be a place of wonders, which anticipates the wondrous story to follow. The localization of the Cyclopes on the island of Sicily is conventional ever since Thucydides.[46] I would like to draw attention to Virgil's divergence from the –more or less– conventional Pindaric version of the myth,[47] according to which it was Typhoeus and not Enceladus who was crashed under mount Aetna.[48] Virgil's use of Enceladus is much more than a random choice of mythological variation; it reinforces the metaliterary texture of Achaemenides' episode, as it offers a subtle allusion to a text of huge poetological impact, namely the prologue of Callimachus' *Aetia*.[49] The geographical localization of Aetna and Virgil's intentional substitution of Enceladus for Typhoeus provides an interesting link with Callimachus' renowned wish to shake off old age from his shoulder in the manner of Enceladus under the burden of Sicily in the prologue of his *Aetia*.[50] The Virgilian reception of Callimachus' reference is further sustained by the description of Polyphemus' eye as an Argive shield,[51] which is echoing a similar reference to the eye of the Cyclops in Callimachus' *Hymn to Artemis* 52–53.[52]

---

[44] Horsfall 2006 on Verg. Aen. 3.570–87 offers a useful tabular summary of the multiple intertextual influences on the Virgilian account of Aetna's volcanic eruption.
[45] Lucr. 1.717 ff.
[46] Horsfall 2006, 406. For the conventional association of the Cyclopes with the island of Sicily, see Eitrem *RE* XI 2, s.v. 'Kyklopen' 2330.63–2331.3; Barchiesi *EV* I, s.v. 'Ciclopi' 778 with bibliography; with Aetna in particular, see Eitrem *RE* XI 2, s.v. 'Kyklopen' 2331.3–41.
[47] For details on the myth and its many variations, see Williams 1962 on Verg. Aen. 3.578ff. and Horsfall 2006 on Verg, Aen. 3.578.
[48] Verg. Aen. 3.578–80: *fama est Enceladi semustum fulmine corpus/ urgeri mole hac, ingentemque insuper Aetnam/ impositam ruptis flammam exspirare caminis.*
[49] So Hollis 1992, 273–74. Apart from Callimachus, Nelis 2001, 50–51 further suggests the possibility of an influence by Apollonius Rhodius' *Argonautica* (description of Typhaon and Phaethon). Paschalis 1997, 138 explains the association of Aetna with Enceladus through their etymological combination of fire (Aetna <αἴθω) with sound (Enceladus< κέλαδος, κελάδω).
[50] Cf. Call. *Aet.* fr. 1.35–36 Pf.: αὖθι τὸ δ' ἐκδύοιμι, τό μοι βάρος ὅσσον ἔπεστι/ τριγλώχιν ὁλοῷ νήσος ἐπ' Ἐγκελάδῳ.
[51] Cf. Verg. Aen. 3.635–37: *fundimur et telo lumen terebramus acuto/ ingens, quod torua solum sub fronte latebat,/Argolici clipei aut Phoebae lampadis instar* with Williams 1962 and Horsfall 2006 *ad loc*. The Callimachean influence on Virgil's representation of the Cyclopes (Aen. 6.630–31, 8.416–53, 8.425) is also noted by Barchiesi *EV* I, s.v. 'Ciclopi' 778–79.
[52] Call. *Dian.* 52–53: πᾶσι δ' ὑπ' ὀφρύν/ φάεα μουνόγληνα, σάκει ἶσα τετραβοείῳ. Callimachus is also present behind *ruptis...caminis* (580) and *mutet latus* (581) in the description of Enceladus crushed by mount Aetna (see Horsfall 2006 *ad loc*.).

Philip Hardie has demonstrated how Virgil manages to portray Polyphemus as a duplicate of Enceladus through an ingenious transference of the qualities of the anthropomorphized mountain to the monstrous Cyclops.[53] This rather unexpected equation of (the Virgilian) Polyphemus with (the Callimachean) Enceladus brings the Virgilian Cyclops right at the heart of the prologue of Callimachus' *Aetia*. In addition, the description of the Cyclopes (and their land) resounds with a plethora of metaliterary markers which ultimately transfigure them into metapoetic analogues of the Callimachean Telchines.[54] Polyphemus is huge (632: *immensus*) and inhabits an enormous cave (617: *uasto in antro*), he is *qualis quantusque* (641), he is so tall that he knocks his head on the stars (619–20: *arduus altaque pulsat/ sidera*), like his brothers (678: *Aetneos fratres, caelo capita alta ferentis*), who are likened with oak trees and cypresses towering up into the air (679–81). Polyphemus is struggling to hold his pace firm because of his huge bodily mass (656: *uasta se mole mouentem*). Virgil's description of the staggering blind Polyphemus through the use of the emphatic homoeoptoton *monstrum horrendum informe ingens* (658) becomes essentially an acute critique of a literary tradition that has gone way out of proportion and is now suffering from its massive size and artistic shortcomings. Polyphemus' gigantic size seems to be echoing the volume of the bountiful Demeter[55] or the Persian kilometer[56] or the fat sacrifice victim[57] of the Callimachean prologue. The enormity of Polyphemus is also evident in the roar he raises to the sky when realizing that Aeneas' fleet is leaving his island unharmed.[58] The immensity of his bellow could perhaps be taken as an analogue for the noise of the asses, as opposed to

---

53 Hardie 1986, 264–65. Cf. also Flores *EV* IV, s.v. 'Polifemo' 165.
54 Verg. *Aen.* 3: *portus...ingens* (570), *uasto in antro* (617), *domus... /... ingens* (618–19), *arduus altaque pulsat/ sidera* (619–20), *manu magna* (624), *immensus* (632), *lumen.../ ingens* (635–36), *qualis quantusque* (641), *Aetneos fratres, caelo capita alta ferentis* (678), *uasta se mole* (656), *monstrum ... ingens* (658), *quales cum uertice celso/ aeriae quercus aut coniferae cyparissi/ constiterunt* (679–81).
55 Call. *Aet.* fr. 1.9–10 Pf.: ἀλλὰ καθέλκει/ πολὺ τὴν μακρὴν ὄμπνια Θεσμοφόρο[ς.
56 Call. *Aet.* fr. 1.17–18 Pf.: αὖθι δὲ τέχνῃ/ κρίνετε,] μὴ σχοίνῳ Περσίδι τὴν σοφίην. The possibility of a reference to the Persian kilometer becomes all the more intriguing in view of the Persian implications behind Achaemenides' name (for the etymological association of Achaemenides with Achaemenes, the founder of the Persian royal house, see Kinsey 1979, 112, 117; Cova *EV* I, s.v. 'Achemenide' 22; O'Hara 1996, 116, 147 with bibliography; Paschalis 1997, 140 n. 106 with bibliography; Hinds 1998, 112, n.22, Papaioannou 2005, 80 n. 9 with bibliography).
57 Call. *Aet.* fr. 1.23 Pf.: ... τὸ μὲν θύος ὅττι πάχιστον.
58 Verg. *Aen.* 3.672–73: *clamorem immensum tollit, quo Pontus et omnes/ contremuere undae penitusque exterrita tellus*. For the Homeric background of Polyphemus' great howl, see Williams 1962 and Horsfall 2006 *ad loc*.

the singing voice of the cicadas in the Callimachean prologue (29–30).[59] A final link between Polyphemus and the Telchines is offered by the fact that the Telchines, like the Cyclops, were closely associated with the sea, since god Poseidon was considered to be their father.[60]

Polyphemus' killing of two of Ulysses' comrades[61] is also packed with metaliterary ambiguity. His huge hand (624: *manu magna*), a vivid metaphor for a poetry of Telchinian pedigree, is threatening the very existence of the epic tradition, as represented by Odysseus and his crew. I am tempted to read the comrades' *corpora* (623) both as body[62] and as text,[63] all the more so, since nuances of taxonomy[64] and metrical rhythm[65] are latent in the use of *numerus* at line 623.[66] Running the risk of over-interpretation, I would further suggest that Virgil's preference for number two (623: *duo...numero*), instead of number six which appears in the Homeric text, constitutes an implicit allusion to the two Homeric epics. The killing of Odysseus' two comrades translates *mutatis mutandis* into the destruction of the *Iliad* and the *Odyssey* by the monstrous hands of the disproportionate offspring of a decadent post-Homeric production.

The metaliterary impact of Polyphemus becomes even more obvious in Virgil's connection of the Cyclopes with three composites of the verb *fateor*, a verb associated with 'declaration' and 'open acknowledgement'. Polyphemus is firstly portrayed by Achaemenides as *dictu affabilis*, a creature not easy to approach or talk to.[67] He also calls the Cyclopes unspeakable (644: *infandi Cyclopes*), and at the sight of the Trojan fleet he expresses the wish to escape the abominable clan (653: *gentem...nefandam*). The Cyclops is mentioned by name only near the end

---

[59] Call. *Aet.* fr.1.29–30 Pf.: ... ἐνὶ τοῖς γὰρ ἀείδομεν οἳ λιγὺν ἦχον/ τέττιγος, θ]όρυβον δ' οὐκ ἐφίλησαν ὄνων.
[60] For more details on the association of the Telchines with Poseidon and the sea in general, see Herter *RE* 5 A.1, s.v. 'Telchinen' 210.44–68 and 211.65–213.6.
[61] Verg. *Aen.* 3.623–25: *uidi egomet duo de numero cum corpora nostro/ prensa manu magna medio resupinus in antro/ frangeret ad saxum, sanieque aspersa natarent*.
[62] *OLD* s.v. 'corpus' 1.
[63] *OLD* s.v. 'corpus' 16.
[64] *OLD* s.v. 'numerus' 11.
[65] *OLD* s.v. 'numerus' 13.
[66] A similar case of ambiguity can be traced behind Achaemenides' reference to the Cyclopean footsteps at line 648 (*prospicio sonitumque pedum uocemque tremesco*). In this case, *pes* can be taken either as bodily or as metrical foot.
[67] Verg. *Aen.* 3.621: *nec uisu facilis nec dictum adfabilis ulli* with Williams 1962 *ad loc.* for problems of interpretation. The line ultimately looks back to Accius' *Philocteta* fr. 538 (Macr. 6.1.55): *quem neque tueri contra neque adfari nequeas* (so Wigodsky 1972, 87–88). Paschalis 1997, 141 notes: 'The cluster *uisu...dictu adfabilis* combines the component –ωψ of Κύκλωψ and the component –φημος of Πολύφημος'.

of Achaemenides' speech (641), which is framed between *fatur* (612) and *fatus erat* (655).⁶⁸ The recollection of the etymological association of Polyphemus with φήμη is unavoidable. However, Polyphemus hindered by his massive volume fails to communicate with Achaemenides, as his head strikes the sky.⁶⁹ Hence, the Cyclops becomes the incarnation of a 'much spoken of' poetry, which unfortunately fails to communicate its art, becomes incomprehensible and ultimately causes revulsion.

Achaemenides' episode reaches its conclusion on the shore, as Polyphemus leaves his cave on the mountain and moves towards the sea (657: *et litora nota petentem*).⁷⁰ Whereas the Odyssean narrative focuses more on the blinding of Polyphemus and less on Odysseus' escape, in Virgil it is the other way round.⁷¹ In the pursuit of the Trojan fleet by the Cyclops (3.655–74) Virgil diverges from his Homeric prototype in that his Cyclops does not stay on shore hurling huge rocks against the ships (*Od.* 9.480–83, 537–40). The Virgilian Cyclops, instead, wades far into the sea until he realizes the futility of his attempt to catch up with the fleeing ships. The accumulation of terms referring to the sea (662: *altos tetigit fluctus*, 662: *ad aequora uenit*, 664: *graditur per aequor*, 665: *fluctus*, 668: *aequora*, 671: *Ionios fluctus*, 672: *pontus*) underlines the metaliterary suggestiveness of the sea as metaphor for literary endeavour. Moreover, the presence of *pontus* (672) combined with the triple repetition of *fluctus* (662, 665, 671), a term often applied to river streams,⁷² implicitly alludes to another Callimachean passage of immense poetological importance, namely the end of the Callimachean *Hymn to Apollo*, where a combination of the sea with river streams also occurs.⁷³ If so, the streams that hit Polyphemus' ribs recall the muddy and filthy streams of the Assyrian river that threaten to contaminate the clear and untroubled open sea (of the Virgilian text). Polyphemus' steps in the sea

---

68 Paschalis 1997, 141. See also Papaioannou 2005, 95.
69 Moskalew 1988, 33 draws an interesting parallel between the description of Polyphemus and the appearance of *Fama* (Φήμη) in book 4. 173–97.
70 For the metaliterariness of *litora nota*, see Papanghelis 1999, 282.
71 So Williams 1962 on Verg. *Aen.* 3. 677–81.
72 *OLD* s.v. 'fluctus' 2a.
73 Call. *Apol.* 105–12: ὁ Φθόνος Ἀπόλλωνος ἐπ' οὔατα λάθριος εἶπεν·/ "οὐκ ἄγαμαι τὸν ἀοιδὸν ὃς οὐδ' ὅσα πόντος ἀείδει."/ τὸν Φθόνον ὡπόλλων ποδί τ' ἤλασεν ὧδέ τ' ἔειπεν·/ "Ἀσσυρίου ποταμοῖο μέγας ῥόος, ἀλλὰ τὰ πολλά/ λύματα γῆς καὶ πολλὸν ἐφ' ὕδατι συρφετὸν ἕλκει./ Δηοῖ δ' οὐκ ἀπὸ παντὸς ὕδωρ φορέουσι μέλισσαι,/ ἀλλ' ἥτις καθαρή τε καὶ ἀχράαντος ἀνέρπει/ πίδακος ἐξ ἱερῆς ὀλίγη λιβὰς ἄκρον ἄωτον." In Book 3 of the *Aeneid* Virgil alludes to the Callimachean *Hymn to Apollo* again in Apollo's oracle to Aeneas on the island of Delos (see Barchiesi 2001, 133–35). For Callimachus' presence at the end of Book 3, see Geymonat 1993.

then could be read as the agonizing attempts of the Telchinian[74] post-Homeric epic to persecute, to rival and emulate (a sense latent in *fluctus aequare sequendo* at line 671[75]) the new Roman epic. The emphatic negation of *nulla...potestas* (670) and *nec potis* (671) ultimately reveals the Cyclops' incompetence and the consequent failure in his pursuit. The image of the Cyclops and his horrible brothers on the shore staring at Aeneas' ship sailing away with propitious wind marks the end of the episode. Polyphemus' failed *hospitium* of Achaemenides gives way to a much more favourable *hospitium* by the Trojans (666–67: *recepto/ supplice*), which in turn signifies the reception of what seems to be an agonizing post-Homeric tradition by the Roman epic.[76]

All these literary and metaliterary exchanges aside, Virgil's description of the Cyclops can also be seen as operating within the wider context of the Romans' visual engagement with Greek epic, in this case through wall-painting. It was during the reign of Augustus that the so-called 'Second Pompeian Style' evolved and offered (among others) exceptional depictions of atmospheric landscapes and scenes from the *Odyssey*. Judging from Vitruvius' comments on mural decorations of Roman houses, Homeric themes must have been a popular choice.[77] Fairly recently Joseph Farrell has acutely drawn our attention to the importance of these visual *'Iliads'* and *'Odysseys'* in Homer's cultural and ideological assimilation in Rome.[78] What is particularly relevant to my discussion is the impressive popularity of the Cyclops theme in these decorations, which makes it a most suitable complement of the Homeric text in Virgil's refiguration of the story.[79]

I would like to conclude this paper with an Ovidian coda. In Ovid's *Metamorphoses* (14.158–440), when the Trojans finally arrive at Italy, they meet a character named Macareus. Macareus, a shipmate of Ulysses, who has also stayed behind, recognizes almost immediately among the Trojan crew Achaemenides, his Greek comrade. This time, however, nothing reminds of Achaemenides' previous

---

[74] The volume of the Cyclops is once again implied by the fact that even though he has gone halfway through in the open sea, still it is only his ribs that receive the blow of the waves.
[75] *OLD* s.v. 'aequo' 11.
[76] Verg. *Aen.* 3.666–67: *nos procul inde fugam trepidi celerare receptor/ supplice sic merito taciti incidere funem*. For Achaemenides' episode as a story of failed hospitality, see Kinsey 1979, 116–17; Moskalew 1988, 30–31 (as a model for Dido's hospitality to Aeneas); Gibson 1999, 364–65.
[77] Vitr. 7.5.1–2.
[78] Farrell 2004, 260–63 offers an excellent discussion of the evidence provided by the so-called *tabulae Iliacae*, the cycle of Odyssean landscapes from the Esquiline, frescoes from Pompeii, the sculpture garden of Spelonga.
[79] For a detailed examination of the Odyssean landscapes and monsters in Roman wall-painting, see Balensiefen 2005.

appearance in the Virgilian text. Achaemenides has been fully restored to his former archaic glory (Ov. *Met.* 14.165–67), and this means that someone, somehow must have taken good care of him on board Aeneas' ship.[80] More importantly, Achaemenides has made his choice, as he proudly declares that he prefers Aeneas' ship to Ithaca and that he reveres Aeneas equally with his father (Ov. *Met.* 169–71). This undeniably constitutes Ovid's bold metaliterary acknowledgment of the deliverance of Homer's legacy by the Virgilian epic.

---

[80] For a detailed discussion of Ovid's highly sophisticated and inherently metapoetic treatment of the encounter between Macareus and Achaemenides in his *Metamorphoses*, see Papaioannou 2005, 79–111.

Boris Kayachev
Scylla the Beauty and Scylla the Beast: A Homeric Allusion in the *Ciris*

'Once we have accepted that the *Ciris* stems from neither Virgil nor Gallus, but was written by a post-Virgilian poetaster...' – with these words R.O.A.M. Lyne, who was later to produce the nowadays standard commentary on the poem,[1] begins his first substantial contribution to the *Cirisfrage*.[2] The quoted passage contains two fundamental statements, one made explicitly and the other only implied. The former is that the *Ciris* postdates Virgil. Although since then it has been argued again that the *Ciris* does stem from Gallus,[3] it need not concern us at present. The latter asserts that the *Ciris* is mediocre poetry. And indeed, throughout the article Lyne is never tired of pointing out in the *Ciris* instances of 'heavy-handed' and 'unskillful' plagiarism.[4] Lyne was, understandably, not alone in this condescending attitude to his object of study, an attitude made fashionable by Housman's passing remark that the *Ciris* 'was indited by a twaddler'.[5] But it was Lyne's commentary, which is indeed, as a reviewer puts it, 'an excellent book on a poem which is less than excellent',[6] that virtually canonized the view of the *Ciris* as a derivative piece of poetry.

Since the publication of Lyne's commentary a number of minor studies on the *Ciris* have appeared, which often make considerable progress in solving individual problems or establishing separate allusions, but still do not attempt a systematic re-evaluation of the poem. Characteristic is the ingenious demonstration by Catherine Connors that the puzzling reference to 'simultaneous hunting and herding' at *Ciris* 299f. (*Cnosia nec Partho contendens spicula cornu/ Dictaeas ageres ad gramina nota capellas*)[7] does not in fact imply actual herding at all, but alludes to the belief 'that goats that had been wounded by a hunter were able to save themselves by seeking out and ingesting dictamnus' (i.e. *gramina nota*).[8] (Indeed, as has been observed by Annette Bartels approaching the poem from a narratological perspective, 'eine Analyse, die den Text mit seinen Eigentüm-

---

[1] Lyne 1978.
[2] Lyne 1971, 233.
[3] Gall 1999.
[4] Lyne 1971, 240, 241, 248.
[5] Housman 1902, 339.
[6] Williams 1980a, 247.
[7] Cf. Lyne 1978, 226–27.
[8] Connors 1991, 558.

lichkeiten ernst nimmt, zeigt, daß die *Ciris* zumindest besser ist als ihr Ruf'.[9]) Still, Connors cautiously admits that the 'display of etymological and scientific *doctrina* associated with dictamnus' may be derived from 'what was presumably the *Ciris* poet's source for the digression, Valerius Cato's *Dictynna*', rather than be original to the poem itself.[10]

Let us briefly adduce some more examples. Heather White has recently produced a plausible explanation for the perplexing comparison of the bird *ciris* with 'Leda's Amyclean goose' (489: *ciris Amyclaeo formosior ansere Ledae*) as referring not to Zeus' transformation into a swan[11] but to that of Leda herself into a goose, as reported by some sources.[12] Jackie Pigeaud has clarified a number of difficult details in the description of Scylla's *metamorphosis* (490–507), in particular the simile comparing it with the development of the embryo within an egg, by pointing out striking parallels in ancient medical writings.[13] Riemer Faber has firmly situated the *peplos ekphrasis* (21–35) within the earlier poetic tradition of embroidered garments as cosmic images,[14] thus vindicating it from Lyne's charge of being a borrowing ill-suited to the new context.[15] Luigi Lehnus and Donato De Gianni have demonstrated the *Ciris* poet's acquaintance with Callimachus' *Hecale* and Euripides' *Hippolytus* respectively, though both were partly anticipated by Atillio Dal Zotto, of whose research they seem to be unaware.[16] Armando Salvatore and Erich Woytek have shed a more favourable light on the *Ciris*' engagement, though not unknown before, with the poetry of Cicero (the former) and Catullus (the latter).[17] Jeffrey Wills has pointed out a suggestive allusion to Apollonius' *Argonautica* and Adrian Hollis to Nicander's *Theriaca* (in studies not primarily concerned with the *Ciris*),[18] both of which we shall have the occasion to consider more closely.

---

[9] Bartels 2004, 62.
[10] Connors 1991, 558.
[11] Cf. Lyne 1971, 246. Lyne 1978, 301 also mentions 'a version in which Leda's Jupiter appeared as a goose', but that still leaves *Amyclaeo* unexplained, since it was Leda and not Zeus who had connections with Amyclae.
[12] White 2006, 180.
[13] Pigeaud 1983. To cite just one example, Pigeaud's interpretation (130) of 499 (*medium capitis discrimen*) as the sagittal suture seems more convincing than Lyne's 1978, 304f., as the hair parting.
[14] Faber 2008.
[15] Cf. Lyne 1978, 109–10.
[16] Lehnus 1975, though earlier than Lyne 1978, but apparently still too late to be taken into account; De Gianni 2010; Dal Zotto 1903, ignored by Lyne.
[17] Salvatore 1984; Woytek 2005.
[18] Wills 1996, 166; Hollis 1998, 171f.

Some (but far from all) of these advances in understanding the *Ciris* are now brought together in a new commentary by Pierluigi Gatti, who also makes further useful observations of his own, such as, for example, noting an allusion to a fragment of Euphorion's *Thrax* at *Ciris* 129–32.[19] But Gatti's commentary is still too limited in scale and ambition to effect a thorough reappraisal of the poem. This is, of course, not the place to offer such a reappraisal, for the obvious reason of space limits; there is, however, enough room to take at least one more step towards it. In what follows I shall discuss a case of Homeric reception in the *Ciris*, which will both shed light on some ambiguities of the text and demonstrate the poem's sophistication in engagement with the literary past.

As pointed out by Craig Kallendorf in a study of allusion as a form of reception, 'there are two readers operating in allusion: the critic who notices an allusion and the author who wrote it'.[20] This underlying isomorphism of the two modes of reception – reading by the critic and reading by the author – often leads to the former's role being assimilated to that of the latter: modern scholarship tends to value the critic's creativity in producing a text's meaning. I would suggest that the reverse perspective is also valid: the author can in a sense be thought of as being as passive in interpreting a predecessor's text as the ideal critic of an earlier generation had to be. This ambivalence of the author's role in appropriating a model, it will be shown, is not merely exemplified in the *Ciris*, but deliberately thematized by the poet.

I propose to begin by reading and discussing a passage of the *Ciris* that embeds – as we shall come to see – a Homeric context, albeit in an implicit way. As a punishment for the betrayal of her father and city, the Megarian princess Scylla, daughter of Nisus, is being dragged through the sea behind Minos' ship, when at last she is pitied by Amphitrite and turned into the *ciris* (478–89):

fertur et incertis iactatur ad omnia uentis,
cumba uelut magnas sequitur cum paruula classis
Afer et hiberno bacchatur in aequore turbo,
donec tale decus formae uexarier undis
non tulit ac miseros mutauit uirginis artus
caeruleo pollens coniunx Neptunia regno.
sed tamen aeternum squamis uestire puellam

---

[19] Gatti 2010, 128, though here too he is anticipated by Latte 1935, 149 n. 35, and Spanoudakis 2004, 39. This allusion may be of some interest for the argument that the *Ciris* is a work of Gallus as in antiquity Gallus was closely associated with Euphorion.

[20] Kallendorf 2006, 68. On the latter's role as a reader, cf. further: 'The alluding author begins the process by reading an earlier text, then working out an interpretation of that text. As he or she begins writing, the new text unfolds in dialogue with the old one.'

*infidosque inter teneram committere pisces
non statuit (nimium est auidum pecus Amphitrites):
aeriis potius sublimem sustulit alis,
esset ut in terris facti de nomine ciris,
ciris Amyclaeo formosior ansere Ledae.*

*Onward she moves, tossed to and fro by uncertain winds
(like a tiny skiff when it follows a great fleet,
and an African hurricane riots upon the wintry sea)
until Neptune's spouse, queen of the azure realm,
suffered it not that such a beauteous form should be harassed by the waves,
and transformed the maiden's sorry limbs.
But even so she decided not to clothe the gentle maid with scales forever,
or place her amid treacherous fishes
(all too greedy is Amphitrite's flock):
rather, she raised her aloft on airy wings,
that she might live on earth as Ciris, named from the deed wrought–
Ciris, more beautiful than Leda's Amyclaean swan.*
(trans. Fairclough/ Goold 2000 with minor adjustments)

It is the figure of Amphitrite and her role in this context that require most attention. As Lyne acknowledges, there seems to be 'no parallel for Amphitrite as the agent of Scylla's transformation, indeed for her playing any prominent part in the Scylla *Nisi* (as opposed to Scylla *monstrum*) story', though he concedes that her entry is 'fairly natural, given that it is in her province that Scylla is suffering'.[21] Shortly we shall see that the main reason for introducing Amphitrite is indeed to create a link with the story of the other Scylla.

Within the quoted passage Amphitrite is named twice: first, by *antonomasia*, as *coniunx Neptunia* at 483; then, directly, at 486. The latter context is peculiar, as Lyne rightly points out: 'Is *Amphitrites* here metonymy or proper name? Neither is particularly easy given that Amphitrite is the subject of the main sentence. I am inclined to think that it is not a metonymy [...]. *pecus A*[*mphitrites*] is a much livelier phrase at any rate if *Amphitrites* is not a metonymy'.[22] We shall see that Lyne is probably right in taking *Amphitrites* literally, but the problem is deeper than Lyne realized.[23] If *Amphitrites* is a metonymy, it reduces the expression *pecus Amphitrites* to a metaphorical periphrasis meaning no more than 'inhabitants of the sea,' which suits the context perfectly. If, however, *Amphitrites* is an actual proper name, it seems natural to take *pecus* literally as well;

---

21 Lyne 1978, 298.
22 Lyne 1978, 300.
23 Other commentators – Némethy 1909, Lenchantin de Gubernatis 1930, Hielkema 1941, Salvatore 1955, Haury 1957, Knecht 1970, Dolç 1984, Gatti 2010 – are no more helpful than Lyne.

but then one cannot help wondering why Amphitrite's sheep, which (one assumes) peacefully graze in pastures of seaweed, should pose a threat even to a small fish such as Scylla would be likely to become.

The passage we are dealing with evokes a context from earlier in the *Ciris*, the section of the proem that announces the poem's plot and also recounts variant stories told about (the other) Scylla (46–91).[24] In a pointed manner, Amphitrite's decision to turn Scylla into a bird rather than fish mirrors the narrator's choice of that particular version of Scylla's *metamorphosis* (note *potius*):

aeriis potius sublimem sustulit alis,	
esset ut in terris facti de nomine ciris.	(487–88)

Rather, she raised her aloft on airy wings,
that she might live on earth as Ciris, named from the deed wrought.

Scylla nouos auium sublimis in aere coetus	
uiderit et tenui conscendens aethera penna	
caeruleis sua tecta super uolitauerit alis.	(49–51)

Scylla saw in the sky aloft strange gatherings of birds,
and, mounting the heavens on slender pinions,
hovered on azure wings above her home.

...potius liceat notescere cirin	
atque unam ex multis Scyllam non esse puellis.	(90–91)

Rather, let Ciris become known,
and not a Scylla who was but one of many maidens.
(trans. Fairclough/Goold 2000 with minor adjustments)

Likewise, the preceding lines (481–86) telling of Amphitrite's general intention to transform Scylla bring to mind the account of alternative versions given in the proem (54–89). That section of the *Ciris* is badly preserved, and the text's meaning is not always clear, but overall features are discernible. The narrator starts by rejecting the variant claiming that it was Scylla the daughter of Nisus who turned into the Homeric Scylla (54–63).[25] Then he considers different alternative versions of the origin of Scylla the monster (64–88). Firstly, she may be the daughter of either Crataeis (so Homer) or some other monster (66 f.). Secondly, she may be a mere fiction, an allegorical image of lust (68 f.). Thirdly, and this is the most relevant version, Scylla may be a beautiful girl with whom Neptune

---

[24] On the different ancient accounts of Scylla(s), see Hopman 2012.
[25] Peirano 2009, 188–92, argues that Callimachus may have been an exponent of this conflated version. On the distinction between, and conflation of, the two Scyllas in Hellenistic and Roman poetry, see Hopman 2012, 195–215.

committed adultery and who in revenge was transformed by Amphitrite into a monster (70–76). Finally, she may be a prostitute who was thus punished for offending Venus (77–88).

The reference to Amphitrite as *coniunx Neptunia* at 483 is not therefore a mere figure of speech, but performs the function of a pointer to that earlier context: unlike the other Scylla who slept with Neptune, Scylla the daughter of Nisus has done nothing wrong to Amphitrite and consequently she is turned (482: *mutauit uirginis artus*, cf. 70: *speciem mutata*) into a beautiful bird rather than a hideous sea monster. But the two contexts have also another, deeper connection. In the idiosyncratic account given by the *Ciris* the attack on Odysseus and his companions is viewed as Scylla's revenge for what Amphitrite did to her (74–76).[26] According to the logic of this variant of the story, Odysseus must be a protégé of Amphitrite's – and so is Scylla the daughter of Nisus. Both suffer at sea: the former is violently attacked (60: *uexasse*) by Scylla the monster, the latter is tossed (481: *uexarier*) by the violent waves,[27] and it is only through Amphitrite's intervention that Nisus' daughter is rescued from the menacing sea beasts (note 451–453 speaking of *aequoreae pristes*).

The most obvious source for the treatment of Scylla the monster in the proem is Homer, the only poetic authority referred to by name (65: *Colophoniaco ... Homero*, cf. 62: *Maeoniae ... chartae*). The mention of Crataeis as Scylla's mother (66: *ipse Crataein ait matrem*) is perhaps the most precise and explicit piece of information that is derived from the *Odyssey* (12.124–25: Κράταιιν,/ μητέρα τῆς Σκύλλης) but far from the only one. The following passage seems particularly relevant (12.95–100):

αὐτοῦ δ' ἰχθυάᾳ, σκόπελον περιμαιμώωσα,
δελφῖνάς τε κύνας τε καὶ εἴ ποθι μεῖζον ἕλῃσι
κῆτος, ἃ μυρία βόσκει ἀγάστονος Ἀμφιτρίτη.
τῇ δ' οὔ πώ ποτε ναῦται ἀκήριοι εὐχετόωνται
παρφυγέειν σὺν νηΐ· φέρει δέ τε κρατὶ ἑκάστῳ
φῶτ' ἐξαρπάξασα νεὸς κυανοπρώροιο.

*She fishes there, eagerly searching around the rock
for dolphins and sea-dogs and whatever greater beast she may happen to catch,
such creatures as deep-wailing Amphitrite rears in multitudes past counting.
By her no sailors yet may boast that they have fled*

---

[26] The idiosyncrasy lies in the fact that the idea of the attack on Odysseus as a means of revenge comes from an analogous story in which Scylla is transformed, for a similar reason, by Circe: as Lyne 1978, 133 points out, 'there is no tradition that Odysseus was ever a favourite of Amphitrite's as he was of Circe's – so Scylla's actions could hardly have piqued her'.
[27] The connection is noted by Skutsch 1901, 101.

> unharmed in their ship; for with each head she carries off a man,
> snatching him from the dark-prowed ship.
> (trans. Murray/ Dimock 1995 with minor adjustments)

This is of course the subtext that underlies the description of Scylla's attack on Odysseus at 59–61, whether it is borrowed from Virgil's *Eclogues* (6.75–77) or is original to the *Ciris*:

> candida succinctam latrantibus inguina monstris
> Dulichias uexasse rates et gurgite in alto
> deprensos nautas canibus lacerasse marinis.
>
> With howling monsters girt about her white waist,
> she often harried the Ithacan ships and in the swirling depths
> tore asunder with her sea dogs the sailors she had clutched.
> (trans. Fairclough/Goold 2000 with minor adjustments)

Scylla's barking (*latrantibus ... monstris*) was mentioned in Homer only a few lines before (12.85: δεινὸν λελακυῖα); *nautas* renders ναῦται (one may also speculate that *timidos*, which in Virgil stands instead of *deprensos*, is a learned translation of ἀκήριοι as 'spiritless' rather than 'unharmed'); and the ambiguous 'sea dogs' (*canibus ... marinis*) can be linked not only to 12.86 (σκύλακος νεογιλλῆς) but also – as we shall see, more correctly – to 12.96 (κύνας).

Now, finally turning to my main point, I would suggest that the phrase *pecus Amphitrites* at 486 picks up this Homeric allusion: 'Amphitrite's sheep' are precisely those 'dolphins, dogs, and other sea beasts' (*infidi pisces* indeed!) ἃ μυρία βόσκει ἀγάστονος Ἀμφιτρίτη, and that is why this *auidum pecus* poses a threat to Scylla the daughter of Nisus. To start with a formal argument, the spondaic ending *Amphitrites* is a 'figure of allusion' pointing to Ἀμφιτρίτη at *Od.* 12.97, positioned likewise at the end of the verse.[28] Furthermore, much as the *Ciris* context leaves in doubt whether *pecus Amphitrites* is to be taken literally or figuratively, so the Homeric one can be, and in fact was, interpreted in both ways. The ambiguity of the Latin phrase is arguably a response to the treatment of this Homeric context in Hellenistic *exegesis*. On the one hand, βόσκειν is a *vox propria* for tending livestock,[29] and at *Od.* 4.413 a point made by Eustathius (2.15 referring to

---

[28] As is observed by Wills 1996, 19: 'a Latin *spondeiazon* can reflect an imitation of a particular Greek *spondeiazon*'.
[29] So Eustathius interprets it as referring to grazing on seaweed (2.15): δῆλον δὲ καὶ ὅτι ἡ τῶν μνίων καὶ φυκίων καὶ βρύων τῶν κατὰ θάλασσαν νομὴ βόσκει τὰ νεμόμενα, ἴσως δὲ καὶ ἑτέρων τινῶν φυτῶν ὡς εἰκὸς θαλαττίων. θύννοι γὰρ ἱστοροῦνται ἐπέκεινα Σικελίας βαλανηφαγεῖν ἀπὸ

1.173) – Proteus, another sea deity, is compared to a herdsman. On the other, as is stressed by Porphyry (ad *Il.* 8.1.86 Schrader), the epithet ἀγάστονος ('much groaning') points to the elemental rather than anthropomorphic embodiment of the sea (in contrast to *Od.* 5.422: οἷά [sc. sea beasts] τε πολλὰ τρέφει κλυτὸς Ἀμφιτρίτη, where the next line also speaks of κλυτὸς ἐννοσίγαιος).[30] Finally, there is also a perfect reason why these *infidi pisces* are a particular threat to Scylla the daughter of Nisus: being constantly preyed on by Scylla the monster, they will be only too glad to take revenge on her fenceless namesake.

Still, a slightly different interpretation is possible and perhaps even preferable. One lesser-known rationalizing explanation of the Homeric monster, fragmentarily preserved in the scholia to Apollonius' *Argonautica*,[31] treats 'dolphins, dogs, and other sea beasts' as an integral part of the dangerous natural phenomenon underlying Homer's depiction of Scylla:[32] according to these scholia, Scylla is a promontory with underwater reefs at its feet, full of fish of prey that attack sailors shipwrecked there. This interpretation is apparently alluded to in the *Aeneid* (3.425: *nauis in saxa trahentem*; there are no reefs in Homer) and it may well be behind the description of the Homeric Scylla in the *Ciris* proem at 60 f.: *uexasse rates et gurgite in alto/ deprensos nautas canibus lacerasse marinis*. As Lyne observes, although at first sight *deprensos* seems to imply being snatched by Scylla, 'such a very literal sense is in fact hard to parallel,' whilst '*deprendo* is in fact almost a *uox propria* of people being caught unaware, at a disadvantage, for one reason or another (usually, obviously, weather) *at sea*.'[33] If so, the passage easily allows of a rationalizing interpretation along the lines suggested by the scholia to Apollonius (note especially *ad* 4.825–831b: εἶτα ἐξιόντες θαλάσσιοι κύνες καὶ ἕτερα διάφορα θηρία ἐσθίουσι τοὺς ἐν ταῖς ναυσὶν ἄνδρας): *deprensos* can be taken to mean 'suffering shipwreck' and *canibus lacerasse marinis* to refer to attack of 'sea dogs' (θαλάσσιοι κύνες, going back to *Od.* 12.96: κύνας), that is either sharks or some other dangerous fish rather than 'real'

δρυαρίων φυομένων κατὰ θάλασσαν – despite the fact that Homer is evidently speaking of fish of prey.

30 Though the last argument can be turned on its head: since at *Od.* 5.422 Amphitrite is clearly a deity rather than element, so it should be at *Od.* 12.97 as well.
31 For texts, see Ressel 2000, 10, n. 12, who also conveniently adduces relevant fragments from Sallust and the scholia to Lycophron's *Alexandra*.
32 Virgil's description of Scylla's lower half as *immani corpore pistrix/ delphinum caudas utero commissa luporum* (*Aen.* 3.427 f.) seems likewise to be interpreting δελφῖνάς τε κύνας τε καὶ εἴ ποθι μεῖζον ἕλῃσι/ κῆτος as part of the monster.
33 Lyne 1978, 128.

dogs.³⁴ Ironically enough, it thus turns out that Scylla the princess is rescued in the end, on some implicit level of meaning, from none other than Scylla the monster. This rescue of one Scylla from the other has apparently also a poetological dimension, for Scylla the daughter of Nisus is indeed saved by the author, through his choice of a particular variant of the myth, from transforming into the Homeric monster.

However, although the version that makes both Scyllas one and the same figure is explicitly rejected already in the proem, and after that Scylla the monster completely disappears from the narrative, on the level of subtexts the danger is never over. As has been suggested by Wills, the passage denouncing Scylla as the ruin of both her father and fatherland (130 f.: *Scylla nouo correpta furore,/ Scylla, patris miseri patriaeque inuenta sepulcrum*) contains an allusion, signalled by the reduplication of *Scylla*, to a context in the *Argonautica* speaking of the other Scylla's parents (4.827–29):³⁵

ἠὲ παρὰ Σκύλλης στυγερὸν κευθμῶνα νέεσθαι
(Σκύλλης Αὐσονίης ὀλοόφρονος, ἣν τέκε Φόρκῳ
νυκτιπόλος Ἑκάτη, τήν τε κλείουσι Κράταιιν)...

Nor to sail by the hideous den of Scylla
(the deadly Ausonian Scylla, whom night-wandering Hecate,
the one called Crataeis, bore to Phorcys).
(trans. Race 2009 with minor adjustments)

And as has been observed by Hollis, the striking comparison of Scylla being dragged behind Minos' ship (478–80, quoted above) to 'a dinghy when towed behind a cargo-boat' seems to originate in an analogous simile from Nicander's *Theriaca* that illustrates 'the crooked motion of a *cerastes*'³⁶ (268–70):

---

34 Furthermore, 59: *succinctam latrantibus inguina monstris* finds a parallel in Sallust (*Hist.* 4.27, a fragment going back to the same common source as the scholia): *caninis succinctam capitibus, quia collisi ibi fluctus latratus uidentur exprimere*.
35 Wills 1996, 166: 'The recombination of the two Scyllas was a poetic favourite, so the reference is not impeded by the fact that Apollonius' Σκύλλη is the sea peril rather than the daughter of Nisus. In fact, the Scylla of the *Ciris* turns out to be just as ruinous (*patris ... sepulcrum*) as the fabled monster (ὀλοόφρυνος). The passage from Apollonius may have had further appeal as a rare mention of the monstrous Scylla's father, since the relationship of father and daughter is at heart of the Latin poem'.
36 Hollis 1998, 171–72. Lyne 1971, 248, explained this simile in the *Ciris* 'as being due to the unskillful plagiarism of our poet' from Stat. *Silv.* 1.4.120–22.

> τράμπιος ὁλκαίης ἀκάτῳ ἴσος ἥ τε δι' ἄλμης
> πλευρὸν ὅλον βάπτουσα, κακοσταθέοντος ἀήτεω,
> εἰς ἄνεμον βεβίηται ἀπόκρουστος λιβὸς οὔρῳ.
>
> *Like the dinghy of a merchantman dipping its whole side*
> *in the brine when the wind is contrary,*
> *as it forces its way to windward.*
> (trans. Gow/ Scholfield 1953)

Though hiding under the surface of the text's literal meaning, this sinister snake cannot but indicate to the attentive reader a far different course of metamorphosing Scylla than that chosen by Amphitrite and the narrator. In this way, I would suggest, the *Ciris* poet acknowledges that, once evoked, a source text can never be completely obliterated; once begun, the process of reception will go on within the new text, sometimes even against the author's will.

As a conclusion, I would like to offer tentatively some further thoughts on the poetological implications of the Scylla myth as treated in the *Ciris*. In a recent discussion of the figure of Scylla in classical Roman and Renaissance English poetry, Philip Hardie has pointed out that the duality of Scylla's nature, which is particularly characteristic of Ovid's version where she is turned into half-maiden and half-monster, reflects the reader's 'more sophisticated response to poetic fictions' that 'is divided between disbelief and the willing suspension of disbelief'; for 'in Ovid's narrative of the actual transformation of Scylla the issue of believability, *credulitas*, is transferred from the poet's readers to the subject of metamorphosis herself'[37] (*Met.* 14.59–63):

> *Scylla uenit mediaque tenus descenderat aluo,*
> *cum sua foedari latrantibus inguina monstris*
> *adspicit; ac primo, credens non corporis illas*
> *esse sui partes, refugitque abigitque timetque*
> *ora proterua canum. sed quos fugit attrahit una.*
>
> *Then Scylla comes and wades waist-deep into the water;*
> *When all at once she sees her loins disfigured with barking monster-shapes.*
> *And at first, not believing that these are parts of her own body,*
> *she flees in fear and tries to drive away*
> *the boisterous, barking things. But what she flees, she takes along with her.*
> (trans. Miller/Goold 1984 with minor adjustments)

Hardie also makes a relevant observation (this time from a slightly different perspective) on what is the dividing plane of Scylla's hybridity: 'it is those parts of

---

[37] Hardie 2009b, 121.

her body that lie beneath the surface of the water poisoned by Circe's drugs that undergo metamorphosis'.[38] I would suggest that, thus interpreted, the quoted Ovidian passage provides an excellent commentary on the way the *Ciris* poet deals with variant images of Scylla(s), whether or not the *Metamorphoses* actually postdate the *Ciris*.[39] Above the water surface, that is, on the literal level, Scylla is a beautiful princess who is turned into a graceful bird; beneath it, that is, on the level of subtexts and hidden meanings, she can be as monstrous and hideous as the Homeric beast. Not only, however, does Ovid explicate this tension between the explicit and the implicit in static terms, he also depicts the dynamics of the reading process: at first the reader can only see what is on the surface, but gradually, often against his own will and to his own disappointment, he also becomes aware of various undertones, potentially sinister and subversive – provided, of course, that he looks beneath the surface at all.

As noted above, both the critic and the author can be thought of as readers, and accordingly this pattern of progressing from the explicit to the implicit is characteristic of both the critic's and the author's engagement with an earlier text. At some point both the critic and the author lose control over the text they are 'reading', which then takes over the initiative in creating –or sometimes destroying– the meaning. How to deal with this Scylla of uncontrollable intertextual associations is a question of great importance, and moreover one that is a central issue for the poetological agenda of the *Ciris*. But to face it, and escape the fate of Odysseus' companions, we need to be better equipped than we are at the moment. In this paper I have tried to produce, by focusing on a single case of Homeric reception, just one more piece of evidence that further demonstrates the importance of taking into account the intertextual dimension of the *Ciris*. For if we ignore it, the *Ciris*, as indeed any poem, will turn into a lifeless –to return to the Ovidian image (14.73)– *scopulum, qui nunc quoque saxeus exstat*.

---

38 Hardie 2009b, 126.
39 Note that the collocation *latrantibus inguina monstris* is only attested at *Ciris* 59, Verg. *Ecl.* 6.75 and Ov. *Met.* 14.60.

Andreas N. Michalopoulos
Homer in Love:
Homeric Reception in Propertius and Ovid

> Macr. *Sat.* 6.3.1: *quod quidem summus Homericae laudis cumulus est, quod, cum ita a plurimis adversus eum vigilatum sit, coactaeque omnium vires manum contra fecerint, "Ille velut pelagi rupes inmota resistit".*
>
> It is the peak of Homer's glory that although he has been the target of a crowd of writers and he has gathered against him this broad coalition, however "like a rock in the sea he remains unshaken".

According to Macrobius this would be the view of Servius, the famous Virgilian commentator, about Homer and the timeless power of his poetry. The Homeric epics have been widely refigured and appropriated in the works of numerous Greek and Roman writers throughout the ages. In Rome a great number of authors working on different literary genres have enriched their works with the use of Homer. Especially interesting is the Homeric reception in Latin love elegy, a genre of which the Romans were particularly proud, considering it to be a national creation surpassing its Greek counterpart (Quint. *Inst.* 10.1.93). As regards its themes and poetics Latin love elegy is generically opposed to epic and claims for itself a clearly defined and independent space among other literary genres. Hence, the treatment of the Homeric reception in such a dissimilar genre is a fascinating challenge.

In this paper I shall attempt to evaluate the reception of Homer in the elegies of Propertius and in Ovid's *Amores*.[1] This is certainly not a new field of research, however it offers a good opportunity for some useful observations. I shall examine which Homeric episodes and characters are more appealing to Propertius and Ovid and why. I shall also explore the type of elegiac context into which Homeric material is assimilated and the way in which this appropriation[2] is achieved. I shall look into the objectives and the (meta)literary goals of the Roman elegists for appropriating Homeric material in their poems, whether it be characters, scenes, episodes or mere allusions. Finally, I shall seek to illustrate the similarities and differences between Propertius and Ovid in their refiguration and reception of the Homeric epics.

---

[1] Tibullus, the other great Roman elegist, is more reserved in his use of Homeric material, with the notable exception of elegy 1.3, which alludes to Odysseus' stay at Alcinous' palace on Phaeacia.
[2] For the terms 'appropriation' and 'refiguration', see Hardwick 2003, 9–10.

Although Ovid was particularly fond of Tibullus,[3] he also believed that he had a lot in common with Propertius (Ov. *Tr.* 4.10.45 f.): *saepe suos solitus recitare Propertius ignes/ iure sodalicii, quo mihi iunctus erat* ('Often Propertius would declaim his flaming verse by right of the comradeship that joined him to me', trans. Wheeler/ Goold 1988[2]). In their books of elegies –in fact at key positions, usually at the beginning and at the end of a book– Propertius and Ovid voice their views about poetry. In these poems there are frequent references to Homer and his poetic value, which offer a clear image as to what the Roman elegists really think of him.

At 1.7.1–76 Propertius acknowledges Homer's supremacy in epic poetry[4] and declares –somewhat humorously, no doubt[5]– that his friend, Ponticus, who is writing a new epic, is competing with the grand master of epic poetry. Nevertheless, Propertius, as a *praeceptor amoris*,[6] clearly states his preference for elegy (cf. also 1.7.13 –19).[7] In a similar manner at 1.9.11 f. Propertius declares Mimnermus' superiority to Homer in love matters[8] and at 2.34.45 f. he asserts that the epic poetry of Antimachus and Homer is useless in love.[9] In 2.1, a typical elegiac *recusatio*,[10] Propertius mentions the Trojan War as a classic epic theme, which, however, he does not have the power to treat, therefore he prefers elegy. By the same token, at 3.1.25 – 34 Propertius –adopting a well-known motif of Greek and Latin literature[11]– claims that the glory of Troy and of the heroes who fought there is due to Homer, who won immortality through his poetry, although even Homer himself would not have become known, had the war just ended.[12]

Ovid in turn at *Am.* 1.15.9 f., defending his choice to write poetry and not to pursue a military or legal career, mentions Homer first in a long list of poets who

---

[3] See Ov. *Am.* 3.9, *Tr.* 2.447 – 64.
[4] See Richardson 1977, *ad loc.*; Fedeli 1980, *ad loc.*
[5] See Baker 2000 on Prop. 1.7.3.
[6] For Propertius' stance as a *praeceptor amoris*, see Fedeli 1980, 186 and Maltby 2006, 147 – 53.
[7] For the opposition between epic and elegy, *duritia* and *mollitia*, in Prop. 1.7, see Fedeli 1980, 186 f. and 231; Kennedy 1993, 31 – 33; Heyworth/Morwood 2011, 31 f. For the Gallan undertones of the polemic between epic and elegy, see Cairns 2006a, 203.
[8] Mimnermus was considered to be the possible inventor of the elegiac distich and of elegy; see Fedeli 1980 on Prop. 1.9.11 – 12. On Mimnermus' erotic poetry, see Szádeczky-Kardoss 1959. On the relation of Mimnermus' poetry to the origins of Latin love elegy, see Cairns 2006b, 72 – 81. For the Callimachean colouring of Propertius' advice to Ponticus, see Syndikus 2010, 65.
[9] On the helplessness of the epic or tragic poet when he falls in love, see Hollis 2006, 102 and Syndikus 2010, 209 n. 440.
[10] Other *recusationes* in Augustan poetry include: Verg. *Ecl.* 6, Hor. *Sat.* 2.1.10–20, *Carm.* 1.6, 2.12, Prop. 1.6, 2.1.39 – 48, 3.9, Ov. *Am.* 1.1. For the *recusationes* in Ovid's *Amores* in particular, see Deremetz 1999, 72 – 74.
[11] See Syndikus 2010, 219.
[12] See Heyworth/Morwood 2011 on Prop. 3.1.25 – 32.

will remain immortal thanks to their works,[13] while in his dirge for Tibullus' death he states that although all poets eventually die, even the great Homer himself, their works remain in eternity (*Am.* 3.9.25–30).

It is clear that both Propertius and Ovid in their 'serious' poems about poetry and poetics fully agree that Homer is the greatest epic poet beyond any doubt, still, this does not alter their steadfast and irrevocable decision to write love elegies. They both have a very good reason for that: this is the only kind of poetry that will enable them to win the love of the *puellae* (the well-established *Nützlichkeit* motif),[14] despite the undeniable fact of course that love is present in the Homeric epics too. There are love triangles (Achilles-Briseis-Agamemnon), illicit, extra-marital affairs (Paris-Helen, Odysseus-Circe, Odysseus-Calypso), and conjugal love (Hector-Andromache, Odysseus-Penelope). This had been noted already in antiquity,[15] while Ovid highlighted the erotic content of the Homeric poems, in order to support his case and defend his own love poetry against Augustus' decision to banish him (*Tr.* 2.1.371–80). With remarkable outspokenness he interpreted the Homeric epics in erotic terms;[16] he summarized the *Iliad* as the dispute between a husband and a lover over an adulterous wife and as the dispute between two leaders over Briseis;[17] he also summarized the *Odyssey* as the story of Penelope's erotic siege by the suitors in the absence of her husband. Moreover, he pointed out that the respectable Homer wrote about the love scan-

---

13 For Homer as the poet *par excellence* in Ovid's poetry, see Skiadas 1965, 95 ff. and McKeown 1989 on *Am.* 1.15.9–10, who cites *Am.* 1.8.61, 3.8.28, 3.9.25 ff., *Ars* 2.279 f., 3.413 f., *Tr.* 4.10.22, *Pont.* 4.2.21 f.
14 Both Propertius and Ovid –Tibullus too (2.4.15–20)– stress the unsuitability of epic poetry, of Homer in particular, for love matters, whereas they emphasize the suitability of elegy for winning their beloved *puellae*. For a comparison of elegy with other forms of poetry and for its prevalence in matters of love, see Stroh 1971. See also Stahl 1985, 48–71 on Propertius' use of the usefulness motif. James 2003, 13–21, 77–79 notes that elegy is a poetry full of flatteries aiming at winning over the beloved and that the *puellae* prefer it to epic. See also Reinhardt 2006, 207; Syndikus 2006, 272 n. 88. For the usefulness motif in Ovid and in particular its use in elegy 2.1, which is inspired by Prop. 1.7, 1.9 and Tib. 2.4, see Booth 1991, 25; McKeown 1998, 2–4; James 2003, 16 f.
15 See Ingleheart 2010 on Ov. *Tr.* 2.371–80, who cites *Priapea* 68, *AP* 9.166.5–6. Other erotic readings of the *Iliad* include: Hor. *Carm.* 2.4.3–12, Prop. 2.1.49–50, 2.8.29–38, Prop. 2.9a.3–14. See Buchheit 1962, 102, n. 1 with bibliography *ad loc.* and 103, n. 3 with examples; Callebat 2012 on *CP* 68.1 with bibliography. See also Ingleheart 2010 on Ov. *Tr.* 2.371–74.
16 According to Ingleheart 2010 on *Tr.* 2.363–468, Ovid does not parody earlier literature to ridicule Augustus' interpretation of the *Ars*, but reworks previous literature to emphasize elements in it which anticipate Latin love elegy.
17 Cf. Hor. *Epist.* 1.2.6 f., 11 ff., 15 f., *Carm.* 2.4.3 f., Prop. 2.8.35 cited by Luck 1977 on Ov. *Tr.* 2.371–4.

dal of Aphrodite and Ares, and about the love of two goddesses, Calypso and Circe, for the mortal Odysseus (*Od.* 5.13ff. and 10.133ff.).[18]

Comparison of the poetic *persona* with Homeric heroes

For reasons of space I shall discuss a particular type of Homeric reception in Propertius and Ovid, namely cases in which the poetic *persona* is compared with a certain Homeric hero.[19] In elegy 2.8 Propertius is mourning, because Cynthia is now with somebody else. The poet is so despaired, that he declares his decision to die after killing her first. He then narrates Achilles' conduct after Agamemnon took Briseis away from him (29–40):

> *ille etiam abrepta desertus coniuge Achilles*
> *cessare in Teucris pertulit arma sua.*
> *viderat ille fuga stratos in litore Achivos,*
> *fervere et Hectorea Dorica castra face;*
> *viderat informem multa Patroclon harena*
> *porrectum et sparsas caede iacere comas,*
> *omnia formosam propter Briseida passus:*
> *tantus in erepto saevit amore dolor.*
> *at postquam sera captivast reddita poena,*
> *fortem illum Haemoniis Hectora traxit equis.*
> *inferior multo cum sim vel matre vel armis,*
> *mirum, si de me iure triumphat Amor?*

> After his sweetheart was abducted, lonely Achilles
> allowed his weapons to lie idle in his hut.
> He saw the Achaeans cut down in flight along the shore,
> the Greek camp ablaze with Hector's torch;
> He saw Patroclus' mutilated body sprawled
> in the dust, his locks matted with blood;
> he endured all this for the sake of beautiful Briseis;
> so cruel the grief when love is wrenched away.
> But after late amends restored the captive to him,

---

[18] Ingleheart 2010 on *Tr.* 2.371–80 juxtaposes Ovid's summaries of the *Iliad* and the *Odyssey* to Horace's corresponding summaries (*Epist.* 1.2.6–16 [the *Iliad*] and 1.2.17–26 [the *Odyssey*]) and notes that Horace's focus 'is narrowly ethical'. Nevertheless, at *Sat.* 1.3.107–8 Horace names Helen's *cunnus* as the cause of the Trojan War.
[19] On a wide variety of possible engagements with Homeric epic in antiquity, see Graziosi 2008a, 32–35.

he dragged the valiant Hector behind his Thessalian horses.
Since I am far inferior to him in birth and battle,
no wonder love can triumph over me!
(trans. Lee 1994 with adjustments)

Propertius portrays Achilles as a lover-fighter, who in the name of love left his fellow Greeks defenceless and even suffered to lose his closest friend, Patroclus.[20] In only ten lines (42–50) Propertius summarizes a very big part of the *Iliad*.[21] On a metapoetic level this compression is very indicative of the transformation and adaptation of the lengthy and grandiose epic into the narrow and humble generic framework of elegy. On the level of the story itself Propertius' argument is based on the arbitrary and clearly elegiac interpretation that Achilles' actions were dictated by his great love for the *formosa* Briseis[22] and not by Agamemnon's huge insult to his personal honour.[23] It is also worth noting that in order to strengthen his argument Propertius calls Briseis the *coniunx* 'wife' of Achilles (2.8.29),[24] whereas she only was his slave, a spoil of war (*Il.* 9.343: δουρικτητή).[25] Nowhere in the *Iliad* is Briseis called the 'wife' of Achilles, except in lines 19.297–99, where Briseis *herself* – but not the poet – recalls Patroclus' promise that Achilles would take her back to Greece as his wife: ἀλλά μ' ἔφασκες Ἀχιλλῆος θείοιο/ κουριδίην ἄλοχον θήσειν, ἄξειν τ' ἐνὶ νηυσὶν/ ἐς Φθίην, δαίσειν δὲ γάμον μετὰ Μυρμιδόνεσσι.[26]

---

20 According to Knoche 1936, 267–68, there are three motifs as points of comparison between Propertius and Achilles: the abduction of the beloved, the pain suffered thereupon and the turn to extreme actions. See also Fedeli 2005 on 2.8.29–38.
21 For this summary of the *Iliad* and the one at Prop. 2.8.29–38, which focuses on Briseis' abduction by Agamemnon and its effect on Achilles and the Achaeans, see Berthet 1980, 144.
22 In the *Iliad* Achilles declares his love for Briseis only once (9.341–43), however this serves his goal to show that losing her is equal to Menelaus' loss of Helen. See Hainsworth 1993 on 9.342. Achilles' relationship with Briseis was eroticized after Homer. Ingleheart 2010 on Ov. *Tr.* 2.373–74 offers several parallels (B. 13.133–37, Prop. 2.8.29–36, Ov. *Tr.* 4.1.15–16, *Am.* 1.9.33–4, 2.8.11, *Her.* 3, *Ars* 2.711–16, *Rem.* 777–84) and cites Nisbet/Hubbard 1978 on Hor. *Carm.* 2.4.3–4.
23 Noted in passing by Syndikus 2010, 132. And this is not the only inaccuracy. As Papanghelis 1987, 117 f. rightly notes, lines 2.8.37 f. presuppose a version of the story with 'un-Homeric emphasis...In the *Iliad* the return of Briseis is not enough to bring Achilles back on the battlefield nor is her return a condition for the latter's reconciliation with Agamemnon'. Cf. also Richardson 1977 on Prop. 2.8.29–38, who attributes Propertius' distortion of the Iliadic account to the 'half-deliberate falsification of his fevered imagination'.
24 Cf. Prop. 2.9.17, where Briseis is listed along with Penelope among the loyal and devoted wives.
25 See Richardson 1977 on 2.8.29.
26 Likewise at *Il.* 9.336 Achilles calls her his ἄλοχον θυμαρέα, however this is a formulaic expression and the term ἄλοχος of Briseis is surprising, 'since the term normally denotes a wife (κουρίδιος

Propertius re-reads and reinterprets the heroic epic through his personal, elegiac viewpoint and transfigures it through the elegiac-erotic system of values. The epic system of values is pushed to the margin or rather is reshaped in elegiac manner. Achilles' personal honour, which suffered badly by Agamemnon and became the main theme of the greatest Greek epic, has no place in the elegiac world. Propertius adjusts the epic system of values to his own case, in order to serve his goal, which is clearly stated at lines 39f. in the form of an *ex minori* argument: since such an important hero and fighter (*armis*) of divine origin (*matre*, Thetis) behaved in this way because of love –or at least this is what Propertius believes and wants *us* to believe– why is it strange for him to become a victim in the triumph of the god Amor?[27]

Propertius returns to Achilles in elegy 2.22a, where he explains to his friend Demophoon that his passion for women neither weakens him nor wears him down; on the contrary, he is ready to take up any kind of erotic challenge. To strengthen his point, he once again draws an *exemplum* from the *Iliad*, this time adding Hector to the picture. Propertius portrays Achilles and Hector as heroes who distinguished themselves in war, despite the fact that they enjoyed the love of Briseis and Andromache respectively before going to battle (2.22a.29–34):

> *quid? cum e complexu Briseidos iret Achilles,*
> *num fugere minus Thessala tela Phryges?*
> *quid? ferus Andromachae lecto cum surgeret Hector,*
> *bella Mycenaeae non timuere rates?*
> *illi vel classes poterant vel perdere muros:*
> *hic ego Pelides, hic ferus Hector ego.*
>
> Think of Achilles when he left Briseis' embrace –
> did the Trojans stop running from his spear?
> Or when fierce Hector rose from Andromache's bed,
> didn't Mycenaean ships fear battle?
> Those heroes could destroy barriers and fleets;
> in my field I'm fierce Hector and Achilles.
> (trans. Lee 1994 with adjustments)

Once again Propertius' appropriation of Homer is clearly elegiac and erotic. On the one hand, he acknowledges the military prowess of the two top fighters of the Greeks and the Trojans, who wreak havoc on their opponents. In this respect

---

is its regular epithet) and is contrasted with δούλη, 'concubine', at 3.409'; see Hainsworth 1993 on *Il.* 9.336. Ovid picks up this relationship in Briseis' letter to Achilles (*Her.* 3.5f., 52).

[27] Whitaker 1983, 122 notes that Achilles' success serves to demonstrate the hopelessness of Propertius' case.

he is consistent with the epic tradition. On the other hand, Propertius associates their bravery and effectiveness in war with their erotic activity, and this is of course unprecedented and subversive. Achilles' and Hector's sexual activity does not affect their military activity in the least; in fact, their military success matches their success in bed. To put it a bit more boldly, their sexual activity actually enhances their military prowess.

To take it even further, one may also detect a sexual innuendo in Propertius' reference to Achilles' military valour. The use of the noun *telum* (30) is perfectly normal for Achilles' arms; at the same time, however, this is a well-established sexual euphemism for 'penis'.[28] Since in the previous line Propertius refers to Achilles' intercourse with Briseis, it is not hard for the Roman readers, who are well-versed in such matters, to make the proper associations and recognize the allusion.

This is a very symptomatic case of the elegiac 'deflation' of heroic epic, especially as regards the top two heroes of the *Iliad*. Nowhere in the *Iliad* is there a reference to the sexual union of Achilles and Briseis[29] or of Hector and Andromache.[30] Far from it, Hector, the protector of Troy, reprimands his brother Paris for indulging in love[31] or for spending his time fondling his armour (6.321 f.) and neglecting his military duties.[32] The conversion of Achilles and Hector into lovers-fighters is their passport into the world of elegy and is achieved through the *militia amoris* motif:[33] the lover is compared with a soldier in the service either of the god Amor or of his beloved. Thanks to this motif epic and elegy, two

---

28 See Adams 1982, 17, 19, 20.
29 According to Otto 1880, 26, the scene of Achilles going to battle from the arms of Briseis may be posthomeric or Hellenistic, whereas Whitaker 1983, 119 assumes that it may have been invented by Propertius' 'humorous ingenuity'. At *Il.* 9.132 – 34 Agamemnon swears that he did not sleep with Briseis.
30 Cf. Andromache's words to Hector at their last meeting (*Il.* 6.407 – 502, in particular 429 f.): Ἕκτορ ἀτὰρ σύ μοί ἐσσι πατὴρ καὶ πότνια μήτηρ/ ἠδὲ κασίγνητος, σὺ δέ μοι θαλερὸς παρακοίτης. Παρακοίτης means 'husband', not 'lover' (*LSJ*[9] s.v.). For this passage, see also Georgopoulou in this volume.
31 Cf. also Prop. 3.8.31 – 34 for Paris' erotic battles with Helen as a detailed development of the theme of *militia amoris*, with Maltby 2006, 159 f.
32 Hector often blames Paris for starting the war and reprimands him for his passiveness and his unwillingness to take part in the battle (*Il.* 3.38 – 57, 6.325 – 31, 13.769 – 73). For these passages, see also Karamanou in this volume.
33 Ovid treats the motif of the *militia amoris* extensively in *Am.* 1.9. For the motif, see Brandt 1911 on Ov. *Am.* 1.9; Spies 1930; La Penna 1951, 193 – 95; Thomas 1964; Baker 1968; Murgatroyd 1975 and 1980 on Tib. 1.10.53 – 56; Lier 1978, 33 f.; Fedeli 1980 on Prop. 1.6.30; Lyne 1980, 71 – 78, 251 – 52; Cairns 1984; Cahoon 1988; Bellido 1989; Maltby 2002 on Tib. 1.1.75 f.

apparently disparate genres, unexpectedly display common features within the cultural and literary landscape of Augustan Rome.

Apart from highlighting Achilles' and Hector's love life, which is bold and innovative as such, Propertius moves a step further. Whereas in the case just discussed (2.8.29–40) he had set up an *ex minori* argument stating that he was inferior to Achilles, now (2.22a.34) he does not hesitate to equate himself with *Iliad's* top heroes. His approach is cheeky and irreverent:[34] he calls himself *ferus Hector* and adopts the epic and grandiose patronymic *Pelides*.

I shall soon get back to Propertius, but for the moment I am going to discuss Homer's reception in Ovid's *Amores*. Writing after Propertius and Tibullus Ovid had the opportunity –and also felt the need– to renovate the genre of love elegy. His novel approach is evident in the way he appropriates and refigures Homeric epic material; a very suggestive example is provided in *Amores* 1.7. Ovid is furious and blames himself for beating his beloved.[35] After noting that even with her disheveled hair, his mistress is most beautiful (he likens her with Atalanta, Ariadne and Cassandra at 1.7.11–18), he denounces his hands as sacrilegious (1.7.27–28) and makes a very interesting comparison (1.7.31–34):

pessima Tydides scelerum monimenta reliquit:
ille deam primus perculit; alter ego.
et minus ille nocens: mihi quam profitebar amare
laesa est: Tydides saevus in hoste fuit.

Diomedes' crime set the worst example:
he first to strike a goddess, second me.
His guilt was less: I harmed the girl I professed to love;
Diomedes raged against his enemy.
(trans. Melville 1990 with minor adjustments)

Ovid compares his crime[36] with Aphrodite's injury by Diomedes, while she was trying to save her son Aeneas from certain death (*Il.* 5.297–351). This is probably the most typical case of sacrilege in literary tradition. In order to imbue his verse with epic colour, Ovid calls Diomedes by the grandiose patronymic *Tydides*.[37] First he equates himself with the great epic hero (31f.), yet another cheeky application of the *militia amoris* motif. Necessary for this equation is the equally bold

---

[34] For Propertius' humour at 2.8.37f., see Papanghelis 1987, 131. Heyworth 2009, 268 picks up Propertius' humorous intention when he calls himself Achilles and Hector in love.
[35] See also Michalopoulos 2003.
[36] For the *peccatorum comparatio*, see McKeown's 1989 detailed discussion on Ov. *Am.* 1.7.31–34.
[37] Cf. Propertius' use of the patronymic *Pelides* for Achilles at 2.22a.34 discussed above.

equation of his beloved *puella* with Aphrodite within the framework of another well-established elegiac motif, the *puella divina* motif.³⁸

Ovid, however, does not stop here. In the following couplet he claims that he is more sacrilegious than Diomedes. His argument is that, whereas the son of Tydeus (*Tydides* again) attacked an enemy –Aphrodite fighting on the Trojan side– he attacked the woman he claimed to love. Through this sophistic exaggeration (*hyperbole*) Ovid portrays himself as history's worst criminal. Humour is effortlessly produced.³⁹

Nevertheless, this is not just another appropriation of Homeric material within a mythological *exemplum*. The comparison between Diomedes and Ovid is also a comparison (and conflict) between two genres, epic and elegy. Ovid (the elegist) is shown to be bolder than Homer (the epic poet); the elegiac writing and way of life (ἐρωτικῶς ζῆν καὶ ἐλεγειακῶς γράφειν) is shown to be more advanced than epic writing and the military world of epic. Elegy surpasses epic and moves into an area where epic had not dared to go. Love and love poetry appear to be more dangerous than epic, which had been the military and violent genre *par excellence* so far. Ovid brings elegy to a higher level.

Before Ovid, Propertius too had shown the will to outdo epic by refiguring it; in fact, he does that in a particularly erotic elegy, 2.14. The poet is excited and celebrates a night of love with Cynthia. The beginning of the poem is really impressive: in four successive couplets, each beginning in a similar or identical way (*non ita* and *nec sic* x3),⁴⁰ Propertius proudly states that his joy surpasses the joy of famous literary persons at the peak of their success (2.14.1– 8):⁴¹

Non ita Dardanio gavisus, Atrida, triumpho's,
cum caderent magnae Laomedontis opes;
nec sic errore exacto laetatus Ulixes,

---

38 See Lieberg 1962, *passim*; Kost 1971 on Musaeus 33; Sabot 1976, 388 ff.; Lyne 1980, 308, n. 20. Cf. also Prop. 1.7.6 (*vel in sanctos verbera ferre deos*) and Ov. Am. 1.7.27 f. (*quid mihi vobiscum, caedis scelerumque ministrae?/debita sacrilegae vincla subite manus*), where Ovid prepares the way for the portrayal of his beloved as a goddess. See Barsby 1979², 83, 85, 87.
39 See McKeown 1989, 164 and Whitaker 1983 on Ovid's flippant irreverent wit. For Propertius' influence on Ovid's *Amores*, see Berman 1972 and 1975; Du Quesnay 1973; Morgan 1977; McKeown 1987, 11–115; Boyd 1997; O'Neill 1999; Heyworth 2009.
40 See Syndikus 2006, 274.
41 Whitaker 1983, 95 points out that the mythological *exempla* at the beginning of the poem are closely associated with Propertius' case, since they illustrate not only his excessive happiness at his erotic success, but also his joy won after 'long hard toil'. Many scholars have rightly noted that these *exempla* are somewhat ambivalent, since the careers of these mythological figures were marred by unpleasant events. See Lyne 1980, 100; Ruhl 2000, 98–99; Syndikus 2006, 275 and 2010, 149; Heyworth 2007, 173.

cum tetigit carae litora Dulichiae;
nec sic Electra, salvum cum aspexit Oresten,
cuius falsa tenens fleverat ossa soror;
nec sic, cum incolumem Minois Thesea vidit,
Daedalium lino cui duce rexit iter;
quanta ego praeterita collegi gaudia nocte:
immortalis ero, si altera talis erit.

Atrides' pride in his triumph over Troy,
when Laomedon's great power collapsed,
Ulysses' delight at the end of his wanderings,
when he touched the beloved shore of Dulichia,
Electra's when she saw her brother Orestes safe,
while she was weeping over his false bones,
Ariadne's when she saw Theseus unharmed, led back
by flaxen thread from his Daedalian quest
-these joys were less keen than my rapture last night;
another such will make me immortal.
(trans. Lee 1994 with adjustments)

In lines 5–8 Propertius treats non-Homeric *exempla:* he states that his joy is greater than Electra's, when she saw her brother Orestes alive, and greater than Ariadne's, when she saw Theseus emerging from the labyrinth. I shall focus on the first two 'Homeric' couplets, which are in any case more important because of their prominent position. Strikingly enough, Propertius measures himself against Agamemnon and Odysseus and claims that his own joy for his intercourse with Cynthia surpasses their joy, when they finally managed to achieve their goals: Agamemnon to capture Troy after ten years of war, and Odysseus to return to Ithaca after twenty years of absence.

This is one of the most characteristic cases of Homeric reception in elegiac context. Once again the reception follows the rules of the 'humbler' genre. Agamemnon and Odysseus, i.e. the *Iliad* and the *Odyssey*, are considered inferior to Propertius, i.e. inferior to elegy itself. Subjectivity, a defining feature of elegy, prevails over epic objectivity. Triumphantly, irreverently and cheekily elegy and Propertius' love life are placed above Homer, his great epics (the *Iliad* and the *Odyssey*) and his great heroes (Agamemnon and Odysseus).

On the whole, the following conclusions may be drawn about the Homeric reception in the elegists Propertius and Ovid:

(i) Although the two genres, epic and elegy, are directly opposed to each other as regards their themes and poetics, Propertius and Ovid frequently appropriate Homeric material in their elegies.

(ii) In their poetological elegies both poets pay their respects to Homer and acknowledge him as an unsurpassable epic poet, avoiding direct comparison

(iii) Despite their respect for Homer and his poetry, Propertius and Ovid do not refrain from adopting and refiguring Homeric characters and episodes with humour, liberty and irreverence. The elegists do not feel inferior to epic; on the contrary, they feel confident to measure themselves against it.[42]

(iv) The elegists compare themselves with emblematic Homeric heroes and prove to be better, superior or sometimes inferior to them. By comparing themselves with the great and famous epic heroes the elegists automatically acquire a higher status.

(v) The confrontation between epic and elegy takes place at the highest level, since the elegists mostly prefer top Homeric heroes, such as Achilles, Agamemnon and Hector.

(vi) Propertius is more reserved towards Homer in his first book of elegies. Then in his second and third book, when he has gained confidence after entering the circle of Maecenas, he feels able to emulate with epic and to highlight both his own poetic power and the power of elegy. On the other hand, Ovid does not display 'self-restraint', because when he starts writing the *Amores* he is already well-established in the literary scene and has acquired his own means of expression and his own particular voice. As a result, Ovid is cheekier and more irreverent than Propertius towards Homeric epics.

(vii) The elegists strive to create their own system of values and ideas within an antagonistic context. They define themselves and their genre through comparison with other genres and writers. The comparison with epic constitutes a means of conquering new literary ground.

(viii) The elegists interpret Homer from the firmly subjective and erotic standpoint of elegy. They accommodate Homeric heroes into their elegies by means of emphasizing their love life rather than their military status. Roman elegy challenges epic conventions and deflates epic values. The epic poem, epic heroes and epic episodes are all being 'elegized'. The actions of Homeric heroes become an example that elegiac lovers and their mistresses should either imitate or avoid.

(ix) The fact that Homeric epics can be appropriated and assimilated into diverse genres and contexts illustrates their superior merit and their classic quality. Through an elegiac and metaliterary reading and by means of lit-

---

[42] On Virgil's similar confidence in his *aemulatio* with Homer, see Armstrong 2006, 137.

erary creativity and innovation Homeric texts can constantly generate new interpretations and meanings.
(x) It is manifest that the elegists enjoy playing with epic, transforming it, re-reading it and reinterpreting it from an elegiac perspective. This is a confrontation of poets, genres, themes and poetics. The elegists are well aware of the fact that they deal with something 'sacred', 'lofty' and ever-present,[43] yet they enjoy using it with liberty and irreverence. This is literary emancipation, artistic creativity and ingenuity at its best.

---

43 Hardwick 2003, 112 rightly claims that reception is proof that classical texts, images and ideas are culturally active presences.

Part VI **Homeric Scholarship at the Intersection of Traditions**

Robert Maltby
Homer in Servius: A Judgement on Servius as a Commentator on Virgil

When the late lamented Professor Harry Jocelyn was asked by a keen research student which was the best commentary on Virgil, he is said to have replied without hesitation: 'Servius'. The purpose of the present paper on Servius' intertextual references to Homer is to show that this magisterial judgement cannot perhaps be accepted without some qualification.

When individual passages of Homer and Virgil are compared in Servius, or in the later scholar known as Servius auctus or Servius Danielis, who augmented his Servius with material found in earlier commentaries, such as that, now lost, of Donatus, the modern reader, especially one well versed in the sophisticated games of contemporary literary criticism, may at first be shocked by the apparent naivety and literal-mindedness of the comments he finds. The reason for this is, I think, two-fold. Firstly, the ancient commentators looked upon the epic narratives of Homer and Virgil as in some real sense historical, rather than mythological. What was important above all in such a context was that the author should get his facts right. The narrative should give a plausible account of events with the correct characters carrying out the right actions in the right order for the right reasons. When passages are compared, an important criterion of literary worth is the historical credibility of the narrative. The second concern of these commentators was one of generic appropriateness. Each genre, as Servius tells us in his prefaces to the *Aeneid* and the *Eclogues* of Virgil, has an appropriate style and content: *humilis* for pastoral, *medius* for the didactic and *grandiloquus* for epic.[1] Failure to make the style and content of a particular passage appropriate to the lofty requirements of epic either on the part of Homer or on the part of Virgil will entail the commentator's censure. The four concrete examples that follow will serve to illustrate these points.

---

[1] Serv. *Aen. praef.* p. 4.8 (Thilo-Hagen): scimus enim tria esse genera dicendi, humile, medium, grandiloquum. Serv. *Ecl. praef.* p. 1.16–18 tres enim sunt characteres: humilis, medius, grandiloquus: quos omnes in hoc inuenimus poeta. nam in Aeneide grandiloquum habet, in georgicis medium, in bucolicis humilem. See further Maltby 2011.

a. A storm at sea

Verg. Aen. 1.92–96:

> extemplo Aeneae soluuntur frigore membra;
> ingemit et duplicis tendens ad sidera palmas
> talia uoce refert: 'O terque quaterque beati,
> quis ante ora patrum Troiae sub moenibus altis
> contigit oppetere!

> Straightaway Aeneas' limbs weaken with chilling dread;
> he groans and stretching his two upturned hands to heaven
> thus cries aloud: 'O three and four times blessed,
> whose lot it was to meet death before their fathers' eyes
> beneath the lofty walls of Troy!'
> (trans. Fairclough/ Goold 1999 with minor adjustments)

Hom. Od. 5.406–07:

> καὶ τότ' Ὀδυσσῆος λύτο γούνατα, καὶ φίλον ἦτορ,
> ὀχθήσας δ'ἄρα εἶπε πρὸς ὃν μεγαλήτορα θυμόν

> Then the knees of Odysseus were loosened and his heart melted,
> and deeply moved he spoke to his own mighty spirit.
> (trans. Murray/ Dimock 1995 with minor adjustments)

> Serv. auct. Aen. 1.92: *reprehenditur sane hoc loco Vergilius, quod improprie hos uersus Homeri transtulerit (Od. 5.406–7) καὶ τότ' Ὀδυσσῆος λύτο γούνατα, καὶ φίλον ἦτορ, / ὀχθήσας δ' ἄρα εἶπε πρὸς ὃν μεγαλήτορα θυμόν. nam 'soluuntur frigore membra' longe aliud est, quam λύτο γούνατα: et 'duplices tendens ad sidera palmas talia uoce refert' molle, cum illud magis altum et heroicae personae πρὸς ὃν μεγαλήτορα θυμόν. praetera quis interdiu manus ad sidera tollit, aut quis ad caelum manum tendens non aliud precatur potius quam dicit 'o terque quaterque beati'? et ille intra se, ne exaudiant socii et timidiores despondeant animo, hic uero uociferatur.*

In his comment on *Aen.* 1.92 comparing Virgil's account of the storm at sea stirred up for Aeneas and his comrades by Aeolus at the bidding of Juno in *Aen.* 1.80 ff. with the storm sent against Odysseus by Poseidon in *Od.* 5.291 ff. Servius auctus[2] draws a detailed comparison with *Od.* 5.406–07 to the disadvantage of Virgil. Virgil, he says, has not translated his original properly (*improprie*). *Soluuntur frigore membra*, 'his limbs dissolved with chill (dread)', is in his view quite differ-

---

[2] Following the convention of Thilo-Hagen edition, comments from Servius auctus are printed in italics to distinguish them from those of Servius himself printed in roman type.

ent from λύτο γούνατα, 'his knees were loosened'. His first criticism of Virgil, then, is one of loose translation. Next, *duplices tendens ad sidera palmas talia uoce refert* ('stretching his two palms to the stars, he cries out thus') is, according to Servius auctus, 'soft' (*molle*) in comparison with Homer's πρὸς ὃν μεγαλήτορα θυμόν, which he sees as higher style (*altum*) and more fitting for a heroic character. His second criticism of Virgil, then, is that he uses the wrong stylistic level. Virgil fails to achieve the lofty tone of his original. Finally the commentator accuses Virgil of lacking narrative credibility. Who in the daytime (*interdiu*), he asks, would lift their hands to the stars! And if you were lifting your hands to the stars, who would say: 'Three and four times lucky were they to die', instead of uttering the expected supplication. Lastly Homer makes Odysseus speak to himself, so his comrades do not hear and become despondent, whereas Aeneas blurts out his pain in front of them. Overall, the comment on *Aen.* 1.92 provides a good illustration of Servius auctus' dual concern for narrative credibility and stylistic appropriateness. Macrobius at a later date compares the same two passages in his *Saturnalia*, but has little to add, apart from the fact that Virgil takes the freezing with fear metaphor from elsewhere in Homer.[3]

Keeping with the storm scene and the question of narrative credibility we turn now to Servius' comment on *Aen.* 1.85 concerning the winds that were blowing. Looking first at Verg. *Aen.* 1.84–86:

> *incubuere mari totumque a sedibus imis*
> *una Eurusque Notusque ruunt creberque procellis*
> *Africus et uastos uoluunt ad litora fluctus.*
>
> They swoop down upon the sea and from its lowest depths
> upheave it all, East wind and South,
> and the African gale, thick with tempests, and shoreward roll vast billows.
> (trans. Fairclough/Goold 1999 with adjustments)

and comparing it with Hom. *Od.* 5.295–96:

> σὺν δ' Εὖρός τε Νότος τ' ἔπεσον Ζέφυρός τε δυσαὴς
> καὶ Βορέης αἰθρηγενέτης, μέγα κῦμα κυλίνδων.
>
> The East Wind and the South Wind clashed together, and the fierce-blowing West Wind
> and the North Wind, born in the bright heaven, rolling before him a mighty wave.
> (trans. Murray/ Dimock 1995 with minor adjustments)

---

3 Macr. *Sat.* 5.3.9: καὶ τότ' Ὀδυσσῆος λύτο γούνατα, καὶ φίλον ἦτορ (*Od.* 5.406) *et alibi*: Αἴας δ' ἐρρίγησε κασιγνήτοιο πεσόντος (*Il.* 15.436 + *Il.* 8.330). *hic de duobus unum fabricatus est: extemplo Aeneae soluuntur frigore membra* (*Aen.* 1.92).

we see that Homer has four winds East (Euros), South (Notos), West (Zephyros) and North (Boreas), one, that is, from each point of the compass, whereas Virgil has only three: Euros and Notos, just like Homer, but then missing out Zephyros, the West wind, which is replaced by Africus, the South West wind, and not mentioning the North wind (Aquilo/Boreas) at all. Servius tells us that the North wind is picked up later by Virgil at *Aen.* 1.102:

> Serv. *Aen.* 1.85: EVRVSQVE NOTVSQVE cardinales quattuor uenti sunt, de quibus nunc tres ponit, paulo post unum quem omiserat reddit: (*Aen.* 1.102) 'stridens Aquilone procella'.

This point is missed by Servius auctus, who comments on the line as follows:

> Serv. auct.. *Aen.* 1.85: *EVRVSQVE NOTVSQVE ET AFRICUS bene modo hos tres uentos inferiores tantum nominauit, qui a sedibus imis mare commouent, Zephyrum et Aquilonem tacuit; Zephyrum qui ad Italiam ducit, Aquilonem qui desuper flat. ideo Homerus de eo Od.* 5.296 καὶ βορέης αἰθρηγενέτης, μέγα κῦμα κυλίνδων.

Modern critics like Austin are not worried by the choice of winds here. According to them, Virgil is just putting together an epic storm without any realistic meteorological considerations on wind direction. The ancients, however, were more literal-minded. Seneca sees the passage as unrealistic, because all these winds could not blow together at the same time (as Aristotle had shown), complaining *hoc non fieri potest*,[4] and this literal view of literary criticism is again reflected in Servius auctus, who this time praises Virgil for omitting the West wind, Zephyr, because it would blow Aeneas back to Italy and the North wind, Aquilo, because it blows vertically down *desuper flat*. This literal approach persists with earlier modern editors, who from the time of Mackail praise Virgil for giving a good description of a Mediterranean cyclone, a view supported by Conway, who gives us a vivid account of his personal experience in suffering one. However wrongminded the Servius auctus comment is here, I offer it as another example of the concern of ancient commentators for narrative credibility.

b. The Cyclopes

A similar case concerns Servius auctus' comments on Aeneas' visit to the land of the Cyclopes and his meeting with one of Odysseus crew, Achaemenides, who

---

[4] On the impossibility of all the winds blowing at the same time, see Arist. *Met.* 364a27: δῆλον ὅτι ἅμα πνεῖν τοὺς μὲν ἐναντίους οὐχ οἷόν τε and Sen. *QN* 5.16.2: *quod fieri nullo modo potest*.

had been left behind when Odysseus and the remainder of the Greeks had sailed away (on this episode, see Ch. Michalopoulos in this volume):

> Serv. auct. *Aen.* 3.590: *CVM SVBITO E SILVIS arguitur in hac Achaemenidis descriptione Vergilius neglegentiae Homericae narrationis; Ulixes enim inter initia erroris sui ad Cyclopas uenit: quemadmodum ergo Aeneas post septimum annum, quem a Troia profectus est, socium Ulixis inuenit? praesertim cum eum tribus mensibus in regione Cyclopum dicat moratum, et mox Aeneas de Sicilia ad Africam uenisse dicatur.*

Here Servius auctus tells us that fault is found (*arguitur*) with Virgil in his description of Achaemenides for ignorance of the Homeric narrative at this point. He does not say who finds fault, but such criticisms may well originate with one of the first century AD commentators on Virgil. Here the problem is one of chronology. Odysseus visited the Cyclopes at the beginning of his journey home from Troy *(inter initia erroris)* according to Homer, whereas according to Virgil Aeneas only reached their land seven years after setting sail from Troy. Achaemenides himself says at *Aen.* 3.645 that he has only been there three months.[5] Similar criticism is found in Servius:

> Serv. *Aen.* 3.623: VIDI EGOMET DVO Homerus (*Od.* 9.289 and 311) quattuor dicit. ergo aut dissentit ab eo, ut etiam in temporibus: nam ante ad Siciliam Aeneas, quam Ulixes uenisse dicitur, aut certe hoc dicit, duo uidisse se, quot autem occiderit, ignorare.

> Serv. *Aen.* 3.678: AETNAEOS FRATRES aut similes aut feritate germanos...nam non sunt Polyphemi fratres, quem Neptuni filium Homerus dicit (*Od.* 1.68 ff.). unde eo occaecato Ulixes pertulit tempestatem, qui ad eum uenit derelicta Calypso, cum qua decem annis fuerat: unde, ut supra (ad 3.623) diximus, Vergilii dictis dissentit temporum ratio.

But Servius here offers a different (and wrong) chronological discrepancy with Aeneas arriving before Odysseus. The criticism here then, as in 3.623 on how many of Achaemenides colleagues were killed and in 3.678 on whether the Cyclopes were brothers, is based on a belief that Homer's version of events is correct and departure from this narrative by Virgil is a sign of negligence. Servius, however, in his notes on both 3.623 and 3.678 makes some attempt to square the Homeric and Virgilian accounts. A possible difference here is emerging between Servius auctus, who, as we saw in his discussion of the storm at sea, is willing to criticise Virgil openly and Servius himself, who in both cases offers Virgil an excuse.

---

5 Verg. *Aen.* 3.645: *(Achaemenides) tertia iam lunae se cornua lumine complent.*

c. Jove threatens Juno

Our third example moves on from arguments about the credibility of narrative to the question of stylistic appropriateness that was touched upon earlier under (a) above.

In this case, in his comment on *Aen.* 9.801 describing Jupiter's threat sent via Iris to Juno not to help Turnus in the fight, Servius argues that Virgil is better than Homer:

> Serv. *Aen.* 9.801: HAVD MOLLIA IVSSA FERENTEM melius quam Homerus (*Il.* 8.402ff.) hunc locum executus est: saluo enim sensu uitauit et fabulosa et uilia; nam ille ipsas minas exsequitur.

The passage from Homer he has in mind is *Il.* 8.402ff., where Zeus sends Iris to warn Athena and Hera not to help the Greeks:

> γυιώσω μέν σφωϊν ὑφ' ἅρμασιν ὠκέας ἵππους,
> αὐτὰς δ' ἐκ δίφρου βαλέω κατά θ' ἅρματα ἄξω·
> οὐδέ κεν ἐς δεκάτους περιτελλομένους ἐνιαυτοὺς
> ἕλκε' ἀπαλθήσεσθον, ἅ κεν μάρπτῃσι κεραυνός·
> (*Il.* 8.402–05)
>
> *I shall maim their swift horses beneath the chariot,*
> *hurl them from the chariot and shatter it to pieces;*
> *nor in ten years' circuit*
> *will they be healed of the wounds which the thunderbolt inflicts.*
> (trans. Murray/Wyatt 1999 with adjustments)

In the Virgil passage in question Jupiter sends Iris with *haud mollia iussa* to Juno without spelling out what these harsh commands are:

> *nec contra uiris audit Saturnia Iuno*
> *sufficere: aeriam caelo nam Iuppiter Irim*
> *demisit, germanae haud mollia iussa ferentem,*
> *ni Turnus cedat Teucrorum moenibus altis.*
> (Verg. *Aen.* 9.802–05)
>
> *And Saturnian Juno did not dare grant him strength to oppose them,*
> *for Jupiter sent Iris down through the sky from heaven,*
> *charged with no gentle commands for his sister,*
> *should Turnus not leave the Teucrians' lofty ramparts.*
> (trans. Fairclough/ Goold 1999 with minor adjustments)

In Homer, however, Zeus is more specific: he will maim the goddesses' swift horses, hurl them from their chariot, smash it to smithereens with his thunderbolt, and inflict such wounds, as will take ten years to heal. Here then Virgil is praised for suggesting horrible punishment without actually spelling it out. For to spell out the threats in the way Homer does is, in Servius' view, to include within the narrative elements that are *fabulosa* and *uilia*, 'difficult to credit' and 'of a low style', not compatible with the dignity of epic. In fact, it could be argued that both Virgil and Homer have plenty of elements that are *fabulosa* and *uilia* throughout their epics, but what is important here is the ancient critics' belief that an appropriately elevated epic style and content should be maintained at all times. Again the positive comments on Virgil tend to come from Servius, rather than Servius auctus, who is happier to relay criticism.

d. Even Homer nods

One of these criticisms comes in Servius auctus' note on 12.538:

> Serv. auct. *Aen.* 12. 538: CRETHEV ...*et quidam reprehendunt poetam hoc loco, quod in nominum inuentione deficitur: iam enim in 9.771 sq. Crethea a Turno occisum induxit, ut 775 'Crethea, Musarum comitem'; sed et Homerus et Pylaemenem et Adrastum bis ponit et alios complures.*

Again, as with the vague *reprehenditur* in his note on *Aen.* 1.92 and with *arguitur* in that on 3.590, here the vague *quidam* seems to refer back to unspecified anti-Virgilian critics of an earlier age. In this case Virgil is guilty of killing off the same warrior twice. Cretheus in fact had already been killed by Turnus at *Aen.* 9.771 and here he is again falling to the same warrior at 12.538. This constitutes a serious slip in narrative credibility, but one which, as even Servius auctus is willing to admit, occurs frequently enough in Homer, as he illustrates with the cases of Pylaemenes, Adrastus and others. This perhaps is one of the inconsistencies Virgil himself would have corrected had he lived long enough to edit the final version of his poem.

The two remaining detailed comparisons of Homer and Virgil in Servius can be treated more briefly.

e. The shields of Aeneas and Achilles

The shield of Achilles is described by Homer as 'shining' or 'flashing', μαρμαρέην (*Il.* 18.480) and μαρμαίροντα (*Il.* 18.617), and this provokes from the commentators on Virgil's description of Aeneas' shield the following comments:

> Serv. *Aen.* 8.527: *non autem mirum est a Venere allatis armis inesse fulgorem: nam Homerus dicit a Thetide oblata arma habere motum quondam et spiritum, quae duo in aqua esse manifestum est. Thetidem autem nouimus nympham esse.*

> Serv. auct. *Aen.* 8.529: *PVLSA TONARE recte arma, quae iisdem ignibus, quibus fulmina, facta sunt, ait tonare pulsa. et hic magis proprie, quam Homerus: ille enim spirare ait et moueri, hic uero armis Aeneae caelestem sonitum dedit, unde ueniebant.*

In a reversal of the trend mentioned above, it is here Servius auctus who finds Virgil's description more fitting than that of Homer. Aeneas' shield thunders when struck, revealing its divine origin in the forge of Hephaestus, maker of thunderbolts. Servius, by contrast, finds good points in both descriptions, with Homer's epithets relating Achilles' shield with his mother Thetis, the shining sea nymph.

A little later in the same passage Servius auctus approves of the fact that Virgil, unlike Homer, does not describe in detail the shield before it is brought to Aeneas. For him, Homer's long description is unconvincing, as it suggests that the shield can be made as quickly as it can be described:

> Serv. auct. *Aen.* 8.625: *sane interest inter hunc et Homeri clipeum: illic enim singularia dum fiunt narrantur, hic uero pro perfecto opere noscuntur: nam et hic arma prius accipit Aeneas quam spectaret, ibi postquam omnia narrata sunt, sic a Thetide deferuntur ad Achillem. opportune ergo fecit Vergilius, quia non uidetur simul et narrationis celeritas potuisse conecti et opus tam uelociter expediri, ut ad uerbum posset occurrere.*

f. The flaming helmets of Aeneas and Diomedes

At *Aen.* 10.270–75 the flames flashing from Aeneas' helmet are likened to the baleful blood-red glow of a comet in the night sky, or to the ill-omened Dog-star (Sirius), which threatens mortals with drought and plague. The shining helmet element of this comparison comes from *Il.* 5.4–6, where Athena causes a bright light to shine from Diomedes' helmet and shield, which is likened to the Dog-star.[6] Servius is correct in seeing that the passage in *Il.* 5.4–6 does

---

[6] On Virgil's fondness for imitating this passage, see Macr. *Sat.* 5.13.35 hoc (i.e. *Il.* 5.4): *miratus*

not mention any baleful effects of the Dog-star, whereas Virgil mentions such effects to foreshadow the doom to be brought by Aeneas on the Rutulians:

> Serv. Aen. 10.270: ARDET APEX CAPITI ... est autem Homeri (Il. 5.4) et locus et comparatio. hoc autem iste uiolentius posuit, quod ille stellae tantum facit comparationem, hic etiam stellae pestiferae, respiciens quas clades Rutulis sit inlaturus Aeneas.

But what the commentator has missed is that Virgil here is combining the Il. 5.4–6 reference with a reference to Il. 22.26–31, where the bronze breast plate of Achilles as he pursues Hector shines like the Dog-star, which brings fever to wretched mortals, in a double allusion technique common in Virgil which we saw mentioned by Macrobius above (n. 3).

All six passages where significant literary comparisons are made between Virgil and Homer in Servius or Servius auctus have now been discussed. These, I think, throw significant light on the differences between modern and ancient concerns in this area, as well as illustrating some interesting, if less fundamental, distinctions between Servius and Servius auctus, with the former on the whole being less willing to criticize Virgil than the latter.

g. Concluding statistics on mentions of Homer in Servius

In order to set the six detailed comparisons discussed above in context, I set out here in descending order of frequency all the types of Homeric reference occurring in Servius and Servius auctus. There are in all some 151 references, in which Homer is actually named in Servius and 37 in Servius auctus. By far the majority of these are concerned with showing that Virgil follows Homer either in plot, e.g:

> Serv. Aen. 1.4: VI SVPERVM uiolentia deorum, secundum Homerum, qui dicit a Iunone rogatos esse deos in odium Trioanorum
>
> Serv. 57 = 38% Serv. auct. 8 = 22%

---

supra modum Virgilius immodice est usus (*Aen.* 9.731 [Turnus]; *Aen.* 7.785, 8.620, 10.270 [Aeneas]).

or in translating a Homeric word or phrase, e.g:

> Serv. *Aen.* 1.379: fama super aethera notus / *Od.* 9.19: καί μευ κλέος οὐρανὸν ἵκει
>
> Serv. 26 = 17% Serv. auct. 10 = 27%

The third most common category in both is where Homer is used to establish some factual point: for example, that Homeric heroes did not recline to eat, but simply sat, or that Hera (Juno) commonly made use of a chariot in war, e. g.:

> Serv. *Aen.* 1.17: CVRRVS aut uere currum quo secundum Homerum in bello utitur (*sc. Iuno*) significat.
>
> Serv. 22 = 15% Serv. auct. 8 = 21%

The detailed literary comparisons which form the main discussion of this paper above come next in frequency. They constitute a relatively low proportion of all Homeric references for Servius 3= 2%, with a much higher proportion (6=16%) coming from Servius auctus, who, as we have seen, is less hesitant about relaying criticism of Virgil.

Next in frequency come comments on differences between Virgil and Homer, which are far fewer than those on similarities, e. g.:

> Serv. *Aen.* 8.670: HIS DANTEM IVRA CATONEM ...et supergressus est hoc loco Homeri dispositionem, siquidem ille Minoem Rhadamanthyn Aeacum e impiis iudicare dicit, hic Romanum ducem innocentibus dare iura commemorat.
>
> Servius 11 = 7% Serv. auct. 2 = 5%

The remaining six categories in descending order of frequency may be classed under the following headings:

(i) Homeric epithets, e.g:

> Serv. *Aen.* 7.550: INSANI MARTIS AMORE Homeri epitheton
>
> Servius 9 = 6% Serv. auct. 1 = 3%

(ii) Homeric imagery, e. g.:

> Serv. *Aen.* 9.435 : 'LASSOVE PAPAVERA COLLO DEMISERE CAPVT: Homeri (*Il.* 8.306f.) et comparatio et figura; nam et ille sic ait, ut multorum unum dicere caput.
>
> Servius 7 = 5% Serv. auct. 1 = 3%

(iii) Homeric calques, e.g.:

> Serv. *Aen.* 1.35: SALIS maris secundum Homerum (cf. Homeric ἅλς)
>
> Servius 6 = 4% Serv. auct. 1 =3%

(iv) natural philosophy, e.g.:

> Serv. *Aen.* 1.93: INGEMIT non propter mortem ingemit ...sed propter mortis genus. graue enim est secundum Homerum perire naufragio, quia anima ignea est et extingui uidetur in mare, id est elemento contrario.
>
> Servius 5 = 3% Serv. auct. 0

(v) morphology/ metre, e.g.:

> Serv. *Aen.* 1.100: SARPEDON et in ultima possumus accentum ponere et in paenultima: nam Homerus et 'Sarpedonis' declinauit et 'Sarpedontis' unde et uarius accentus est (= 10.471).
>
> Servius 3 = 2% Serv. auct. 0

(vi) etymology, e.g:

> Serv. *Aen.* 6.132: Cocytusque: fluuius inferorum est, dictus ἀπὸ τοῦ κωκύειν, id est lugere: nam Homerus sic posuit *Od.* 10.514
>
> Servius 2 = 1% Serv. auct. 0

Information under the final three headings may have originated in the Homeric scholia, but this must remain for the present the subject of another paper.

The focus on Homer in this paper should not obscure the fact that the main aim of Servius' commentary is to instruct his pupils on points of Latin language by using Virgil's text as a source of *exempla*.[7] Whereas two notes in every three focus on Virgil's language, only one note in seven is concerned with the broader literary, mythological and historical background.[8]

In conclusion, we can say that Servius' interest in the Homeric background to Virgil's epic, though an important element, is not his main focus of attention, which is directed towards Virgil's use of the Latin language. Furthermore, the way in which the Homeric literary background is discussed in the ancient commentators differs considerably from approaches found in modern criticism. Both Homer and Virgil are expected to abide by ancient ideas of narrative credibility

---

7 On this function of the commentary, see in particular Uhl 1998.
8 Figures in Kaster 1988, 170.

and stylistic appropriateness. Most detailed literary comparisons between the two authors are centred on a consideration of these two criteria. More often than not, especially in Servius auctus, it is Homer who is held up as the model and Virgil who fails to live up to his expertise, but both commentators are willing to concede that on occasion it is the Roman poet who surpasses his teacher. Servius comes at the end of a long tradition of scholarly commentaries and, although he himself may not have had direct knowledge of Alexandrian Homeric scholia, the methodology and much of the technical terminology to be found in Servius clearly has its origins in the Greek scholarship of that period as transferred to the Latin tradition by earlier scholars, such as Valerius Probus of Beirut writing in the Flavian period.[9] The emphasis on a clear and credible narrative expressed in a style appropriate to the epic genre, which has been shown as central to Servius' literary critical approach to both Homer and Virgil in his comparisons of the two, derives ultimately from Aristarchus and his fellow Greek commentators on Homer.

---

9 Maltby 2011, 72–73.

Ivana Petrovic
On Finding Homer: The Impact of Homeric Scholarship on the Perception of South Slavic Oral Traditional Poetry

That Homer was not a person but an embodiment of a bardic institution, the anthropomorphization of the epic tradition, is an idea with ancient roots. Questions regarding the origin and ancestry of Homer were notorious in the Ancient world. Not only did many Greek states vie for the honour of being his native-city, he also received cultic honours in many of them.[1] Ascribing divine origins or heroic status to Homer in Antiquity can be interpreted as a way to acknowledge the impact and importance of his poetry, but also as an expression of doubt regarding his existence as a historical character.

Flavius Josephus (*Contra Apionem* 1.2) first raised the question whether writing actually existed in the ninth-century BC Greece, the traditional date for Homer, and thus laid the foundations of the oral-traditional theory (for Homeric orality, see also Papaioannou, Efstathiou and Michelakis in this volume). In the 18th century, several scholars promulgated the idea that Homer was neither a historical person nor the author of the *Iliad* and the *Odyssey*, but that the epics were a result of compilation of older traditional poetry.[2] François Hédelin, abbé d'Aubignac was the first modern scholar who argued that the Homeric poems were collections of shorter songs stitched together by a compiler (*Conjectures académiques ou dissertation sur l'Iliade d'Homère*, written in 1670 and published in 1715, forty years after the author's death).[3] In 1730 Giambattista Vico published a second edition of his monumental and influential book *Scienza nuova*. In a chapter entitled 'The discovery of the New Homer', Vico advanced the thesis that Homer was not a person, but an idea created by the Greeks.[4] However, it was the classicist Friedrich August Wolf whose theories about Homer turned out to be the most influential. In his *Prolegomena ad Homerum*, published in 1795, Wolf argued that the process of composing the Homeric poems was exceptionally complex. According to Wolf, Homer lived in an illiterate age; his poems were the product of a long tradition of oral composition and compilation, finally

---
[1] On the status of Homer in the ancient world, see Porter 2004b with bibliography. On the cults of Homer, Petrovic 2006, 19–22 (with bibliography).
[2] Grafton 1981.
[3] On D'Aubignac, see Porter 2004b, 330.
[4] Porter 2004b, 329–30.

collected and edited under Peisistratus or his sons. Wolf saw the *Iliad* and the *Odyssey* as a collection of popular songs, a multi-layered text containing lays from different periods, and the task of a philologist in detecting the older, genuinely Homeric parts of the songs from younger parts of poems, which, according to Wolf, were a product of later tradition and inferior bards.[5]

The Homeric question gained renewed momentum in the twentieth century, with the work of Harvard linguist Milman Parry, who argued that Homeric language is fundamentally traditional in character. According to Parry, the epic poet was a craftsman who skilfully manipulated the stock of metrically suitable phrases he inherited from his predecessors. Fieldwork in the countries of former Yugoslavia was of crucial importance for Parry's hypothesis and had focused the attention of international scholarly community on the local Yugoslavian forms of oral traditional poetry. While Parry was working on his PhD at the Sorbonne, his supervisor, eminent linguist Antoine Meillet, introduced him to Matija Murko, an expert in Slavic philology. Murko was at the time studying the local oral epic traditions in Bosnia and had even made recordings of Bosnian bards. Since Parry was interested in the ways bards use formulaic expressions, he decided to learn Serbian and to visit Yugoslavia in order to observe traditional singers at work. Between 1933 and 1935 Parry made two trips to Yugoslavia, where he studied and recorded local oral traditional poetry with the help of his assistant Albert Lord. As a result of their fieldwork, Parry introduced the hypothesis that the formulaic character of Homeric style is to be explained as characteristic of oral composition. Parry's pupil Albert Lord further expanded and refined his teacher's theory.[6]

The orthodox view of the impact of Parry-Lord hypothesis is that it had established not only a new way of contextualizing and understanding Homeric poetry, but that it had also paved the way for a new branch of literary studies—comparative approach to the study of traditional epics from all over the world. The assessment and understanding of many different branches of local oral traditional literature changed dramatically as a result of Parry and Lord's hypothesis: once they were perceived as akin to Homeric poetry, many local traditional texts were elevated in status and became objects of keen scholarly attention. 'World literature' was born as a genre, with Homer as its figurehead.[7]

---

[5] See introduction to Wolf 1985, Grafton 1981, Fowler 2004 and Porter 2004b.
[6] Lord 1960 and 2000^2; Parry 1971. The texts of South Slavic lore and the recordings of bards Parry and Lord made in Yugoslavia are part of the Milman Parry Collection kept in Harvard: http://www.chs.harvard.edu/mpc.
[7] On the impact of Homeric studies on the creation of world literature, see general discussions in Graziosi/Greenwood (eds.) 2007 and Haubold 2007 (with bibliography). Recent samples of comparative approach to oral poetry are Foley 2002 and 2005, as well as Martin 2005 (with bibliography).

In this paper I shall question this orthodoxy and posit that Wolf's work already had a decisive influence on the establishment, preservation and assessment of world literature— at least in the Balkan area. It is a little known fact that the most famous and influential collection of the South Slavic oral traditional lore was compiled, edited and published partly as a result of Wolf's theories. Even in Serbia, where the editor of this collection, Vuk Stefanović Karadžić has the status of father of the nation (so much so, he is universally known by his forename only), the impact of Wolf's theories on his activity as collector and editor is little known.

I shall demonstrate that Homeric scholarship exercised an indirect but crucial influence on Vuk's activity as compiler and editor of Serbian traditional literature. Furthermore, Homer, as a figure of international renown, the fountainhead of European literature, was repeatedly employed by Vuk in order to bestow authority to the collection of folk poems he edited. In his theoretical writings Vuk defended his work as collector and publisher by calling upon Homer, the highest possible poetic authority in Europe. As collector and editor of Serbian traditional literature, Vuk made conscious attempts to illustrate his editions with depictions of bards similar to Homer. This strategy had an immediate impact even on the way the local, Serbian population came to view its own poetic tradition. More than a century before Parry and Lord commenced their fieldwork in Yugoslavia, local bards were represented in the visual arts as resembling the traditional portrait of Homer. Last but not least, the figure of Homer was employed as a shield, in order to counter the ban on circulation of Vuk's collection in Europe, where traditional Serbian poems celebrating recent uprisings against the Turks were seen as potentially dangerous and politically charged material.

a. Homeric scholarship and the first systematic collection of Serbian oral literature

Vuk was born in 1787 in a poor peasant family in a Serbian village, which then belonged to the territory of the Ottoman Empire. He lived in tumultuous times and had survived two bloody uprisings against the Turks. Vuk contributed his survival to his physical impediment (he was lame), which prevented him from taking an active part in the battles, and to his desire for learning, which repeat-

---

For criticism of Parry/ Lord hypothesis, de Vet 1996, 2005 and 2008. The objective of my paper does not concern the validity of the theory *per se*, but the impact of Homeric scholarship on the perception of South-Slavic traditional poetry and on the formation of written collections.

edly drew him beyond the boundaries of Serbia.[8] A crucial event in Vuk's life was his arrival at Vienna, where he met the Imperial censor dealing with Slavonic subjects Jernej Kopitar in 1813. Kopitar was an astonishingly versatile and well-educated scholar. Politically he supported Austroslavism, a doctrine that sought to create a unity of Slavic peoples within the Austrian empire.[9] Austria was interested in strengthening the national pride of its Slav subjects mostly because it saw it as the best defence against the strong Russian influence in the Balkan area. An important part of this policy was the encouragement of Slav populations to develop and strengthen their national identities. Special efforts were made to encourage the development of national literature. As a linguist by education and a true child of his times profoundly influenced by Herder, Kopitar emphasized the importance of language and popular literature as expressions of national spirit. It was Kopitar's idea that Vuk adopted as his lifework: he took it to himself to comprise a grammar and a dictionary of Serbian language and to collect and publish Serbian popular songs, folk-tales and proverbs. Vuk never subscribed to Kopitar's political agenda and often actively opposed it, but he nevertheless wholeheartedly, unreservedly and with great acknowledgement and gratitude adopted Kopitar's literary programme.

Whereas Serbian educational establishment saw it as necessary and urgent to produce a grammar and a dictionary of Serbian language, collecting and editing Serbian folk poetry and prose was in the eyes of many a futile and useless endeavour. In this respect, Vuk was going against the grain. In the early 19th century, oral tradition was very much alive in the Balkans. As Vuk wrote himself, gusle, the instrument that was used to accompany epic performance, could in his time be found in every house in Bosnia, Hercegovina, Montenegro and the southern parts of Serbia. The art of performing was widespread, especially in the villages, away from urban centres. Apart from amateur performers, there also existed a guild of professional singers, usually those who were blind or otherwise physically disabled and could not support themselves and their family by farming. This is how Vuk described performers of male or heroic songs in the preface to the first edition of his collection:

In the districts mentioned, where heroic songs are still most often sung, there will not be anyone who does not know a number of songs (if not completely, at least in part) and there will be some who know more than fifty, perhaps even up to a hundred. Now, anyone who knows fifty different songs, if he has any gift for it, will easily be able to compose a new one. [...] Heroic songs are

---

8 There is a plethora of scholarly literature on Vuk's oeuvre in Serbian. A well-researched and accessible monograph on Vuk's life and times in English is Wilson 1970.
9 On Vuk and Austroslavism, Bonazza 1988.

circulated mainly by blind men, travellers and hajduks.[10] *The blind men go begging from house to house right round the country. In front of every house they sing a song, and then ask for something to be given to them. When something is offered, they will sing more. On holidays they go to the monasteries and churches for the services and sing the whole day long. Again when a traveller arrives at a house for lodging, it is usual to ask him to sing to the gusle, so that travellers sing and listen in the evening. Then the hajduks in winter [...] drink and sing to the gusle all night, mainly songs about hajduks.*[11]

Professional singers were not revered by their community; on the contrary, they were beggars, usually living in poverty. This is the reason why the epic stories of the past were also called 'songs of beggars' in Serbian. Those inhabiting urban centres dismissed them as low, peasants' songs and perceived them as possessing no literary value. Consequently, Vuk's attempts to collect and publish them were viewed with suspicion and ridicule by the intellectual establishment of his native land. Nevertheless, Vuk worked tirelessly and had under great financial strain managed to publish the first systematic collection of Serbian folk songs, tales, riddles and proverbs in the following order:
- *A Small Simple-Folk Slavonic-Serbian Songbook*, Vienna 1814
- *Serbian Folk Song-Book* (Vols. I–IV, Leipzig edition, 1823–33; Vols. I–IV, Vienna edition, 1841–62)
- *Serbian Folk Tales* (1821, with 166 riddles; and 1853)
- *Serbian Folk Proverbs and Other Common Expressions* (1834)
- A book of '*Women's Songs*' from Herzegovina (1866), which was collected by Karadžić's collaborator and assistant Vuk Vrčević; Vuk Karadžić prepared them for publication just before his death.

The preface to the first volume, *A Small Simple-Folk Slavonic-Serbian Songbook*, published in 1814 and partially quoted above is a fascinating document where Vuk also outlines the reasons for embarking on his project and provides valuable information about the dispersion and categories of Serbian oral lore. Most puzzling is the following passage:

I am publishing these; someone else could perhaps work to collect similar songs in Srem and others still in Bačka, Banat, Slavonia, Croatia and Dalmatia; and, if fate wills, someone could collect further songs in Serbia, Bosnia, Hercegovina and Montenegro. And then perhaps a man will be found, whom God has endowed with gifts of poetry and who has had the chance

---

10 Hajduks were local brigands. See also below.
11 From Vuk's introduction to book I of his 'Leipzig collections' of Serb Popular songs 1824. In Appendix E of his monograph, Wilson (1970, 395–400) provides the English translation of most important passages.

> *of learning its rules in the Latin or German tongue; he may try to sift all these collections and write some poems himself according to the taste and manner of his race, and thus out of all these small collections create one big whole.*[12]

This passage betrays the Janus-faced character Vuk intended for his collection. Not only was the collection of oral traditional poetry meant to serve as a model for the standardization and establishment of the reformed Serbian language, these poems were also meant to provide poetic material for foreign audiences. Paradoxically, whereas there was very little interest in the traditional oral lore amongst Serbian intellectuals, in the European literary circles traditional 'national' poetry was very much in vogue. Especially popular were the works of James Macpherson, such as *Fragments of Ancient Poetry collected in the highlands of Scotland and translated from the Galic* [sic] *or Erse language*, a collection of 16 poems which he published in 1760 claiming that it was a translation of lays adapted from old Irish songs. Two subsequently published 'translations' of poems Macpherson attributed to Ossian, a Gaelic bard who was allegedly active in the third century. Whereas the scholarly community denounced these translations as extremely free adaptations of popular songs or even inventions, literary Europe was enchanted by Ossian. Editions and translations of various local traditional poems appeared *en masse*, bringing fame to the nations that produced them. Kopitar and Vuk had very probably hoped that Serbian folklore would also attract the attention of some enthusiastic European poet like Macpherson. However, the idea of making one big whole out of individual local lays betrays some knowledge of modern philological theories, especially Wolf's ideas on Homer.

Commenting on this passage, Wilson astutely notes that it may be 'an indirect reference to current theories of Homeric scholarship, with which he (sc. Vuk) could have become acquainted through Kopitar' (1970, 95). Wilson also notes that Kopitar, as one of the leading intellectuals in Vienna, must have been aware of Wolf's *Prolegomena ad Homerum*.[13]

In fact, we have definitive evidence not only that Kopitar was aware of Wolf's work, but that they knew each other and even collaborated. Kopitar and Wolf had met in Vienna in 1810 and corresponded from 1811 to 1819.[14] At that time, Wolf was editing three dialogues of Plato and had asked Kopitar for help with manuscripts form the Vienna library.[15] In 1819 Kopitar wrote to Wolf, in order

---

[12] Trans. Wilson 1970, 91–94.
[13] Wilson 1970, 195.
[14] Seleškovic 1968.
[15] In the preface to the *Platonis dialogorum delectus*, which Wolf had published in 1812, he thanks Kopitar for his help with the manuscripts.

to draw his attention to the four German translations of South Slavic poetry from Vuk's collection, which he probably completed himself. The reason why these should interest Wolf he explained as follows:

> Nirgends gibt es heut zu Tage treffender Pendants zu Ihren Homeriden, als in Serbien und Bosnien. Ein Exemplar von (Hormayr's) hier erscheinendem Journal: Archiv fur Geographie, Historie, Staats- und Kriegskunst mag doch auch Berlin erreichen? Dort habe ich nun vier Rhapsodien aus dem Freyheitskriege von 1804 übersetzt [...]. Par curiosité sehen Sie's doch an. Im illyrischen Original sind auf meine Veranslassung bereits 2 Bde solcherley serbischer Volkspoesie heraus, 2 neue liegen druckfertig; in allem könnten 10 voll werden.

Kopitar's comparison of Serbian bards with Homeric rhapsodes is a first known instance of comparative approach to the study of South Slavic oral traditional poetry. In my opinion, even the choice of poems for translation into German was Kopitar's bow to Wolf's theories: out of many poems Vuk had already gathered by 1818, Kopitar had picked four lays depicting the recent Serbian uprising against the Turks and the events spanning from 1804 to 1809; one depicting its very origins and tracing the history of the Turkish rule from the battle of Kosovo in 1389 and the other three, ordered chronologically and celebrating the decisive battles which took place in 1806 and 1809. All four were noted down from one bard, Philip Višnjic.[16] Taken together, these four poems convey an impression that a large-scale, continuous narrative depicting the origins and the development of the uprising could originate either in the hands of one skilful traditional poet or, as Vuk suggests in his preface quoted above, in the hands of a gifted foreigner and that 'one big whole' could be created 'out of all these small collections'. Kopitar's translation into German was probably published with the intention of attracting the attention of German scholars, who were familiar with Wolf's ideas and could be inclined to compare his Homerids with the Serbian illiterate blind singers. This would not only lend support to Wolf's theory, but would, in turn, also support the Serbian national cause, for surely a tradition capable of producing someone like Homer was worthy of being considered a nation in the first place. Furthermore, all four lays were noted down from the same bard, one who was already groomed to become a Serbian Homer, as I shall argue below.

However, anyone truly familiar with the Serbian oral traditional poetry like Vuk —who, after all, not only had an expert knowledge of the tradition as a collector, but knew it intimately having grown up in the area where the tradition was very much alive—knew that Serbian songs fall naturally into cycles, but do not tend to exceed 500–700 lines. These cycles roughly correspond to the early history of the Serbian

---

16 On Philip Višnjic, see below.

Empire. The oldest strata of Serbian oral poetry accessible in Vuk's time he called the 'Poems of the earliest days'. They depict the Serbian rulers before the Battle of Kosovo (1389), the building of cities, churches and monasteries, royal weddings, quarrels and minor wars. Due to the historical importance of the battle of Kosovo, a whole cluster of poems centred on it and was called 'The Kosovo Cycle'. These poems commemorate the Serbian Empire's defeat at the hands of the Turks in the late fourteenth century; all are grouped around the historic decisive battle, but most depict events preceding the battle and the aftermath. Most famous among these are 'The fall of the Serbian Empire', 'The mother of the Jugovici' and 'The maiden of Kosovo'. One of the most popular characters of Serbian traditional poetry was Marko Kraljević. There is a whole cycle dedicated to him, a plethora of poems from various times depicting the exploits of prince Marko, who 'came too late to the battle of Kosovo'. Marko was in fact a historic character and a vassal of the Turkish sultan, but the figure of Marko from popular lore stubbornly resists the Turks and dedicates his life to defending the orthodox population. Jakob Grimm, who followed Vuk's work from the very beginning and paved the way for the reception of his collection in Germany by publishing a very influential and favourable review,[17] was struck by the Marko cycle and had asked Vuk whether it might be possible to construct one continuous epic on Marko out of all these. Doubtlessly, Grimm too was influenced by Wolf's *Prolegomena*. Also popular was the cycle of poems depicting the exploits of 'Hajduci', Serbian brigands. Finally, the last cycle, contemporary with Vuk, was the group of poems about the uprising against the Turks.

In a society with no local courts, such as Serbia under the Ottoman Empire, there were no aristocrats who would reward the singers for their praise. There was no native-speaking ruling class with enough leisure for listening to old songs and stories. Traditional storytelling took place in private houses, and the art of singing traditional poems was usually transmitted from father to son. In Bosnia, however, the situation was quite different. In the parts of the country where Muslim religion spread and became dominant, local aristocrats embraced the oral tradition and the heroes of the poems changed places; the Muslim lords became the heroes, and the orthodox populace the enemy. Rich Muslim aristocrats supported the singers and awarded them generously. This is the reason why Muslim culture developed songs much longer than Christians,

---

[17] The review by Jakob Grimm of book III of Vuk's Leipzig collection of Serb popular songs was published in *Göttingsche Gelehrte Anzeigen* 177–78, 5 November 1823. Wilson 1970, Appendix D provides a full English translation.

and this was the area where Parry and Lord were to find their 'Yugoslav Homer' in the early twentieth century.

Consequently, there was no reason to expect a monumental epic of Homeric proportions to originate in Serbia. This state of affairs did little to prevent Vuk and Kopitar from searching for Homer among Serbian bards. One guslar proved to be a particularly good fit for the role. It was the blind singer Philip Višnjić, whom Vuk met in the monastery Šišatovac and described in the following way:

> Philip Višnjić crossed into Serbia in 1804, the summer that the Serbian forces retreated over the Drina, and from then until 1813 he lived only in the Serbian camps around the Drina [...] In 1813 when the Turks reconquered Serbia, he fled with his family to the Srem and settled in the village of Grk. I had heard that he knew some good songs, particularly about the times of Karadjordje[18], and got him to come to Šišatovac in 1815 [....] I then took down from him not only the songs here printed but also a further three from Karadjordje's time,[19] which I have left over to make a fifth book with, if God grant me health. By and large, I think that Philip himself composed all those new songs of the times of Karadjordje. He told me that he had become blind as a young man as a result of smallpox and then went around the whole Pashalik (province) of Bosnia and right down to Skadar begging and singing to the gusle.[20]

The blindness of the bard, his journeys and the subject matter of his poems instantly reminded both Vuk and Kopitar of Homer. It is not a surprise that the portrait of Višnjić was meant to illustrate the whole collection. In March 1817 Vuk wrote to Lukijan Mušicki, eminent poet and archimandrite of the monastery Šišatovac, specifically requesting a portrait of Višnjić to be taken, but to no avail.[21] Due to unfortunate circumstances, no portrait was made of Višnjić during his lifetime. However, the most popular depiction of the bard both in Serbia and abroad, one that is nowadays also used as an emblem of the *Oral Tradition* journal, is meant to represent Višnjić. As argued by Vojislav Jovanović in 1954, this portrait had nothing to do with Višnjić, but presents an idealized representation of a type called 'Serbian Homer', an image which Jovanovic aptly calls 'apocryphal icon'. It was painted by the Croatian artist Josip Danilovic in 1901 and was

---

18 Karadjordje was the leader of the First Serbian uprising against the Turks (1804–13). After the failure of the uprising, he was forced to leave the country and was assassinated upon his return in 1817, probably upon the order of the new Serbian ruler, Miloš Obrenović.
19 Visnjic's most famous poems were the 13 compositions commemorating historical events he witnessed himself, such as *Početak bune protiv dahija* (The Beginning of the Revolt against Dahijas), *Boj na Čokešini* (Battle of Čokešina), *Boj na Mišaru* (Battle of Mišar).
20 Wilson's translation 1970, 111 of Vuk's preface to the Book IV of the Leipzig collection of popular songs published in 1833.
21 The letter is quoted in Jovanović 1954, 3.

immediately accepted as the exemplary portrait of a bard. The similarities of this presentation with the blind Homer type (as presented by Raphael or Mattia Preti) are immediately obvious.

An image of Višnjić was not destined to adorn Vuk's edition of Serbian traditional poetry, but Kopitar and Vuk did not abandon the idea of linking Homer to the collection visually. In 1823 Kopitar sent an illustration of the instrument gusle to Vuk and wrote with regard to the cover illustration of the Leipzig edition:

> *I think, however, that we should provide a group-scene—perhaps a Homer surrounded by listeners young and old.*[22]

At the end, a lithography was made of a guslar surrounded by listeners. The model for the bard was not Višnjić, but probably Vuk himself.[23] However, the idea of a traditional Serbian guslar resembling Homer somehow took roots. In 1839 a famous painter Katarina Ivanović published a lithograph in a Serbian literary magazine with wide circulation called 'Srpski narodni list'. It depicts a bard with gusle surrounded by an admiring audience, a maiden in the right corner and two young men in the left corner of the picture. What is most interesting about this representation of a bard is the title: Srpski Omir, 'Serbian Homer'. By providing her lithography meant for popular circulation with such a title, Katarina Ivanović must have been stating what had by that time become obvious to Serbian educated audiences.

b. Homer as a shield in the creation of Serbian national identity

The year is 1842. By that time, Vuk was an eminent scholar in his 50s, who had almost single-handedly created the basis for a national literature, and yet, he was repeatedly forced to defend his endeavour from bitter critical attacks. As the first systematic collection of Serbian oral literature Vuk's edition played a central role in the development of Serbian literature; it was translated into German and French very soon after its original publication and had a major impact on European literature. Jakob Grimm, Goethe, Alexander Puškin, Prosper Mérimée, Walter Scott and many other European scholars and writers admired Serbi-

---

22 *Ibid.* 4.
23 *Ibid.* 6.

an poetry,²⁴ but, at home, Vuk encountered less enthusiasm for his editorial work. The new Serbian state soon established an uneasy peace with the Ottoman Empire, and the publishing of Vuk's editions was banned on Serbian territory. By their very nature, since they depicted the recent uprising, these poems were capable of stirring patriotism and inciting Serbs to new uprisings. The new ruler of Serbia, Miloš Obrenović found personal offence in the publication of the poems depicting recent political events, since they did not celebrate his own role enough, and glorified instead the leader of the first uprising, Karadjordje.²⁵

The second wave of opposition came from Serbian intellectuals, who perceived folk poetry as unworthy of scholarly attention, being a product of illiterate peasants. They complained about Vuk's striking practice of writing down the poems precisely as he heard them, without correcting the grammar or changing the lines to comply with the standards of poetry composed with the aid of writing. A formidable opponent of Vuk's language reforms, Metropolitan of Karlovci Stefan Stratimirović remarked: 'If we see a drunken man stumble and fall, we would help him rise again',²⁶ thus suggesting that Vuk ought to have changed the grammar and language of the common folk, in order to closer resemble the written discourse. Furthermore, Vuk was slighted for publishing the songs of 'blind beggars'. In his response to the critics published in 1842, Vuk defended his collecting methodology and the editing programme on the whole. Vuk's collecting method was in fact exemplary even by modern standards—as a member of the oral society he fully understood the nature of the songs and their contextual importance and had made transcriptions, which were completely faithful to the song as sung. When accepting transcriptions from others, he insisted on verifying himself that the song in question was actually sung that way among the folk. In his defence Vuk argued that the songs of the common people which he had published were not less worthy, simply because some singers were blind and reduced to begging, and wrote: 'Whoever has any sense and critical acumen will understand upon reading these poems that there is no shame at all in the fact that they are performed by blind beggars. In fact, in this respect, the Serbs should be no more ashamed than the Greeks, who are certainly not

---

24 On the international reception of Vuk's edition, see Wilson 1970.
25 Wilson (1970, 181) provides an English translation of Miloš Obrenović's letter to Vuk from 1824, where the new ruler of Serbia is expressing his dissatisfaction with the way he has been portrayed in contemporary oral poetry. The following passages illustrate his point sufficiently: 'All of us, who were present at these events and witnessed them, were disgusted at the lies in your (*sic!*) songs, which ought to have been founded on truth, seeing that they are about my own times [...] I shall not permit you to circulate among our people lies about my exploits'.
26 Quoted in Karadžic 1842, 127a.

ashamed of the fact that their Homer was a blind beggar. In fact, were he alive now, kings and emperors would pay him heed'.[27] Vuk goes on to argue that the language used in the Serbian oral poems is the best possible example of Serbian and should become a standard and serve as a measuring rod due to its purity and simple beauty of the vernacular.

By this time, Homer had already served as a very useful point of defence for Kopitar as well. In 1824 the highest Austrian police authorities viewed the circulation of poems glorifying recent Serbian uprising with suspicion and feared, similarly to the Serbian establishment, a renewed stirring up of anti-Turkish sentiment. It was Kopitar's duty as censor for Slavonic languages to express an opinion regarding the circulation of the book. Kopitar argued in favour of the circulation advancing the policy of Austroslavism and comparing Vuk to Homer:

> *The fruits which this book will bear, in providing the Serbs with their own independent and much-loved literature (which will soon outstrip the Russian in favour, since it will rally them around a national centre), would easily outweigh through the spirit and tendency on the whole collection any objections against individual and temporarily perhaps harmful details [...] Given that this collection is part of a three-volume edition with quite different contents and a purely scientific tendency (as shown in the preface to the Dictionary), the censor already advised by competent critics of the author (who is recognized as the Illyrian Homer, Ossian etc.) found no difficulty in approving it...*[28]

Kopitar's defence was successful, and the circulation of Vuk's collection in Austria was allowed.

In the age that had produced many attempts to renounce Homer's very existence, he needed to be drafted, in order to defend his fellow oral poets. The modern enlightened Europe in the 18th and 19th century killed Homer only to immediately resurrect him. To use a popular modern phenomenon as an illustration: Homer became the vampire king of European literature. He represents the end of Ancient Greek oral tradition that, once written down, ceased to exist in its previous form as a composition in performance. Once written down, it embarks on an after-life as a relatively stable, unchangeable written text. Comparing a living and existing local oral tradition with Homeric poetry brings to it renown and prestige, but, ultimately, as it is written down, it too ceases to exist in its natural form. It dies as an oral text, only to be resurrected as a written one, from then on remaining forever unchanged. Comparing a local tradition with Homer is thus a kiss of death—but a kiss from a vampire, since it brings with it both death and, in its final *metamorphosis*, immortality. The *metamorphosis* from traditional oral lit-

---

27 Karadžic 1842, 127b.
28 Translation: Wilson 1970, 184.

erature to a published manuscript affiliated with Homeric poetry brings renown and prestige both to local traditional poetry and to the people that created it. The political repercussions of affiliating local poetic traditions to Homer were vast. Comparison of Serbian bards with Homer were consciously employed, in order to bestow a hitherto little known Serbian nation with renown and prestige. Once an analogy with Homer was made, Serbian traditional poetry became part of the family of European literature. The nation that gave birth to it came to be perceived as a part of Europe, too. The way was paved for the Serbian state to emerge from the Ottoman Empire and take its place in the European family.

Finally, more than a century after Vuk's collection was published, it was Homeric scholarship again that exercised an impact in the way South Slavic poetry was perceived in the Western world. This time it was not Serbia, but a relatively new country, Yugoslavia, that profited from association with Homeric poetry.[29] Lord and Parry completed what Wolf had started: though they placed a roof on the house of world literature, it was Wolf who had laid its foundations.

---

29 See on this Graziosi 2007, 132–42.

Part VII **Homer on the Ancient and Modern Stage**

Katerina Mikellidou
Aeschylus reading Homer: The Case of the *Psychagogoi*

Aeschylus' fragmentarily preserved *Psychagogoi* has at its core, possibly as its theme, a dramatized adaptation of a well-known Homeric episode – the *Nekyia*. The meagre surviving fragments suggest that in broad strokes the story goes as follows[1]: Odysseus travels to a 'fearsome' lake (frr. 273, 273a.2 R.; cf. 276 R.) and, under the guidance of local necromancers (frr. 273, 273a R.), contacts Teiresias who gives him a prophecy about his death (fr. 275 R.). The subject-matter *per se* points to a by definition 'Homerizing' play; Book 11 of the *Odyssey* is used as a source text and a point of departure. The aim of the present paper is to investigate this intertextual network between the Homeric *Nekyia* and its Aeschylean version. As will emerge, Aeschylus opens a persistent dialogue with the epic text and establishes a network of competitive dynamics. Yet, as well as persistently recalling his archetype, he also makes a systematic attempt to revise it by endowing this distinctively Homeric episode with a diametrically opposite meaning; while in Homer necromancy unfolds the full proportions of Odysseus' boldness, courage and extraordinariness, in its Aeschylean adaptation it is part of a process of bringing him closer to the ordinary man. The normalization of Odysseus is carried out both by his prophesied death, which is ignominious and trivial (fr. 275 R.), and by the introduction of realistic and familiar elements into the necromantic ritual. Though the practice registers some exotic features and retains a degree of its Homeric outlandishness, it is in many respects brought closer to reality. As we shall see, the reduced exoticism of necromancy and the concomitant detachment of the Aeschylean Odysseus from the fantastic atmosphere of the *Odyssey* produce some very complex effects.

---

[1] On this play, see the edition of P.Köln 3.125 (= fr. 273a R.) in Kramer 1980, 11–23 and the discussions in Gelzer 1981; Lloyd-Jones 1981; Katsouris 1982, 47–51; Rusten 1982; Henrichs 1991, 187–92; Bardel 2005, 85–92; Cousin 2005; Dios 2008, 665–72. Discussions prior to Kramer's edition are useful (see Leeuwen 1890, 72–73; Mette 1963, 127–29), but they ignore the existence of fr. 273a R. The date of the play is uncertain. The abbreviation R. stands for the numbering of Aeschylean fragments in Radt 2009².

a. The prediction of Odysseus' death

The deconstruction of Odysseus' Homeric presentation is first and foremost evident in fr. 275 R., which is delivered by the summoned Teiresias and preserves a prophecy about Odysseus' death. The motif clearly derives from the Homeric *Nekyia*, where the seer concludes his predictions about the hero's *nostos* (on the Odyssean *nostos* motif, see Jacob and Thliveri in this volume) and the due propitiatory activities by referring to the end of his life (*Od.* 11.134–37). As he says, a very gentle death will come to him *ΕΞΑΛΟC*, when he reaches old age. According to the ancient scholia, this prophecy lends itself to a double interpretation depending on the rendering of *ΕΞΑΛΟC*. Odysseus may die 'away from the sea' (ἔξαλος) or 'from the sea' (ἐξ ἁλός), namely a marine death. The poet of *Telegony* presents us with a version that relies upon the inherent ambiguity of the Homeric passage, as it actually combines both interpretations: Odysseus is killed on dry land by Telegonus' arrow, whose edge is made by the spine of a stingray (κέντρον τρυγόνος). Aeschylus chooses to differentiate himself from both epics and put forward his own distinctive version (fr. 275 R.):[2]

> ἐρωδιὸς γὰρ ὑψόθεν ποτώμενος
> ὄνθῳ σε πλήξει νηδύος χαλώμασιν·
> ἐκ τοῦδ' ἄκανθα ποντίου βοσκήματος
> σήψει παλαιὸν δέρμα καὶ τριχορρυές.
>
> For a heron in flight
> will strike you from above with its dung when it opens its bowels;
> and from this the barb of a sea-creature
> will rot your aged, hairless skin.
> (trans. Sommerstein 2008)

The Aeschylean prophecy echoes the Homeric idea of the peaceful death in old age, as well as the Telegonian motif of κέντρον τρυγόνος. However, in this version a heron flying overhead will strike and infect Odysseus' aged skin with his dung that will contain a fatal spine of fish.[3] In this way, Aeschylus keeps the authority of the epic narrative, but at the same time adjusts it to serve his own dramatic ends.

---

[2] For the different versions of Odysseus' death, see Hartmann 1917, 106–12; Severyns 1928, 54f., 412–15.
[3] The uniqueness of the Aeschylean version is underlined in scholium V on *Od.* 11.134 (Dindorf): Αἰσχύλος δὲ ἐν Ψυχαγωγοῖς ἰδίως λέγει 'ἐρρωδιὸς γὰρ...τριχορρυές'.

In the *Odyssey* the hero may not meet a glorious death in the battlefield, but the rhetoric used by Teiresias elevates his predicted peaceful end to an ideal incident. As the seer puts it, Odysseus' death will be 'very gentle (*Od.* 11.135: ἀμβληχρὸς μάλα) and will come when the hero is overcome with 'sleek old age' (*Od.* 11.136: γήρᾳ ὕπο λιπαρῷ ἀρημένον) and his people will 'dwell in prosperity' around him (*Od.* 11.137: ὄλβιοι ἔσσονται). The adjective λιπαρός qualifies this old age as wealthy and healthy-looking, strengthening the notion of the perfect death.[4] In contrast, the prophecy in fr. 275 R. gives an ignominious twist to the Homeric model by introducing the factor of the dung and by presenting old age in a negative light. The Homeric λιπαρὸν γῆρας gives way to παλαιὸν δέρμα καὶ τριχορρυές that conjures up the image of a scrawny and wretched old man. The Homeric echoes of ὄνθος are suggestive. There are only three occurrences of the term in the *Iliad*, all in the context of the footrace between Odysseus, Ajax, and Antilochus during the funeral games in honour of Patroclus. There, Athena, wanting to help Odysseus, intervenes and makes Ajax slip on the dung of the sacrificed bulls as he runs. The irony is obvious. While in the Homeric passage ὄνθος grants an athletic victory to Odysseus in Troy, in the Aeschylean play it causes him a totally unheroic and almost ridiculous death. The application of the epic language to describe a reality that opposes the epic grandeur underscores the distance from the epic world.[5] The process of sepsis caused by the dung trivialises the hero's death yet more.

Aeschylus' departure from the Homeric archetype with reference to Odysseus' death must have resulted in diverse and complex effects. On the one hand, this is the kind of bridging of the divide between heroic past and contemporary present, which finds expression in a whole range of tragic effects, most notably but not exclusively anachronism. Part of the result is an enhanced sense of the relevance of what happens in the play to the world of the audience rather than a dramatization of a closed and distant past. At the same time, the ignominious end reflects and further develops some aspects of Odysseus' tragic profile; as well as making him more ordinary and contemporary it also undermines his heroic status and undercuts his dignity. We may even have something of the belittling of Odysseus later found in Sophocles' *Philoctetes*. The Aeschylean version of the hero should be understood as part of a larger tragic tendency to underscore the less elevated aspects that surrounded Odysseus' character, experience, and behaviour from the start and were already magnified in the archaic

---

4 Cf. Heubeck/ Hoekstra 1989, 86.
5 See Cousin 2005, 150.

period.⁶ This is not to say that the reduction of Odysseus' heroic status is a dramatic end in itself. As will be noted below, it may be a means of exploring larger issues, such as the idea of human limitations.

b. The institutionalization of necromancy

The proximity of Odysseus to the audience is enhanced by the 'normalization' of necromancy. This process is mostly achieved through the institutionalization of the practice, which distances the episode from the impromptu and mythical nature of the Homeric source text and presents us with an Odysseus who now engages not in a dangerous and bold mission at the edge of the Ocean, but rather in an officially prescribed ritual within historical and recognizable surroundings. There exist two indications that point to the institutionalization of necromancy: the locale of the ritual and the introduction of professional practitioners.

Let us take the parameter of the locale first. The main features of the spot where necromancy is performed can be deduced from fragments 273, 273a, and 276 R.:

Fr. 273 R.:

> Ἑρμᾶν μὲν πρόγονον τίομεν γένος οἱ περὶ λίμναν
>
> We, the folk that dwell around the lake, honour Hermes as our ancestor.

Fr. 273a R.:

> ἄγε νυν, ὦ ξεῖν', ἐπὶ ποιοφύτων
> ἴστω σηκῶν φοβερᾶς λίμνας
> ὑπό τ' αὐχένιον λαιμὸν ἀμήσας
> τοῦδε σφαγίου ποτὸν ἀψύχοις
> αἷμα μεθίει   5
> δονάκων εἰς βένθος ἀμαυρόν.
> Χθόνα δ' ὠγυγίαν ἐπικεκλόμενος
> χθόνιόν θ' Ἑρμῆν πομπὸν φθιμένων
> αἰτοῦ χθόνιον Δία νυκτιπόλων
> ἑσμὸν ἀνεῖναι ποταμοῦ στομάτων,   10
> οὗ τόδ' ἀπορρὼξ ἀμέγαρτον ὕδωρ
> κἀχέρνιπτον
> Στυγίοις νασμοῖσιν ἀνεῖται.

---

6 See Stanford 1954, 90–117; cf. Deforge 1986, 259, n. 106; Cousin 2005, 137–38.

*Come now, stranger, stand on the grassy
precincts of the fearful lake and,
when you have cut the throat
of this victim, let fall the blood for the lifeless ones
to drink
into the dim depths of the reeds.
Invoking ancient Earth,
and chthonian Hermes, conveyor of the dead,
implore chthonian Zeus to send up
the swarm of the night-wanderers from the mouths of the river,
the river whose branch, this unenviable water
which washes no hand,
is sent forth by the streams of the Styx.*

Fr. 276 R.:

σταθεροῦ χεύματος

of stagnant current
(trans. Bardel 2005 with slight adjustments)

The geomorphology and hydrography of the landscape are modeled upon the topographical instructions of Circe (*Od.* 10.513–15).[7] This is particularly noticeable with reference to the dominant role of water, which becomes the hallmark of this unusual place and evokes the Homeric description of the infernal rivers. A series of *oxymora* employed for the description of the setting presage the abnormal reversion of the natural order that necromancy inherently involves. For instance, in fr. 273a R. the notion of fertility denoted by ποιοφύτων σηκῶν is countered by the reeds (δονάκων) that can only be found in marshy stagnant waters and are here closely connected with death and the Underworld;[8] the water, a natural source of life-giving and purification, is unenviable (ἀμέγαρτον)[9] and ἀχέρνιπτον,[10] namely unsuitable for ritual use; and in fr. 276 R. the lake is described as a 'stagnant current' (σταθεροῦ χεύματος),[11] combining contradictory qual-

---

[7] See Ogden 2001a, 47–48; Cousin 2005, 139–46. Compare also σηκύς (fr. 273a.2 R.) to πέτρη (*Od.* 10.515). In Python's *Agen* the landscape of necromancy seems to be very similar (cf. fr. 1.1 Sn.: κάλαμος, fr. 1.2 Sn.: ἄορνον).
[8] Reeds often form part of infernal vegetation; cf. Polygnotus' painting in Paus. 10.28.1; Elpenor vase (Boston 34.79, *ARV*² 1045.2.). On the vegetation in the *Psychagogoi* see Cousin 2005, 146.
[9] τομεγαρτουδωρ emended to ἀμέγαρτον ὕδωρ by Kramer 1980, 21–22.
[10] According to the necromantic traditions, the lake of Avernus exhaled noxious fumes that killed birds. See Rusten 1982, 36–38; Ogden 2010, 108; cf. Paus. 8.18.4f.; Call. fr. 407.110 Pf.
[11] For the meaning of this contradictory phrase, see Cousin 2005, 144–45.

ities. Also, terms that denote death (ἀψύχοις, φθιμένων, σφαγίου αἷμα) and fear (φοβερά) or belong to the linguistic field of the Underworld (Χθόνα ὠγυγίαν, χθόνιον, χθόνιον, Στυγίοις, ἀμαυρόν, νυκτιπόλων) endow the landscape with strong infernal connotations.[12]

Notwithstanding these numinous elements of otherworldliness and the awfulness that the description of the setting involves, the Aeschylean Odysseus is unambiguously on the surface. The upward movement of the souls (ἀνεῖναι) and the water (ἀνεῖται) cancels the Homeric blurring of necromancy and *katabasis* and locates the activities of the hero in the world of the living, removing a modicum of their boldness and dangerousness. Also, the Aeschylean Odysseus no longer operates 'off the map' and outside the world of human experience, as the necromantic incident seems to have been relocated from its literal eschatological position at the end of the Ocean to a more realistic environment, even though the place is not explicitly specified. This transfer of the *Nekyia* into historical surroundings may also be dictated by the nature of the tragic genre, as it tends to favour the unfolding of the action in existing locations. In the Aeschylean plays, in particular, the first speaking character reveals the spatial coordinates of the plot, which, even though they are not always familiar to the audience, are still geographically identifiable.[13]

If the existence of the professional necromancers clearly points to an institutionalized framework, the lake (frr. 273, 273a.2 R.) which constitutes the focal point of the ritual gives clues for the identification of the place with a real-life *nekyomanteion*-site. Indeed, the lake is a distinct topographical trait of two important historical oracles of the dead, the Acheron and Avernus *nekyomanteia*.[14] Each identification has its supporters,[15] but arguing for the former or the latter is, I think, pointless. What really matters is the fact that Aeschylus deviates from the Homeric example by locating his *Nekyia* in a remote, albeit historical, spot. Even if we as-

---

12 See Cousin 2005, 148–49.
13 See *Ag.* 24; *Ch.* 3 (corrupted text); *Eum.* 11, 16; *Pers.* 15–16; *PV* 1–2; *Supp.* 15; *Th.* 1.
14 See Ogden 2001a, 43–74 and 2001b, 173–78.
15 Acheron oracle: Katsouris 1982, 47, n. 3; Ogden 2001a, 48, 2001b, 176 and 2002, 26; Cousin 2005, 114. Avernus oracle: Max. Tyr. 8.2; Wilamowitz-Moellendorf 1914, 246, n. 1; Hartmann 1917, 109; Wikén 1937, 126; Phillips 1953, 56; Hardie 1977, 284; Kramer 1980, 18; Gelzer 1981, 122f.; Rusten 1982, 34f.; Dunbar 1995, 711; Hurst/Kolde 2008, 202. For further bibliography, see Ogden 2001a, 49, n. 23. A scholium on Ar. *Ra.* 1266 makes the Chorus inhabit near the lake Stymphalus in Arcadia, where Hermes was widely worshipped. Lloyd-Jones 1981, 22 and Dover 1993 on *Ra.* 1266 were convinced by this, but Wilamowitz-Moellendorf 1914, 246, n. 1 rightly rejected it as 'modern'. Indeed, lake Stymphalus is not a *nekyomanteion*-site, and Hermes was not there worshipped as a chthonic deity or as *psychopompos*. Besides, this lake could not be reached by ship.

sume that by Aeschylus' time the specific *nekyomanteion* fell into disuse, from the audience's viewpoint it would still form part of their cultural landscape and would be connected with a real-life, identifiable and accessible location. In such surroundings, the practice loses a great deal of its exceptional character, something that certainly pulls Odysseus and his heroic world closer to the audience.

Let us now move on to the identity of the Chorus, which is an additional piece of evidence for the localization of the ritual at a *nekyomanteion*-site and its resultant institutionalization. Ancient testimonia support the existence of a resident staff at the oracles of the dead, who were often called ψυχαγωγοί,[16] while Maximus of Tyre explicitly locates this institutionalized group of professional necromancers at Avernus.[17] In the *Psychagogoi* the title of the play is evidently borrowed from the identity of the Chorus.[18] One could perhaps argue that their designation as *psychagogoi* derives from their specific activities in the narrow context of the dramatic plot rather than their actual and regular profession. In this case, their instructive role, as can be seen in fr. 273a R.,[19] would parallel that of *Choephoroi*; just as the women instruct Electra on how to offer the libations, so do the *choreutai* here guide Odysseus in the process of ghost-raising. However, fr. 273 R. suggests that the members of the Chorus actually profess expertise in this ritual practice.[20] This fragment is recited or sung by the Chorus and, since it contains a self-introductory statement, it must be located near the opening of the play, perhaps at the beginning of the first *stasimon*.[21] It would seem that the Chorus consists of native people, who live by the shore of the lake and honour Hermes as their ancestor. The formal overtones of the verb τίομεν, the designation of the group as a 'race', as well as their self-presen-

---

[16] See Ogden 2001b, 182–83.
[17] Max. Tyr. 8.2; cf. Ephor. *FGrH* 70 F 134; Plu. *Mor.* 560e 9–560f 2. According to tradition, Italian *psychagogoi* were called to Sparta, in order to lay the restless soul of Pausanias and release the city from the plight (see Plu. *Mor.* 560e 9–560f 2; fr. 126 Sandbach). On this episode, see Burkert 1962, 49; Faraone 1991, 184–88; Ogden 2001a, 100–05.
[18] The titles of the Aeschylean plays very often denote the Chorus' identity or performative activities (e.g. *Choephoroi, Eumenides, Suppliants, Persae*).
[19] Noteworthy is the fact that fr. 273 R. belongs to those few examples of tragic verses delivered in hexameters (see West 1982, 98). This metrical pattern adds to the formality of the Chorus' language, but it also points to the subversive attitude of Aeschylus toward Homer; epic style is adopted only to be employed by a Chorus that corresponds to one of the most conspicuous innovations in the dramatization of the Homeric *Nekyia*.
[20] Besides, in ancient accounts ψυχαγωγός, the term used to define the identity of the Chorus, often points to a regular and official profession rather than a one-off activity. See e.g. Phryn. *PS* 127.12; schol. in E. *Alc.* 1128 (Schwartz); Paus. 3.17.7. See also the oracular tablet from Dodona (Evangelidis 1935, no. 23): 'Shall we hire Dorios the *psychagogos* or not?'
[21] See Mette 1963, 128.

tation with reference to Hermes imply that the Chorus is constituted by official attendants that preside over the operation of the sanctuary, which is explicitly mentioned in fr. 273a.2 R. (σηκῶν).

Aeschylus, therefore, introduces a Chorus of specialized necromancers, who reside in and attend the operation of a lake *nekyomanteion*, possibly located at Cumae. This choice is not accidental. The dramatist could well remain close to the epic source text by presenting a Chorus of sailors accompanying Odysseus in his necromantic activities. However, the insertion of professionals reduces the exotic element and contributes to the construction of less mythic and more real surroundings. The fact that Odysseus now acts under their official authority and practical assistance not only distances him from the fairytale world of the Homeric *Nekyia*, but it also subtracts from him part of his boldness. This controlled and guided performance of the ritual differs from the Homeric version of the episode, in which Odysseus had a leading role. There, even though he followed Circe's instructions, he was certainly helpless and unprotected, for Circe was physically absent throughout the ritual.

It is tempting to suppose that Aeschylus, in line with the complex intertextuality that he develops with the Homeric text, assigns the role of the *psychagogoi* to the Homeric Cimmerians. Just as the Homeric necromancy takes place at the 'land and city of the Cimmerians' (*Od.* 11.15 ff.), so its Aeschylean dramatization is spatially related to this tribe. In fact, the Chorus represents the native population of the place; from their viewpoint, Odysseus is a stranger (fr. 273a.1 R.: ὦ ξεῖνε), and they call themselves a 'race' (γένος). In Ephorus' account (4th century BC), the mythical Cimmerians are explicitly associated with the lake Avernus,[22] but germs of this tradition may be traced back to Sophocles' time, if we assume that frr. 1060 R. and 682 N.^{2} belong to the same play. The latter refers to an oracle of the dead at Aornos lake, probably meaning the lake Avernus, and comes either from *Odysseus Acanthoplex* or from *Euryalus*.[23] The former preserves the name Κερβέριοι, which is in all likelihood an alternative designation of the Cimmerians. The association of the Cimmerians with the oracle of the dead at Avernus seems reasonable enough in view of the growing tendency to attribute an Italian background to Odysseus' adventures. The localization of the Cimmerians in Italy turned out to be considerably influential, and it might well be the case that Aeschylus was the first to initiate it.[24] If the tragic Chorus was indeed composed of representatives of this race, this would lend further support to the al-

---

[22] See Ephor. *FGrH* 70 F 134a.
[23] See Phillips 1953, 56 and n. 29.
[24] See Plin. *HN* 3.61; Silius Italicus 12.132; Lactantius *Diu. Inst.* 1.6.9; *Origo Gentis Romanae* 10.2; Lyc. 695; [Orph.] *A.* 1125 ff.

ready stated assumption that Aeschylus draws on his epic model with a view to subverting it. The Cimmerians, like Odysseus, would be displaced into real surroundings and their exotic 'land and city' would become identifiable to a spot, which, albeit remote, would still be accessible to an ordinary man.

c. The profile of the dead

The above analysis shows that Aeschylus reworks the theme of Homeric necromancy in a variety of ways. Inasmuch as he departs from it by imbuing it with realistic elements, he also recalls it by employing some distinctively Homeric features. Aeschylus' debt to Homer is evident also in the profile of the dead. The Aeschylean dead are defined as ἄψυχοι. In post-Homeric literature, the term *psychē* acquires an expanded semantic field. While in Homer it denotes the spirit that abandons the body at death, outside the epics it is also loaded with the sense of the Homeric *phrēn*, *noos*, and *thymos*, qualities that refer to the seat of emotions or the emotions themselves.[25] In this vein, a post-Homeric terminology is used to bring to the fore the Homeric concept of the senseless shadows that lack φρένες (*Od.* 10.494–95) and μένος (*Od.* 10.521, 11.29, 49: ἀμενηνὰ κάρηνα). Lloyd-Jones' acute remark that the adjective here contrasts with πάμψυχος in Sophocles' *Electra* (839–40) corroborates this view;[26] as opposed to Amphiaraus who exceptionally retains his consciousness in Hades, the Aeschylean souls are here deprived of it. It is not surprising that ἀψύχοις appears closely connected with the motif of blood-drinking (ποτὸν ἀψύχοις),[27] which itself presupposes the idea of the witless shadow; as in the Homeric *Nekyia*,[28] the witless dead need the blood in order to regain their mental faculties. However, in an episode that draws so heavily on Homer, *psychē* is expected to retain to some extent its initial meaning, creating an ostensible and purposeful paradox: the same dead that are mentioned throughout the Homeric *Nekyia* as ψυχαί are here defined as ἄψυχοι.[29] This contradiction, which denies the dead the very essence of their existence, stresses even more their insubstantiality.

The designation of the dead as νυκτίπολοι and the description of their gathering in terms of a ἑσμός function as additional indications of their weakness. Henrichs

---

[25] See Solmsen 1984, 265–74; Sullivan 1989, 241–62; Bremmer 1994, 91–94.
[26] Lloyd-Jones 1981, 21. See also Henrichs 1991, 188.
[27] See Henrichs 1991, 188–89.
[28] See Sourvinou-Inwood 1995, 81–83; Ogden 2001a, 173; Heath 2005.
[29] Contrast Bremmer 1983, 77, n. 10 and Henrichs 1991, 188, n. 60, who endeavour to prove that the contradiction is only superficial.

argues that the adjective νυκτίπολος alludes to the nocturnal activities of the dead in the terrestrial world and thus illuminates their alternative, more active dimension.[30] He bases his assumption on the fact that in its pre-Hellenistic occurrences the term bears Dionysiac, ritualistic and mystic connotations that allow its transference from the nighttime mystic celebrations to the nocturnal wanderings of the dead in the world of the living under the guise of dream-apparitions.[31] Although Henrichs' interpretation is possible, it is more likely that in the framework of the Aeschylean *Nekyia* νυκτίπολοι refers to the inactive wanderers in the sunless and gloomy Underworld.[32] The term ἑσμός, along with the plural of their representation (ἀψύχοις, φθιμένων, νυκτιπόλων), sheds light on another aspect of the witless and weak dead – their impersonal collectivity.[33] This recalls the Homeric references to massive and indiscriminate swarms of ψυχαί that rush toward the blood (*Od.* 10.529–30, 11.36–37, 42–43, 632–33) or are likened to birds (*Od.* 11.605–06; cf. S. *OT* 175) and throngs of bats (*Od.* 24.6–9).[34] In addition, given that in Aeschylus' *Suppliant Women* (223–24) the term is used to convey the state of the frightened Danaids, it may here qualify the dead as skittish and cowardly. This idea is further corroborated by the term ἄψυχος, as in some contexts *psychē* can acquire the meaning of courage.[35] Last but not least, the emphatic use of the blood sacrifice is consistent with the concept of the weak and witless dead who need blood to restore their mental faculties.

The 'Homerized' profile of the dead not only reflects the resourcefulness with which Aeschylus interacts with the Homeric text, but also shows the flexibility with which he refigures the same motif in different plays. The dead, as described in the *Psychagogoi*, are far removed from the delineation of Darius, the other Aeschylean summoned dead. These multiple and insubstantial souls

---

30 Henrichs 1991, 190.
31 So Rusten 1982, 36, n. 10 and Henrichs 1991, 190–92. On the association between dreams and the nether powers, see e.g. *Od.* 24.11–13; A. *Ch.* 32–41, 532–35; *Pers.* 219–23; S. *El.* 406–10, 453; E. *Hec.* 70–71; *IT* 1262–69; *TrGF* II fr. adesp. 375 Kn.-Sn.; Ar. *Ra.* 1331–32; cf. *Od.* 11.207–08, 222 (see Van Lieshout 1980, 34–37; Padel 1992, 79–81). For the dead in dreams, see e.g. *Il.* 23.65–107; Pi. *P.* 4.159–64; A. *Eum.* 94–139; *Pers.* 197–99; E. *Alc.* 354–55; *Hec.* 1–58.
32 Cf. S. *OC* 1558. See Cousin 2005, 146 and n. 34.
33 On the association of this collectivity with a purposeless and insignificant infernal life, see Bremmer 1994, 101; cf. Henrichs 1991, 194f.
34 Rusten (1982, 35f.) assumes that S. fr. 879 R. (βομβεῖ δὲ νεκρῶν σμῆνος, ἔρχεταί τ' ἄνω) must have drawn on the Aeschylean perception of the souls. On the comparison of the dead to bats, bees, and birds, see Ogden 2001a, 221–24. For the concept of the winged soul, see Vermeule 1979, 18f., 231, n. 13.
35 On *psychē* as 'courage', see e.g. Ar. *Eq.* 457; Th. 2.40.3; cf. E. *Alc.* 642, 696, 717, 956.

that seem to be without power have nothing in common with the fearsome and awe-inspiring Darius who commands the stage in the *Persians*. This discrepancy between two plays composed by the same dramatist not only reflects the diverse treatments to which the necromantic motif can be subjected or the fluidity of its adjacent eschatology, but also shows that there is no single Aeschylean model of necromancy; the dramatist varies the motif from play to play and manipulates it creatively to serve his purposes.

Concluding remarks

Aeschylus employs the *Nekyia*, a distinctively Homeric episode, to achieve an effect which is the opposite of that achieved in the Homeric source text; Odysseus, the cleverest of men, is met with his limitations and human nature. Of course, as pointed out above, this cannot just be about Odysseus. The play touches upon broader issues, whose nature can be guessed at, even though we lack the evidence to fully support our assumptions. The normalization of Odysseus is perhaps the concomitant of the line the play takes about heroism, human potential and human boldness. Aeschylus brings the symbol of ultimate endurance and intelligence closer to the ordinary man and invites us to look at heroism in a different way; even the greatest have limits. This idea is consistent with readings of myth in fifth-century tragedy, which tend to place the emphasis as much on limit as on potential and achievement. In the Sophoclean corpus Oedipus, the cleverest of men, is unable to escape his destiny; in Aeschylus' *Myrmidons* (fr. 132c R.) Achilles is threatened with stoning by the army; in Euripides' *Medea* (1386–88) Jason is destined to be killed by part of his ship. Similarly, the normalization of Odysseus in the *Psychagogoi* probably initiates the audience into the larger idea of human limits. At the same time, the *Psychagogoi* exemplifies the resourcefulness of Aeschylus' interplay with and manipulation of the Homeric source text.

Daniel J. Jacob
Symbolic Remarriage in Homer's *Odyssey* and Euripides' *Alcestis**

The reunion between Admetus and Alcestis at the end of Euripides' *Alcestis* has often been described as a symbolic remarriage of the royal couple of Pheres.¹ Capitalizing on this view, Halleran (1988) maintained that the text offers several clues of this symbolic *matrimonium*,² since it suggests the ritual in which a father, in legal possession of the bride, delivers her to the groom (ἐγγύη), along with the ἀνακαλυπτήρια, that is, the unveiling of the bride in front of the groom and the guests. This view is further supported by the fact that the unveiling was normally accompanied by the bride's silence, as I have suggested elsewhere,³ which is in agreement with the heroine's silence at the end of the play, although the cause of the silence there, is, as we shall see, different. Even if we are not prepared, however, to accept Halleran's view, there is a strong sense of the beginning of a new life, that is, a symbolic remarriage, at the end of the play. In what follows, I shall try to show that this marriage creatively alludes to Homer's *Odyssey*, which is not in itself surprising, if we consider that Euripides, like so many other poets, is deeply indebted to Homer.⁴

Alcestis can be characterized as a play of *nostos*,⁵ in that it displays the typical phases of plays about a character's return and reintegration into the family: separation, hardship/struggle, recognition, reunion.⁶ In the play under discussion, of course, the type of *nostos* in question is singular and strange, namely,

---

* A version of this paper was delivered at the international conference on the *Homeric Receptions in Literature and the Performing Arts* organized by the History Department of the Ionian University, 7–9 November 2011. My warmest thanks go to the organizers of the conference, Athanasios Efstathiou and Ioanna Karamanou, for the invitation; to David Konstan for his generous comments in reading a draft of this paper; and to Antonios Rengakos, Stavros Frangoulidis, Yannis Tzifopoulos and Evangelos Karakasis for their valuable help.
1 For relevant bibliography, see Halleran 1988, 124, n. 8.
2 The opposite view was formulated by Telò 2002, 57–71, as well as Parker 2007 and Seeck 2008 in the relevant comments of their respective commentaries on the play.
3 See Jacob 2010a, 25.
4 See Lange 2002. Lange demonstrated the intertextual debts of Euripides to Homer in the so-called plays of *nostos*. In pp. 223 ff. he parallels Alcestis' death with the demise of Patroclus and Hector in the *Iliad*, but he does not discuss at all the theme of the symbolic marriage in the play.
5 On the topic, apart from the aforementioned book by Lange, see the monograph by Alexopoulou 2009.
6 Cf. Lange 2002, 25 and Hölscher 1988, 228.

the heroine's return from Hades and her restoration to the palace. Its strangeness is also underlined by an additional feature, the fact that the separation is not long-lasting, as happens in analogous cases. As a result, the recognition does not require specific signs (γνωρίσματα) to confirm the identity of the person who returns. This is due also to the fact that, according to the well-known dramatic convention, the play maintains the unity of time, that is, the confinement of the action within a single day, which is that of the queen's death and burial.[7] The recognition takes place at once, and it is superfluous to pose over subtle questions as to why Admetus did not recognize his veil-wearing wife by her clothes[8] and the jewelry with which he had buried her earlier on. The king, of course, realized that the figure and the age of the stranger matched his wife's appearance –and this accounts for his persistent refusal to receive her to his palace– but, understandably enough, he fails to perceive that the dead woman has come back to life. Admetus in his lament had already stressed that the presence outside the palace of a company of women having the same age as Alcestis will cause him sorrow (951–52), let alone, I might add, the continuous presence in the palace of a woman so similar to his wife.

The stranger offers Heracles the chance to organize a well-intentioned game at his host's expense. In this way, the saviour of Alcestis exacts his revenge, concealing the identity of the veiled woman just as Admetus had earlier concealed the identity of the dead person he was mourning in the palace,[9] each time by means of ambiguous phrases. This game results to a dramatic retardation that is necessary for the king to adjust to the presence of the stranger. During the entire conversation with Admetus, Heracles ambiguously argues that he was awarded the woman as a prize in an athletic match, a fact which only partly corresponds to the truth, as it was not a public and common athletic contest but rather a personal struggle with Thanatos.[10] In addition, he refers to a new marriage, though implying, of course, the reunion of Admetus with Alcestis.[11] The king is certainly not able to decode the ambiguous words of his friend and ter-

---

[7] In the *Helen*, where the separation lasts for years –17 years have passed since the breakout of the Trojan War– the meeting, recognition and escape of the spouses take place on the crucial day of the impending wedding of the heroine to Theoclymenus.
[8] In the *Odyssey* Arete understands that the clothes Odysseus wears must have been given to him by Nausicaa. But there the clothes perform a different function. Cf. Hölscher 1988, 124.
[9] For this mirror scene, see Jacob 2009.
[10] Here too one should not ask logical questions, for example, why the guest, Heracles, suddenly decided to abandon the palace and what urged him to take part in athletic games. In any case, Admetus does not doubt or regard his friend's words as impossible.
[11] Halleran (1988, 126) points out that Heracles repeatedly uses the word γυνή in both its meanings: woman and wife.

rified he copes with, obviously ironically, the eventual settlement of the stranger in the marital room, which would actually amount to a second marriage (1055).

However, it turns out that this remarriage involves the same woman, just as in the case of the *Helen*, where Menelaus meets the very same Helen who remained pure in Egypt. The cause is a strange phenomenon: Hera created an idol or image of Helen, which Paris fetched to Troy. The stunning similarity of the two women initially causes comic awkwardness,[12] as Menelaus recognizes his real wife only when it is announced to him that 'Helen' who had been carried from Troy was an idol and had dematerialized in the air. Here, the play between truth and appearances reaches the limits of absurdity, as it leads the spectator to conclude that a ten-year war with thousands of victims on both sides was conducted for the recovery of a non-existent person. In any case, a death occurs in the *Helen* as well, the difference being that it is only verbal, as in the case also of Orestes in Aeschylus' *Choephori* and in Sophocles' *Electra*. In the eve of her unwanted marriage to Theoclymenus, the heroine announces the death of her first husband and expresses her wish to pay him the last tribute. In this manner, she manages to escape with Menelaus on the ship assigned to her for the ceremony. The so-called death leads to a reversal, the reunion of the spouses in a symbolic remarriage.[13] Another reunion, not of spouses but of a brother and a sister, occurs in the *Iphigenia in Tauris*, where the Greeks believe that Iphigenia is dead (*IT* 8), while she is still living in Tauris. All three plays are conditioned by a common theme, the miracle: return from Hades, duplication of a person, mysterious disappearance of the victim from the altar.

But let us return to the *Alcestis*. An immediate meeting of Admetus with his resurrected wife would not only cause him surprise but also great confusion, since Heracles would not have had enough time to give his friend the necessary explanations. That an immediate recognition of the dead Alcestis would be psychologically damaging is further evidenced by the meeting of Odysseus and Laertes in the *Odyssey* (24.224 ff.). Odysseus finds his father alone in the garden. Devastated by years of suffering, the old man is unwashed and poorly-dressed, as his son observes, a sign that has given up the daily care of himself, because it no longer affords him any pleasure. It is noteworthy that Laertes' appearance is transformed after the recognition of his son. The hero oscillates between two plans, as the poet explicitly indicates (24.235 ff.): either to immediately disclose

---

[12] See Seidensticker 1982, 177 ff.
[13] See *Hel.* 722 for the renewed ὑμέναιον. It is worth noting that Heracles' expected reunion with Deianeira in their marital home (S. *Tr.* 206) is joyfully received by the Chorus; but, as it often happens in Sophoclean drama, it will be annulled by the death of the protagonists (see Davies 1991, 105). For a conflation of marital and funeral customs, see Rehm 1994.

his identity to his father or to test his father's reactions first. He goes for the second plan, apparently out of fear that a sudden recognition might have dangerous psychological repercussions.[14] Therefore, he gives a false genealogy and origin and claims to have offered hospitality to Odysseus some time ago, in order to familiarize the old man with the idea of his son's return; the fact that Odysseus is still alive is a positive indication. The old man bursts into tears. At this point, Odysseus yields to the sight of his devastated father and decides to disclose his identity. The old man asks for incontestable signs confirming the stranger's claim. Odysseus shows him the scar,[15] a sign also used in previous recognitions in the *Odyssey*, and, additionally, mentions the kind and the exact number of trees Laertes offered him when Odysseus was a child. Hence, the moving recognition of father and son takes place.

A further example is offered by Chariton's *Callirhoe* (3.1), a novel with which I am dealing below. Dionysius, convinced that Callirhoe has turned down his marriage proposal, decides to starve himself to death. Plangon, however, suddenly announces to him that Callirhoe has accepted his proposal. Overwhelmed by the good news, he falls senseless to the ground and the servants believe that he is dead. Odysseus knows from the beginning whom he is talking with, as is also the case with Heracles and the spectator, who are both aware of the stranger's identity. All can see that a certain period of time has to lapse, so that unwelcome side-effects resulting from unexpected joy are avoided. Coming back from Hades is an extremely rare event. The Chorus had already underlined that such a return was impossible: νῦν δὲ βίου τίν' ἔτ' ἐλπίδα προσδέχωμαι; (130), οὐδ' ἔστι κακῶν ἄκος οὐδέν (135).[16] From this perspective, the heroine's silence is also justified. Adjustment to the world of the living requires time and, above all, a rite of passage, which, even if not foreseen, is completely understandable and expected. Certainly, the playwright was not interested in describing this ritual more precisely and for this reason postpones it for three days, a number with obvious religious connotations. It is also worth mentioning that Heracles speaks of ἀφαγνισμός (1146), while Thanatos had used the verb ἁγνίζω, indicating that Alcestis definitely belongs to Hades (76).[17] I believe that views like those of Naiden

---

14 See scholia Q on line 24.242 (Dindorf): ἵνα μὴ τῆι αἰφνιδίωι χαρᾶι ἀποψύξει ὁ γέρων, ὥσπερ καὶ ὁ κύων ἀπώλετο. Compare Heubeck 1981; Danek 1998, 487 ff.; Wöhrle 1999, 112–13.
15 For the scar, see Hölscher 1988, 64 ff.
16 The ghost of Darius in Aeschylus' *Persians* points out how rarely the Underworld gods consent to a dead person's exit from Hades (688–89).
17 See Naiden 1998, 82, n. 26. Halleran 1982 found a further correspondence between Alcestis' farewell to life and her return to it: the use of *antilabe* with lexical similarities. Objections against Halleran were raised by Telò 2002, 65–66.

(1998) eliminate the autonomy of poetry and undermine its 'logic', because they attempt to define with precision the nature of the resurrected Alcestis, that is, whether she is a ghost or a body still dead, able to move but not yet able to speak. What matters is the fact that the heroine returns to life and not the actual circumstances of this return: namely how Heracles manages to free the queen's shadow from the arms of Thanatos and bring it back to the dead body lying in the grave. Similar realistic problems concern neither the poet nor the spectator. Alcestis' silence is, therefore, imposed by religion[18] and is complementary to the bride's silence during the ἀνακαλυπτήρια, as I mentioned above. The view that Alcestis' silence expressly betrays her disappointment, coldness and, probably, her anger also against her selfish husband is groundless. The interpretation is in opposition to the heroine's personal and explicit statement that she sacrificed herself, because she could not continue her life with their orphan children on her own, in separation from Admetus forever (287–88). Of course, a few lines earlier (285–86) she had claimed that she could remarry the husband of her choice, who would not only be well-off, but would also have royal status. It is apparent, however, that this is an *ad hoc* statement to stress the magnitude of her sacrifice, because the law, at least in fifth-century Athens, did not provide for a choice of husband by a widow. After all, it would be contradictory on her part to impose a stepfather on her children, once she has demanded that Admetus should avoid imposing a stepmother on them (305). There is, therefore, no indication that Alcestis' attitude to her husband has changed, let alone that it has turned negative.

Heracles, as already observed, recovers Alcestis after a struggle with Thanatos of a kind which, as a rule, leads to the acquisition of a wife or her retrieval in case of separation, the difference being that in our play the recovered wife is assigned to her husband by the winner, in return for his generosity and hospitality. This development is necessitated by the plot, as Heracles was the only one[19] who

---

[18] See Trammel 1941/1942 and Betts 1965. Compare Riemer 1989, 93–103.
[19] This unique event evokes the archery contest in book 21 of the *Odyssey*, where, as we shall see, Odysseus is the only one able to stretch the bow (compare Hölscher 1988, 69). In both cases the result is the same: the reunion of the couple. Lesky (1925, 55) cites the view of Maas only to reject it (1895, 151, n. 48): according to Maas, the invincible Admetus, as the etymology of his name suggests, fights with Thanatos and thus rescues his wife. However, such a version would run counter to the plot of the drama. On the husband's combat with his rival, see Hölscher 1988, 61 and 64. Admetus, of course, wishes he had Orpheus' melodic voice, in order to descend to Hades and bring his wife back to life (357 ff.); nonetheless, his unfulfilled wish stresses the infeasibility of the undertaking. Assael 2004 claims that the play includes references to mystic rites. In my opinion, the characterization of Alcestis as μάκαιρα δαίμων (1003) might refer to the apotheosis of the dead known from later golden tablets. See Jacob 2010b.

had the ability to descend to Hades and return alive –he is to repeat this achievement after the accomplishment of his last deed, carrying Cerberus' back up to the earth. An example of a similar recovery on the husband's part is offered in Menelaus' conflict with the Egyptians on the ship at the moment of the escape (*Hel.* 1592 ff.); the hero had previously expressed his wish to fight with Theoclymenus (843–50), but his duel is cancelled after the plot against the Egyptian king has been planned.

Two instances of 'wife-acquisition' after a struggle are cited below. They deviate from the classical procedure, in which the bride's father invites the suitors to perform a feat or solve a difficult riddle, in order to be given her hand, because marriage is by no means the initial goal of the deeds.[20] The first comes up as early as in book 6 of the *Iliad*. In the belief that Bellerophon has tried to rape his wife, Anteia, Proetus commissions a relative of his to kill the presumed culprit (160 ff.). Proetus' father-in-law, wishing to avoid defiling his hands with human blood, orders Bellerophon to murder the Chimaera, believing that this attempt will cost Bellerophon his life. However, he kills the Chimaera and successfully performs further exploits, such as his battle with the Solymoi, the Amazons and, finally, the elite Lycians who had ambushed him. Then the king of the Lycians, convinced of the hero's innocence, gives him his daughter as a wife, along with half of his kingdom. In other instances, a successful outcome has tragic consequences. In the prologue of Euripides' *Phoenissae*, Jocasta informs us that she has been given to Oedipus as a wife along with the kingdom, because he was the only one who was able to solve the enigma of the Sphinx and free Thebes from her predations (50 ff.).

In my opinion, the case of Alcestis directly alludes to the archery contest in the *Odyssey*. Penelope postpones an undesirable marriage with one of the suitors for quite a long time, by using various tricks. After her delaying tactics are revealed, she is obliged to choose a second husband. For this purpose she suggests, upon Athena's advice, that the suitors perform a deed entirely compatible with the occasion: to stretch Odysseus' bow and make the arrow pass through twelve axes (21.1 ff.). Penelope states that, even if Odysseus, disguised as a beggar, manages to stretch the bow, she is not going to marry him (21.310 ff.), thus nullifying the deeper narrative reason for this contest in advance. The ironic cor-

---

[20] On the motif in question and its use in the *Odyssey*, see Krischer 1992. Krischer conclusively remarks that it is not about a simple archery contest: it is instead about a concrete attempt of the suitors to stretch Odysseus' bow, so that a suitor having a potential equivalent to that of the missing hero would be chosen. Accordingly, the event betrays psychological motives. The main deviation, of course, lies in the fact that the contest is not organized by the bride's father but by the bride herself, who is about to have a second marriage.

respondences with the *Alcestis* are obvious: the disguised Odysseus corresponds to the veiled heroine, and Penelope's rejection of Odysseus the beggar has its parallel in Admetus' refusal to welcome the unknown woman. Both situations result in a happy reunion: the unknown figure to be rejected is revealed to be no other than the spouse. The reunion in *epos* is postponed because of the intervening narrative of *mnēstērophonia*, whereas in the *Alcestis* the reunion of the couple is immediately achieved: Heracles' struggle with Death underlies the short and vague comment that he participated in an athletic contest and is not described in an elaborate messenger's *rhēsis*, due to Heracles' well intentioned deception of Admetus. As in the *Odyssey*, in the *Helen* too, the heroine is on the threshold of a new and unpleasant marriage cancelled at the last minute, when the separated spouses are reunited.

In the *Alcestis* the new marriage, of which Heracles speaks persistently and ironically, eventually proves to be identical with the first one, in contrast with both previously cited instances. What constitutes a real threat in the *Odyssey* and the *Helen* is in the *Alcestis* only a seeming danger. The reason is that the proposal for a new marriage comes from a trusted friend of Admetus, who is by no means willing to harm his companion. Heracles is one of those loyal friends also known from other Euripidean plays: Pylades in the *Electra* and, above all, in the *Orestes* and in the *IT*, as well as Theseus in the *Heracles*. At this point, it is worth noting that the friend either accompanies his comrade or appears as the crisis reaches its peak. In the *Alcestis*, in particular, the guest Heracles learns the truth about the identity of the dead woman too late, but his intervention turns out to be beneficial. Thus, what seems to be a violation of Admetus' promise to his wife, namely that he will never remarry, ends up as a happy reunion with her. Furthermore, one more characteristic reversal is to be observed: the person who is subjected to Heracles' noble yet at the same time ironical pressure to remarry is this time not a woman (Penelope, Helen), but a man who accepts the proposal and is reunited with his wife.

In the *Alcestis*, therefore, the typical phases of *nostos* are present: separation, more precisely the final separation due to death, trial (here represented by Heracles' struggle with Thanatos for the reasons I mentioned above), recognition and reunion. This thematic sequence recurs later in the Hellenistic novel. A typical example appears in an early example, namely Chariton's *Callirhoe*,[21] which presents some notable similarities with the *Alcestis*.[22] Chaereas

---

[21] See Reardon 1996. A list of parallels between Chariton and other Greek novels is offered by Garin 1909, 423–27.

22 On *Callirhoe*'s relation to tragedy, see in general Trzaskoma 2010, 219, n. 2 with earlier bibliography. On *Callirhoe*'s relation to the *Alcestis*, see Alvares 2002, 113–14. Alvares points out two similarities between the novel and the drama: Admetus' wish that the dead Alcestis may appear in his dreams (*Alc.* 354–56, compare *Callirhoe* 2.1) and Alcestis' wish that Admetus should not impose a stepmother on their children (*Alc.* 305 ff., compare *Callirhoe* 8.4). The latter similarity had already been observed by Hirschberger (2001, 169), but, like Alvares, she too is unaware of the fact that the concern of the heroine, as is also the case with Alcestis in her prayers to Hestia (163 ff.), is her child's marriage, and, what is more, that in the novel the bride is known in advance: it is the orphan daughter of Dionysius. I also do not believe that Hirschberger (2001, 169) is right in maintaining that Hermocrates' claim concerning his daughter's wish that Chaereas may outlive her (1.5.7) alludes to the *Alcestis*, because the issue is not her sacrifice for her husband but the longevity of Chaereas after her death as well. Her view (2001, 172) that the Chorus refers to the means of Admetus' suicide (227–30) is also groundless. The Chorus comes to realize that the situation is so desperate that it can only be cured by suicide. This realization, however, which also occurs in other dramas as a rhetorical way to describe despair, is not directly associated with Admetus. On the contrary, Hirschberger correctly believes (2001, 172) that Pheres' accusation that Admetus killed his wife (696) is repeated in Dionysius' allegation against Chaereas (*Callirhoe* 5.8.5), as well as that the beautiful woman in Arados can make up for the loss of Callirhoe, just as a new marriage can console Admetus (1087, compare *Callirhoe* 8.1.6). Finally, Hirschberger (2001, 172) correctly points out that the veiled stranger Chaereas meets in Arados (8.1.6–7), who upsets him because of her similarity with Callirhoe, refers to the veiled Alcestis at the end of the play (1061–69). Of course, we must note that Callirhoe is unescorted and alive and it is she who recognizes Chaereas by his voice and accordingly reveals her identity. In any case, it is thanks to this strange ἀνακαλυπτήρια that the reunion of the separated spouses is attained in the novel as well. However, I believe that further similarities exist: Callirhoe's assumption that the gods of the Underworld are summoning her, when she regains her senses in the grave (1.9), evokes the hallucinations which the dying heroine experiences in the drama (*Alc.* 253 ff.). In 5.9, after the unexpected meeting of Chaereas and Callirhoe in the court, the heroine wonders whether what she saw was simply the ghost of Chaereas recalled by some Persian magus. Admetus also similarly wonders about Alcestis' return to life (*Alc.* 1027–28). In contrast, however, to the silent Alcestis, Chaereas not only speaks, but is also aware of the relevant facts. It is notable that Dionysius, even after receiving Callirhoe's letter, still believes that the child is his, as also happens with Xuthus in Euripides' *Ion* (see Ruiz-Montero 1996, 51). Two further, yet stereotyped, passages may also be informed by the *Alcestis*. When blaming Polycharmus for preventing him from killing himself during Callirhoe's burial (6.2), Chaereas is reminiscent of Admetus accusing the Chorus of not letting him fall into his wife's grave (897 ff.). After Callirhoe and Chaereas have fled to Syracuse, Artaxerxes announces that he is not able to give him Callirhoe, although he wants to, and therefore assigns him power over Ionia (8.5). Heracles also appeals to the same inability, but, ironically, the veiled Alcestis is by his side (1072 ff.). The similarities between *Callirhoe* and the *Alcestis* lead to the hypothesis, which, however, cannot be elaborated in the present paper, that the change from the painful events in the first books of the novel to the happy end, which is foretold at the beginning of book 8, draws its origin from the Euripidean play. The difference, of course, is due to the fact that in the *Alcestis* Apollo prophesies the rescue of the heroine as early as in the prologue, whereas in the novel the hardships of the protagonists constitute simple fiction. For the relation of Chariton to theatre, see Tilg 2010, 137–40. Tilg (2010, 144) describes Chariton as a prisoner

and Callirhoe get married out of mutual love at first sight. Chaereas falls victim of an intrigue of his wife's former suitors and thinks that Callirhoe is cheating on him. Out of jealousy he kicks the pregnant Callirhoe[23] and she loses her senses. Believing her to be dead, Chaereas lays Callirhoe to rest, but the heroine regains her senses in the tomb and is then abducted by grave-robber pirates. This causes her separation from her husband, her being sold as a slave to Dionysius and her remarriage to him, which results in the birth of Chaereas' child. When he finds out that Callirhoe is alive, Chaereas commits himself to the quest for her. He arrives at Miletus and is close to discovering her, but his triremes are set on fire and he himself is captured and sold as a slave to Mithridates, the satrap of Caria. Callirhoe is informed of his arrival, but misinformation makes her believe that Chaereas and his comrades have been killed, so she builds a cenotaph in his honour. Mithridates is accused of adultery by Dionysius, as he believes that Chaereas' letter to Callirhoe, which arrived from Caria, is fake and betrays the satrap's own erotic interest in Callirhoe. In the trial in front of the Great King, Artaxerxes, Mithridates brings along Chaereas, who is still alive, and thus he is found not guilty. The spouses finally meet each other during the trial, but their reunion is postponed. While Artaxerxes sets a new trial date to decide to which of the husbands he will adjudge Callirhoe, a mutiny of the Egyptians from Persia breaks out, and Chaereas joins them as an admiral and crushes the Persian fleet. He gains possession of the island Arados, where Artaxerxes has left the women and children. There unexpectedly he comes across Callirhoe and they happily return to Syracuse.

This is not the place to discuss the problematic hermeneutics that the plot of this novel presents. I merely limit myself to those elements which suggest various analogues between the novel and drama in general and therefore constitute the starting point for any interpretative approach of this novel.

(i) The various hardships the couple goes through are due to Aphrodite's anger at Chaereas for abusing his wife, which is congruent with the notion of divine wrath triggering a tragic development (cf. for instance Euripides' *Hippolytus*).[24] After the repeated predicaments of the couple have assuaged the anger of the goddess, the spouses are reunited. This means that Callir-

---

of prose. Personally, I would argue that just as Isocrates' encomiastic/rhetorical speeches are prose equivalents to Pindaric epinician poetry, Chariton's novel, in a similar manner, may be viewed as a prose equivalent to Euripidean drama. From this perspective, it is not coincidental that Tilg often characterizes *Callirhoe* as tragicomedy (2010, 246, 276), a term which defines Euripidean plays closing with a happy ending.

23 For historical parallels of cruel conduct, see Tilg 2010, 48.
24 See the passages collected by Helms 1996, 115–17.

hoe's marriage to Dionysius must also be dealt with from this perspective, namely as part of Chaereas' punishment, and not as Callirhoe's adultery; likewise, Odysseus' seven-year sojourn with Calypso is not assessed negatively, since the hero, like Callirhoe, has the constant, painful and fervent wish for *nostos*.

(ii) Callirhoe is the central figure of the novel and, as Helen in the homonymous Euripidean play,[25] she blames her beauty for making her the object of desire of many important figures, including the Great King.

(iii) Finally, Polycharmus is Chaereas' friend, faithful and inseparable to death (an exact equivalent to Pylades, who accompanies Orestes to the exotic land of Taurians), and will marry his friend's sister (8.8), just as Pylades will marry Electra.[26]

Certainly, the comparison of the novel with drama does not indicate a direct dependence; the birth of the Hellenistic novel is an extremely complex phenomenon, coming into existence via various sources, not always exclusively Greek according to some scholars,[27] and presenting multiple combinations. I am simply pointing to the use of common story-patterns with intertextual references to tragedy and other earlier literary texts, including the so-called tragic historiography and the biographical tradition.[28] There is, of course, no doubt that the novel has more realistic antecedents than tragic theatre. That is why the heroine does not die, but she is simply placed senseless in the grave. It is thus characteristic that 'rational' critics of Euripides, such as A.W. Verrall,[29] surmised that no real death occurs in the *Alcestis* either. In the case under discussion, however, one should

---

25 For bibliography on *Callirhoe* and *Helen*, see Trzaskoma 2010, 219, n. 2.
26 Cf. E. *El.* 1249 and *Or.* 1658–59. It is noteworthy that both Helms 1966 and Billault 1996 in their specialized studies on the characters of the novel leave out Polycharmus' characterization, albeit without justification. I believe that Polycharmus is Chaereas' *alter ego*, insomuch as he represents his friend's innermost thoughts, functioning in fact as his extension. For example, when claiming that the sacrifice of their lives, on account of their siding with the Egyptian rebels against Artaxerxes, is preferable to Chaereas' suicide without a tangible result, Polycharmus brings to mind Pylades' suggestion to Orestes, namely to lose their lives after having murdered Helen (*Or.* 1105 ff.). Surely, Chaereas himself could have had this very thought. In other words, Polycharmus, like Pylades in the play (cf. especially *Ch.* 900–02, where Pylades, silent throughout the play, utters the crucial three lines encouraging his friend to commit matricide), constitutes the outward expression of Chaereas' inner world, a fact that renders unnecessary Polycharmus' characterization as an independent person.
27 See for instance Whitmarsh 2010.
28 On this, see Ruiz-Montero 1996, 49–51 (especially for Euripidean drama).
29 Verrall 1895, 1–128.

consider both the fairy-tale origin of the plot of the drama and its divine direction evoking the *Ion* and the *Helen*, in that the homonymous heroes are also under the invisible protection of the gods.

From this perspective, one is justified, I believe, in maintaining that Euripides did have in mind the Odyssean remarriage; yet, he developed it with notable deviations. Alcestis settles again in the palace as queen, after coming back from Hades, which is the place also 'visited' by Odysseus before his *nostos*, without, however, losing his life. This conclusion, in conjunction with a variety of alterations pointed out in the case of the aforementioned tragedies (belonging, according to Lange, to the plays of *nostos* 'conversing' with the *Odyssey*), proves, with all the clarity one might desire, how flexible and multivalent the story-patterns are (in this case, the *nostos* theme); or, even more precisely, how flexible and multivalent the various subtextual basic thematic units are (here: separation, hardship/struggle, recognition, reunion), which interconnect and add up forming a story characterized by a concrete, functional and architecturally structured arrangement and specific content. Despite the demonstrable intertextual relations, there is no slavish imitation here. It is more like a palimpsest, in which parts of the earlier text may be read through the overwritten text. In particular, the way the separation is brought about, the beneficial intervention and struggle of the humans (which requires, as a rule, the assistance of the gods), the kind of struggle and the type of opponent, the time of and the means used for the reunion– all these elements vary, creating multivalent and, in some cases, unexpected relations. More precisely, the *Alcestis* includes:

(i) Reversals: a) a new marriage is proposed for a man and not a woman, b) the victor of the contest is not wedded to the woman functioning as his prize, but gives her back to her husband, who is also his friend.
(ii) The second marriage is identical to the first, not a union with an unwelcome person that is finally avoided.
(iii) The superhuman nature of the rivals: the contest of the semi-god Heracles with a supernatural figure, Thanatos.
(iv) *Nostos:* a return from the world of the dead, not from a place on earth.

In conclusion, Euripides in the *Alcestis* refigured the reunion of Odysseus and Penelope in the *Odyssey*, which plays an archetypal role in similar instances; then again, the fairy-tale prehistory of the play, on the one hand, and the flexible dynamics of the *nostos* story-pattern, on the other, contributed to the literary processes shaping the transformation of the epic source text into dramatic plot.

Ioanna Karamanou
Euripides' 'Trojan Trilogy' and the Reception of the Epic Tradition

In 415 BC Euripides produced the *Alexandros, Palamedes* and *Trojan Women* followed by the satyr-play *Sisyphus*.[1] All three tragedies draw on the Trojan myth, display unity of locale with Troy as the place of action and share dominant themes, concepts and dramatic characters. Consequently, scholarly consensus from Gilbert Murray till now, including the influential monograph by Ruth Scodel, regards this Euripidean production as presenting the features of a 'connected trilogy'.[2] My purpose is, firstly, to contribute to the argumentation in favour of the thematic and ideological connection of these plays, which, I shall argue, is of a different nature than that of Aeschylean trilogies (it is for this reason that I shall be using the term 'Trojan trilogy' in inverted commas). Secondly, I shall explore the generic transformation of the epic material into tragedy in the light of fifth-century intellectual and ideological contexts, which could yield insight into the cultural processes filtering the Euripidean reworking of the Homeric source text.[3]

The *Alexandros* treats the *nostos* of the ill-omened exposed baby Alexandros/ Paris to the palace of Troy, following his athletic triumph in the funeral games held in his memory, a failed murder-attack against him by his mother Hecabe, in ignorance of his true identity, and a speech of prophetic frenzy by Cassandra foretelling the future disaster of Troy and of Priam's royal *oikos*. The second tragedy, the *Palamedes*, presents the victimization of the homonymous hero by Odysseus at Troy, Palamedes' trial before Agamemnon as a judge and his sub-

---

1 Schol. Ar. *Vesp.* 1326b (Koster); Ael. *VH* 2.8.
2 Murray 1932, 645–56 and 1946, 127–48 (cf. earlier Schöll 1839, 47 ff. conjecturing that this was a firmly connected trilogy; Krausse 1905, 178–84; Wilamowitz 1906², 259–63); Schmid/ Stählin 1940, 474–80; Menegazzi 1951, 190–91; Pertusi 1952, 251–73; Friedrich 1953, 61–75; Mason 1959, 86–88; Scarcella 1959, 66–70; Webster 1966, 208–13; Wilson 1967, 221–23; Stössl 1968, II 232–33, 288–89; Lee 1976, x-xiv; Scodel 1980, 64–121; Jarkho 1982, 241–45; Barlow 1986, 27–30; Sopina 1986, 117–30; Ritoók 1993, 109–25; Hose 1995, 33–57; Kovacs 1997, 162–76; Falcetto 2002, 21–37 (with rich bibliography on this matter); Cropp 2004, 47–48; Sansone 2009, 193–203; Di Giuseppe 2012, 12–13. Cf. the scepticism expressed in Planck 1840, 25–35; Koniaris 1973, 85–122; Conacher 1967, 132–34.
3 On the investigation of contexts as a fundamental concept of classical reception theory, see Martindale 1993, 11–18; Hardwick 2003, esp. 1–2, 107–13; Hardwick/ Stray 2008, 1–5; see further 'Introduction' (this volume).

sequent unjust condemnation to death.[4] The *Trojan Women* concludes the Trojan War by presenting its repercussions from the side of the defeated and, in particular, of the Trojan womenfolk.

The first obvious connecting link between these three tragedies is the unity of locale with Troy as the place of action. Moreover, the third tragedy of this production, the *Trojan Women*, contains scenes reflecting and recalling earlier events from the previous plays, following the technique of the 'mirror scenes' of Aeschylean trilogies.[5]

A striking mirror scene aiming at illustrating the antithesis before and after the reversal of fortune for Troy is the Cassandra episode in *Tr.* 308–461, which reflects Cassandra's scene of prophetic frenzy in the *Alexandros* (frr. 62e–h K.[6]). Her prophecies in the *Trojan Women* involve an inversion of her earlier foretellings in the *Alexandros*, in that in the latter she foretells disaster out of prosperity, while in the former she prophesies victory out of defeat.[7] The ironic antithesis between seeming and being is clear in both cases, and Euripides seems to be exploiting Cassandra and the implications of her prophecies (seemingly unbelievable, albeit true) as a means of highlighting this very contrast. In both cases, her prophetic madness is described as *baccheia* (*Tr.* 307, 341, 348–49, 366–67, 408, 414–15, *Alexandros* fr. 62e K.).[8] I would note that this term seems to be particularly nuanced; it not only alludes to bacchic frenzy, but also to the collective character of bacchic cult, not least because Cassandra's prophecies affect the whole Trojan community.[9] Apart from the visual and thematic links between the two scenes already noted by Ruth Scodel,[10] it should be added that Cassandra's virginal modesty in the *Alexandros*, as expressed in fr. 17.33 J. of Ennius' *Alexander*, which was evidently modelled upon the homonymous Euripidean

---

[4] On the plot of the *Alexandros*, see the hypothesis preserved in P.Oxy. 3650. 1–32. On the *Palamedes*, see schol. E. *Or.* 432 (Schwartz); Hyg. *fab.* 105; [Apollod.] *Epit.* 3.8.
[5] On this Aeschylean technique, see Taplin 1977, 100–03, 357–59 and on its exploitation in Euripidean drama, see Strohm 1957, 165–82; Mastronarde 2010, 68–77; Burnett 1971, 37–38, 42, 61–62, 163, n. 9, 169–73; Dingel 1967, 192–95; Steidle 1968, 15–17; Halleran 1985, 86–87.
[6] The abbreviation K. stands for the numbering of Euripidean fragments in Kannicht 2004.
[7] Scodel 1980, 69; Webster 1966, 210–11. See also Mazzoldi 2001, 138–65; Croally 1994, 228–31; Mossman 2005, 359–60; Gartziou-Tatti 1997, 322–23.
[8] See Scodel 1980, 69–70; Karamanou 2015, 392–94.
[9] On the communal dimension of bacchic rites, see, for instance, Segal 1997², 328f., 363–69, 389–91; Guettel-Cole 2007, 334–38; Henrichs 1982, 137–60.
[10] See Scodel 1980, 70.

play,[11] provides an ironic antithesis to her imminent status as Agamemnon's mistress in *Tr.* 310 ff. Moreover, the torch imagery foreboding the Trojan disaster in her prophecies in the *Alexandros* (Ennius *Alexander* fr. 17.41–42 J.) is employed antithetically in the third tragedy of this production to allude to the wedding torch as a means of her avenging the injustice done to herself, her family and Troy (*Tr.* 308–325, 353–364).

Hecabe's ritual lamentation for Astyanax in *Tr.* 1156–1255 seems to recall a possible earlier ritual lamentation for the exposed baby Alexandros at the beginning of the homonymous play, as I have argued in a publication.[12] More specifically, fr. 46a, col. ii K. of the *Alexandros* contains the choral cry ἒ ἒ (l. 41), as well as a reference to γόοι (l. 35: 'grieving cries'), which are typical of ritual lamentations revolving around a hero's death. This scene is consistent with the testimony of the hypothesis (hyp. *Alexandros:* P.Oxy. 3650, col. i, 8–10) referring to Hecabe's mourning for the apparent loss of her baby and with the consolation addressed to her by the Chorus-leader (frr. 44–46 K.) earlier in the play. Accordingly, the possible lament for the seemingly dead baby boy in the *Alexandros* could be interestingly mirrored in the actual funeral of Hecabe's grandchild in the third tragedy of the 'Trojan trilogy'; ironically enough, the fate of Astyanax is sealed with Alexandros' survival.

In addition, the indirect evidence for the *Alexandros* (Hyginus *fab.* 91, in conjunction with a group of Etruscan mirror-back relief-representations dated to the fourth and third century BC: *LIMC* I, 'Alexandros', figg. 21–23) suggests that Alexandros sought refuge at an altar to escape the attack against him organized by Hecabe with the assistance of her son Deiphobus, in ignorance of his true identity.[13] Hyginus (*fab.* 91) mentions that this was the altar of Zeus Herkeios. This detail recurs only in a Coptic textile medallion (Hermitage Museum, inv. nr. 11507), which is dated to the fifth century AD[14] and could have either been modelled upon an earlier (and now lost) artistic representation or may have drawn on an intermediary literary work, such as Hyginus' handbook, which was a common source for mythological lore in Late Antiquity. It is worth bearing

---

11 On Ennius' use of the Euripidean *Alexandros* as a source text, see Snell 1937, 59; Jocelyn 1967, 204; Timpanaro 1996, 6–69; Jouan/ van Looy 1998, 46 ff.; Skutsch 1968, 161; Collard/ Cropp/ Gibert 2004, 36; Collard/ Cropp 2008, I 38; Di Giuseppe 2012, 160–70. The abbreviation J. refers to the numbering of Ennius' fragments in Jocelyn 1967.
12 Karamanou 2012, 403–04.
13 On the plotting scene between Hecabe and Deiphobus (fr. 62d. 24–30 K.), see Huys 1986, 9–36. For more detail on the relation of Hyg. *fab.* 91 and the Etruscan mirror-back relief-representations to the *Alexandros*, see Karamanou 2013, 415–28.
14 See Kannicht 2004, I 178, Nauerth 1986, pl. 7.1.

in mind, however, that though the Roman mythographer's account largely reflects elements which are congruent with the evidence for the Euripidean *Alexandros*, it is not a hypothesis and, therefore, does not necessarily report every aspect of this tragic plot with accuracy. Nonetheless, if the possible implications of this piece of information are investigated with due caution, then Alexandros' conceivable flight to the particular altar of a domestic god protecting blood ties[15] may acquire special dramatic significance within the framework of this production. Alexandros' supplication at this altar and, in turn, his rescue and recognition with his family signpost the beginning of the Trojan disaster ironically reaching its climax in the *Trojan Women*, where Priam's slaughter is mentioned to have taken place at the very same altar of the god who protected blood kinship and the integrity of his *oikos* (*Tr.* 16–17, 481–83). As the altar of Zeus Herkeios stands in the courtyard, that is, at the crossroads between private and public sphere, it serves to represent the connection of the *oikos* with the *polis*;[16] in both the *Alexandros* and the *Trojan Women* the events of the household (the repercussions of Paris' rescue and Priam's slaughter respectively) affect directly the city of Troy, which collapses along with its royal *oikos*.

As has already been noted,[17] particular characters in the *Trojan Women* are closely connected with incidents or characters in the previous plays of this production, which I shall briefly mention. Andromache's entry in a carriage with Hector's son and Hector's armour, as well as her focus on her life with him in her speech (*Tr.* 643–56, 673–78), recalls Hector's role in the *Alexandros*, which will be explored below. Helen as the cause of the Trojan War in *Tr.* 914 ff. mirrors the figure of Alexandros in the first play. Her particular reference to the crown which she demands for her alleged contribution to the Greek victory (*Tr.* 937) alludes to the crowned winner Alexandros in the homonymous play (fr. 61d.6 K.). Alexandros' brother Deiphobus appears as his athletic rival in *Alexandros* fr. 62a–b K. (see also hyp. P.Oxy. 3650. 22–25) and is referred to as an erotic rival in *Tr.* 959–60. Odysseus' ruse and malice are brought forward in both the *Palamedes*[18] and *Tr.* 281–91, 713–25, 1224–25, whereas the satyr-play of this production bears the name of Sisyphus, Odysseus' father, according to a branch of the tradition adopted by Euripides.[19] The figure of Si-

---

15 On the cult of Zeus Herkeios, see *Il.* 11.771–75; *Od.* 22. 335; Hdt. 6. 68; S. *Ant.* 487 with the notes of Jebb 1900³, 96 and Griffith 1999, 350; schol. Pl. *Euthd.* 302d (Greene); Harpocration s.v. Ἕρκειος Ζεύς p. 134 Dindorf; Nilsson 1967³, I 125; Burkert 1985, 255.
16 For the spatial connotations of the altar of Zeus Herkeios in tragedy, see Rehm 2002, 106, 117, 122, 171.
17 See especially Scodel 1980, 68–72.
18 See above, n. 4.
19 See *Cyc.* 104 and *IA* 524, 1362.

syphus, therefore, is associated with the previous plays by means of his relation to Odysseus, as well as by his incarnating the very theme of deception and ambiguity deriving from the antithesis between seeming and being, which permeates this production, as mentioned above: in the first tragedy, Alexandros is not the low-born herdsman that he seems to be, but a royal son, and the seemingly happy ending of his return designates the beginning of Trojan disaster; Palamedes appears to be a traitor, without really being one; and the Greeks seem to have won the war, while they are in fact defeated.[20]

The latter remark sets a challenge to explore the connecting links among these plays not only in terms of theme but with regard to concept, as well. It is noteworthy that all three tragedies are named after the victims, whether they are actual victims, as Palamedes and the women of Troy, or near victims as Alexandros.[21] Both Alexandros and Palamedes fall victims of their opponents' *phthonos* (that is, resentful envy or indignation at one's prosperity).[22] I would observe that this idea culminates at the *Trojan Women*, where punishment is also instigated by *phthonos* and, in this case, divine *phthonos*,[23] since the insolent behaviour of the Greeks towards the gods incurs divine wrath (*Tr.* 65–97). As Gilbert Murray noted, the *Alexandros* and the *Palamedes* provided a sketch of the main Trojan and Greek characters respectively, alluding to their fate, while the third play, the *Trojan Women*, encompasses the fate of both the Greeks and the Trojans.[24] Moreover, it should be pointed out that in the three trial-debates of these tragedies, the accused is perceived as an enemy of the community. The first agon in the *Alexandros* presents the clash of the royal son who has been raised as a herdsman with his fellow herdsmen. In this trial-debate Alexandros is accused of haughty behaviour towards the other shepherds before Priam as a judge (frr. 48, 50, 56, 60, 61 K. and hyp.: P.Oxy. 3650. 15–21). Subsequently, Palamedes is falsely regarded as a betrayer of the Greek army (fr. 588 K.), while Helen is held responsible for communal damage and claims to be innocent albeit guilty (*Tr.* 860–1059). The idea of the clash with the community in all three plays is a factor suggestive of the political implications of this production, which, interwoven with the opposition of seeming and being pervading these debates, evidently

---

[20] See also Murray 1946, 127–48.
[21] Scodel 1980, 73–76 notes that these three tragedies present 'the murder of the innocent'.
[22] See Scodel 1980, 75; for Odysseus' *phthonos* against Palamedes, see schol. E. *Or.* 432 (Schwartz); Gorg. *Pal.* DK 82 B11a.3; for an analysis of Deiphobus' *phthonos*, see Karamanou 2011, 44–46.
[23] For the features of *divine phthonos*, see Walcot 1978, 22–37, 41–51; Bulman 1992, 31–36; Milobenski 1964, 36–37; Lloyd-Jones 1983^2, 55–58.
[24] Murray 1946, 128–48 and 1932, 645–56 followed by Barlow 1986, 30; Dunn 1996, 112–13; Shapiro/ Burian 2009, 9.

reflects the socio-political ambiguity of that period. The brutality and vagueness of contemporary warfare, as well as the abusive power of the mighty over the weaker (an idea recalling the Melian Dialogue in Th. 5.84–116 with reference to events which broke out in 416 BC), are suggestive of a social and ideological crisis. In the *Trojan Women* Euripides seems to have aimed at conveying a strong anti-war message, whilst powerfully illustrating throughout this dramatic production the ambiguity and frailty of human judgment in that troubled period.[25]

Hence, the unity of the 'Trojan trilogy' does not rest upon a tightly constructed continuity of plot, which is represented in most trilogies of Aeschylus. As argued above, this production displays thematic and conceptual coherence, as well as structural links among the plays, such as the aforementioned mirror scenes. Its unity may thus be perceived not as a tight sequence of plot, as in Aeschylean trilogies, but rather as a sequence of thought.

In his 'Trojan trilogy' Euripides largely draws his mythical material from the cyclic epics of the seventh and sixth century BC. In more specific terms, the subject-matter of the *Palamedes* is provided in the *Cypria* (fr. 30 Bernabé), having also been treated in the *Palamedes* tragedies by Aeschylus and Sophocles, and that of the *Trojan Women* mainly derives from the cyclic poem *Iliou Persis*. Similarly, the *Alexandros* contains elements narrated in the *Cypria*, such as Cassandra's foretelling of the disaster which is to be caused by Alexandros[26] and her probable reference to the Judgment.[27] Yet, the theme of Alexandros' exposure and reunion with his family, which is treated in the *Alexandros* tragedies by Euripides and Sophocles, does not occur in Proclus' brief summary of the *Cypria*. The earliest evidence for the exposure motif in this legend is found in early fifth-century iconography depicting Alexandros' recognition and reunion with his natal family.[28] Due to the fragmentary state of Pindar's *Paean* VIIIa fr. 52i (A) 14–25 Sn.-M., there is no concrete literary reference to the boy's exposure before

---

[25] See Murray 1946, 126f., 141–48; Hose 1995, 35–36, 47–57; Falcetto 2002, 32–37 (with rich earlier bibliography); Croally 1994, 232–33; Goff 2009, 27–35; Mastronarde 2010, 77–78; Shapiro/ Burian 2009, 4–7. For the events of that period, see Kagan 1981; Rhodes 2011², 53–59, 75–76; Hornblower 1983, 140–42.

[26] See hyp. *Alex.*: P.Oxy. 3650. 27–28, E. *Alexandros* frr. 62e–h K., Ennius *Alexander* frr. 17, 25, 26 J. and Procl. *Chrest.* 93–94; nonetheless, in Proclus' summary of the *Cypria* Cassandra foresees the impending disaster at the point of Alexandros' departure for Greece to gain Helen (cf. similarly Pi. *Paean* VIIIa, fr. 52i (A) 7–25 Sn.–M. and schol. ad 52i (A) 1–9) and not within the context of the reunion with his natal family, as in Euripides.

[27] See Ennius *Alexander* fr. 17. 47–49 J. and Procl. *Chrest.* 86–90; cf. also West 2013, 59–60, 75–79, 83–85. On the tragic reception of the Epic Cycle, see most recently Sommerstein 2015, 461–86.

[28] See *LIMC* I, s.v. 'Alexandros', figg. 16 and 17 dated to 485 and 470 BC respectively.

fifth-century tragedy, apart from a description of Hecabe's ill-omened dream preserved in this Pindaric passage.²⁹

Although Euripides does not treat Homeric episodes as such in this production, it is particularly interesting that he tends to reiterate Homeric characterization and ideology. His appropriation of Homeric ideology probably rests upon the widely held assumption that Homer's epics superseded the other epic traditions through an adaptation of the heroic tradition to the new self-image of Greek culture and the shaping of collective memory towards the end of the archaic period.³⁰ The epic tradition of the Trojan myth thus crystallized into the Homeric poems, which became an indisputable frame of reference and an inseparable part of classical Greek identity.

Basic Homeric features appropriated and refigured by Euripides in his 'Trojan trilogy', such as the anthropomorphic gods and the character-sketching of Hecabe, Helen, Odysseus and Andromache, have already been the subject of much study.³¹ My purpose is to focus selectively on less studied and even unexplored aspects of Homeric reception by Euripides from the standpoint of his tragic rhetoric, which enables him to approach elements of the epic tradition through late fifth-century spectacles.

In an earlier paper I argued that the fragmentary material from the *Alexandros* preserves parts of an interesting second agon clearly signposted as an ἅμιλλα λόγων between Hector and his brother Deiphobus before their mother Hecabe as a judge.³² The objective of this formal debate, which takes place after the athletic triumph of the herdsman Alexandros, is Hector's disagreement with his brother's intention to have the unknown herdsman eliminated. Deiphobus resents the encroachment on his royal status by the socially inferior herdsman, who deprived him of the prize at the games, which the prince regards as his legitimate privilege and rightful possession. As I mentioned above, Deiphobus' emotion could be best described as *phthonos*, which involves the resentment

---

29 See also Robert 1881, 233–39; Snell 1937, 58; Stinton 1965, 56–57; Guidorizzi 2000, 341; Collard/ Cropp/ Gibert 2004, 43; Tsagalis 2008c, 83–84. On the other hand, Jouan 1966, 135–37 favoured the possibility that the exposure motif originates in the *Cypria*.
30 See Finkelberg 2007, 169–88; Graziosi 2002, 235–54, esp. 240 and on the vast importance of Homer for tragedy, see, for instance, Griffin 1998, 56; Easterling 1997, 25; Davidson 2012, esp. 245–46. For Euripides' dialogue with Homer, see Lange 2002; Croally 1994, 17–21; Mossman 1995, esp. 19–47; Davidson 1999–2000, 117–28.
31 See Poole 1976, 280–81; Desch 1985; Barlow 1986, 19, 26–27; Garner 1990, 165–67; Hardwick 1992, 236–37; Croally 1994, 227–34; Easterling 1997, 173–77; Worman 1997; Xanthakis-Karamanos 1998, 32–36; Davidson 1999–2000, 126–28; Davidson 2001; Worman 2002, 120–22; Canavero 2004, 171–85; Dimock 2008, 76–80; Montiglio 2011, 3–12; Marshall 2012.
32 For the substantiation of this scene as an agon, see Karamanou 2011.

one feels against people who rise above themselves, violating the status rules of a highly class conscious society,[33] and is also closely related to athletic prowess.[34] His ethical stance follows the requirements of a shame culture and the attention which must be paid to acknowledge one's honour.

Homeric ethics form part of the ideological nexus of a shame culture, according to which a man pursues the expressed ideal norm of society, whilst internalizing the anticipated judgments of others on himself (on the distinction between shame culture and guilt culture and their implications for Homeric reception in the classical period, see also Volonaki and Mantzouranis in this volume).[35] In the *Iliad* Deiphobus participates in the battle in 13.156 ff., 413–16 and asserts his honour by killing Hypsenor to avenge the death of Asius and vaunting that a payment in honour for honour has been made.[36] After Homer, he is also mentioned by Alcaeus (*SLG* fr. S262.12) to have been killed during the sack of Troy and is given prominence by Euripides as rival and near-murderer of Alexandros in the homonymous play.[37] Deiphobus' feeling of *phthonos* due to his defeat by the herdsman Alexandros in Euripides rests upon an ideal self-image which is placed under threat and an awareness of the standards under which he is liable to be criticized.[38] Accordingly, he disparages Hector's moderate attitude towards the herdsman's victory, accusing his brother of being conspicuous to the Trojans as inferior to a slave (fr. 62a.14 K.). The Homeric *persona* of Deiphobus is thus appropriated by Euripides and presented to commend the traditional competitive values of honour and fame of the Iliadic shame culture. His persistence in reasserting his honour by going as far as attempting to eliminate the triumphant herdsman makes him an unsympathetic character in the Euripidean play.

In this formal debate Deiphobus' *phthonos* is brought into sharp contrast with Hector's *sōphrosynē* (fr. 62a.7–8, 11–12, 16 K.) and sense of justice towards the herdsman's well-earned victory (fr. 62b.10–13 K.).[39] His justice and moderation are co-operative excellences and constituent features of a quiet moral behaviour commended in late fifth-century Athens. The Euripidean depiction of Hector's moderation draws

---

[33] Arist. *Rh.* 1387b 22–1388a 24; *EE* 1233b 19 f.; *EN* 1108b 3–5; see Ben-Ze'ev 2003, 106–12; Konstan 2003, 13–14 and 2006, 125–28.
[34] See Scodel 1980, 75.
[35] The term 'shame culture' was coined by Dodds 1951, 28–63. See also Hammer 2007, 155–58; Redfield 1994², 113–16; Adkins 1960, 154–58, 185–89.
[36] See Wilson 2002, 27, 154; Kyriakou 2001, esp. 256–57.
[37] Deiphobus is employed thereafter as a character in later literature, as in the *Posthomerica* (6.318, 507–08, 8.300, 9.149, 167 ff., 223 ff., 11.340, 13.354 ff.) by Quintus of Smyrna.
[38] For a further description of the features of shame culture, see Cairns 1993, 14–26; Silk 2004², 62.
[39] Karamanou 2011, 44–45.

on his Homeric portrait. In the *Iliad* Hector, who is perceived as representing Troy at its best, combines the traditional qualities of high birth and valour (6.403, 444–46, 7.215–18, 24.214–16, 258–59) with co-operative excellences, such as justice and moderation; he has a strong sense of duty towards his family and homeland, while, at the same time, his mild temper emerges from his human attitude towards Helen by not allowing her to be mistreated (24.767–75) and from his moderation towards furious Achilles in 22.256–57.[40] Hence, the Euripidean agon between Hector and Deiphobus seems to showcase the continued existence of competitive values along with co-operative excellences in late fifth-century Athens,[41] and Euripides exploits the polarity of the argumentation of these Homeric characters to allude to this period of ideological transition.

In the *Iliad* Hector's heroic *ēthos* is clearly defined in contrast with the less heroic character of Alexandros/Paris. In books 3 (30 ff., 264 ff.), 6 (280–85, 325–31, 523–25) and 13 (769–73), Hector strongly disapproves of Paris' reluctance to fight and his military weakness.[42] Alexandros/Paris seems to display an almost unsocialized attitude, in that he is insensitive to the moral disapproval of others, including Helen, who expresses her low opinion of him in books 3 (428–36) and 6 (349–53).[43] Accordingly, I would suggest that in the *Alexandros* Euripides seems to have taken up the Homeric idea of Paris' clash with his social context, as Alexandros/Paris comes to conflict with his foster-environment, that is, the group of his fellow-herdsmen in the aforementioned first agon of the play, in which he is accused of haughty behaviour. In the argumentation employed in this trial-debate, Alexandros is rebuked for his fondness for the noble class (fr. 50 K.) and for his arrogance, which is described as useless and vile (fr. 48 K.), arousing the hostility of his fellow-herdsmen. This accusation displays his anti-social attitude and bears serious implications in a period in which one's usefulness to the household and the *polis* was regarded as a cardinal virtue of the good citizen.[44]

---

40 For Hector's moderation, see also Aeschylus' *Phrygians* or *The Ransoming of Hector* fr. 264 R. (and Sommerstein 2008, 267).
41 On the coexistence of competitive and co-operative excellences towards the end of the fifth century, see Cairns 1993, 265–342; Adkins 1960, 156–68.
42 See also the delineation of Hector's virtue by Priam as compared to his other sons (including Paris) in 24.248–54. For Paris' unheroic portrait, see, for instance, Gartziou-Tatti 1992, 73–80, 85–90.
43 See Redfield 1994², 113–15.
44 Dover 1974, 296–98; Fouchard 1997, 194–99; Adkins 1972, 115 ff.; Bryant 1996, 151–68, 205; Pearson 1962, 181–82.

Unlike Hector and Andromache, who are presented particularly in book 6 of the *Iliad* as embodying virtue and loyalty to their household and homeland,[45] the figures of Alexandros/Paris and Helen are displayed as representing calamity and social disorder. I shall argue that book 6 also seems to provide the main material for Euripides' reception of Helen's figure in his 'Trojan trilogy'. In fact, it may not be fortuitous that Euripides regularly draws on this very book for issues of characterization and ideology, particularly with regard to Helen, Hector and Andromache. As has been observed, book 6 of the *Iliad* succeeds in arousing the tragic emotions of pity and fear, by underscoring the clash between individual needs and social expectations and delineating the psychological complexity of the characters, as well as divine detachment,[46] thus providing ample material for the shaping of a tragic plot.

Eustathius was the first to note that this book includes a manipulative —and almost seductive (according to Graziosi and Haubold)— speech of Helen addressed to Hector in front of Paris.[47] To appease Hector's anger towards his brother, she addresses him with soothing, 'honey-sweet words' (6.343: μύθοισι ...μειλιχίοισι), which may well be paralleled to the honeyed, dangerously seductive manner of the Sirens in book 12 of the *Odyssey* (12.187: μελίγηρυν).[48] Helen attributes her abduction to the will of the gods and sides with Hector, isolating herself from Paris whom she regards as morally insensitive, as he does not bear the burden of his shameful acts (6.344–58). At the same time, she seems to be guilt-ridden and remorseful, wishing that she had died in infancy,[49] and even employs a rhetoric of self-abuse, through which she finally succeeds in gaining sympathy and deflecting blame by others.[50] Hector's reaction to her speech is self-controlled, though he clearly describes her tactics as involving the rhetoric of persuasion (6.360: οὐδέ με πείσεις).

---

45 See Redfield 1994², 122 ff.; Schein 1984, 173–77; Graziosi/Haubold 2010, 29–31; Katz 1981; Grethlein 2006, 246, 250.
46 See Redfield 1994², 69–98; Graziosi/Haubold 2010, 26.
47 See Eust. schol. *Il.* 6.354–55, 360–62 (Vol. II 328 van der Valk) describing Helen's attitude towards Hector as flattering and wheedling; see especially II 328, 9–10 (van der Valk): Ἑλένη μὲν κολακεύουσα τὸν Ἕκτορα, 17–18: ἔοικε δὲ Ἕκτωρ ἐν τούτοις ὑποπτεύειν τὸ τῆς Ἑλένης αἱμύλον and 22: κολακευτικῶς ἡ σοφὴ Ἑλένη ἐναβρύνεται. Cf. Graziosi/Haubold 2010, 43–44.
48 See also Katz 1981, 28–29.
49 Cf. similarly *Il.* 3.173–75, 24.763–64; see Maguire 2009, 113–14.
50 See Worman 2007, 156–57; Day 2008, 83–98.

I suggest that Helen's speech in the *Iliad* seems to be echoed in her *adikos logos* in the formal debate in E. *Tr.* 914–65.[51] Her dangerously polite and softening words towards Menelaus at the beginning of the agon (*Tr.* 895–900, 903–04) recall her soothing approach of Hector in the Homeric passage. Following her Homeric *persona* and appropriating Homeric argumentation, Helen in *Tr.* 935–37 refers to her ill reputation and casts herself to the role of the victim of divine will and Paris' actions (*Tr.* 919–31, 940–50), in order to be released from blame. Nonetheless, unlike her Iliadic remorseful self, Helen's *persona* is transformed by Euripides, in that she goes as far as explicitly and shamelessly denying her culpability (*Tr.* 916–65). The denial of her personal responsibility is the main line of argumentation also in Gorgias' famous defence of Helen, which serves to illustrate the power of rhetorical ability.[52] Her seductive stance and manipulative approach based on her beauty and her soothing use of words, which do not mislead Hector in the Iliadic passage, are appropriated in her unjust rhetoric and provocative appearance with the purpose of luring Menelaus in the Euripidean agon, and are strongly reprimanded by Hecabe and the female Chorus-leader (*Tr.* 966–68, 1022–28). The latter is not taken in by Helen's rhetorical skill, which she regards as employed at the expense of truth and justice (*Tr.* 967–68: πειθὼ διαφθείρουσα τῆσδ', ἐπεὶ λέγει/ καλῶς κακοῦργος οὖσα), echoing Hector's aforementioned remark about her rhetoric in the Homeric passage. Furthermore, in the Iliadic scene Helen sets up a triangle among herself, Paris and Hector, noting their fame in future poetry (6.357–58);[53] the triangle-pattern is reconfigured in two levels within the Euripidean formal debate: among herself, Menelaus and dead Paris throughout her speech, as well as among herself, Paris and his rival Deiphobus at a particular point of her rhetorical narration (*Tr.* 959–60).

Euripides' reception of Helen's seductive and manipulative rhetoric of persuasion in the Iliadic passage may also be explored from the viewpoint of audience response. To gain sympathy, the Homeric Helen blames herself, whilst taking, at the same time, a fatalistic view of the plight which has been caused. In Homer she is the daughter of Zeus (3.171, 199, 228, 418, 426) and as such she is released from the blame of others, being presented as the means of implementing Zeus' *nemesis* (3.164–65).[54] Helen's theocentric position in the *Iliad* is trans-

---

[51] For Helen's *adikos logos*, see Basta Donzelli 1986, 389–409; De Romilly 1976, 311–21; Croally 1994, 142–49; Gellie 1986; Conacher 1998, 51–57; Lloyd 1984, 307–09; Meridor 2000, 16–29; Gregory 1991, 171–73.
[52] Gorg. *Hel.* DK 82 B11.6–7; see Worman 1997; Consigny 2001, 60–94, 104–07; Ballif 2001, 65–99; Bergren 1983, 82–86.
[53] See Graziosi/Haubold 2010, 43.
[54] Cf. *Cypria* fr. 1 Bernabé; see Austin 1994, 26–32 and 2007, 34–36; Roisman 2006, 5–20.

planted into the Euripidean play and put into criticism within the context of the agon and, in turn, before the audience. The dramatist introduces Hecabe as Helen's rhetorical opponent and enters into a 'dialogue' with aspects of the latter's Homeric *persona* and the surrounding ideology. Hecabe's rationalistic refutation of Helen's position unveils the injustice concealed in the latter's rhetorical elaboration and the unscrupulousness hidden behind her manipulative stance. Accordingly, in the eyes of the fifth-century audience, divine influence as such does not seem to count as an excuse, since passion may be involuntary, that is, god-sent, but one's response is not.[55] Therefore, the theocentric argumentation employed by Helen would have been questionable in everyday life and tends to be commonly associated in tragedy with characters whose attitude is immoral, as the Nurse in *Hipp.* 433–81 and Pasiphae in *Cretans* fr. 472e K.[56] At the end of the debate the irony is palpable, since Helen's power of words and appearance—also stressed by Gorgias (DK 82 B11.8–14, 16–19)— leads to her actual victory in the agon, in that she manages to escape death, whereas Hecabe is the 'moral' winner in the eyes of the audience.[57]

Consequently, Euripides' response to the epic tradition in his 'Trojan trilogy' does not merely involve the tragic shaping of the mythical legacy of early *epos*. Rather, the dramatist engages in a complex dialogue with Homeric characterization and ideology, whilst regularly embedding his epic referents within agonistic contexts, in accordance with the sophistic doctrine of *dissoi logoi*. In the *Alexandros* the distinction between Homeric competitive values and fifth-century co-operative excellences is eloquently drawn in the Hector-Deiphobus agon. At the same time, the anti-social Iliadic portrait of Alexandros/Paris seems to be appropriated in the first formal debate of the same play and is opposed to the cardinal fifth-century virtue of usefulness. Furthermore, Helen's Homeric *persona* is refigured and challenged in the trial-debate of the *Trojan Women*. In the agon heroic values tend to be confronted with new modes of thought,[58] and Euripides often juxtaposes aspects of traditional and contemporary ideology within the rhetorical framework of his formal debates. Likewise, in the famous debate of the *Antiope* between Zethus and Amphion representing the *vita activa* and *vita contemplativa* respectively, Euripides draws a sharp contrast between the traditional

---

[55] On this fifth-century ideological position, see Adkins 1960, 14–16, 22–25, 120–27; Guthrie 1971, 228–30; Lloyd-Jones 1983², 150–51; Dodds 1951, 185–86.
[56] Barrett 1964, 238–48; Gregory 1991, 67–70; Dolfi 1984, 125–38; Reckford 1974, 319–28; Rivier 1975, 48–60.
[57] See Dubischar 2001, esp. 342–48; Barlow 1986, 207–08.
[58] See Croally 1994, 135–37; Goldhill 1997, 148–49; Vernant/Vidal-Naquet 1986, 21–31; Lloyd 1992, 104–05; Kamerbeek 1958, *passim*.

competitive values and the quieter virtues of late fifth century.[59] Euripides thus refigures aspects of Homeric ideology, by juxtaposing them to late fifth-century ethics; the dynamics of his tragic rhetoric give ample scope for a dialogue which brings to the fore the dialectic, as well as the tension between the virtues of the epic tradition and the values of his own era.

---

[59] On this debate, see Carter 1986, 163–73; Gibert 2009, 26–34; Slings 1991; Kerferd 1981, 84–85. Famous comic parallels of the clash between traditional and contemporary ideology representing the common theme of 'New vs Old' are provided in the agon scenes of Ar. *Nu.* 889–1114 and *Ra.* 830–1481 (see Dover 1968, lxii-lxiii and 1972, 183–89).

Varvara Georgopoulou
Andromache's Tragic *Persona* from the Ancient to the Modern Stage

This essay aims at exploring the reception of the Homeric figure of Andromache within the dramatic genre across cultural contexts. The transformation of the Homeric material by Euripides, Seneca, Racine, Jean Giraudoux and Akis Dimou could provide an overview of the key stages in the reception history of this legend in theatre, as well as of the cultural processes shaping its refiguration over a wide time-span and within different intellectual and artistic contexts.[1]

Although Andromache's appearance in the *Iliad* occupies a rather small space, she has become a symbolic figure in world literature. This is mainly due to the moral and aesthetic function of the famous meeting of Hector and Andromache at the walls of Troy in the Iliadic passage (6.390–493). Within the ominous war atmosphere culminating at the duel of its two protagonists (Achilles and Hector), the peaceful and harmonious encounter of the couple in a military epic is an impressive indication of Homer's knowledge of human nature, focusing on human needs as against social norms (on the sixth book of the *Iliad* and its reception, see also Karamanou in this volume). Andromache, the daughter of the great Eetion, king of Cilician Thebes (6.395), enjoyed the honour of becoming the wife of brave Hector and a noblewoman of Troy. The serenity and happiness of her home were suddenly overturned by the invasion of the Achaeans which deprived her violently of her paternal family. As she says to Hector: Ἕκτορ ἀτὰρ σύ μοί ἐσσι πατὴρ καὶ πότνια μήτηρ/ ἠδὲ κασίγνητος, σὺ δέ μοι θαλερὸς παρακοίτης (6.429–31; see also A. Michalopoulos in this volume). One cannot help but admire their feelings for each other and Hector's warm sympathy expressing his anxiety about her fate (6.429).[2] Andromache's fears are soon to be justified: as she is preparing Hector's bath to relieve his exhausted body after the battle, Achilles' horses are dragging his corpse (22.448). Andromache rushes out of her house μαινάδι ἴση (22.461), as she sees the terrible sight she swoons, and, when she comes to her senses again, she bursts into a heart-rending lament (22.477–514), τὴν δὲ κατ' ὀφθαλμῶν ἐρεβεννὴ νὺξ ἐκάλυψεν (22.466).[3]

---

[1] On the significance of the exploration of these complex processes in the field of classical reception studies, see, for instance, Hardwick 2003, esp. 3–11; Hardwick/ Stray 2008, 1–5; Martindale 2007, 297–311.
[2] On this scene, see Schein 1984, 173–77; Graziosi/ Haubold 2010, 29–31.
[3] For more detail, see Segal 1971, 33–57; Grethlein 2006, 247–51; Dué 2006, ch. 1

An eloquent contrast may be drawn between the dark atmosphere of the Homeric farewell scene between husband and wife and Sappho's *epithalamium* preserved in fr. 44.24–34 L.-P., which describes the arrival of the two newlyweds at Troy. The latter scene is perfectly structured in both content and form reflecting social and artistic contexts, the outer and inner world of the poetess.[4] The *persona* of Andromache, the noblewoman and the model wife and mother of Homeric heritage losing everything and becoming a captive and a slave-concubine, was to be taken over by the tragic Muse, who continued her story, appropriating, as well as deviating from the Homeric source text.

Greek and Roman tragedy constitute key phases in the reception history of Andromache's *persona*, not least because they provide insight into those aspects of the Homeric legend which were refigured in later theatre. Of the three great tragic poets Euripides innovated in the description of human passions and of female psychology. The political circumstances of the Peloponnesian War and the social resonances of the sophistic movement formulate the key lines of the framework within which his plays may be located and assessed.[5] Euripides transformed the Homeric Andromache presenting her as the protagonist in the tragedy of the same title and as a secondary character in the *Trojan Women*.

The *Andromache* was produced in the 420s (possibly in 425 BC)[6] and treats the events following the Trojan War. The title-heroine lives in Phthia as a captive and concubine of Neoptolemus, the son of Achilles who was her husband's murderer. Neoptolemus is absent and his lawful wife, Hermione, threatens to kill Andromache along with the little son whom she has borne to Neoptolemus. Andromache has fled as a suppliant to Thetis' altar. Her character in this play, as it emerges from her formal debate with Hermione, is consistent with her Homeric figure, as far as wisdom, patience and maternal love are concerned (*Andr.* 147–273). At the same time, Euripides reshapes Andromache's *persona*, in that she employs rhetorical elaboration and solid argumentation. This agon is most interesting not least because it touches on issues of female psychology by presenting two diametrically opposite views of the female role. The haughty behaviour and female independence of Hermione as a high-born wife are eloquently contrasted to Andromache's representation of the submissive, devoted and tolerant wife. As the latter advises the arrogant Spartan Hermione: φίλτρον δὲ καὶ τόδ'· οὐ τὸ κάλλος, ὦ γύναι, ἀλλ' ἀρεταὶ τέρπουσι τοὺς ξυνευνέτας (*Andr.* 207–08: 'it is not our beauty but our virtues that fascinate our bed-partners'). This onstage conflict between the two rivals disputing over their

---

4 See Bowra 1961, 236–39.
5 See, for instance, Conacher 1998; Egli 2003, 136–216; Vellacott 1975, ch. 6.
6 See Stevens 1971, 15–18; Lloyd 1994, 11–12.

twin beds, which is an innovation in the treatment of this legend, is a significant piece of evidence for Euripidean ideology, aesthetics and approach to matters of gender.[7] Euripides also exploits this particular dramatic situation to implicitly criticize the Spartans, as well as to challenge the widely held polarity between Greeks and 'barbarians' and the unjustified bragging of the Greeks. Andromache constantly stresses that she still regards Hector as her husband and that she was coerced to become Neoptolemus' concubine.[8]

In the ensuing dialogue with Menelaus Andromache deviates from the Homeric standards of female virtue and argues so strongly before the Spartan king, that the Chorus-leader accuses her: ἄγαν ἔλεξας ὡς γυνὴ πρὸς ἄρσενας (*Andr.* 364: 'you said a lot to men, you being a woman'). Then, in her lament when Menelaus threatens to kill her son if she does not leave the altar, she is presented as the affectionate and death-stricken mother we have seen in Homer; this theme recurs in the *Trojan Women*.[9] Instead of erotic enchantment and sensuality, the barbarian Andromache pleads for prudence and continence, which is a dominant idea in Euripides' critical and poetical reflection. This tragedy displays certain peculiarities not only with regard to its diverse plot-structure, but also in terms of Andromache's elegiac lamentation in the Doric dialect (*Andr.* 103–16). This lament, which is the only example of elegiac metre in extant Greek tragedy, has led some critics to assume that it may originate in a lost tradition of threnodic elegy.[10]

The *Trojan Women* was produced later in 415 BC, when the Athenians were preparing for the Sicilian expedition and had already invaded the island of Melos (in the previous year), which they occupied, having slaughtered the men and enslaved children and women. The fate of the Homeric heroine has been interpreted as an implicit Euripidean criticism of the aggressive Athenian policy and of the effects of war on human condition.[11] In the second episode of the *Trojan Women* (*Tr.* 577–779) Andromache maintains her Homeric profile, consisting chiefly of female wisdom, dignity and companionship, which however enhance her misery, as they inspire Achilles' son, Neoptolemus, with the desire to take her with him to Greece. Andromache cries bitterly because she would rather die than betray Hector with another man, but Hecabe advises her to submit herself to her new master and forget her dear late husband, in the hope of helping the future resurrection of

---

[7] See also Allan 2000, *passim*; Gould 1980, 56; Lloyd 1994, 6–9; Conacher 1967, 167–69.
[8] See McClure 1999, ch. 5; Mastronarde 2010, 275–79.
[9] See Lloyd 1994, 124–35.
[10] See particularly Page 1936, 206–30; contra Bowie 1986, 22.
[11] See Murray 1932, 645–46; Croally 1994, 232–33; De Romilly 1986, ch. 5; Shapiro/Burian 2009, 4–7; Delebecque 1951, 254ff.; Goossens 1962, 520ff.

Troy perhaps through her offspring (*Tr.* 577–683).[12] However, a new lamentation of Andromache follows Talthybius' announcement that Odysseus has decided to have Astyanax thrown down from the walls of Troy (*Tr.* 709–779). The image of Andromache, clasping her little son on her bosom, has been recorded in world art as a symbol of maternal affection, as well as of the brutality of war (on the cinematic reception of the *Trojan Women*, see Bakogianni in this volume).

In his own *Troades* Seneca innovates compared to Euripides' *Trojan Women* and *Hecabe*, which are his main source texts.[13] According to his aesthetic predilections, he increases the *pathos* of his drama by adding to Astyanax's execution the repulsive sacrifice of the Trojan princess Polyxena on Achilles' tomb. Andromache becomes totally obsessed with fear and lies to Odysseus about Astyanax's fate, as her maternal love makes her abandon her regal dignity: 'Show me flames, wounds and the terrible art of tortures, hunger, cruel thirst, several punishments. All kinds of irons in my suffering flesh, a prison with suffocating darkness and everything that a victor dares to do when he is angry or afraid. A mother's soul is not scared' (*Tro.* 582–88). As with most of her literary refigurations, Andromache is seeing the dead Hector in Astyanax: 'In my son, Hector, I love only you. Make him live, so that you will live again' (*Tro.* 646–48). Virgilian echoes (*Aen.* 2.270–97) are evident in her wish that her son lives to create a new Troy.[14]

In the context of French Classicism, Racine returns to Virgil, whilst bringing erotic passion to the fore. Jean Racine's *Andromaque* (1667) is one of his early plays helping him to establish himself on the Parisian stage and emerge as a worthy rival of Pierre Corneille, the dominant poet of that period. Despite his young age, Racine was already experienced in treating human passions. According to his own account given in the prologue he had written for his play (Racine 1994, 15–16), he derived the dramatic locale, the plot and heroes from the third book of Virgil's *Aeneid*, except for Hermione, who originates in Euripides. He studied and admired the plays of the latter in the humanistic environment of the Port-Royal monastery, where he had been raised and educated. Still, in the same prologue he emphatically draws attention to his conscious deviation from the Euripidean plot: in contrast to Euripides' *Andromache*, who had a son by Pyrrhus, his own Andromache 'does not recognize another husband besides Hector and has no other son besides Astyanax' (*ibid.* 19). Racine defends poetic freedom in his handling of the legend and focuses on the manner in

---

12 See Barlow 1986, 190–91; Dué 2006, 13–14.
13 For more detail, see Schiesaro 2003, 190–202; Fantham 2011, 457–74; Ahl 1986, 35–40; Calder 1970.
14 See Schiesaro 2003, 195.

which a poet adapts the available material to his subject, thus highlighting the complexity of the reception process.[15] He mainly draws on Virgil, presenting Andromache as married to another son of Priam, the seer Helenus, who grabbed from Aeacus' son, Pyrrhus, his wife and royal power (*Aen.* 3.294–504); thus, 'Andromache came again into the possession of a paternal husband' (3.297). Racine retains chiefly from Virgil Andromache's devotion to Hector, which characteristically emerges from her description as 'wife of Hector' (3.488: *coniugis Hectoreae*), and the transfer of Troy to her new country symbolized by Hector's cenotaph and the false Simoens (3.300–05).[16]

The French dramatist places unrequited love and passion to the core of his tragedy, raising issues of gender and female character-sketching: his Andromache continues to be in love with her dead Trojan husband and, albeit a captive and a slave, does not dare to reciprocate the love of her master, Pyrrhus. The latter is enamoured of her, despising Hermione provocatively. Hermione is madly in love with Pyrrhus and rejects the love of Orestes, her childhood friend, who is eager to commit crimes for her sake. Of this group of love-stricken people, only Andromache has enjoyed mutual love and wants to remain faithful to Hector's memory by adoring her son, Astyanax, whom she identifies with Hector, thus enraging Pyrrhus: 'She always talked about Hector. In vain did I guarantee her son's safety; "he is Hector", she said and clasped her offspring his hands, "his lips, his courage, I recognize it's you my precious husband, the one I am now touching". What is she thinking? That I am going to leave her son with her to keep the flame of her love alive?' (Act 2, Scene 5, 650–56).

Racine's characters talk incessantly about the object of their love, change moods and feelings all the time contradicting themselves;[17] only Andromache remains stable and clear-minded. In her eyes Pyrrhus is the violent and bloodthirsty conqueror, who killed her brothers and sisters during the fatal night when Troy fell, and nothing can erase this memory. Hector's image is dominant in her thoughts, which she interrupts only to address him, talking to him as if he were alive. The memories of the fall of Troy, of the violent extinction of her compatriots and the atrocities of the conquerors are always present for her, and by visiting Hector's cenotaph she is searching for a solution to her dilemmas, when Pyrrhus' threat to kill her son becomes oppressive. Eventually, she decides to commit suicide immediately after the wedding, in order to save her son and at the same time remain faithful to Hector. Nonetheless, fate works in her favour:

---

[15] See, for instance, Goodkin 1989.
[16] See Martinez-Cuadrado 1986, 159–214; Otis 1964, 253–61; Berthelot 1992; Couprie 1996; Décélé 2005; Elliott 1969, *passim*; Defaux 1977, 22–31.
[17] See De Romilly 1995, 36–37; Racevskis 2008, 75–85.

Pyrrhus' unexpected death releases her from her gnawing dilemma and makes her a queen. Once more the Trojan woman has the divine favour of fulfilling her desire to remain faithful to her true love.

Racinean passion is a substitute for God or Fate, is all-powerful and thus destructive. The lovelorn Pyrhhus says: 'Love wins and uproots perniciously' (Act 4, Scene 5, 1297). He has totally succumbed to the erotic spell, which leads him to confront Trojans and Greeks, and before dying he crowns Andromache as Queen. In Racine's plays madness and passions are dominant: Pyrrhus and Hermione die, Orestes loses his mind. Through Andromache's literary *persona* Racine reaffirms Trojan merit, identity and status, as legend has it that French people descend from them.[18]

Some centuries later, Jean Giraudoux, the most prominent French playwright of Interwar years, revisited Andromache appropriating the Homeric legend to correspond to his antiwar visions. Giraudoux had an excellent classical education and was also trained theoretically and practically in the school of war – he was wounded in World War I and decorated for bravery. Subsequently, he had a solid theatrical presence, especially through his co-operation with a famous man of the theatre, Louis Jouvet, who staged almost all of his plays. In 1936 Jouvet produced, directed and played in Giraudoux's *The Trojan War Will Not Take Place* in the Théâtre de l'Athénée. Giraudoux drew his material from ancient myths, in order to express the humanistic quests of his turbulent times. This play presents prominent features of his dramaturgy: humanism, the conflict with destiny, dilemmas concerning the choice between two opposite options, the emergence of simplicity in complexity and of the extraordinary in the ordinary. Giraudoux was a master of style at a time when theatre directing was taking precedence and made stage language a sublime tool of expression.[19]

Giraudoux chose Andromache in the opening scene of his play, in order to express his ideological position –based on wish and hope at the same time – when she announces to the prophetess Cassandra that 'The Trojan War will not take place' (Act 1, Scene 1). As always, Andromache is Hector's beloved and loyal wife and is pregnant with his son, to whom she sees Hector, as she did earlier in Euripides, Seneca and Racine: 'I am interested in him because he is yours'. Her question to Hector, 'Do you love war?' (Act 1, Scene 3) reveals the pervasive influence of war on human conscience and the contradictory feelings towards the enemy. Andromache is constantly defending peace, refuting

---

[18] For this legend, see for instance Bizer 2011, ch. 1.
[19] See Brockett 1995, 482; Body 1986, esp. ch. 1; Reilly 1978; Moraud 1936, 13–29; Le Sage 1958; Mercier-Campiche 1954.

Priam's arguments: 'You always die for your country, when you have lived as a worthy, active, wise man' (Act 1, Scene 6).

Giraudoux's idiosyncratic irony, which makes him resemble the playwrights of the Absurd,[20] demystifies the love affair between Paris and Helen as much as the marital harmony between Andromache and Hector: 'Hector is my direct opposite. He does not share any of my tastes. We spend every day either by beating one another or by sacrificing ourselves. Happy spouses do not have clear faces'. In his portrayal of the couple Giraudoux follows the dramatic path opened by August Strindberg's incessantly fighting couples, which will be later taken over by the hostile couples of the Absurd. Andromache represents ordinary and peaceful life and is aware of destiny, whose sound and echo dominate in the play,[21] giving a tragic dimension even to humoristic scenes. 'I do not know what destiny is', Andromache confesses to Cassandra, whose very figure encapsulates destiny (Act 1, Scene 1). The only power against almighty destiny is love. Perhaps love is the only thing worthy of a war, so 'Helen must love Paris, since no one, not even destiny itself, can attack destiny light-heartedly' (Act 2, Scene 8) is Andromache's argument towards the unrepentant Helen.

Modern Greek theatre widely receives and reshapes ancient tragic myths starting with the *Iphigenia* written by the Cephalonian dramatist Petros Katsaitis in 1720. Systematic refigurations of tragic legends appear from the Interwar period onwards reaching their peak in Postwar times (on the transformation of ancient myths in modern Greek theatre, see also Petrakou in this volume). The playwrights of that era enter into a creative dialogue with their ancient tragic models often deviating consciously from their source texts, as in Iakovos Kambanellis' trilogy *O Deipnos* (*The Last Supper*, 1993).[22]

The monologue *Andromache or Landscape of a Woman in the Height of the Night* (1999) written by the Greek playwright Akis Dimou is embedded within the context of postmodernist trends towards radical reworkings of ancient myths, which developed at the end of the 20th and the start of the 21st century. Dimou is a main representative of postmodernism in modern Greek theatre, and his production belongs to the genre of poetic drama. The dominant features of all his plays are intertextual dialogue and female presence.[23]

In the prologue the dramatist mentions that he has selected Virgil's version, according to which Neoptolemus gave Andromache to Helenus, Hector's brother, who is a seer and ended up being a captive and a slave like her. She finds refuge

---

20 See Kofidou 2004, *passim*.
21 See Frois/ Lesot 1998, 21–24; Albérès 1957; Robichez 1976.
22 On the contexts of these refigurations, see Chasapi-Christodoulou 2002, *passim*.
23 See Georgopoulou 2009, 537–45.

in a place in Epirus and settles there in a quasi Trojan landscape, an imitation of Troy, watered by an equally artificial river, Simoens, a tributary of Scamander (Dimou 2006, 244). Dimou's heroine has experienced deportation, male deception and violence in every possible way. Hence, she imagines and 'creates' a false reality, to which she totally adjusts and with which she identifies herself: 'This city is me, away from cities' (*ibid.* 246). In vain does she seek in Greek language 'a language that can bear the horrible burden of memory' (*ibid.* 245).

Andromache's words reflect insufferable memories full of bloodshed and violent loss: native country, husband, child, her bodily and moral freedom, her womanhood. The ideal vehicle to convey her despair is associative illogical speech, going far and deeply into the dreams and the subconscious and even reaching at some moments a real delirium. Gradually, however, the memories fade and the feelings become blunted: 'I say Helen and I think that I am calling an old friend' (*ibid.* 247). Her female nature claims its rights, as she becomes obsessed with the matter of her erotic deprivation: 'No man has touched me since the first darkness of the world'. This isolation leads her imagination to her first and perhaps one and only erotic interest: 'In the last summer before the war, her erotic instinct woke up and she felt a strong desire for a man who was bathing singing' (*ibid.* 251). This remembrance gives her some stamina and she reveals her suppressed female nature: 'I am a woman and my knowledge, what is left in the mirror's teeth, a lock of my plaits, an edge of my worn out glance' (*ibid.* 256).

Realizing all these, she becomes stronger and comes out of the inertia of ignorance and agony to plunge into conscious action. The weak Andromache at last makes up her mind: 'Forget the promised epic, ignore that they have you as a model, gallop deeply inside yourself, so that the doctrines of time will not touch you' (*ibid.* 257). She is no more the fallen princess of Troy, the devoted wife and affectionate mother. An outcast and isolated, she has found her own self and the strength to manifest it and decide upon her own fate: 'I shall draw vespers, I shall let no one forget' (*ibid.* 258). Dimou's *Andromache* draws on the Iliadic Andromache and the farewell scene, sharing the theme of male cruelty with its epic model. At the same time, features drawn from the Homeric myth are interwoven with everyday episodes and games of the imagination and the subconscious.

Andromache's route from the walls of Troy to the postmodern paths of the subconscious makes her an authentic and everlasting symbol, whose destiny has been shaped by the polarity between love and war. Key themes of the ancient dramatic treatments of Andromache's legend, such as gender issues involving female otherness as defined by war-violence and militarism, are refigured in later theatre under varying historical and socio-cultural circumstances. Andromache as the protagonist in the Euripidean tragedy of the same title and as a secondary character in the *Trojan Women* is appropriated by Euripides to criticize war by castigating the militarism of the Athenian empire and the violence of human nature. At the same time, Andromache's rhetorically elaborate argumentation in her agon with Hermione succeeds in revealing diverse views of the female role. Subsequently, Seneca amplifies the elements of revenge and bloody violence according to his aesthetic predilections, by adding to Astyanax's execution the repulsive sacrifice of Polyxena on Achilles' tomb. Racine brings erotic passion and unreciprocated love to the fore, in conjunction with gender relations, within the literary contexts of French Classicism. Later, on the eve of the Second World War, Jean Giraudoux conveys an anti-military message in his play *The Trojan War Will Not Take Place*. Andromache becomes his mouthpiece expressing his pacifistic ideas and, at the same time, his belief in the power of fate. In the postmodern monologue of the Greek playwright Akis Dimou *Andromache or Landscape of a Woman in the Height of the Night* Andromache appears as stripped of her mythical past and as shaping a new identity. The ending of Dimou's *Andromache*, perhaps the saddest of all Andromaches, concludes the literary route of this figure through time, whilst mirroring all her earlier *personas:* 'I do not know another chain except for love that holds the other so absolutely bound... in this way, born victors become slaves and the defeated triumph' (*ibid.* 248).

Kyriaki Petrakou
Odysseus Satirical: The Merry Dealing of the Homeric Myth in Modern Greek Theatre

The title is playing with a common type of ancient satyr-play titles, the different spelling naturally indicating a different genre. Odysseus' figure as a Homeric intertext in post-antique sources makes its debut in Dante's *Commedia Divina*, in which Odysseus does not return to Ithaca. Subsequently, he appears in Renaissance tragedies drawing on the Trojan War: Robert Garnier's *La Troade* (1579), Shakespeare's *Troilus and Cressida* (1602), Joost van der Vondel's *Palamedes* (1625), Racine's *Iphigénie* (1674).[1] His figure is then employed in a whole series of plays, none of which, however, are comedies. By contrast, in Greek antiquity Odysseus was a popular character in satyr-plays (Aeschylus' *Circe*, Aristias' *Cyclops* and Euripides' *Cyclops* – the only extant play). He also appeared regularly in old comedy, as in Epicharmus' *Cyclops*, *Odysseus the Deserter*, *Odysseus Shipwrecked*, *Sirens*, in Cratinus' *Odysseis*, in Theopompus' *Sirens, Penelope, Odysseus* and in Philyllius' *The Washing Women or Nausicaa*[2] (on Odysseus' parodic refigurations in other genres, see Alexandrou in this volume). In modern theatre, a bitter parody of the Odysseus myth occurs in Jean Giraudoux's *The Trojan War Will Not Take Place* (1935) (on this play, see Georgopoulou in this volume). This subject recurs to this day, not only in drama but also in other forms of contemporary theatre, such as dance theatre and performance.[3]

Mythological comedy or parody, influenced by the French operetta and vaudeville, appeared in modern Greek theatre during the 1870s, when neo-classical tragedy was the dominant genre in drama. Alexandros Rizos Ragavis wrote *Zeus' Visit* (1874) and Spyridon Vasiliadis *Zeus' Love Affairs* or *Semele* (1874). The majority of plays of ancient subject-matter written in that period were serious or tragic.

Most of the plays with Odysseus as the pivotal character, serious or comic, treat his return to Ithaca and the murder of Penelope's suitors.[4] The first play of the comic genre which will be further explored was also staged (rather an exception to the majority of plays written during the 19th century and being destined only for dramatic contests or publication[5]). It was Panagiotis Zanos' 'tragic

---
1 See Grammatas 1994.
2 See, for instance, Revermann 2013, 109–13 and n. 34.
3 Puchner 2005, 328–29.
4 See Chasapi-Christodoulou 2002, 1113–56.
5 See Petrakou 1999.

comedy', as he named it, entitled *Penelope's Suitors and Odysseus' Homecoming* (Zanos 1884). It mainly follows the Homeric plot, while the comic element is provided by the suitors, the slaves and the folk people. It supports the idea that Odysseus is within his rights in imposing the traditional royal power as a divine prerogative. The author dedicated the play to Queen Olga, who accepted the dedication. It was quite a success and remained for more than 15 years in the repertory of several theatrical companies, who performed it in Greece and in Greek communities abroad (Constantinople, Smyrna and perhaps elsewhere).

In the first part of the 20th century satirical Odysseus seems to have appeared as a dramatic subject only in dramatic contests[6] and in the shadow puppet theatre.[7] From the Interwar years to the present, many plays of ancient subject-matter have been written, most of which with contemporary connotations. The preference of the playwrights, however, is for serious content. Of a total of 130 plays written from 1930 to 1980 only 20 use the ancient myth with the purpose of satirizing it.[8] The satirical-political treatment of the myth started during the German Occupation and the Civil War with a focus on the Trojan War and Odysseus-subjects. The playwrights of farce wrote some opportune and bold plays, as *The Trojan War* (1948) by Alekos Sakellarios and Christos Giannakopoulos, in which the three great ancient leaders, Achilles, Agamemnon and Odysseus (representing Churchill, Roosevelt and Stalin) suppress the rights of the peoples. Since the Second World War, a series of satirical plays have been produced by several Greek playwrights, containing criticism of modern social and political contexts in open or disguised connotations, like Iakovos Kambanellis' *Odysseus, Come Home* (1952) and *The Last Act* (1997), Manolis Skouloudis' *Odyssey* (1961), Demetris Christodoulou's *Hotel Circe* (1966), Giorgos Charalambidis' *Penelope's 300*. These and other plays will be analyzed along with their critical reception, with the purpose of exploring the contemporary allusions and nuances of this very popular archetypal myth, as well as the function of Odysseus' refigurations within different socio-political contexts.[9]

The first play of this case-study is the aforementioned comedy *The Trojan War*, which is thought to be a farce (the text has been lost, but its writers are usually labelled as farce-playwrights). On the basis of the reviews it may be inferred that it had contemporary political implications. They cannot have been very radical, however, as the censorship of the time did not ban it.

---

6 Petrakou 1999, *passim*.
7 Chatzipantazis 1984, 105–07.
8 Chasapi-Christodoulou 2002, 1107.
9 On the critical analysis of performances as an essential tool of exploring their reception, see Hardwick 2003, 51–56; Bennett 1990, 86–165; Pavis 2003, 7–52.

Kambanellis' *Odysseus, Come Home*, on the other hand, written in 1950/1952, could not be published or staged until 1966 and then it was understood as political by the majority of the critics of its many productions. In this play Odysseus does not really wish to return to Ithaca and regularly misleads his companions, who regularly rebel against him, but in the end they succumb to his lies. He is far from resembling the divine Homeric hero—he is short, unattractive, worn out. Not even the Trojan Horse was his own invention: he stole the idea from a common soldier named Nikias, who appears in the play, but has no ambition to reveal the truth. Odysseus has arrived at an island whose irresponsible queen, Nefeli, was identified by many critics as the real queen of Greece, Frederica. Penelope and the prime minister of Ithaca do not want him back, as he is obviously lesser than his myth and will damage the profits from tourism, so they replace him with Elpenor, his stupid but handsomer and more virile companion. Odysseus tells the truth and at first the trick works with the people, who embrace him as an anti-hero and as one of them, but the government puts him away and erects his statue instead. For the first production of the play by Karolos Koun's Art Theatre in 1966 Kambanellis gave assurances (in the programme of the production) that his target was not to demystify and downgrade our heroes and ancestors. He really wanted to make a play about those who started out for their own Troy following their dreams and ideals. They succeeded, became famous, but time transformed them into 'merchants of their own glory'.[10] The dramatic time is defined as 'twenty years after the second Trojan War.[11] In general, the playwright stressed its existential content in his statements for several productions of the play, although its political dimension was not ignored either by the critics of its first production or of its second by the National Theatre in 1980. However, in the productions which followed the fall of the seven-year dictatorship (1967–1974), many of them interpreted the hints as aimed also at the Left.[12] Kambanellis himself wrote that the absurd element of the play lies in the collective situations, especially those which deviated from the original intentions of their heroes and were transformed into something different, even the reverse of their expectations, a statement that could be interpreted in a simplified way as the defeat of the ideals of the Left. Later he explained that he used the myth in order to say something about contemporary times and he thought that the well-known ancient myth could be a vehicle for effective communication.[13] There have been more productions – it is a very popular play.

---

10 Kambanellis 1979, 208.
11 Kambanellis 1979, 213.
12 Petrakou 2007, 245.
13 Kambanellis 1980.

Skouloudis' *Odyssey*, labeled as a 'theatrical tragic-satirical trilogy', was published and staged in 1961. Each of the three plays has in fact the length of an act of a rather long three-act play and it is in verse. The suitors pursue Penelope cynically, in order to acquire the royal power and then discard her. Penelope is sorry for her incompetence as a ruler, which is also the case with Telemachus, even if he does not realize it. Odysseus, although he is as unattractive as Kambanellis' hero, manages to seduce Circe and Calypso, while Penelope is still dreaming of him. Odysseus finishes the play by killing the suitors, and this conventional ending, combined with the subversive lines of the text, perplexed the critics. In fact, this play had been commissioned from the playwright by the radio authorities, on the condition that he would not deviate from the Homeric tradition.[14] Homer appears in it as the narrator and the characters are more or less our familiar Homeric heroes. In the first play the slave Melantho conspires with her lover, Eurymachus, so that the latter can marry Penelope, kill Telemachus and keep her as his mistress forever. The other suitors are equally cynical. In the second part Odysseus and his companions are on Circe's island. Circe is rather disappointed in him and transforms the companions into pigs, but he arouses her desire by pretending to be erotically unwilling. Odysseus has a little chat with Homer about existential philosophy and the atomic theory. Homer finds the human race funny, but Odysseus warns him not to say that openly. Then he has his affair with the nymph Calypso, abandons her and travels to Corfu, where he seduces Nausica. Penelope has a dream in which she quarrels with her three rivals, which the critics interpreted as a conflict of her three egos. Odysseus returns to Ithaca and kills the suitors after the disgusting Eurymachus has killed Melantho.

In his introduction at the programme for the production (actually extending to a whole essay) Skouloudis explained that a contemporary writer who wants to use 'the immortal Homeric material' has inevitably assimilated the dogmas of Judaism and Christianity. He may have satirized the Homeric epics, but in fact he adores them. However, he disregarded this idolization and turned to satire, in order to amuse the audience and help it overcome outdated social and tyrannical symbols. His message is that man can create his own destiny. His critics had differing opinions. Angelos Terzakis liked *Odyssey* and was happy that it had no political implications.[15] Alkis Thrylos was rather surprised that a talented adaptor of dramatic texts like Skouloudis did not do better in the text. Thrylos believed that Skouloudis really meant to satirize contemporary events and

---

14 Skouloudis 1961, 5.
15 Terzakis 1961.

situations.¹⁶ Considering Skouloudis' statements, Oikonomidis regarded his dramatic intentions as too ambitious in the composition of a play containing realism, materialism, idealism, surrealism, academicism in the way they co-existed in those crucial times. He considered the play to be really innovative: starting from Euripides' challenges, which still preoccupy human thought, he enriches them with contemporary issues like space travels. Nonetheless, the play can somewhat confuse the audience, despite its perfect structure. Still, it is a step of progress in modern Greek dramatic production.¹⁷ Klaras praised it as expressing the essence of Hellenism, although the Homeric material is unsuitable for a theatrical adaptation.¹⁸ We could infer rather the opposite, to judge from the number of plays that it has inspired all over the world. Most of the critics enjoyed the ironical-satirical tone of the play, its theatricality, its dramatic composition, whilst approaching with some circumspection the too complex ideological parameters and their multi-dimensional treatment.¹⁹

The play *Hotel Circe* (1966) of the poet Dimitris Christodoulou is described by its author as 'a satirical drama taking place in contemporary times'. The dramatic space is (again) Circe's island, on which she is running a hotel with totalitarian methods. It is not difficult to interpret it as an allegory of the islands used as places of exile for the communists.²⁰ Her general manager is Cerberus (Pluto's dog in Hades), who is in love with Circe. He interrogates the clients and, according to their answers, puts them in the basement, in an ordinary room or in the penthouse. The servants either do not understand what is happening or they pretend not to. Circe is looking forward to Odysseus' arrival, in order to get involved into an affair with him and in the meantime transforms his companions into pigs. Odysseus comes, rejects her advances and her politics, re-transforms the pigs into human beings and persuades the servants and the folk people to rebel, build a ship and go away with him to freedom.

The political implications are so obvious, that the fact that it was produced in 1966 and then again in 1972 is rather puzzling. Few critics wrote about it, perhaps in order to protect the playwright and the theatrical company from being sent to a Circe's island by the government of defection or the threatened dictatorship, of which everybody spoke. The notoriously right-wing critic Alkis Thrylos delivered the verdict that Christodoulou's dramatic talent was not equal to his remarkable poetic skill.

---

16 Thrylos 1980.
17 Oikonomidis 1961.
18 Klaras 1961.
19 Koukoulas 1961; Varikas 1961; Kokkinakis 1961.
20 On Greek prison islands and the particular theatrical activity developed there, see recently Van Steen 2011, esp. 1–29.

The style of the work is in-between the theatre of the absurd and the orthodox theatre (meaning realistic), as well as being absolutely indifferent and disappointing.[21] Varikas wrote a serious aesthetic analysis in which he understandably avoided deciphering the specific political implications. He characterized it as 'a theatrical allegory' corresponding to Christodoulou's poetry, often inspired by ancient Greek myths and symbols. According to him, Odysseus and Circe represent two rival powers: Circe symbolizes violence, while Odysseus represents the free spirit which comes to wake up the vision of freedom and dignity in the souls of the slaves, making them realize their strength and rebel. Cerberus stands for the organized violence used by the central power, whereas the two cleaning-women embody the simple and uncorrupted folk. It is a miniature of contemporary society which depicts the tragic deadlock in which people live today, as well as cherishing the hope for a new and better world. Although it is a rather weak play dramaturgically, it is nevertheless a promising first attempt of the poet to write drama; its merit lies not only in its lofty ideological target and questioning, but also results from its general concept containing many strong points.[22]

George Charalambidis' *Penelope's 300*[23] is written in a very different tone, full of comical impulse. It was a great success when it was produced in the middle of the seven-year dictatorship (1970–71), although it is possible that it was banned by the censorship the following year. Subsequently, a series of productions by the same and other theatre companies followed. The title seems to imply the three hundred members of the Greek parliament. Ithaca is presented as a totally corrupted country, to which a cunning Cephalonian comes pretending to be Odysseus and the others pretend to believe him. The suitors try to appear as protectors of the people, while the Cephalonian manages to win the people by means of his rhetoric. Telemachus is fatalistically ready to succumb to the rich shipowner who wants to help Ithaca financially, but is really aiming at exploiting its natural resources, particularly the oil of the Ionian Sea. We learn that the suitors are Americans, British and Russians and they all want the same thing. The Cephalonian and Telemachus somehow manage to overpower them and Homer tries to understand what is going on.

The playwright stated in a preliminary press conference that his play used material from Aristophanes, the Greek shadow puppet theatre (Karaghiozis) and folk culture in order to deal with the present situation satirically.[24] The playhouse was always packed mainly by university students. At first the production

---

21 Thrylos 1981.
22 Varikas 1966.
23 Charalampidis 1972.
24 Charalambidis 1971.

escaped the notice of the regime, perhaps because it was considered to be a satire of the parliamentary system. Later someone may have interpreted the Cephalonian as a caricature of the opportunist dictator (Papadopoulos) and it was banned. (It is difficult to reconstruct the true story, as the newspapers did not publish such news at the time.) A prominent critic commented that Charalambidis obviously aimed at political satire, but the play was really confused (and confusing). It seemed to follow the Brechtian model, though not very successfully. Other critics just dismissed it as naïve or indifferent, but one of them regarded it as a very timely allegory of universal politics: powerful governments pursue their own interests either by pretending to protect the weak by stirring up riots that render their intervention necessary or by causing mortal conflicts among the weak, of whom they take advantage. The playwright had composed a merry comedy on these very crucial issues.[25]

Then, in 1997 Kambanellis decided to write a sequel to his first *Odysseus*. He wrote *The Last Act*, in which Odysseus returns to Ithaca in a state of psychological break-down, where everyone has forgotten him and only a young journalist thinks that she could exploit the subject. Penelope and Telemachus have invited a second-rate theatre company to play the roles of the main figures of the Odysseus-myth, hoping to get him out of his amnesia. The director has a long speech about Odysseus' adventures and extraordinary abilities, composing a political personality comparable only to Eleftherios Venizelos among real politicians. Odysseus escapes secretly from his room, in order to stay incognito for a while in a room which the journalist visits disguised as a call-girl, in order to extract information out of him. Not only that: the younger generation is eager to listen to stories about struggles and heroes of the past, even though half of them are untrue. Odysseus finally does come out of his stupor, only to follow the itinerant actors and play out his own story with them: he wants to be the interpreter of his own life.

The playwright stated that he was inspired to write a kind of sequel to his *Odysseus, Come Home* as he was watching its second production by the Art Theatre in 1990. He felt that he had left his Odysseus on Circe's island in abeyance and he should really send him back to Ithaca to see what would happen. The dramatic time of this second play is 'time present', showing all the developments of the historical-social context depicted in the previous one of the Fifties and Sixties (the time of first writing and first production). Perhaps it is not clear from this concise narration of the plot that Odysseus as a dramatic character never appears. In the play-dance drama *Par-Odyssey* (1999) written and performed by the students of Art Theatre drama school, Odysseus was also non-existent:

---

25 Doxas 1971.

he was a small moving light. *The Last Act* had two productions, one in Thessaloniki (1997–98) and another one in Athens by a different theatre company (2001), but its existential core did not seem to instigate many reviews except for theoretical critics.[26] Puchner analyzed it as an appendage of *Odysseus, Come Home*. In the first play, Odysseus becomes marble –along with his myth – and his statue gets smeared in the course of time by the droppings of birds. The somehow Pirandellian questioning about the conflict between the ego and society ends with the victory of society.[27] In the second play Odysseus defines himself as he likes. Almost all characters in this play turn to art in order to give a new meaning to the events of their lives: Penelope, Telemachus, Odysseus himself (another Pirandellian idea), while the media intervene to create a story that will interest the audiences and establish the journalist's career. Here Kambanellis reduces the political satire and draws emphasis on another contemporary phenomenon: the power of persuasion exerted by the media.[28]

Apart from the aforementioned plays, there are some more, less well-known and unstaged. Stavros Melissinos wrote *Odysseus' Helmet* (1961) based on *Iphigenia in Aulis* and parodying the homosexual tendencies of the ancients (exclusively?), because of which Iphigenia is sacrificed contrary to the oracle. Odysseus and the wise Nestor organize things, so that the leaders' misconduct does not become known. As well as ridiculing the licentiousness of the leaders, the play criticizes the scandalously unfair tax system. The text is imbued with Aristophanic obscenities and contemporary implications. The play *Penelope and her Suitors* (1984) by the Cypriot Kostas Sokratous also has certain Aristophanic targets, which he expresses by means of sexual jokes, a facetious atmosphere and a modern denouement: the suitors stay alive and Penelope, like a modern feminist woman, punishes Odysseus for his prolonged absence and his more than certain infidelities, by demanding that he should help with the housework. Charis Sakellariou with *The Sleep of the Lotus-Eaters* (1990) offered a new and fanciful interpretation of the familiar myth. The latter cannot be understood without the author's prologue, in which he interprets lotus eating as a hypothetical regime of a socialist nature in a North African country, where the citizens lived in freedom and equality with social welfare etc. Odysseus got lost and his companions returned to Ithaca and established such a regime there. The old aristocracy, in an effort to get its privileges back, presents a vagabond as Odysseus, Penelope accepts him and the bard Phemius composes an epic poem.

---

26 See Pefanis in Kambanellis 1998, 369–71.
27 Puchner 2005, 326.
28 Puchner 2005 and 2010, 766–67, 778.

According to a contemporary critic, the literary myth functions in three ways as regards its mythical background: subjectively, when one of its elements is selected and given prominence; comparatively, when new and strange elements are added to the mythical material; and deductively, when some part of the myth is eliminated or minimized.[29] Perhaps all those deductions, additions or selections can be freely used in an adaptation for a novel, as well as in poetry, since a poem can be either brief or extensive. However, in the conventional performance length of a play (extending to two hours approximately) all these three functions are present. In our own topic, it is usually the central mythical figure (Odysseus) who is also the pivotal character, even when he is absent, as in the two chronologically subsequent plays mentioned. In modern Greek and European drama, the Trojan cycle provides most of the subjects.[30] Odysseus is a universally favoured character, who is appropriated mainly to pose challenges to serious, existential issues related to the present.

On the basis of this brief —in terms of the real extension of the subject— and unavoidably indicative examination of the satirical or 'parody-like' handling of the Homeric Odysseus-myth in drama, it can be deduced that the majority of these plays belong to the Postwar era and to Greek playwrights. There are numerous literary *personas* of Odysseus in prose works, poetry and drama within ancient, ancient-like, timeless or contemporary contexts. The lampooning style, however, is rather a Greek contribution with the exception of the most famous of all, Leopold Bloom in Joyce's *Ulysses*, which contains sparse humoristic resonances.

During the 19th century the dominating ideology in Greece mostly aimed at national and social cohesion having the proof of the continuity of Hellenism through its long and mostly unbroken history, which stemmed from ancient Greece and had its culture as its objective. There is hardly any play making fun of this issue: only some weak points in public life were targets. Zanos' play was fully appreciated, because his satire aimed at those who tried to overthrow the government, and there was a '*catharsis*' which was attained according to Homeric ideology, by means of the punishment of the conspirators and the restoration of the *status quo*. In fact, a previous play by the same author staged a few months before his *Penelope's Suitors*, in which he handled an ancient myth much more subversively, was severely attacked by the critics (among whom the poet Kostis Palamas) as sacrilegious towards ancient ideals. As a result, Zanos never published that play and in the next one (*Penelope's Suitors*) he changed

---

29 Durand 1987, 17–28.
30 Chasapi-Christodoulou 2002, 1113.

the focus of his satire, making it consistent with the official ideology, which resulted in the great success of his play.

In the course of the 20th century this ideology changed completely and became subversive in most of the plays and almost never supportive of the essence of the myth. Among the plays discussed here, the most important is Kambanellis' *Odysseus, Come Home*, on which less emphasis was given in this survey, as it has been so widely discussed and explored. If the beginning of the dramatic current of satirical Odysseus with a focus on political satire was *The Trojan War* by Sakellarios-Giannakopoulos, the real turning-point came through Kambanellis, who produced a much more subversive play with Odysseus as its hero and, at the same time, fertile as regards the difficult issues he wanted to touch on. Considering that it was written immediately after the Greek Civil War, this was a very difficult, even dangerous, attempt depending on the perception of the censor. The majority of modern Greek playwrights belong to or lean towards the Left. At the same time, less politically committed playwrights wanted to write about certain crucial issues, as well. The farce playwrights managed to pass off some subjects that were not really politically harmless, but the plays were considered light theatre and the censors did not pay as much attention to them as to the plays of 'serious' writers, even if they were comedies. Kambanellis later stated that he found authentic material in those farces[31] and that through the character of the prime-minister of Ithaca (Evandros) he really wanted to satirize the Greek prime minister of that period.[32] Contemporary theoretical critics may use various textual or other methods as tools in their analyses, but the press reviews especially of the time of the first production spotted better the political implications about persons, events and situations, when this was possible.

In this chronologically successive survey the influence of Kambanellis' *Odysseus* on subsequent plays is made quite evident, both in terms of their handling of the myth and their contemporary connotations. They reflect Postwar political conditions in Greece, cautiously distorted, and point symbolically and cryptically—but not unrecognizably—to the deception and exploitation of the people, the persecution of the Left, the intrigues of the palace, the incompetence and perhaps the double game of the progressive parties, the use of information as a means of guidance and suppression, the confusion of political leaders and other official factors trapped in conflicting financial, class interests and ideologies and the need to anticipate the political tricks and reversals which must be counteracted. One can see that Odysseus appears as a regular, larger-than-life hero in Zanos' play, in which he wins

---

31 Kambanellis 1990b, 49.
32 Petrakou 2007, 556.

and restores social order according to his interests, while the playwright does not dispute his role. In the 20th century, however, after the Second World War and the Greek Civil War, Odysseus was demystified and became a genuine anti-hero. His achievements are frauds (*Odysseus, Come Home*), he is a leader of the people (*Hotel Circe*), he is a false person (*Penelope's 300*, *The Sleep of the Lotus-Eaters*), non-existent (*The Last Act*, *Par-Odyssey*) and ridiculous (*Penelope and her Suitors*). Still, he is dominant in his environment even when his presence is a void: the figures surrounding him need to occupy themselves with him either to make him conform to the new circumstances or because it is simply impossible for them to forget him and thus eliminate his imposing, even devastating presence. Nikos Kazantzakis considered Odysseus to be a concrete symbol of the Western man and employed him as the hero of a tragedy, a long epic and a short poem. Many other writers also seem to regard him as a fundamental figure capable of conveying eternal as well as contemporary ideas. Only writers who based satirical plays on Odysseus (with the exception of the aforementioned farce writers, the others did not usually write comedies) depicted him as an illusion of humanity about the value of the leaders (essentially an anarchic message) and a utopia tending towards oblivion, although peoples do not seem capable of handling their own fate. The divine and resourceful Odysseus, the most attractive and ever-present Homeric figure, has been totally transformed, yet he is a very good bearer of a contemporary anti-myth.

Part VIII **Refiguring Homer in Film and Music**

Pantelis Michelakis
The Reception of Homer in Silent Film*

Discussions of the reception history of Homer in cinema usually begin with the earliest commercially available films on the subject which date back to the 1950s. Earlier films on *The Fall of Troy* and on Odysseus' travels and return to Ithaca are usually dismissed as 'non-Homeric' or are confined to passing references in online filmographies and in the footnotes of scholarly books and articles. However, by the advent of synchronised sound in the late 1920s, more than a dozen films had been produced across Europe and North America on, or at least had evoked, Troy and Odysseus. Some of them are now lost, but those that have survived, together with press reviews, posters, production stills and other ephemera testify to a whole chapter in the cinematic history of Homer that has hitherto been neglected. What follows is an attempt to situate silent films concerned with Homer's poems in relation to the larger reception of Homeric epic but also in relation to the cinematic genre of film epic.

Silent films on early Greek epic vary in length from the one-minute *Judgment of Paris* which was produced in France in 1902 (*Le jugement de Pâris*, dir. Georges Hatot) to the forty-minute *Odyssey*, produced in Italy in 1911 (*Odissea*, dir. Francesco Bertolini, Giuseppe de Liguoro and Adolfo Padovan), and the more than three-hour-long *Helen*, produced in Germany in 1924 (*Helena*, dir. Manfred Noa). The earliest among these films, the *Judgment of Paris* and the *Island of Calypso: Ulysses and the Giant Polyphemus* (*L'île de Calypso: Ulysse et le géant Polyphème*, France, 1905, dir. Georges Méliès) can be seen as examples of how early cinema uses classical mythology as a platform for the display of optical tricks. Themes such as a journey, revenge, or marital life are central to the half-dozen films whose titles evoke the *Odyssey* and Odysseus but whose subject is distinctively modern: *An Odyssey of the North* (USA, 1914, dir. Hobart Bosworth), *A Polynesian Odyssey* (USA, 1921, dir. Burton Holmes), *Circe, the Enchantress* (USA, 1924, dir. Robert Z. Leonard) and the two films entitled *The Return of Odysseus* produced in 1918 (*Die Heimkehr des Odysseus*, Germany, dir. Rudolf Biebrach) and 1922 (*Die Heimkehr des Odysseus*, Germany, dir. Max Obal) respectively. At least two films demonstrate the strong impact on early cinema of theatre: the 1909 *Return of Ulysses* (*Le Retour d'Ulysse*, France, dir. André Calmettes) and the 1913 *King Menelaus at the Movies* (*König Menelaus im Kino*, Austria, 1913, dir. Hans Otto Löwenstein). And two films use parody and burlesque to revisit the

---

* A different version of this paper appeared in Michelakis/ Wyke (eds.) 2013, 145–68.

associations of Greek epic in early cinema with action and romance: *King Menelaus at the Movies* and *The Private Life of Helen of Troy* (USA, 1927, dir. Alexander Korda). A single chapter cannot do justice to the many issues raised by this diverse body of films, but under the headings of epic film and Homeric epic it can at least begin to explore how silent film based on Homeric themes challenges common assumptions both about epic as a film genre and about the reception history of Homer.

a. Epic film

The films which stand out in terms of their artistic ambition, monumental scale and wide distribution in numerous countries across Europe and North America are the Italian *Fall of Troy* of 1911 (*La caduta di Troia*, dir. Luigi Romano Borgnetto and Giovanni Pastrone), the Italian *Odyssey* of the same year and the German *Helen* of 1924 (both mentioned above). Scenes with hundreds of extras, massive sets, siege engines, naval battles, aerial shots of chariot races and special effects ranging from artificial rain to man-eating monsters dominate the three films from beginning to end. In *Helen* the title character arrives at Troy on a chariot drawn by lions, and in *The Fall of Troy* she is transported through the ether in a giant, Botticelli-style seashell pulled by little Cupids. The strong presence of spectacle, however, does not detract from the romance which in all three cases plays an instrumental role in the construction of the narrative. As the foreword in the press book of *Helen* puts it: 'While presenting to you Homeric combats on land and at sea with mighty warriors and engines of war, in scenes and settings on a scale so colossal as to defy description, yet throughout the wonderful love story of Helen and Paris predominates'.[1]

The scale and ambition of these films have an aggressive and sensational publicity campaign to match. 'Never in the history of the film business', concludes a review of *The Odyssey*, 'has such an elaborate advertising campaign been outlined... We have no hesitancy in saying that no motion picture has ever been so thoroughly advertised and never was so much well-designed advertising matter placed at the disposal of the state right buyer.'[2] The advertising campaign for *The Odyssey* was assigned to no other than Frank Winch, the publicity organizer of the Buffalo Bill show, who was now invited to transfer his en-

---

[1] From the 'Foreword' of the press book of the film held in the collections of the British National Film Archive.
[2] *The Moving Picture World*, 17 February 1912, 590.

trepreneurial skills to the new and promising film industry.³ Twenty million pieces of printed matter were claimed to have been produced 'for the exploitation of *The Odyssey*', which included programmes, music scores, illustrated souvenir booklets with the story of the *Odyssey*, paperback, cloth and leather-bound copies of 'the greatest epic poem in all literature' in Greek or English, postcards announcing the playing date of *The Odyssey* and even printed copies of a lecture to accompany the screen viewing.⁴ The advertising campaign also included lobby displays of life-size photos as well as grottoes, stucco effects, lighting effects, plaster busts of Homer, Grecian costumes for lecturers and glass-front folding frames.⁵ In addition to all this, there were letters collected 'from every university president in America commending the *Odyssey* as a masterpiece of world's literature', and a nationwide essay competition was launched, with 'a cash prize of $100 for the best thousand-word essay on the greatest of all epic poems', in which a hundred thousand students were supposed to have taken part.⁶ As an advertisement in a trade journal put it, probably without irony and certainly without exaggeration, 'there is no limit to the advertising possibilities that you may take advantage of'.⁷

It may be tempting to see the issues of length, spectacle, romance and publicity as defining the early cinematic reception of Homer in the way that they shaped 'the epic film' of the Hollywood industry of the 1950s and 1960s or the European low-budget, 'sword-and-sandal' films of the same period, or even the more recent revival of epic cinema since Ridley Scott's *Gladiator* (2000). However, this would be both anachronistic and reductive, doing little justice not only to the many films mentioned above, that would be excluded from such an interpretative scheme, but also to those that would be included. American film audiences first saw the journeys of Odysseus and *The Fall of Troy* in imported European productions, which predated the cinemascope epics of Hollywood by half a century. In the period before the emergence of the historical epics of D.W. Griffith, this encounter with imported productions generated enthusiasm and admiration, rather than the derision customarily levied at non-American cold-war attempts to deal with epic on film. Generically too, the diversity of the films under consideration speaks in favour of a more inclusive and flexible definition of the terms 'Homeric' and 'epic' than those provided by epic film

---

3 *Ibid.*
4 Quotes from *The Moving Picture World*, 24 February 1912, 706.
5 *Ibid.*
6 *The Moving Picture World*, 17 February 1912, 584.
7 *The Moving Picture World*, 10 February 1912, 504.

(whether old or new). The term 'epic' was first introduced as a generic title for films in 1911,[8] a year when the novelty and ambition of multi-reel films was thematically channeled not through great historical events of the past, but directly through a literary tradition of epic poems stretching back to ancient Greece.

In the first three decades of cinema 'Homer' not only meant a combination of the monumental, the antiquarian and the ethical (i. e. the trademark qualities of what was to become 'film epic').[9] 'Homer' also embraced trick cinematography, eroticism, fantasy and, on occasion, parody and burlesque. In silent cinema, the great civilizations of the past communicated not only 'via the peaks', as Deleuze writes about film epics, drawing on Nietzsche's conception of history as a series of great moments.[10] They also communicated via the troughs of the mundane, the contingent and the everyday. Consider, for instance, the search for a lost manuscript entitled 'Helen of Troy' in *The Target of Dreams* (USA, 1916, Knickerbocker Star Features) or the presence of a manicurist possessing the beauty of Helen of Troy in *Rigadin and the Pretty Manicurist* (*Rigadin et la jolie manicure*, France, 1915, dir. Georges Monca) or even the extended use of the word 'Odyssey' to describe the adventures of a countryman in a metropolis (*Odyssée d'un paysan à Paris*, France, 1905, dir. Charles-Lucien Lépine), of an entomologist in the army (*L'Odyssée d'un savant*, Pathé, France, 1908), of a spaceship (*L'Odyssée de la voiture astral*, France, 1905, dir. Georges Méliès) and even of a meal (*Odissea di una comparsa*, Italy, 1909, dir. Romolo Bacchini).

In terms of narrative development too, the 'free-wheeling approach to plot material from the *Iliad*'[11] and the *Odyssey* is striking when compared to classical Hollywood or more recent attitudes of film epic towards authenticity and fidelity. For instance, in *The Private Life of Helen of Troy*, Helen's return to Sparta at the end of the film is only the beginning of new erotic adventures for her and of a decision by Menelaus to ignore her. In *The Fall of Troy* the central Homeric heroes Achilles, Agamemnon and Odysseus are all made irrelevant and they are not even introduced by name. In *Helen* Achilles and Hector are both in love with Helen, Patroclus is in love with Achilles, Paris unsuccessfully tries to kill Priam with the poisoned arrows meant for Achilles, and, as Troy is in flames, Priam attempts to poison Helen to appease the gods before drinking the poisonous potion himself. Moving beyond play with the Homeric source material, in

---

[8] On the origins of the use of the term 'epic' as a generic label in film criticism, see Hall/ Neale 2010, 23. On film epic between history and the canon of Western literary epic, see Paul 2013.
[9] See especially Deleuze 1986, 152–55; Sobchack 1990; Burgoyne 2011a.
[10] Nietzsche [1874] 1980.
[11] Winkler 2007, 205 with reference to the 1931 *Queen of Sparta* (USA).

what follows I offer two particularly telling examples of how silent films related to Homer challenge homogenizing assumptions about epic as a film genre.

Epic films are often seen as vehicles for community-building narratives, especially for national narratives as 'expressions of the myth-making impulse at the core of national identity'.[12] More often than not, they are perceived as 'effective instruments of ideological control which, through spectacular and engaging historical reconstructions, manipulate their audiences to assent to a celebratory model of national identity'.[13] Historical epics of the silent era are not always exempt from this as the hegemonist tendencies of Giovanni Pastrone's *Cabiria* (Italy, 1914) and D. W. Griffith's *Intolerance* (USA, 1916) suggest. Manfred Noa's *Helen* (1924) can be seen as participating in a similar search for a national epic through the ancient Greeks, a distinctly German epic in this case, such as those we find in the works of G.W.F. Hegel and Richard Wagner, associated with the Hellenization of 'the entire genre of epic and, through this, German national identity'.[14] However, *Helen* does not produce a nostalgic longing for heroic achievements of a glorious past. The intertitles convey a sense of being spoken for everyone, 'from a stance of sure knowledge'[15] of the kind associated with the epic narrator of later epic films. Yet, at the same time, they also convey a sense of doom not normally expected from the epic narrator. In this sense, *Helen* envisages history as tragedy rather than romance, with its motivating forces being guilt, ambition, hate and fear. Grave mistakes are committed out of the best motives and personal decisions turn out to have unintended and uncontrollable consequences for the community: Menelaus forces Helen against her will to travel to the games in honour of the most beautiful Greek woman, which leads to his own rivalry with Achilles and to the night that Helen spends with Paris in the temple of Aphrodite. Helen sleeps with Paris persuaded she gives herself to a god and fails to listen to his warnings that he is a simple shepherd. She then follows Paris to Troy out of shame for having slept with him, rather than out of love. Paris kills Achilles not because he wants to – in fact Helen asks him not to – but because Helen is the reward for which other archers are keen to shoot Achilles if he does not. Paris does not alert the celebrating Trojans to the Greeks inside the Trojan horse, in order to prove to Helen that, for once, he can do what she asks him to do. Priam's role as the patriarch who holds absolute power over the life of his children and subjects, Paris' Oedipal relation with him, Helen as an object of desire and the death and devastation with which the film ends

---

12 Burgoyne 2011b, 83.
13 Wyke 1997, 22.
14 Foster 2010, 34.
15 Burgoyne 2011a, 10.

play out a complex web of intergenerational and gender relations that are in crisis.

The film was made during a time when the aftershocks of the German defeat and loss in the Great War were felt most strongly. Like other German films of the period, it can be seen as 'part of a widespread discourse that sought to work through the traumatic experience of war and national defeat',[16] evoking 'fear of invasion and injury', and exuding 'a sense of paranoia and panic'.[17] If epic films of both the silent era and of later periods commonly help celebrate an imperial and expansionist national identity, *Helen* does not provide its spectators with symbolic solutions to troubling experiences brought about by war and military defeat. Although, like other war films or history films of the period, it is interested in authenticity, and, like war films, adventure films or melodramas, it plays with generic formulas in various ways, it also features expressionistic and futuristic costumes, harsh lighting effects, fragmented or unexpected story lines and extreme psychological states triggered by defeat, deceit and betrayal. Offering a strong sense that decline is inevitable, it provides a preoccupation with national history which is openly political, yet focused on the 'grandeur of doom',[18] devoid of the celebratory political tone usually associated with the canon of film epic.

If epic films are often seen as vehicles for community-building narratives, and their critical success depends on their ability to appeal to critics normally keen to rehearse arguments for their 'political bad faith and cultural vulgarity',[19] their commercial success depends largely on their ability to appeal to broader, international audiences. Accounting for both critics and international audiences can cause considerable friction between (and within) film narratives and the promotional discourses that surround them. The critical acclaim and international success of the 1911 *Odyssey* provides a notable exception to this rule. 'The outlook is for an indefinite run for these reels', reads a report from a cinema in Boston on the phenomenal success of the film in the USA.[20] The film appeals equally 'to mass and class', notes another review from New York.[21] All types of spectators were targeted by the film's immense publicity discussed above, from right-holders and exhibitors to academics, librarians, 'lovers of sensational melodrama'

---

16 Kaes 2009, 146.
17 *Ibid.* 3.
18 See Kracauer 2004^2, 88.
19 Burgoyne 2011a, 3.
20 *The Moving Picture World*, 11 May 1912, 552.
21 *The Moving Picture World*, 30 March 1912, 1194.

and, last but not least, 'schools and colleges, the churches and lyceums'.[22] According to the film's publicity, invitations to the American premiere of the film were sent even to 'President Taft, Col. Roosevelt, Attorney General Wickersham and the Principals of Yale, Harvard, Princeton, Cornell and Columbia Universities'.[23]

In a review article published in *The Moving Picture World*, the American film lecturer and trade journal critic W. Stephen Bush undertook to explain how a foreign film could meet with such critical acclaim and commercial success.[24] Bush claims that *The Odyssey* provides education in a very broad sense that combines entertainment and instruction. He argues that, as such, the film appeals to different communities of spectators, including 'readers' and 'students' of Homer on the one hand and 'the masses' or 'general public' on the other hand, in a way that 'leaves the critic silent in admiration'. The agency of the film is powerful, he claims, marking 'a new epoch in the history of the motion picture as an actor in education'. But Bush also makes the film mediate invisibly between 'every human being' and 'the genius of Homer' through 'feeling', 'influence' and the 'beauty of form'. And he proceeds by establishing an analogy between the 'primitive' audience of Homer 'who knew nothing of libraries and of all the aids of modern education and who had to be moved chiefly by the beauty of form' and 'the masses of the people today', making a case for the power of aesthetics to move peoples across social divides, ages and art forms. On top of these broad claims and generalizations, Bush makes the even bolder claim that Homer, in his cinematic guise, is the educator of all America. That such a claim about the educational power of cinema could be made with the help of a foreign film that was setting the benchmark for the nascent national industry is quite unique in the history of American cinema. There is no room here for the ambivalence shown by critics towards cinema's preoccupation with history and its aspirations to cultural authority that we find in the post-Second World War period. Nor do we find here any of the Postwar derision of European epics for their 'inauthenticity' and 'betrayal of European high-art traditions' or scorn for their transnational orientation.[25]

The 1911 *Odyssey* does not focus thematically on the national motifs of much epic cinema, such as 'the legend of a people, the battles and treaties that define a sacred landscape and the emergence of particular heroic and sainted figures'.[26]

---

22 *The Moving Picture World*, 24 February 1912, 666; 30 March 1912, 1193; 2 May 1914, 643.
23 *The Moving Picture World*, 10 February 1912, 486.
24 *The Moving Picture World*, 16 March 1912, 941–42.
25 Burgoyne 2011a, 9.
26 Burgoyne 2011b, 83.

Instead it features themes related to the individual, to travelling to foreign lands, to family values and homecoming. Free of geographically or culturally-specific references, it becomes suitable for circulation across and beyond national and cultural boundaries. It is precisely through the fact that this silent epic does not showcase a glorious national history or a common religion, language or ethnic background that it becomes central in debates about cinema and its ability to bring together a socially and culturally heterogeneous body of spectators in the name of a common past and a shared identity.

b. Homeric epic

Silent films related to Homer challenge homogenizing assumptions not only about epic as a film genre but also about Homer's poems and the history of their interpretation. The generic diversity of early cinema breaks down the totalizing and canonical work of Homer into component parts that are spread across and reconfigured within a number of artistically and culturally contingent cinematic modes and forms. Homer's name can perform a number of different functions in relation to the complex process of reception that situates early films within and against Homer's history of interpretation: it can symbolize this process, but it can also ignore or conceal it. As in antiquity, the name 'Homer' can be used not only for the Homeric poems themselves but also for other narratives of the myth of the Trojan War.[27] A purist strategy would reject as non-Homeric films on the Trojan War that break down and broaden the spatial and temporal framework of the *Iliad* and the *Odyssey* or downplay the primacy of their narratives in favour of formal and thematic preoccupations more familiar from other poems of the Epic Cycle, including action, romance, the exotic and the miraculous.[28] An alternative approach would be to question the possibility or usefulness of a clear distinction between Homer's *Iliad* and *Odyssey* and other poems of the Epic Cycle which may have served as sources of inspiration for the films under consideration or which can be used as a basis for intertextual analysis. For instance, one could explore the reasons for which the authority of Homer features so prominently in the publicity of films which may have otherwise taken little interest in the plots or characters of his poems.

---

27 On the name 'Homer' applied indiscriminately to both the Homeric poems and the poems of the so-called 'Epic Cycle' already in pre-classical Greece, see Burgess 2001.
28 See, for instance, Solomon 2007. On the uniqueness of Homer's poems in relation to the Epic Cycle, see Griffin 1977.

Another possibility would be to challenge the priority of the dialogue between films and ancient texts over a dialogue between films and their modern contexts, from novels, theatre plays and paintings to wider historical, technological and ideological practices and processes associated with the culture of modernity and its fascination with Homer. The French *Return of Ulysses* of 1909 interacts not only with the *Odyssey* but also with other dramatic and non-dramatic works inspired by it, works which its screenwriter, Jules Lemaître, composed around the same period. Similarly, *The Private Life of Helen of Troy* invites us to think not only of Homer's poems but also of John Erskine's almost contemporary novel which shares with the film its title and on whose success the film sought to capitalize (despite its many differences from it). And the film *Helen* draws not on a humanistic, classicizing Homer, but on the 'strange, brutal and threatening' Homer of Friedrich Nietzsche,[29] anticipating Sigmund Freud's pessimistic reading of the *Iliad* in his *Civilization and its Discontents* by several years.[30]

The Homer of early cinema is not only a canonical figure of the Western literary tradition. *The Fall of Troy* begins with a white-bearded bard holding a lyre in his hands reciting in front of an attentive audience. The image of the bard performing in front of an audience reappears in the films *Odyssey* and *Helen*. This image engages with a pictorial, rather than literary, tradition for the representation of the epic bard in performance that goes back to antiquity. What is static in paintings can now be made more vivid and lifelike, being set literally in motion. And what is only a script in the literary tradition, awaiting its performance and interpretation by readers, can now appear at the moment of its realization, complete with a bard and an audience. At one level, of course, this plays with the paradoxes of translating words into images inherited from the pictorial tradition. At a different level, however, early cinema claims for itself not just the visuality of pictorial representations of Homer's poetry but also the textuality of written epic (not least through intertitles). Even more importantly, it claims for itself the orality of Homeric poetry, the sense of a performative event associated with the bard's recital of epic poetry in front of an audience. Silent film returns to processes of pre-literary production and dissemination of knowledge associated with orality, not because of any interest in how alien they are for a post-literary culture, but because of their perceived relevance to it. Like epic bards, silent cinema adopts a 'rhetoric of traditionality' that facilitates the interplay between film viewing and audience.[31]

---

29 Porter 2004a, 15.
30 Porter 2004b, 332–35.
31 On the rhetoric of traditionality and on the interplay between oral performer and audience, see Scodel 2002.

What attracts early cinema to this image of the epic bard in recital is not its potential contribution to the vision of film as a universal pictorial language. Orality holds the promise of recovering not the lost indexicality of language but a whole process of artistic production and dissemination based on the liveness of performance, repetition and the fostering of a sense of a community. In this sense, the appeal for early cinema of the oral performative tradition of archaic epic is quite different from the appeal for cinema of the pictorial languages of ancient Egypt, Israel and Babylon. Ong speaks of a post-literary form of orality which 'has striking resemblances to the old in its participatory mystique, its fostering of a communal sense, its concentration on the present moment and even its use of formulas [...] Like primary orality, secondary orality has generated a strong group sense, for listening to spoken words forms hearers into a group, a true audience .'[32] Early cinema's instantaneity and complexity, then, must be viewed 'as the spatio-temporal equivalent of Ong's "sounded word", which "exists only when it is going out of existence... [and] is not simply perishable but essentially evanescent and sensed as evanescent"'.[33] Ong's examples of secondary orality include media such as the telephone, radio and television. However, early cinema too illustrates ways in which, in a post-literary world, orality is remediated through a technologically based but performance-oriented event of images and sounds.

In fact, one could go so far as to argue that early film does not simply represent the orality of archaic Greek epic, but also helps define it (on Homeric orality, see also Papaioannou, Efsthathiou and I. Petrovic in this volume). There is no more obvious way to illustrate this than considering very briefly Milman Parry's research into South Slavic heroic songs, to which the role of storage and retrieval technologies of sound and vision was central (on South Slavic oral poetry, see also I.Petrovic in this volume). Parry's audio recordings and his 1935 film footage of the Yugoslav singer Avdo Medjedovic, one of 'the earliest ethnographic films' ever made, have received little attention in this respect.[34] The way, however, in which they helped define the content they were supposed to document is profound, informing as they did the very rhythm and structure of versification (octosyllabic when dictated, as opposed to decasyllabic when sung).[35] From Parry's 'kino' to recent scholarly work discussing epic formulas in terms of 'the cuts

---

32 Ong 1982, 136.
33 Joyce 2002, 336 quoting Ong 1982, 32.
34 Sound recordings by Milman Parry and what his fieldnotes refer to as a 'kino' can be found in the CD that accompanies Parry 2000. They are also available in the Online Database of Harvard's Milman Parry Collection of Oral Literature. On Parry's 'kino', see Mitchell/ Nagy 2000, vii.
35 Scaldaferri 2011, 20.

of montage or as a kind of zooming in on a particular feature of a larger scene',[36] film technologies, practices and techniques have served as an often 'transparent' or 'natural' feedback loop for the scholarship on Homeric orality.

There is another aspect of early cinema as a subject of historical enquiry that can be associated with Homer's epic poetry. The material specificity of early films challenges the fixity and rigidity of the cinematic artwork in ways that raise methodological issues similar to those associated with the multiformity of the Homeric texts. Some of the films in question are lost, others damaged, shortened or re-edited for distribution in different contexts. Some exist in multiple copies, and each copy is different not only in terms of its condition of preservation, but also in terms of overall length, number and order of scenes, and number, subject matter and language of intertitles. The drive to police the boundaries of the filmic narrative and to protect the interests of right holders is well documented in trade journals: 'William J. Burns, the world's most noted detective, announced a new departure in his work – he has entered the film industry, throwing his power and prestige into the protection of a company controlling a reproduction of Homer's *Odyssey.*'[37] But similarly well documented are the fluidity and the shifting, open-ended and evanescent boundaries of film narratives as they circulate through time and space. Noa's *Helen* reappeared in Germany four years after its original release in a shortened version under the title *The Hero of the Arena* (*Der Held Der Arena*, 1928). Seven years later it was re-released in the USA, under the Italian title *La Regina di Sparta* (*The Queen of Sparta*). The sets and costumes of *The Private Life of Helen of Troy* were recycled, at least in part, in *Vamping Venus*, and its plot reappears in Manu Jacob's French novel of the same name, which was published in the immediate aftermath of the film's release (a novel, then, based on a film that, in its turn, draws on a novel and a play which engage with various stories around the Trojan War).[38]

Film archivists often draw on the critical methods of recension and emendation to analyze the complex genealogy of film prints. Consider, for instance, the use of a stemma to provide the genealogy of existing prints for *The Fall of Troy* in Marotto/ Pozzi 2005, 111. However fascinating technically and aesthetically restorations of films such as *The Odyssey* and *Helen* might be, they should not be confused with the quest for a 'definitive' or 'original' version, nor should they detract from the rich and adventurous history of the films' dissemination. On the one hand, there is the archival drive to fix films through storage, retrieval and

---

36 Elmer 2009, 48.
37 *The Moving Picture World*, 10 February 1912, 486.
38 Jacob 1929.

digital or other forms of preservation. On the other hand, to speak of early films on Homer as 'capturing the imagination' of a whole nation or as 'being forgotten' by film-makers for several generations are not just turns of phrase, but attempts to situate them within a cultural framework based on memory, rather than history, and on repetition through variation.

Anastasia Bakogianni
Homeric Shadows on the Silver Screen: Epic Themes in Michael Cacoyannis' Trilogy of Cinematic Receptions*

Michael Cacoyannis' (1922–2011) three cinematic receptions of Greek tragedy: *Electra* (1961–62), *The Trojan Women* (1970–71) and *Iphigenia* (1976–77) were created in the shade of the Homeric epics.[1] Cacoyannis' trilogy is modelled on Euripides' *Electra* (between 422 and 413 BC), *Troades* (415 BC) and *Iphigenia in Aulis* (406/5 BC). However, other 'hidden' or 'masked' layers of reception open up channels that lead further back to the Homeric epics themselves. This discussion focuses on the debt that Cacoyannis owes to the Homeric poems and the ways in which the epics shaped his directorial vision, both on the visual plane, as well as on the level of narrative and characterization.

Michael Cacoyannis' three cinematic receptions construct a complex and multi-layered relationship with ancient Greece. They operate at a closely interwoven nexus of multiple strands of reception that demonstrates the sophistication of their response to the classical past within a modern Greek context. Cacoyannis openly acknowledged his debt to Euripidean dramaturgy, but his debt to the Homeric epics can be described by using a metaphor that also applies to the medium of cinema itself: 'flickering shadows on a silver screen'.[2] Cacoyannis' Euripidean trilogy can thus be classified as a 'masked' reception of the Homeric epics.

What makes this particular case study worth examining is precisely the indirect nature of its dialogue with the epics.[3] While on the face of it Cacoyannis'

---

* This paper is dedicated to the memory of Michael Cacoyannis, who passed away on 25 July 2011. With sincere thanks to Ioanna Karamanou and Athanasios Efstathiou for their editorial assistance during the revision process. I would also like to acknowledge the generous help of Mike Edwards (Roehampton University), Lorna Hardwick (The Open University) and Gonda Van Steen (University of Florida).
1 I am paraphrasing Rick's title *The Shade of Homer* (1989). MacKinnon argues against labelling the three films a trilogy (1986, 74–75). More recently Michelakis is equally sceptical (2013, 42–43). I would counter that there are enough commonalities to warrant their consideration as one. Moreover, the extent of the debt these films owe to the Homeric epics can only be fully appreciated if they are examined as a unit. Karalis in his *A History of Greek Cinema* also applies the label (2012, 183).
2 http://wcclibraries.wordpress.com/2011/10/18/flickering-shadows-on-a-silver-screen.
3 The range of receptions of the Homeric epics, some of which are showcased in the present volume, is both rich and varied. Some further representative examples of scholarship from

Euripidean trilogy is defined by its open dialogue with another ancient literary genre, that of tragedy, it also enjoys a less obvious, 'masked' relationship with ancient epic that enriches and to a large extent determines the overall shape and content of the three films. This is Greek tragedy mediated through the lens of the Homeric epics, an anachronistic inversion of the traditional chronological narrative of the relationship between ancient Greek epic and tragic poetry that leads us to re-examine our assumptions about the connections between these two ancient genres and their dialogue with the modern world.

In methodological terms this particular case study of the dialogue between past and present falls under the purview of what Martin Winkler classifies as 'classical film philology' (2009, 13). Indeed, a close analysis of the filmic text is required, in order to discover the 'epic' elements that exist hidden under the 'tragic' label that Cacoyannis assigned to his reception, thus making his link to Greek tragedy explicit, but disguising his debt to the Homeric epics. 'Tragedy' and 'epic' are slippery terms, however, our relationship to them is continuously renegotiated.[4] For the purposes of this paper I am focusing in particular on the ways in which they can contribute to the project of unpicking the reception of these two ancient genres in Cacoyannis' cinematic trilogy, but also in problematizing that very process. Because ultimately, these filmic receptions move beyond anything found in the ancient sources, whether tragic or epic, to offer a unique modern amalgamation of both ancient genres reimagined for a cinematic audience.

Cacoyannis' status as an *auteur* is particularly relevant to this discussion. An *auteur* is defined as a film director who is not a mere craftsman working within a formula or simply an adaptor, but one who utilises the medium to develop and express personal creativity. Eisenstein's theory of the dialectic of montage[5] emphasized the control that a director can exert over his film, making his role analogous to that of the author of a work of literature.

Reader/viewer response theory, however, complicates this equation by acknowledging the role of the reader/spectator in the creation of meaning. Cacoyannis' receptions were created in the popular medium of cinema, but appealed mostly to art-house audiences interested in alternative types of films and to classical

---

this fast-growing area: Graziosi/ Greenwood (eds.) 2007; Latacz/ Greub/ Blome/ Wieczorek (eds.) 2008; Vandiver 2010.

4 Paul's discussion of 'epic' as a 'cultural' phenomenon (2013, 4) is relevant here, as is her discussion of the difficulties of classification and the importance of demarcating the boundaries of one's own project (1–35).

5 This refers to the process of editing a film: the director chooses particular shots, in order to construct a montage sequence that creates the desired meaning (Kolker 1998, 15–17). See also Eisenstein 1991.

scholars who analyze films with ancient themes and use them as pedagogical tools.⁶ As a member of the latter category my reading of Cacoyannis' trilogy is conditioned by my ongoing search for classical themes in modern culture. I would argue, however, that the epic echoes in the trilogy would also resonate particularly strongly with a large section of Cacoyannis' intended audience, modern Greek spectators (to which group I also belong).⁷ The Homeric epics have remained a cornerstone of the educational system in the modern state and have cast a long shadow over its cultural products. Cacoyannis' trilogy allows a knowledgeable audience, familiar with the Homeric poems, the opportunity to form connections with the epic tradition.⁸ Non-knowledgeable audience members, who are, however, familiar with the 'sword and sandal' genre, could also discover epic resonances in terms of Cacoyannis' cinematic style.⁹ Vrasidas Karalis criticizes *Iphigenia* for being 'heavy with the Hollywood aesthetic of the grand spectacle', but as I hope to demonstrate below, this emphasis on spectacle is not confined to the last film in the trilogy. Rather, it forms part of the director's thoughtful response to the dominant cinematic idiom of the time. Cacoyannis creatively borrowed elements of the Hollywood style and reconfigured them for use in his own personal vision of the classical past (Bakogianni 2011, 162–66). Furthermore, the distinction I have drawn between knowledgeable and non-knowledgeable audiences has to be dismantled, at least in part, because of the intersections in the membership of these groups. Such is the glamour and impact of the medium of cinema in modern society that films provide a common point of reference, a new type of *lingua*

---

6 For analysis of Cacoyannis' trilogy from the perspective of classical film philology, see Bakogianni 2008, 119–67; 2009, 45–68; 2011, 153–94; 2013a, 207–33 and 2013b, 225–49; MacKinnon 1986, 74–96; McDonald 1983 and 2001, 90–117; McDonald/ Winkler 2001, 72–89; Michelakis 2001, 241–57; 2004, 199–217; 2006, 219–26 and 2013, 46–51 (*Electra*), 140–48 (*Iphigenia*), 193–99 (on the use of ruins). For the use of film as a pedagogical tool by classicists, see McDonald 2008, 327–41 and Paul 2008, 303–14.
7 The language of *Electra* and *Iphigenia* is Greek, which potentially limits the film's appeal to non-Greek speaking viewers to those prepared to watch a subtitled film. Both films did reach foreign audiences, particularly *Electra* which won the award for best screen adaptation at the Cannes and was nominated for an Oscar in the Best Foreign Film category. *Iphigenia* was also presented at Cannes in 1977, but was less well received. Even *The Trojan Women* with its international cast, which necessitated the use of English, would only appeal to spectators prepared to engage in a film that openly acknowledges its debt to Greek tragedy.
8 I am using the term 'tradition' here in the way that Paul defines it, stressing the importance of 'textual relationships' (2013, 23).
9 A distinction should be drawn here between contemporary cinema audiences, whose point of reference would have been the 'sword and sandal' epics of the 1950s and 60s, and modern audiences, who have also experienced the renaissance of the genre in the new millennium ushered in by *Gladiator* (2000).

franca, which allows the viewer to build multiple bridging points between the Homeric epics and Cacoyannis' trilogy.

This picture is further complicated by the 'Homeric question'. If 'Homer' is a sign that stands for the collective efforts of a number of ancient *rhapsodes* (Kahane 2005, 6), who created the oral tradition on which the surviving written version of the ancient epics is based, then this destabilizes further the category of 'author/*auteur*' and his/her purported control over the finished product. My reading of Cacoyannis' Euripidean trilogy brings to the surface its 'hidden' epic elements. It reads counter to the director's claim to authenticity that relies on his acknowledged relationship with Greek tragedy and undermines his directorial control of the intended meaning of his trilogy. In other words, I argue that Cacoyannis, like a number of other modern Greek artists, produced his reception of Greek tragedy in the long shadow of Homer, but chose not to explicitly acknowledge this debt.

a. Visual echoes

In the predominantly visual medium of cinema Cacoyannis' debt to the Homeric epics operates most accessibly on the level of the visual. The opening of his *Trojan Women* transports his cinematic audience to the ruins of Troy and the world of the *Iliad*. The film was shot in a ruined castle in Spain, as the director was in a state of exile from Greece, to escape the censorship imposed by the Greek military dictatorship that was ruling the country (1967–74).[10] Cacoyannis' decision to excise the divine prologue that opens Euripides' play and to replace it with a large-scale night scene, starring a large cast of Trojan prisoners being herded by Greek soldiers, signals the director's desire to set an 'epic' tone for his reception. He used the freeze-frame technique to create brief, but significant pauses in the narrative flow of the film: focusing the viewer's attention on shots of the ruined walls of the citadel, the enslaved women and the carts loaded with the Greeks' war booty.

These opening scenes establish an 'epic' tone for Cacoyannis' cinematic reception of Euripides' tragedy, but also one that destroys the distancing effect of Euripides' original divine prologue. Instead, the audience is guided by an 'omnis-

---

[10] The Greek military dictatorship, known as the 'Χούντα', banned Cacoyannis' *The Trojan Women:* Goff 2009, 85–86. The modern trend of interpreting the play as an anti-war statement was one that Cacoyannis embraced, in order to reflect contemporary concerns: Bakogianni 2009, 60–64. As Hall demonstrates, this was part of the radicalization of Greek tragedy: Hall 2004, 1–9.

cient narrator' (Winkler 2009, 8) into viewing the fall of Troy in political terms. This authorial voice tells the spectators that Helen was just an excuse. The Greeks went to war because they coveted Trojan gold. The director is thus guiding his audience towards a particular interpretation of his source text, one that is set in an 'epic' register that helps to bring to the surface the political dimension of the tragedy.

In the popular imagination the citadel of Mycenae has become a potent and widely recognizable visual symbol of the Homeric epics themselves (Wiener 2011, 535). Cacoyannis' decision to set the prologue of his *Electra* in the ruins of the ancient citadel and to have his Agamemnon (Theodoros Demetriou) walk under that famous Lion Gate sets the tone for his reinterpretation of the Euripidean source text. Cacoyannis' choice of setting for these added scenes demonstrates how his view of ancient drama was transfigured through the prism of the Homeric epics. The prologue thus serves a dual function. It sets the scene and tone of Cacoyannis' first cinematic reception and it explains the backstory of Agamemnon's return and subsequent murder to non-knowledgeable audience members. The shock of Euripides' choice of the peasant's hut as the setting for his *Electra* is thus destroyed by Cacoyannis' decision to delay the scenes set at this humble dwelling to a later point in the filmic narrative. Cacoyannis thus privileges the 'epic' rather than the 'tragic' register in the opening scenes of his first cinematic reception.

In *Iphigenia* we first encounter the heroine and her mother at Mycenae when they receive Agamemnon's letter informing them of the false news of the proposed marriage to Achilles designed to lure them to Aulis. This scene forms part of an added prologue that creates a sharp contrast between Agamemnon's *oikos* and life in the Greek encampment. In this third film the ruins of Mycenae represent a happy domestic world which Iphigenia (Tatiana Papamoskou) and Clytaemestra (Irene Papas) leave behind to journey to the Greek military camp at Aulis. These two key scenes in *Electra* and *Iphigenia* help to construct a world of 'epic' proportions and to locate Cacoyannis' trilogy visually in a grand heroic past. They establish an 'epic' register for Cacoyannis' cinematic receptions of Greek drama that is not actually present in Euripides.

A larger visual analogy can usefully be drawn from the comparison of Cacoyannis' cinematic receptions to the narrative of the Homeric epics. Cacoyannis' filmic technique combines wide-shots of large-scale scenes with the use of the more intimate close-up during key dramatic moments. He thus adapts for the modern medium of cinema the Homeric poems' alternation of large-scale scenes with a big cast of characters with more intimate moments focusing on particular individuals. One could indeed argue that the Homeric narrative is ideally suited to being discussed in 'cinematographic' terms.[11] The same does not hold true of Greek tragedy, which was confined to the performance space of ancient open-air theatres and restricted by the genre's rules about the number of actors (2–3) and Chorus members (12–15) allowed.

An illustrative example of Cacoyannis' affinity for this element in the Homeric epics is the opening scene of his *Iphigenia*, in which he establishes the scale of the Greek expedition by a tracking shot of the ships culminating in a wide shot of a mass of soldiers on the beach. In Euripides' play the army remains off-stage, so Cacoyannis' vision of the Greek expeditionary force more closely echoes passages in the *Iliad*, such as the extended simile that describes the Achaeans 'as the multitudinous nations of birds winged... so of these the multitudinous tribes from the ships and/ shelters poured to the plain of Skamandros, and the earth beneath their/ feet and under the feet of their horses thundered horribly' (*Il.* 2.459–66: τῶν δ', ὥς τ' ὀρνίθων πετεηνῶν ἔθνεα πολλά/ [...] ὣς τῶν ἔθνεα πολλὰ νεῶν ἄπο καὶ κλισιάων/ ἐς πεδίον προχέοντο Σκαμάνδριον· αὐτὰρ ὑπὸ χθὼν/ σμερδαλέον κονάβιζε ποδῶν αὐτῶν τε καὶ ἵππων). This wide-shot of the Achaean army in the epic is contrasted with close-ups of their leaders, in this particular scene Agamemnon (*Il.* 2.477). In *Iphigenia* the camera also comes to focus on Agamemnon after the opening shots of the army at Aulis. Cacoyannis emphasizes Agamemnon's struggle to retain control over the soldiers and to prevent their descent into anarchy and mob rule.[12] The application of this cinematic technique throughout the trilogy and the added/modified prologues of all three films are some of the means by which the 'epic' register of Cacoyannis' cinematic receptions is established.

b. Epic themes

These visual elements are reinforced by the narrative thematic connections that underlie the plot of Cacoyannis' receptions and connect them to the Homeric epics. One of the overarching concerns of Cacoyannis' Euripidean trilogy is the emphasis he places on the price of war that echoes the exploration of this theme in the *Iliad*. Cacoyannis' *The Trojan Women* and *Iphigenia*, in particular,

---

[11] My discussion of this particular Homeric narrative technique using the language of film studies is indebted to Nick Lowe (Royal Holloway College, University of London). For the visual impact of the epics, see also Greenwood 2007, 146 and in particular 158–71.
[12] The negative role that the army plays in the development of the plot of *Iphigenia* reflects contemporary political concerns about the key role that the military played during the dictatorship: Bakogianni 2013b, 228–29.

reflect the ancient epic's emphasis on the darker aspects of the war, the loss of life and the impact on the civilian population. Two well-known passages that exemplify the Iliadic exploration of this theme are the death of Sarpedon (*Il.* 16.462–505) and Hector's moving but brief reunion with Andromache (*Il.* 6.369–502).[13] Both Greeks and Trojans faced the possibility of death in battle, but for the Trojans defeat also meant the enslavement of non-combatants. The meeting between husband and wife foreshadows Andromache's fate in Euripides' *Troades*; enslaved and without a protector she is utterly helpless to prevent the murder of her son Astyanax. In his *Trojan Women* Cacoyannis dramatized this scene for contemporary cinematic audiences expanding on the feelings of empathy that the epic engenders for the doomed Trojans (on the transformations of this Iliadic scene, see also Karamanou and Georgopoulou in this volume).

The *Iliad* balances this awareness of the consequences of war with the desire of the warriors to achieve *aretē* and to win *kleos*.[14] Achilles' choice of a short but glorious life over a long peaceful one, a choice to which he recommits after Patroclus falls in battle (*Il.* 18.88–126), encapsulates the epic concept of heroism. In the justification of the heroic code provided by Sarpedon (*Il.* 12.310–28) a warrior is motivated by both a desire for the material gains that he can win in battle, as well as the glory that allows a hero's reputation to outlive him (Chiasson 2009, 187–88). Cacoyannis, however, disrupted this balance between the benefits and the cost of war in the epic. His films stress the negative impact the war had on the non-combatants and diminish the *kleos* it confers. He thus subverts both his epic and tragic sources. In order to understand his approach to this key theme his cinematic receptions must be considered within their contemporary context.

Cacoyannis created his trilogy during the turbulent decades of the 1960s and 1970s, when wars and conflicts around the world gave rise to an increasingly vocal peace movement. Cacoyannis, too, raised his voice in protest and as an act of resistance (Bakogianni 2009). He had personally experienced the toll that modern warfare takes on the civilian population. He lived through the Blitz in London during World War II and he documented the Turkish invasion of his home island of Cyprus in 1974. In response to these political upheavals and their human cost Cacoyannis focused not on the glory of war but on its price. *The Trojan Women* accentuate the tragedy of the fallen city of Troy symbol-

---

[13] Sarpedon is portrayed sympathetically in the epic, so his death at the hands of Patroclus is 'tragic', but it is also necessary if he is to achieve heroic status: Janko 1992, 371–75. Hector speaks first of his duty to his family and city (ll. 441–46) and only gradually reveals how deep his feelings for Andromache run and how the thought of her future suffering (ll. 450–65) makes his imminent death more acceptable to him: Graziosi/ Haubold 2010, 204–13.
[14] For a discussion of the popularity of the theme in more recent films, see Paul 2013, 70–80.

ized by the fate of its former queen Hecuba (Katherine Hepburn), who desperately and unsuccessfully tries to hold the last remnants of her family together. Over the course of Cacoyannis' film, as in Euripides' play, the audience watches her lose her daughter Cassandra, learn the news of Polyxena's sacrifice and stand by unable to aid her daughter-in-law Andromache and her grandson Astyanax, who is thrown to his death from the walls. Cacoyannis' sympathies lie with Hecuba as demonstrated in the *agon* scene in which she wins the argument on a rational basis, but Helen ultimately triumphs by using her seductive charms to manipulate Menelaus.

Cacoyannis' *Iphigenia* followed and explored in more detail the causes of the Trojan War. This film was released three years after the invasion of Cyprus. The director returned home when this news reached him, in order to create a record of these dark events. His documentary *Attila 74* explores the causes that precipitated the Turkish invasion as well as its tragic aftermath. Cacoyannis visited the refugee camps and captured on film first-hand accounts of the experience of the displaced, focusing in particular on the suffering of grieving mothers and the bewilderment and pain of children. *Iphigenia* portrays its heroine as an innocent girl betrayed by her male relatives for the sake of their political and military ambitions. Cacoyannis' second Clytaemestra is also a much more sympathetic character, whose hatred of Agamemnon is made comprehensible to the audience. In her grief at the loss of her daughter she becomes the Greek counterpart of the Trojan Hecuba and a symbol for all Cypriot mothers mourning their dead children (Bakogianni 2013a, 216–17).

Cacoyannis' preoccupation with the importance of family life and domesticity reflects similar themes in the *Odyssey*. Cacoyannis emphasized the importance of home and family in his cinematic receptions by demonstrating the disruptive effect that war has on them. *The Trojan Women* accomplishes this by stressing the women's feelings of loss. The men of Troy are already dead. Domestic harmony has been destroyed and now lives on only in the memory of mothers, wives and daughters. In *Iphigenia*, on the other hand, Cacoyannis explores the gradual destruction of familial bonds. The director provided a glimpse of happy domesticity in the scenes between mother and daughter at Mycenae, mentioned above, and on their trip to Aulis, only to show how the royal family breaks apart when Clytaemestra and Iphigenia learn the true purpose of Agamemnon's request that his daughter joins him at Aulis. The tragic results of the wedge this drives between husband and wife are demonstrated in Cacoyannis' *Electra* when Clytaemestra murders Agamemnon in the prologue and thus irrevocably destroys the last ties that bind the family together. As the heir to his father's throne Orestes is smuggled away to safety and the rift between mother and daughter widens. The audience has already witnessed the young Electra of the prologue brush off her mother's hand from her shoulder, but her contempt becomes hatred after the murder of her father. In another scene added by Cacoyannis the audience sees Clytaemestra forcing her daughter, now embodied by Papas, to marry the peasant against her wishes. The relationship portrayed in this scene is one of conflict. Mother and daughter should be *philoi*,[15] but in Cacoyannis' reception they are clearly *echthroi*. This is demonstrated again in the *agon*, when they verbalize their two diametrically opposite positions.

A theme related to the exploration and validation of the importance of family life and domesticity is that of *nostos*. Odysseus' ten-year long quest to return to his *oikos* is contrasted with Agamemnon's fatal early return (Heubeck/West/Hainsworth 1998, 16–17). Cacoyannis explores Agamemnon's *nostos* in the first and third film of his trilogy. In the prologue of his *Electra* Cacoyannis demonstrated to his audience the unsuccessful culmination of Agamemnon's *nostos*. The spectators act as witnesses to Agamemnon's murder by Clytaemestra and Aegisthus in the bath. It is this crime that provides the springboard for the revenge plot that follows and Cacoyannis accentuates this point by allowing his film audience to view the murder. In contrast, the Agamemnon of Cacoyannis' third film is not a returning hero murdered by an evil wife as in his *Electra*. As embodied by Costas Kazakos, Agamemnon is a weak man responsible for destroying his own family by his ambition to lead the Greek army against Troy. The last scene of the film in which Clytaemestra gazes at the departing fleet with hatred in her eyes brings the audience full circle back to the first film in the trilogy and Cacoyannis' portrayal of the murder of Agamemnon (McDonald 2001, 100). Unlike Odysseus, his *nostos* was unsuccessful as his ghost reveals to his old comrade (*Od.* 11.405–34). In his third film Cacoyannis lays the blame for Clytaemestra's betrayal squarely at Agamemnon's feet. Despite trials and tribulations, Odysseus achieves his longed-for goal, which is to restore domestic harmony and order to his *oikos*. In contrast, Cacoyannis presented his audience with an Agamemnon who had irrevocably destroyed his family by sacrificing his daughter on the altar of his ambitions and could therefore never really return to it.

c. Heroic values and characterization

Iliadic values underpin Cacoyannis' characterization of many of his heroes and heroines. His three main female protagonists, Electra, Hecabe and Iphigenia display

---

[15] For an exploration of the problematic nature of *philia* in Euripides' *Electra*, see Konstan 1985, 176–85.

strong Homeric qualities such as their preoccupation with *timē* (honour) and *kleos* (glory/reputation). In his adaptation of a Euripidean play Cacoyannis created an idealized and sympathetic Electra who fights for justice and the restoration of the rightful succession. The royal *oikos* was brutally violated and its workings disrupted by Aegisthus' and Clytaemestra's murder of Agamemnon. Electra is determined to help her brother Orestes restore order to their family and to the city, but ultimately the siblings fail and are obliged to go into exile. Cacoyannis thus creates an 'epic' version of Electra that contrasts sharply with Euripides' more prosaic tragic heroine worried about her status and inheritance (*El.* 303–22).

The Trojan Women emphasizes the nobility of Hecabe in particular, but also that of Andromache (Vanessa Redgrave) and the other Trojan survivors. It portrays them as heroic, in their capacity to endure and to adapt to their tragic change of fortune. An illustrative example is Andromache's heroic but ultimately doomed attempt to protect Astyanax from the Greeks' decree of death. In the film she actively tries to resist by hugging her son to herself and trying to prevent Talthybius (Brian Blessed) from seizing him and sending him to his death. Hecabe and the Chorus surround her in a loose circle supporting her emotionally. In the end, however, the tragic mother is forced to relinquish her son, but she does so in a dignified manner that condemns the cruelty of the Greek perpetrators. Cacoyannis drives this point home by allowing his audience to glimpse the murder of Astyanax. He is shown at the walls of Troy accompanied by a Greek soldier and a dizzying montage of the rocks below suggests his fall. The ability to survive thus becomes a heroic quality in Cacoyannis and an act of resistance in itself. In contrast, the Greeks are portrayed as weak, unjust and downright cruel, which further enhances the heroic qualities of the Trojan women.

In *Iphigenia* Cacoyannis explains the young heroine's change of heart as a patriotic sacrifice, so that the Greek army can avenge the insult of Helen's abduction. She realizes that she cannot save herself, but she can choose the manner of her death and how she is remembered. Prompted by her love for her father and aware of the threat posed by the Greek army to her family she chooses a glorious death that prefigures Achilles' own choice. The epic hero reconsiders his decision after his quarrel with Agamemnon (*Il.* 9.308–429), but ultimately he recommits to it after the death in battle of Patroclus. Cacoyannis thus created an Iphigenia that was a fitting partner to this epic Achilles, even though their marriage never actually took place. However, Iphigenia's decision indirectly leads to the death of Achilles and it destroys her own family as well as the city of Troy.

Despite the good intentions of Cacoyannis' heroines, however, their decisions have terrible consequences. Revenge comes at the cost of matricide in *Electra* and Iphigenia's heroic decision is shown to be manifestly misguided in Cacoyannis' reception of the problematic text of the *Iphigenia in Aulis*. Moreover, the happiness of domestic life, briefly portrayed in the early scenes of the prologue of *Electra* and more extensively in the depiction of the loving and nurturing relationship between Clytaemestra and Iphigenia, is utterly destroyed by the heroine's actions, however noble in intent. Iphigenia's decision also leads directly to the destruction of Hecabe's world. The tragic queen loses her last links to her past life over the course of the film, which ends with her and the Chorus walking away from the ruins of Troy and heading towards the Greek ships that will bear them away to a life of slavery. Cacoyannis portrays the traditional concept of heroism with its emphasis on honour, glory and a good reputation in a negative light. He valorizes instead the courage of the victim (McDonald 1983, 132).

Many of Cacoyannis' male characters retain a heroic presence reminiscent of that of the warriors of epic, rather than of the ambiguous protagonists of Euripides' dramas. The director modifies the ancient concept of heroism based on military prowess by introducing modern concerns such as the responsibility of a leader to rule justly and romantic love. The director's first conception of Agamemnon, as the audience sees him in the silent prologue of his *Electra*, is as the returning conqueror of Troy. In the film his mantle is gradually assumed by his son Orestes (Yannis Fertis). His is a journey from *ephebe* to full heroic warrior status, similar to Telemachus' trajectory in the *Odyssey*. Nestor in fact holds up Orestes as a role model for the prince of Ithaca (*Od.* 3.304–10).[16] In Cacoyannis' reception the audience watches Orestes grow in stature over the course of the film from an unsure youth to an active participant and shaper of the plot. Pylades, Electra and the old retainer guide him, but he takes the lead in the killing of Aegisthus at the feast and afterwards. His most heroic action by far, however, is to go into voluntary exile at the end of the film, because he has lost the support of the people after committing matricide (Bakogianni 2011, 190–91). In the closing scenes of the film he even gives up on the companionship of Pylades silently commanding him to follow Electra instead. Cacoyannis' Orestes can now stand alone and stoically accept the consequences of his actions. It is this new type of heroism that is valorized by Cacoyannis.

Achilles in *Iphigenia* (played by Panos Mihalopoulos) is also presented as a heroic, if rather rash warrior. This more closely resembles his portrayal in the epic than in Euripides' more ambiguous and questioning version of the Homeric hero (McDonald 1983, 156). Cacoyannis portrays the Achaeans' greatest warrior as willing to defend Iphigenia, even if that entails opposing the will of the Greek army. Cacoyannis added a scene in which Achilles' own troops throw

---

16 The epic marginalizes the matricide and, instead, stresses the rightful killing of Aegisthus: Heubeck/West/ Hainsworth 1998, 181.

stones at him and refuse to help him defend Iphigenia. He is thus a sympathetic figure whose arrogance is tempered by his courage. Cacoyannis also adds romantic love as a facet of his portrayal of the hero.[17] In the film, as in the play, his agreement to defend Iphigenia after Clytaemestra's supplication is motivated by his sense that his honour has been impugned. When, however, Iphigenia and Achilles do meet later in the film, Cacoyannis suggests that his young protagonists fall in love at first sight (MacKinnon 1986, 90 and Bakogianni 2013a, 229). This romantic love coupled with her love for her father and family forms the bedrock of the motivation that leads Cacoyannis' young heroine to decide to submit to the sacrifice demanded of her.

Concluding remarks

In Michael Cacoyannis' trilogy of films the close connection between the Homeric epics and Greek tragedy is performed in the modern medium of cinema. Cacoyannis inverts the traditional relationship between these two genres by re-heroizing Euripides (MacKinnon 1986, 94). The director's purportedly 'Euripidean' trilogy is in fact infused with 'epic' elements in terms of its visual language, as well as of narrative and characterization. However, in contrast to other cinematic adaptations whose claim of being modelled on one of the Homeric epics can be more explicitly constructed,[18] Cacoyannis' relationship with the epics is a more indirect, implicit one. Moreover, it is one that needs to be carefully disentangled, like Penelope's un-weaving of the shroud of Laertes at night.

---

[17] Wolfgang Petersen in his *Troy* (2004) also added romantic love as an essential element in his portrayal of Achilles. His love for Briseis is a powerful force that drives his heroism, particularly at the end of the film when he dies in order to save her. For an exploration of this theme in the film, see Chiasson 2009, 188–203. See also Allen (2007, 156–62) and Blondell on the emphasis the film places on the Achilles-Briseis romance (2009, 9).

[18] For the reception of the Homeric epics in the cinema, see Solomon 2001, 103–11 and Paul 2013, 36–92. In the new millennium Wolfgang Petersen's film *Troy* (2004) is one such reception that inscribes its claim to have been 'inspired' by the *Iliad* in its opening credits.

Hara Thliveri
'Travelling to the Light, Aiming at the Infinite': The *Odyssey* of Mikis Theodorakis

There are many elements in common between Mikis Theodorakis[1] and Homer, from their birth on the same island, Chios, to their being claimed by many cities. The most important is that Theodorakis, the most famous modern Greek composer active during the last eighty years, managed to elevate poetry to a continuing narrative of national Greek myth. The objective of the present study is to explore Theodorakis' refiguration of the idea of Homeric *nostos* in his most recent song-cycle entitled *Odyssey* with poetry by Kostas Kartelias. The work was set to music in 2006 and was recorded as a CD by Legend Recordings in 2007 with Maria Farandouri as a soloist and orchestration by Irina Velentinova.[2] The official press conference to launch the CD took place on 20 March 2007 at the Pallas Theatre in Athens, in the presence of the composer.[3]

I shall start by pointing out the significance of the photograph used on the cover of the CD, in which the composer is depicted at the age of twelve, at the

---

[1] I am grateful to Mikis Theodorakis for his reading of my text and for his suggestions, which led, I hope, to a better overall structure. Many thanks to Theodorakis' assistant Rena Parmenidou; to the poet Kostas Kartelias for his invitation to attend the performance of *Canto General* at the Herodeion on 12 July 2012; to the painter Nikolas Klironomos for his collaboration and his permission to publish one of his paintings of Theodorakis; to the company Legend Recordings for permission to reproduce the cover of the *Odyssey*; to Maria Hatzara for the information from the archive of Maria Farandouri; and to Alexandra Sgouropoulou from the Orchestra "Mikis Theodorakis". I warmly thank Professor Gail Holst-Warhaft for her support and her permission to use extracts from her translation of the *Odyssey* of Kartelias and also the painter Jannis Psychopedis for his permission to publish a photograph of his painting *Lower Limbs – History Lesson* (Figure 3). Finally, I am obliged to Dr Ioanna Karamanou and Dr Thanasis Efstathiou for their invitation to participate in the Homeric Receptions Conference in Corfu (7–9 November 2011) in a session entitled 'Refiguring Homer in Film and Music'.
[2] The premiere of the *Odyssey* took place on 20 June 2007 at Kyme, Euboea, at an event in honour of the poet Kostas Kartelias; see http://www.cuma.gr/content/blogcategory/68/145/20/160/. It was preceded by the live performance of two songs ('Beautiful Helen' and 'The Song of the Sirens') during a concert by Maria Farandouri in Munich on 25 September 2006, at a time when the CD had not yet come out; on 30 January 2008, a substantial part of the work was presented at the Megaron Mousikis (Concert Hall) in Athens with Maria Farandouri and the Berliner Instrumentalisten as part of a tribute to Mikis Theodorakis.
[3] For the entire press conference, see http://www.youtube.com/watch?v= QYnEg0Jlzm4 (Part 1 to Part 6b).

Figure 1. The cover of the *Odyssey*, Legend Recordings 2007. Photograph of Mikis Theodorakis at the age of twelve in 1937. Published by permission of Legend Recordings.

time when he lived in Patras with his family (Figure 1).⁴ In his autobiography Theodorakis described his two-year stay in the Achaean capital (1937–38) as 'carefree years'⁵ and states that the main event of that period, which determined his later course, was his enrolment in the Odeion of Patras and his decision to involve himself in music.⁶ The publication of the childhood photograph becomes an important element adding to the autobiographical significance of the *Odyssey*, as a means of mythologizing the personal history of the composer. Theodo-

---

4 The picture dates from 1937 and is part of a family photograph in which, apart from the young Mikis, appear his father, Georgios Theodorakis, his mother, Aspasia, and his younger brother, Yannis; see Theodorakis 1993, 10.
5 Theodorakis 1986, 75.
6 Theodorakis 1986, 78; see also the painting *Patras* of Klironomos in Figure 2 following.

rakis is here portrayed as the central figure of the myth, as another Odysseus who wishes to return to his own Ithaca. On this basis, I shall attempt to show that the setting of the *Odyssey* to music represents the completion of the composer's personal *nostos*. Then:

> *Odyssey* could mean the long journey of Mikis Theodorakis in the Sea of Music, which he started when he wrote his first song in Patras in 1937 at the age of 12, continuing until the most recent stop, in April 2006 at the age of 81, when he composed the 14 songs of this *Odyssey*.[7]

At the same time, Theodorakis' *Odyssey* provides an incentive to explore the reception of the Odyssean *nostos* in popular discourse,[8] by posing the question of how ancient symbols feed collective memory (on the archetypal Odyssean *nostos* and its reworkings, see also Jacob in this volume). Theodorakis himself, at the age of eighty one, when he composed his *Odyssey*, gave his own answer by realizing the failure of social and cultural values to re-build a better world for the advocacy of which he has spent most of his life. His *Odyssey* leads to a heterotopian environment, a lonely performing *topos*, which cannot exist anywhere else but at 'the depths of our being'. As such, Theodorakis highlights the end of a whole era —mainly of the 20th century— which was characterized by the dramatic endeavours of the Greek people for territorial stability, the establishment of democracy and political independence.[9] The new age is that of crushing people by isolation, hard working conditions, lack of free time, cheap cultural prototypes for consumption and lack of spirituality:

> We are living the end of utopia, which was, as now, our capacity to live together with the 'other'. The awareness of such a great tragedy is that which desiccates us all the more. Consequently, salvation is found at least in the emotional return to the depths of our 'being', in case we find the water we lack and slake our thirst.[10]

Towards this direction, I shall demonstrate that Theodorakis' *nostos* is not static; it rather signifies the setting for a new orientation. Self-knowing becomes the first step of an inner-outer process which reaches the linking of man, primarily,

---

7 From the leaflet included with the CD of the *Odyssey*, Legend Recordings 2007.
8 On the features of Homeric *nostos* and its reception, see Taplin 1977, 124–125; Haubold 2000, 105–106, 192–193; Zajko 2004, 322. On the persistence of this motif throughout ancient as well as Modern Greek literature, see Alexopoulou 2009, esp. ch. 2 and Appendix; Alexopoulou 2006, 1–9.
9 On the appropriation of classical models for socio-political purposes, see the examples discussed in Hardwick 2003, 99–107; van Steen 2011, esp. 1–63; Hardwick 2013, 18–23.
10 From the leaflet included with the CD of the *Odyssey*, Legend Recordings 2007.

with himself and, secondarily, with his external cosmic environment. This type of *return* already developed by the poet Angelos Sikelianos (1884–1951) presents a *new mythology* of facing the world through the deliverance of poetry:

> *Returning is at the core of Sikelianos' poetry, from the opening words of his first major poem ('Alaphroiskiotos'), to the great works of his maturity [...] Return is associated by Sikelianos with rebirth and rejuvenation; the poetic process is a form of resurrection, and ancient myth and texts are given a new lease of life through their reworking in new poems.*[11]

In the course of elucidating Theodorakis' perception of *nostos*, it will be worth comparing it with the contemporary paintings of Jannis Psychopedis included in his exhibition *Nostos*, which was held in Athens in 2008. I shall argue that Psychopedis' view is totally different; it rather seems to highlight the gap between *then and now* in order to reveal the contradictory relationship of the ancient past and the present. His view, bare, critical but also nostalgic, aspires to portray social degradation, and his *nostos* suggests that 'the idea-value-principle exists minus its ultimate receiver'.[12] The symbols of antiquity, statues and myths, typical elements of morality and humanistic development, are 'trapped' in a way that signals a non-*return* direction in the future:

> *The Greece of today, the wounded environment, the neglected values, the debased —to a large extent— cultural heritage of Greece, the forgotten tradition, sybaritism, the imitation of unworthy models. In the end, as well as at the very beginning, it is Greece, from which we have turned away our gaze.*[13]

a. The *nostos* of childhood

The depiction of the young Theodorakis on the cover of the CD (Figure 1) is noteworthy to the extent that it determines the external time of his life journey and the features of his personal *nostos*. The fourteen songs of the *Odyssey* are identified, as much emotionally as expressively, with the deepest and purest facets of the composer's soul.[14] The *Odyssey* then concerns a return to the first starting-

---

11 Ekdawi, 2002, 115.
12 Takis Mavrotas in Psychopedis 2008, 25.
13 *op.cit.*, 24–25.
14 The titles of the songs are: 1. 'Beside the Sea', 2. 'The Song of the Companions', 3. 'Shipwreck', 4. 'The Song of the Sirens', 5. 'In the Underworld', 6. 'On Calypso's Isle', 7. 'Beautiful Helen', 8. 'Circe', 9. 'Like a Beast', 10. 'The Love God', 11. 'Sea Witch', 12. 'To Nausica', 13. 'Pe-

point of life and to the settings to music of that period. Theodorakis himself has acknowledged that his artistic nature 'was the creation'[15] of his youthful period, and, most importantly, he has recognized the *Odyssey* songs as a recollection of the musical enquiries of his childhood (1937–43).[16] Morphologically, the style here follows the composer's turn in the 1980s towards utmost lyricism and melody with harmony without populist elements.[17] It is music with even greater spirituality. The piano, the violin, the cello, the percussion, the mandolin, the saxophone, the guitar and the clarinet are the main instruments, while the absence of the bouzouki can be explained as a conscious return to childhood sounds.[18] Theodorakis enthrals us with the density of the motifs and the overall strength of the composition, so that the *Odyssey* comes to denote another stage in the evolution of the so-called *popular art song*, which emerged in the 1960s with the *Epitaphios* of Yannis Ritsos.[19]

In the case of Theodorakis, the journey of life constitutes a crooked line through a large number of places in which the composer lived during his childhood: Chios (1925), Mytilene (1925–28), Syros and Athens (1929), Ioannina (1930–32), Argostoli (1933–36), Patras (1937–38), Pyrgos (1938–39) and Tripolis (1939–43).[20] The young Theodorakis followed his family moves, because of his father, who, serving as a high civil servant, had undertaken several unwelcome moves because of his pro-Venizelos views.[21] The year 1943, one year before the liberation of the country from the Germans, constitutes a new page in Mikis' life, as he settles in Athens and begins his systematic involvement in music.

---

nelope's Song', 14. 'Without Identity'. For a wider approach to the song-cycle, see Koutoulas 1998, 426.
15 Theodorakis 2002, 62.
16 Theodorakis at the press conference on the *Odyssey*, 20 March 2007, Pallas Theatre, Athens (Part 2); see above, n. 3.
17 Theodorakis' gradual move towards lyricism is initiated in 1978 with his setting to music poetry of Tasos Livaditis entitled *The Lyrics*, followed more firmly with his setting to music poetry of Dionysis Karatzas and more specifically: *The Faces of the Sun* (1987), *Like an Ancient Wind* (1987), *Beatrice in Zero Street* (set to music in 1986, recorded in 1994), and *The More Lyrical* (1996). For the significance of melody in the music of Theodorakis overall, see Lazaridou-Elmaloglou 2004, Part 1, 64–65.
18 Theodorakis used the bouzouki and elements of *rembetika* for the first time in the *Epitaphios* of Yannis Ritsos in 1960; see Mouyis 2010, 30 ff.
19 On the *Epitaphios*, see Mouyis 2010, 28–43, especially 31; see also Beaton 1999, 223–26.
20 Theodorakis 1986, 16; see also Giannaris 1973, 3–26.
21 Theodorakis 1986, 50, 70, 82.

The constant displacements of Theodorakis' family during the period 1925–43 made this period significant for moulding the composer's personality. As has already been noticed:

> *Perhaps there might be, sometime in the future, seriously focused studies to show what he himself (i.e. Theodorakis) implies, that there is a relationship of his initial wanderings with other subsequent creative wanderings and pursuits.*[22]

Going through Theodorakis' autobiography of his first eighteen years, one understands quite easily that in his case the geographical wandering leads to another version of the *persona* of Odysseus. Theodorakis bears the stigma of the 'self-imprisoned'[23] and self-exiled, as the severance from his many homes carries the meaning of exclusion from the world of those who live without travelling. With the features of the outsider (ξένος), the young Mikis felt barely accepted in each new city that he moved to:

> *I was always the outsider. In Ioannina, an Athenian; in Argostoli, an Epirote; in Patras, a Cephalonian and so on.*[24]

> *Because, in contrast to the child who lives permanently in the village or the town and has a steady reference point – even though low and inadequate -, the child who is uprooted constantly does not manage to absorb anything.*[25]

Theodorakis' diverse experiences in the Greek provinces constituted a source of inspiration for the painter Nikolas Klironomos, who created a series of ten impressive paintings naming them after the towns where the composer lived (see Figure 2). The paintings of Klironomos were presented first in 2007 in an exhibition of the painter in Athens entitled *His childhood years ... a journey*.[26] In 2008 the works were exhibited at the 'Mikis Theodorakis Museum' in Zatouna, Arcadia, as part of the celebrations of the 40th anniversary of Theodorakis' exile in Zatouna, and in December 2010 they were lent to the Evgenidou Foundation during the celebration of the 85th birthday of the composer. Klironomos' work, a kind of 'wall newspaper' of photographs, sketches, newspaper clippings, manuscripts and musical notes, exploits elements of the composer's autobiography by defin-

---

22 Kouyoumoutzakis 2007, 44.
23 Theodorakis 1986, 97.
24 Theodorakis 1986, 34. All extracts from Theodorakis are translated by the author.
25 op. cit., 64.
26 The exhibition took place in the Gallery 'Ekfrasi-Yianna Grammatopoulou'; see Klironomos 2007 (Catalogue); Hermann 2008, 80, 82–83, 261.

ing his private space, the bedrooms of his childhood which, acting as a colourful fantasy 'shell', protected him from the 'hostile' outside world.

The prerequisite for the perpetuation of the figure of Odysseus, though, is not the journey but his capacity to return. In its core, *nostos* is schismatic, as the breakup of the primordial image of the *cosmos* —through alternations of places, traits and people— causes fateful divisions as much with the external environment as with the self. The basic question about the *Odyssey* of Mikis Theodorakis is, then, under which presuppositions does his *nostos* become possible.

b. The reconstruction of the lost prototype

In setting the *Odyssey* to music Theodorakis claims his spiritual locality in Patras at the age of twelve years old. The reconnection with childhood sixty-nine years later (1937– 2006) attains the significance of the highest challenge, as long as the signs of familiarity which unite him with the starting-point and erase the losses of the journey must be recognized.[27] Overcoming the inertia of nostalgia, the attainment of *nostos* in the *Odyssey* manages to bridge the distance between the present and the past.[28] The transparency of feelings and the deferential congruence of music with the poetic word are two distinct elements which fascinate us, so that we can say that the 'true' Ithaca is reached by the person who has built himself on the mythology of childhood and who never lost faith in the aesthetic world throughout his life. In Theodorakis' *Odyssey*, I would say that what occurs is what Odysseus Elytis writes in *Εν λευκώ (Carte Blanche)*:

> The way to speak about the past, without becoming suspected of nostalgia, has not yet been found. Nevertheless, it is one thing to load time and to carry it together with your wrinkles and another to circulate within it, backwards-forwards, with the easiness that only poetry allows you.[29]

The poetry of Kartelias, with its expressive austerity and emotional innocence, becomes the vehicle for Theodorakis' reconnection with his youthful inspiration. In other words, poetry creates the premises for the performing of *nostos*. Besides,

---

[27] For his arduous process of composition especially after the age of seventy, see the press conference on the *Odyssey* (Part 1); see above, n. 3.
[28] An opposite example could be the 'Return of the Emigrant' by Giorgos Seferis (*Deck Diary A*, 1938), who upon returning to his homeland feels the greatest loss of the past, because he cannot harmonize the signs of the present in his memory.
[29] Elytis 2006^6, 300–01.

Theodorakis started as a songwriter with the members of his own family as his audience:

> It is not well-known that I started as a songwriter. Besides, this was the only thing that we could do in the provinces. We did not have a piano, we did not have school orchestras, we only sang. So, at the age of twelve (this is the reason for this photograph, it is exactly in Patras when I was twelve) I compose my first song.[30]

The composer's first song is entitled 'The Boat' and was written in 1937.[31] The connection to the *Odyssey* is an emotional, stylistic and semiological association, as in this most recent song-cycle the return to the harbour and the deliverance from the early memories are achieved. It is worth referring to Klironomos' painting entitled *Patras* (Figure 2), in which the young Mikis' room is depicted

Figure 2. Nikolas Klironomos, *Patras*, work VII, mixed techniques on canvas, paper and cardboard, 100 x 180 cm, 2005–2006. Published by permission of Nikolas Klironomos.

with his first violin on the left side of his desk and his first handwritten score of the aforementioned song hanging on the wall above the lamp.[32]

---

30 Theodorakis, press conference on the *Odyssey* (Part 2; see above, n. 3); Theodorakis 1986, 81.
31 Theodorakis 1993.
32 Klironomos 2007, 35.

Setting the *Odyssey* to music evokes the preparatory phase of the composer between 1937 and 1943,[33] when he started to set to music poems of the leading Greek poets found in school text-books. Dimitris Karvounis, who conducted the choral teaching of forty youthful songs of Theodorakis, points out that in these songs 'there is a finished compositional proposal with a morphological balance, an aesthetic and perfectly artistic result'.[34]

The exceptional value of the first songs is that they constitute the 'core of the musical self'[35] of Theodorakis, representing also his psychological need to express himself during the lonely years of family travels. In sum, the *Odyssey* encapsulates an analogous need of Theodorakis to recognize his childhood dream for reasons which, as we shall see, are not far distant from those of his youth. In this manner, the ring-composition of the Homeric journey is displayed, in that the start becomes the end and the end forms a new beginning.

c. The anti-journey of utopia

The poet Kostas Kartelias is another version of the wandering Odysseus, who leaves his birthplace in Athens during his childhood and establishes himself with his father in Euboea:

> I would say that loneliness characterizes my childhood. The loneliness of few words. My siblings and cousins, whom I loved and used to talk to, had left for Athens to study. Conversations and life in the village were very poor. Imagination was insufficient and dangerous in daily life. I wanted to leave.[36]

And here, the return to Ithaca is reconstructed on an inner field, which reveals the harmony of the individual with himself after a struggle and the liberation from external circumstances. The writing of Kartelias breathes warmth and unpretentious familiarity and manages to approach man as a suffering sensuous being.

In the poem 'Beside the Sea'[37] Ithaca becomes synonymous with the very centre of existence, 'the depths of my soul', which takes on perspective and 'horizon' through the fulfillment of feelings. The Cavafy-like didacticism does not apply:

---

[33] Cf. Theodorakis, http://int.mikis-theodorakis.net/index.php/article/archive/8/; Koutoulas 1998, 406–07.
[34] Karvounis 2005, 124; cf. Theodorakis 1993.
[35] Theodorakis 1993, 8; cf. Theodorakis 2005, *First Songs*, Intuition (CD).
[36] http://www.cuma.gr/content/view/248/145/; see also Kartelias 2007.
[37] Cf. translation by Holst-Warhaft 2012.

> Laistrygonians, Cyclops,
> angry Poseidon—don't be afraid of them.³⁸

Odysseus, speaking in the first person, admits that the only way to find solace escaping 'the fury of Poseidon' and 'the anger of the winds', is through love. The 'fire in my breast', as he writes, is 'a sign of return to an Ithaca that I must return to/ on my life's long journey'.

In 'The Song of the Companions' the intrinsic human powers engender a type of poetic *nostos* towards an Ithaca perceived as 'the open sea', challenging us to 'journey into danger'. 'Greetings, sacred danger', Sikelianos writes similarly in 'The Song of the Argonauts', while subsequently:

> Silent virgin peace, in which journey you will immerse us
> now that our effort blossomed wings!³⁹

In these circumstances, *eros* is a powerful impetus of a route which leads against any prevailing restraint and manipulation. As a result of this process, the poetic *nostos* manages to raise life to a more genuine, non-materialistic level, in which imagination and perceptible understanding play a primary role. The following excerpt is from the 'The Song of the Companions':

> The world always
> finds new rulers
> and we lonely poets
> will remain.

Being consistent with this outlook, Theodorakis records how solitude (as a result of the constant childhood moves) set him on the road to music as a kind of defence against external circumstances:

> My pathological absorption in and pursuit of music, which happened [...] in 1938–39, at Pyrgos in Elis, had as its basis a psychological motivation, a personal answer of my own – a kind of escape but also of liberation – from the imaginary walls which I had raised around me, refusing even to stroll in the community of people.⁴⁰

The progress towards the poetic *nostos* is the anti-journey within the journey and the self-conscious placing against all conventionalism of life. It concerns also the

---

38 Keeley/ Sherrard 1995, 15 ('Ithaka' by C. Cavafy).
39 Sikelianos 2003⁴, 65; extract translated by Hara Thliveri.
40 Theodorakis 1986, 65–66.

dynamics towards utopia, the search for the ideal, the metaphysical passage to freedom, which surpasses adversities. Theodorakis writes:

> I was pleased when in 1947 and 1948 they 'travelled' us on their say-so, so as to send us into exile. On the beach my parents were wailing, and even though I was bound with handcuffs, I was trying with difficulty to hide the wave of joy flaring up within me, because soon we would set sail, aiming at piercing the horizon – the journey![41]

This liberating vision was the fundamental ideological motivation for Theodorakis all his life, during his youth, as well as later through his personal stance in political and social struggles. He himself admits that:

> Facing problems –social and national– became, at least on my part, in one way dream-like, ideological and not at all realistic.[42]

d. Return to the *first self*

In 1943, in a period of spiritual searching during his stay in Tripolis, Theodorakis moulds his theory of Universal Harmony,[43] which conveys his existential striving for the detection of the bonds of man with the *cosmos* and the 'pursuit of the Ideal':

> that is, of the significant centre, which is found very deep within us and at the same time far away, because it is the law of the Cosmos, of the Beginning and the End.[44]

Theodorakis' conception of Universal Harmony, which is extended to the ability of art to reproduce the notional links within the cosmic environment,[45] reflects, in my opinion, a mental kinship with the views of Angelos Sikelianos, who already in 'The Visionary' ('Alaphroiskiotos', 1909) bases the theory of the return to the *first self:*

---

[41] Theodorakis 1986, 20; cf. Theodorakis 2002, 89–90: 'a journey to the light, aiming at the infinite', which inspired the title of this article.
[42] Theodorakis 2002, 133.
[43] For an overview of Universal Harmony, see Theodorakis 1986, 98 ff.; Theodorakis 2007, 77– 102; Lazaridou-Elmaloglou 2004 (Part I) 57 ff.; Mouyis 2010, 80–94.
[44] Theodorakis 1986, 98.
[45] Theodorakis 1986, 141; cf. Mouyis 2010, 83: 'Art was the only power that could create within us a microcosm in perfect parallel with the *Cosmos*. It could transfer the Laws that define Universal Harmony inside us'.

> *At this outset my entire Being is situated from the beginning, biologically unbreakable, as the principal core of a clear experience of the cosmic consciousness of life.*[46]

Sikelianos and Theodorakis reinforce the nostalgia for the attainment of the one intrinsic centre, which constitutes the sole umbilical bond of man with the universe. They both regard the youthful years as enabling the individual to become a receiver of cosmic pulse through poetics and senses. In the 'Hymn of the Great Nostos' of Sikelianos, the *first self* is the biological unity revealing the indisputable bond of man with the universe:

> *And as the armed Eros descends before me*
>   *the depths of heaven,*
> *without my seeking it, I leap and dance in turn*
>   *with my mind's armour!*[47]

For the young Theodorakis the linking of man with the *cosmos* occurs through music, as music transfers to man the *Law of the Universe*, which happens also to be the *Law of Total Creation*.[48] The composer highlights the influence of Palamas, who 'believed that rhythm in poetry —the rhythmic stride— symbolizes the rhythm that governs the Universe'.[49] In another, more metaphysical, manner, Sikelianos considers that:

> *The oral Poetic World [...] represents [...] the fundamental tone of the deep biological and psychological Unity of the Universe and of man with the Universe and man.*[50]

Here I argue that the aforementioned views of Sikelianos and Theodorakis demonstrate the greatest capacity of the poetic *nostos* to attain hyper-realistic perception within the bounds of human life. They both consider the period of youth to bring out the strongest spiritual powers of man. As Theodorakis says:

> *Perhaps the composer at that time, between the ages of 12 and 16, is more genuine. He speaks more with himself, with the Universe, with his inspiration.*[51]

---

46 Sikelianos 1999⁵, 23.
47 Sikelianos 2003⁴, 104; extract translated by Hara Thliveri.
48 Theodorakis 1986, 140–41; see also Theodorakis 2002, 146.
49 Theodorakis 1986, 140–41.
50 Sikelianos 1981, 148.
51 See Koutoulas 1998, 408.

Consequently, the return of Theodorakis through his *Odyssey* to his *first self*, as fulfilment of his poetic *nostos*, renders the power of man to capture the catholic essence of life, the essence, that is, which joins the spiritual experience with the apparent world. In 'The Visionary' of Sikelianos, the young Odysseus is met sleeping on some seashore of his homeland after his return.[52] In this way, through the hypnosis of the mind and the awakening of the senses, the poet lays the ground for the opening of his poetic inspiration.[53]

The metaphysics of the senses likewise play a role in the poetry of Kartelias. In 'The Song of the Sirens',[54] 'the wind blows a song that seems endless', and the sound of the sea is fragmented into 'a thousand voices'. Within a boundless sea setting, there is 'no mast to be tied to and no rope'. The ties with the material world are halted and the dilemma of Odysseus is not how to avoid 'so much music', but which of all to choose. The Sirens, in contrast to the fearsome Homeric monsters we know, represent the enchanting call of the art leading beyond the borders of the world of experience:

When the ocean starts singing,
there's so much music to bear,
a thousand voices, so you don't know
how to choose and there's no mast to be tied to
and no rope.
I'll soar on my wings
that I'll spread
over the strange islands of paradise.

The conception of this moving boat refers to a kind of ritual mystery-process in which the artist (as a mediator himself between the earth and the universe) liberates his inspiration by soaring *on his wings*. The repetition at the end 'untie your hair, so I can see you' shows that this transforming —more or less erotic — power of art towards freedom is the only path to the salvation of man, offering people an escape from 'the endless desert':

Untie your hair, so I can see you, know you
in the blind alleys of the world,
in the endless desert of the world.
Untie your hair, so I can come and speak to you.

---

[52] Sikelianos 1999⁵, 85 ('Return') translated in Keeley/Sherrard 1980, 11; Anagnostopoulos 1995, 121–31; Ekdawi 2002, 115–19, esp. 118.
[53] The return of Odysseus to Lefkada implies a sense of autochthony in view of the origin of Sikelianos; cf. Ricks 1989, 63.
[54] Holst-Warhaft 2012.

Elsewhere, Theodorakis refers to a 'mysterious calling, an erotic expectation':

> *For me this heart's longing, this leap of the heart, which I felt each time I crossed the sea by boat is exactly the same that I feel each time I decide to write a piece. A mysterious calling, an erotic expectation of the elusive.*[55]

e. The parameter of national awareness

According to Theodorakis, the poem 'In the Underworld' has 'historical, social and ultimately autobiographical content', and for this reason he chose to sing it himself.[56] The beloved dead, the dead fellow-combatants, themselves also spectres of an invisible world, are the shades which Odysseus meets in Hades. To keep *nostos* alive, one must endure remembering. In this way, with the feelings brightly burning, he can maintain his lyrical humidity, so as not to be alienated by 'society's filth'. Oblivion kills the living, the dead and makes nations disappear.

Born in 1925, of Cretan descent,[57] Mikis Theodorakis belongs to a generation which was scarred by the experiences of the Second World War, the Occupation, the National Resistance against the Germans (1941–44) and the Civil War (1946–49). Maintaining throughout his life the patriotic ideals of the National Liberation Front (EAM),[58] Theodorakis reaches manhood in a period in which Greece claims association with the achievements of 1821 and distances itself from the national defeat of the Asia Minor Catastrophe (1922). Theodorakis, then, brings back the topography of the *Odyssey* from the shores of Asia Minor,[59] and his birthplace in Chios, to the Eptanisa and the so-called 'Old Greece'. From his first hearing 'the practised choirs or the bands'[60] in Argostoli and his first setting to music of poems of Solomos, Valaoritis, Palamas and Drosinis in Patras, Pyrgos and Tripolis, Theodorakis reunites the scattered elements of Hellenism and lays the foundation for the reunification of the national body; in other words, he lays the foundation for the completeness and recollection of national *nostos*.

---

[55] Lazaridou-Elmaloglou 2004, Addendum II, 33.
[56] Theodorakis, press conference on the *Odyssey* (Part 2; see above, n. 3).
[57] For a recent overview of the biography of Theodorakis, see Mouyis 2010, 14–20.
[58] Hamilakis 2007, 207–10.
[59] The composer's parents and mother's family were victims of the Asia Minor Catastrophe of 1922. Cf. the antiheroic prototype of Odysseus in Seferis; Ricks 1989, 119–34.
[60] Theodorakis 1986, 66: 'From Argostoli, when I heard the practised choirs or the bands, that is, melody with harmony, which in the end produced the Greek Art Song, I felt an inexplicable attraction'.

But, what are the popular connotations of *nostos* today, in the second decade of the 21st century? Is there a common *topos* of return and how does *nostos* nurture national imagination?[61] The received cultural acquisitions show but a museum character, unless they inspire fruitfully the present. As befits the circumstances of personal awakening, on a collective level a nation owes it to itself to resist the declining memory of its past and to recognize its own familiar traces through the course of time. In this way, the emancipation of the literary prototypes —such as the Homeric ones— aligns the present with the past and brings out the *contemporary mythical heroes*.[62]

In 2008, a year after the premiere of the *Odyssey* of Theodorakis, a dynamic contribution was made by the exhibition of the painter Jannis Psychopedis entitled *Nostos* at the Museum of Cycladic Art in Athens. In the exhibition a critical approach to modern Greek physiognomy was imprinted, by contemplating the interrelation of the present with the recent historic past:

> *Nostos*, the homeward journey of Odysseus from Troy, exhibits Psychopedis' intellectual bravado and obsession with constantly balancing on a tightrope, with his eyes turning to the timeless forms of the art of the ancient Greek civilization or immersing himself in the contemplation of contemporary reality.[63]

In their conception, the *Odyssey* of Theodorakis and the *Nostos* of Psychopedis represent two different receptions: the reception of the first, as said, looks forward to utopia, while that of the latter is dominated by a realistic, critical mood insisting on the memories of a mutilated past which seeks confirmation. In the *Fragmented Memory*[64] the cutting of the ancient statue stresses the weakness of our epoch to reformulate archetypal forms, being also suggestive of the misleading effect of memory within time. Additionally, in the *Lower Limbs–History Lesson* (Figure 3)[65] one understands that the greater the distance in time, the greater the alienation, the harder the dialogue of the extremes and the familiarity of the allusions among themselves. To conclude, the *nostos* of Psychopedis is unfulfilled; it involves a nightmarish dialectical discourse with the present, which, unfortunately, does not ensure a further promising co-existence.

The last song of the *Odyssey* entitled 'Without Identity' adds new elements, which are brought together in the realism of Psychopedis and in the fluid atmos-

---

61 For national imagination as the 'nostalgia for the whole', see Hamilakis 2007, 282, 290–93.
62 Theodorakis 2002, 318.
63 Takis Mavrotas in Psychopedis 2008, 24.
64 Psychopedis 2008, 140 (Plate).
65 Psychopedis 2008, 91 (Plate).

Figure 3. Jannis Psychopedis, *Lower Limbs–History Lesson*, 40 x 52 x 50 cm., 1996. Reproduced by permission of Jannis Psychopedis.

phere of the time. In contrast with the previous thirteen poems, Odysseus is here portrayed as a wanderer within a faceless urban environment. Nothing recalls the excitement of travelling and the natural setting of 'The Song of the Companions' or 'The Song of the Sirens'. Odysseus introduces himself as 'Nobody', an unknown person who exists 'in the crowd in a city I do not know'. In Theodorakis' eyes, the modern era marks an equivalent period of isolation. Alienation is a new circumstance of globalization and the devaluation of national ideals. Thirty-seven years after he set to music the 'Spiritual March' ('Pnevmatiko Emvatirio') of Sikelianos during his exile in Zatouna, the 'accomplished' Greece seems to have lost its heirs. It is a period of degradation, which becomes apparent, as the composer observes, in the division between the popular and art elements recurring in these days after the great advances of the decades after 1960.[66] He also confesses:

> I stopped feeling the presence of others around me. Sometimes I have the impression that I am alone, banished in a waste land [...] So, whom do I write about? About those who don't see and about those who don't listen to me?[67]

f. A personal performing *topos*

The *Odyssey* of Mikis Theodorakis prescribes the *nostos* to a personal performing *topos*. As 'a journey into danger', the Homeric return must end with the target of self-realization, i.e. the state of affirmation which leads to the bonds with childhood. For this attainment, forgetfulness must be overcome; however difficult the circumstances, Odysseus cannot exist as *Nobody*, 'without identity and name among people'. The meeting-point of Kartelias and Theodorakis is poetry, where poetry is regarded as the disposition of elevating life to a more self-knowing level. Theodorakis asserts:

> The 'person', that is ourselves, must ultimately live the idea that Ithaca does not exist and that he must be grasped by his own pathos and his own sentiments, in order to stay on the surface of the rough sea which is life.[68]

At the end of this journey, Ithaca is not poor; it makes up for the empirical losses of memory. Music comes to socialize the person, and the poet-composer seeks 'to come and speak to you'. The hieratic, fervent voice of Maria Farandouri anchors the lyri-

---

[66] Cf. Theodorakis' views on the predominant music scene: Theodorakis 2002, 81, 83, 85 – 86, 154, 294 – 95.
[67] Theodorakis 2002, 118.
[68] From the leaflet included with the CD of the *Odyssey*, Legend Recordings 2007.

cism which never wavers. The melody, albeit nostalgic, does not expose us to melancholy. There is a progressive climax towards an emotional profusion and a cyclical retrieval of feelings. Ultimately, the music of the *Odyssey* is liberating. It is not the memory-trauma, but the memory-idea through the art-music. The latter unites the perceptive dimension with the ostensible world. Theodorakis' *Odyssey* is transformed into a musical *iconotopia*. The composer performs what he sees when he sits on a 'fantastic hammock'[69] at the edge of the universe. There are no Homeric monsters, but only the immersion in the world of music and the senses. The search of 'the depths of my soul' becomes the prospect of man rejoining with his outward environment in a dramatic attempt to amplify human limits. And in this way, the human course is tamed within the bounds of *cosmos*.

Overcoming fortune is the destiny of heroes. Each one who manages to keep the measure of himself and not to fall into the over- or under-estimation of time is also an Odysseus. The journey of Theodorakis-Odysseus is the placement of man in the universe. For this journey there is an axiom to learn, that the childhood home is not just a place, but 'those who love us'.[70]

---

[69] Theodorakis 2002, 88.
[70] Theodorakis 1986, 136: 'My homeland was my house. My parents. Those who loved us'.

Bibliography

Accorinti, D./ Chuvin, P. (eds.) (2003), *Des Géants à Dionysos*, Alessandria.
Acosta-Hughes, B./ Kosmetatou, E./ Baumbach, M. (eds.) (2004), *Labored in Papyrus Leaves: Perspectives on an Epigram Collection Attributed to Posidippus (P.Mil.Vogl.VIII 309)*, Washington/ Cambridge (Mass.).
Adams, J.N. (1982), *The Latin Sexual Vocabulary*, Baltimore.
Adkins, A.W.H. (1960), *Merit and Responsibility: A Study in Greek Values*, Oxford.
— (1971), "Homeric Values and Homeric Society", *JHS* 91, 1–14.
— (1972a), *Moral Values and Political Behaviour in Ancient Greece*, London.
— (1972b), "Truth, ΚΟΣΜΟΣ, and ΑΡΕΤΗ in the Homeric Poems", *CQ* 22, 5–18.
Aélion, R. (1983), *Euripide héritier d' Eschyle*, Vols. I-II, Paris.
Agosti, G. (2003), *Nonno di Panopoli, Parafrasi del Vangelo di San Giovanni, Canto Quinto*, Florence.
— (2005), "Interpretazione Omerica e creazione poetica nella tarda Antichità", in: A. Kolde/ A. Lukinovich/ A.L. Rey (eds.), 19–32.
Ahl, F. (1986), *Trojan Women by Lucius Annaeus Seneca*, Ithaca.
Albérès, R.M. (1957), *Esthétique et morale chez Jean Giraudoux*, Nizet.
Alexandrou, M. (2016), "Mythological Narratives in Hipponax", in: C. Carey/ L. Swift (eds.), 210–28.
Alexandrou, M./ Carey, C./ D' Alessio, G. (eds.) (forthcoming), *Song Regained: Working with Greek Poetic Fragments*, Berlin.
Alexopoulou, M. (2006), "Nostos and the Impossibility of a 'Return to the Same': From Homer to Seferis", *New Voices in Classical Reception Studies* 1, 1–9.
— (2009), *The Theme of Returning Home in Ancient Greek Literature:The Nostos of the Epic Hero*, Lewiston.
Allan, W. (2000), *The Andromache and Euripidean Tragedy*, Oxford.
Allen, A. (2007), "Briseis in Homer, Ovid, and Troy", in: M.M. Winkler (ed.), 148–62.
Allen, R. E. (1998), *The Dialogues of Plato*. Vol. III, New Haven.
Allen, T. (1899), "Ludwich's Homervulgata", *CR* 13, 39–41.
— (1912), *Homeri Opera*, Vol. V, Oxford.
Alvares, J. (2002), "Love, Loss and Learning in Chaereas and Callirhoe", *CW* 95, 107–15.
Anagnostopoulos, J. (1995), "An Introduction to the Poetry and the Poetics of Angelos Sikelianos", *Kotinos to Angelos Sikelianos* (Κότινος στον Άγγελο Σικελιανό), *Tetradia Euthinis* 11, 118–36.
Annas, J. (1981), *An Introduction to Plato's Republic*, Oxford.
— (1982), "Plato on the Triviality of Literature", in: J.M.E. Moravcsik / P. Temko (eds.), 1–28.
Anton, J.P. (ed.) (2002), *70 Years since the First Delphic Festivals: Ancient Drama in Delphi from Angelos Sikelianos till Today* (70 Χρόνια από τις πρώτες Δελφικές Εορτές. Το αρχαίο δράμα στους Δελφούς από τον Άγγελο Σικελιανό έως τις μέρες μας), European Cultural Centre of Delphi, Conference Proceedings (Delphi, 16–20 July 1997), Athens.
Anton, J.P./ Preus, A. (eds.) (1989), *Essays in Ancient Greek Philosophy III: Plato*, New York.
Arafat, K.W. (1996), *Pausanias' Greece: Ancient Artists and Roman Rulers*, Cambridge.

Archimandritis, G. (2011), *Mikis Theodorakis: My Life (Μίκης Θεοδωράκης: Η ζωή μου)*, Athens.
Armstrong, R. (2006), "The *Aeneid:* Inheritance and Empire", in: M.J. Clarke/ B.G.F. Currie/ R.O.A.M. Lyne (eds.), 131–57.
Arnold, B. (1994–95), "The Literary Experience of Vergil's Fourth *Eclogue*", *CJ* 90.2, 143–60.
Ashmole, B./ Yalouris, N. (1967), *Olympia: The Sculpture of the Temple of Zeus*, London.
Assael, J. (2004), "La resurrection d'Alceste", *REG* 117, 37–58.
Athanassaki, L./Nikolaides, A./Spatharas, D. (eds.) (2014), *Private Life and Public Speech in Greek Antiquity and Enlightenment: Studies in Honour of Ioanna Yatromanolaki (Ιδιωτικός βίος και Δημόσιος Λόγος στην Ελληνική Αρχαιότητα και στον Διαφωτισμό. Μελέτες αφιερωμένες στην Ιωάννα Γιατρομανωλάκη)*, Herakleion.
Atwood, M. (2007), *The Penelopiad: The Play*, London.
Austin, C./ Bastianini, G. (2002), *Posidippi Pellaei quae supersunt omnia*, Milan.
Austin, N. (1994), *Helen of Troy and her Shameless Phantom*, Ithaca.
—— (2007), "The Helen of the *Iliad*", in: H. Bloom (ed.) (2007a), 33–54.
Austin, R.G. (ed.) (1977), *P. Vergili Maronis Aeneidos, liber sextus*, Oxford.
Ayres, L. (ed.) (1995), *The Passionate Intellect: Essays on the Transformation of Classical Traditions Presented to Professor I. G. Kidd*, New Brunswick.
Bailey, C. (ed.) (1936), *Greek Poetry and Life: Essays Presented to G. Murray*, Oxford.
Baker, R.J. (1968), "*Miles annosus:* The Military Motif in Propertius", *Latomus* 27, 322–49.
—— (2000), *Propertius I*, Warminster.
Bakogianni, A. (2008), "All is Well that Ends Tragically: Filming Greek Tragedy in Modern Greece", *BICS* 51, 119–67.
—— (2009), "Voices of Resistance: Michael Cacoyannis' *The Trojan Women* (1971)", *BICS* 52, 45–68.
—— (2011), *Electra Ancient and Modern: Aspects of the Tragic Heroine's Reception*, London.
—— (2013a), "Annihilating Clytemnestra: The Severing of the Mother-Daughter Bond in Michael Cacoyannis' *Iphigenia* (1977)", in: K.P. Nikoloutsos (ed.), 207–33.
—— (2013b), "Who Rules this Nation? (Ποιός κυβερνά αυτόν τον τόπο;): Political Intrigue and the Struggle for Power in Michael Cacoyannis' *Iphigenia* (1977)", in: A. Bakogianni (ed.), Vol. I, 225–49.
—— (2013c), "Introduction: In Dialogue with the Past", in: A. Bakogianni (ed.), Vol. I, 1–9.
—— (ed.) (2013), *Dialogues with the Past: Classical Reception Theory and Practice*, Vols. I-II (*BICS* Suppl. 126), London.
Bakola, E./ Prauscello, L./ Telò, M. (eds.) (2013), *Greek Comedy and the Discourse of Genres*. Cambridge.
Balaban, O. (2011), "The Moral Intellectualism of Plato's Socrates: The Case of *Hippias Minor*", *Bochumer Philosophiches Jahrbuch für Antike und Mittelalter* 13.1, 1–14.
Balensiefen, L. (2005), "Polyphem-Grotten und Skylla-Gewässer: Schauplätze der *Odyssee* in römischen Villen", in: A. Luther (ed.), 9–31.
Ballif, M. (2001), *Seduction, Sophistry and the Woman with the Rhetorical Figure*, Illinois.
Balot, R. (2004), "Courage in the Democratic Polis", *CQ* 54, 406–23.
Banašević, N. (1964), "Ranija I novija nauka I Vukovi pogledi na narodnu epiku", *Prilozi* 30, 3–4.
Baragwanath, E. (2008), *Motivation and Narrative in Herodotus*, Oxford.

Barchiesi, A. (2001), *Speaking Volumes: Narrative and Intertext in Ovid and Other Latin Poets* (ed. and trans. M. Fox and S. Marchesi), London.
—— (1984a), *La traccia del modello: effetti omerici nella narrazione virgiliana*, Pisa.
—— (1984b), "Ciclopi", in: *Enciclopedia Virgiliana* I, Rome, 778–79.
—— (1999), "Representations of Suffering and Interpretation in the *Aeneid*", in: P. Hardie (ed.), 324–44.
Bardel, R. (2005), "Spectral Traces: Ghosts in Tragic Fragments", in: F. McHardy / J. Robson / D. Harvey (eds.), 83–112.
Barfield, R. (2011), *The Ancient Quarrel Between Philosophy and Poetry*, Cambridge.
Barlow, S.A. (1971), *The Imagery of Euripides*, London.
—— (1986), *Euripides: Trojan Women*, Warminster.
Barnes, J. (1982), *The Presocratic Philosophers: The Arguments of the Philosophers*, London/ Boston/ Melbourne/ Henley.
Barrett, W.S. (1964), *Euripides: Hippolytos*, Oxford.
Barsby, J. (1979²), *Ovid Amores I*, Oxford.
Bartels, A. (2004), *Vergleichende Studien zur Erzählkunst des römischen Epyllion*, Göttingen.
Bartol, K. (1993), *Greek Elegy and Iambus: Studies in Ancient Literary Sources*, Poznań.
Bassi, K. (2003), "The Semantics of Manliness in Ancient Greece", in: R.M. Rosen/ I. Sluiter (eds.), 25–58.
Basta Donzelli, G. (1986), "La Colpa di Elena: Gorgia ed Euripide a confronto", in: L. Montoneri/ F. Romano (eds.), 389–409.
Baumbach, M./ Petrovic A./ Petrovic I. (eds.) (2010), *Archaic and Classical Greek Epigram*, Cambridge.
Beaton, R. (1999), *An Introduction to Modern Greek Literature*, Oxford.
Beisinger, M./ Tylus, J./ Wofford, S. (eds.) (1999), *Epic Traditions in the Contemporary World: The Poetics of Community*, Berkeley/ Los Angeles.
Belfiore, E. (1985), "Lies Unlike the Truth: Plato on Hesiod, *Theogony* 27", *TAPhA* 115, 47–57.
—— (2006), "A Theory of Imitation in Plato's Republic", in: A. Laird (ed.), 87–114.
Bellido, J.A. (1989), "El motivo literario de la *militia amoris* y su influencia en Ovidio", *EClás* 31, 21–32.
Benakis, L. (2012), *Ἰαμβλίχου Προτρεπτικὸς ἐπὶ φιλοσοφίαν*, Athens.
Benardete, S. (1963), "Some Misquotations of Homer in Plato", *Phronesis* 8, 173–78.
Bennett, S. (1990), *Theatre Audiences: A Theory of Production and Reception*, London.
Benson, H.H. (ed.) (2006), *A Companion to Plato*, Chichester.
Ben-Ze'ev, A. (2003), "Aristotle on Emotions towards the Fortune of Others", in: D. Konstan/ N.K. Rutter (eds.), 99–121.
Berg, W. (1974), *Early Virgil*, London.
Bergren, A. (1983), "Language and the Female in Early Greek Thought", *Arethusa* 16, 69–95.
Berman, K.E. (1972), "Some Propertian imitations in Ovid's *Amores*", *CPh* 67, 170–77.
—— (1975), "Ovid, Propertius and the Elegiac Genre: Some Imitations in the *Amores*", *RSC* 23, 14–22.
Bernabé, A. (1996²), *Poetarum Epicorum Graecorum Testimonia et Fragmenta*, Pars I, Stuttgart/ Leipzig.
Berthelot, A. (1992), *Andromaque de Racine*, Paris.
Berthet, J.F. (1980), "Properce et Homère", in: A. Thill (ed.), 141–53.
Betts, G. (1965), "The Silence of Alcestis", *Mnemosyne* 18, 66–67.

Betts, J.H./ Hooker, J.T./ Green, J.R. (eds.) (1986), *Studies in Honour of T.B.L. Webster*, Vols. I-II, Bristol.
Bieler, L. (1935/1936), *Theios Anēr: Das Bild des "göttlichen Menschen" in Spätantike und Frühchristentum*, Darmstadt.
Billault, A. (1996), "Characterization in the Ancient Novel", in: G. Schmeling (ed.), 115–29.
Bing, P. (2002/2003), "Posidippus and the Admiral: Kallikrates of Samos in the Epigrams of the Milan Papyrus (P.Mil.Vogl.VIII.309)", *GRBS* 43, 243–66.
–– (2009), *The Scroll and the Marble: Studies in Reading and Reception in Hellenistic Poetry*, Ann Arbor.
Bing, P./ Bruss, J.S. (eds.) (2007), *Brill's Companion to Hellenistic Epigram*, Leiden/ Boston.
Binns, J.W. (ed.) (1973), *Ovid*, London/ Boston.
Bishop, P. (ed.) (2004), *Nietzsche and Antiquity: His Reaction and Response to the Classical Tradition*, New York.
Bittlestone, R./ Diggle, J./ Underhill J. (2005), *Odysseus Unbound: The Search for Homer's Ithaca*, Cambridge.
Bizer, M. (2011), *Homer and the Politics of Authority in Renaissance France*, Oxford.
Blondell, R. (2002), *The Play of Character in Plato's Dialogues*, Cambridge.
–– (2009), "'Third Cheerleader from the Left': from Homer's Helen to Helen of Troy", *CRJ* 1:1, 4–22.
Bloom, H. (ed.) (2007a), *Homer's The Iliad* (updated edition), New York.
–– (ed.) (2007b), *Homer* (updated edition), New York.
Blundell, M.W. (1992), "Character and Meaning in Plato's *Hippias Minor*", in: J.C. Klagge / N.D. Smith (eds.), 131–72.
Boardman, J. (1985), *Greek Sculpture: The Classical Period*, London.
Bobas, C. (ed.) (2009), *D'une frontière à l'autre: Mouvements de fuites, mouvements discontinus dans le monde Néo – Hellénique*, Athens.
Body, J. (1986), *Jean Giraudoux: la légende et le secret*, Paris.
Boedeker, D. (2003), "Pedestrian Fatalities: The Prosaics of Death", in: P. Derow/ R. Parker (eds.), 17–36.
Bogner, H. (1934), "Die Religion des Nonnos von Panopolis", *Phil.* 89, 320–33.
Bonazza, S. (1988), "Vuk Stefanović Karadžić und der Austroslavismus", *Europa Orientalis* 7, 361–71.
Booth, J. (1991), *Ovid Amores II*, Warminster.
Booth, J./ Maltby, R. (eds.) (2006), *What's in a Name? The Significance of Proper Names in Classical Latin Literature*, Wales.
Borg, B. (2010), "Epigrams in Archaic Art: The 'Chest of Kypselos'", in: M. Baumbach/ A. Petrovic/ I. Petrovic (eds.), 81–99.
Bossi, F. (1986), *Studi sul Margite*, Ferrara.
Bosworth, A. B. (2000), "The Historical Context of Thucydides' Funeral Oration", *JHS* 120, 1–16.
Bouzakis, M./ Papavasiliou, E. (eds.) (2005), *Mikis Theodorakis: The Man, the Artist, the Musician, the Politician, the Cretan and the Ecumenical (Μίκης Θεοδωράκης: Ο άνθρωπος, ο δημιουργός, ο μουσικός, ο πολιτικός, ο Κρητικός και ο οικουμενικός), Conference Proceedings (Chania, 29–31 July 2005)*, Chania.
Bowie, A.M. (1993), *Aristophanes: Myth, Ritual and Comedy*, Cambridge.
–– (2007), *Herodotus: Histories, Book VIII*, Cambridge.

Bowie, E.L. (1986), "Early Greek Elegy, Symposium and Public Festival", *JHS* 106, 13–35.
— (2001), "Early Greek Iambic Poetry: The Importance of Narrative", in: A. Cavarzere/ A. Aloni/ A. Barchiesi (eds.), 1–27.
— (2002), "Ionian ἴαμβος and Attic κωμῳδία: Father and Daughter, or Just Cousins?", in: A. Willi (ed.), 33–50.
— (2010), "Epigram as Narration", in: M. Baumbach/ A. Petrovic/ I. Petrovic (eds.), 313–77.
Bowra, C.M. (1961), *Greek Lyric Poetry: From Alcman to Simonides*, Oxford.
Boyancé, P. (1937), *Le culte des Muses chez les philosophes grecques: études d' histoire et de psychologie religieuse*, Paris.
Boyd, B.W. (1995), "*Non enarrabile textum:* Ecphrastic Trespass and Narrative Ambiguity in the *Aeneid*", *Vergilius* 41, 71–90.
— (1997), *Ovid's Literary Loves: Influence and Innovation in the Amores*, Ann Arbor.
Boys-Stones, G./ Haubold, J. (eds.) (2010), *Plato and Hesiod*, Oxford.
Bradley, K. / Cartledge, P. (eds.) (2011), *The Cambridge World History of Slavery*, Vol. I: *The Ancient Near East and Mediterranean World to AD 500*, Cambridge.
Brandt, P. (1911), *P. Ovidi Nasonis Amorum Libri Tres*, Leipzig.
Brandwood, L. (1976), *A Word Index to Plato*, Leeds.
Braswell, B.K. (1988), *A Commentary on the Fourth Pythian Ode of Pindar*, Berlin/ New York.
Breitenberger, B. (2007), *Aphrodite and Eros: The Development of Erotic Mythology in Early Greek Poetry and Cult*, New York/ London.
Bremer, J.M./ Radt, S.L./ Ruijgh, C.J. (eds.) (1976), *Miscellanea Tragica in Honorem J.C. Kamerbeek*, Amsterdam.
Bremer, J.M. / Van den Hout, Th.P.J. / Peters, R. (eds.) (1994), *Hidden Futures: Death and Immortality in Ancient Egypt, Anatolia, the Classical, Biblical and Arabic-Islamic World*, Amsterdam.
Bremmer, J.N. (1983), *The Early Greek Concept of the Soul*, Princeton.
— (1994), "The Soul, Death, and the Afterlife in Early and Classical Greece", in: J. M. Bremer / Th.P.J. van den Hout / R. Peters (eds.), 91–106.
Broadie, S. (1991), *Ethics with Aristotle*, New York.
Brockett, O. (1995), *History of the Theatre*, Boston.
Brockliss, W./ Chaudhuri, P./ Haimson Lushkov, A./ Wasdin, K. (eds.) (2012), *Reception and the Classics: An Interdisciplinary Approach to the Classical Tradition*, Cambridge.
Brockliss, W./ Chaudhuri, P./ Haimson Lushkov, A./ Wasdin, K. (2012), "Introduction", in: W. Brockliss/ P. Chaudhuri/ A. Haimson Lushkov/ K. Wasdin (eds.), 1–16.
Brook, T. (1986), "Review of Jonathan D. Spence, *The Memory Palace of Matteo Ricci* (1984)", *The Journal of Asian Studies* 45.4, 831–33.
Brosius, M. (2000), *The Persian Empire from Cyrus II to Artaxerxes II*, LACTOR 16, London.
Brown, C.G. (1988), "Hipponax and Iambe", *Hermes* 116, 478–81.
— (1997), "Iambos", in: D.E. Gerber (ed.), 11–88.
Bryant, J.M. (1996), *Moral Codes and Social Structure in Ancient Greece*, New York.
Buchheit, V. (1962), *Studien zum Corpus Priapeorum*, Munich.
Budelmann, F./ Michelakis, P. (eds.) (2001), *Homer, Tragedy and Beyond: Essays in Honour of P.E. Easterling*, London.
Budelmann, F. (ed.) (2009), *The Cambridge Companion to Greek Lyric*, Cambridge.
Buffière, F. (1952), *Les mythes d' Homère et la pensée grecque*, Paris.
Bulman, P. (1992), *Phthonos in Pindar*, Berkeley/ Los Angeles.

Bundy, E.L. (1962), *Studia Pindarica*, Berkeley.
Burgess, J. (2001), *The Tradition of the Trojan War in Homer and the Epic Cycle*, Baltimore/ London.
Burgoyne, R. (2011a), "Introduction", in: R. Burgoyne (ed.), 1–16.
— (2011b), "Bare Life and Sovereignty in *Gladiator*", in: R. Burgoyne (ed.), 82–97.
— (ed.) (2011), *The Epic Film in World Culture*, New York.
Burkert, W. (1962), "Γόης: zum griechischen 'Schamanismus'", *RhM* 105, 36–55.
— (1972), "Die Leistung eines Kreophylos: Kreophyleer, Homeriden und die archaische Heraklesepik", *MH* 29, 74–85.
— (1985), *Greek Religion* (trans. J. Raffan), Oxford.
Burn, A.R. (1984^2), *Persia and the Greeks: The Defense of the West 548–478 BC*, London.
Burnet, J. (1900), *The Ethics of Aristotle*, London.
Burnett, A.P. (1971), *Catastrophe Survived: Euripides' Plays of Mixed Reversal*, Oxford.
— (2008), *Pindar*, Bristol.
Burnyeat, M.F. (1971), "Virtues in Action", in: G. Vlastos (ed.), 209–34.
Cadell, H. (1998), "À quelle date Arsinoé II Phildelphe est-elle décédée?', in : H. Malaerts (ed.), 1–3.
Cahoon, L. (1988), "The Bed as Battlefield: Erotic Conquest and Military Metaphor in Ovid's *Amores*", *TAPhA* 118, 293–307.
Cairns, D. L. (1993), *Aidōs: The Psychology and Ethics of Honour and Shame in Ancient Greek Literature*, Oxford.
Cairns, F. (1984), "The Etymology of *Militia* in Roman Elegy", in: L. Gil/R.M. Aguilar (eds.), 211–21.
— (2006a), *Sextus Propertius: The Augustan Elegist*, Cambridge.
— (2006b), "Propertius and the Origins of Latin Love-elegy", in: H.-C. Günther (ed.), 69–95.
Caizzi, F. (1966), *Antisthenis Fragmenta*, Milan.
Calame, Cl. (2004), "Deictic Ambiguity and Auto-Referentiality: Some Examples", in: N. Felson (ed.), 415–43.
Calboli, G. (ed.) (1969), *Cornifici rhetorica ad C. Herennium*, Bologna.
Calder, W. (1970), *Originality in Seneca's Troades*, Chicago.
Callebat, L. (2012), *Priapées*, Paris.
Campbell, D. A. (2001), *Greek Lyric III: Stesichorus, Ibycus, Simonides, and Others*, Cambridge (Mass.)/ London.
— (2002), *Greek Lyric I: Sappho and Alcaeus*, Cambridge (Mass.)/ London.
Campbell, M. (1981), *A Commentary on Quintus Smyrnaeus' Posthomerica XII*, Leiden.
Canavero, D. (2004), "Ripresa ed evoluzione: Andromaca ed Ecuba nelle *Troiane* di Euripide", in: G. Zanetto/ D. Canavero/ A. Capra/ A. Sgobbi (eds.), 171–85.
Caplan, H. (1954), *Rhetorica ad Herennium*, London.
Caprara, M. (1999), "Nonno e gli Ebrei: Note a *Par.* IV, 88–121", *SIFC* 17, 195–215.
Carey, C. (1991), "The Victory Ode in Performance: The Case for the Chorus", *CPh* 86, 192–200.
— (1995), "Pindar and the Victory Ode", in: L. Ayres (ed.), 85–103.
— (2000), *Aeschines*, Austin.
— (2005), "Propaganda and Competition in Athenian Oratory", in: K.A.E. Enenkel/ I.L. Pfeijffer (eds.), 65–100.

— (2007a), "Epideictic Oratory", in: I. Worthington (ed.), 236–52.
— (2007b), *Lysiae Orationes cum Fragmentis*, Oxford.
— (2008), "Hipponax Narrator", *Acta Antiqua Academiae Scientiarum Hungaricae* 48, 89–102.
— (2009), "Iambos", in: F. Budelmann (ed.), 149–67.
— (forthcoming), "Embedded Fragments", in: M. Alexandrou/ C. Carey/ G. D' Alessio (eds.).
Carey, C./ Swift, L. (eds.) (2016), *Iambus and Elegy*, Oxford.
Carney, E. (2006), *Olympias: Mother of Alexander the Great*, London.
Carruthers, M. (1990), *The Book of Memory*, Cambridge.
Carruthers, M./ Ziolkowski, J. (2002), *The Medieval Craft of Memory: An Anthology of Texts and Pictures*, Philadelphia.
Carter, L. B. (1986), *The Quiet Athenian*, Oxford.
Cartledge, P. / Harvey, F. (eds.) (1990), *Crux: Essays presented to G.E.M. de Ste. Croix on his 75th Birthday*, Exeter.
Cavarzere, A./ Aloni, A./ Barchiesi, A. (eds.) (2001), *Iambic Ideas: Essays on a Poetic Tradition from Archaic Greece to the Late Roman Empire*, Lanham.
Chantler, A./ Dente, C. (eds.) (2009), *Translation Practices: through Language to Culture*, Amsterdam/ New York.
Chantraine, P. (1942), *Grammaire Homérique*, Vol. I, Paris.
— (1968–1980), *Dictionnaire étymologique de la langue grecque*, Paris.
Charalabopoulos, N.G. (2012), *Platonic Drama and its Ancient Reception*, Cambridge.
Charalambidis, G. (1971), "Press Review", *Vradyni*, 9 Oct. 1971.
— (1972), *Penelope's 300*, Athens.
Chasapi-Christodoulou, E. (2002), *Greek Mythology in Modern Greek Drama. From Cretan Theatre to the End of the 20th Century* (Η ελληνική μυθολογία στο νεοελληνικό δράμα. Από την εποχή του Κρητικού Θεάτρου έως το τέλος του 20ού αιώνα), Vols. I-II, Thessaloniki.
Chatzipantazis, Th. (1984), *Karaghiozis' Invasion in Athens in 1890* (Η εισβολή του Καραγκιόζη στην Αθήνα του 1890), Athens.
— (2003), *Greek Comedy and its Models in the 19th century* (Η ελληνική κωμωδία και τα πρότυπά της στον 19ο αιώνα), Herakleion.
Chiasson, C.C. (2009), "Redefining Homeric Heroism in Wolfgang Petersen's *Troy*", in: K. Myrsiades (ed.), 186–207.
Christiansen, B./ Thaler, U. (eds.) (2013), *Ansehenssache. Formen von Prestige in Kulturen des Altertums*, Munich.
Christodoulou, D. (1966), *Hotel Circe*, Athens.
Clarke, M. (2004), "Manhood and Heroism", in: R.L. Fowler (ed.), 74–90.
Clarke, M.J./ Currie, B.G.F./ Lyne, R.O.A.M. (eds.) (2006), *Epic Interactions: Perspectives on Homer, Virgil and the Epic Tradition Presented to Jasper Griffin by Former Pupils*, Oxford.
Clarke, W. (1978), "Achilles and Patroclus in Love", *Hermes* 106, 381–96.
Clausen, W. (1994), *Virgil: Eclogues*, Oxford.
Clauss, J.J./ Cuypers, M. (eds.) (2010), *A Companion to Hellenistic Literature*, Oxford.
Clay, D. (1988), "The Archaeology of the Temple to Juno in Carthage", *CPh* 83, 195–205.
— (2000), *Platonic Questions: Dialogues with the Silent Philosopher*, University Park, Pennsylvania.
— (2004), *Archilochos Heros: The Cult of Poets in the Greek Polis*, Cambridge (Mass.).

Coleman, R. (1977), *Vergil: Eclogues,* Cambridge.
Collard, C./ Cropp, M. J./ Gibert, J. (2004), *Euripides: Selected Fragmentary Plays,* Vol. II, Oxford.
Collard, C./ Cropp, M.J. (2008), *Euripides: Fragments,* Vols. I-II, Cambridge (Mass.)/ London.
Combellack, F. M. (1965), "Some Formulaic Illogicalities in Homer", *TAPhA* 96, 41–56.
Conacher, D.J. (1967), *Euripidean Drama: Myth, Theme and Structure,* Toronto.
— (1998), *Euripides and the Sophists,* London.
Connors, C. (1991), "Simultaneous Hunting and Herding at *Ciris* 297–300", *CQ* 41, 556–59.
Consigny, S. (2001), *Gorgias: Sophist and Artist,* South Carolina.
Cook, E. (2001), *Achilles,* London.
Cooper, J. M. (ed.) (1997), *Plato: Complete Works,* Indianapolis.
Cormack, M. (2006), *Plato's Stepping Stones: Degrees of Moral Virtue,* London.
Cornford, F.M. (1941), *Plato: Republic,* Oxford.
Couprie, A. (1996), *Racine, Andromaque: résumé, personnages, thèmes,* Paris.
Cousin, C. (2005), "La *Nékuia* homérique et les fragments des *Evocateurs d'âmes* d'Eschyle", *Gaia,* 9, 137–52.
Cousland, J.R.C./ Hume, J.R. (eds.) (2009), *The Play of Texts and Fragments. Essays in Honour of Martin Cropp,* Leiden.
Cova, P.V. (1984), "Achemenide", in: *Enciclopedia Virgiliana* I, Rome, 22–23.
Coventry, L. (1989), "Philosophy and Rhetoric in the *Menexenus*", *JHS* 109, 4–10.
Crawley, R./ Wick, T.E. (1982), *Thucydides: The Peloponnesian War,* New York.
Creed, L.J. (1973), "Moral Values in the Age of Thucydides", *CQ* 23, 213–31.
Croally, N.T. (1994), *Euripidean Polemic: The Trojan Women and the Function of Tragedy,* Cambridge.
Cropp, M.J./ Lee, K.H./ Sansone, D. (eds.) (1999–2000), *Euripides and Tragic Theatre in the Late Fifth Century,* Urbana.
Cucchiarelli, A. (2012), *Le Bucoliche,* Roma.
Dal Zotto, A. (1903), *La Ciris e le sue fonti greche,* Feltre.
Dalby, A. (1995), "The *Iliad,* the *Odyssey* and their Audiences", *CQ* 45.2, 269–79.
Danek, G. (1998), *Epos und Zitat: Studien zu den Quellen der Odyssee,* Vienna.
Daskalopoulos, D. (2009), "Allusions to the Fortune of Odysseus in Modern Greek Poetry", in: Th. Pylarinos (ed.), 71–77.
Davidson, J. (1999–2000), "Euripides, Homer and Sophocles", in: M.J. Cropp/ K.H. Lee/ D. Sansone (eds.), 117–28.
— (2001), "Homer and Euripides' *Troades*", *BICS* 45, 65–79.
— (2012), "The Homer of Tragedy: Epic Sources and Models in Sophocles", in: A. Markantonatos (ed.), 245–62.
Davies, M. (1991), *Sophocles: Trachiniae,* Oxford.
Davis, G. (2008), "Reframing the Homeric: Images of the *Odyssey* in the Art of Derek Walcott and Romare Bearden", in: L. Hardwick/ C. Stray (eds.), 401–14.
Davreux, J. (1942), *La légende de la prophétesse Cassandre,* Liège.
Day, J.W. (1989), "Rituals in Stone: Early Greek Grave Epigrams and Monuments", *JHS* 109, 16–28.
Day, L.K. (2008), *'Bitch that I am': An Examination of Women's Self-Deprecation in Homer and Virgil,* Diss. Arkansas.

De Gianni, D. (2010), "La nutrice di Scilla e la nutrice di Fedra: ispirazioni euripidee nella *Ciris*", *Vichiana* 12, 36–45.
De Jong, I.J.F. (1997), "Homer and Narratology", in: I. Morris/ B. Powell (eds.), 305–25.
De Jong, I.J.F./ Bowie, A./ Nünlist, R. (eds.) (2004), *Narrators, Narratees and Narratives in Ancient Greek Literature*, Leiden.
De Romilly, J. (1976), "L'excuse de l'invincible amour dans la tragédie grecque", in: J.M. Bremer/ S.L. Radt/ C.J. Ruigh (eds.), 309–21.
–– (1986), *La modernité d'Euripide*, Paris.
–– (1995), *Tragédies grecques au fil des ans*, Paris.
De Stefani, C. (2002), *Nonno di Panopoli, Parafrasi del Vangelo di s. Giovanni: canto I*, Bologna.
De Vet, T. (1996), "The Joint Role of Orality and Literacy in the Composition, Transmission, and Performance of the Homeric Texts: A Comparative View", *TAPhA* 126, 43–76.
–– (2005), "Parry in Paris: Structuralism, Historical Linguistics and the Oral Theory", *Cl.Ant.* 24.2, 257–84.
–– (2008), "Context and the Emerging Story: Improvised Performance in Oral and Literate Societies", *Oral Tradition* 23.1, 159–79.
Décélé, M. (2005), *Le mythe grec et sa mythopoïèse dans Andromaque et Iphigénie de Racine*, Diss. Athens.
Defaux, G. (1977), "Culpabilité et expiation dans l'*Andromaque* de Racine", *Romanic Review*, Janvier 1977, 22–31.
Deforge, B. (1986), *Eschyle, poète cosmique*, Paris.
Degani, E, (1984), *Studi su Ipponatte*, Bari.
–– (1991), *Testimonia et fragmenta*, Stuttgart.
Degani, E./ Burzacchini, G./ Nicolosi, A. (2007), *Ipponatte: Frammenti*, Bologna.
Delatte, A. (1915), *Études sur la littérature pythagoricienne*, Paris.
Delebecque, E. (1951), *Euripide et la guerre du Péloponnèse*, Paris.
Deleuze, G. (1968), *Différence et Répétition*, Paris.
–– (1986), *Cinema 1: The Movement Image*, London.
Denniston, J.D. (1954²), *The Greek Particles*, Oxford.
Dentith, S. (2000), *Parody: The New Critical Idiom*, London.
Deremetz, A. (1999), "Visages des genres dans l'élégie ovidienne: *Amores* 1.1 et 3.1", in: J. Fabre-Serris/ A. Deremetz (eds.), 71–84.
Derow, P./ Parker, R. (eds.) (2003), *Herodotus and his World: Essays for a Conference in Memory of George Forrest*, Oxford.
Desch, W. (1985), "Die Hauptgestalten in Euripides' *Troerinnen*", *GB* 12, 65–100.
Deslauriers, M. (2003), "Aristotle on *andreia*, Divine and Sub-Human Virtues", in: R. M. Rosen / I. Sluiter (eds.), 187–211.
Destrée, P./ Herrmann, F.G. (eds.) (2011), *Plato and the Poets*, Leiden/ Boston.
Detienne, M. (1962), *Homère, Hesiode et Pythagore, Collectio Latomus* 57, Brussels.
Dewald, C./ Marincola, J. (eds.) (2006), *The Cambridge Companion to Herodotus*, Cambridge.
Di Giuseppe, L. (2012), *Euripide: Alessandro*, Lecce.
Di Luzio, A. (1969), "I papyri omerici d' epoca tolemaica e la constituzione del testo dell' epica arcaica", *RCCM* 11, 3–152.

Dickey, E. (2007), *Ancient Greek Scholarship: A Guide to Finding, Reading, and Understanding Scholia, Commentaries, Lexica and Grammatical Treatises*, Oxford/ New York.
Dillon, J. (2010), "Iamblichus of Chalcis and his School", in: L.P. Gerson (ed.), Vol. I, 359–74.
Dimock, W.C. (2008), "After Troy: Homer, Euripides, Total War", in: R. Felski (ed.), 66–81.
Dimou, A. (2006), *Dramatic Works*, Vols. I-II, Athens (Άπαντα: Τα Θεατρικά, Αθήνα).
Dingel, J. (1967), *Das Requisit in der griechischen Tragödie*, Diss. Tübingen.
Dinter, M. (2005), "Epic and Epigram – Minor Heroes in Virgil's Aeneid", *CQ* 55, 153–69.
Dios, J. M. L. de (2008), *Esquilo: Fragmentos, Testimonios*, Madrid.
Dodds, E.R. (1951), *The Greeks and the Irrational*, Berkeley/ Los Angeles.
Dodson, D.S. (2009), *Reading Dreams: An Audience-Critical Approach to the Dreams in the Gospel of Matthew*, London.
Dolç, M. (1984), *Elegies a Mecenas, l'Agró, Minúcies, l'Almadroc, últims poemes*, Barcelona.
Dolfi, E. (1984), "Su *I Cretesi* di Euripide: Passione e Responsabilità", *Prometheus* 10, 121–38.
Dornseiff, F. (1921), *Pindar*, Leipzig.
Dover, K.J. (1968), *Aristophanes: Clouds*, Oxford.
— (1972), *Aristophanic Comedy*, Berkeley/ Los Angeles.
— (1974), *Greek Popular Morality in the Time of Plato and Aristotle*, Berkeley/ Los Angeles.
— (1978), *Greek Homosexuality*, London.
— (1987–88), *The Greeks and their Legacy*, Vols. I-II, Oxford.
— (1988), "Greek Homosexuality and Initiation", in: K.J. Dover (1987-88), Vol. II, 115–34.
— (1993), *Aristophanes: Frogs*, Oxford.
Doxas, A., "*Penelope's* 300", *Eleftheros Kosmos*, 14 Oct. 1971.
Drachmann, A.B. (1903–27), *Scholia Vetera in Pindari Carmina*, Vols. I-III, Leipzig.
Du Quesnay, I. M. Le M. (1973), "The *Amores*", in: J.W. Binns (ed.), 1–48.
Dubischar, M. (2001), *Die Agonszenen bei Euripides*. Stuttgart.
Dué, C. (2001), "Achilles' Golden Amphora in Aeschines' *Against Timarchus* and the Afterlife of Oral Tradition", *CPh* 96, 33–47.
— (2006), *The Captive Woman's Lament in Greek Tragedy*, Austin.
Dué, C./ Ebbott, M. (2010), *Iliad 10 and the Poetics of Ambush: A Multitext Edition with Essays and Commentary*, Washington DC.
Dunbar, N. (1995), *Aristophanes: Birds*, Oxford.
Dunn, F. (1996), *Tragedy's End: Closure and Innovation in Euripidean Drama*, New York/ Oxford.
Durand, G. (1987), *Le mythe et le mythique*, Paris.
Dyson, M. (1988), "Poetic Imitation in Plato's *Republic* 3", *Antichthon* 22, 42–53.
Easterling, P.E. (ed.) (1997), *The Cambridge Companion to Greek Tragedy*, Cambridge.
— (1997a), "Constructing the Heroic", in: C. Pelling (ed.), 21–37.
— (1997b), "Form and Performance", in: P.E Easterling (ed.), 151–77.
— (1999), "Actors and Voices: Reading between the Lines in Aeschines and Demosthenes", in: S. Goldhill/ R. Osborne (eds.), 154–66.
Easterling, P.E./ Hall, E. (eds.) (2002), *Greek and Roman Actors: Aspects of an Ancient Profession*, Cambridge.
Edmondson, J. / Keith, A. (eds.) (2008), *Roman Dress and the Fabrics of Roman Culture*, Toronto.

Edmundson, M. (1995), *Literature Against Philosophy, Plato to Derrida: A Defence of Poetry*, Cambridge.
Edwards, A.T. (1993), "Homer's Ethical Geography: Country and City in the *Odyssey*", *TAPhA* 123, 27–78.
Edwards, M. (1991), *The Iliad: A Commentary* (General Editor: G.S. Kirk), Vol. V: Books 17–20, Cambridge.
Efstathiou A. (2014), "Το ιδιωτικό και το δημόσιο στη δοκιμασία ρητόρων στην Αθήνα των κλασικών χρόνων (Private and Public in the dokimasia of *rhētores*)", in: L. Athanassaki/ A. Nikolaides/ D. Spatharas (eds.), 231–54.
Egan, R.B. (1996), "Corydon's Winning Words in *Ecl.* 7", *Phoenix* 50, 233–39.
Egli, F. (2003), *Euripides im Kontext zeitgenössischer intellektueller Strömungen*, Munich/ Leipzig.
Eisenstein, S.M. (1991), *Selected Works*, Vol. II: *Towards a Theory of Montage* (ed. M. Glenny and R. Taylor, trans. M. Glenny), London.
Eitrem, S. (1922), "Kyklopen", in: *RE* XI 2, Stuttgart, 2328–47.
Ekdawi, S. (2002), "The Myth of Eternal Return", in: J. Anton (ed.), 115–24.
Elderkin, G.W. (1941), "The Akanthos Column at Delphi", *Hesperia* 10.4, 373–80.
Elliger, W. (1975), *Die Darstellung der Landschaft in der griechischen Dichtung*, Berlin/ New York.
Elliot, R. (1969), *Mythe et légende dans le théâtre de Racine*, Paris.
Elliott, J. (2013), *Ennius and the Architecture of the Annales*, Cambridge.
Elmer, D.F. (2009), "Presentation Formulas in South Slavic Epic Song", *Oral Tradition* 24.1, 41–59.
Elsner, J. (1995), *Art and the Roman Viewer: The Transformation of Art from the Pagan World to Christianity*, Cambridge.
Elytis, O. (2006⁶), *Carte Blanche (Εν λευκώ)*, Athens.
Emlyn-Jones, C. (2008), "Poets on Socrates' Stage: Plato's Reception of Dramatic Art", in: L. Hardwick/ C. Stray (eds.), 38–49.
Emlyn-Jones, C./ Hardwick, L./ Purkis, J. (eds.) (1992), *Homer: Readings and Images*, London.
Enenkel, K.A.E./ Pfeijffer I.L. (eds.) (2005), *The Manipulative Mode: Political Propaganda in Antiquity*, Leiden.
Erler, M./ Kramer, B. / Hagedorn, D. / Hübner, R. (eds.) (1980), *Kölner Papyri (P.Köln)* 3, Opladen.
Evangelidis, D. (1935), "Ἠπειρωτικαὶ ἔρευναι: Ι. Ἡ ἀνασκαφὴ τῆς Δωδώνης, ΙΙ. Ἀνασκαφὴ παρὰ τὸ Ῥαδοτόβι", *Ἠπειρωτικὰ Χρονικά*, 10, 193–264.
Faber, R. (2008), "The Woven Garment as Literary Metaphor: The *Peplos* in *Ciris* 9–41", in: J. Edmondson/ A. Keith (eds.), 205–16.
Fabre-Serris, J./ Deremetz, A. (eds.) (1999), *Élégie et épopée dans la poésie Ovidienne (Héroïdes et Amours). En hommage Simone Viarre*, Lille.
Fairclough, H.R./ Goold, G.P. (1999), *Virgil*, Vol. I: *Eclogues, Georgics, Aeneid 1–6* (1st ed. by H.R. Fairclough, London 1916, revised by G.P. Goold), Cambridge (Mass.)/ London.
Fairclough, H.R./ Goold, G.P. (2000), *Virgil*, Vol. II: *Aeneid VII-XII, Appendix Vergiliana* (1st ed. by H.R. Fairclough, London 1918, revised by G.P. Goold), Cambridge (Mass.)/ London.
Falcetto, R. (2002), *Il Palamede di Euripide*, Alessandria.
Fantham, E. (2011), *Roman Readings: Roman Response to Greek Literature from Plautus to Statius and Quintilian*, Berlin/ New York.

Fantuzzi, M./ Hunter, R.L. (2004), *Tradition and Innovation in Hellenistic Poetry*, Cambridge.
Fantuzzi, M. (2005), "Posidippus at Court: The Contribution of the Ἱππικά of P. Mil.Vogl. VIII 309 to the Ideology of Ptolemaic Kingship", in: K. Gutzwiller (ed.), 249–68.
Fantuzzi, M./ Tsagalis, C. (eds.) (2015), *The Greek Epic Cycle and its Ancient Reception: A Companion*, Cambridge.
Faraone, C.A. (1991), "Binding and Burying the Forces of Evil: The Defensive Use of 'Voodoo Dolls' in Ancient Greece", *Cl.Ant*, 10, 165–205.
— (2002), *The Rise and Fall of the Afterlife*, London/ New York.
Farrell, J. (2004), "Roman Homer", in: R. L. Fowler (ed.), 254–71.
Fedeli, P. (1980), *Properzio: Il primo libro delle elegie*, Florence.
— (2005), *Properzio: Elegie, Libro II*, Cambridge.
Felski, R. (ed.) (2008), *Rethinking Tragedy*, Baltimore.
Felson, N. (ed.) (2004), *The Poetics of Deixis in Alcman, Pindar and Other Lyric*, Arethusa Special Edition 37, no. 3.
Ferrari, G.R.F. (1989), "Plato and Poetry", in: G. A. Kennedy (ed.), 92–148.
— (ed.) (2007), *The Cambridge Companion to Plato's Republic*, Cambridge.
Ferri, R. (ed.) (2011), *The Latin of Roman Lexicography*, Pisa/ Rome.
Finkelberg, M. (2007), "Homer as a Foundation-Text", in: H. Bloom (ed.) (2007b), 169–88.
— (ed.) (2011), *The Homer Encyclopedia*, Malden/ Oxford.
Fisher, N. (2001), *Aeschines: Against Timarchos*, Oxford.
Flores, E. (1988), "Polifemo", in: *Enciclopedia Virgiliana* IV, Rome, 164–66.
Floridi, L. (2014), *Lucillio: Epigrammi*, Berlin/ Boston.
Foer, J. (2011), "Secrets of a Mind Gamer", *The New York Times Sunday Magazine*, 22/2/2011.
Foley, H.P. (ed.) (1981), *Reflections of Women in Antiquity*, New York/ London.
Foley, J.M. (2002), *How to Read an Oral Poem*, Urbana/ Chicago.
— (ed.) (2005), *A Companion to Ancient Epic*. Malden/ Oxford.
Ford, A. (1999), "Reading Homer from the Rostrum: Poems and Laws in Aeschines' *Against Timarchus*," in: S. Goldhill/ R. Osborne (eds.), 231–56.
Foster, D.H. (2010), *Wagner's Ring Cycle and the Greeks*, Cambridge.
Fouchard, A. (1997), *Aristocratie et Démocratie*, Paris.
Fowler, D. (1992), "Narrate and Describe: The Problem of *Ekphrasis*", *JRS* 82, 24–34 (reprinted in: D. Fowler, *Roman Constructions: Readings in Postmodern Latin*, Oxford 2000, 64–85).
— (2002), *Lucretius on Atomic Motion: A Commentary on De rerum natura 2.1.332*, Oxford.
Fowler R.L. (1987), *The Nature of Early Greek Lyric: Three Preliminary Studies*, Toronto.
— (1990), "Two More New Verses of Hipponax (and a Spurium of Philoxenus?)", *ICS* 15, 1–22.
— (2004), "The Homeric Question", in: R.L. Fowler (ed.), 220–32.
— (ed.) (2004), *The Cambridge Companion to Homer*, Cambridge.
— (2006), "Herodotus and his Prose Predecessors", in: C. Dewald/ J. Marincola (eds.), 29–45.
Foxhall, L./ Gehrke, H.-J./ Luraghi, N. (eds.) (2010), *Intentionale Geschichte: Spinning Time*, Stuttgart.
Fraenkel, E. (1950), *Aeschylus: Agamemnon*, Vols. I-III, Oxford.
Fraser, P.M. (1972), *Ptolemaic Alexandria*, Vols. I-III, Oxford.
Frazer, J.G. (1913^2), *Pausanias' Description of Greece*, Vols. I-VI, London.

Friedländer, P. (1964), *Plato: The Dialogues*, Vol. II (trans. H. Meyerhoff), New York.
Friedrich, P. (1978), *The Meaning of Aphrodite*, Chicago/ London.
Friedrich, W.H. (1953), *Euripides und Diphilos*, Munich.
Frois, É./ Lesot, A. (1998), "Analyse critique", in: J. Giraudoux, *La guerre de Troie n' aura pas lieu*, Paris, 11–65.
Furbank, P.N. (1992), "On Reading Homer without knowing any Greek", in: C. Emlyn-Jones/ L. Hardwick/ J. Purkis (eds.), 33–46.
Gadamer, H.G. (1975), *Truth and Method* (trans. G. Barden and J. Cumming), New York.
Gagarin, M. (1987), "Morality in Homer", *CPh* 82, 285–306.
Gaines, R. (1982), "Qualities of Rhetorical Expression in Philodemus", *TAPhA* 112, 71–81.
Gaisser, J. (2002), "The Reception of Classical Texts in the Renaissance", in: A. J. Grieco/ M. Rocke/ F. Gioffredi Superbi (eds.), 387–400.
Gall, D. (1999), *Zur Technik von Anspielung und Zitat in der römischen Dichtung: Vergil, Gallus und die Ciris*, Munich.
Garin, F. (1909), "Sui romanzi greci", *SIFC* 17, 423–60.
Garner, R. (1990), *From Homer to Tragedy: The Art of Allusion in Greek Poetry*, London.
Garrison, D. H. (1978), *Mild Frenzy: A Reading of the Hellenistic Love Epigram*, Wiesbaden.
Gartziou-Tatti, A.(1992), "Pâris-Alexandre dans l' *Iliade*", in: A. Moreau (ed.), 73–92.
—— (1997), "Χορός και Τελετουργία στις *Τρῳάδες* του Ευριπίδη", *Dodone* 26, 313–34.
Gatti, P.L. (2010), *Pseudo Virgilio: Ciris*, Milano.
Gellie, G. (1986), "Helen in the *Trojan Women*", in: J.H. Betts/ J.T Hooker/ J.R. Green (eds.), I 114–21.
Gelzer, T. (1981), "Neue Kölner Papyri", *MH* 38, 120–24.
—— (1985), "*Μοῦσα αὐθιγενής*: Bemerkungen zu einem Typ pindarischer und bacchylideischer Epinikien", *MH* 42, 95–120.
Genette, G. (1982), *Palimpsestes: La Littérature au Second Degré*, Paris.
Georgopoulou, V. (2006), "Women's Chorus: from Juliet to Andromache (Χορός Γυναικών: Από την Ιουλιέττα στην Ανδρομάχη)", in: A. Dimou, *Dramatic Works* (Άπαντα: Τα Θεατρικά), Vol. I, Athens, 362–66.
—— (2009), "Excesses and Variations of Love in the Dramaturgy of Akis Dimou (Υπερβάσεις και παρεκκλίσεις του έρωτα στο θεατρικό έργο του Άκη Δήμου)", in: C. Bobas (ed.), 537–45.
Georgousopoulos, K. (1984) (review of 1971), "*Penelope's 300*", in: *Keys and Codes of Theatre* (Κλειδιά και Κώδικες Θεάτρου), Athens, Vol. II, 13–17.
Gerber, D. (1987), "Pindar's Olympian Four: A Commentary", *QUCC* n.s. 25, 7–24.
Gerber, D.E. (ed.) (1984), *Greek Poetry and Philosophy: Studies in Honour of Leonard Woodbury*, Chico.
—— (ed.) (1997), *A Companion to the Greek Lyric Poets*, Leiden.
—— (1999), *Greek Iambic Poetry: From the Seventh to the Fifth Centuries BC*, Cambridge (Mass.).
Gerson, L.P. (ed.) (2010), *The Cambridge History of Philosophy in Late Antiquity*, Vols. I-II, Cambridge.
Geymonat, M. (1993), "Callimachus at the End of Aeneas' Narration", *HSPC* 95, 323–31.
Giangrande, G. (1968), "Sympotic Literature and Epigram", *L'Épigramme Grecque* (*Entr. Fond. Hardt* 14), 91–178.
Giannaris, G. (1973), *Mikis Theodorakis: Music and Social Change*, New York.

Gibert, J. (2009), "Euripides' *Antiope* and the Quiet Life", in: J.R.C. Cousland/ J. R. Hume (eds.), 23 – 34.
Gibson, R.K. (2007), *Excess and Restraint: Propertius, Horace and Ovid's Ars Amatoria* (*BICS* Suppl. 89), London.
Gil, L./ Aguilar, R.M. (eds.) (1984), *Apophoreta Philologica Emmanueli Fernandez-Galiano a Sodalibus Oblata*, Madrid.
Gill, C. (1993), "Plato on Falsehood—not Fiction", in: C. Gill/ P. Wiseman (eds.), 38 – 87.
Gill, C./ Wiseman, P. (eds.) (1993), *Lies and Fiction in the Ancient World*, Exeter.
Giraudoux, J. (1998), *La guerre de Troie n'aura pas lieu*, Paris.
Glenn, J. (1972), "Virgil's Polyphemus", *G&R* 19.1, 47 – 59.
Godley, A.D. (1920 – 25), *Herodotus: The Persian Wars*, Vols. I-IV, London.
Goff, B. (2009), *Euripides: Trojan Women*, London.
Goldhill, S. (1991), *The Poet's Voice: Essays on Poetics and Greek Literature*, Cambridge.
—— (1997), "The Language of Tragedy: Rhetoric and Communication", in: P.E. Easterling (ed.), 127 – 50.
—— (2001) (ed.), *Being Greek under Rome: Cultural Identity, the Second Sophistic and the Development of Empire*, Cambridge.
—— (2010), "Cultural History and Aesthetics: Why Kant is no place to start Reception Studies", in: E. Hall/ S. Harrop (eds.), 56 – 70.
Goldhill, S./ Osborne, R. (eds.) (1999), *Performance Culture and Athenian Democracy*, Cambridge.
Goldhill, S./ von Reden, S. (1999), "Plato and the Performance of Dialogue", in: S. Goldhill/ R. Osborne (eds.), 257 – 89.
Goodkin, R.E. (1989), *Autour de Racine: Studies in Intertextuality*, Yale.
Goossens, R. (1962), *Euripide et Athènes*, Brussels.
Gould, J. (1980), "Law, Custom and Myth: Aspects of the Social Position of Women in Classical Athens", *JHS* 100, 38 – 59.
Gould, T. (1964), "Plato's Hostility to Art", *Arion* 2, 70 – 91.
—— (1990), *The Ancient Quarrel between Poetry and Philosophy*, Princeton.
Gow, A.S.F. (1952^2), *Theocritus*, Cambridge.
Gow, A.S.F./ Scholfield, A.F. (1953), *Poems and Poetical Fragments: Nicander of Colophon*, Cambridge.
Gow, A.S.F./ Page, D. L. (1965), *The Greek Anthology: Hellenistic Epigrams*, Vols. I-II, Cambridge.
Grafton, A. (1981), "Prolegomena to Friedrich August Wolf", *Journal of the Warburg and Courtauld Institutes* 44, 101 – 29.
Grammatas, Th. (1994), *From Tragedy to Drama. Essays of Comparative Theatrology* (Από την τραγωδία στο δράμα. Μελέτες συγκριτικής θεατρολογίας), Athens.
Grant, A. (1885), *The Ethics of Aristotle*, London.
Graziosi, B. (2002), *Inventing Homer: The Early Reception of Epic*, Cambridge.
—— (2007), "Homer in Albania: Oral Epic and the Geography of Literature", in: B. Graziosi/ E. Greenwood (eds.), 120 – 42.
—— (2008a), "The Ancient Reception of Homer", in: L. Hardwick/ C. Stray (eds.), 26 – 37.
—— (2008b), "Review of R. Bittlestone/ J. Diggle/ J. Underhill, *Odysseus Unbound: the Search for Homer's Ithaca*", *JHS* 128, 178 – 80.

—— (2010), "Hesiod in Classical Athens: Rhapsodes, Orators, and Platonic Discourse", in: G. Boys-Stones /J. Haubold (eds.), 111–32.
Graziosi, B./ Greenwood, E. (eds.) (2007), *Homer in the Twentieth Century: Between World Literature and the Western Canon*, Oxford.
Graziosi, B./ Haubold, J. (2003), "Homeric Masculinity: ΗΝΟΡΕΗ and ΑΓΗΝΟΡΙΗ", *JHS* 123, 60–76.
Graziosi, B./ Haubold, J. (2009), "Greek Lyric and Early Greek Literary History", in: F. Budelmann (ed.), 95–113.
Graziosi, B./ Haubold, J. (2010), *Homer: Iliad Book 6*, Cambridge.
Greenwood, E. (2007), "Logue's Tele-Vision: Homer from a Distance", in: B. Graziosi/ E. Greenwood (eds.), 145–76.
Greenwood, L.H.G. (1961), *Aspects of Euripidean Tragedy*, London.
Gregory, J. (1991), *Euripides and the Instruction of the Athenians*, Ann Arbor.
—— (ed.) (2005), *A Companion to Greek Tragedy*, Oxford/ Malden/ Victoria.
Grenfell, B.P./ Hunt, A.S. (1897), *Greek Papyri, Series* II, Oxford.
Grethlein, J. (2006), *Das Geschichtsbild der Ilias*, Göttingen.
—— (2008), "Memory and Material Objects in the *Iliad* and the *Odyssey*", *JHS* 128, 27–51.
Grieco, A.J./ Rocke, M./ Gioffredi Superbi, F. (eds.) (2002), *The Italian Renaissance in the Twentieth Century*, Florence.
Griffin, J. (1977), "The Epic Cycle and the Uniqueness of Homer", *JHS* 97, 39–53.
—— (1992), "Theocritus, the *Iliad* and the East", *AJPh* 113, 189–211.
—— (1998), "The Social Function of Attic Tragedy", *CQ* 48, 39–61.
Griffith, M. (1999), *Sophocles: Antigone*, Cambridge.
Griswold, C. L. (2012), "Plato on Rhetoric and Poetry", in: *The Stanford Encyclopedia of Philosophy* (Spring 2012 Edition).
Griswold, Jr. C. L. (1985), "Plato's Metaphilosophy: Why Plato Wrote Dialogues?", in: D. O'Meara (ed.), 143–67.
Grube, G.M.A. (1992), *Plato: Republic* (revised by C.D.C. Reeve), Indianapolis/ Cambridge.
Grzybeck, E. (1990), *Du calendrier macédonien au calendrier ptolémaique: problèmes de chronologie hellénistique*, Basel.
Guettel-Cole, S. (2007), "Finding Dionysus", in: D. Ogden (ed.), 327–41.
Guichard, L.A. (2004), *Asclepíades de Samos: Epigramas y fragmentos*, Bern.
Guidorizzi, G. (2000): *Igino: Miti*, Milan.
Günther, H.C. (ed.) (2006), *Brill's Companion to Propertius*, Leiden.
Guthrie, W.K.C. (1962–1981), *A History of Greek Philosophy*, Vols. I-VI, Cambridge.
—— (1971), *The Sophists*, Cambridge.
Gutzwiller, K.J. (1992), "The Nautilus, the Halcyon, and Selenaia: Callimachus's Epigram 5Pf. = 14G.-P.", *Cl.Ant.* 11, 194–209.
—— (1997), "The Poetics of Editing in Meleager's Garland", *TAPhA* 127, 169–200.
—— (1998), *Poetic Garlands: Hellenistic Epigrams in Context*, Berkeley/ Los Angeles/ London.
—— (ed.) (2005), *The New Posidippus: A Hellenistic Poetry Book*, Oxford.
—— (2010), "Heroic Epitaphs of the Classical Age: The Aristotelian *Peplos* and Beyond", in: M. Baumbach/ A. Petrovic/ I. Petrovic (eds.), 219–49.
Habicht, C. (1985), *Pausanias' Guide to Ancient Greece*, Berkeley.
Hainsworth, B. (1993), *The Iliad: A Commentary* (General Editor: G.S. Kirk), Vol. III: Books 9–12, Cambridge.

Hall, E. (1995), "Lawcourt Dramas: The Power of Performance in Greek Forensic Oratory", *BICS* 40, 39–58.
— (2008), *The Return of Ulysses: A Cultural History of Homer's Odyssey*, Baltimore.
Hall, E./ Harrop, S. (2010), *Theorising Performance: Greek Drama, Cultural History and Critical Practice*, London/ New York.
Hall, E./ Macintosh, F./ Wrigley, A. (eds.) (2004), *Dionysus since 69: Greek Tragedy at the Dawn of the Third Millennium*, Oxford.
Hall, S./ Neale, S. (2010), *Epics, Spectacles and Blockbusters: A Hollywood History*, Detroit.
Halleran, M. (1982), "Alcestis Redux", *HSCP* 86, 51–53.
— (1985), *Stagecraft in Euripides*, Kent/ Sydney.
— (1988), "Text and Ceremony at the Close of Euripides' *Alcestis*", *Eranos* 86, 123–29.
Halliwell, S. (1996), "Plato's Repudiation of the Tragic", in: M.S. Silk (ed.), 332–49.
— (1997), "The *Republic*'s two Critiques of Poetry", in: O. Höffe (ed.), 313–32.
— (2000), "The Subjection of *Muthos* to *Logos*: Plato's Citations of the Poets", *CQ* 50, 94–112.
— (2006), "Plato and Aristotle on Denial of Tragedy", in: A. Laird (ed.), 115–41.
Hamilakis, Y. (2007), *The Nation and its Ruins: Antiquity, Archaeology and National Imagination in Greece*, Oxford.
Hammer, D. (2007), "Toward a Political Ethic", in: H. Bloom (ed.) (2007a) 155–80.
Hanink, J. (2014), *Lycurgan Athens and the Making of Classical Tragedy*, Cambridge.
Harder, M. A. (2007), "Epigram and the Heritage of Epic", in: P. Bing/J.S. Bruss (eds.), 409–28.
Harder, M.A / Regtuit, R.F. / Wakker, G.C. (eds.) (1998), *Genre in Hellenistic Poetry*, Groningen.
Harder, M.A./ Regtuit, R.F./ Wakker, G.C. (eds.) (2006), *Beyond the Canon*, Leuven.
Harder, M.A./ Regtuit, R.F./ Wakker, G.C. (eds.) (2012), *Gods and Religion in Hellenistic Poetry*, Leuven.
Hardie, A. (2007), "Juno, Hercules and the Muses at Rome", *AJPh* 128, 551–92.
Hardie, C. (1977), "The Crater of Avernus as a cult-site", in: R.G. Austin (ed.), 279–86.
Hardie, P. (1985), "Imago Mundi: Cosmological and Ideological Aspects of the *Shield of Achilles*", *JHS* 105, 11–31.
— (1986), *Virgil's Aeneid: Cosmos and Imperium*, Oxford.
— (ed.) (1999), *Virgil: Critical Assessments of Classical Authors*, Vol. III: *The Aeneid* (trans. R. Lauglands), London.
— (2009a), *Lucretian Receptions: History, The Sublime, Knowledge*, Cambridge.
— (2009b), "The Self-Divisions of Scylla", *Trends in Classics* 1, 118–47.
Hardwick, L. (1992), "Convergence and Divergence in Reading Homer", in: C. Emlyn-Jones/ L. Hardwick/ J. Purkis (eds.), 227–48.
— (1997), "Reception as Simile: The Poetics of Reversal in Homer and Derek Walcott", *IJCT* 3.3, 326–38.
— (2002), "Classical Texts in Post-Colonial Literatures: Consolation, Redress and New Beginnings in the work of Derek Walcott and Seamus Heaney", *IJCT* 9.2, 236–56.
— (2003), *Reception Studies*, Oxford.
— (2009), "Playing around Cultural Faultlines: The Impact of Modern Translations for the Stage on Perceptions of Ancient Greek Drama", in: A. Chantler/ C. Dente (eds.), 167–84.

— (2011), "Fuzzy Connections: Classical Texts and Modern Poetry in English", in: J. Parker/ T. Matthews (eds.), 39–60.
— (2013), "Against the 'Democratic Turn': Counter-texts, Counter-contexts, Counter-arguments", in: L. Hardwick/ S. Harrison (eds.), 15–32.
Hardwick, L./ Harrison, S. (eds.) (2013), *Classics in the Modern World: A Democratic Turn?* Oxford.
Hardwick, L./ Stray, C. (2008), "Introduction: Making Connections", in: L. Hardwick/ C. Stray (eds.), 1–9.
Hardwick, L./ Stray, C. (eds.) (2008), *A Companion to Classical Receptions*, Oxford/ Malden.
Harrison, E.L. (1986), "Achaemenides' Unfinished Account: Vergil *Aeneid* 3.588–691", *CPh* 81.2, 146–47.
Harrison, S. (2007), *Generic Enrichment in Vergil and Horace*, Oxford.
Harrison, T. (2000), *Divinity and History: The Religion of Herodotus*, Oxford.
Hartmann, A. (1917), *Untersuchungen über die Sagen vom Tod des Odysseus*, Munich.
Harvey, F. (1990), "Dona Ferentes: Some Aspects of Bribery in Greek Politics", in: P. Cartledge/ F. Harvey (eds.), 76–117.
Haslam, M. (1997), "Homeric Papyri and Transmission of the Text", in: I. Morris /B. Powell (eds.), 55–100.
Haubold, J. (2000), *Homer's People: Epic Poetry and Social Formation*, Cambridge.
— (2007), "Homer after Parry: Tradition, Reception, and the Timeless Text", in: B. Graziosi/ E. Greenwood (eds.), 27–46.
Haury, A. (1957), *Ciris: Edition critique*, Bordeaux.
Häusle, H. (1979), *Einfache und frühe Formen des griechischen Epigramms*, Innsbruck.
Havelock, E. (1963), *Preface to Plato*, Oxford.
Hawkins, S. (2013), *Studies in the Language of Hipponax*, Bremen.
Heath, J. (2005), "Blood for the Dead: Homeric Ghosts Speak up", *Hermes* 133, 389–400.
Heinze, R. (1993), *Virgil's Epic Technique* (trans. H. and D. Harvey and F. Robertson, with a preface by A. Wlosok), Stuttgart.
Helms, J. (1966), *Character Portrayal in the Romance of Chariton*, The Hague/ Paris.
Henrichs, A. (1982), "Changing Dionysiac Identities", in: B.F. Meyer/ E.P. Sanders (eds.), 137–60.
— (1991), "Namenlosigkeit und Euphemismus: Zur Ambivalenz der chthonishen Mächte im attischen Drama", in: H. Hofmann/ M.A. Harder (eds.), 161–201.
Hermann, H. (2008), *Mikis Theodorakis: Der Rhythmus der Freiheit*, Berlin.
Herrman, J. (2004), *Athenian Funeral Orations*, Newburyport.
— (2009), *Hyperides: Funeral Oration*, Oxford.
Hershkowitz, D. (1991), "The *Aeneid* in *Aeneid* 3", *Vergilius* 37, 69–76.
Herter, H. (1934), "Telchinen", in: *RE* V A.1, Stuttgart, 197.9–224.56.
Hesk, J. (1999), "The Rhetoric of Anti-rhetoric in Athenian Oratory", in: S. Goldhill/ R. Osborne (eds.), 201–30.
— (2000), *Deception and Democracy in Classical Athens*, Cambridge.
Heubeck, A. (1981), "Zwei homerische πεῖραι (ω 205ff. – B 53ff.)", *ZAnt* 31, 73–83.
Heubeck, A./ West, S./ Hainsworth, J.B. (1988), *A Commentary on Homer's Odyssey*, Vol. I, Oxford.
Heubeck, A./ Hoekstra, A. (1989), *A Commentary on Homer's Odyssey*, Vol. II, Oxford.
Heyworth, S.J. (2007), *Cynthia: A Companion to the Text of Propertius*, Oxford.

— (2009), "Propertius and Ovid", in: P.E. Knox (ed.), 265–78.
Heyworth, S.J./ Morwood, J.H.W. (2011), *A Commentary on Propertius, Book 3*, Oxford.
Hielkema, H. (1941), *Ciris: quod carmen traditur Vergilii*, Diss. Utrecht.
Hill, J./ Church Gibson, P. (eds.) (1998), *The Oxford Guide to Film Studies*, Oxford/ New York.
Hinds, S. (1998), *Allusion and Intertext: Dynamics of Appropriation in Roman Poetry*, Cambridge.
Hintzen-Bohlen, B. (1995), *Die Kulturpolitik des Eubulos und des Lykurg: Die Denkmäler-und Bauprojekte in Athen zwischen 355 und 322 v.Chr.*, Berlin.
Hirschberger, M. (2001), "Epos und Tragödie. Ein Beitrag zur Intertextualität des griechischen Romans", *WJA* 25, 157–86.
Hobbs, A. (2000), *Plato and the Hero: Courage, Manliness and the Impersonal Good*, Cambridge.
Hoekstra, A. (1957), "Hésiode et la tradition orale", *Mnemosyne* 10, 193–225.
Hoerber, R.G. (1962), "Plato's *Lesser Hippias*", *Phronesis* 7, 121–31.
Höffe, O. (ed.) (1997), *Platon: Politeia*, Berlin.
Hofmann, H./ Harder, M.A. (eds.) (1991), *Fragmenta Dramatica*, Göttingen.
Hollis, A.S. (1992), "Hellenistic Colouring in Virgil's *Aeneid*", *HSCP* 94, 269–85.
— (1994), "Nonnus and Hellenistic Poetry", in: N. Hopkinson (ed.), 43–62.
— (1998), "Nicander and Lucretius", *PLILS* 10, 169–84.
— (2006), "Propertius and Hellenistic Poetry", in H.-C. Günther (ed.), 97–125.
Hölscher, U. (1988), *Die Odyssee: Epos zwischen Märchen und Roman*, Munich.
Holst, G. (1980), *Theodorakis: Myth and Politics in Modern Greek Music*, London.
Holst-Warhaft, G. (2012), "*Odyssey* by Kostas Kartelias translated by Gail Holst-Warhaft", *Per Contra: An International Journal of the Arts, Literature, and Ideas*, Spring issue 2, http://www.percontra.net/issues/23/poetry/odyssey/
Holub, R.C. (2003²), *Reception Theory: A Critical Introduction*, London.
Hope, R. (1960), *Aristotle: Metaphysics*, Ann Arbor.
Hopkins, D. (2010), *Conversing With Antiquity*, Oxford.
Hopkinson, N. (1984), *Callimachus: Hymn to Demeter*, Cambridge.
— (ed.) (1994), *Studies in the Dionysiaca of Nonnus*, Cambridge.
Hopman, M.G. (2012), *Scylla: Myth, Metaphor, Paradox*, Cambridge.
Hornblower, S. (1983), *The Greek World: 479–323 BC*, London.
— (2004), *Thucydides and Pindar: Historical Narrative and the World of Epinician Poetry*, Oxford.
Horsfall, N. (2006), *Virgil, Aeneid 3: A Commentary*, Leiden.
Hose, M. (1995), *Drama und Gesellschaft*, Stuttgart.
Housman, A.E. (1902), "Remarks on the *Culex*", *CR* 16, 339–46.
Howes, G.E. (1895), "Homeric Quotations in Plato and Aristotle", *HSCP* 6, 153–237.
Hunt, P. (2011), "Slaves in Greek Literary Culture", in: K. Bradley/ P. Cartledge (eds.), 22–47.
Hunter, R.L. (1999), *Theocritus: A Selection*, Cambridge.
— (2004), "Homer and Greek Literature", in: R.L. Fowler (ed.), 235–53.
— (2010), "Language and Interpretation in Greek Epigram", in: M. Baumbach/ A. Petrovic/ I. Petrovic (eds.), 265–88.
Hurst, A./ Kolde, A. (2008), *Lycophron: Alexandra*, Paris.
Hutton, W. (2005), *Describing Greece: Landscape and Literature in the Periegesis of Pausanias*, Cambridge.

Huys, M. (1986), "The Plotting Scene in Euripides' *Alexandros*", *ZPE* 62, 9–36.
Ingleheart, J. (2010), *A Commentary on Ovid, Tristia, Book 2*, Oxford.
Irwin, T.H. (1999²), *Aristotle: Nicomachean Ethics*, Indianapolis.
— (2010), "The Sense and Reference of *Kalon* in Aristotle", *CPh* 105, 381–96.
Iser, W. (1978), *The Act of Reading: A Theory of Aesthetic Response*, Baltimore/ London.
Jacob, D.J. (1993), "Die Stellung des *Margites* in der Entwicklung der Komödie", *Hellenica* 43, 275–79.
— (2009), "Die Spiegel der Alkestis", in: E. Karamalengou/ E. Makrygianni (eds.), 179–87.
— (2010a), "Euripides' *Alcestis* as Closed Drama", *RFIC* 138, 14–27.
— (2010b), "Milk in the Gold Tablets from Pelinna", *Trends in Classics* 2, 64–76.
Jacob, M. (1929), *La vie privée d'Hélène de Troie*, Paris.
Jacoby, F. (1945), "Athenian Epigrams from the Persian Wars", *Hesperia* 14, 185–211.
James, S.L. (2003), *Learned Girls and Male Persuasion: Gender and Reading in Roman Love Elegy*, Berkeley/ Los Angeles.
Janaway, C. (1995), *Images of Excellence: Plato's Critique of the Arts*, Oxford.
— (2006), "Plato and the Arts", in: H.H. Benson (ed.), 388–400.
Janko, R. (1992), *The Iliad: A Commentary* (General Editor: G.S. Kirk), Vol. IV: Books 13–16, Cambridge.
Jarkho, V. (1982), "Besprechung von R. Scodel, *The Trojan Trilogy of Euripides*", *Gnomon* 54, 241–45.
Jauss, H.R. (1982), *Toward an Aesthetic of Reception* (trans. T. Bahti), Minneapolis.
Jebb, R.C. (1900³), *Sophocles: The Antigone*, Cambridge.
Joachim, H. H. (1951), *Aristotle: The Nicomachean Ethics. A Commentary*, Oxford.
Jocelyn, H.D. (1967), *The Tragedies of Ennius*, Cambridge.
Jones, C. (2010), *New Heroes in Antiquity: From Achilles to Antinoos*, Cambridge (Mass.)/ London.
Jouan, F. (1966), *Euripide et les légendes des Chants Cypriens*, Paris.
Jouan, F./ van Looy, H. (1998), *Euripide: Les fragments*, Vol. I, Paris.
Jovanović, V.M. (1954), "O liku Filipa Višnjića I drugih guslara Vukova vremena", *Zbornik Matice Srpske za književnost I jezik, Novi Sad* 2, 67–96.
Jowett, B. (1953⁴), *The Dialogues of Plato*, Vols. I-V, Oxford.
Joyce, M. (2002), "No One Tells You This: Secondary Orality and Hypertextuality", *Oral Tradition* 17.2, 325–45.
Kaes, A. (2009), *Shell Shock Cinema: Weimar Culture and the Wounds of War*, Princeton.
Kagan, D. (1981), *The Peace of Nicias and the Sicilian Expedition*, Ithaca.
Kahane, A. (2005), *Diachronic Dialogues: Authority and Continuity in Homer and the Homeric Tradition*, Lanham.
Kahn, C.H. (1963), "Plato's Funeral Oration: The Motive of the *Menexenus*", *CPh* 58, 220–34.
— (1981), "Did Plato Write Socratic Dialogues?", *CQ* 31, 305–20.
— (1998), *Plato and the Socratic Dialogue: The Philosophical Use of a Literary Form*, Cambridge.
Kallendorf, C. W. (2006), "Allusion as Reception: Virgil, Milton, and the Modern Reader", in: C. Martindale/ R.F. Thomas (eds.), 67–79.
— (2007), "Introduction", in: C.W. Kallendorf (ed.), 1–4.
— (ed.) (2007), *A Companion to the Classical Tradition*, Oxford/ Malden.
Kambanellis, I. (1979), "*Odysseus, Come Home*", in: *Theatre*, Vol. II, Athens, 213–95.

—— (1990a), "Author's note", in: Programme of *Odysseus, Come Home*, National Theatre, Athens.
—— (1990b), *From the Stage and from the Auditorium* (Από σκηνής και από πλατείας), Athens.
—— (1998), "*The Last Act*", in: *Theatre*, Vol. VII, Athens, 167–241.
Kambylis, A. (1965), *Die Dichterweihe und ihre Symbolik: Untersuchungen zu Hesiodos, Kallimachos, Properz und Ennius*, Heidelberg.
Kamerbeek, J.C. (1958), "Mythe et realité dans l'oeuvre d'Euripide", *Entr. Ant. Clas.* 6, 1–41.
Kannicht, R. (1988), *The Ancient Quarrel Between Philosophy and Poetry: Aspects of the Greek Conception of Literature*, Canterbury.
—— (2004), *Tragicorum Graecorum Fragmenta*, Vol. V 1–2: *Euripides*, Göttingen.
Kantzios, I. (2005), *The Trajectory of Archaic Greek Trimeter*, Leiden.
Karadžić, V.S. (1842), "Pravi uzrok i početak skupljanja našijeh narodnijeh pjesama", *Peštansko-budimski skoroteča* 20/21, 118–28 (reprinted in Vuk Karadžić, Izabrani Spisi o jeziku I književnosti, priredio B. Nikolić, Belgrade 1969).
Karalis, V. (2012), *A History of Greek Cinema*, New York/ London.
Karamalengou, E./ Makrygianni, E. (eds.) (2009), *Ἀντιφίλησις. Studies on Classical, Byzantine and Modern Greek Literature and Culture in Honour of J. T. A. Papademetriou*, Stuttgart.
Karamanou, I. (2011), "The Hektor-Deiphobos Agon in Euripides' *Alexandros* (frr. 62a-b K.: P.Stras. 2342,2 and 2343)", *ZPE* 178, 35–47.
—— (2012), "Allocating fr. 46a K. within the Plot of Euripides' *Alexandros*: A Reinspection and Reassessment of P.Stras. 2342,1", in: P. Schubert (ed.), 399–405.
—— (2013), "The Attack Scene in Euripides' *Alexandros* and its Reception in Etruscan Art", in: A. Bakogianni (ed.), Vol. II, 415–31.
—— (2015), "Torch Imagery in Euripides' *Alexandros* and *Trojan Women*", in: *Balkan Light 2015 Conference Proceedings* (Acropolis Museum, 16–19 September 2015), Athens, 392–97.
Kartelias, K. (2007), *The Glass* (Το γυαλί: σχέδιον γ), Athens.
Karvounis, D. (2005), "Mikis Theodorakis' Children's Songs", in: M. Bouzakis/ E. Papavasiliou (eds.), 122–29.
Kaster, R.A. (1988), *Guardians of the Language: The Grammarian and Society in Late Antiquity*, Berkeley/ Los Angeles.
Katsouris, A. (1982), "Aeschylus' 'Odyssean' Tetralogy", *Dioniso* 53, 47–60.
Katz, M.A. (= M.B. Arthur) (1981),"The Divided World of *Iliad* VI", in: H.P. Foley (ed.), 19–44.
Kavanagh, P. (2005), *Collected Poems* (ed. A. Quinn), Harmondsworth.
Kazazis, J.N./ Rengakos, A. (eds.) (1999), *Euphrosyne: Studies in Ancient Epic and its Legacy in Honour of Dimitris N. Maronitis*, Stuttgart.
Keeley, E./ Sherrard, P. (1980), *Angelos Sikelianos: Selected Poems*, London.
—— (1995), *A Bilingual Collection of Poems by C.P. Cavafy*, London.
Keith, A.M. (1994), "Elegiac Poetics and Elegiac *Puellae* in Ovid's *Amores*", *CW* 88.1, 27–40.
Kelly, M. (ed.) (1966), *For Service to Classical Studies: Essays in Honour of F. Letters*, Melbourne/ Canberra/ Sydney.
Kennedy, D.F (1993), *The Arts of Love: Five Studies in the Discourse of Roman Love Elegy*, Cambridge.
Kennedy, G.A. (ed.) (1989), *The Cambridge History of Literary Criticism*, Vol. I, Cambridge.
—— (1994), *A New History of Classical Rhetoric*, Princeton.
Kerferd, G.B. (1981), *The Sophistic Movement*, Cambridge.

Keulen, A.J. (2001), *L. Annaeus Seneca: Troades*, Leiden.
Kindstrand, J.F. (1973), *Homer in der zweiten Sophistik,* Uppsala.
King, K.C. (1987), *Achilles: Paradigms of the War Hero from Homer to the Middle Ages*, Berkeley/ Los Angeles.
Kinsey, T.E. (1979), "The Achaemenides Episode in Virgil's *Aeneid* III", *Latomus* 39, 110–24.
Kirk, G. S. (1985), *The Iliad: A Commentary*, Vol. I: Books 1–4, Cambridge.
Klagge, J.C./ Smith, N.D. (eds.) (1992), *Methods of Interpreting Plato and his Dialogues*, Oxford.
Klaras, B. (1961), "The *Odyssey* in a Satirical Trilogy by Skouloudis", *Vradyni*, 2 Nov. 1961.
Klironomos, N. (2007), *His Childhood Years...A Journey: Paintings inspired by Mikis Theodorakis' Childhood. A Painter's Offer to the Great Composer* (Τα παιδικά του χρόνια... ένα ταξίδι : Έργα εμπνευσμένα από τα παιδικά χρόνια του Μίκη Θεοδωράκη, προσφορά του ζωγράφου στο μεγάλο συνθέτη), Athens.
Knauer, G.N. (1964), *Die Aeneis und Homer*, Göttingen.
— (1981), "Vergil and Homer", in: H. Temporini et al. (eds.), *ANRW* XXXI 2, 870–918.
Knecht, D. (1970), *Ciris: authenticité, histoire du texte, édition et commentaire critiques*, Brugge.
Knight, V.H. (1995), *The Renewal of Epic: Responses to Homer in the Argonautica of Apollonius*, Leiden.
Knoche, U. (1936), "Zur Frage der Properzinterpolation", *RhM* 85, 8–63.
Knox, P.E. (ed.) (2009), *A Companion to Ovid,* Malden/ Oxford.
Koch, G. (ed.) (1986), *Studien zur frühchristlichen Kunst* III, *Göttinger Orientforschungen* 2, Göttingen.
Kofidou, A. (2004), *Confluences thématiques et techniques chez J. Giraudoux et E. Ionesco*, Diss. Thessaloniki.
Kokkinakis, G. (1961), "*Odyssey*. A Satirical Comedy by Manolis Skouloudis", *Acropolis*, 5 Nov. 1961.
Kolde, A./ Lukinovich, A./ Rey, A.L. (eds.) (2005), *Κορυφαίῳ ἀνδρί: Mélanges offerts à André Hurst*, Geneva.
Kolker, R. P. (1998), "The Film Text and Film Form", in: J. Hill/ P. Church Gibson (eds.), 11–29.
Koniaris, G.L. (1973), "*Alexander, Palamedes, Troades, Sisyphus*—A Connected Tetralogy? A Connected Trilogy? ", *HSCP* 77, 85–124.
Konstan, D. (1985), "*Philia* in Euripides' *Electra*", *Phil.* 129, 176–85.
— (2003), "Before Jealousy", in: D. Konstan/ N.K. Rutter (eds.) 7–28.
— (2006), *The Emotions of the Ancient Greeks*, Toronto/ London.
Konstan, D./ Rutter, N.K. (eds.) (2003), *Envy, Spite and Jealousy,* Edinburgh.
Kost, K. (1971), *Musaios: Hero und Leander*, Bonn.
Kotzia-Panteli, P. (2002), "Forschungsreisen. Zu Iamblichus' *Protreptikos* 40, 1–11 Pistelli", *Phil.* 146, 111–32.
Koukoulas, L. (1961), "*Odyssey*", *Athinaiki*, 4 Nov. 1961.
Koutoulas, A. (1998), *Theodorakis the Musician* (Ο μουσικός Θεοδωράκης. Κείμενα – Εργογραφία – Κριτικές 1937–1996), Athens.
Kouyoumoutzakis, Y. (ed.) (2007), *Universal Harmony, Music and Science in Mikis Theodorakis* (Συμπαντική αρμονία, μουσική και επιστήμη στον Μίκη Θεοδωράκη), Herakleion.
— (2007), "Mikis Theodorakis: The Journey", in: Y. Kouyoumoutzakis (ed.), 43–72.

Kovacs, D. (1997), "Gods and Men in Euripides' *Trojan Trilogy*", *Colby Quarterly* 33, 162–76.
Kracauer, S. (2004²), *From Caligari to Hitler: A Psychological History of the German Film*, Princeton.
Kramer, B. (1980), "Schülerübung; Anapäste (Aischylos, *Psychagogoi?*)", in: M. Erler / B. Kramer / D. Hagedorn / R. Hübner (eds.), 11–23.
Krausse, O. (1905), *De Euripide Aeschyli Instauratore*, Jena.
Krischer, T. (1991), "Rezension: W. Mader, *Die Psaumis-Oden Pindars (O. 4 and O. 5)*, Innsbruck 1990", *AAHG* 44, 158–59.
—— (1992), "Die Bogenprobe", *Hermes* 120, 19–25.
Kronick, J.G. (2006), "The Ancient Quarrel Revisited: Literary Theory and the Return to Ethics", *Philosophy and Literature* 30.2, 436–49.
Kuhrt, A. (2007), *The Persian Empire: A Corpus of Sources from the Achaemenid Period*, Vol. I-II, London.
Kyriakidis, S. (2007), *Catalogues of Proper Names in Latin Epic Poetry*, Newcastle upon Tyne.
Kyriakou, P. (2001), "Warrior Vaunts in the *Iliad*", *RhM* 144, 250–76.
La Penna, A. (1951), "Note sul linguaggio erotico dell' elegia latina", *Maia* 4, 187–209.
—— (2000), "L'Ordine delle raffigurazioni della guerra Troiana nel tempio di Cartagine (*Aeneid* I 469–493)", *Maia* 52, 1–8.
Labarbe, J. (1949), *L'Homère de Platon*, Liège.
Lada-Richards, I. (2002), "The Subjectivity of Greek Performance", in: P.E. Easterling/ E. Hall (eds.), 395–418.
Laird, A. (ed.) (2006), *Oxford Readings in Classical Studies: Ancient Literary Criticism*, Oxford.
Lamberton, R. (1986), *Homer the Theologian: Neoplatonist Allegorical Reading and the Growth of the Epic Tradition*, Berkeley/ Los Angeles.
Lamberton, R./ Keaney, J.J. (eds.) (1992), *Homer's Ancient Readers: The Hermeneutics of Greek Epic's Earliest Exegetes*, Princeton.
Lampert, L. (2002), "Socrates' Defence of Polytropic Odysseus: Lying and Wrong-doing in Plato's Lesser Hippias", *The Review of Politics* 64.2, 231–60.
Lange, K. (2002), *Euripides und Homer: Untersuchungen zur Homernachwirkung im Elektra, Iphigenie im Taurerland, Helena, Orestes und Kyklops*, Stuttgart.
Lasserre, F./ Sulliger, J. (eds.) (1976), *A. Rivier: Études de littérature grecque*, Geneva.
Latacz, J./ Greub T./ Blome P./ Wieczorek A (eds.) (2008), *Homer: Der Mythos von Troia in Dichtung und Kunst*, Munich.
Latte, K. (1935), "Der Thrax des Euphorion", *Phil.* 90, 129–55.
Lattimore, R. (1951), *The Iliad of Homer*, Chicago.
Lausberg, H. (1960), *Handbuch der literarischen Rhetorik: eine Grundlegung der Literaturwissenschaft*, Vols. I-II, Munich.
Lazaridou – Elmaloglou, I. (2004), *Mikis Theodorakis: His Symphonic Works in the Period 1937–1960 (Μίκης Θεοδωράκης: το συμφωνικό έργο της περιόδου 1937–1960)*, Diss. Athens.
Le Sage, L. (1958), *L'oeuvre de Jean Giraudoux*, University Park, Pennsylvania.
Leach, E.W. (1966), "Nature and Art in Vergil's Second *Eclogue*", *AJPh* 87, 427–45.
Lear, G.R. (2004), *Happy Lives and the Highest Good: An Essay on Aristotle's Nicomachean Ethics*, Princeton.
—— (2011), "Mimesis and Psychological Change in *Republic* III", in: P. Destrée/ F.G. Herrmann (eds.), 195–216.

Lee, G. (1980), *Virgil: The Eclogues*, London.
— (1994), *Propertius: The Poems*, Oxford.
Lee, K.H. (1976), *Euripides: Troades*, London.
Leeuwen, J. van (1890), "Quaestiones ad Historiam Scenicam pertinentes", *Mnemosyne* 18, 68–75.
Lehnus, L. (1975), "Una scena della *Ciris* (vv. 220 ss.): Carme e l'*Ecale* di Callimaco", *RIL* 109, 353–61.
Lenchantin de Gubernatis, M. (1930), *P. Vergili Maronis Ciris*, Torino.
Lesky, A. (1925), *Alkestis: Der Mythus und das Drama*, Vienna.
Levin, S.B. (2001), *The Ancient Quarrel Between Philosophy and Poetry Revisited: Plato and the Greek Literary Tradition*, Oxford.
Lévystone, D. (2005), "La figure d'Ulysse chez les Socratiques. Socrate polytropos", *Phronesis* 50, 181–214.
Liddel, P. (2008), "Scholarship and Morality: Plutarch's Use of Inscriptions", *Acta of the 7th International Plutarch Society Congress*, Rethymno, 125–37.
Liddel, P. / Low, P. (eds.) (2013), *Inscriptions and their Uses in Greek and Latin Literature*, Oxford.
Lieberg, G. (1962), *Puella divina: die Gestalt der göttlichen Geliebten bei Catull im Zusammenhang der antiken Dichtung*, Amsterdam.
Lier, B. (1978), *Ad topica carminum amatoriorum symbolae*, New York/ London.
Lipka, M. (2001), *Language in Vergil's* Eclogues, Berlin/ New York.
Livrea, E. (2000), *Nonno di Panopoli, Parafrasi del Vangelo di S. Giovanni, Canto B*, Bologna.
Lloyd, M. (1984), "The Helen Scene in Euripides' *Troades*", *CQ* 34, 303–13.
— (1992), *The Agon in Euripides*, Oxford.
— (1994): *Euripides: Andromache*, Warminster.
Lloyd-Jones, H. (1981), "Notes on P.Köln III 125 (Aeschylus *Psychagogoi?*)", *ZPE* 42, 21–22.
— (1983^2), *The Justice of Zeus*, Berkeley/ Los Angeles/ London.
— (1987), "A Note on Homeric Morality", *CPh* 82, 307–10.
Lobel, E./ Roberts, C.H./ Wegener, E.P. (1952), *The Oxyrhynchus Papyri*, Vol. XX, London.
Lombardo, S. (2000), *Homer: Odyssey* (introduction by S. Murnaghan), Indianapolis.
Long, A. A. (1997), "Morals and Values in Homer", *JHS* 90, 121–39.
Longley, M. (2006), *Collected Poems*, London.
Loraux, N. (1986), *The Invention of Athens: The Funeral Oration in the Classical City* (trans. A. Sheridan), Cambridge (Mass.)/ London.
Lord, A.B. (2000^2), *The Singer of Tales* (re-edited with an introduction by S. Mitchell and G. Nagy; 1st ed. 1960), Cambridge (Mass.).
Lorenz, K. (2010), "Dialectics at a Standstill", in: M. Baumbach/ A. Petrovic/ I. Petrovic (eds.), 131–48.
Lowenstam, S. (1993), "The Pictures of Juno's Temple in the *Aeneid*", *CW* 87, 37–49.
Lowry, E. (1991), *Thersites: A Study in Comic Shame*, Diss. Harvard.
Luck, G. (1977), *P. Ovidius Naso Tristia*, Vol. II: *Kommentar*, Heidelberg.
Ludwich, K. (1898), *Die Homervulgata als voralexandrinisch erwiesen*, Leipzig.
Lumpp, H.M. (1963), "Die Arniadas-Inschrift aus Korkyra: Homerisches im Epigramm – Epigrammatisches im Homer", *Forschungen und Fortschritte* 37, 212–15.
Luraghi, N./ Foxhall, L. (2010), "Introduction", in: L. Foxhall/ H.-J. Gehrke/ N. Luraghi (eds.), 9–14.

Luther, A. (ed.) (2005), *Odyssee-Rezeptionen*, Frankfurt.
Lyne, R.O.A.M. (1971), "The Dating of the *Ciris*", *CQ* 21, 233–53.
— (1978), *Ciris: A Poem Attributed to Vergil*, Cambridge.
— (1980), *The Latin Love Poets from Catullus to Horace*, Oxford.
Maass, E. (1895), *Orpheus*, Munich.
Mac Góráin, F. (2012–13), "Apollo and Dionysus in Virgil", *Incontri di filologia classica* 12, 191–238.
Macan, R.W. (1908), *Herodotus: The Seventh, Eighth and Ninth Books*, London.
MacCoull, L.S.B. (2003), "Nonnus (and Dioscorus) at the Feast: Late Antiquity and After", in: D. Accorinti/ P. Chuvin (eds.), 489–500.
Maciver, C.A. (2012), *Quintus Smyrnaeus' Posthomerica: Engaging Homer in Late Antiquity*, Leiden/ Boston.
Mackay, E.A. (ed.) (1999), *Signs of Orality: The Oral Tradition and Its Influence in the Greek and Roman World*, Leiden.
Mackie, H. (2003), *Graceful Errors: Pindar and the Performance of Praise*, Ann Arbor.
MacKinnon, K. (1986), *Greek Tragedy into Film*, London.
Mader, W. (1988), *Die Psaumis-Oden Pindars (O. 4 und O. 5): Ein Kommentar*, Innsbruck.
Maguire, L.E. (2009), *Helen of Troy: From Homer to Hollywood*, Oxford/ Malden.
Mahon, D. (1979), *Poems 1962–1978*. Oxford.
— (1990), *Selected Poems*, London.
— (2005), *Harbour Lights*, Oldcastle Co. Meath.
Makris, C. (2001), *Porphyry's De Vita Pythagorica (Πορφύριου Πυθαγόρου Βίος)*, Athens.
Malaerts, H. (ed.) (1998), *Le Culte du souverain dans l' Égypte ptolémaïque au IIIe siècle avant notre ère*, Leuven.
Maltby, R. (2002), *Tibullus: Elegies*, Cambridge.
— (2006), "Major Themes and Motifs in Propertius' Love Poetry", in: H.-C. Günther (ed.), 147–81.
— (2011), "Servius on Stylistic Register in his Virgil Commentaries", in: R. Ferri (ed.), 63–74.
Manolea, C.P. (2004), *The Homeric Tradition in Syrianus*, Thessaloniki.
Markantonatos, A. (ed.) (2012), *Brill's Companion to Sophocles*, Leiden.
Markantonatos, A./ Tsagalis, C. (eds.) (2008), *Ancient Greek Tragedy: Theory and Practice (Αρχαία Ελληνική Τραγωδία: Θεωρία και Πράξη)*, Athens.
Markle, M.M. (1976), "Support of Athenian Intellectuals for Philip: A Study of Isocrates' *Philippus* and Speusippus' Letter to Philip", *JHS* 96, 80–99.
Marotto, A./ Pozzi, D. (2005), "*La caduta di Troia* e la sua rinascita: La documentazione del restauro dell' edizione italiana del 1911", *Cinegrafie* 18, 103–30.
Marshall, B. (ed.) (1980), *Vindex Humanitatis: Essays in Honour of J.H. Bishop*, Armidale.
Marshall, C.W. (2012), "Homer, Helen and the Structure of Euripides' *Trojan Women*", in: D. Rosenbloom/ J. Davidson (eds.), 31–46.
Martin, R.P. (2005), "Epic as Genre", in: J.M. Foley (ed.), 9–19.
Martindale, C. (1993), *Redeeming the Text: Latin Poetry and the Hermeneutics of Reception*, Cambridge.
— (2006), "Introduction: Thinking through Reception", in: C. Martindale/ R.F. Thomas (eds.), 1–13.
— (2007), "Reception", in: C. Kallendorf (ed.), 297–311.

– (2010), "Performance, Reception, Aesthetics: or why Reception Studies need Kant", in: E. Hall/ S. Harrop (eds.), 71–84.
– (2013), "Reception—a New Humanism? Receptivity, Pedagogy, the Transhistorical", *CRJ* 5:2, 169–83.
Martindale, C./ Thomas, R.F. (eds.) (2006), *Classics and the Uses of Reception*, Oxford/ Malden/ Victoria.
Martinez-Cuadrado, J. (1986), *Ensayo Critico sobre Andromaque de Racine*, Murcia.
Marusic, J. (2011), "Poets and Mimesis in the *Republic*", in: P. Destrée/ F.G. Herrmann (eds.), 217–40.
Mason, P.G. (1959), "Kassandra", *JHS* 79, 80–93.
Masson, O. (1962), *Les fragments du poète Hipponax*, Paris.
Mastronarde, D.J. (2010), *The Art of Euripides: Dramatic Technique and Social Context*, Cambridge.
Mazzoldi, S. (2001), *Cassandra, la vergine e l' indovina*, Pisa/ Rome.
McClure, L.K. (1999), *Spoken Like a Woman: Speech and Gender in Athenian Drama*, Princeton.
– (2003), *Courtesans at Table: Gender and Greek Literary Culture in Athenaeus*, New York/ London.
McDonald, M. (1983), *Euripides in Cinema: The Heart Made Visible*, Philadelphia.
– (2001), "Eye of the Camera, Eye of the Victim: Iphigenia by Euripides and Cacoyannis", in: M.M. Winkler (ed.), 90–117.
– (2008), "A New Hope: Film as a Teaching Tool for Classics", in: L. Hardwick/ C. Stray (eds.), 327–41.
McDonald, M./ Winkler, M.M. (2001), "Michael Cacoyannis and Irene Papas on Greek Tragedy", in: M.M. Winkler (ed.), 72–89.
McHardy, F. /Robson, J./ Harvey, D. (eds.) (2005), *Lost Dramas of Classical Athens*, Exeter.
McKeown, J. C. (1987), *Ovid: Amores*, Vol. I: *Text and Prolegomena,* Liverpool.
– (1989), *Ovid: Amores*, Vol. II: *A Commentary on Book One*, Leeds.
– (1998), *Ovid: Amores*, Vol. III: *A Commentary on Book Two*, Leeds.
McLoughlin, K. (2011), *Authoring War: The Literary Representation of War from the Iliad to Iraq*, Cambridge.
Melissinos, S. (1961), "*Odysseus' Helmet*", in: *Aristophanic Comedies Strictly for Adults*, Athens, 1–52.
Melville, A.D. (1990), *Ovid: The Love Poems*, Oxford.
Menegazzi, B. (1951), "L'*Alessandro* di Euripide", *Dioniso* 14, 172–97.
Mercier-Campiche, M. (1954), *Le théâtre de Giraudoux et la condition humaine*, Paris.
Meridor, R. (2000), "Creative Rhetoric in Euripides' *Troades*", *CQ* 50.1, 16–29.
Mette, H. J. (1963), *Der verlorene Aischylos*, Berlin.
Meyer, B.F./ Sanders, E.P. (eds.) (1982), *Jewish and Christian Self-Definition* III: *Self Definition in the Greco-Roman World,* London.
Meyer, E. A. (1993), "Epitaphs and Citizenship in Classical Athens", *JHS* 113, 99–121.
Michalopoulos, A.N. (2003), "The Intertextual Fate of a Great Homeric Hero: Diomedes in Vergil (*Aen.* 11.252–93) and Ovid (*Rem.* 151–67)", *Acta Ant. Hung.* 43, 77–86.
Michel, C. (2014), *Homer und die Tragödie: zu den Bezügen zwischen Odyssee und Orestie-Dramen (Aischylos: Orestie; Sophokles: Elektra; Euripides: Elektra)*, Tübingen.

Michelakis, P. (2001), "The Past as a Foreign Country? Greek Tragedy, Cinema and the Politics of Space", in: F. Budelmann/ P. Michelakis (eds.), 241–57.
—— (2002), *Achilles in Greek Tragedy*, Cambridge.
—— (2004), "Greek Tragedy in Cinema: Theatre, Politics, History", in: E. Hall/ F. Macintosh/ A. Wrigley (eds.), 199–217.
—— (2006), "Reception, Performance and the Sacrifice of Iphigenia", in: C. Martindale/ R. F. Thomas (eds.), 219–26.
—— (2013), *Greek Tragedy on Screen*, Oxford.
Michelakis, P./ Wyke, M. (eds.) (2013), *The Ancient World in Silent Cinema*, Cambridge.
Mikalson, J.D. (2005), *Ancient Greek Religion*, Oxford/ Malden.
Miller, F.J. and Goold, G. (1984^2), *Ovid: Metamorphoses*, Vols. I-II, London.
Milobenski, E. (1964), *Der Neid in der griechischen Philosophie*, Leiden.
Minchin, E. (1999), "Describing and Narrating in Homer's *Iliad*", in: E.A. Mackay (ed.), 49–64.
—— (2001), *Homer and the Resources of Memory: Some Applications of Cognitive Theory to the Iliad and the Odyssey*, Oxford.
—— (2007), *Homeric Voices*, Oxford.
Miralles, C. (1981), "L'iscrizione di Mnesiepes (Arch. test. 4 Tarditi)", *QUCC* 38, 29–46.
—— (1988), *The Poetry of Hipponax*, Rome.
Miralles, C./ Pòrtulas J. (1983), *Archilochus and the Iambic Poetry*, Rome.
Mitchell, S./ Nagy, G. (2000^2), "Introduction to the Second Edition", in: A. B. Lord (ed.), vii–xxix.
Mitscherling, J. (1982), "Xenophon and Plato", *CQ* 32, 468–69.
—— (2005), "Plato's Misquotation of the Poets", *CQ* 55, 295–98.
Monoson, S.S. (1998), "Remembering Pericles: The Political and Theoretical Import of Plato's *Menexenus*", *Political Theory* 26, 489–513.
Montiglio, S. (2011), *From Villain to Hero: Odysseus in Ancient Thought*, Ann Arbor.
Montoneri, L./ Romano, F. (eds.) (1986), *Gorgia e la sofistica*, Catania.
Moraud, Y. (1936), "Notice", in: Jean Giraudoux, *La guerre de Troie n'aura pas lieu*, Paris, 13–29.
Moravcsik, J.M.E. (1986), "On Correcting the Poets", *OSAP* 4, 35–47.
Moravcsik, J.M.E./ Temko, P. (eds.) (1982), *Plato on Beauty, Wisdom, and the Arts*, Totowa.
Moreau, A. (ed.) (1992), *L' Initiation: Actes du Colloque International de Montpellier 11–14 Avril 1991*, Montpellier.
Morgan, K. (1977), *Ovid's Art of Imitation: Propertius in the Amores*, Leiden.
Morris, I./ Powell, B. (eds.) (1997), *A New Companion to Homer*, Leiden.
Morrison, A.D. (2007), *The Narrator in Archaic Greek and Hellenistic Poetry*, Cambridge.
Moss, J. (2007), "What is Imitative Poetry and Why is It Bad?", in: G.R.F. Ferrari (ed.), 415–44.
Mossman, J. (1995), *Wild Justice: A Study of Euripides' Hecuba*, Oxford.
—— (2005), "Women's Voices", in J. Gregory (ed.), 352–65.
Most, G.W. (2006), *Hesiod: Theogony, Works and Days, Testimonia*, Cambridge (Mass.)/ London.
—— (2011), "What Ancient Quarrel between Philosophy and Poetry?" in: P. Destrée/ F.G. Herrmann (eds.), 1–20.
Most, G.W./ Norman, L.F./ Rabau, S. (eds.) (2009), *Révolutions homériques*, Pisa.

Mouyis, A. (2010), *Mikis Theodorakis: Finding Greece in his Music*, Athens.
Mulhern, J.J. (1968), "Τρόπος and πολυτροπία in Plato's *Hippias Minor*", *Phoenix* 22, 283–88.
Murdoch, I. (1977), *The Fire and the Sun: Why Plato Banished the Artists*, Oxford.
Murgatroyd, P. (1975), "*Militia amoris* and the Roman Elegists", *Latomus* 34, 59–75.
—— (1980), *Tibullus I*, Pietermaritzburg.
Murray, A.T./ Dimock, G.E. (1995), *Homer: The Odyssey*, Vols. I-II (1st ed. by A.T. Murray, London 1919, revised by G.E. Dimock), Cambridge (Mass.)/ London.
Murray, A.T./ Wyatt, W.F. (1999), *Homer: Iliad*, Vols. I-II (1st ed. by A.T. Murray, London 1924–25, revised by W.F. Wyatt), Cambridge (Mass.)/ London.
Murray, G. (1932), "The Trojan Trilogy of Euripides (415 BC)", *Mélanges Gustave Glotz*, Paris, Vol. II, 645–56.
—— (1946), "Euripides' Tragedies of 415 BC: The Deceitfulness of Life", *Greek Studies*, Oxford, 127–48.
Murray, P. (1996), *Plato: On Poetry (Ion; Republic 376e-398b9; Republic 595–608b 10)*, Cambridge.
—— (2011), "Tragedy, Women and the Family in Plato's *Republic*", in: P. Destrée/ F.G. Herrmann (eds.), 175–94.
Muth, S. / Petrovic, I. (2013), "Medientheorie als Chance – Überlegungen zur historischen Interpretation von Texten und Bildern", in: B. Christiansen/ U. Thaler (eds.), 281–318.
Mylonopoulos, J. (ed.) (2010), *Divine Images and Human Imaginations in Ancient Greece and Rome*, Leiden.
Myrsiades, K. (ed.) (2009), *Reading Homer: Film and Text*, Madison.
Nagy, G. (1983), "Sema and Noesis: Some Illustrations", *Arethusa* 16, 35–55.
—— (1990), *Pindar's Homer: The Lyric Possession of an Epic Past*, Baltimore/ London.
—— (1996), *Homeric Questions*, Austin.
—— (2009), *Homer the Classic*, Cambridge (Mass.)/ Washington DC.
Naiden, F.S. (1998), "Alcestis the Ghost", *Lexis* 16, 77–85.
Natsina, Ch. (2012), "The Debt towards Aphrodite: Female Dedicators and their Interrelations with the Goddess in Votive Epigrams of the *Greek Anthology*", in: M. A. Harder/ R. F. Regtuit/ G. C. Wakker (eds.), 249–79.
Nauerth, C. (1986), "Szenen eines verlorenen euripideischen Dramas auf einem koptischen Stoff", in: G. Koch (ed.), 39–47.
Nehamas, A. (1982), "Plato on Imitation and Poetry in Republic 10", in: J.M.E. Moravcsik/ P. Temko (eds.), 47–78.
Neitzel, H. (1975), *Homer-Rezeption bei Hesiod*, Bonn.
Némethy, G. (1909), *Ciris: epyllion pseudovergilianum*, Budapest.
Nicolosi, A. (2007), *Ipponatte, 'Epodi di Strasburgo', Archiloco, 'Epodi di Colonia' (con un' appendice su P. Oxy. 69, 4708)*, Bologna.
Niditch, S. (1983), "Oral Tradition and Biblical Scholarship", *Oral Tradition* 18.1, 43–44.
Niehoff, M.R. (ed.) (2012), *Homer and the Bible in the Eyes of Ancient Interpreters*, Leiden.
Nietzsche, F. ([1874] 1980), *On the Advantage and Disadvantage of History for Life* (trans. P. Preuss), Indianapolis.
Nightingale, A.W. (1995), *Genres in Dialogue: Plato and the Construct of Philosophy*, Cambridge.
Nikoloutsos, K.P. (ed.) (2013), *Ancient Greek Women in Film*, Oxford.
Nilsson, M.P. (1967^3), *Geschichte der griechischen Religion*, Munich.

Nisbet, R.G.M./ Hubbard, M. (1978), *A Commentary on Horace: Odes, Book II*, Oxford.
Nisetich, F. (1989), *Pindar and Homer*, Baltimore.
Nisters, T. (2000), *Aristotle on Courage*, Frankfurt am Main.
O'Connor, D. (2007), "Rewriting the Poets in Plato's Characters" in: G.R.F. Ferrari (ed.), 55–89.
O'Hara, J.J. (1996), *True Names: Vergil and the Alexandrian Tradition of Etymological Wordplay*, Ann Arbor.
O'Meara, D.J. (ed.) (1981), *Studies in Aristotle*, Washington DC.
— (ed.) (1985), *Platonic Investigations*, Washington DC.
O'Neill, K.N. (1999), "Ovid and Propertius: Reflexive Annotation in *Amores* 1.8", *Mnemosyne* 52, 286–307.
Ober, J. (1989), *Mass and Elite in Democratic Athens: Rhetoric, Ideology, and the Power of the People*, Princeton.
Ober, J./ Strauss, B. (1990), "Drama, Political Rhetoric and the Discourse of Athenian Democracy", in: J. Winkler/ F. Zeitlin (eds.), 237–70.
Ogden, D. (1996), *Greek Bastardy*, Oxford.
— (2001a), *Greek and Roman Necromancy*, Princeton/ Oxford.
— (2001b), "The Ancient Greek Oracles of the Dead", *Acta Classica*, 44, 167–95.
— (ed.) (2007), *A Companion to Greek Religion*, Oxford/ Malden/ Victoria.
Oikonomidis, K. (1961), "*Odyssey* by M. Skouloudis", *Ethnos*, 2 Nov. 1961.
Olson, S.D. (1988), "The 'love duet' in Aristophanes' *Ecclesiazusae*", *CQ* 38, 328–30.
Ong, W.J. (1982), *Orality and Literacy: The Technologizing of the Word*, London.
Ophuijsen, J.M./ Stork, P. (1999), *Linguistics into Interpretation: Speeches of War in Herodotus VII 5 & 8–18*, Leiden.
Oswald, A. (2011), *Memorial*, London.
Otis, B. (1964), *Virgil, a Study in Civilized Poetry*, Oxford.
Otto, A. (1880), *De fabulis Propertianis*, Part I, Diss. Bratislava.
Ovink, B.J.H. (1931), *Philosophische Erklärung der Platonischen Dialoge* Meno und Hippias Minor, Amsterdam.
Owens, J. (1981), "The Καλόν in the Aristotelian Ethics", in: D.J. O'Meara (ed.), 261–77.
Padel, R. (1992), *In and Out of the Mind: Greek Images of the Tragic Self*, Princeton.
Page, D. L. (1936), "The Elegiacs in Euripides' *Andromache*", in: C. Bailey (ed.), 206–30.
— (1979), *Sappho and Alcaeus: An Introduction to the Study of Ancient Lesbian Poetry*, Oxford.
Papaioannou, S. (2005), *Epic Succession and Dissension: Ovid, Metamorphoses 13.623–14.582, and the Reinvention of the Aeneid*, Berlin/ New York.
Papanghelis, Th. D. (1987), *Propertius: A Hellenistic Poet on Love and Death*, Cambridge.
— (1995), *From Bucolic Eutopia to Political Utopia* (Από τη βουκολική ευτοπία στην πολιτική ουτοπία), Athens.
— (1999), "*relegens errata litora*: Virgil's Reflexive 'Odyssey'", in: J.N.Kazazis/ A. Rengakos (eds.), 275–90.
Papanghelis, Th./ Harrison, S./ Frangoulidis, S. (eds.) (2013), *Generic Interfaces in Latin Literature: Encounters, Interactions and Tranformations*, Berlin/ New York.
Pappas, N. (1989), "Socrates' Charitable Treatment of Poetry", *Philosophy and Literature* 13, 248–61.

Parker, J./ Matthews, T. (eds.) (2011), *Tradition, Translation, Trauma: The Classic and the Modern*, Oxford.
Parker, L. (2007), *Euripides: Alcestis*, Oxford.
Parmentier, L. (1925), "Les Troyennes", in: H. Grégoire/ L. Parmentier (eds.) *Euripide*, Vol. IV, Paris.
Parry, M. (1971), *The Making of Homeric Verse: The Collected Papers of Milman Parry* (ed. by Adam Parry), Oxford.
Partee, M.H. (1981), *Plato's Poetics: The Authority of Beauty*, Utah.
Paschalis, M. (1997), *Virgil's Aeneid: Semantic Relations and Proper Names*, Oxford.
Paton, W. R. (1916–1918), *The Greek Anthology with an English Translation*, Vols. I-V, Cambridge (Mass.)/ London.
Paul, J. (2008), "Working with Film: Theories and Methodologies", in: L. Hardwick/ C. Stray (eds.), 303–14.
–––– (2013), *Film and the Epic Classical Tradition*, Oxford.
Pavis, P. (2003), *Analyzing Performance: Theater, Dance and Film* (trans. D. Williams), Ann Arbor.
Pearson, L. (1962), *Popular Ethics in Ancient Greece*, Stanford.
Peirano, I. (2009), "*Mutati artus:* Scylla, Philomela and the End of Silenus' Song in Virgil *Eclogue* 6", *CQ* 59, 187–95.
Pelling, C. (2006), "Homer and Herodotus", in: M.J. Clarke/ B.G.F. Currie/ R.O.A.M. Lyne (eds.), 75–104.
Pelling, C. (ed.) (1990), *Characterisation and Individuality in Greek Literature*, Oxford.
–––– (ed.) (1997), *Greek Tragedy and the Historian*, Oxford.
Penzel, J. (2006), *Variation und Imitation: ein literarischer Kommentar zu den Epigrammen des Antipater von Sidon und des Archias von Antiocheia*, Trier.
Peraki-Kyriakidou, H. (2006), "Antonomasia and Metonymy in the Proem to Virgil's *Georgics*", in: J. Booth/ R. Maltby (eds.), 83–99.
–––– (2010), "Dionysus in the Service of Virgil's Bucolic Poetry (Ο Διόνυσος στην υπηρεσία της βουκολικής ποιητικής του Βιργιλίου)", in: S. Tsitsiridis (ed.), 555–82.
–––– (2013), "Virgil's *Eclogue* 4.60–63: A Space of Generic Enrichment", in: Th. Papanghelis/ S. Harrison/ S. Frangoulidis S. (eds.), 217–230.
–––– (2014), "The Smile of Acanthus as an Indicator of Poetics: Virgil *Ed.* 4.20 (Το γέλιο του ακάνθου ως δείκτης ποιητικής: Βιργιλίου *Εκλογή* 4.20)", in: M. Voutsinou-Kikilia/ A. Michalopoulos/ S. Papaioannou (eds.), 91–99.
Perlman, S. (1964), "Quotations from Poetry in Attic Orators of the Fourth Century BC", *AJPh* 85, 155–72.
Perris, S. (2011), "Proems, Codas and Formalism in Homeric Reception", *CRJ* 3.2, 189–212.
Pertusi, A. (1952), "Il significato della trilogia troiana di Euripide", *Dioniso* 15, 251–73.
Perysinakis, I.N. (2004), "Homer's *Iliad* I: A Reading in the Poet's Language (Ομήρου *Ιλιάδα* Ι: Μια ανάγνωση με τη γλώσσα του ποιητή)", *Seminario* 30, 157–74.
–––– (2006), "Archaic Moral Values and Political Behaviour in the Early and Middle Dialogues of Plato and in the *Laws* (Αρχαϊκές ηθικές αξίες και πολιτική συμπεριφορά στους πρώιμους και μέσους διαλόγους του Πλάτωνα και τους *Νόμους*)", *Ariadne* 12, 69–92.
–––– (2009), "The Reception of Ancient in Modern Greek Literature: An Itinerary", in: Th. Pylarinos (ed.), 195–216.

Petrain, D. (2006), "Moschus' *Europa* and the Narratology of *Ecphrasis*", in: M.A. Harder/ R.F. Regtuit/ G.C. Wakker (eds.), 249–70.
Petrakou, K. (1999), *The Theatrical Contests: 1870–1925 (Οι Θεατρικοί Διαγωνισμοί: 1870–1925)*, Athens.
–– (2007), *Theatrical Turning Points and Courses (Θεατρικές (σ)τάσεις και πορείες)*, Athens.
Petrovic, A. (2007), *Kommentar zu den Simonideischen Versinschriften*, Leiden/ Boston.
–– (2013), "Inscribed Epigrams in Orators and Epigrammatic Collections", in: P. Liddel/ P. Low (eds.), 197–213.
Petrovic, I. (2006), "Delusions of Grandeur: Homer, Zeus and the Telchines in Callimachus' Reply (*Aitia* Fr. 1) and *Iambus* 6", *A&A* 52, 16–41.
Pfeiffer, E. (1933), *Virgil's Bukolika: Untersuchungen zum Form-problem*, Stuttgart.
Pfeiffer, R. (1949), *Callimachus*, Vol. I, Oxford.
Pfeijffer, I.L. (2004), "Pindar and Bacchylides ", in: I.J.F. De Jong/ A. Bowie/ R. Nünlist (eds.), 213–32.
Phillips, E. D. (1953), "Odysseus in Italy", *JHS* 73, 53–67.
Phillips, J. (1987), "Plato's Use of Homer in the *Hippias Minor*", *Favonius* 1, 21–30.
–– (1989), "Xenophon's *Memorabilia* 4.2", *Hermes* 117, 365–70.
Pickard-Cambridge, A. (1988²), *The Dramatic Festivals of Athens* (revised with a new supplement by J. Goold and D.M. Lewis), Oxford.
Pigeaud, J. (1983), "La Métamorphose de Scylla (*Ciris* 490–507)", *LEC* 51, 125–31.
Pirenne-Delforge, V. (1996), "Les Charites à Athènes et dans l' île de Cos", *Kernos* 9, 195–214.
–– (2010), "Greek Priests and 'Cult Statues': In How Far are they Unnecessary?", in J. Mylonopoulos (ed.), 121–41.
Pistrick, E./ Scaldaferri, N./ Schwörer, G. (eds.) (2011), *Audiovisual Media and Identity Issues in Southeastern Europe*, Newcastle upon Tyne.
Planck, H. (1840), *De Euripidis Didascalia Troica*, Göttingen.
Planinc, V. (2003), *Plato through Homer: Poetry and Philosophy in the Cosmological Dialogues*, Missouri.
Poole, A. (1976), "Total Disaster: Euripides' *The Trojan Women*", *Arion* 3, 257–87.
Poole, W. (1990), "Male Homosexuality in Euripides", in: A. Powell (ed.), 108–50.
Porter, J.I. (2004a), "Nietzsche, Homer and the Classical Tradition", in: P. Bishop (ed.), 7–26.
–– (2004b), "Homer: The History of an Idea", in: R.L. Fowler (ed.), 324–43.
Powell, A. (ed.) (1990), *Euripides, Women and Sexuality*, London.
Pozzi, D. /Wickersham, J. (eds.) (1991), *Myth and the Polis*, Ithaca.
Pratt, L.H. (1993), *Lying and Poetry from Homer to Pindar: Falsehood and Deception in Archaic Greek Poetics*, Ann Arbor.
Prince, C. Kerr (2008), "Poeta sovrano? Horizons of Homer in Twentieth-Century English–Language Poetry", in: *The Homerizon: Conceptual Interrogations in Homeric Studies*, Washington Center for Hellenic Studies.
http://chs.harvard.edu/publications.sec.classics.ssp
Psychopedis, J. (2008), *Nostos* (N.P. Goulandris Foundation, Museum of Cycladic Art), Athens.
Pucci, P. (1987), *Odysseus Polutropos: Intertextual Readings in the Odyssey and the Iliad*, Ithaca.
Puchner, W. (2005), *Courses and Turning-points: Ten Theatrological Essays (Πορείες και Σταθμοί: Δέκα Θεατρολογικά Μελετήματα)*, Athens.

— (2010), *Landscapes of the Soul and Myths of the City: Iakovos Kambanellis' Theatrical Universe* (*Τοπία ψυχής και μύθοι πολιτείας: το θεατρικό σύμπαν του Ιάκωβου Καμπανέλλη*), Athens.
Purkis, J. (1992), "Reading Homer Today", in: C. Emlyn-Jones/ L. Hardwick/ J. Purkis (eds.), 1–18.
Putnam, M. (1998), *Virgil's Epic Designs*, New Haven.
Pylarinos, Th. (ed.) (2009), *Greek Antiquity and Modern Greek Literature* (*Ελληνική αρχαιότητα και νεοελληνική λογοτεχνία*), Ionian University, Department of History, Conference Proceedings (Corfu, 30 October-1 November 2008), Corfu.
Quinn, K. (1968), *Vergil's Aeneid: A Critical Description*, London.
Race, W. H. (1990), *Style and Rhetoric in Pindar's Odes*, Atlanta.
— (2009), *Apollonius Rhodius: Argonautica*, Cambridge (Mass.)/ London.
Racevskis, R. (2008), *Tragic Passages: Jean Racine's Art of the Threshold*, New Jersey.
Racine, J. (1994), *Andromache* (trans. into Greek by S. Paschalis), Athens.
Radt, S. (2009^2), *Tragicorum Graecorum Fragmenta (TrGF)*, Vol. III: *Aeschylus*, Göttingen.
Ramminger, J. (1991), "Imitation and Allusion in the Achaemenides Scene (Vergil, *Aeneid* 3.588–691)", *AJPh* 112.1, 53–71.
Ramphos, S. (1978), *The Exile of Poets: A Platonic Paradox* (*Η εξορία των ποιητών: ένα πλατωνικό παράδοξο*), Athens.
Raubitschek, A.E. (1968), "Das Denkmal-Epigram", *L'Épigramme Grecque* (Entr. Fond. Hardt 14), 1–27.
Rayor, D.J. (2004), *The Homeric Hymns*, Berkeley/ Los Angeles/ London.
Reardon, B. (1996), "Chariton", in: G. Schmeling (ed.), 309–35.
Reckford, K.J. (1974), "Phaedra and Pasiphae: The Pull Backward", *TAPhA* 104, 307–28.
Redfield, J.M. (1994^2), *Nature and Culture in the Iliad*, North Carolina.
Rehm, R. (1994), *Marriage to Death: The Conflation of Marriage and Death Rituals in Greek Tragedy*, Princeton.
— (2002), *The Play of Space: Spatial Transformation in Greek Tragedy*, Princeton.
Reilly, J.H. (1978), *Jean Giraudoux*, Boston.
Reinhardt, T. (2006), "Propertius and Rhetoric", in: H.-C. Günther (ed.), 199–216.
Rengakos, A. (1993), *Der Homertext und die hellenistischen Dichter*, Stuttgart.
— (1994), *Apollonios Rhodios und die antike Homererklärung*, Munich.
Ressel, M. (2000), "Le metamorfosi del mito di Scilla", *Myrtia* 15, 5–26.
Revermann, M. (2013), "Paraepic Comedy: Points and Practices", in: E. Bakola/ L. Prauscello/ M. Telò (eds.), 101–28.
Reynolds, M. (2011), *The Poetry of Translation: From Chaucer and Petrarch to Homer and Logue*, Oxford.
Rhodes, P.J. (1981), *A Commentary on the Aristotelian Athenaion Politeia*, Oxford.
— (2011^2), *A History of the Classical Greek World: 478–323 BC*, Oxford/ Malden.
Richardson, L. Jr. (1977), *Propertius: Elegies I-IV*, Norman.
Richardson, N. J. (1974), *The Homeric Hymn to Demeter*, Oxford.
— (1993), *The Iliad: A Commentary* (General Editor: G.S. Kirk), Vol. VI: Books 21–24, Cambridge.
Ricks, D. (1989), *The Shade of Homer: A Study in Modern Greek Poetry*, Cambridge.
Riemer, P. (1989), *Die Alkestis des Euripides: Untersuchungen zur tragischen Form*, Frankfurt.
Rieu, E.V. (1950), *The Iliad*, Harmondsworth.

Ritoók, Z. (1993), "Zur Trojanischen Trilogie des Euripides", *Gymnasium* 100, 109–25.
Rivier, A. (1975), "Euripide et Pasiphae", in: F. Lasserre/ J. Sulliger (eds.), 43–60.
Robert, C. (1881), *Bild und Lied*, Berlin.
Robert, L. (1966), "Sur un decret et sur un papyrus concernant des cultes royaux", in : A.E. Samuel (ed.), 175–211.
Roberts, M. (1985), *Biblical Epic and Rhetorical Paraphrase in Late Antiquity*, Wiltshire.
Robertson, N. (1999), "The Stoa of the Hermes", *ZPE* 127, 167–72.
Robichez, J. (1976), *Le théâtre de Giraudoux*, Paris.
Rocha-Pereira, M.H. (1989–90²), *Pausaniae Graeciae Descriptio*, Vols. I-III, Leipzig.
Rogers, K. (1993), "Aristotle's Conception of Τὸ Καλόν", *Ancient Philosophy* 13, 355–71.
–– (1994), "Aristotle on the Motive of Courage", *Southern Journal of Philosophy* 32, 303–13.
Roisman, H.M. (2006), "Helen in the *Iliad:* Causa Belli and Victim of War", *AJPh* 127, 1–36.
Rolley, C. (1994), *La Sculpture Grecque: 1. Des origines au milieu de Vème siècle*, Paris.
Roochnik, D. (1990), "The Quarrel Between Philosophy and Poetry: Studies in Ancient Thought", *Ancient Philosophy* 10, 301–04.
Rose, M.A. (1979), *Parody/ Metafiction: An Analysis of Parody as a Critical Mirror to the Writing and Reception of Fiction*, London.
–– (1993), *Parody, Ancient, Modern, and Post-modern*, Cambridge.
Rose, P.W. (2012), *Class in Archaic Greece*, Cambridge.
Rosen, R.M. (1987), "A Poetic Inspiration Scene in Hipponax?", *AJPh* 109.2, 174–79.
–– (1988), "Hipponax, Boupalos and the Conventions of the Psogos", *TAPhA* 118, 29–41.
–– (1990), "Hipponax and the Homeric Odysseus", *Eikasmos* 1, 11–25.
–– (2007), *Making Mockery: The Poetics of Ancient Satire*, Oxford.
Rosen, R.M./ Sluiter, I. (eds.) (2003), *Andreia: Studies in Manliness and Courage in Classical Antiquity*, Leiden.
Rosen, R.M./ Sluiter, I. (eds.) (2008), *Kakos: Badness and Anti-value in Classical Antiquity*, Leiden.
Rosen, S. (1988), *The Quarrel Between Philosophy and Poetry: Studies in Ancient Greek Thought*. New York.
Rosenbloom, D./ Davidson, J. (eds.) (2012), *Greek Drama IV: Texts, Contexts, Performance*, Oxford.
Rotstein, A. (2010), *The Idea of Iambos*, Oxford.
Rubin, D.C. (1995), *Memory in Oral Traditions: The Cognitive Psychology of Epic, Ballads and Counting-out Rhymes*, New York.
Rudolph, K.C. (2010), "Homeric Criticism in the *Hippias Minor*", https://camws.org/meeting/2010/program/abstracts/06B1.Rudolph.pdf.
Ruhl, M., (2000), *Die Darstellung von Gefühlsentwicklungen in den Elegien des Properz*, Göttingen.
Ruiz-Montero, C. (1996), "The Rise of the Ancient Novel", in: G. Schmeling (ed.), 29–85.
Rundin, J. (1996), "A Politics of Eating: Feasting in Early Greek Society", *AJPh* 117, 179–215.
Russell, D. (1990), "Ethos in Oratory and Rhetoric", in: C. Pelling (ed.), 197–212.
Russo, J./ Fernández-Galiano, M./ Heubeck, A. (1992), *A Commentary on Homer's Odyssey*, Vol. III, Oxford.
Rusten, J.S. (1982), "The Aeschylean Avernus: Notes on P. Köln 3.125", *ZPE* 45, 33–38.
Rutherford, R.B. (1996), *Homer*, Cambridge.

Sabot, A.F. (1976), *Ovide, poète de l'amour dans ses œuvres de jeunesse*, Paris.
Sakellariou, Ch. (1990), *The Sleep of the Lotus-Eaters*, Athens.
Salkever, S.C. (1993), "Socrates' Aspasian Oration: The Play of Philosophy and Politics in Plato's *Menexenus*", *American Political Science Review* 87, 133–43.
Salvatore, A. (1955), *Studi sulla tradizione manoscritta e sul testo della Ciris II: Commentario e testo critico*, Napoli.
— (1984), "Echi degli *Aratea* nella *Ciris*", *Ciceroniana* 5, 237–41.
Samuel, A.E. (ed.) (1966), *Essays in Honor of C.Bradford Welles*, New Haven.
Sansone, D. (2009), "Euripides' New Song: The First Stasimon of *Trojan Women*", in: J.R.C. Cousland/ J.R. Hume (eds.), 193–203.
Saunders, T. (2008), *Bucolic Ecology: Virgil's Eclogues and the Environmental Literary Tradition*, London.
Scaldaferri, N. (2011), "A Tool for Research, a Source for Identity Construction: Considerations and Controversies on the Use of Audiovisual Media", in: E. Pistrick/ N. Scaldaferri/ G. Schwörer (eds.), 14–36.
Scarcella, A.M. (1959), "Letture Euripidee: Le *Troade*", *Dioniso* 22, 60–70.
Scarth, E.A. (2008), *Mnemotechnics and Virgil: The Art of Memory and Remembering*, Saarbrücken.
Schein, S.L. (1984), *The Mortal Hero*, Berkeley/ Los Angeles.
— (ed.) (1995), *Reading the Odyssey: Selected Interpretive Essays*. Princeton.
Schiesaro, A. (2003), *The Passions in Play: Thyestes and the Dynamics of Senecan Drama*, Cambridge.
Schmeling, G. (ed.) (1996), *The Novel in the Ancient World*, Leiden/ New York/ Cologne.
Schmid, W./ Stählin, O. (1940), *Geschichte der griechischen Literatur*, Vol. I 3, Munich.
Schmitz, Th. (1992), "Datierung und Anlaß der vierten Olympischen Ode Pindars", *Hermes* 120, 142–47.
— (1994), "Noch einmal zum Mythos in Pindars vierter olympischer Ode", *RhM* 137, 209–17.
Schöll, A. (1839), *Beiträge zur Geschichte der griechischen Poesie*, Berlin.
Schubert, P. (ed.) (2012), *Proceedings of the 26th International Congress of Papyrology*, Geneva.
Scodel, R. (1980), *The Trojan Trilogy of Euripides*, Göttingen.
— (1992), "Inscriptions, Absence and Memory: Epic and Early Epitaph", *SIFC* 10, 57–76.
— (2002), *Listening to Homer: Tradition, Narrative and Audience*, Ann Arbor.
Scourfield, J.H.D. (ed.) (2007), *Texts and Culture in Late Antiquity*, Wales.
Seeck, G.A. (2008), *Euripides Alkestis*, Berlin/ New York.
Segal, C. (1971), "Andromache's *anagnorisis:* Formulaic Artistry in *Iliad* 22.437–476", *HSCP* 75, 33–57.
— (1978), "The Myth was Saved: Reflections on Homer and the Mythology of Plato's *Republic*", *Hermes* 106, 315–36.
— (1997²), *Dionysiac Poetics and Euripides' Bacchae*, New Jersey.
Seidensticker, B. (1982) *Palintonos Harmonia: Studien zu komischen Elementen in der griechischen Tragödie*, Göttingen.
Seleškovic, M.T. (1968), "Kopitareva prepiska sa Fridrihom Volfom", *Kovčežić* 8, 109–13.
Sens, A. (2011), *Asclepiades of Samos: Epigrams and Fragments*. Oxford.
Severyns, A. (1928), *Le Cycle épique dans l'École d'Aristarque*, Liège/ Paris.

Shapiro, A./ Burian, P. (2009), *Trojan Women by Euripides*, Oxford.
Sharrock, A./ Morales, H. (2000), *Intratextuality: Greek and Roman Textual Traditions*, Oxford.
Sickle, J. van. (1975), "The new erotic fragment of Archilochus", *QUCC* 20, 125–56.
Sikelianos, A. (1980), *Prose (Πεζός λόγος)*, Vol. II, Athens.
— (1981), *Prose (Πεζός λόγος)*, Vol. III, Athens.
— (1999⁵), *Lyric Life (Λυρικός βίος)*, Vol. I, Athens.
— (2003⁴), *Lyric Life (Λυρικός βίος)*, Vol. II, Athens.
Silk, M.S. (ed.) (1996), *Tragedy and the Tragic*, Oxford.
— (2004²), *Homer: The Iliad*, Cambridge.
Skiadas, A. (1965), *Homer im griechischen Epigramm*, Athens.
Skouloudis, M., (1961), *Odyssey*, Athens.
Skouteropoulos, N.M. (1995), *Plato: Hippias Minor (Πλάτωνος Ιππίας Ελάττων)*, Athens.
Skutsch, F. (1901), *Aus Vergils Frühzeit*, Leipzig.
Skutsch, O. (1968), *Studia Enniana*, London.
— (1985), *The Annals of Quintus Ennius*, Oxford.
Slings, S. R. (1991), "The Quiet Life in Euripides' *Antiope*", in: H. Hofmann/ M.A. Harder (eds.), 137–52.
Small, J.P. (1995), "Artificial Memory and the Writing Habits of the Literate", *Helios* 22.2, 159–66.
— (1997), *Wax Tablets of the Mind: Cognitive Studies of Memory and Literature in Classical Antiquity*, London/ New York.
Smith, A. (2010), "Porphyry and his school", in: L.P. Gerson (ed.), I 325–57.
Smith, R.A. (1997), *Poetic Allusion and Poetic Embrace in Ovid and Virgil*, Ann Arbor.
Snell, B. (1937), *Euripides Alexandros und andere Strassburger Papyri mit Fragmenten griechischer Dichter*, Hermes Einzelschr. 5, Berlin.
Sobchack, V. (1990), "Surge and Splendor: a Phenomenology of the Historical Epic", *Representations* 29, 24–49.
Sokratous, K. (1984), *Penelope and her Suitors*, Nicosia.
Solmsen, F. (1984), "*Phren, kardia, psyche* in Greek Tragedy", in: D. E. Gerber (ed.), 265–74.
Solomon, J. (2001), *The Ancient World in Cinema*, New Haven/ London.
— (2007), "The Vacillations of the Trojan Myth: Popularization and Classicization, Variation and Codification", *IJCT* 14.3–4, 482–534.
Sommerstein, A. H. (2007), *Aristophanes: Ecclesiazusae*, Warminster.
— (2008), *Aeschylus: Fragments*, London/ Cambridge (Mass.).
— (2015), "Tragedy and the Epic Cycle", in: M. Fantuzzi/ C. Tsagalis (eds.), 461–86.
Sopina, N.R. (1986), "New Light on the *Alexander* of Euripides and its Place in Euripidean Drama", *Vestnik Drevnej Istorii* 176, 117–30.
Sotiriou, M. (1998), *Pindarus Homericus*, Götttingen.
Sourvinou-Inwood, C. (1995), *'Reading' Greek Death*, Oxford.
Spanoudakis, K. (2004), "Adesp. Pap. Eleg. *SH* 964: Parthenius?", *APF* 50, 37–41.
Spence, J.D. (1984), *The Memory Palace of Matteo Ricci*, New York.
Spies, A. (1930), *Militat omnis amans*, Diss. Tübingen.
Sprague, R. K. (1962), *Plato's Use of Fallacy*, New York.
Stahl, H.-P. (1985), *Propertius: "Love" and "War": Individual and State under Augustus*, Berkeley.
Stanford, W.B. (1954), *The Ulysses Theme*, Oxford.

—— (1959), *Homer: Odyssey Books I-XII*, Bristol.
Stansbury- O' Donnell, M. (1989), "Polygnotos's *Iliupersis*: A New Reconstruction", *AJA* 93, 203–15.
—— (1990), "Polygnotos's *Nekyia*: A Reconstruction and Analysis", *AJA* 94, 213–35.
Stegemann, V. (1930), *Astrologie und Universalgeschichte: Studien und Interpretationen zu den Dionysiaka des Nonnos von Panopolis*, Leipzig.
Steidle, W. (1968), *Studien zum antiken Drama unter besonderer Berücksichtigung des Bühnenspiels*, Munich.
Stein, H. (1889), *Herodotos, vierter Band: Buch VII*, Berlin.
Steiner, D.T. (2008), "Beetle Tracks: Entomology, Scatology and the Discourse of Abuse", in: R.M. Rosen/ I. Sluiter (eds.), 59–117.
—— (2010), *Odyssey: Books XVII-XVIII*, Cambridge.
Stephens, S. (2004), "For you, Arsinoe…", in: B. Acosta-Hughes/ E. Kosmetatou/ M. Baumbach (eds.), 161–76.
Stevens, P.T. (1971), *Euripides: Andromache*, Oxford.
Stewart, A. (1990), *Greek Sculpture: An Exploration*, London/ Yale.
Stewart, J. A. (1892), *Notes on the Nicomachean Ethics of Aristotle*, Oxford.
Stinton, T.C.W. (1965), *Euripides and the Judgement of Paris*, London.
Stössl, F. (1968), *Euripides: Die Tragödien und Fragmente*, Vol. II, Zurich.
Strauss Clay, J. (forthcoming), "Homer's Epigraph: *Iliad* 7. 87–91", *Phil.* 159.
Stroh, W. (1971), *Die römische Liebeselegie als werbende Dichtung*, Amsterdam.
Strohm, H. (1957), *Euripides: Interpretationen zur dramatischen Form*, Munich.
Struck, P.T. (2004), *Birth of the Symbol: Ancient Readers at the Limits of Their Texts*, Princeton.
Sullivan, S.D. (1989), "The Extended Use of *Psyche* in the Greek Lyric Poets", *La parola del passato* 44, 241–62.
Swanger, D. (1997), "The Metaphysics of Poetry: Subverting the 'Ancient Quarrel' and Recasting the Problem", *Journal of Aesthetic Education* 31.3, 55–64.
Syndikus, H.P. (2006), "The Second Book", in H.-C. Günther (ed.), 245–318.
—— (2010), *Die Elegien des Properz*, Darmstadt.
Szádeczky-Kardoss, S. (1959), *Testimonia de Mimnermi Vita et Carminibus* (*Acta Universitatis Szegedinensis, Sectio Antiqua 1959, Minora Opera ad studium antiquitatis pertinentia* 2), Szeged.
Tanner, S. (2010), *In Praise of Plato's Poetic Imagination*, Lanham.
Taplin, O. (1977), *The Stagecraft of Aeschylus: The Dramatic Use of Exits and Entrances in Greek Tragedy*, Oxford.
—— (1980), "The Shield of Achilles within the *Iliad*", *G&R* 27, 1–21.
—— (1992), *Homeric Soundings*, Oxford.
—— (2007), "Some Assimilations of the Homeric Simile in Late Twentieth- Century Poetry", in: B. Graziosi/ E. Greenwood (eds.), 177–90.
Tar, I./ Mayer, P. (eds.) (2005), *Studia Catulliana: In memoriam Stephani Caroli Horvath (1931–1966)*, Szeged.
Tarrant, D. (1951), "Plato's Use of Quotation and Other Illustrative Material", *CQ* 45, 59–67.
Taylor, A.E. (1926), *Plato: The Man and his Work*, London.
Taylor, C.C.W. (1991), *Plato: Protagoras*, Oxford.
—— (2006), *Nicomachean Ethics: Books II-IV*, Oxford.

Telò, M. (2002), "Per una grammatica dei gesti nella tragedia greca I", *MD* 48, 9–75.
Terzakis, A. (1961), "*Odyssey* by M. Skouloudis", *To Vima*, 5 Nov. 1961.
Theodorakis, M. (1986), *The Ways of the Archangel (Οι δρόμοι του Αρχαγγέλου)*, Vol. I, Athens.
— (1993), *40 Songs for Children (40 τραγούδια για παιδάκια και παιδιά)*, Athens.
— (1997), *Poetry Set to Music: Songs (Μελοποιημένη ποίηση: Τραγούδια)*, Vol. I, Athens.
— (2002), *Where can I find my Soul ? (Πού να βρω την ψυχή μου)*, Athens.
— (2007), "Universal Harmony (Συμπαντική Αρμονία)", in: Y. Kouyoumoutzakis (ed.), 75–102.
Thill, A. (ed.) (1980), *L'élégie romaine. Enracinement, Thèmes, Diffusion*, Mulhouse.
Thomas, E. (1964), "Variations on a Military Theme in Ovid's *Amores*", *G&R* 11, 151–65.
Thomas, R. (2000): *Herodotus in Context: Ethnography, Science and the Art of Persuasion*, Cambridge.
Thomas, R.F. (1983), "Virgil's Ecphrastic Centrepieces", *HSCP* 87, 175–84.
— (1988), *Virgil: Georgics*, Vol. I: Books I-II, Cambridge.
— (1998) "Melodious Tears: Sepulchral Epigram and Generic Mobility", in: M.A. Harder/ R.F. Regtuit/ G.C. Wakker (eds.), 205–23.
Thrylos, A. (1980) (review of 1961), "M. Skouloudis: *Odyssey*, a Satirical Comedy in Three Parts", *Greek Theatre (Ελληνικό Θέατρο)*, Vol. IX (1962–63), Athens, 13–14.
— (1981) (review of 1966), "D. Christodoulou: *Hotel Circe*, a Play in Two Parts and Five Pictures", in: *Greek Theatre (Ελληνικό Θέατρο)*, Vol. X (1964–66), Athens, 387–89.
Tilg, S. (2010), *Chariton of Aphrodisias and the Invention of the Greek Love Novel*, Oxford.
Timpanaro, S. (1996), "Dall' *Alexandros* di Euripide all' *Alexander* di Ennio", *RFIC* 124, 5–70.
Todd, S. C. (2000), *Lysias*, Austin.
— (2007), *A Commentary on Lysias, Speeches 1–11*, Oxford.
Trammel, E. (1941/42), "The Mute Alcestis", *CJ* 37, 144–50.
Trümpy, C. (2010), "Observations on the Dedicatory and Sepulchral Epigrams and their Early History", in: M. Baumbach/ A. Petrovic/ I. Petrovic (eds.), 167–80.
Trzaskoma, S. (2010), "Chariton and Tragedy: Reconsiderations and New Evidence", *AJPh* 131, 219–31.
Tsagalis, C. (2008a), *Inscribing Sorrow: Fourth-century Attic Funerary Epigrams*, Berlin/ New York.
— (2008b), *The Oral Palimpsest*, Cambridge (Mass.).
— (2008c), "Transformations of Myth: The Trojan Cycle in the Three Great Tragic Poets (Μεταμορφώσεις του Μύθου: Ο Τρωικός Κύκλος στους Τρεις Μεγάλους Τραγικούς)", in: A. Markantonatos/ C. Tsagalis (eds.), 33–115.
Tsitsiridis, S. (ed.) (2010), *Parachoregema: Studies on Ancient Theatre in Honour of Professor Gregory M. Sifakis*, Herakleion.
Uhl, A. (1998), *Servius als Sprachlehrer: zur Sprachrichtigkeit in der exegetischen Praxis des spätantiken Grammatikerunterrichts*, Göttingen.
Urmson, J.O. (1982), "Plato and the Poets", in: J.M.E. Moravcsik/ P. Temko (eds.), 125–36.
Usher, S. (1990), *Isocrates' Panegyricus and To Nicocles*, Warminster.
— (1999), *Greek Oratory: Tradition and Originality*, Oxford.
— (2007), "Symbouleutic Oratory", in: I. Worthington (ed.), 220–35.
Usher, S./ Najock, D. (1982), "A Statistical Study of Authorship in the Corpus Lysiacum", *Computers and the Humanities* 16, 85–105.

Ussher, R.G. (1973), *Aristophanes: Ecclesiazusae*, Oxford.
Valakas, K. (1987), *Homeric Mimesis and the Ajax of Sophocles*, Diss. Cambridge.
Van der Valk, M. (1963–64), *Researches on the Text and Scholia of the Iliad*, Vols. I-II, Leiden.
Van Lieshout, R.G.A. (1980), *Greeks on Dreams*, Utrecht.
Van Steen, G. (2001), "Playing by the Censors' Rules: Classical Drama revived under the Greek Junta (1967–74)", *Journal of the Hellenic Diaspora* 27.1–2, 133–94.
—— (2011), *Theatre of the Condemned: Classical Tragedy on Greek Prison Islands*, Oxford.
Vandiver, E. (2010), *Stand in the Trench, Achilles: Classical Receptions in British Poetry of the Great War*, Oxford.
Varikas, V. (1961), "The *Odyssey* on stage", *Ta Nea*, 15 Nov. 1961.
—— (1966), "*Hotel Circe*", *Ta Nea*, 3 May 1966.
Vasaly, A. (1993), *Representations: Images of the World in Ciceronian Oratory*, Berkeley.
Vellacott, P. (1975), *Ironic Drama: A Study of Euripides' Method and Meaning*, Cambridge.
Venuti, L. (2011), "The Poet's Version; or An Ethics of Translation", *Translation Studies* 4.2, 230–47.
Vermeule, E. (1979), *Aspects of Death in Early Greek Art and Poetry*, Berkeley.
Vernant, J.P./ Vidal-Naquet, P. (1986), *Mythe et tragédie en Grèce ancienne*, Paris.
Verrall, A.W. (1895), *Euripides the Rationalist: A Study in Art and Religion*, Cambridge.
Vian, F. (1990), *Nonnos de Panopolis, Les Dionysiaques*, Vol. IX: Chants XXV-XXIX, Paris.
Vlastos, G. (ed.) (1971), *Philosophy of Socrates*, New York.
—— (1991), *Socrates: Ironist and Moral Philosopher*, Ithaca.
Vollgraff, G. (1921), "Ἐκ μύρτου κλαδί", *Mnemosyne* 49, 246–50.
Voutsinou-Kikilia, M./ Michalopoulos, A./ Papaioannou, S. (eds.) (2014), *Rideamus igitur: Humour in Latin Literature (Rideamus igitur: Το Χιούμορ στη Λατινική Γραμματεία)*, Athens.
Vox, O. (1975), "Epigrammi in Omero", *Belfagor* 30, 67–70.
Wade-Gery, H.T. (1933), "Classical Epigrams and Epitaphs: A Study of the Kimonian Age", *JHS* 53, 71–104.
Walcot, P. (1973), "The Funeral Speech: A Study of Values", *G&R* 20, 111–21.
—— (1978), *Envy and the Greeks: A Study of Human Behaviour*, Warminster.
—— (1996), "Continuity and Tradition: The Persistence of Greek Values", *G&R* 43, 169–77.
Walcott, D. (1990), *Omeros*, London.
—— (1993), *The Odyssey: A Stage Version*, London.
Wallace, M.B. (1984), "The Metres of Early Greek Epigrams", in: D.E. Gerber (ed.), 303–15.
Walters, K.R. (1980), "Rhetoric as Ritual: The Semiotics of the Attic Funeral Orations", *Florilegium* 2, 1–27.
Webb, R. (2009), *Ekphrasis, Imagination and Persuasion in Ancient Rhetorical Theory and Practice*, Farnham/ Burlington.
Webster, T.B.L. (1966), "Euripides' Trojan Trilogy", in: M. Kelly (ed.), 207–13.
Weil, R. (1955), "Éschine lecteur de Platon", *REG* 68, xii.
Weiss, R. (1981), "Ὁ Ἀγαθός as Δυνατός in the *Hippias Minor*", *CQ* 31, 287–304.
Wells, J.B. (2009), *Pindar's Verbal Art: An Ethnographic Study of Epinician Style*, Cambridge (Mass)/ London.
Wendel, C. (1958²), *Scholia in Apollonium Rhodium vetera*, Berlin.
West, D. (1990), *Virgil: The Aeneid*, London.

—— (2002), *Horace: Odes III*, Oxford.
West, M. L. (1966), *Hesiod: Theogony*, Oxford.
—— (1974), *Studies in Greek Elegy and Iambus*, Berlin.
—— (1982), *Greek Metre*, Oxford.
—— (1989–1992²), *Iambi et Elegi Graeci*, Vols. I-II, Oxford.
—— (1998–2000), *Homerus: Ilias*, Vols. I-II, Stuttgart/ Leipzig.
—— (2013), *The Epic Cycle: A Commentary on the Lost Troy Epics*, Oxford.
West, S. (1967), *The Ptolemaic Papyri of the Iliad*, Cologne/ Opladen.
—— (1987), "And it came to pass that Pharaoh dreamed: Notes on Herodotus 2.139, 141", *CQ* 37, 262–71.
—— (1988), *A Commentary on Homer's Odyssey*, Vol. I: Introduction and Books I-VIII, Oxford.
Wheeler, A.L./ Goold, G.P. (1988²), *Ovid: Tristia, Epistulae ex Ponto*, Cambridge (Mass.).
Whitaker, R. (1983), *Myth and Personal Experience in Roman Love-elegy*, Göttingen.
Whitby, M. (2007), "The Bible Hellenized: Nonnus' *Paraphrase* of St John's Gospel and Eudocia's Homeric Centos", in: J.H.D. Scourfield (ed.), 195–231.
White, H. (1985), *New Essays in Hellenistic Poetry*, Amsterdam.
—— (2006), "Studies in the Text of Latin Poets of the Golden Age", *Minerva* 19, 175–92.
Whitman, C.H. (1958), *Homer and the Heroic Tradition*, Cambridge.
Whitmarsh, T. (2010), "Prose Fiction", in: J.J. Clauss/ M. Cuypers (eds.), 395–412.
Wiener, M.H. (2011), "Mycenae", in: M. Finkelberg (ed.), 535–38.
Wigodsky, M. (1972), *Vergil and Early Latin Poetry*, Wiesbaden.
Wikén, E. (1937), *Die Kunde der Hellenen von dem Land und den Völkern der Apenninenhalbinsel bis 300 v. Chr.*, Lund.
Wilamowitz-Moellendorf, U. von (1906²), *Griechische Tragödien*, Vol. III, Berlin.
—— (1914), *Aischylos: Interpretationen*, Berlin.
Willcock, M. (1997), "Neoanalysis", in: I. Morris/ B. Powell (eds.), 174–89.
Willi, A. (ed.) (2002), *The Language of Greek Comedy*, Oxford.
Williams, B. (1993), *Shame and Necessity*, Berkeley.
Williams, F. (1978), *Callimachus, Hymn to Apollo: A Commentary*, Oxford.
Williams, G. (1983), *Technique and Ideas in the Aeneid*, New Haven/ London.
Williams, R.D. (1962), *P. Vergili Maronis Aeneidos Liber Tertius*, Oxford.
—— (1980a), " Review on Lyne 1978", *JRS* 70, 247.
—— (1980b), "Virgil and Homer", in: B. Marshall (ed.), 170–76.
Wills, J. (1996), *Repetition in Latin Poetry: Figures of Allusion*, Oxford.
Wilson, D. (1970), *The Life and Times of Vuk Stefanović Karadžić 1787–1864: Literacy, Literature and National Independence in Serbia*, Oxford.
Wilson, D.F. (2002), *Ransom, Revenge and Heroic Identity in the Iliad*, Cambridge.
Wilson, J.R. (1967), "An Interpolation in the Prologue of Euripides' *Troades*", *GRBS* 8, 205–23.
Winkler, J. / Zeitlin, F. (eds.) (1990), *Nothing to do with Dionysos? Athenian Drama in its Social Context*, Princeton.
Winkler, M.M. (ed.) (2001), *Classical Myth and Culture in the Cinema*, New York.
—— (ed.) (2007), *Troy: From Homer's Iliad to Hollywood Epic*. Malden/Oxford.
—— (2007), "The Trojan War on the Screen: An Annotated Filmography",in: M.M. Winkler (ed.), 202–15.
—— (2009), *Cinema and Classical Texts: Apollo's New Light*, Cambridge.

Wöhrle, G. (1999), *Telemachs Reise. Väter und Söhne in Ilias und Odyssee oder ein Beitrag zur Erforschung der Männlichkeitsideologie in der homerischen Welt*, Göttingen.
Wolf, F.A. (1985), *Prolegomena to Homer, 1795* (trans. and ed. by A. Grafton/ G.W. Most/ J.E.G. Zetzel), Princeton.
Woodruff, P. (1982), "What Could Go Wrong with Inspiration? Why Plato's Poets Fail", in: J.M.E. Moravcsik / P. Temko (eds.), 137–50.
Wooten, C. (1987), *Hermogenes' On Types of Style*, Chapel Hill.
Worman, N. (1997), "The Body as Argument: Helen in Four Greek Texts", *Cl.Ant.* 16, 151–203.
—— (2002), *The Cast of Character: Style in Greek Literature*, Austin.
—— (2007), "The Voice which is not One: Helen's Verbal Guises in Homeric Epic", in: H. Bloom (ed.) (2007b), 149–68.
Worthington, I. (2003), "The Authorship of the Demosthenic Epitaphios", *MH* 60, 152–57.
—— (ed.) (2007), *A Companion to Greek Rhetoric*, Malden.
Woytek, E. (2005), "Anmerkungen zur Catull-Rezeption in der Ciris", in: I. Tar/ P. Mayer (eds.), 77–89.
Wyke, M. (1997), *Projecting the Past: Ancient Rome, Cinema and History*, New York.
—— (2002), *The Roman Mistress: Ancient and Modern Representations*, Oxford.
Wypustek, A. (2013), *Images of Eternal Beauty in Funerary Verse Inscriptions of the Hellenistic and Greco-Roman Periods*, Leiden/ Boston.
Xanthakis-Karamanos, G. (1998), "Homer and Euripides: The *Cyclops* and the *Troades*", *Platon* 50, 28–38.
Yates, F.A. (1966), *The Art of Memory*. London.
Young, D.C. (1983), "Pindar *Pythians* 2 and 3: Inscriptional ποτέ and the Poetic Epistle", *HSCP* 87, 31–48.
Zajko, V. (2004), "Homer and Ulysses", in: R.L. Fowler (ed.), 311–23.
Zanetto, G./ Canavero, D./ Capra, A./ Sgobbi, A. (eds.) (2004), *Momenti della ricezione omerica: Poesia arcaica e teatro*, Milan.
Zanker, P./ Ewald, B.C. (2013), *Living with Myths: The Imagery of Roman Sarcophagi* (trans. J. Slater), Oxford.
Zanos, P. (1884), "*Penelope's Suitors and Odysseus' Homecoming*", in: *Greek Theatre* (Ελληνικό Θέατρο), Vol. I, Athens, 1–140.
Zeitlin, F. (2001), "Visions and Revisions of Homer", in: S. Goldhill (ed.), 195–266.
Zembaty, J.M. (1989), "Socrates' Perplexity in Plato's *Hippias Minor*", in: J.P. Anton/ A. Preus (eds.), 51–70.
Ziolkowski, J. (1981), *Thucydides and the Tradition of Funeral Speeches at Athens*, New York.
Zissos, A. (2008), *Valerius Flaccus' Argonautica: Book 1*, Oxford.

Notes on Contributors

Margarita Alexandrou (UCL) is completing her doctoral thesis, a commentary on the fragments of the iambic poet Hipponax. Her research interests lie primarily in archaic Greek poetry and its reception across the spectrum of Greek and Roman literature. She has a growing interest in Greek literary papyrology and is currently co-editing a volume on the methodology of working with literary fragments.

Karim Arafat is Emeritus Reader in Classical Archaeology at King's College London, where he taught for many years before moving to Athens. He now teaches at Deree, the American College of Greece. He has published extensively on Classical art, particularly vase-painting, the relations between art and literature and Pausanias. His books include *Pausanias' Greece: Ancient Artists and Roman Rulers* (Cambridge 1996); *Classical Zeus: A Study in Ancient Art and Literature* (Oxford 1990).

Anastasia Bakogianni is Visiting Fellow at the Institute of Classical Studies, University of London. Her research and publications focus on the reception of Greek Literature in the modern world, especially in the performance culture of modern Greece. She is the author of *Electra Ancient and Modern: Aspects of the Tragic Heroine's Reception* (Institute of Classical Studies 2011), editor of *Dialogues with the Past: Classical Reception Theory and Practice* (ICS 2013) and co-editor of *War as Spectacle: Ancient and Modern Perspectives on the Display of Armed Conflict* (Bloomsbury 2015).

Chris Carey taught at the University of St Andrews, the University of Minnesota, Carleton College and Royal Holloway, the University of London, before becoming Professor of Greek at University College London. He has published on Greek lyric, Homer, tragedy and comedy, Greek law and politics and the Attic orators. He is currently writing a commentary on Book VII of Herodotus for Cambridge University Press, a book on Thermopylae for Oxford University Press and a book of essays on Pindar's *Olympian Odes*.

Athanasios Efstathiou is Associate Professor of Ancient Greek Language and Literature at the Department of History of the Ionian University. He obtained his first degree in Classics and his MA in Classics and Byzantine Studies from the Department of Philology (Aristotle University of Thessaloniki). Subsequently he attended as a non-award student the MA course on Late Antiquity and Byzantium at King's College London, while he acquired his PhD in Classical Oratory at Royal Holloway College (University of London). His research interests cover the subjects of rhetoric and oratory of the Classical and Byzantine period, historiography, attic law, Athenian democracy, papyrology, palaeography, history of Greek language.

Varvara Georgopoulou is Assistant Professor of Modern Greek Theatre at the Department of Theatre Studies of the University of the Peloponnese. Her research interests include theatre criticism, the revival of ancient Greek drama, as well as gender issues in drama. She has taken part in many conferences in both Greece and abroad. She is the author of *Theatre Criticism in Mid War Athens* (2 Vols., Athens 2008–09), *The Theatre in Cephalonia 1900–1953* (Athens 2010), *Female Routes: Galateia Kazantzaki and the Theatre* (Athens 2012) and *The Mirrors of Dionysus: History and Ideology in Modern Greek Theatre, 1920–1950* (Athens 2016).

Lorna Hardwick is Professor Emerita in Classical Studies at the Open University, UK and director of the Reception of Classical Texts research project. With Professor James Porter she is Series Editor of *Classical Presences* (Oxford University Press) and she was the founding editor of the *Classical Receptions Journal*. She has published books and articles on Homer, Athenian cultural history and on modern translations and adaptations of classical material, especially poetry and drama.

†Daniel Jacob (1947–2014) was Professor of Greek at the Department of Classics of the Aristotle University of Thessaloniki since 1992. His main research interests focused on Pindar, Greek tragedy, especially Euripides, Aristotle's *Poetics* and the reception of ancient Greek literature. He was the author of seven books, including *Pindar's Pythian Odes* (Herakleion 1994), *The Poetics of Greek Tragedy* (Athens 1998), for which he received an honourary award by the Academy of Athens, *Issues of Literary Theory in Aristotle's Poetics* (Athens 2004) and a two-volume commentary on Euripides' *Alcestis* (Athens 2012), for which he received a second honourary award by the Academy of Athens. He published extensively in Greek and international scholarly journals and collective volumes.

Maria Kanellou is a Research Fellow of the Academy of Athens, an Honourary Research Fellow at UCL and a Teaching Fellow of OUC. She is currently revising for publication her PhD thesis entitled *Erotic Epigram: A Study of Motifs*. The thesis studies the development and generic features of the literary epigram, especially of its erotic subtype, from the Hellenistic to the early Byzantine period through the close analysis of the life-cycle of recurrent themes. She is also preparing the publication of two collective volumes on ancient Greek epigram arising out of two international conferences held at UCL.

Ioanna Karamanou (MPhil Cambridge, PhD University College London) is Assistant Professor of Greek Drama at the Department of Theatre Studies of the University of the Peloponnese. Her research interests focus on Greek tragedy and its reception, tragic fragments, papyrology and ancient literary criticism. She is the author of *Euripides: Danae and Dictys* (*BzA* 228, Munich/Leipzig 2006, K.G. Saur/ De Gruyter) and has published a number of articles in international peer-reviewed journals and chapters in international collective volumes. She is currently completing an edition and commentary on Euripides' *Alexandros*.

Boris Kayachev has recently obtained a doctorate from the University of Leeds with a thesis on the pseudo-Virgilian *Ciris*. His current interests include Apollonius' *Argonautica* and its use of non-Homeric epic, Latin elegy and its engagement with Hellenistic models, as well as a number of texts outside the classical canon.

Robert Maltby is Emeritus Professor of Latin Philology at the University of Leeds. His research interests include Latin Language, Roman Comedy and Roman Elegy. Apart from numerous periodical articles in these areas, his publications include *A Selection of Latin Love Elegy* (Bristol 1980), *A Lexicon of Latin Etymologies* (Leeds 1991), *Tibullus: Elegies* (Cambridge 2002), *Terence: Phormio* (Oxford 2012) and, with K. Belcher, *Wiley's Real Latin* (Malden, MA 2014).

Christina-Panagiota Manolea (BA in Classics, University of Athens 1992, PhD in Classics, University College London 2002) is lecturing on Greek Civilization (Hellenic Open University). She has worked on the reception of ancient Greek literary tradition in Neoplatonism and the reception of ancient Greek rhetoric in Byzantine and Modern Greek writers. She is currently editing *Brill's Companion to the Reception of Homer from the Hellenistic Age to Late Antiquity*.

Kleanthis Mantzouranis is a Teaching Fellow in Classics at the University of St Andrews. He has previously taught at UCL and Birkbeck College. He received his PhD from UCL in 2012 and is currently working on turning his thesis into a monograph. His specialist interests lie in Aristotle and the history of Greek ethical and political thought.

Andreas N. Michalopoulos is Associate Professor of Latin at the University of Athens. He is the author of *Ancient Etymologies in Ovid's Metamorphoses: A Commented Lexicon* (Leeds 2001), *Ovid, Heroides 16 and 17: Introduction, Text and Commentary* (Cambridge 2006), and *Ovid, Heroides 20 and 21: Introduction, Text, Translation and Commentary* (Athens 2014). His research interests include Augustan poetry, ancient etymology, Roman drama, Roman novel and the modern reception of Classical literature.

Charilaos N. Michalopoulos is Assistant Professor of Latin at the Department of Greek Philology of the Democritus University of Thrace. His research interests include Augustan poetry, gender studies and classics and the modern reception of Latin literature. He has published on Ovid, Seneca and Martial and is the author of *Myth, Language and Gender in the Corpus Priapeorum* (Athens 2014).

Pantelis Michelakis is Reader in Classics at the University of Bristol. He is the author of *Greek Tragedy on Screen* (OUP 2013), *Euripides' Iphigenia at Aulis* (Duckworth 2006) and *Achilles in Greek Tragedy* (CUP 2002). He has also co-edited *The Ancient World in Silent Cinema* (CUP 2013), *Agamemnon in Performance, 458 BC to AD 2004* (OUP 2005) and *Homer, Tragedy and Beyond: Essays in Honour of P.E. Easterling* (SPHS 2001).

Katerina Mikellidou (BA Athens, MA Oxford) completed her PhD (2014) on the encounters between the living and the dead in fifth-century drama under the supervision of Professor Chris Carey (UCL). She has taught Intermediate Latin in UCL and Modern and Ancient Greek in the University of Cyprus. She is currently teaching 'Philosophical Texts' (University of Cyprus) and the postgraduate course 'Theoretical Approaches to Ancient Greek Literature' (Open University of Cyprus). She is mainly interested in Greek Drama, eschatology, ritual and archaic poetry.

Sophia Papaioannou is Associate Professor of Latin literature at the National and Kapodistrian University of Athens. Her principal areas of research include ancient epic, the literature and culture of the Age of Augustus and Roman Comedy. Her main publications include books on Ovid's *Metamorphoses*, Plautus, Terence and New Comedy. Part of her current research is a book on the influence of Homeric orality in the structure and poetics of Virgil's *Aeneid*.

Helen Peraki-Kyriakidou is a retired Assistant Professor of Latin Literature at the Aristotle University of Thessaloniki. Her main areas of interest are Virgil's *Eclogues* and *Georgics*, Roman epic and historiography. She has also published a number of articles on ancient etymology and etymologizing. Together with Stelios Phiorakis she has written a book on *The Law Code of Gortyn* (Herakleion 1973).

Ioannis N. Perysinakis is Professor Emeritus of Ancient Greek Literature at the Department of Philology of the University of Ioannina. His teaching and research interests focus on ancient Greek Literature with an emphasis on moral values and political behaviour from Homer to Plato and Aristotle, the re-evaluation of archaic values and the reception of ancient Greek in Modern Greek Literature. He has written extensively on Homer, Hesiod, lyric poetry, Greek tragedy, Plato and Modern Greek Literature. His publications include (in Greek) *The Concept of Wealth in Herodotus* (Ioannina 1998²) and *Archaic Lyric Poetry* (Athens 2012). He is currently working on the ancient quarrel between philosophy and poetry.

Kyriaki Petrakou is Professor at the Department of Theatre Studies of the University of Athens. Her research focuses on Modern Greek Theatre from the mid-nineteenth century onwards. She is the author of seven books, including *The Drama Competitions 1870–1925* (Athens 1999), *Theatrological Miscellanea* (Athens 2004), *Kazantzakis and the Theatre* (Athens 2005), *The Impact of Modern Greek Theatre Abroad: Translations – Performances* (Athens 2005), *Theatrical Attitudes and Courses* (Athens 2007). She has taught in the Universities of Vienna (2000), Silesia (2002) and in the Open University of Cyprus (2011–2013).

Andrej Petrovic is Senior Lecturer at the Department of Classics and Ancient History of Durham University. His research interests and publications concern Greek Epigraphy and Religion. His published work on early Greek epigram includes the monograph *Kommentar zu den Simonideischen Versinschriften* (Brill 2007) and *Archaic and Classical Greek Epigram* (co-edited with M. Baumbach and I. Petrovic, CUP 2010).

Ivana Petrovic is Senior Lecturer in Greek literature at the Department of Classics and Ancient History of Durham University. Her book *Von den Toren des Hades zu den Hallen des Olymp: Artemiskult bei Theokrit und Kallimachos* (Brill 2007) studies contemporary religion in Hellenistic poetry. She has co-edited volumes on the Roman triumph (Stuttgart 2008) and on Greek archaic epigram (CUP 2010). She has also published papers on Greek poetry, Greek religion and magic. Her forthcoming monograph, co-written with Andrej Petrovic, discusses the phenomenon of inner purity in Greek religion.

Margarita Sotiriou is Lecturer of Classical Philology at the University of the Peloponnese. She is the author of *Pindarus Homericus* (Göttingen 1998). Her publications concern archaic lyric poetry, mainly choral song, its poetics, performance and reperformance, as well as its reception within antiquity and intertextuality. Her current main project is a commentary on the Epinician Odes of Bacchylides.

Hara Thliveri (PhD King's College London) has taught at the Department of Greek and Latin at UCL, at the University of London MA programme 'The classical past in Modern Greece' and at the Open University. Her publications include 'The Discobolos of Myron: Narrative Appeal and Three-dimensionality' in: F. Macfarlane/ C. Morgan (eds.) *Exploring Ancient Sculpture* (London 2010); 'Towards a Modern Understanding of *Topos* and *Logos:* The Olympia of Angelos Sikelianos', *Skepsis XXII/ii* (2012); 'Art and Poetics in Nikos Engonopoulos' in: A. Bakogianni (ed.) *Dialogues with the Past* (London 2013). In 2013 she edited a volume in honour of the composer Mikis Theodorakis.

Eleni Volonaki (MA, PhD Royal Holloway, University of London) is Assistant Professor at the Department of Philology, University of the Peloponnese. She has also taught at the Department of Classics, Royal Holloway (1995–2004), at the Open University UK (2003–2007) and at the Hellenic Open University (2006–2014). She is the author of *A Commentary on Lysias' Speeches Against Agoratos and Against Nicomachos* (Athens 2010) and has published in international journals and in collective volumes in the fields of ancient Greek law and rhetoric, Greek values and epic poetry and Hellenistic rhetoric. She is completing a commentary on Lycurgus' speech *Against Leocrates*, which is to be published in *BICS* Supplements.

Maria Ypsilanti obtained her first degree from the Department of Greek Literature of the University of Athens (1991–1995). She studied at King's College London (MA in Classics, 1996–1997) and at University College London (PhD in Classics, 1998–2003); PhD thesis: *An Edition with Commentary of Selected Epigrams of Crinagoras*, forthcoming (revised and enriched with the rest of Crinagoras' poems) in Oxford University Press. Since 2004 she teaches Ancient Greek Literature at the University of Cyprus. Her research interests include Hellenistic poetry, poetry of Late Antiquity, epigram, tragedy and textual criticism.

General Index

Achaemenides 7, 263–275, 306 f.
Achilles 15–17, 21 f., 58, 75, 98–106, 108–111, 115, 117, 119 and n. 62, 123, 128, 147–151, 153–155, 157, 163, 167, 170, 184 f., 210 f., 228, 231, n. 20, 252–257 with nn. 17 and 18, 260, 291–296 with nn. 20 and 22, 296 with nn. 34 and 37, 299, 310 f., 341, 363, 369–372, 377, 380, 396 f., 409, 411, 414–416 and n. 17
adaptation 8, 26 f., 59 and n. 2, 68 f., 117, 123, 216 f. and n. 5, 223 f., 293, 320, 331, 361, 383, 387, 407, n. 7, 414, 416
Admetus 343–345 and n. 10, 347 and n. 19, 349 f. and n. 22
Aeneas 251–257 with nn. 12, 14 and 17, 260 f., 263 and n. 3, 267–269 and n. 28, 271, 273–275 and nn. 73, 76, 296, 304–307, 310 f. and n. 6
Aeschines 5, 93–107, 109–123
– *Against Ctesiphon* 93 and n.1, 112, 114, 116, 122 f.
– *Against Timarchus* 93 and n. 1, 96, 98, 103, 112, 122 f.
– *On the False Embassy* 93, 104, n. 28, 112, 116, n. 52, 121
Aeschylus 8, 73, 77, 79, 101 f., 122, 218, 331–333, 336–341 and n. 19, 345, 346, n. 16, 360, 363, n. 40, 379
– *Choephori* 345
– *Myrmidones* 101 f., 341
– *Nereides* 101
– *Persians* 73, 79, 341, 346, n. 16
– *Phrygians* 101, 363, n. 40
– *Psychagogoi* 8, 331, 333, 335, n. 8, 340 f.
– *Suppliants* 337, n. 18, 340
Agamemnon 74 f. and n. 10, 115 f., 148, 169 and n. 14, 208, 211, 291–295 with nn. 21, 23 and 29, 298 f., 355, 357, 380, 396, 409 f., 412–415
agathos 125–128 with nn. 3, 8 and 9, 145, 153, 156–159
agon 359, 361 and n. 32, 363, 365–367 and n. 59, 370, 377, 412 f.

Ajax 116, n. 52, 147 f., 155, 166, 179 f. and n. 22, 333
Alcestis 343–348 with nn. 4, 17 and 19, 350, n. 22, 353
Alcinous 36, 61, 229–233, 235, 289
Alexandros/ Paris 179 f., 191, n. 5, 291, 295 with nn. 31 and 32, 345, 355, 357–364 with nn. 26 and 42, 365 f., 375, 393 f., 396 f.
allegory 9, 154, 178, n. 13, 182, 383–385
allusion 7, 18, 24, 31, 38 f., 46, n. 3, 51, 103, n. 27, 112, 120, 165–168 and n. 12, 200 f., nn. 39 and 42, 203, 216, 224, 241, n. 50, 263, 265, 268 and n. 34, 270, 272, 277–279 and n. 19, 283, 285, 289, 295, 311, 380, 431
Amphitrite 279–284 with nn. 26 and 30, 286
analogue 271, 351
andragathia 143 and n. 74, 145
andreia (courage) 128, 163–173
Andromache 9, 54–57 and n. 31, 291, 294 f. and n. 30, 358, 361, 364, 369–377, 411 f. and n. 13, 414
Antipater of Sidon 199
Aphrodite 6, 65, 101, 189, 191–202, 204, 209, 244, 292, 296 f., 351, 397
Apollo 23, 97, n. 13, 202, 209 f. and n. 8, 212, 237, 238, n. 40, 244 f., 273 and n. 73, 350, n. 22
Apollonius Rhodius 219, 223, n. 36, 263, 268, n. 34, 270, n. 49, 278, 284, 285, n. 35
– *Argonautica* 268, n. 34, 270, n. 49, 278, 284 f.
appropriation 2–8, 11, 15, 39, 42, 45, n. 1, 46, 50, n. 15, 51, 53 f. and n. 28, 68, 93, 103, 123, 152, 163, 173, 175 f., 249, 267, 279, 289 and n. 2, 294, 296–299, 361 f., 365 f., 370, 374, 376, 387, 419, n. 9
Archedike 56–58
archetype 8, 189, 201, n. 40, 265, 331, 333
Archilochus 31, 43, 101, 119, n. 64, 204

aretē 5, 66, 125–127 and n. 3, 130 f., 133–138 and n. 44, 140–145 and n. 70, 153, 156–158, 411
Aristarchus 93, n. 2, 110 and n. 40, 175 and n. 1, 314
Aristias 379
– *Cyclops* 379
Aristophanes 121, 191, 384, 386
Aristotle 6, 42, n. 30, 56, 71, 94, 104, 118 f. and n. 60, 152, 155, 157 f. and n. 29, 160 f., 163–173, 175, 184, n. 46, 306
– *Metaphysics* 152, 429
– *Nicomachean Ethics* 94, 160, 163, 166, n. 9
– *Poetics* 42, n. 30, 71, n. 4, 119, 155, 157
– *Rhetoric* 5, n. 13, 56, n. 36, 94, 111, 142, n. 73, 171, 362, n. 33
Astyanax 357, 372 f., 377, 411 f., 414
asyndeton 66
Athena 34 f., 47, 62, 179 f. and n. 22, 189, n. 1, 193–195 with nn. 14 and 22, 210, 265, 308, 310, 333, 348
Atossa 73
Atwood, Margaret 21 f.
audience 1, 4–6, 11, 15, 21 f., 32 f. with nn. 8 and 9, 42, 65, n. 15, 67–69, 73, 76, 85, 87, 95, 99 f. and n. 20, 102–104, 106, 112, 117, 119, 121, 130, 134 f., 137, 154, 165, 183, 185 f., 191, 217, 220, 222, 249, 251, 254–256 and n. 14, 320, 324, 333 f., 336 f., 341, 366, 382 f., 386, 395, 397–399, 401 f. and n. 31, 406–409 with nn. 7 and 9, 411–415, 424
audience response 4, 6, 9, 365
auteur 406, 408
authority 4–6, 8, 11, 31, 41, 67, n. 25, 69, 72, 93, 98, 101, 114, 122, 165, 173, 183, n. 43, 205, 207 f., 266, 282, 317, 332, 338, 399 f.

Bacchini, Romolo: *Odissea di una comparsa* 396
bards 252, 316 f. and n. 6, 321, 323, 327, 401
Bertolini, Francesco et al.: *Odissea* 393
Biebrach, Rudolf: *Die Heimkehr des Odysseus* 393

Borgnetto, Luigi Romano and Pastrone, Giovanni: *La caduta di Troia* 394
Bosworth, Hobart: *An Odyssey of the North* 393
Briseis 208, 291–295 with nn. 21–24, 26 and 29, 416, n. 17
bucolic poetry 7, 227 f., 239, 241 and n. 50
Bupalus 32 and n. 4, 35–38
burlesque 191, 393, 396

Cacoyannis, Michael 10, 405–416 with nn. 6 and 10
– *Electra* 10, 405, 407 with nn. 6 and 7, 409, 412–415 and n. 15
– *Iphigenia* 10, 405, 407 with nn. 6 and 7, 409 f., 412–416 and n. 12
– *Trojan Women* 10, 405, 407 f. with nn. 7 and 10, 410–412, 414
Callimachus 44, 119, 177, n. 9, 195, 197, 216, n. 4, 270 f. with nn. 49 and 52, 273, n. 73, 278, 281, n. 25
– *Aetia* 270 f.
– *Hecale* 216, n. 4, 278
– *Hymn to Apollo* 97, n. 13, 273 and n. 73
– *Hymn to Artemis* 270 and n. 52
Callinus 205
Calmettes, André: *Le retour d' Ulysse* 393
canon 267, 396, n. 8, 398
Cassandra 179 f. and n. 22, 296, 355 f., 360 and n. 26, 374 f., 412
censorship 8, 11, 380, 384, 408
Chaeremon 117
– *Achilles Thersitoktonos* 117
Charalambidis, Giorgos: *Penelope's 300* 380, 384
Chariton 346, 349–351 with nn. 21 and 22
– *Callirhoe* 346, 349–352 with nn. 22 and 25
Charybdis 39, 269
Choeroboscus 42 and n. 31
choliambic metre 32, 43
Chorus 336–338 with nn. 15, 18, 19 and 20, 345 f., 350, n. 22, 357, 365, 371, 410, 414 f.
Christianity 217, 382
Christodoulou, Dimitris: *Hotel Circe* 380, 383 f., 387

General Index — 483

cinema 10, 393–404, 405–416
cinematic reception 10, 372, 395, 405, 408–412
Circe 35, 120, 180, 282, n. 26, 287, 291f., 335, 338, 379f., 382–385, 389, 393, 420, n. 14
classical film philology 406, 407, n. 6
Clytaemestra 409, 412–416
Colluthus 216
commentary 3f., 8, 11, 26, 41, 175, 217, 256, 303, 313
competitive excellences 125–127 and n. 8, 133, 136, 138, 143f., 362f. and n. 41, 366f.
contexts (of reception) 1–11, 15, 23, 26, 36, 63, 125, 126, n. 9, 218, 231, 282, 299, 340, 355 and n. 2, 366, 369f., 375, n. 22, 377, 380, 387, 401, 403
Cook, Elizabeth 16, 22
co-operative excellences 125, 127, 138, 362f. and n. 41, 366
Corneille, Pierre 372
correspondences 264
Cratinus 119, n. 64, 379
– *Odysseis* 379
Creophylus 176f. with nn. 9 and 10
critical analysis 9, 380, n. 9
Croesus 52–54 and n. 27, 57f.
cultural process 9, 355, 369
culture 2, 6, 8, 10, 16, 26, 96, 122, 125, 153, 169, n. 15, 236f., 239, 245, 247, n. 70, 249, 264 and n. 15, 322, 361f. with nn. 35 and 37, 384, 387, 401, 407
Cyclops 7, 38, 263, 265–267, 269–274 and n. 74, 426
Cynthia 292, 297f.
Cypria 206, 253, 360f. with nn. 26 and 29, 365, n. 54
Cypso 32, n. 4, 36, 39, n. 23

Dante, *Commedia Divina* 379
Darius 72f., 79, n. 27, 340f., 346, n. 16
Deiphobus 357–359 with nn. 13 and 22, 361–363 and n. 37, 365f.
Deleuze, Gilles 3, 17, 396
dēmos 100, 113, 123, 126, 141

Demosthenes 93, 96, 100 and n. 20, 112–114, 116–123 with nn. 52, 54 and 72, 138–141 with nn. 56 and 64, 144
– *Epitaphios* 138–140
– *On the Crown* 93, 120–121, 122, n. 72
– *On the False Embassy* 96, 122, n. 72
Derrida, Jacques 16
descriptio 7, 249–261 with nn. 5, 13, 14 and 16, 310
dialogue 3f., 7–10, 18, 83, 279, n. 20, 331, 361, n. 30, 366f., 375, 401, 405f., 431
Dimou, Akis: *Andromache or Landscape of a Woman in the Height of the Night* 9, 369, 375–377
Diomedes 54, n. 28, 163, 170, 173, 253–256 and n. 17, 260, 296f., 310
Dionysus 236–238 with nn. 40 and 43
dissemination 199, 250, 401–403
distortion 32, n. 4, 43, 95, 114, 137, n. 50, 293, n. 23
diversity 1f., 10, 77, 151, 395, 400
Donatus 303

Eisenstein, Sergei 406 and n. 5
ekphrasis 213, 249–251 and n. 5, 254–257 with nn. 14, 16 and 17, 261, 278
Elytis, Odysseus 423 and n. 29
Empedocles 181f.
emulation 5, 7f., 11, 58, 163, 227–247
Ennius 239f., 264, n. 13, 356f. and n. 11, 360 with nn. 26 and 27
– *Alexander* 356f., 360 with nn. 26 and 27
– *Annales* 239
Epic Cycle 87, 98 and n. 15, 116, n. 52, 252–254, 360, n. 27, 400 with nn. 27 and 28
epic film 394f., 397f.
Epicharmus 379
– *Cyclops* 379
– *Odysseus Shipwrecked* 379
– *Odysseus the Deserter* 379
– *Sirens* 379
epigram 4, 6, 45–58, 81, 112f., 115, 122, n. 73, 158, n. 29, 177, n. 9, 189–204, 243
epinician poetry 59–69, 351, n. 22
epitaphios (funeral oration) 125–145

epitymbia 45–58
epos 4–11, 31, 35, 38–39 with nn. 20 and 23, 41f., 44, 45, n. 1, 46, 228, n. 7, 349, 366
equivalent/ equivalence 5, 7, 68, 89, 99, 141, 222, 251, n. 5, 348, n. 20, 351f. and n. 22, 402, 433
Erginus 60f., 63f. and n. 14, 67f.
Eriphyle 209f.
eros 98, 199–203 and n. 39, 220, n. 23, 426, 428
etymology 116, n. 55, 222, 237, 313, 347, n. 19
Euripides 9f., 93, 96f. and n. 8, 122, 216, n. 4, 278, 341, 343–353, 355–367, 369–372, 374, 376, 379, 383, 405, 408–416
– *Alcestis* 9, 343–353
– *Alexandros* 9, 355–367
– *Andromache* 9, 370–371, 372, 376–377
– *Antiope* 366
– *Cretans* 366
– *Cyclops* 379
– *Electra* 10, 349, 352, 405, 407 with nn. 6 and 7, 409, 412–415 and n. 15
– *Helen* 344, n. 7, 345, 349, 352, n. 25, 353
– *Hippolytus* 278, 351
– *Iphigenia in Aulis* 10, 386, 405, 414
– *Iphigenia in Tauris* 345, 349
– *Medea* 341
– *Orestes* 349
– *Palamedes* 355, 356, n. 4, 358–360 and n. 22
– *Phoenissae* 348
– *Sisyphus* 355, 358
– 'Trojan trilogy' 9, 355–367
– *Trojan Women* 9f., 355–367, 370–372, 376, 405, 407, n. 7, 408 and n. 10, 410–412, 414
Euryalus 61–63, 191 and n. 4, 338
Eustathius, archbishop of Thessalonica 182, 221 and n. 29, 222f. and n. 36, 283 and n. 29, 364 and n. 47
exegesis 6, 11, 186, 216, 222, 283
exemplum 69, n. 38, 110, 294, 297

figura etymologica 223
film 2, 8, 10, 393–416
first person statement 66f.
formal debate 9, 361f., 365f., 370
formula 15, 17, 25, 39, 46 and n. 4, 51, 55, 95, 97, 109, 127, 166, 189 and n. 1, 201, 215, 217, 224, 231, 233, 267, 293, n. 26, 316, 398, 402, 406
French Classicism 9, 372, 377
Freud, Sigmund 401

Garnier, Robert: *La Troade* 379
gender 9, 371, 373, 376f., 398
genre 1f., 5–7, 10, 20, 27, 31, 33, 41f., 44, 46f. and n. 2, 48, 50 and n. 14, 89, 132 and n. 32, 142, 192, 200, 204, 215, 227, 235, 289, 296–300, 303, 314, 316, 336, 369, 375, 379, 393f., 397, 400, 406f. and n. 9, 410, 416
Giraudoux, Jean: *The Trojan War Will Not Take Place* 9, 369, 374f., 377, 379
Gorgias 134, 144, 150, 365f.
– *Encomium of Helen* 365f.
– *Epitaphios* 134 and n. 35

Hades 147, 184, 219, 339, 344–348 with nn. 16 and 19, 353, 383, 430
Hatot, Georges: *Le jugement de Pâris* 393
Hecabe 355, 357 and n. 13, 361, 365f., 371f., 413–415
Hector 15, 45–58, 85f., 105–107, 109, 136 and n. 45, 148, 163, 169, n. 14, 170, 173, 253, 260, 291–296, 299, 311, 343, n. 4, 358, 361–366, 369–375, 396, 411 and n. 13
Helen 47, n. 7, 72, n. 6, 108, 181f., 200f. and n. 40, 291, 292, n. 18, 293, n. 22, 295, n. 31, 344, n. 7, 345, 349, 352 and n. 26, 358–361 and n. 26, 363–366 with nn. 47 and 51, 375f., 393f., 396–398, 401, 403, 409, 412, 414, 417, n. 2, 420, n. 14
Hera 207, 220, 228, 308, 312, 345
Heracles 82, 85, 208, 236, 344–347 with nn. 10, 11 and 13, 349f. and n. 22, 353
Hermes 23, 33–35, 208, 210f., 334–338 and n. 15

Hermione 370, 372–374, 377
Herodas 44
Herodotus 4f., 71–89, 205f., 208
Hesiod 43, 93f., 96, n. 8, 101, 112, n. 47, 122f., 178, 205–207, 220
– *Theogony* 205
hexameter 6, 15, 39 and n. 23, 42, 44, 46, 51, n. 19, 53, n. 25, 97, 215f. and n. 1, 337, n. 19
Hipponax 4, 31–44
Holmes, Burton: *A Polynesian Odyssey* 393
Homer See Index of Homeric Passages
Homeric Hymns 191, n. 5, 194, n. 17, 220
Homeric question 250 and n. 3, 316, 408
Homeric scholarship 1, 7f., 177, n. 10, 206, 315, 316f. and n. 7, 320, 327, 403
Homerids 321
Horace 18, 292, n. 18
hybrid 286
hybris 126, 158, 232
hyperbole 75, 190f. and n. 6, 193, n. 13, 198–200, 202–204, 297
Hypereides 114, 141–145 and n. 63
– *Epitaphios* 141–144
hypertext 31, nn. 1 and 2, 261
hypotext 31 and n. 2

Iamblichus 6, 175–186
– *De Mysteriis* 176, 185f. and n. 49
– *De Vita Pythagorica* 176–184, 185f.
– *Protrepticus* 176, 184–186
iambos 31f. and n. 3, 38, n. 20, 43f. and n. 31
Ibycus 101, 190–192 with nn. 5 and 8, 198f., 202
identity 4, 9, 11, 53, 59, 67, 100, 111, 123, 127, 144, 207, 235, 337 with nn. 18 and 20, 344, 346, 349f. and n. 22, 361, 374, 377, 400, 421, n. 14, 431, 433
– national identity 324, 397f.
Iliou Persis 180, n. 22, 360
imagery 6, 40 and n. 26, 45, n. 1, 216, n. 6, 220, 224, 229 and n. 13, 235, 239, 241, 243, 258, 312, 357
imitatio 26, 31, 135, 155f. and n. 24, 216, 224, 266, 283, n. 28, 353, 376, 420

intertext/ intertextuality 4, 7–9, 19, 31f. and n. 1, 33 and n. 9, 39–44, 46, 59, 74, 76, 94f., 181, n. 30, 194, n. 17, 263f., 268–270 and n. 44, 287, 303, 331, 338, 343, n. 4, 352f., 375, 379, 400
Interwar period 9, 374–375, 380
Irus 34
Ithaca 67, 207, 229, 265, 267f. and n. 32, 275, 283, 298, 379, 381f., 384–386, 388, 393, 415, 419, 423, 425f., 433

Jauss, Hans Robert: 2
– aesthetics of reception 2
– horizon of expectations 2, 5, 10f.
Jouvet, Louis 374

kakos 125, n. 3, 158f.
Kambanellis, Iakovos 10, 375, 380–382, 385f., 388
– *Odysseus, Come Home* 10, 380, 381, 385–386, 388–389
– *The Last Act* 380, 386, 389
– *The Last Supper* 375
Katsaitis, Petros 375
Kavanagh, Patrick 19f.
Kazantzakis, Nikos 389
kleos 4f., 18, 48, 50, 71, 81–83, 127f., 411, 414
Korda, Alexander 394
– *King Menelaus at the Movies* 393f.
– *The Private Life of Helen of Troy* 394, 396, 401, 403
Koun, Karolos 381

Laertes 234f., 345f., 416
Laodamas 61–63
Leonard, Robert: *Circe, the Enchantress* 393
Leonidas 82–85 with nn. 29, 31 and 34
Lépine, Charles-Lucien: *Odyssée d'un paysan à Paris* 396
literacy 50, 249–251 and n. 1, 259
literary criticism 31, n. 1, 175, 209, 250, 303, 306
Logue, Christopher 20, 22, 24, 27
Longley, Michael 19–21
Lord, Albert 250, n. 3, 316f. with nn. 6 and 7, 322f., 327

Löwenstein, Otto: *König Menelaus im Kino* 393
Lycurgus 93, 96, 122 f. and n. 72
– *Against Leocrates* 93, 96, 122, n. 72
Lysias 134–138, 144
– *Epitaphios* 134–136, 144

Macrobius 239, 289, 305, 311
Mahon, Derek 17 f.
Marathon 73, 76, 114, 142, n. 72
Margites 44, 118 f. with nn. 61, 63 and 64, 123
Meleager 149, 191, n. 5, 202–204, 209, 243
Méliès, Georges 393, 396
– *L'île de Calypso: Ulysse et le géant Polyphème* 393
– *L' Odyssée de la voiture astral* 396
Melissinos, Stavros: *Odysseus' Helmet* 386
Memnon 210, 253, 254, n. 14, 260
Menelaus 84, 181, 293, n. 22, 345, 348, 365, 371, 393, 396 f., 412
metapoetry 4, 7, 11, 26, 31, 42 f., 44, 203, 236, 244, 251, 257, 271, 275, n. 80, 293
mimēsis 5, 153 f., 156 f.
Mimnermus 290 and n. 8
Minchin, Elizabeth 22 f.
mirror scenes 344, n. 9, 356, 360
model 8, 15 f., 26, 39, 51, 58 f., 63, 65, n. 15, 76, 78, 119, 135, 144, 151, 156, 163, 206 f., 227, n. 3, 238, n. 43, 239–241, 243, 250, 257, 263, 264, n. 15, 274, n. 76, 279, 314, 320, 324, 333, 339, 341, 375 f., 385, 397, 415, 419, n. 9, 420
Modern Greek theatre 8 f., 375–377, 379–389
Monca, Georges: *Rigadinet la jolie manicure* 396
morphology 45, 313, 421, 425
motif 4, 6 f., 9 f., 39, 45, 64 f., 67–69 with nn. 34 and 38, 74, 76, 78, 80, 83, 89, 115, 120, n. 66, 121, 189–191, 193, n. 14, 198–200, 202–204 and n. 50, 216, 218, n. 12, 219, 224, 250, 290 f. and n. 14, 293, 295 and n. 33, 296 f., 332, 339–341, 348, n. 20, 360, 361, n. 29, 399, 419, n. 8, 421
Murko, Matija 316

narrative 5, 7 f., 10 f., 17, 19, 20, n. 14, 24, 26, 34–41, 43 f., 45 and n. 1, 50 f. with nn. 15 and 17, 54 f., 58, 60, 64 f. and n. 15, 67 f., 69 with nn. 38 and 39, 71, 73 f. and n. 10, 75 with nn. 14 and 17, 76–78, 80, 82–85, 87, 89, 135, 141, n. 66, 155, 200, n. 39, 208, 216, 220, 224, 231 f. and n. 23, 249–257, 259–261, 269, 273, 285 f., 303, 305–309, 313 f., 321, 332, 348 f., 394, 396–398, 400, 403, 405 f., 408–410 and n. 11, 416, 417
– focalized narrative 252
narrator 4, 32 and n. 6, 33 f., 38 and n. 20, 41, 44, 67 and n. 30, 68 f. with nn. 32 and 38, 71, 75, n. 14, 83 f. and n. 31, 89, 161, 250 f., 257, 281, 286, 382, 397, 409
– primary narrator 4, 33, 59, 67
Nausicaa/Nausica 43, 189, n. 1, 191, n. 6, 265, 344, n. 8, 379, 382, 420, n. 14
necromancy 8, 331, 334 f. and n. 7, 336, 338 f., 341
Nekyia 8, 232, 331 f., 336–341
neoanalysis 250 and n. 2
Neoptolemus 179, 370 f., 375
New Testament 215 and n. 1
Nicander 278, 285
– *Theriaca* 278, 285
Nietzsche, Friedrich 396 and n. 10, 401
Noa, Manfred: *Helena* 393, 397, 403
Nonnus of Panopolis 6, 215–224
Nossis 192–194, 204
nostos 9 f., 332, 343 and n. 4, 349, 352 f., 355, 413, 417, 419 f. and n. 8, 423, 426, 428–431, 433
novel 20, 58, 213, 247, 296, 346, 349–352 with nn. 21, 22 and 26, 387, 401, 403

Obal, Max: *Die Heimkehr des Odysseus* 393
Odysseus 8, 10, 21 f., 31, 33–38 and n. 18, 40 f., 43, 61 f., 63 f. with nn. 9 and 14, 67–69 with nn. 28–31, 115 f., 147–152, 155, 180, 182 f., 189, n. 1, 212, 234 f.,

267, 269, 272 f., 282 f. and n. 26, 287, 289, n. 1, 291 f., 298, 304–307, 331 f. and n. 2, 333 f., 336–339, 344, n. 8, 345 f., 347 f. with nn. 19 and 20, 349, 352 f., 355, 358 f. and n. 22, 361, 372, 379–389, 393, 395 f., 413, 419, 422 f., 425 f., 429–431 with nn. 53 and 59, 433 f.
oikos   355, 358, 409, 413 f.
orality   7, 10 f., 93, 232, n. 23, 249–261, 315–327, 401–403
oratory   5, 64, n. 12, 93–145, 258 and n. 20
Orestes   298, 345, 352 and n. 26, 373 f., 412, 414 f.
Orpheus   206, 347, n. 19
Oswald, Alice   24–27
Ovid   7, 266, 274 f., 286 f., 289–300
– Amores   289 f. and n. 10, 296 f. and n. 39, 299
– Metamorphoses   266, n. 22, 274 f. and n. 80, 287

paideia   5, 99, 137, 139, 142
Palamedes   355, 359 and n. 22, 379
paradigm   5 f., 17, 139, 143, 149, 163 and n. 1
paraphrase   6, 24, 94, 98, 104, 106, 122, 215–224
Paris (see above, Alexandros/Paris)
parody   10 f., 31 and n. 1, 36 and n. 17, 39 and n. 24, 42 and nn. 29–30, 137 and n. 46, 191, n. 7, 201, n. 40, 291, n. 16, 379, 386 f., 393, 396
Parry, Milman   250, n. 3, 316 f. with nn. 6 and 7, 323, 327, 402 and n. 34
pathos   86, 201, 372, 433
Patroclus   58, 84, 98–108, 110 f., 123, 128, 138, 181 and n. 27, 292 f., 333, 343, n. 4, 396, 411 and n. 13, 414
Pausanias   6, 48, n. 8, 118, 205–213, 337, n. 17
Peisistratus   56, 58, 114, 316
Peloponnesian War   131, 134, 370
Penelope   21, 180, 184, 189, n. 1, 201 and n. 40, 210, 291, 293, n. 24, 348 f., 353, 379–382, 384–387, 389, 416
Penthesilea   253 f. and n. 14, 260

performance   4, 9, 16, 18 f., 22 f., 25, 39, n. 22, 59 and n. 5, 67, 69, 93, 98 and n. 15, 117, 121, 131, 136, n. 45, 138 f., 153, 163, 250 f. and n. 5, 261, 318, 326, 338, 379 f. and n. 9, 387, 401 f., 410
– performance history   9
– performative 'I'   67
Pericles   129, n. 20, 131–133 with nn. 29 and 30, 136 f. and n. 46, 144
peripeteia   81
Persian Wars   5, 71, 137 and n. 50
persona   4, 7, 9, 32, 67, 197, 292, 362, 365 f., 369 f., 374, 377, 387, 422
phēmē ('report')   96 f.
philosophy   1, n. 1, 5, 147–186, 259, 313, 382
Philostratus   6, 182, 212 f.
Philyllius: The Washing Women or Nausicaa   379
phthonos   359 with nn. 22 and 23, 361 f.
Pindar   4, 59–69, 79, n. 27, 205, 211 f., 351, n. 22, 360
– Eighth Paean   211
– Fourth Olympian   4, 59–69
– Paean VIIIa   360 and n. 26
Plato   5 f., 93, 101 f. and n. 22, 110, 119, 128, 136–138, 144, 147–161, 163 and n. 1, 164 f. with nn. 4 and 7, 173, 175, 177 f. with nn. 9 and 14, 179, 184 and n. 46, 185 f., 219, 320
– Apology   110, 151, 153
– Hippias Major   151
– Hippias Minor   5, 147–161
– Ion   93 f., 152, 154
– Menexenus   128, 136–138
– Protagoras   102, n. 22, 153, 159 f., 165, n. 7
– Republic   153–160, 165, n. 5, 178, 184
– Symposium   101, 157
Plutarch   56 f. and n. 39, 64, n. 12, 110, n. 41, 114 and n. 49, 118, 141, 182 and n. 35
polis   358, 363
polytropia   151
Polyxena   191, n. 6, 372, 377, 412
popular culture   10

Porphyry   6, 175 f. with nn. 1 and 3, 178 f. and n. 11, 181 f. with nn. 30 and 34, 185 f., 284
– *Quaestiones Homericae*   175
Poseidon   180, 210, 220, n. 21, 272 and n. 60, 304, 426
Posidippus   195 with nn. 20 and 22, 197 f. with nn. 28–30
Postwar period   9 f., 375, 387 f., 399
praise   4 f., 49, 51 f., 56 f., 59–61, 65 f. and n. 22, 68 f., 78, 81, 126, 128–137, 139–145, 155, 159, 172, 189 f. and n. 1, 192, 193, n. 14, 194, 197, n. 30, 198–202, 204, 246, 306, 309, 322
Priam   21, 88, 147, 179, 223, 254, 260, 355, 358 f., 363, n. 42, 373, 375, 396 f.
Propertius   7, 289–299
prototype   100, 103, 119, 205–207, 273, 419, 423, 430, n. 59, 431
Psaumis   59 f., 64, n. 14, 66 and n. 19, 67 f.
Psychopedis, Jannis   417, n. 1, 420, 431 f.
Pythagoras   176–178, 180 f. and n. 29, 182 f. and n. 43, 184 and n. 46

Quintilian   215, 259, n. 23
Quintus Smyrnaeus   216 and n. 5, 219, 362, n. 37
quotation   5, 8, 93 and n. 2, 94–96, 98, 104, 106–109, 110 and n. 41, 111 f., 122, 166, 176, 181, n. 30, 185

Racine, Jean   9, 369, 372–374, 377, 379
– *Andromaque*   372–374
– *Iphigénie*   379
receiving text   2–4, 8, 11, 26, 31, 175
reception   1–11 with nn. 1, 2 and 8, 15–20, 23 f., 26 f., 31, 38, 40–42, 44, 46, 53, 59, 64, 68 f., 93, 102, 113 f., 123, 132, 149, 153, 160 f., 163–165, 175, 184, 186 f., 189, 200, 202, 204, 215 f., 224, 235, 249 f. and n. 4, 263 f. and n. 15, 270, 274, 279, 286 f., 289, 292, 296, 298, 300, n. 43, 322, 325, n. 24, 343, 355, n. 3, 360, n. 27, 361 f., 364 f., 369, n. 1, 372 f., 380 and n. 9, 393, 395, 400,
405 f. and n. 3, 408–410, 411–415, 416, n. 18, 419 and n. 8, 431
– reception history   3, 9 f., 369 f., 393 f.
recognition   15, 235, 245, 267, n. 28, 343 f. and n. 7, 345–346, 349, 353, 358, 360
refiguration   2, 6, 9 f., 67, 274, 289 and n. 2, 369, 372, 375, n. 22, 379 f., 417
Renaissance   286, 379, 407, n. 9
repetition   3, 15, 17–19, 21, 23–27, 106, 232, n. 23, 240, 257, 267 and n. 28, 273, 402, 404, 429
representation   6 f., 23, 45 and n. 1, 52 f. and n. 27, 102, 117, 126, 136, 156, 163, 171, 173, 196, 235, 251, 261, 270, n. 51, 323 f., 340, 357, 370, 401
reworking   1–3, 7, 9, 11, 26, 44, 64, 110, 114, 131, 269, 355, 375, 419 f.
rewriting   16, 18, 26, 117, 151, n. 12, 215
rhapsodes   22, 321, 408
Rhesus   39 f., 253 f. and n. 10, 260
Rhetorica ad Herennium   258 and n. 22, 259 f. and n. 23
rhetoric   9, 68, 76, 93–123, 134, 136 f. and n. 44, 140, 144, 153 f. and n. 20, 333, 361, 364–367, 384, 401 and n. 31
Rieu, Emile Victor   19
ritual   178, 223, 243, 331, 334–338, 343, 346, 357, 429
Royal Shakespeare Company   21

Sakellarios, Alekos and Giannakopoulos, Christos: *The Trojan War*   380, 388
Sakellariou, Charis: *The Sleep of the Lotus-Eaters*   386
Salamis   76, 80
Sappho   190, 194, 210, 370
satire   39, 201, 382, 385–388
satyr-play   355, 358, 379
scholia   8, 47, nn. 6 and 7, 49 f. with nn. 11 and 14, 55–57, 149, 175, 284 f. with nn. 31 and 34, 313 f., 332, 346, n. 14
Scylla   7, 277–287
second sophistic   6, 206
self-reference   65
Semonides   31
Seneca: *Troades*   9, 306, 369, 372, 374, 377
Serbia   2, 7 f., 316–327

Servius 8, 254f. and n. 15, 256 and n. 17, 267, n. 27, 289, 303–314
shadow puppet theatre 380, 384
Shakespeare, William: *Troilus and Cressida* 379
shame culture 125, 169, n. 15, 362 and nn. 35 and 38
Sikelianos, Angelos 420, 426–429, 433
silent film 10, 393–404
simile 17, 19f. and n. 14, 21, 24f., 84–86, 166–168 and n. 12, 227, 278, 285 and n. 36, 307, 410
Simonides 81, 83, n. 30, 155, 159, 257
Sirens 120f., 123, 211, 364, 379, 417, n. 2, 420, n. 14, 429, 433
Skouloudis, Manolis: *Odyssey* 380, 382f.
Socrates 93, 102, 110, 136f., 147–154, 157–161, 163, n. 1
Sokratous, Kostas: *Penelope and her Suitors* 386
sophists 100, 152f.
Sophocles 122, 208, 333, 338f., 345, 360
– *Electra* 339, 345
– *King Oedipus* 208, 341
– *Philoctetes* 333
sōphrosynē 135, 138f., 142, 144, 362
source text 1–11, 31, 41, 59, 65, n. 15, 69 and n. 39, 165, 186, 215, 235, 286, 331, 334, 338, 341, 353, 355, 357, n. 11, 370, 372, 375, 409
South Slavic oral poetry 316, n. 6, 317–327, 402
Stefanović Karadžić, Vuk 317–327
Steiner, George 15f.
Stesichorus 46, n. 5, 205
St. John's Gospel 6, 215–224
story-pattern 352f.
subtext 250, 283, 285, 287, 353
subversion 4, 41, 44, 50
supplication 21, 254 and n. 13, 260, 263, 265, 305, 358, 416

Talthybius 372, 414
Tantalus 182f., 232
Telemachus 34, 63, 229, 382, 384–386, 415
Terzakis, Angelos 382

theatre criticism 9
Theocritus 7, 231, n. 14, 235f., 238, n. 43, 241, 243
Theodorakis, Mikis: *Odyssey* 10, 417–434
Theopompus:
– *Odysseus* 379
– *Penelope* 379
– *Sirens* 379
Thermopylae 81, 83, 89
Thersites 115–117, 123
Thetis 105, 109f., 218, n. 17, 294, 310, 370
Thrylos, Alkis 382–384
Thucydides 56f., 97, n. 13, 129, n. 20, 131–133, 137 and n. 46, 144, 270
Tibullus 289–291 with nn. 1 and 14, 296
timē 126–128, 414
topos 21, 100, 182, 268, 419, 431, 433
tradition 6–8, 17–20, 24, 27, 40, 42–44, 46, 50f., 57, 59, 69, n. 39, 72, 74, 81, 88, 93f., 103, 110f. and n. 40, 123, 127, 129, 137, 139, 175f., 177f. with nn. 10 and 13, 180, 182, 216, 236, 244, 249f. and n. 1, 251f., 255, n. 15, 259f., 264, n. 12, 265–267, 269, 271f., 274, 278, 295f., 301, 314, 315–318, 321–323, 326f., 355, 358, 361, 366f., 371, 382, 396, 399, 401f., 407f. and n. 8, 420
transformation 1–3, 5–10, 38f., 46, n. 4, 153, 189, 198, 204, 222, 225, 263, 278, 280, 286, 293, 353, 355, 369, 375, 411
translation 18–20, 24, 26, 147, 205, 264, 283, 305, 320f.
transmission 2, 7, 15, 94f., 123, 177 and n. 10, 184f., 267
transplantation 5, 11, 18, 25
Triphiodorus 216
Trojan War 5, 71f., 88, 113f., 123, 180 and n. 22, 207, 210, 251–253 and n. 10, 255f. and n. 15, 260, 290, 292, n. 18, 344, n. 7, 356, 358, 370, 374, 377, 379–381, 388, 400, 403, 412
Troy 15, 54, 72, 86–88, 103f., 113f., 139 and n. 59, 170, 207, 252, 256, 260, 290, 295, 298, 304, 307, 333, 345, 355–359, 362f., 369f., 372f., 376, 381, 393–397, 401, 403, 408f., 411–416, 431

Ulysses   263, 265, 267f. and n. 27, 272, 274, 298, 387, 393, 401

van der Vondel, Joost: *Palamedes*   379
variation   55, 68, n. 34, 108, 110f., 122, 190, 196, 215, 217, 219–223, 270 and n. 47, 404
Verse Theater Manhattan   22
version   8, 15, 21f., 26, 38, 43, 79, 103, 105, 109, 111, 139, 208, 231, 235, 250, 255f., 260, 270, 278, n. 11, 281 and n. 25, 285f., 293, n. 23, 307, 309, 331–333, 338, 347, 375, 403, 408, 414f., 422, 425
Virgil   7f., 20, 227–247, 249–261, 263–275, 277, 283f. and n. 32, 289, 299, n. 42, 303–314, 372f., 375
– *Aeneid*   7f., 249–261, 263–275, 284, 303 and n. 1, 372
– *Eclogues*   7, 227–247, 283, 303

– [Virgil] *Ciris*   7, 277–287
visual arts   264, 317

Walcott, Derek   15, 19, 20f. and n. 14, 26
wall-paintings   208 and n. 7, 210, 264, 274 and n. 79
Wolf, Friedrich August   8, 315–317, 320–322, 327
World War II   19, 377, 380, 389, 399, 411

Xerxes   73–75, 77–81, 83–88

Zanos, Panagiotis: *Penelope's Suitors and Odysseus' Homecoming*   379f., 387f.
Zeus   59f., 65f., 74f., 85, 87, 101, 104, 170, 179, 209f., 219f., 228, 234, 278 and n. 11, 308f., 335, 357f. with nn. 15 and 16, 365, 379

Index of Homeric Passages

Iliad:

1.57   223, n. 36
1.162   217
1.169–71   147
1.226   183, n. 45
1.497   218, n. 17
1.557   218, n. 17

2.16–34   74, n. 11
2.41   217
2.53   223
2.85   183, n. 45
2.93–94   97
2.105   183, n. 45
2.119–22   171, n. 20
2.144–52   25
2.210   219
2.212–24   115
2.221   116
2.243   183, n. 45
2.254   183, n. 45
2.281   217
2.295–98   171, n. 20
2.391–93   169, n. 14
2.459–66   410
2.463   219
2.477   410
2.548   25
2.552–54   113 f.
2.695–702   24
2.772   183, n. 45
2.788–89   223
2.867–69   76, n. 21

3.1–9   77, n. 21
3.8–9   165, n. 6
3.30 ff.   363
3.38–57   295, n. 32
3.64   193, n. 15
3.144   139
3.156–58   47
3.164–65   365
3.171   365

3.173–75   364, n. 49
3.178–80   47
3.199   365
3.200–02   47
3.228   365
3.264 ff.   363
3.418   365
3.426   365

4.114   217
4.173   183, n. 45
4.176   183, n. 45
4.242–46   171, n. 20
4.376–81   87

5.30   53, n. 25
5.35   53, n. 25
5.297–351   296
5.355   53, n. 25
5.427   193, n. 15
5.529–32   171, n. 18
5.696   219
5.787   171, n. 18
5.792   165, n. 6
5.830   53, n. 25
5.904   53, n. 25

Book 6   348, 364
6.90   221, n. 32
6.146–51   25
6.255   36, 217
6.280–85   363
6.325–31   295, n. 32, 363
6.343   364
6.344–58   364
6.357–58   365
6.360   364
6.369–502   411
6.381–502   136, n. 45
6.390–493   369
6.403   363
6.407–502   295, n. 30
6.429   369
6.429–31   369

6.444–46   363
6.454–59   55, n. 34
6.459–65   54 f.
6.460–61   48, 55, n. 32
6.523–25   363

7.84–91   48
7.89–90   48, 50
7.215–18   363
7.411   220

8.13–14   219
8.146–50   170
8.161–66   171, n. 19
8.228   171, n. 18
8.402–05   308
8.535–36   171, n. 17

9.132–34   295, n. 29
9.239   54, n. 28
9.308–13   147
9.308–429   414
9.312–13   147
9.336   293 f., n. 26
9.341–343   293 and n. 22
9.357–63   147
9.389   193, n. 15
9.497   185
9.571   218
9.601–05   171, n. 19
9.618–19   148
9.650–55   147
9.663   222

10.274 ff.   40
10.329   220

11.11–12   166, n. 8
11.67–71   17
11.86–91   86
11.90–91   171, n. 17
11.305–06   232, n. 21
11.313–15   171, n. 20
11.407–10   171, n. 17
11.558–65   166
11.762–64   171, n. 17

12.235   220
12.309–28   80
12.310–21   171, n. 19
12.310–28   411
12.421–25   19
12.432–38   85, n. 35

13.13   182
13.154   220
13.156 ff.   362
13.240   222, n. 33
13.276–86   171, n. 17
13.389–93   240
13.390   227
13.413–16   362
13.471–74   168, n. 12
13.769–73   295, n. 32, 363

14.11   213

15.36–37   207
15.127   53, n. 25
15.142   53, n. 25
15.191   219
15.293   220
15.561–64   165, n. 6
15.594–95   166, n. 8

16.88   220
16.344   219
16.462–505   411
16.482–85   20
16.482–86   227, 240
16.483   227
16.528–29   166, n. 8
16.765–70   240
16.765–71   227
16.806–15   181, n. 27

17.1–6   84, n. 33
17.51–60   181
17.210–13   54, n. 29

18.73–77   105
18.79–93   105
18.88–126   411
18.90–93   105

18.95–96   105
18.95–99   109 f.
18.98–126   105, 110
18.128–37   105
18.245   223
18.246   223
18.324–29   104
18.333–35   106 f.
18.478   257
18.478–608   210
18.481–82   193, n. 14
18.550–60   17
18.590–604   211

19.87   218
19.164–66   165, n. 6
19.282   189, n. 1, 193, n. 15

20.129   217
20.421   219

21.199   219
21.350–52   228
21.573–80   167

22.99–110   170
22.147–57   86
22.256–57   363
22.268–69   171, n. 17
22.448   369
22.461   369
22.466   369
22.470   193, n. 15
22.477–514   369

23.65–68   105
23.69–92   105
23.77–91   105, 107 f.
23.114 ff.   227, n. 3
23.200   232
23.859   67, n. 28

24.214–16   363
24.248–54   363, n. 42
24.258–59   363
24.260   54, n. 28
24.498   54, n. 28

24.675   222
24.699   189, 193, n. 15
24.763–64   364, n. 49
24.767–75   363
24.790   223, n. 36

Odyssey:

1.111   221, n. 28
1.320–22   165, n. 6

2.92–95   184
2.150   223
2.209   201, n. 41

3.215   217
3.304–10   415

4.14   189
4.123   222, n. 33
4.221   181
4.413   283
4.563   232
4.567   232
4.602–04   229
4.607   229
4.681   201, n. 41

5.13 ff.   292
5.295–96   305
5.406–07   304
5.422   284, n. 30

6.15–17   191, n. 6
6.16   189, n. 1
6.149–57   189, n. 1
6.149 ff.   43

7.53 ff.   36
7.96–97   221, n. 32
7.112   230
7.112–13   235, n. 27
7.112–32   230
7.113   230
7.124   231
7.125   231
7.129–30   232

7.132   231

8.1–96   61
8.24   223, n. 36
8.97–253   61
8.100   64
8.145   63
8.153   63
8.158   63
8.184   64
8.185   63
8.202   63
8.205   63
8.206   63
8.214   63
8.215–18   63
8.229–31   63
8.335–37   23
8.337   193, n. 15
8.342   193, n. 15
8.362–66   191, n. 5

9.52   218, n. 17
9.177–566   263
9.480–83   273
9.537–40   273

10.275–301   35
10.494–95   339
10.513–15   335
10.521   339
10.529–30   340

Book 11 (*Nekyia*)   8, 331f., 336, 337, n. 19, 338–341
11.15ff.   338
11.29   339
11.36–37   340
11.42–43   340
11.49   339
11.134–37   332
11.135   333
11.136   333
11.137   333
11.271–73   208
11.327   209
11.489–90   184

11.582–92   182
11.588–90   232
11.591–92   233
11.605–06   340
11.632–33   340

12.39–54   120
12.85   283
12.86   283
12.95–100   282f.
12.96   283f.
12.97   283f. and n. 30
12.124–25   282
12.158–200   120
12.187   364

13.102–12   175
13.397–403   265
13.430–38   265

14.144–45   183
14.180   201, n. 41

15.105   221, n. 32
15.180   220

16.78–81   34, n. 11
16.78–85   34
16.96   217

17.37   189, n. 1, 193, n. 15
17.578   93, n. 3

18.28   34, n. 12
18.99   201, n. 41
18.190–96   189, n. 1
18.292   221, n. 32

19.54   189, n. 1

21.1ff.   348
21.174   201, n. 41
21.232   201, n. 41
21.310ff.   348

22.88   219
22.386   221

22.439   221, n. 28
22.453   221, n. 28
22.465–72   21

23.790–91   63, n. 9

Book 24   233, 235
24.6–9   340
24.224 ff.   345

24.235 ff.   345
24.244–50   233 f., 235
24.318–19   166, n. 8
24.331   234
24.333–44   234 f.
24.336   243
24.337–39   235
24.340–41   234
24.421   223, n. 36

www.ingramcontent.com/pod-product-compliance
Lightning Source LLC
Chambersburg PA
CBHW051200300426
44116CB00006B/389